SAILS AND STEAM
IN THE MOUNTAINS

SAILS AND STEAM
IN THE MOUNTAINS

A Maritime and Military History of
Lake George and Lake Champlain

Russell P. Bellico

PURPLE MOUNTAIN PRESS
Fleischmanns, New York

To Jane and Bill

Sails and Steam in the Mountains:
A Maritime and Military History of Lake George and Lake Champlain

Published by
PURPLE MOUNTAIN PRESS, LTD.
Main Street, P.O. Box E3, Fleischmanns, New York 12430-0378
914-254-4062, 914-254-4476 (fax), Purple@catskill.net

First edition published in 1992.
Second, third, and fourth printings with minor changes: 1993, 1995, 1998.

Copyright © 1992 by Russell P. Bellico

Library of Congress Cataloging-in-Publication Data

Bellico, Russell P. (Russell Paul) 1943-
     Sails and steam in the mountains : a maritime and military history
of Lake George and Lake Champlain / Russell P. Bellico. -- 1st ed.
          p.   cm.
     Includes bibliographical references and index.
     ISBN 0-935796-33-9. -- ISBN 0-935796-32-0 (pbk.)
     1. George, Lake, Region (N.Y.)--History, Military. 2. George,
Lake, Region (N.Y.)--History, Naval. 3. Champlain, Lake, Region-
-History, Military. 4. Champlain, Lake, Region--History, Naval.
     I. Title
F127.L3B45   1992
974.7'5--dc20   92-25010
                                                                      CIP

Manufactured in the United States of America.
Printed on acid-free paper.

Front cover: Engagement on Lake Champlain on October 13, 1776.
E. Newbold Smith Collection (Philadelphia Maritime Museum).

Contents

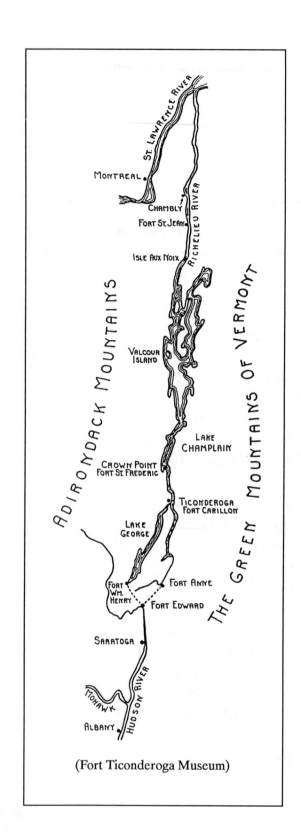

(Fort Ticonderoga Museum)

Acknowledgments

I AM INDEBTED TO MANY INDIVIDUALS for their assistance with my research on Lake George and Lake Champlain that extended for two decades. To begin with, I am especially appreciative of my father's interest in history which resulted in a vacation trip to Lake George and Fort Ticonderoga in 1952. As a nine-year-old, I was thoroughly impressed by my first real contact with tangible American colonial history. Two years later, the observation of the ongoing archaeological excavation at the site of Fort William Henry and another visit to Fort Ticonderoga solidified my life-long interest in the history of the two lakes. When I began my diving excursions to the lakes in the late 1960s, Frank Pabst, a well-known entrepreneur in Plattsburgh, helped renew my interest in the maritime history of the two lakes with his wealth of information on the war fleets. Nearly 20 years later, Pabst, then operator of the tour boat *Juniper*, was the first to suggest that I write a book on the maritime history of Lake Champlain.

Special appreciation is due to the staffs of the many libraries that helped me ferret out a variety of historical materials. The following libraries were primarily useful in my investigation: The New York State Library and Archives in Albany; the University of Massachusetts at Amherst; the Bailey/Howe Memorial Library at the University of Vermont; the Benjamin F. Feinberg Library at SUNY, Plattsburgh; the Boston Public Library; the National Archives of Canada in Ottawa; the Massey Library of the Royal Military College at Kingston, Ontario; the National Archives in Washington, D.C.; the Connecticut State Library in Hartford; the Crandall Library of Glens Falls; the Starr Library at Middlebury College; the Fort Ticonderoga Museum Library; the Bixby Library of Vergennes; the Amherst College Library; the Lake George Historical Association; the American Antiquarian Society at Worcester, Massachusetts; the Massachusetts Historical Society in Boston; the Ticonderoga Historical Society; the Nimitz Library of the U.S. Naval Academy; and the town libraries of Essex, Port Henry, Westport, and Willsboro, New York.

I owe a singular debt of gratitude to Helen Lent, an administrative assistant at Westfield State College, whose support, endless corrections of my manuscript, and typing were crucial to the completion of the project. In addition, special thanks are due to the many work-study students at the college for their diligent transcription of my handwritten draft onto a word

1

processor. Proofreading by Professors Stephen Sossaman, Wallace Goldstein, and Frank Ciarleglio was essential in detecting errors and recommending changes. Credit is also due Catherine Handy, reference librarian at Westfield State College, for her persistent attention to my requests for interlibrary loans. Support for the project from the Committee on Professional Development and a sabbatical leave from Westfield State College enabled me to complete the research and writing of the manuscript. Advice on photography and the printing of my black and white photographs by John Morytko, director of photographic services at the college, is gratefully acknowledged. I also appreciate the help provided by Kenneth Haar and Deborah Samwell who transferred the manuscript onto disks at the college's computer center.

Vital historical information from Betty Ahearn Buckell, Gary Zaboly, Hudson Hagglund, George Bray, and Robert Benway and oral history from Captain Marty Fisher, Captain Gordon Burleigh, Captain Merritt Carpenter, Harmel Burton, and Peter Smith helped piece together the history of the two lakes. The diligent efforts of artists Montserrat Centeno and Gary Zaboly to comply with my requests for illustrations are gratefully recognized.

I received valuable help and encouragement from Joseph Zarzynski, executive secretary of Bateaux Below, Inc. Research assistance by Marilyn Mazzeo and Grace MacDonald of the Lake George Historical Association and support for the book from the board of directors are greatly appreciated. William Cowan's advice and knowledge of the book publishing market proved to be invaluable, and I am grateful to *American History Illustrated* in permitting me to reprint excerpts from my 1985 article.

I am appreciative for having been included in the side-scan sonar expeditions with three separate teams in the 1980s on Lake Champlain in search of Benedict Arnold's lost gondola. The sound archaeological work on Lake Champlain shipwrecks carried out in recent years by the Lake Champlain Maritime Museum deserves credit for breathing renewed interest in the long history of these freshwater fleets. Similar efforts by Bateaux Below have also created a new emphasis on the preservation of historic vessels. I am also exceedingly grateful to diving associates who were willing to pose for my underwater photographs on numerous expeditions in search of shipwrecks. Fellow members of the *Land Tortoise* project at Lake George are deserving of special recognition for their efforts in documenting a unique vessel in American history.

Finally, I owe thanks to my wife, Jane, for her proofreading, encouragement, and patience. I also appreciate my twelve-year-old son's occasional suggestions during the project. In particular, his discovery that young Paul Revere served at Fort William Henry in 1756 provided an assurance that interest in the history of the two lakes will transcend generations.

Introduction

No LAKES HAVE A GREATER CLAIM to a place in American history than Lake George and Lake Champlain. While visitors to the lakes today gaze upon tranquil waters filled with pleasure boats, three wars fought between 1755 and 1814 saw deadly cannon fire, vessels engaged in devastating attacks, and the French and English empires ascend and decline. Most military histories of the lakes are limited to these wars, but numerous raids by both the French and English occurred via the lakes during the seventeenth century and three major English expeditions reached the lake valleys in 1690, 1709, and 1711. These distant events in time have been recorded and passed on by history-minded residents and tourists for new generations in oral and written chronicles and have been kept alive in part by the forts that line their shores and the shipwrecks lying on the bottom of the lakes. The lakes are the common element of the past that provide the foundation for the retelling of historic events. They are special places that generations have embraced both for their beauty and history.

In their first two centuries of European habitation, the Lake George - Lake Champlain valleys witnessed a continual struggle for control of their strategic waterways in a period when the only viable means of transportation was by water. Some of the initial chapters of this book, covering the early expeditions and the French and Indian War, deal extensively with land engagements; however, these events are integral to the total history of the lakes and are interwoven with their maritime activity. In each of these cases, land battles were the consequence of the larger struggle over control of the water route. The long navigable lakes were the logical entrance from Canada into the center of the English colonies. Expeditions and forts were continually raised in defense of rival claims to the water highway of the two lakes. In nearly all of these early battles, large armies were transported on the lakes in massive fleets of bateaux accompanied by radeaux, row galleys, schooners, and sloops. The most extensive naval battles, on the other hand, would await the American Revolution and the War of 1812. Although the hastily constructed Champlain fleet in 1776 under Benedict Arnold went down in defeat at the hands of a more heavily armed British armada, the presence of the American fleet delayed the British advance and ultimately changed the course of the American Revolution. The clouds of war were to engulf Lake

3

Champlain once again in a renewed rivalry with Great Britain over control of the strategic Champlain waterway during the War of 1812. The decisive defeat of the British flotilla at Plattsburgh Bay in 1814 by the American fleet under Thomas Macdonough was instrumental in bringing the war to a conclusion with the Treaty of Ghent.

How accurately can we recount these events, some of which occurred over two centuries ago? Surprisingly, there may be more written documents on these military campaigns than from some expeditions during twentieth-century wars. Without modern technology most military communications were written down and carried by messengers. Often several letters by different authors were written describing the same event. The soldiers themselves, realizing that they were making history, carried journals and diaries in their packs. Although the journals manifest rudimentary spelling, punctuation, and grammar, they provide a means of untangling fact from myth and have added a firsthand dimension to the narrative of the book. The history of these events can be clarified but will never be final since other documents will surely be uncovered and events reinterpreted in the future.

Following the wars, a commercial period initiated a new era in the history of Lake George and Lake Champlain. Before railroads and trailer trucks, the water highway of the lakes provided the only economical means of transporting cargoes of pulpwood, iron ore, coal, granite, marble, graphite and lumber from the resource-rich areas of the north to the marketplaces of the middle-Atlantic and New England states. Lake Champlain was a natural trade route from Canada to the United States which increased in importance with the building of the Champlain Canal in New York with its connection to the Hudson River and the Chambly Canal in Canada. Schooners, canal boats, and majestic steamboats plied the water passageway of Lake Champlain for more than a century. The luxurious steamers of Lake George conveyed cheerful passengers to scores of major summer hotels along the lake or to the stagecoaches (later railroad) at the northern landing which transported passengers to the steamer landing on Lake Champlain at Ticonderoga. The steamboat epoch is replete with dramatic tales of steamer disasters and the modern search for and discovery of their remains.

The book is not only a testament to the past but closely ties the historic events to the exciting archaeological discoveries of the present. True underwater exploration of wreck sites in the lakes began with a survey of the Revolutionary War flagship *Royal Savage* by a commercial diver in 1909 and the subsequent examination and raising of that vessel and the gondola *Philadelphia* by Colonel Lorenzo Hagglund in the 1930s. At the same time a crude diving apparatus enabled a diver in Lake George to investigate bateau wreck sites from the French and Indian War.

By the 1950s and 1960s, with the availability of modern scuba diving equipment, the exploration of shipwrecks in the lakes became a popular sport for hundreds of individuals. Unfortunately, many archaeological sites were quickly torn apart for souvenirs. Many wooden and iron artifacts retrieved from these wrecks deteriorated and were eventually thrown away. Likewise, some of the vessels raised from the depths of Lake Champlain in the twentieth century, including one of Benedict Arnold's gondolas, Amherst's brig *Duke of Cumberland*, and the 1809 *Vermont*, were allowed to deteriorate after exposure to the elements. Fortunately, several vessels did survive their salvage from the lakes, such as a French and Indian War bateau in the Adirondack Museum, the Revolutionary War gondola *Philadelphia* in the Smithsonian, and the War of 1812 schooner *Ticonderoga* on display at Whitehall.

By the 1980s a new era of conservation and preservation of wrecks had begun in the lake valleys. In the first half of the decade the Champlain Maritime Society in Burlington provided the leadership in sound archaeological studies on a variety of shipwreck sites. Many groups, including the New York State Divers Association, now recognize that these wrecks are finite resources that need to be preserved for future generations to enjoy. In the 1980s the widespread deployment of side-scan sonar resulted in the discovery of major intact shipwrecks in Lake Champlain. Following several significant underwater discoveries, the state of Vermont initiated a number of successful underwater historic preserves for visiting divers which have resulted in the reorientation of the diving public toward the concept of preservation. The discoveries have renewed interest in the history of the lake basins and encouraged a re-examination of their maritime heritage. Widespread support has enabled the Lake Champlain Maritime Museum at Basin Harbor to collect artifacts from Lake Champlain's maritime history and build full-size replicas of a bateau from Lake George and Benedict Arnold's 1776 gondola *Philadelphia*. Likewise, the 1990 discovery in Lake George of the intact 1758 radeau *Land Tortoise* has focused attention on the archaeological treasures of the lakes.

After more than 20 years of searching and photographing wreck sites in both lakes, I am encouraged by the new interest in conservation of these vessels by diverse groups of history enthusiasts and divers.

Drawing by Gary Zaboly

1. Years of Conflict

LAKE GEORGE AND LAKE CHAMPLAIN, intertwined by history and geography, rank as two of the most significant water routes in the settlement of North America. Melting glaciers thousands of years ago left the lake basins with a myriad of deep channels, islands, towering palisades, and rock outcroppings surrounded by lofty mountain peaks. While the receding ice gave Lake George its present shape, the Champlain Valley was inundated by salt water forming the Champlain Sea. Remnants of the oceanic past, including marine fossils, bones of walruses, and a skeleton of a whale have been discovered along the shoreline of Lake Champlain. As the land in the north uplifted, cutting the inlet from the St. Lawrence, the waters of Lake Champlain gradually changed from salt to freshwater. Fish such as the ling, sheepshead, and sturgeon trace their origin to this earlier sea. Both Lake George and Lake Champlain drained south to the Hudson River during the last period of glaciation, but later the geological rise of the surrounding land mass caused the water to empty to the north for both lakes.

Today Lake Champlain is the largest body of deep freshwater in the United States exclusive of the Great Lakes. Champlain spans 120 miles from Whitehall, New York, at the southern end to its northern outlet in the Richelieu River. At the widest point, it reaches 12 miles across with a maximum depth of 400 feet. The lake's nearly 500 square miles encompass 71 islands. Over 90 percent of the water in Champlain comes from tributaries that drain into its basin. Lake George, by contrast, receives most of its water from springs. The 32 miles of Lake George, surrounded by steep mountain sides reaching heights of 2,500 feet along the middle of the lake, resemble a pristine fjord. The 172 islands that dot its clear water coupled with its breathtaking scenery have endeared the lake to visitors of the region throughout history.

The lakes have not always been tranquil, however. These now placid waterways were the sites of three wars and many violent shipwrecks during their turbulent history, producing a legacy of stories of the American past. They were the scenes of heroic acts of courage, deeds of treachery and torture, and perilous Indian encounters. The interest in the history of these stormy events stems not from a glorification of war but from a fascination with the lakes as special places whose beauty and past are interwoven. The names of islands and landmarks often reflect the historic incidents of the wartime period: Floating Battery Island, Sabbath Day Point, Rogers Rock, Prisoners Island, Arnold's Bay, Carleton's Prize, Schuyler Island, etc. As part of a natural water route from Canada to the Hudson River and the Atlantic Ocean, Lake Champlain and Lake George were of strategic importance to rival colonial powers. Colonel Louis Antoine de Bougainville, pondering strategy during the French and Indian War while at Ticonderoga, noted in his journal in 1758 that "the lakes and rivers are the only outlets, the only open roads in this country."[1] Bougainville, like many military leaders who would follow, concluded that "the only way to assure ourselves the possession of Lake Champlain. . .is by a strong naval force."[2] Radeaux, brigs, sloops, row galleys, and gunboats would become a familiar part of the scenery during war periods. When peace finally arrived in the nineteenth century, it was time for new fleets of commercial schooners, steamboats, canal boats, and horse boats to once again follow the natural water route that the lakes provided.

Although most of the early history of Lake George and Lake Champlain has been written from the ethnocentric view of the European inhabitancy, there is ample evidence that native civilizations had occupied the area for thousands of years. Stone points discovered at Highgate, Vermont (east of Maquam Bay), indicate the presence of a hunting society of Paleoindians about 9300 B.C. The archaic period in Vermont, rooted in a broad-based hunting and gathering culture, has been dated from 3500 B.C. to perhaps 2000 B.C. based upon relics uncovered at two sites along Otter Creek (Vergennes). Artifacts from the Woodland period found at the Winooski River, Swanton, and East Creek range in dates from 60 A.D. to after 1000 A.D. East Creek, lying on the Vermont side across from Fort Ticonderoga, was the apparent site of a large village for many years before the Iroquoian tribes or Europeans arrived at Lake Champlain. During the 1930s an excavation of a site on East Creek by the Museum of the American Indian yielded pottery, 15-inch spearpoints, arrowheads, and strings of copper beads. The creek marshes had teemed with muskrat, beaver, and water fowl, while the adjacent north slopes of Mount Independence held the best source of flint in the lake valleys. The flint at East Creek was so good that Henry Knox delivered a substantial quantity to George Washington, along with the cannon from Ticonderoga, during the British siege of Boston in the Revolutionary War.

The Iroquois migrated to New York from the lower Mississippi, perhaps as early as 2,000 years ago, and eventually spearheaded one of the most important confederacies of North American Indians known as the Five Nations (after 1713 Six Nations). The Iroquois had an agriculture-based economy with corn as the staple crop. Their well-developed political structure included councils composed of democratically elected members which met in long, bark-covered communal houses. Fine pottery, mats of husk corn, baskets, and orchard fruits were produced and traded, utilizing wampum as a medium of exchange. Wampum was usually made from parts of shells strung on threads that were often worn as bracelets or necklaces. More importantly, wampum, in the form of belts, was a symbolic record of intertribal transactions as well as a way of recording historic events.

Evidence of a village site on the Ticonderoga peninsula, alternately occupied by both Algonquin and Iroquois tribes, had included large quantities of tools and arrowheads. Likewise, a village site on Missisquoi Bay where 1,000 artifacts have been unearthed may have been inhabited both by Iroquois and Abnaki Indians (Algonquin Confederacy). By 1575 the Algonquin and Iroquois tribes were mortal enemies vying for control of the region. The Iroquois laid claim to the western shore of Lake Champlain while the Algonquin tribes held the eastern shore. Many of the place names along the lake are Europeanized versions of the original Indian names.[3]

While there is limited evidence that other European travelers may have seen Lake Champlain first, the honor of discovery by a European goes to 39-year-old Samuel de Champlain who named it after himself in 1609. Prior to that, Champlain had fought in France to drive the Spanish invaders out. Five years later, in 1599, he made his first Atlantic voyage to the Caribbean and Central America as a guest aboard his uncle's ship. After several more voyages to North America in the early years of the seventeenth century, Champlain established himself as a map maker and explorer as well as a successful fur trader. His ability to build friendly relations with the Indian tribes along the St. Lawrence established France in the region and enhanced the lucrative fur trade. Return trips to France found Champlain eagerly seeking backing for new expeditions to North America. Champlain's goal through his many voyages was to locate a Northwest Passage to the Orient; to this end he explored the waters of Lake Huron, Lake Ontario, the Ottawa River, and perhaps the Oswego and Genesee rivers. Champlain spent a brutal fourth winter of 1608-1609 in North America at present-day Quebec City. Twenty of the 28 French explorers died; Champlain himself contracted scurvy. The following summer he met along the St. Lawrence River with the Algonquin and Huron who had been driven north by the Iroquois. They persuaded him to join in a campaign against their enemies at a lake to the south (Lake Champlain). Since Champlain needed the Huron for the fur trade and geographic information on the region, he felt obligated to participate in the expedition or risk compromising France's harmonious relations with the northern tribes.

In July 1609 Champlain and his crew traveled as far as the Richelieu River in a "shallop" or small sailing galley. Encountering the rapids in the Richelieu, Champlain and two Frenchmen transferred to Indian canoes. The war party of Algonquin, Huron, and Montagnais proceeded in 24 canoes up "the River of the Iroquois" or Richelieu. Upon entering the lake, Champlain saw "four beautiful islands" but spent more time describing a five-foot fish "as big as my thigh, and had a head as large as my fists, with a snout two feet and a half long, and a double row of very sharp, dangerous teeth. Its body has a good deal the shape of the pike."[4] His description has led to some controversy whether he had simply seen a garpike or the illusive Lake Champlain monster.[5]

The Indians informed Champlain that the place where they anticipated meeting their Iroquois enemies had a "rapid" [falls at Ticonderoga] and beyond that area lay a "lake which is some nine or ten leagues [Lake George]."[6] Traveling at night to avoid detection, Champlain and the Indians met a party of Iroquois paddling in canoes at ten o'clock on July 29, "at the extremity of a cape which projects into the lake on the west side."[7] There has been some debate over the years regarding the location of the cape where Champlain and the Iroquois met. Some writers suggest that the cape was Crown Point while others insist that it was the Ticonderoga peninsula on which the fort stands today. Since there is ample evidence that the Ticonderoga area had once been an Indian camp and that Champlain later observed the "rapid" at Ticonderoga, it is probable that this is the cape rather than Crown Point.

Both Indian parties began yelling at each other with the Iroquois withdrawing to their camp on the shore. Champlain had encountered a Mohawk party of the Iroquois Nation. The Mohawk onshore began cutting trees to form a barricade or circular stockade as a defense while the Algonquin or Huron pulled their canoes together offshore. The Indians

with Champlain sent a contingent in two canoes to the Mohawk to ask if they wished to fight. The Indians onshore affirmed their desire to engage the Algonquin, but persuaded them to await daylight in order to distinguish one from another. During the rest of the night both parties traded verbal insults while the Mohawk danced and sang. The next morning, Champlain prepared his arquebus (a matchlock musket) with four balls, put on his armor, and went ashore with the Indians. Until that point Champlain had not been seen by the Mohawk. Two hundred Mohawk with three "chiefs," identified by the big plumes in their headdress, walked out of their stockade as Champlain and the Indians advanced. The chiefs were probably only war captains since chiefs did not participate in battle and would have worn horns, not feathers.[8] Champlain recorded what was probably the first engagement involving Europeans in the lake valley: "When I saw them make a move to draw their bows upon us, I took aim with my arquebus and shot straight at one of the three chiefs, and with this shot two fell to the ground and one of their companions was wounded who died thereof a little later."[9]

Arrows thickened the air from both sides amid the loud shouts of the combatants. The Mohawk, according to Champlain, used shields made of wood woven together with cotton thread. These were no match for the arquebus, however, as one of Champlain's two companions who had hidden in the trees fired into the Mohawk. Frightened by the blast of this unknown weapon, the Mohawk finally fled deep into the forest. In addition to the Mohawk dead, ten to twelve were taken prisoner and later tortured. Champlain's Indians had 15 to 16 wounded with arrows, but their wounds healed swiftly, according to Champlain.

ABOVE. The 1609 battle of Samuel de Champlain and the Mohawk, drawing from the 1613 edition of his *Voyages*.
LEFT. Samuel de Champlain, from *The Summer Paradise in History* by Warwick Stevens Carpenter . (The Delaware and Hudson Company)

The Algonquin gathered up the abandoned shields and corn, departing northward within three hours. Champlain modestly noted in his journal that "where this attack took place is in 43° and some minutes of latitude, and was named Lake Champlain."[10] After several days of travel, Champlain returned to Quebec with the Montagnais Indians.

Champlain's encounter with the Iroquois has been linked to the collision course with the Six Nations in later years. Although some Iroquois tribes would side with the French during the French and Indian War, for the most part they remained enemies. Champlain would subsequently return to North America several more times and fight two more battles with the Iroquois. Between 1603 and 1632 Champlain would have four volumes of his adventures published with maps and illustrations. The primary result of his exploration in 1609, however, would be the discovery of a route through Lake Champlain and Lake George to the Hudson River — a route that would probably be the most contested waterway in North America during wars that would span the seventeenth, the eighteenth, and early nineteenth centuries.

Shortly after Champlain's voyage into Lake Champlain, Henry Hudson, supported by the Dutch East India Company, sailed into New York's coastal waters in September of 1609. During the next month, Hudson, also searching for a Northwest Passage, explored the Hudson River as far as present-day Albany in his 80-ton vessel *Half Moon*. His career in North America, however, was much shorter. The following year Hudson made his final voyage in the English ship *Discovery*, during which his vessel became frozen in the winter ice of Canada's Hudson Bay while searching for the Northwest Passage. After a bitter winter of deprivation, the crew mutinied, sending Hudson, his son and seven others adrift in a small boat, never to be seen again. Four years after Hudson's exploration of the river, the Dutch concluded a treaty with the Iroquois and established a trading post at Fort Orange (Albany). The Dutch would dominate the economy of southern New York for the next half century.

The French during the seventeenth century were largely engaged in the fur trade with the Canadian Indians, exporting as many as 150,000 skins a year. Large felt hats, made from beaver pelts, were the basic fashion of the day for European men. The French in this period tried to convert the Indians to Christianity, beginning with four missionaries who accompanied Champlain to Canada in 1615. Ten years later, the order of Jesuit priests arrived in Quebec to provide instruction in Christian faith and doctrine to the Huron. Father Isaac Jogues, perhaps the most famous Jesuit missionary, had spent six years with the Huron before being captured by an Iroquois war party in August of 1642. Although he might have escaped, Father Jogues rushed to the aid of two lay brothers who had been wounded. The Mohawk took their captives back to their villages, stopping the first night at Isle La Motte in northern Lake Champlain and later on "Jogues Island" (near present-day Westport, N.Y.). On the latter island the captives were forced to submit to the "salvo, which consists in having the prisoners pass between two rows [of Indians], each discharging upon them blows from sticks."[11]

Whether the war party transported the brutalized Jogues through "Lake Andiatarocte" (an Indian name meaning "place where the lake closes" or present-day Lake George) or through southern Lake Champlain is subject to some debate. Upon reaching their villages along the Mohawk River, Father Jogues had all but two of his fingernails pulled out, knuckles smashed, and his remaining fingers mutilated into stumps. The next year, while accompanying the Iroquois, Jogues was a few miles from the Dutch settlements on the

Hudson. Arendt Van Corlaer, a Dutch merchant friendly with the Mohawk, and a Dutch Reformed minister, Jan Megapolensis, after learning of Father Jogues' tortured captivity, assisted his escape from the Indians. He returned to France after being shipwrecked on the coast of England.

After receiving special permission from the Pope to celebrate mass with his mutilated hands, Jogues returned to Canada and was sent as an ambassador on a peace mission to the Mohawk with two Algonquin and Sieur Bourdon, a French engineer. Father Jogues stopped at Isle La Motte and Otter Creek before reaching "Lake Andiatrocte." Upon viewing the lake in 1646, Jogues christened it "Lac du Saint-Sacrement," a name that was used until the English changed it to Lake George in 1755. Upon reaching the Iroquois villages along the Mohawk River, Father Jogues set the stage for peaceful relations with the French, leaving gifts and religious articles before departing for Canada on June 16. He returned to Canada with an invitation to establish a mission at the Mohawk villages. Upon approval by the Jesuits, the 39-year-old Jogues returned with René-Jean LaLande in late August. By early October after caterpillars had consumed the Mohawk's grain and an epidemic had occurred, Jogues was charged with bringing the "Evil Spirit" to the village and was murdered. On October 18, 1646, Jogues and LaLande had their decapitated heads mounted on stakes at the Mohawk village. Father Jogues was canonized a saint in 1930; his statue today gazes upon the waters of Lake George from Battlefield Park in Lake George Village.

As the colonial powers vied for trade outlets, the potential for conflict increased. By the middle of the seventeenth century the English were ready to challenge the Dutch presence in North America. Between 1652 and 1675 three periods of warfare between the two rival commercial powers occurred. In 1664 the Dutch colony on the Hudson River was captured by the English, but subsequently retaken by the Dutch in 1673. It was quickly seized again by the English. By 1675 the Dutch were permanently driven from North America. The Dutch colonists, however, remained in the Hudson River settlement retaining their cultural and religious heritage.

The elimination of the Dutch and the growth of New France ultimately led to a collison course between the French and English colonial empires in North America. Under King Louis XIV in 1661, France revived its interest in the economic potential of North America. Under several effective governors of New France, ambitious plans for settlement and trade alarmed England and its colonists. Three wars, King William's War (1689-1697), Queen Anne's War (1702-1713), and King George's War (1744-48), would ensue before the final confrontation of the French and Indian War (1755-1763). Each war escalated the size of the armies and the ferocity of battle as each nation attempted to oust the other from North America.

Initially the conflict began with the Iroquois challenge to the French settlements and forts along the St. Lawrence River. At the mouth of the Richelieu River, the French built Fort Richelieu in 1641 which was burned five years later by the Iroquois. By 1663 the Iroquois had grown bolder, attacking farms and towns in Canada which spread fear throughout New France. The threat led to the rebuilding of Fort Richelieu and construction of several other fortifications along the St. Lawrence and Richelieu Rivers. A regiment of the tough French Carignan-Sallieres regulars, who had achieved fame in the wars against the Turks, landed in Quebec in 1665 to establish the military power of New France.

Although an Iroquois peace ambassador visited Canada in December, the new gover-nor-general of New France, Daniel de Courcelles, planned a daring raid in mid-winter against the Mohawk villages in New York. On January 9, 1666, Courcelles, carrying his own 25-30 pound pack, led nearly 600 troops wearing snowshoes over Lake Champlain, then overland to the Hudson. However, as early as the third day of the expedition, ears, fingers, noses, and knees of some of the men had become frozen. By February 14 the troops, who had become lost following their Indian guides, found themselves near the Dutch village of Schenectady instead of the Iroquois settlements along the Mohawk River. The troops had only a minor skirmish with Mohawk. Arendt Van Corlaer, who had earlier helped Father Jogues, came to the rescue with provisions of peas and bread. The Dutch also offered shelter, but Courcelles refused, fearing that his troops might desert once they got next to a fireplace. For his help, Lieutenant General de Courcelles invited Van Corlaer to Canada.* The French party retreated northward but were forced to march all night in a blinding snowstorm. Pursued by Mohawk, sixty soldiers died of starvation and exposure or were taken prisoner before the army returned to Canada on March 8.

Courcelles and Canadian Viceroy Marquis de Tracy did not abandon the plan to crush the Iroquois villages. To this end, they sent Captain de la Motte and the regiment of regulars to an island in Lake Champlain to build a fourth fort. The outpost, called Fort St. Anne, was completed by July 26, 1666, on the northwest end of present-day Isle La Motte. The 144-foot fort with four log bastions was abandoned as a fortified outpost around 1671, but its remnants were still clearly observable in the late nineteenth century.

By summer a peace offer from ambassadors of the Five Iroquois Nations, meeting with the French in Quebec, seemed to offer the hope of a durable accord. But within a few days the news that a captain in the Carignan Regiment and nephew of Governor de Tracy had been killed by the Mohawk set the stage for another French expedition to the Iroquois villages. September 28, 1666, was set for a rendezvous of French forces involved in the operation. Both General Courcelles and Governor Tracy led the 1,300-man expedition in 300 vessels "consisting partly of very light batteaux,** and partly of bark canoes."[12] The army paddled south on Lake Champlain, left some troops with provisions to build a stockaded fort at Ticonderoga, portaged to Lake George, and proceeded to its southern shore where the French hid their vessels for the return trip. The French army marched to the Mohawk River and burned four Iroquois villages consisting of 100 large sturdy cabins with "a triple palisade, surrounding their stronghold, twenty feet in height and flanked by four bastions."[13] In the spring of 1667, to the surprise of the small garrison at Fort St. Anne, several Iroquois ambassadors appeared, requesting peace with the French and asking for missionaries. On May 22, 1667, ten Iroquois ambassadors met in Quebec with the French to conclude a treaty of peace.

By the 1680s rising tension over land claims by the French and English was the harbinger of future conflict. Beginning in 1684, land patents north of Fort Orange (Albany) by the governor of New York, Colonel Thomas Dongan, were the first in a succession of grants that moved the English closer toward areas claimed by the French. The French believed

---

* The following year Van Corlaer drowned "crossing a great bay" during a storm on Lake Champlain. While there is some debate regarding where he actually drowned, the bay south of Port Kent, New York, adjacent to Schuyler Island is named Corlaer Bay.
** Bateaux were flat-bottomed vessels 27-36 feet in length used for carrying men and cargo on inland waters (see chapter 2).

the English were arming the Iroquois and secretly encouraging them to break the peace which resulted in additional raids against the Iroquois. Marquis de Denonville, the Canadian governor, proposed a strategy in 1688 to extend French influence with a garrisoned outpost at the "end" of Lake Champlain which meant Crown Point in that period.

For several years Denonville and other French officials developed elaborate proposals to attack the English through Lake Champlain, Lake George, and the Hudson to New York City. The plan, similar to those devised in later wars, would be aimed at dividing the English colonies. By June of 1689, Louis XIV, the king of France, approved the plan. "He has the more readily consented thereto since he knows that the English inhabiting that country have contemplated of late years, exciting the Iroquois nations, his Majesty's subjects, with a view to oblige them to make war on the French."[14] In addition, the king charged the English with usurping trade in territories belonging to New France. Before the plan was put into action, 1,300 Mohawk in 250 canoes invaded Canada, totally destroying the village of La Chine on the island of Montreal, murdering its residents, and taking 130 captives.

The response to the La Chine raid was combined with a long-range plan of attack on the English colonies. Several French attacks on northern New England and New York villages would signify an escalation of the conflict with the first direct assault on the English. Although the leadership had once again changed in New France with the recall of Denonville and the reappointment of the vigorous 69-year-old former governor, Count de Frontenac, the military and political objectives remained the same. The long-planned attack on New York finally commenced with a scaled-down force at the beginning of February 1690. The expedition consisted of 210 men which included 96 Indians. After the Indians balked at the proposed assault on Fort Orange, the raiding party diverted to Schenectady, which resulted in the burning of the village and massacre of 60 men, women, and children. The significance of this action along with two other raids on New Hampshire and Maine was to engulf the colonies in the larger European wars. King William's War (1689-1697), part of a larger war fought by Europe's Grand Alliance against France, would initiate a conflict that would last on and off for the next 73 years culminating with the decisive end of the Seven Years' War.

A more ambitious invasion through the Champlain Valley was planned for the spring by Governor Frontenac of New France. In the meantime, the officials of New York were not idle, sending Captain Jacobus de Warm from Albany in March 1690 with 12 English troops and 20 Mohawk to establish a base near Crown Point. The contingent constructed "a little stone fort" on Chimney Point across the lake from Crown Point.[15] Another small English party was subsequently sent to Otter Creek and later to Fort Chambly on the Richelieu River. Lieutenant Governor Leisler of New York busily corresponded with other colonies in an effort to mount a defense against the rumored French invasion.* After meeting with delegates from Massachusetts and Connecticut, a strategy was put in motion to assemble an 800-man army in Albany along with the Mohawk to invade Canada through Lake Champlain. Coinciding with the Champlain offensive, a naval expedition would attack Quebec. Following a lengthy debate, Fitzjohn Winthrop of Connecticut, who had some military experience in England, was chosen to lead the army. Winthrop, the son of former Connecticut Governor John Winthrop and a grandson of the first Massachusetts Bay governor, would later become a governor of Connecticut.

---

* Lieutenant governors during the seventeenth and eighteenth centuries often handled most of the actual work in administering the colonies.

Arriving in Albany in late July 1690, Major General Winthrop "found the designe against Canada poorly contrived and little prosecuted, all things confused and in noe readiness or posture for martching the forces towards Canada."[16] Despite these problems, the army, which approximated 750 troops and an equal number of Mohawk, advanced toward Lake Champlain in early August. Winthrop, nearing Saratoga on August 2, received dispatches from Boston and Connecticut that the fleet was ready to sail against Canada. By August 6 the army reached Wood Creek at the very southern end of Lake Champlain in present-day Whitehall, New York.

After a few days, the lack of provisions and canoes along with smallpox which had infected the army made the problems of the ill-planned expedition all the more obvious. The expedition attempted to make canoes on the site, but "the tyme being soe far spent, the barke would not peele, and soe noe more canooes could be made."[17] The area around Whitehall in that period had mostly elm rather than birch trees. Since it was too late in the season for elm bark to be peeled, the expedition was doomed. After a council of war lasting two days with the Indians and officers, Winthrop noted in his journal on August 15 that the lack of provisions and canoes made it "adviseable to returne with the army."[18] The expedition, however, did not entirely end with Winthrop's withdrawal. Captain John Schuyler, brother of the mayor of Albany and grandfather of General Philip Schuyler of Revolutionary War fame, dissatisfied with the council's reticence to proceed, called for volunteers to raid the French outposts in Canada. During the month of August, Schuyler's party of 29 militia and 120 Mohawk raided La Prairie near Montreal, returning to Albany with 19 prisoners by the end of the month. While the raid was not much of a military victory, it served notice on the French that the colonists of New England could strike deep into French territory.

The second prong of the expedition toward Canada had even worse luck. Sir William Phips, a provincial from Maine who achieved knighthood for his salvage of a sunken Spanish treasure ship in the West Indies, captured Port Royal in Acadia for the English in 1690. Phips returned to Boston triumphant in time to take charge of the fleet that had been assembled to invade Quebec. After a late start, Phips succeeded in maneuvering his fleet through the difficult stretches of the St. Lawrence. Phips engaged in a cannon duel with shore batteries at Quebec City and landed 2,000 men, but failed to take the city and returned to Boston.[19]

Although plans were formulated during subsequent years for major expeditions, including French schemes to invade Boston and Manhattan, the period of the 1690s consisted mainly of raiding parties. Finally, the Peace of Ryswick in 1697 created a temporary cessation of hostilities in the region. Peace was unfortunately short-lived as the War of Spanish Succession in Europe resulted in Queen Anne's War (1702-1713) in North America. The French in Canada planned to destroy all the colonial settlements along the New England frontier. Following a route through Lake Champlain, 250 French and Indians destroyed Deerfield, Massachusetts, in February 1704, killing 47 villagers and taking 112 prisoners. The little village, situated near the Connecticut River, was portrayed as a fort with soldiers when the successful raid was reported by the Canadian governor to authorities in France. After several years of raids on New England settlements, the English developed a plan for conquest of French territories in North America. The military plans and outcome were similar to the 1690 English expeditions toward Canada. The war in North America would be ineffectual, with armies mustered and dissolved. Years of bloodshed along the frontier and one tragic naval catastrophe would end with another stalemate.

The 1709 British strategy involved a campaign through Lake Champlain with a naval force attacking Quebec from the St. Lawrence River. In late May the lieutenant governor of New York chose Colonel Francis Nicholson as the commander-in-chief of the new expedition against Canada. His orders included building canoes and boats at Wood Creek on Lake Champlain and to "cut a road from Albany to the Wood Creek for the marching of the men and carrying of the provisions."[20] Nicholson would also serve at various times as a governor or lieutenant governor of five different colonies. Colonel Nicholson began his military career as a young ensign in Flanders before going to Tangier as a lieutenant in 1680. After service in England, the authoritarian officer was transferred to North America.[21] Two veteran officers of King William's War, Peter and John Schuyler, would also join the expedition to Canada. The expeditionary force of approximately 1,600 men made it as far as Wood Creek by July. A road was cut from present-day Schuylerville along the east side of the Hudson to Fort Edward and over to Wood Creek. Along the way, three forts or outposts were also built. At Wood Creek about 100 bateaux and many canoes were constructed to move the troops on Lake Champlain. The army at Wood Creek was ravaged by disease as it awaited news of the English fleet that was to be sent against Quebec.

Meanwhile, the governor of New France, Philippee de Rigaud Vaudreuil, raised 1,500 troops for a campaign on Lake Champlain to oppose Nicholson's army. Aside from a few skirmishes, the main French army never left Chambly on the Richelieu River to engage the English expedition. By October Nicholson learned that the promised warships had been sent instead to Lisbon, Portugal. With an army ravaged by smallpox and dysentery, the discouraged army burned their bateaux, canoes, and forts before marching back to Albany. Governor Vaudreuil soon learned from his Indian scouts that the English had burned their "forts and bateaux." His report to French officials, however, attributed the retreat of the English troops and the evacuation of the Mohawk villages to the threat of the French army: "so great was the terror among the enemy on account of my encampment at Chambly, that the Mohawk had left their village and retired to Corlar [Schenectady]."[22]

The following winter Francis Nicholson and Peter Schuyler along with four Mohawk chiefs went to England to seek aid for a renewed expedition against New France. It was not until 1711 that the expedition came to fruition, however. The plan again called for a force to attack through Lake Champlain while a naval fleet with marines would assault Quebec by way of the St. Lawrence River. Sir Hovendon Walker, a relatively obscure naval commander, was chosen to lead a convoy of 70 ships from Boston with 6,400 English soldiers and 1,500 provincial troops commanded by Brigadier General Jack Hill. The Admiral sailed with his vessels at the end of July.

Francis Nicholson, now a lieutenant general, was again the commander-in-chief of the forces in New York. Two thousand troops from the colonies were assembled at Albany where nearly 600 flat-bottomed bateaux were built for the trip to Canada. The plan in 1711 was nearly identical to that of 1709 except for a change to the Lake George route, which was thought to be healthier for the troops than Wood Creek. The militia first reached the ruins of Fort Schuyler, destroyed in the 1709 retreat. Nicholson's troops rebuilt and renamed the outpost Fort Anne. By September, as some of the advance units of the army reached Lake George, Nicholson at Fort Anne heard the news of the disaster that struck the British naval fleet in the St. Lawrence River.

By August 18 the massive fleet had reached Gaspé before entering the St. Lawrence River. Ignoring the warnings of a seasoned French navigator, Admiral Walker sailed into the tricky waters of the St. Lawrence without knowledge of the proper bearings. Sailing past Anticosti Island at the mouth of the St. Lawrence, the fleet ran into a heavy fog on August 20. When land was sighted, Walker misunderstood the sighting and ordered a tack in the wrong direction before going to bed. In a short period of time, Walker, in his night clothes, was called to the deck since the wind was blowing the fleet toward the rocky shores of the St. Lawrence. Most of the ships were able to anchor, but eight transports and two supply ships smashed on the rocks. Walker, shaken by the catastrophe, abandoned the expedition and sailed back to England.

Upon hearing the news of the end of the naval expedition on the St. Lawrence, Nicholson, having little choice, abandoned the campaign, burned Fort Anne, and again returned with his troops to Albany. The Treaty of Utrecht in 1713 brought peace to Europe and in turn to North America. The treaty established the boundary between New France and English New York at Split Rock on Lake Champlain (between present-day Westport and Essex, N.Y.). The boundary, however, was never completely accepted by the French. The years of uneasy peace would only lead to an inevitable struggle.

The years following the treaty brought relative quiet to the region. John Lydius, a Dutch trader from Albany, after a long period of successful trade with Canada, was exiled from New France in 1730. The next year he built a stockaded trading post at the "Great Carrying Place" (present-day Fort Edward) on the Hudson River to continue his business. At the same time (1730) Charles de Beauharnois, governor of New France, sent a 30-soldier detachment under Michel Dagneaux to drive out the English traders who had penetrated Lake Champlain to trade with the Indians. On October 15, 1730, Beauharnois sent a letter to the king of France with a recommendation to build a fort at Crown Point on Lake Champlain. Beauharnois wrote, "When in possession of Crown Point the road will be blocked on the English should they wish to pass over our territory. . .whilst, seizing on the fort we could harass them by small parties, as we have done from 1689 to 1699 when we were at war with the Iroquois."[23] On May 8, 1731, Louis XV approved the construction of a log stockaded fort that would later be rebuilt with stone.

A few French families might have settled at Chimney Point across from Crown Point before French troops arrived in 1731.[24] The Chimney Point settlement may have utilized some of the materials remaining from the small fortification built there by the English in 1690. The evidence, including a map, points to 1731 as the construction date of the first fort in the Crown Point area which was actually located across the lake at Chimney Point.[25] Governor Beauharnois sent Hertel de la Fresnie and 20 workmen and soldiers from Montreal on August 16, 1731, to build the stockaded fort. By September 22 the outpost at "Pointe a la Chevelure" was completed including the interior buildings.

By November of 1731 the English began to protest the fort as an encroachment on their territory. The protests fell on deaf ears and the king approved the building of a "redoubt" in 1734 that eventually became the fort on the opposite shore. By 1737 the stone fort on the western shore was substantially complete and named after Frédéric de Maurepas, the secretary of state for the marines. By tradition most French forts were given the prefix Saint (Fort St. Frédéric). The fort with only four usable cannon needed considerable work in 1740 as Chevalier de Beauharnois, the nephew of the governor noted: "fortifications without ditches and without ramparts. . .no barracks, guard-rooms on the third floor, no cells, no

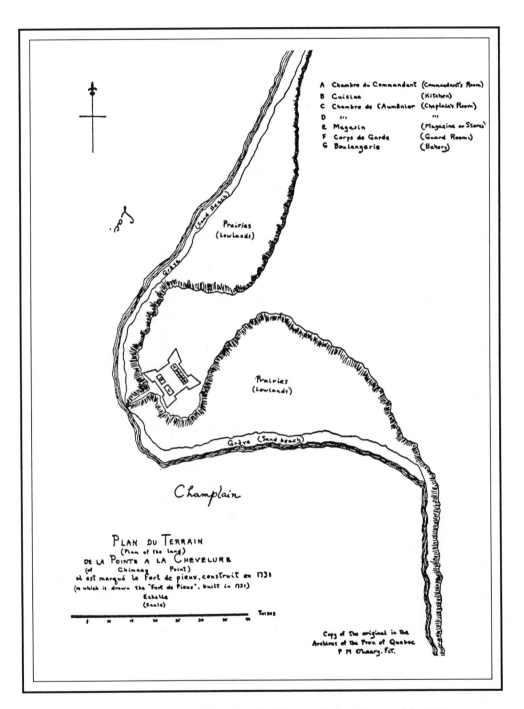

Outpost at "Pointe a la Chevelure" (Chimney Point, Vermont) in 1731.
Reconstruction of a map by Guy Omeron Coolidge.

prison."[26] Fort St. Frédéric underwent additional construction which enlarged the fort. The walls had risen higher and a four-story citadel became a fort within a fort. Stone barracks and a church within the walls were also completed using limestone from a nearby quarry. By 1742 Fort St. Frédéric, in size and armament, was second only to the stronghold at Quebec. The fort building on Lake Champlain was only part of the larger picture of English-French rivalry for control of North America.

In 1742 the first major sailing vessel on Lake Champlain was built at Crown Point. A sloop of 45 tons was built by the Corbin brothers ("Kings Carpenters") of Quebec.[27] The captain of the vessel was Joseph Payant St. Onge, who supervised its construction and later became known as the "Admiral of Lake Champlain." The vessel, which might have been named *St. Frederic*, made regular trips between Fort St. Jean on the Richelieu River and Crown Point well into the 1750s. General William Johnson in 1755 noted that the French "have a Vessell which sails and brings all sorts of Supplys from Crown Point."[28]

England and France by 1744 were once again at war in Europe (War of the Austrian Succession) which became known as King George's War (1744-1748) in North America. Fort St. Frédéric would serve as a base of operations and staging area for military forays into the surrounding region. Before St. Frédéric became an important base during the war, however, the large French fortification of Louisbourg on Cape Breton Island became the focus of attention. After years of construction, Louisbourg, with its 116 cannon, was a formidable military structure by 1744. John Bradstreet, an English officer at Nova Scotia who also owned a small trading schooner, was captured and sent to Louisbourg after the small English fishing port where he had been assigned was seized. Bradstreet, who would later play a role in the Lake George and Lake Champlain campaigns of the French and Indian War, was paroled and sent to Boston. In Boston he was able to provide specific information about Louisbourg to Governor William Shirley of Massachusetts who organized an expedition of New England militia to capture the fortress. With little military training, the 4,300-man army, after a month and a half siege, forced the surrender of the fortress on June 15, 1745. Historian Edward Hamilton would later conclude that the expedition "gave the Yankee colonists confidence in their own abilities, and it was a training ground for the leaders of the two wars yet to come, the last French war and the Revolution."[29]

In the fall of 1745 French raids from their stronghold at Fort St. Frédéric on New England and New York intensified. Lieutenant Colonel Michel Marin, who had arrived at St. Frédéric following the French defeat at Louisbourg, headed a party of 509 regulars and Indians in a late November attack on Saratoga. The village was burned and 109 prisoners were taken. On the return trip the French also burned the trading post of John Lydius at the "Great Carrying Place." Lydius subsequently went to Boston to plead for military action against the French at Fort St. Frédéric. Although Governor Shirley of Massachusetts formulated plans for an assault on St. Frédéric, nothing came of the plans in the immediate period. Large-scale raids continued in 1746 and 1747 from Fort St. Frédéric, but no English expedition ever materialized.

France and England in 1748 signed the Treaty of Aix-la-Chapelle which ended the war. Louisbourg was returned to the French while the northern boundaries along Lake Champlain and Lake George remained unclear. Fort St. Frédéric remained a French stronghold with troops periodically camped as far south as Lake George. The Iroquois were quite displeased with the performance of their English allies but valued the trade with them enough to maintain the alliance. In his letter to the governor of Canada on May 9, 1749, Governor Shirley protested French settlers at Fort St. Frédéric as an intrusion on English territory.[30] The French response was to send the army out with lead plaques to be installed along the frontier that France recognized.

Fort St. Frédéric remained the bastion of French strength in the lake valleys. In the summer of 1749, Peter Kalm, a Swedish professor traveling in North America, described the French fortress: "The fort is built on a rock, consisting of black-lime or slate. . .It is nearly square, has high, thick walls made of the same limestone. . .On the eastern part of the fort, is a high tower, which is proof against bomb-shells, provided with very thick and substantial walls, and well stored with cannon from the bottom almost to the very top."[31]

Governor George Clinton of New York in 1750 sent an observer to size up the fort. Captain Benjamin Stoddard noted ramparts and bastions, high thick stone walls, a dry ditch with a drawbridge and a subterranean passage to the lake, and a citadel "four story high each turned with arches, mounts twenty pieces of cannon and swivels. . .The walls of the citadel are about ten foot thick the roof high and very taut covered with shingles."[32]

By 1754 the French renewed their raids with an assault on Fort Number 4, the northernmost English settlement near Charlestown, New Hampshire. Subsequent events in 1755 would lead to another planned expedition to capture Fort St. Frédéric. The most involved and bloodiest war with the French and Indians would follow. The stage was set for the final showdown in North America.

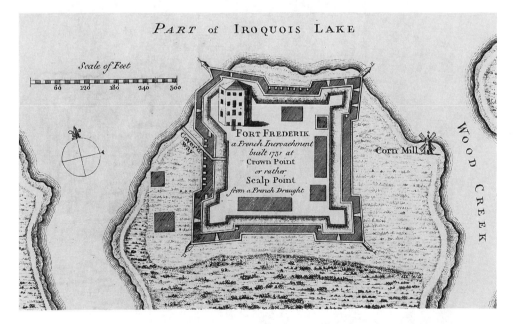

Early drawing of Fort St. Frédéric at Crown Point showing the four-story citadel.
(Library of Congress)

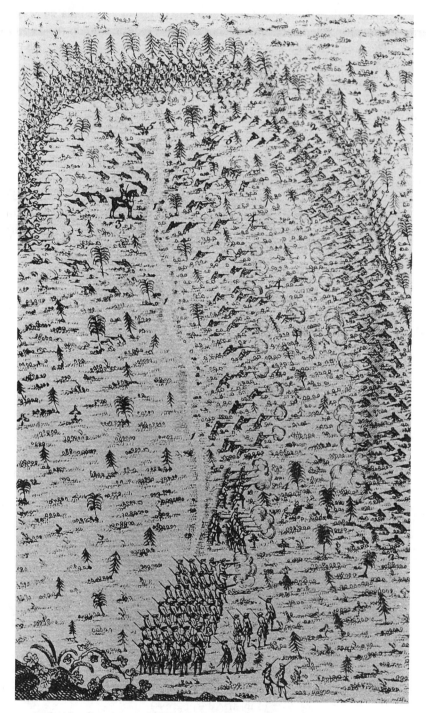

Ambush of troops under Colonel Ephraim Williams on September 8, 1755, from "A Prospective-Plan" by Samuel Blodget. (American Antiquarian Society)

2. Battle of Lake George

AFTER 1750 THE BALANCE OF POWER between Britain and France in North America was undermined by the rapid increase of population in the English colonies. From a quarter million people in 1700, the population of the English colonies soared to 1.2 million by 1750. Population pressure led to the formation of land companies which began to infringe on territories claimed by the French.

One crucial issue was control of the strategic Ohio Valley which the French considered an essential link between their Canadian and Louisiana territories. The French built a series of forts and trading posts along the Mississippi, Ohio, and St. Lawrence rivers which protected their frontiers. Subsequently, the English land dealers and traders were dislodged from the Ohio Valley by the French, and Fort Duquesne was established at the junction of the Ohio, Allegheny, and Monongahela rivers (modern-day Pittsburgh). George Washington, then a 22-year-old lieutenant colonel in the Virginia militia, was dispatched in 1754 to reinforce British claims in the area. With only 300 men at a hastily constructed entrenchment called Fort Necessity, following heavy rains, Washington was forced to surrender to a larger French detachment, leaving the valley in the control of the French.

That same year a congress was called at Albany, attended by delegates from seven colonies, to establish a collective plan for the impending war and to win the Iroquois Nation to the British side. Neither objective, however, was met despite a well-conceived plan by Benjamin Franklin. By late 1754 decisions leading to an ultimate confrontation in America would be made in London and Paris with the assignment of several thousand troops to North America by each side. A conference of governors called in April 1755 by Major General Edward Braddock, the British commander-in-chief, endorsed plans to oust the French from Forts Duquesne, Niagara, St. Frédéric, and Beauséjour (Nova Scotia).

General Braddock, a 60-year-old professional officer, would initiate the first part of the plan by leading troops to capture Fort Duquesne, while Governor William Shirley of Massachusetts was to attack Fort Niagara on Lake Ontario (north of present-day Buffalo). The latter campaign, which was to advance through Oswego, New York (southeast shore of Lake Ontario), would cut communications between Canada and the French forts and settlements in the west. The assignment to lead the militia to Lake George and Lake

Champlain would go to William Johnson, a New York entrepreneur who held the rank of colonel in the Albany County militia. Last, the leadership of the Acadian (Nova Scotia) expedition would be given to an experienced regular officer, Lieutenant Colonel Robert Monckton.

The opening campaign under Braddock began on June 10 with a long, slow march of regular and provincial soldiers to Fort Duquesne. Although Lieutenant Colonel Thomas Gage led a party of advance troops, Braddock's army was surprised and ambushed by French troops and Indians on July 9, 1755, just before reaching its objective. The panic-stricken British forces, not accustomed to forest warfare, were annihilated by French troops and Indians hidden in the brush and trees. The valiant Braddock had four horses shot from under him before he fell with a mortal wound. Colonel George Washington, a militia aide to Braddock, had two horses shot from under him and four musket balls tear through his clothes. Governor Shirley's oldest son, also an aide to Braddock, was not as lucky and died in the battle. The ensuing war for control of the colonial empires in America, later called the French and Indian War (often dated from 1754-1763), would be the North American phase of the Seven Years' War (1756-1763).

Following the death of Braddock, Governor William Shirley was commissioned the commander-in-chief of all British and provincial forces in North America. Governor Shirley, a major force in the Louisbourg campaign of King George's War (1744-1748), was a lawyer by profession without formal military training. Although Shirley's contribution to colonial politics and military campaigns would later be recognized by historians, his handling of financial matters would be highly criticized. Shirley's personal fortunes increased in wartime, with additional patronage distributed among his supporters in the colonial legislature. War created an abundance of military commissions, supply contracts, credit, and hard currency in colonial America.[1] Ultimately, this would prove the undoing of Shirley with his recall to England in 1756 under suspicion of misconduct. Audits of his financial embroilments would not be settled until 1763.

Shirley's Niagara campaign of 1755 never proceeded farther than Oswego. Departing with a smaller force than planned, Shirley's troops became bogged down with short provisions and an expected attack of French troops from Fort Frontenac which lay across the lake from Oswego. Shirley, tragically, suffered the loss of a second son in the 1755 campaign with the death of Captain John Shirley at Oswego due to disease. The campaign under Monckton in Acadia, however, achieved its objectives. Unfortunately for the Acadians, thousands were forcibly deported from their homes.

The expedition sent to Lake George and Lake Champlain under William Johnson would have the only real military success of 1755. Although Johnson, like many other militia officers, had no military training, he had successfully worked with the Iroquois during King George's War and had been appointed Colonel of the Six Nations in April 1755. Since the expedition would take place in the colony of New York, Johnson's appointment as a major general of the Massachusetts militia by Governor Shirley would assure cooperation from the New Yorkers. His commission stated that the army under his command was "to be employed in an attempt to erect a strong fortress upon an eminence near the French fort at Crown Point, and for removing the encroachments of the French on His Majesty's land there."[2] Second-in-command, Phineas Lyman, a major general in the Connecticut militia, was actually a Yale-educated lawyer who also had no formal military training. The 39-year-old Lyman was an energetic and competent politician who founded one of Connecticut's first law schools at his home in Suffield. Despite his business and scholarly background, Lyman would prove to be an effective officer under fire. The lack of experience by Johnson and Lyman, however, was compensated for by a number of seasoned officers who served in King George's War and the siege of Louisbourg in 1745.

Since this was to be an expedition of colonial or provincial troops, the colonial governments solicited volunteers to join the foray to liberate Lake Champlain from the French. Connecticut raised 1,000 men, New Hampshire 500, Rhode Island 400, Massachusetts 1,200, and New York provided 500 and paid for 300 troops supplied by Connecticut.[3] By June many of the colonial militia began to assemble near Albany. After a review of the troops by Governor Shirley and General Johnson in early July, Phineas Lyman with a contingent of New Englanders tried to clear a wagon trail for the rest of the army to the north over the rugged terrain. The Lyman party, battling mosquitoes and black flies, alternatively moved supplies by river in bateaux and on land, advancing about 50 miles to a sharp bend in the Hudson River called the "Great Carrying Place" or portage.

At the portage Lyman began construction of a rudimentary fort called Fort Lyman that would later (September 21, 1755) be named Fort Edward by Willam Johnson after the grandson of the British king. By August 14, Johnson, with the rest of the army, had managed to reach the camp at the portage with additional supplies, bateaux, and artillery.* Johnson, upon arrival, ordered a halt to construction of a road to Wood Creek on Lake Champlain. After a council of war with the militia officers, a new road, far more practical than the Wood Creek route, was started to Lake George. At the end of August the provincial army had grown to 3,100, with 250 Indians and 21 pieces of artillery.

In all probability, the most essential piece of equipment for the expedition to successfully reach Fort St. Frédéric at Crown Point was the bateau. The bateau was the workhorse of the military during the French and Indian War, the American Revolution, and was even used during the War of 1812 on Lake Champlain. Provisions and light military supplies were often moved by bateaux, but their most important function was to carry troops. The typical bateau on Lake George during this period was 25-35 feet long and held approximately 22 soldiers with provisions. The vessel was a flat-bottomed, double-ended boat with oak frames (ribs) and bottoms of pine planks. While the vessels were usually rowed or perhaps poled in the shallow water, sails were improvised if the wind was blowing in the right direction. One or two "steersman" would control the direction of the bateau from the stern by use of a long sweep (oar). Later British and provincial expeditions on Lake George (1758) would mark each bateau with a regimental number. The origin of the bateau remains somewhat of a mystery. Apparently, English colonists did not bring the flat-bottomed construction from England. However, as early as Queen Anne's War (1702-1713), the colonials were constructing bateaux in the Mohawk Valley. Six hundred bateaux were built in Albany in

---

* At Fort Lyman one lingering squabble concerned the campfollowers or prostitutes who had trailed the Rhode Island and New York regiments from Albany. While this was a typical occurrence with armies of the period, some officers were particularly worried about the consequences of "immoralities." Major General Lyman wrote to Johnson complaining that "I perceive that there is a number of women coming up with the York forces and Rhode Island which gives a great uneasiness to ye New England troops."[4] On July 27 Johnson wrote from Albany to Lyman regarding the "bad women" in camp, "I hope we shall not soil the Justice of our Cause with a Conduct rebellious against that Almighty Power upon whose Favour depends the Success of all human Enterprises."[5] The issue reached a turning point at the council of war on August 18. Lyman made a motion that all the "Women in the Camp should be removed from the same and forbid to return."[6] Several days later they were sent off to Albany.

1711 alone. The name implies a French origin, but there is evidence that the influence was actually Dutch. The French, in any event, used "light batteaux" in the 1666 expedition on Lake Champlain.[7]

The Dutch controlled the Hudson River from its date of discovery in 1609 until 1674. The first permanent settlement in 1624, Fort Orange (later Albany), was Dutch. Dutch boatbuilders had developed vessels strikingly similar to the Lake George bateaux nearly two centuries earlier for the fishing trade in Europe. Albany was still essentially a Dutch community when hundreds of bateaux were constructed during the years of the French and Indian War.[8] The Lake George bateau construction is well documented with archaeological surveys in 1960, 1965, and 1987 (see chapter 4).

In 1755 each colony except New Hampshire brought bateaux with them to Albany, but the inadequate number and size forced construction of several hundred additional vessels in Albany. In fact, carpenters were summoned from as far as Boston to build the bateaux. In early September Johnson ordered at least 200 bateaux from Fort Lyman. However, the lack of a sufficient number of wagons to carry bateaux to Lake George was one of the factors that ultimately compromised the expedition's goal to capture Crown Point.

By August 28, 1755, Johnson, with 1,500 troops and 40 Indians, had reached the virgin shores of Lake St. Sacrement, the first sizable English force to ever reach the lake. Johnson, an astute politician, promptly changed the name to Lake George, after King George, and sent word of his action to Britain. While the army was busy cutting down all the trees around the camp, the teamsters were hauling supplies needed for the expedition. On September 4 and 5 the army began construction of a storehouse and "Laid out the foart" at Lake George.[9]

According to Johnson, the army immediately faced problems at the lake. The hired wagon drivers threatened to leave the army unless they had more guards to protect them along the crude road from Fort Lyman. Johnson complained that the wagoners discarded cannonballs, plundered provisions, and deserted; "in short they are a set of great Rascals."[10]

The New York and Connecticut companies threatened to leave the army unless they were paid. Johnson, presuming that they would have no place to spend it at the lake, had originally agreed to defer payment until the troops returned. The troops had other ideas which caused Johnson to quickly dispatch a request for the compensation to be sent to Lake George. Johnson repeatedly expressed his disappointment with his men: "the Troops & the officers with few Exceptions a set of low lifed Ignorant people, the Men lazy, easily discouraged by Difficulties."[11] On top of this he suspected an officer of conspiring with one of his soldiers to sell rum to the Indians. At the council of war on September 5, Johnson informed the officers that his orders had not been obeyed since "Rum was constantly and plentifully sold to the Indians who were in great numbers daily made Drunk."[12]

Meanwhile at Fort St. Frédéric, the French with the knowledge of the approach of the British expeditionary force were not idle. Baron de Dieskau, born in the German duchy of Saxony, prepared to intercept the provincial army. The 54-year-old Dieskau was the most experienced professional soldier in the northern theater. In August General Dieskau had arrived in Montreal and without delay proceeded to Fort St. Frédéric. He had examined the captured papers of the defeated Braddock which outlined the British plan to take Fort St. Frédéric. By late August, Dieskau had an army of 774 regulars, Canadian militia and colonial troops of 1,585, artillerymen of 67, and nearly 700 Indians at Crown Point.[13] In quick order, the General mounted an expedition to cut the supply lines of the intruders.

Indian scouts brought an English prisoner to Dieskau while the French were camped at Carillon (Ticonderoga).* The prisoner skillfully fabricated a story that only 500 men were at Fort Lyman with the remaining provincial force retreating back to Albany.

Based on this information and other considerations, Dieskau left a sizable portion of his troops, estimated by the Canadian governor at more than 1,800 men, at Carillon. Dieskau would later suggest that the small size of his expeditionary force was needed to move swiftly through the wilderness. In addition, a lack of provisions and the fact that the British had

Sir William Johnson.
(New York State Library, Albany)

King Hendrick, Mohawk Chief.
(Albany Institute of History and Art)

only colonial militia who were "the worst troops on the face of the earth" helped make the decision to leave so many troops at Carillon.[14] Dieskau embarked with 600 Indians, 680 Canadians, and 220 regulars on September 4 to surprise the troops at Fort Lyman, according to the second-in-command of the expedition, Adjutant General M. de Montreuil.[15] One hundred twenty troops were left to guard the vessels at South Bay while the main force

* Carillon translates to a chime of bells which was probably derived from the cascade of water at the outlet of Lake George in present-day Ticonderoga. Ticonderoga was the Indian name for the noise of falling waters. Other derivations of Ticonderoga include the Iroquois term for two rivers flowing into each other and the place of rocks dividing the water.

followed an Indian trail toward Fort Lyman. The French camped less than four miles from the fort.

On the afternoon of September 7, Johnson received information from Indian scouts of the French advance. One wagoner, Jacob Adams, volunteered to warn the garrison at Fort Lyman, while a makeshift breastwork of logs and stumps was hurriedly constructed at Lake George by the soldiers. After a brief meeting, many of the other hired wagon drivers, apprehensive over the imminent attack, bolted from the camp without notice and headed for Fort Lyman with their wagons.

The messenger sent by Johnson, unfortunately, was tortured and killed. Some of the other wagon drivers who had also been captured apparently provided Dieskau with an accurate account of the provincial forces. Still confident of victory, the French general gave orders to attack Fort Lyman the next morning. The Caughnawaga Indians with Dieskau, however, absolutely refused to move against the fort, which influenced the Algonquin and Abenaki Indians to take the same stance. The main issue concerning the Indians was the probability of facing cannon at the fort. Many of them had seen a single cannonball cut a tree in half or smash down a wall and were sure the English had a great many cannon there. While they would not attack the fort, they agreed to assault Johnson's camp at the lake even though by this time they were aware of the actual forces there. The Indians suggested to Dieskau that they were unwilling to attack Fort Lyman along the Hudson River since it was "on territory rightfully belonging to them," whereas the Lake George camp was on Indian territory.[16]

Nine of the deserting wagoners returned to Johnson's camp with two Indian scouts and two soldiers about midnight. They had heard Adams pleading for mercy, which meant that the garrison at Fort Lyman had not been warned of an impending attack. The next morning, September 8, a council of war voted to detach 1,000 men and 200 Indians to intercept the enemy retreating from the presumed attack on the garrison at Fort Lyman. The 1,000 troops were sent under the command of Colonel Ephraim Williams of Deerfield, Massachusetts, and 200 Indians under King Hendrick, the 75-year-old Mohawk chief.* The provincial soldiers and Indians departed between eight and nine o'clock in the morning, anticipating the French to be close to Fort Lyman about 13 miles away. But Dieskau, learning of the provincial advance from his scouts, had deployed his forces in the shape of a hook along both sides of the rough road that connected Lake George to Fort Lyman. Williams' troops had only gone three to four miles from the base camp when they found themselves in a French trap along a ravine formed by French Mountain. Williams had not sent out scouts, even though Braddock's army a month earlier in Pennsylvania had been similarly ambushed in a heavily wooded area.

King Hendrick paused to inform Williams that he had scented Indians. Soon musket fire by the Indians pierced the silence. Dieskau was enraged that the Indians had sprung the ambuscade too quickly, convinced that the Caughnawaga (Iroquois nation) had purposely fired early (reportedly in the air) to warn their relatives among the Mohawk.[18] Dieskau had harbored negative feelings toward the Iroquois from the beginning. Following the battle at Lake George, he wrote to the governor of Canada, M. de Vaudreuil, "I

---

* The old, heavily scarred leader of the Mohawk was the most influencial of Johnson's Indians among the Iroquois. King Hendrick was born a Mohican Indian in Westfield, Massachusetts, around 1680 and served as a warrior, statesman, and preacher. Hendrick was one of the four Mohawk chiefs who went with Peter Schuyler to England in 1710.[17]

prophecied to you, Sir, that the Iroquois would play some scurvy trick; It is unfortunate for me that I am such a good prophet."[19] The Massachusetts troops were nearly in the trap when the entire French force opened fire from behind trees and bushes. The musket fire, pouring in from an unseen enemy, devastated the ranks of the provincial troops. Hendrick had a horse shot from under him and was bayoneted by a French grenadier. Williams, at the head of his regiment, tried gallantly to rally the militia but was swiftly cut down with a shot through the head.* The provincial troops soon fell into a panic, wildly retreating back to the lake. Lieutenant Colonel Nathan Whiting now assumed command of the troops and established some defense as they retreated. The sounds of heavy gunfire were heard at the Lake George camp an hour and a half after Williams' detachment had left. The camp immediately "beat to arms"; as the fire came closer, Johnson sent Lieutenant Colonel Edward Cole of Rhode Island with 300 men to cover the retreat of the detachment. The provincial force retreated to a small pond about two miles from the Lake George camp where they made a brief stand before continuing their retreat to the lake. At ten o'clock the vanguard of the surviving troops under Whiting began to rejoin Johnson's army at Lake George.

Hearing the musket fire coming closer and closer, the soldiers at Lake George continued to prepare for the oncoming French assault by desperately adding wagons and bateaux to their rudimentary barricade of logs and stumps. Several field pieces and heavy cannon were put in place behind the breastwork with one field piece placed in a strategic position on the high ground of the left flank. The onslaught was slowed, however, as the Indians stopped to scalp the dead, disobeying Dieskau's order to postpone scalping until the provincials had been defeated. The French commander's plan was to follow the retreating provincials closely, rushing with them into Johnson's camp in the confusion of the returning detachment. However, as the Indians and Canadians approached the breastwork, a few cannonades sent them scurrying for cover. According to Johnson, the French regulars appeared in sight before noon "and marched along the road in very regular order directly upon our center: They made a small halt about 150 yards from our breastwork, when the regular troops (whom we judged to be such by their bright and fixed bayonets) made the grand and center attack."[20] The Indians and Canadians beseeched Dieskau for time to rest and care for their wounded before assaulting the provincial entrenchment. But Dieskau was undeterred in his strategy. The Indians pleaded, "Father! you have lost your reason—listen to us!"[21] But Dieskau was intent on seizing the moment to crush the provincials. Some of the Indians with Dieskau belonged to the same Iroquois Confederacy, as did the Mohawk with Johnson, which may account for some of their reluctance in the fight.

By noon the renewed battle heated up. Behind the rough barricade, the provincial troops, untested under fire, grew panicky upon hearing the Indian war whoops and musket fire. The rout of the Williams' detachment had likewise unsettled the fresh recruits. The retreating Williams' detachment passed through the fresh troops causing the men at the

---

*In Albany preceding the campaign to Lake George, Ephraim Williams wrote a will bequeathing his land to the town of Williamstown, Massachusetts, with the condition that the money would be used for the establishment of a free school. The school, incorporated in 1773, adopted the name of Williams College in 1793. After the Battle of Lake George, the body of the 41-year-old Williams was hidden by his men to prevent mutilation. Later he was buried by the side of the military road four miles from Lake George at a site marked by a large irregular stone (west side of Route 9 today). In 1854 Williams College alumni erected a marble monument to mark the location where Colonel Williams had been shot (east side of Route 9).

barricades to turn and run after them. General Phineas Lyman of Connecticut ordered the officers to stop them. When the troops did not respond, Lyman himself ran after them, ordering one soldier "to the front and march up and defend it or I would kill him in a minute. . .they all marched back and the fight came on right before me."[22] With brave resolution Dieskau advanced against the provincials who, in the main, held their ground. Captain William Eyre, the director of artillery, used grapeshot, mortar, and cannon effectively to keep the camp from being overrun by the French. The Canadians and Indians besieged the provincials in a disorganized fashion from the woods. This left the frontal assault to the vastly outnumbered French regulars. Johnson, while directing operations early in the battle, received a musket ball in the "fleshy part of his thigh" and later retired to his tent for at least part of the battle.[23] General Lyman, however, aggressively guided the provincial recruits throughout the entire conflagration. The French advance of regulars, firing by platoons in a line six across, was brought to a halt far from the breastwork.

The blast of cannon and bellow of musket fire became persistent. The cannon fire was actually heard in distant Saratoga. Thomas Williams, a Massachusetts surgeon and brother of Colonel Ephraim Williams, described the battle as "the most awful day my eyes ever beheld. . .there seemed to be nothing but thunder & lightning & perpetual pillars of smoke."[24] The cannon fire finally forced the grenadiers to seek shelter behind trees and stumps. Mortar bombs lobbed into the position of the Indians on the flanks also caused them to pull back further. The casualties, however, were mounting on both sides after several hours of devastating fire that had raked both armies. As the wounded provincial troops were carried back from the breastworks, even some of the heretofore uncommitted wagoners stepped foward with muskets to continue the fight.

In an effort to revitalize his troops, Dieskau apparently risked exposure and was subsequently wounded through the leg a short distance from the provincial lines. Dieskau's adjutant, Pierre Andre de Montreuil, despite a musketball to his own arm, washed Dieskau's wound with brandy. Dieskau, however, was hit again in the leg. Two Canadians were called to rescue him, but one was killed immediately. At this point, Dieskau refused to be moved and was propped up against a tree where he ordered Montreuil to organize a final assault on the provincial entrenchment.

By five o'clock the French forces had been shattered while the provincials were flush with self-confidence. The provincial troops and Indians leaped over the breastworks and rushed the French, sending them dashing in retreat; "our men sprang over the breastwork and followed them like lions and made terrible havoc and soon brought arms full of guns, laced hats, cartridge boxes."[25] Many of the French were slaughtered and a number of prisoners were taken in the turbulent withdrawal. In the ensuing havoc, General Dieskau was left behind. An advancing provincial soldier pointed his musket at Dieskau, while the French general gestured wildly not to shoot. But the soldier, apparently thinking that Dieskau might have a pistol, fired a shot that "traversed both my hips."[26] The provincial soldier who had emigrated from Canada spoke French to Dieskau. Dieskau shouted, "You rascal, why did you fire at me? You see a man lying on the ground bathed in his blood, and you fire, eh?"[27] Eight provincial soldiers finally carried Dieskau to a cot in Johnson's tent.

A party of Canadians and Indians, who had earlier left the battle scene, were busy looting and scalping the dead provincial troops near the scene of the morning ambush of Williams' men when a detachment of 120 New Hampshire and 90 New York troops from Fort Lyman surprised them. A deadly fight resulted in the remnants of Dieskau's force retreating to their bateaux at South Bay. Tradition has it that many of the Canadian and Indian bodies where thrown into the pond since named "Bloody Pond" located on Route 9 today.

According to Johnson, the whole engagement and pursuit by the provincial troops had ended by seven o'clock. The wounds of Johnson and Dieskau were attended to by surgeons in Johnson's tent. While in the tent that evening, a group of Mohawk quarreled with the provincial commander. When they departed, Dieskau inquired about the wishes of the Indians. Johnson retorted that they wanted him to turn over his prisoner "in order to burn

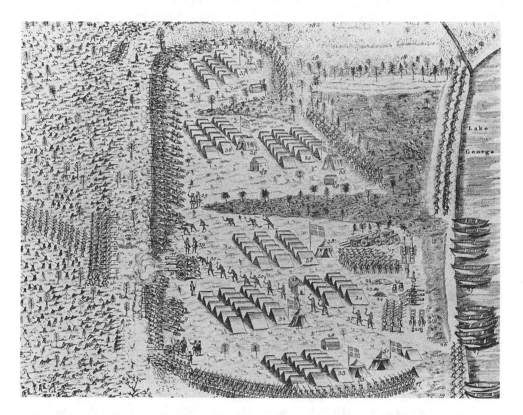

"A Prospective-Plan" of the Battle of Lake George, September 8, 1755, by Samuel Blodget. Blodget was an eyewitness to the battle who first published the "Plan" in Boston in 1755 with the engraving by Thomas Johnston. The "Plan" was republished in London the following year by Thomas Jeffreys. (American Antiquarian Society)

you in revenge for the death of their comrades."[28] Dieskau was obviously relieved that their wishes were not accommodated. Johnson assigned a detachment of 50 soldiers and a captain to escort Dieskau to another tent. Despite these steps, an officer barely prevented a Mohawk from stabbing Dieskau the next morning.

The badly wounded Dieskau, shot through the bladder, remained at the Lake George camp until September 16. A mutual respect developed between the rival commanders.

Johnson referred to Dieskau as "a man of Quality, a soldier & a Gentleman."[29] Later Johnson had the French general stay at his own house where he was cared for by his sister whose husband had been killed at Lake George. Dieskau, writing in October from Albany, expressed "gratitude which I owe for all your kind favors."[30]

The number of losses suffered by both sides has been subject to wide variation in different accounts. Johnson's initial report of the battle gave the provincial loss at 130 killed and 60 wounded with the French casualties at 500-600 men.[31] However, Thomas Williams, the camp surgeon, reported 216 provincials buried and 96 wounded with 400-500 French losses, while the French reported a loss of 132 killed and 400 wounded.[32] The wounded often died of convulsions or shock from amputations as the large, lead musket balls made devastating injuries. In addition, the musket balls found in the bullet pouches of the dead French soldiers were thought to be poisoned with copper and yellow arsenic. The lack of modern medicines further jeopardized recovery.

According to Seth Pomeroy, a provincial lieutenant colonel, the day after the battle the army began "ye malencoly work of burring our Dead."[33] The grisly burials continued for three days after the engagement. At the same time the Indians were busy scalping those killed on the French side, "already near 70, and were employed after the battle last night, and all this afternoon, in bringing in scalps; and great numbers of French and Indians yet left unscalped," Johnson reported on September 9.[34] The practice of scalping became widespread during the French and Indian War since the French offered bounties for British scalps while the British raised the ante by offering bounties for both French and Indian scalps. Rather than bring back live prisoners, it was more efficient to bring back scalps tied to a belt. The economic incentive, though, created short cuts for the Indians. A good-sized scalp could be cut and trimmed by the Indians to produce two or even three scalps.

Some of the provincials engaged in looting the enemy bodies before burial. It was a common practice to loot bodies of the enemy since the only safe place to carry one's possessions or money was on oneself. Surprisingly, the French supplies included British muskets that the French had taken after Braddock's defeat in Pennsylvania. The belongings collected from the French bodies, however, were never distributed to the men. The Mohawk Indians had gotten most of it and departed rapidly from Johnson's camp.

Rather than the army being buoyed by the victory over the French, the camp at Lake George was described by Seth Pomeroy as "a Meloncolly Place [with] So many of our near Frinds taken away."[35] Shortly thereafter, Pomeroy fell ill and noted that sickness was prevalent in the camp. Nine days after the engagement, Johnson observed that, "our sick daily increase."[36] After ten days there were so many sick that wagonloads of men were sent home. The troops at Lake George were not seasoned regulars of the British army, but fresh recruits from small villages across New England who had never experienced the emotional impact of the conflagration of battle. By October 20, the minutes of the council of war indicated that nearly one third of the army was "Sick and unfit for duty their spirits Exhausted ."[37]

Part of the malaise of the army was probably caused by the death of relatives and friends in the battle. Colonial militia were often composed of neighbors and family members. The saddest task was to write home of the loss. Surgeon Williams' letter to his wife unhappily reported the death of his brother Ephraim as well as the severe wounding of his brother Josiah. Seth Pomeroy also had the heavyhearted duty to write his sister-in-law of his brother Daniel's death in the engagement.

The main mission of the army was to drive the French from Crown Point. Although there were still two hours of daylight after the main engagement had ended on September 8, Johnson did not allow the army to pursue the retreating French, nor did he attempt to intercept them the following day. Johnson had the army remain at Lake George since Dieskau indicated that the French had more troops nearby, there was a lack of information about the total size of the French forces at Fort St. Frédéric, there were insufficient bateaux to transport troops, and sickness and exhaustion pervaded the provincial troops. After the defeat at Lake George, the French retreated to their camp at Ticonderoga by September 11. Dieskau's second-in-command, Pierre Andre de Montreuil, was left in charge of the French troops there. M. de Rigaud Vaudreuil, governor of New France, ordered a fort to be built at Ticonderoga. The work on the four-bastioned fortress under the inexperienced Canadian engineer, Michel de Lotbinière, continued for the rest of the season.* French officers were later critical of the fort since it was located too far from the narrows of the lake, which later required the building of a redoubt or second small fort closer to the water.

William Johnson's decision to remain at Lake George and construct a fort renewed a smoldering conflict between Johnson and William Shirley, the Massachusetts governor and commander of all the British forces in North America. In a letter to Lieutenant Governor Thomas Pownall of New Jersey before the Lake George engagement, Johnson complained that Shirley had the "Insolence of a man drunk with power, envenomed by Malice and burning with Revenge — his Arguments are weak and confused they bear the evident marks of Passion overruling reason — he asserts facts notoriously false."[39]

Apparently, the dispute originated over Shirley's negative representation of Johnson to some of the Indians and a conflict over Johnson's appointment by General Braddock as the sole Superintendent of Indian Affairs. Shirley was upset over Johnson's failure to provide 100 Indians to escort him to Oswego and his unhappiness with Johnson's progress in attacking Crown Point. When Johnson refused to send the Indians to guide Shirley to Oswego, Shirley commissioned John Lydius, owner of the trading post at the "Great Carrying Place" (Fort Lyman). The appointment of Lydius infuriated Johnson, who considered him a duplicitous character. When Johnson wrote his long, detailed report to Shirley on September 9 of the engagement at Lake George, he sent duplicate letters to the governors of the colonies but did not directly send the letter to Shirley. Apparently, Shirley received a copy of the letter in New York sent to the lieutenant governor of Massachusetts, Spencer Phips, with instructions "to despatch a copy of this letter to General Shirley; my time and circumstances won't permit my writing to him immediately."[40] The letter was an interesting summary of the events of September 8, but omitted any credit to General Lyman of Connecticut for his part in the battle.

Although Shirley urged that the French be driven from Ticonderoga, Johnson was not inclined to move northward with the army. General Lyman and others, however, wanted to get on with the expedition while the French were disorganized. Johnson's immediate plans included building a fort at the site of the camp at Lake George. The type of fort, however, became a debatable point among the men at the lake. At the council of war on September 14, Johnson and Captain William Eyre, the chief engineer, pushed for a strong fortification with earthen bastions, but temporarily yielded to the wishes of the other officers who wanted

* Lotbinière made a fortune on Fort Carillon with a franchise on the profitable canteen, the only entertainment for the garrison. Lotbinière also profited by using teams of horses that he owned to haul sand for the mortar.[38]

a simple picketed fort of logs. Their decision was based on the views of the officers and troops who had "an Aversion to digging."[41]

In subsequent letters from Lake George, Johnson complained of the "Obstinacy and Ignorance" of the officers regarding the issue of a more elaborate fort and the "averseness of Labour" of the troops building it.[42] Upon hearing of the fort, General Shirley immediately wrote to Johnson, disagreeing with the project; "the Fort, you design to build at the End of the Lake will be of little or no utility for carrying on another Expedition," and in a second letter, "I can by no means adopt your engineer's opinion of the urgent necessity of immediately erecting a strong fort at Lake George."[43] Johnson, however, simply ignored Shirley's opinion.

Before he made any move, Johnson would call a council of war with his officers. In this respect, the provincial army was run somewhat democratically, if not efficiently. On September 22, 1755, Johnson called a council of war in his tent to seek his officers' opinions on proceeding toward Crown Point. The unanimous opinion of the officers advised Johnson to arrange to proceed as soon as reinforcements and provisions arrived. Shortly thereafter (September 25), Shirley again wrote to Johnson, telling him to send General Lyman against the French army at Ticonderoga if Johnson himself couldn't go. On the 27th, one soldier was put in confinement for stating that the expedition to Crown Point would not go forward that year since General Johnson had stopped General Lyman from proceeding. On September 30 Johnson ordered his aide, Captain Peter Wraxall, to deliver to the governors of the colonies the minutes of the council of war and other reports in order to seek advice regarding proceeding with the expedition. Upon hearing of the materials sent to the governors, Shirley criticized the action on October 14 since by the time all the opinions were gathered by Johnson it would be "the End of November which will be Extreamly late for me to send you Directions."[44]

There were many reasons for Johnson's hesitancy. The musket ball that wounded Johnson in what was diplomatically called "the thigh" had never been extracted and continued to bother him. By early October Johnson was stricken "By a violent Inflamation in my head and ear, I have been for some days mostly confined to my bed wholly to my tent." He was "bled, blistered and purged" which did not alleviate the illness, for good reason.[45] Obviously, his personal illness, which confined him to his tent for nearly three weeks along with the sickness among the troops, affected his judgment to proceed north.

One major problem for the expedition was the failure to bring the bateaux from Fort Edward (called Fort Lyman until September 24). By the end of October there were only 85 fit for service at the lake. More importantly, the artillery boats that Johnson ordered built in September had never been completed. Two days before the September 8 battle, Private James Hill from Newbury, Massachusetts, had been assigned to cut timber for "Flabots" that were "about 40 feet Long and to ro With 20 oars, to Cairee the artillere."[46] At the end of September, although he had ordered 100 carpenters to work on the scows or flat-bottomed boats, not one had been finished.

Since the report on the failure to finish the vessels was included in the council of war minutes sent to the governors, the issue of the vessels became an additional point of concern for the governors who wanted to know why they weren't finished. By early October Stephen Webster, the captain of the carpenters, formally replied to Johnson. Webster maintained that the problem was Johnson's orders to build the fort, which left the garrison without enough carpenters to construct the boats. However, one vessel was completed, two partly caulked, and another had been half-built. On October 22 Johnson wrote to the governor of New York that he had renewed the orders for work to continue on the artillery scows. What these vessels actually looked like is not quite certain. However, a detailed set of instructions for a large "float" had been sent by John Dies, a ship outfitter from New York City, to Johnson in late August. Dies proposed a vessel with a bottom of "squared loggs 8 or nine inches thick,. . .trunnel'd together, the sides of this flatt should be Raisd, high Enough for a Breast work to Cover the Men with portholes cut. . . Mount Some of your Field Pieces, Man'd with 40 or 50 men."[47] Variants of this type of vessel would later be called a radeau or floating battery. The radeau was a wide, partially enclosed floating barge with both sails and oars, mounting heavy guns which would be used in defense of a fleet of bateaux (see chapter 4).

Johnson's own hesitancy to proceed was reflected in his perception of the circumstances at Lake George. By late September he noted that most of the troops wanted to return home. He also worried about the adequacy of provisions, complaining that the reinforcements, especially from Connecticut, ate the provisions as fast as the wagons delivered them, which would handicap an advance to Ticonderoga or Crown Point. With his Indian scouts drifting away, troops still weary from the September engagement, the inadequacy of supply wagons, and the near universal insubordination at Lake George, Johnson had a multitude of reasons for not pressing north. Following the advice of Governor Charles Hardy of New York to make an effort to proceed or at least give the appearance of proceeding, Johnson, sensing the loss of resolution of the army after many delays, called a council of war on October 9. General Lyman presided since Johnson was still sick in his tent at the time. Johnson's charge to the council was whether the army should move against the French and if the advice were in the negative, the reasons should be given for not moving. The council was "Unanimously of Opinion that in the present Circumstances of this Army an immediate attempt upon Tionderogo. . . is not adviseable." The reasons were "The Want of sufficient Number of Men and sufficient Quantity of Provisions."[48] They also suggested that the work cease on the flat-bottomed boats in order to finish the fort. At the time there were about 3,600 men at the lake, 500 at Fort Edward, and 2,500 recruits in Albany or in transit.

Nine days later Johnson asked for a council of war to consider sending a detachment to attack the French at the northern end of Lake George. Lyman again presided over the council, which postponed consideration on the detachment until further scouting reports and deferred Johnson's request to proceed with building more of the flat-bottomed boats. On the 20th, the council with Lyman presiding, again answered Johnson's question about proceeding with the expedition by voting in the negative because of a lack of supplies, the danger of ice, and the sickness of the army. Essentially, Johnson was pressing for an answer on proceeding to Crown Point from the council that he already knew would be negative due to the lost initiative and lateness of the season. He was, in effect, using the council to transfer the criticism for the inaction of the army onto their shoulders.

While the army vacillated at the lake, two Indian scouts mistakenly reported a large French army on the east side of the Narrows. Captain Robert Rogers and his Rangers, on the other hand, put the French at Ticonderoga. Johnson, panicky over an impending French attack, wrote to Shirley on November 11, asking that the reinforcements at Albany be sent up with all possible dispatch. Rogers was correct; no attack occurred. Robert Rogers with his New Hampshire volunteers quickly established a reputation for the bravado of their scouting forays into French territory. The first naval engagement on Lake George occurred between Rogers, using bateaux mounting small swivel cannon, and French troops in vessels at Isle of Mutton (Prisoners Island) in the fall of 1755.

After being ignored all during the fall, General Shirley called a council of several governors and provincial officers in Albany on November 17, 1755, which recommended "that the Army under the Command of Major General Johnson, do advance against the Enemy."[49] At the same time the Connecticut troops insisted on their dismissal from the army at the lake. By the 21st of November the minutes of the Albany meeting reached Lake George. Johnson reported the Albany decision was "next to an absolute Order for this Army proceeding forthwith against the Enemy, he would recommend that an attempt be made with the utmost Dispatch and Vigour."[50] The provincial officers were not intimidated,

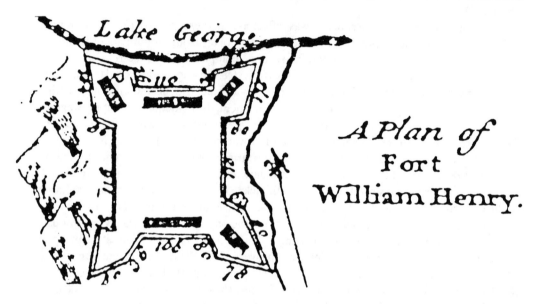

A plan of Fort William Henry, from "A Prospective-Plan" by Samuel Blodget.
(American Antiquarian Society)

voting again not to go forward and adjourned the meeting until the next morning when they would state their reasons. The following morning the officers saved time by referring to the reasons given at the council of war in October. They were, however, able to add cold weather as a new rationale. The next day Johnson wrote a short letter to Shirley informing him that if he ordered the men to go forward, the majority would flatly refuse; the officers and men simply wanted to go home. This ended the 1755 expedition.

The fort, nevertheless, was substantially completed by late fall. At the council of war on September 29, the provincial officers finally had approved Johnson and Eyre's plan for a strong earthern fort that could hold a 500-man garrison. By the beginning of November the four bastions and ramparts were finished, and most of the parapet and magazines were completed, as well as one of the barracks while a second one was nearly ready. Captain Nathaniel Dwight of Belchertown, Massachusetts, noted in his 1755 journal the detailed dimensions of the fort which included a 30-foot thick main wall, two-story barracks, storehouses, magazines, and a large encampment protected by a breastwork lying to the east of the fort.[51] Johnson named Fort William Henry after a grandson of the king. By the middle of the month the artillery was moved to the fort; the two barracks were completed and timber for a third had been cut. Although the mission of challenging Fort St. Frédéric had not occurred in 1755, nonetheless the foothold at Lake George had advanced the British frontier significantly northward.

What happened to the main protagonists in the Lake George battle? After a month's stay in Albany, General Dieskau was sent to New York City where he was further treated for his wounds. Still a prisoner in 1757, he sailed for England where he remained until the end of the war in 1763. Four years after returning to France, he died from the wounds suffered at Lake George. William Johnson, however, received accolades and rewards for his role in the battle. The victory at Lake George, coming after Braddock's fiasco, led Britain to award him the title of baronet, one of only three ever issued to a colonial, and parliament granted him 5,000 pounds for his service. Sir William Johnson was then appointed the Royal Indian Agent and Superintendent of the Six Nations by King George. He would play a prominent role in the years of the French and Indian War as the most competent Indian agent of the British. Phineas Lyman, who never received credit for his role during the battle at Lake George, was to serve with dedication each year of the northern campaigns from 1756-1760, despite more lucrative business and legal opportunities in Connecticut.[52]

The setting in the fall of 1755 of death and destruction on a primitive lake in the wilderness is in odd contrast to the resort that Lake George has become in the twentieth century. In 1755 only bateaux were on the lake, laboriously hauled to this backcountry. If these provincial soldiers could gaze today upon the lake and observe the flotilla of pleasure boats, tour ships, waterskiers, and parasail riders, what would they make of it?

Louis Antoine de Bougainville.
(National Archives)

3. Defeat at Fort William Henry

THE SPRING OF 1756 saw a solidifying of positions in the valleys of Lake George and Lake Champlain. The Crown Point expedition, rekindled in 1756, again failed to move northward, largely due to the problems caused by a change in the commander-in-chief of the British forces in North America. General Shirley's command in June was turned temporarily over to General Daniel Webb and then to General James Abercromby. Sir William Johnson, Lieutenant Governor James De Lancey of New York, and William Pownall, lieutenant governor of New Jersey, had successfully discredited Shirley among their influential friends in England. The new commander-in-chief, John Campell, Earl of Loudoun, was an experienced officer from the British upper class. Lord Loudoun's personal belongings alone virtually filled a whole transport on the voyage to America. In July he arrived in New York with sixteen servants and his mistress.

Loudoun had developed a distrust for Shirley before arriving in the colonies. Upon reaching New York, Loudoun heard additional criticism of inefficiency, profiteering and irregular commission purchases involving Shirley. The problem of insubordination among the provincial officers was, to Loudoun's mind, Shirley's fault. In 1756 Shirley appointed John Winslow, an experienced provincial officer from Massachusetts, as commander of a new expedition against the French position on Lake Champlain. To raise the provincial troops for another Crown Point campaign, Shirley promised that the soldiers would serve within a limited geographical region and solely under the provincial officers who enlisted them.

Shirley had placed limited emphasis on the official "Rules and Articles of War" laid down by the British army. Under these regulations, all provincial officers of company grade would be junior to regular officers of the same rank in the British army. Majors and colonels, for example, would only rank as "eldest captains" when marching with British regular officers. Just before Loudoun had actually taken command, General Abercromby had queried General Winslow, in command of the provincial troops, concerning the integration of the regulars with the provincial army. After a council of war at Fort Edward, Winslow's provincial officers held that any change in the arrangement under which the troops had been raised would end the Crown Point expedition. The officers replied that "it is our opinion that the effect will be a dissolution of the greater part of the army and have a direct tendency to prevent the raising [of] any provincial troops for his majesty's service for the future."[1]

Loudoun, however, intended to firmly place the colonial troops and officers in a subordinate position. Loudoun, meeting with Shirley in late July, blamed him for the insubordination and mutinous conditions that existed among the provincial troops during the period of his service as commander-in-chief. Shirley contacted General Winslow and wrote to Loudoun in an attempt to explain the views of the provincial officers. After arriving at his new headquarters in Albany on July 31, Loudoun summoned General Winslow from Lake George but, not receiving Shirley's earlier ominous letter, Winslow thought the invitation was merely a social call and declined. Loudoun perceived the refusal as evidence of insubordination. A second order to appear caused Winslow and his officers to immediately ride the 60 miles to Albany. Apparently Winslow did not alter his initial viewpoint of the arrangements and purpose of the provincial army. In a reply to a letter written by Loudoun the day after their meeting in Albany, Winslow stated that his officers were willing " to act in conjunction with his majesty's troops. . .so that the terms and conditions agreed upon and established by the several governments to whom they belong and upon which they were raised, be not altered."[2]

While agreeing to follow the orders of Loudoun, as commander-in-chief, Winslow had stood his ground by reasserting the conditions under which the provincial troops had been raised. Not having enough regulars to do without the provincials, Loudoun did not integrate the regulars with the provincials. Winslow remained in command of the troops at Lake George. However, further squabbles with the civil authorities of Albany over quartering troops there and problems with provincial arrangements for supplies compromised any further advance toward the French forts on Lake Champlain. Loudoun finally decided that America was a lawless country without rules, "but rule every man pleases to lay down to himself."[3] These differences would ultimately provide the roots of a rebellion 20 years later. He resolved that the provincial troops were useless and were not to be trusted.

The turning point in the 1756 campaign came during the summer with capitulation of the Oswego garrisons to 3,000 French regulars and 250 Indians. Following a siege, using cannon captured from Braddock a year earlier, nearly 1,600 troops, laborers, and women surrendered at the three Oswego forts. As many as 100 British prisoners were butchered by the Indians before the French troops intervened, a portent of the massacre to come at Fort William Henry in 1757. Loudoun had decided to attack Ticonderoga in 1756, but after the news of the Oswego disaster, ordered Winslow in late August to assume a defensive position. Despite a force twice the size of the French, the plans to move northward on Lake George to attack the French forts were once more tabled for the duration of the season. Governor Shirley was recalled to England in the fall of 1756 where he faced questions of his intricate financial dealings and military affairs. Although he later missed the governorship of Jamaica, he did become governor of the Bahamas. Shirley returned to Boston in 1769, where he spent the last two years of his life.

For the men at Lake George, scarcely a shot was fired during the 1756 season. Most of the provincial troops, including 21-year-old Paul Revere, swatted mosquitoes for most of the summer at Fort William Henry. The fort, however, was strengthened and a large number of bateaux as well as several sloops were constructed at the edge of the lake. According to the report of Lieutenant Colonel Ralph Burton, who had been sent by Loudoun to inspect

Fort William Henry, Lake George had a considerable fleet in the summer of 1756: "They have two small Sloops of about Twenty Tons each, have four Swivels mounted on each, one Sloop of 30 Tons launched the 23d Instant, another of the same size to be launched in a few days, they propose having in each of those Vessells, four small Cannon or Royals—Two large Scows, and one a Building, a good many whaleboats, and more building."[4] The first sloop was "nam'd the Earl of Loudon" and the second was apparently called the *George* according to a depiction on a powder horn of a provincial recruit at Lake George.[5] French scouts, after observing the activity at the fort reported that the British had "two armed vessels on the lake, two others on the ways, and about two hundred bateaux."[6]

Meanwhile, Captain Robert Rogers with his Rangers made forays northward to gain intelligence of the French position. According to Rogers, as many as 4,000 men occupied Fort Carillon with 150 bateaux pulled onshore. By September the French had 5,300 men at Carillon and at their advanced posts. The fortress at Ticonderoga with its massive labor force had taken shape by that summer. The French had also built a redoubt and two bastions at the northern end of Lake George at "the Little Carrying Place" which was garrisoned by 670 soldiers. The fortification was later named Fort Vaudreuil after the Canadian governor. The Rangers observed the comings and goings of canoes, bateaux, and a schooner of 40 tons on Lake Champlain during this period.

The action during the 1756 season consisted of skirmishes between scouting parties. In one action in July, Rogers reported pursuing two vessels, "lighters" or "shallops" (probably small sailing galleys), which were sunk with their cargoes near Button Bay on Lake Champlain.[7] In early October, the French found four "barges" abandoned in a little cove on the eastern shore above Crown Point; one "mounted with three swivels."[8] The French were totally confused as to where the vessels came from. Actually, the vessels were whaleboats that were hidden by Rogers after a scout to St. Jean on the Richelieu River in late August. The vessels had been laboriously carried over the mountains on the east side of Lake George near present-day Huletts Landing to Lake Champlain. However, another trail at Glenburnie to Lake Champlain, known to the British in 1756, would have been an easier route.

The relative calm was broken in January 1757 when Rogers with 74 Rangers captured seven French prisoners and three sleighs on Lake Champlain. Pursued by a force of 179 French regulars, Canadians, and Indians, the Rangers were overtaken at a ravine near Ticondergoa which resulted in a bloody engagement known as the "Battle of La Barbue Creek." After a harrowing escape and heavy losses, Rogers and his men returned to Fort William Henry on January 23, 1757.

In March 1757, on the heels of the La Barbue Creek battle, Fort William Henry became the object of a major French assault. Marquis de Vaudreuil, Governor of French Canada, sent a force of 1,600 men to surprise the small garrison at Fort William Henry. The command of the expedition was given to the governor's brother, Francois-Pierre de Rigaud de Vaudreuil, an appointment that outraged other regular French officers. Rigaud, however, had experience as a veteran officer of the "troupes de la marines." The French army remained at Carillon from March 9 to March 15 to organize rations and to await more favorable weather. Every fourth man was given a five-foot scaling ladder that could be pieced together to make a ladder three times the original length. Twelve days' rations to be transported on sleds were issued and combustible materials supplied to burn the British fort. On March 16 the army of regulars, Canadian troops, and Indians camped below Sugar

Fort Ticonderoga. Photo by the author.

Loaf Mountain in the vicinity of present-day Huletts Landing. The next night the men camped on the ice without making fires near Northwest Bay. At eleven o'clock in the evening of March 18 the army left for the "Bay of Niacktaron," which would be the depot for the provisions and sleds several miles from Fort William Henry.

Meanwhile the Fort William Henry garrison of 346 men and 128 invalid troops was not aware of the impending attack. According to John Stark, captain of the Rangers at the fort, the troops were planning a celebration for St. Patrick's Day. Stark had commanded the sutler to issue no rum without a written order, but the Irish troops which composed most of the garrison except the Rangers still proceeded with "a drunken carouse" in the desolate outpost.[9] The Rangers, however, remained sober and an alert sentry noticed the French party before they arrived.

After an assessment by several officers of the difficulty in assaulting the fort, the Indians and Canadians were sent out early on March 19 to burn the buildings and bateaux on the outside of the fort. The fort's cannon roared their welcome to the invading men. Troops from the fort were dispatched to extinquish the fires but were driven back with a number of losses. During the day the French continued their attack with musket fire that did little damage to the fort. That evening two hundred additional Canadian militia were sent to help burn the vessels, bateaux, and storehouses. Two sloops that were trapped in the ice and a large number of bateaux on shore were burned.

About noontime on March 20, the French force paraded across the ice, prominently displaying their scaling ladders in an attempt to intimidate the small garrison. The army stopped at a safe distance from the fort; subsequently, several men walked foward with a red flag.* Chevalier de Mercier, a Canadian officer, was sent into the fort blindfolded to demand the surrender of the garrison. Mercier presented a lengthy surrender proposal that included a guarantee that the troops would be allowed the honors of war and could keep their valuables except for something to appease the Indians from whom the British had nothing to fear! If the British did not surrender, the French warned of dire consequences. Major William Eyre, the fort's commander and chief of artillery in the 1755 engagement at Lake George, consulted with his officers before returning his short answer, "That it was his fixed resolution to defend his Majesty's fort to the last extremity."[10] The extra time allowed the fort's garrison to pull the roof off the storehouses so that the fires set by the French would not spread to the rest of the fort. The French renewed the attack against the fort but retired late in the day.

That night another attack occurred, but the purpose was simply to burn the British outbuildings and boats. Little occurred in the next two days because of bad weather. On the night of the second day (March 22), twenty volunteers from the French regulars finally succeeded by eleven o'clock in burning "a vessel pierced for sixteen guns" that was on its stocks.[11] In total the French reported burning hundreds of bateaux, four larger vessels, two storehouses, the sawmill, the Ranger huts, wood planks, and a small fort (probably the hospital).[12] Contemporary French accounts describe the destruction of 350 bateaux and "four brigantines of 10 & 14 guns."[13] Fort William Henry, surrounded by a sea of fire for several days, was the only structure left standing by the time the French were finished. Although the French force outnumbered the garrison at Fort William Henry by a four to one margin, the French troops finally trudged northward on March 23, exhausted after more

---

* A red flag was used as a flag of truce instead of a white one since the French flag was white.

than a week without shelter. Governor Vaudreuil's report to his superiors in France praised his brother's expedition as a feat of accomplishment at a considerable risk. The casualties on both sides were light; Captain John Stark was grazed by a musket ball, the only time he was wounded in the French and Indian War or the Revolution.

The early summer of 1757 brought feverish activity at Fort Carillon as the French prepared to make a renewed attack on Fort William Henry. Bateaux with white-coated regulars, vessels with cannon and supplies, and Indians in canoes were arriving daily at the fort on Lake Champlain. Although the British knew of the intention of the French to capture Fort William Henry in 1757, the fort had a relatively small garrison since Lord Loudoun had diverted many of the troops for an ill-fated expedition to attack the reoccupied French base of Louisbourg on Cape Breton Island. The British preparations for the Louisbourg expedition involved sending a good portion of the troops for a lengthy campaign, first to New York City and then after weeks of delay to Nova Scotia. The tardy advance allowed the French time to prepare; reinforcements at Louisbourg and a large French fleet mounting 1,360 cannon forced the British to abort their attack in August. In the meantime, New York had lost some of its best troops, including Robert Rogers and a good part of his Rangers. The French, however, knew of the diversion of the British troops and decided to move on the fortification at Lake George. A contemporary account written by Louis Antoine de Bougainville, a French officer and aide to the French commander, the Marquis de Montcalm, in June 1757 noted, "In order to take advantage of the absence of Lord Loudoun, who has lead away the best troops, . . .the Marquis de Vaudreuil has determined to lay siege to Fort George, called by the English William Henry."[14]

After receiving reports of the heightened French activities from scouts, a large reconnaissance force was dispatched toward Ticonderoga in late July to attack some of the French outposts and burn the sawmill at the outlet of Lake George. Colonel John Parker was sent with a provincial force, mainly of the well-equipped and trained New Jersey regiment, which consisted of "350 men, 5 captains, 4 lieutenants, and an ensign in twenty-two barges, two of them under sail."[15] After a French reconnaissance bateau under the command of Lieutenant de St. Ours had been attacked by British provincials at "Isle de la Barque" (Harbor Islands) on July 20, a large detachment of Indians was sent by the French to entrap the provincials. On July 22 Bougainville noted that "Three hundred men, Indians and Canadians are now lying in ambush, part in canoes, part on land, and plan to capture them."[16] After the French viewed six provincial vessels near "Isle de la Barque," Bougainville reported that 450 additional men under Sieur de Corbière, mostly Indians, were sent, "to lay an ambush among the islands with which this part of the lake is covered."[17] At nightfall Corbière observed "twenty barges and two skiffs" of the provincials (Colonel James Montresor listed the vessels as whaleboats; bateaux and whaleboats were usually called "barges" in contemporary French military journals).[18]

At daybreak on July 24, the French and Indians captured three vessels without firing a shot. Apparently, the provincial fleet was widely separated since the next three vessels, unaware of the ambush, were also captured. The provincial prisoners later reported to the French "that they had separated in the course of the night."[19] The remaining flotilla of 16 vessels similarly fell into the trap. As the Indians darted out of the green foliage, screaming and firing muskets at the unsuspecting soldiers, the provincials tried to retreat southward but were stopped by a flotilla of Indian canoes at their rear. Nearly all of the vessels were sunk or captured. Parker and 60 men escaped in a few whaleboats. One hundred sixty-one

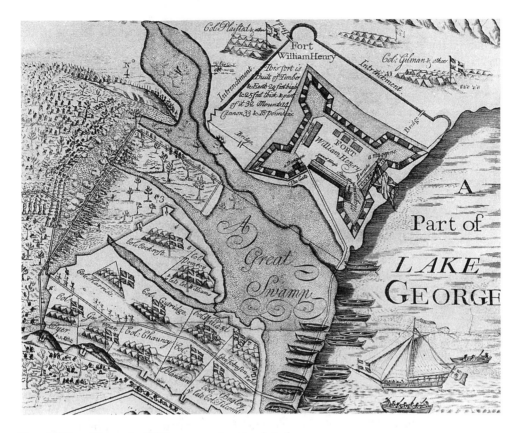

Fort William Henry in 1756, engraved and printed
by Thomas Johnston in Boston, April 1756.

BELOW. Detail of above showing the sloop
Earl of Loudoun or the sloop *George*.
(American Antiquarian Society)

prisoners were taken, but many provincials drowned in the mayhem. Bougainville recounted the battle: "the Indians jumped into the water and speared them like fish, and also sinking the barges by seizing them from below and capsizing them. . . The English, terrified by the shooting, the sight, the cries, and the agility of these monsters, surrendered almost without firing a shot."[20]

The exact location of the attack on Parker's vessels has always been subject to some uncertainty. Various secondary historical accounts have placed the attack at the Harbor Islands, Odell Island, or Sabbath Day Point. One of the earliest secondary British accounts of the battle was written by Thomas Mante in 1772. This version, based on a contemporary letter, differs somewhat from the original French journals. Mante places Parker and his men on an unnamed island overnight. Before daybreak, Parker sent three vessels to the mainland to reconnoiter the enemy by whom they were captured. From the intelligence gained from the provincial prisoners, the French posted 300 men in ambush behind a point where Parker planned to land. The French put their own men back in the provincial boat where they were to "lie on their oars" as a signal for Parker to land. When Parker and his men landed they were surrounded by the French and Indians. [21] This story, however, is slightly at odds with the information taken from the provincial prisoners.

Most evidence points to Sabbath Day Point as the location of the Parker battle. The Pennsylvania archives, for example, did include a "List of Killed, Wounded and Missing at Sabbath-day Point, 26th July, 1757."[22] The most definitive location of the battle comes from a letter in the Pennsylvania archives written at the camp at Lake George on July 14, 1758. The letter was written a year after the Parker disaster following the Abercromby expedition to Ticonderoga in 1758 (chapter 4): "At 6 o'clock in the evening we had already arrived at Sabbath-day Point, 24 miles, a spot famous by the unfortunate defeat last year of Colonel Parker, who lost there 300, out of a detachment of 350 men, he had under his command. We beheld there its melancholy remains, both in the water and on the shore."[23]

The captives of the Parker detachment were taken back to the Indian camp for a feast that evening. The rum from the captured vessels was consumed by the Indians and at least three of the provincials were "put in the pot and ate."[24] Father Roubaud, a Jesuit missionary priest who had originally accompanied the Abnakis Indians of St. Francis to Carillon, observed the Ottawa Indians "eating, with a famished avidity, this human flesh. . .drinking skullfuls of human blood."[25] Roubaud carefully approached a young Ottawa to dissuade him from cannibalism, but instead the young warrior offered the priest "a piece of the broiled Englishman."[26] After meeting a provincial officer, Father Roubaud beseeched an old Ottawa to purchase the freedom of the captive but was rebuffed in a threatening tone. The rest of the prisoners were taken to Fort Carillon where the Indians made "touching" visits to them, bringing white bread, according to Bougainville, but "Just the same, they ate one of them up at this camp."[27] On July 26 the remaining provincials were sent as prisoners of the Indians to Montreal on a schooner. In early September the prisoners were ransomed by the French from the Indians, sent to Quebec, and then on to Halifax, Nova Scotia.

Hearing of the engagement, Major General Daniel Webb, the commander at Fort Edward, called for reinforcements without delay, "the situation here is degenerating. Two-thirds of Colonel Parker's detachment of three companies either killed or captured in an ambush on the lake."[28] A week after the ambush, an advance party of French and Indians observed the remnants of the victory, with abandoned vessels thrown on shore as well as mutilated bodies of the provincial troops on the banks and scattered in the woods.

By the end of July 1757, the French were ready to embark on the largest military expedition up to that time in the region with the destruction of Fort William Henry as its goal. At the command of the French forces at Fort Carillon was the Marquis de Montcalm, one of the finest French generals in the French and Indian War. Montcalm at 45 years old was a warm, enthusiastic leader who inspired his men and had the strong allegiance of the Indians. He had been appointed to command the French forces in 1756, when he demonstrated his military ability by successfully attacking the British outpost at Oswego. In addition to Montcalm's military prowess, his second-in-command, Chevalier de Lévis, was another excellent officer who would later become marshal of France. Other distinguished officers who would prove themselves in the northern theater included Louis Antoine de Bougainville and Sieur de Bourlamaque.

Montcalm assembled a massive force of 3,081 French regulars, 2,946 Canadian militia, 188 artillery men, and 1,806 Indians.[29] Some of the officers that participated in the March 1757 offensive against Fort William Henry, including Rigaud de Vaudreuil and Sieur Mercier, were back for another try. The unusual part of the expedition was the representation of 40 Indian nations, which included more than half from the Great Lakes and the Mississippi River. Why would so many come so far to help the French? They believed that the French were there to help the Indians. The French had not tried to settle the land as extensively as the English colonists had. In a grand council of the 40 Indian nations held at the portage in Ticonderoga on July 27, Kisensik, the famous Nipissing chief, addressed the nations of the far West: "We domesticated Indians thank you for having come to help us defend our lands against the English who wish to usurp them."[30] Montcalm responded that "The great King has without doubt sent me to protect and defend you."[31] Nearly all of the Indians were convinced of the importance of the mission and cooperated with the French fully.

Since the French did not have enough bateaux to move the entire army by water, a separation was made whereby one division would follow an old Mohawk trail along the west side of Lake George while the main force would follow by water. On the morning of July 30, a detachment of 2,488 men which included approximately 500 Indians began their trek along the virgin shores of the lake. Meanwhile the army had labored for the previous six weeks to bring the artillery, bateaux, and provisions from Carillon to the departure point on northern Lake George. Five hundred workmen continued the portaging of supplies all night. Supplies were kept to a minimum, with soldiers taking only one coat, a blanket, weapons, and only three tents per company. Montcalm himself did not bring a mattress along. The cannon and mortars, mounted on their carriages, were held on a platform between two bateaux. Thirty-one of these "pontoons" were utilized.[32] Bateaux were also used for provisions and a few had crude tent-like canopies for the priests.

On August 1 Montcalm with his main force in 250 bateaux set out at two o'clock in the afternoon. The Indians had departed a day earlier in more than 150 canoes. The bateaux fleet covered the lake with a blanket of swiftly paddling soldiers in their varied-colored dress. South of Bald Mountain (later called Rogers Rock) a severe storm near a "cape" (probably Anthony's Nose) brought the fleet to a temporary halt. Resuming the voyage, the bateaux and canoes maneuvered through the green islets and majestic slopes of the Narrows as darkness descended. At two in the morning the fleet approached the end of Tongue Mountain, which was later named Montcalm Point on early Lake George maps. After observing the prearranged signal of three fires on the dark hillside of present-day Bolton

Landing, Montcalm continued across Ganousky Bay (Northwest Bay) at three o'clock in the morning to rendezvous with Lévis and his army. The armies reunited somewhere on the Bolton Landing shore at daybreak.

At ten o'clock in the morning of August 2, Brigadier Lévis renewed his march southward, while Montcalm departed at noon for the southern part of the lake. The bateaux now hugged the bays and indentations of the western shoreline to avoid detection by the British. The fleet halted at "Great Sandy bay" about nine miles from the southern end of the lake. The journey southward was soon renewed with a final disembarkation at Lévis's camp at a point

Lake George at the Narrows. Photo by the author.

of land that jutted out into the lake several miles north of Fort William Henry. At ten that night two vessels on a scout from the fort approached the area where the Indians had pulled their canoes ashore. According to Father Roubaud, 1,200 Indians gave chase to the two vessels, one of which was captured with some of the men massacred; the other crew made their escape back to the fort.[33] The prisoners were able to give Montcalm important information about the position and numbers of troops at Fort William Henry. In the middle of the night Montcalm issued orders for the army to move toward the fort at daybreak. Suddenly, a single cannon shot from the fort echoed up the lake, a signal to arms that one of the prisoners had divulged earlier to Montcalm.

At dawn the French army began marching toward the fort, apprehensive that the British might be preparing to intercept their position, but still optimistic that the British could be defeated outside the fort thus avoiding a long siege. The force under command of Lévis established a position on the west side of the road to Fort Edward, opposite the entrenched camp of the British and on the south side of the fort. The French army, preparing to besiege the fort from the northwest side, began making fascines (bundles of sticks fastened together like wicker baskets) that would be filled with dirt to build earthworks. At five in the morning the Indians in 120 canoes had formed a chain across the lake while yelling war cries to frighten the fort's garrison. Cannon mounted on platforms between two bateaux fired at the fort but were too far away to be effective. The rest of the day, the Indians fired their muskets from behind tree trunks in the cleared land near the fort.

At three on the afternoon of August 3, Montcalm sent one of his aides, Sieur Fonvive, with a message calling for the British garrison to surrender, warning that the fort was surrounded by the French army, superior artillery, and savages whose cruelty had already been experienced by a detachment from the fort. Montcalm used the Indians to threaten the garrison: "I have it yet in my power to restrain the savages, and to oblige them to observe a capitulation, as none of them have been as yet killed."[34] The commander at the entrenched camp and Fort William Henry, Lieutenant Colonel George Monro of the 35th Regiment, a resolute Scotch veteran, replied that he was determined to defend the fort to the last man.

The fort in 1757 appeared to be an irregular square with four bastions and ramparts of heavy logs set in cross tiers like cribs with dirt sandwiched between. Barracks for approximately 500 men, storehouses, casemates, and a magazine were inside the fort. The thick log walls, about 17 feet high, were strong enough to resist infantry and light artillery, but vulnerable to heavy siege guns. The fort was protected by chevaux-de-frise (standing rows of logs with sharpened ends), a dry moat on the sides facing the land, and by a swamp on the east. The Fort had 18 cannon, 1 howitzer, 2 mortars, and 17 swivel guns. To the southeast of the fort lay the entrenched camp on higher ground bordering the road to Fort Edward. The entrenched camp, where Dieskau had been defeated in 1755, had a breastwork of logs, stumps, rocks, six cannon, and a few swivel guns, with the land cleared a substantial distance around. What were conditions inside Fort William Henry during the French and Indian War? A year earlier, Lieutenant Colonel Ralph Burton had written to Lord Loudoun about the "dirty" conditions at the garrison where sickness and daily burials were prevalent: "The fort stinks. . .their necessary houses, kitchens, graves and places for slaughtering cattle, all mixed through the encampment."[35]

The number of men at Lake George by early August was clearly outnumbered by the French army. General Daniel Webb in command of Fort Edward on the Hudson River had visited Fort William Henry on July 25, returning to Edward on the 29th. Shortly thereafter, a scouting party under Israel Putnam of the Rangers had observed the movement of Montcalm's flotilla on Lake George. Webb wrote to the governor of New York for reinforcements and suggested that "I am determined to march to Fort William Henry with the whole army under my command as soon as I shall hear of the farther approach of the enemy."[36] A few days later Webb dispatched 800 Massachusetts provincials under Colonel Joseph Frye and 200 regulars under Lieutenant Colonel John Young to Fort William Henry. The French were aware of this reinforcement on August 2 when they questioned the prisoners captured from the bateaux late that night. The total number of troops at Lake George after Webb's reinforcements were approximately 2,300 effectives, with 1,600 remaining at Fort Edward. Most of the troops were stationed at the entrenched camp while the fort normally contained about 500 soldiers.

During the siege Colonel Monro sent several letters to Webb asking for more reinforcements. The first at nine o'clock on August 3 and the second at six o'clock that evening pressed for help. George Bartman, Webb's aide-de-camp, forwarded a letter late in the afternoon of August 3 to Monro that "every thing will be done for the best on yours and Colonel Youngs part, and is determin'd [Webb] to assist you as soon as possible with the whole army if requir'd."[37] Webb instead sent letters to the governors of the New England colonies asking for immediate reinforcements which, of course, could never arrive in time. The next day Monro sent two more messages: "I make no doubt that you will soon send us a reinforcement."[38] This was to no avail since the French had killed Webb's messenger along the Fort Edward road. In the lining of the messenger's jacket was a letter dated August 4 at noon which informed Monro that General Webb "does not think it prudent (as you know his strength at this place) to attempt junction, or to assist you till reinforc'd by the Militia of the Colonies" and that a Canadian recently captured told him that the French army was 11,000 strong.[39] Webb believed his 1,600 men would prove useless in trying to help the beleaguered garrison and suggested surrender.

By August 4 the French had further solidified their position in preparation for the siege. A decision was made to place the two main batteries on the northwest side of the fort so that cannon fire would cross onto the ramparts. The pontoon arrangement of bateaux with the artillery was finally brought up to the small cove on the southwest shore of the lake after nightfall. Twelve cannon and a few mortars were unloaded. The little inlet later became known as "artillery cove," which was also the supply depot for the trenches that the French had dug for the siege. While the Indians continued to fire away at the fort during the day, the troops inside were busy taking off the roofs of wooden shingles from the barracks and storehouses and throwing them into the lake. This was to inhibit the spread of fire in an attack. The Indians, fearing that they might be throwing something of value away, asked Montcalm for troops to stop it.

Eight hundred men assigned to the trench digging continued working all night, nearly completing the left battery by daybreak on August 5. At four o'clock in the morning the night shift of trench diggers was relieved by the day workers. Some of the French troops who had camped too close to Fort William Henry were pulled back since some had been killed in their tents from cannonballs and mortar bombs from the fort. One thousand workers that night completed the trenches for the left battery and brought the cannon from the lakeside. At six o'clock that morning, a battery of eight cannon, including three large 18-pounders and a 9-inch mortar, commenced firing on the west side of the fort and the north side facing the lake, and upon the vessels below. When a shot that cut the pulley for the fort's flag was accompanied by cheers from the French, a brave volunteer rehoisted the flag but in "doing this had his head Shot off with a Ball."[40] Again during the night (August 6), 500 workers labored to complete the right battery. The elaborate digging and maneuvering in trenches seems an eerie forerunner of the debilitating trench warfare to come over 150 years later in World War I. Finally at six o'clock in the morning on August 7, the right battery with its two 18-pounders, five 12-pounders, one 8-pounder, two howitzers and a mortar began firing on the fort; some shells ricocheted on the entrenched camp. Some of the same cannon, captured from Braddock in 1755, had been used by the French to besiege Oswego in 1756.

After a double salvo from both batteries, Montcalm sent Bougainville under a flag of truce accompanied by a drummer along with 15 grenadiers with the captured letter written by General Webb from Fort Edward. Fifteen British soldiers and several officers met Bougainville outside the fort where they "blindfolded me, led me first to the fort, and then to the entrenched camp where I handed to the commandant the letter of the Marquis de

Montcalm and that of General Webb."[41] Monro thanked Bougainville for the French politeness and the generosity. The letter obviously was a devastating psychological blow to the garrison. They were outnumbered by more than three to one by the French with no hope for reinforcements. After the detachments went back to their respective lines, the cannonades resumed with thundering echoes reverberating from French Mountain. The steadfast Monro issued orders to the garrison "that if any person proved cowardly or offered to advise giving up the Fort that he should be immediately hanged over the walls of the Fort."[42]

The distant cannon firing from Fort William Henry could be heard each day by General Webb at Fort Edward. "I have not yet received the least reinforcement," Webb complained to Lord Loudoun, "but I fear it cannot long hold out against so warm a cannonading if I am not reinforced by a sufficient number of militia to march to their relief."[43] Two thousand militia did arrive at Fort Edward shortly thereafter, but to Webb it was too little and in hindsight too late. Sir William Johnson, after learning of the siege of Fort William Henry, marched to Fort Edward with 800 provincials, Mohawk, and Mohican (by August 12, there were 4,239 milita encamped at Fort Edward). General Webb, however, was unmoved when Johnson pressed him to advance against the French lines. Before reinforcements came to Fort Edward, Webb, sustained by a council of war, had planned to abandon Fort Edward. While Webb seemed more willing to entertain the idea of reinforcing Fort William Henry after the arrival of fresh troops, serious preparations for such an advance were never made. While a letter on August 6 to Monro suggested that the troops at Fort Edward were ready to "set out in the night with the whole join'd together," two days later another letter postponed the promised assistance "owing to the delay of the Militia."[44] William Johnson later described Webb as a "coward" who "was nearly beside himself with physical fear after the fall of Fort William Henry. His army was in good spirits and anxious to fight. The general alone was panic stricken."[45]

About midnight on August 7, some of the volunteer Canadian militia with their Indians made a sniping attack on the entrenched camp at Fort William Henry whereby a contingent of 300 provincial and regular troops left the barricade to counterattack. Twenty-one Canadians and Indians were killed in the exchange. The French reported 60 English soldiers killed in the battle.

That night the French continued their trench making closer to the fort. The following day of August 8 the diggers worked on an elaborate "wet ditch" or causeway over the marshy areas northwest of the fort. Two hundred workers continued their toil during the early morning hours of August 9. By that time the predicament of the encircled garrison had reached a critical stage. In addition to the several hundred killed or wounded, smallpox had spread throughout the fort. Only seven small-bore cannon were left in operation, according to Colonel Frye of the Massachusetts militia; all the large cannon and mortars had burst or had been disabled by enemy fire.[46] It was common for cannon to burst from metal fatigue after repeated firings.

After a recommendation of surrender to Colonel Monro from a council of war in the early morning of August 9, a white flag was raised. With drums beating repetitiously, Lieutenant Colonel Young rode on horseback to Montcalm's tent. A lengthy set of terms involving nine articles was agreed to by Colonel Monro. The British garrison was to march out with the usual honors of war with their guns, all artillery and military provisions were to be turned over to the French, none of the troops could serve against the French or Indians

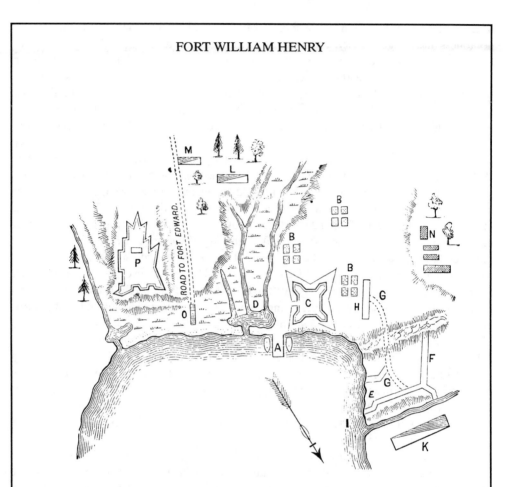

FORT WILLIAM HENRY

A. Dock
B. Garrison gardens
C. Fort William Henry
D. Morass
E. Montcalm's 1st battery
F. Montcalm's 2nd battery
G. Montcalm's approaches
H. Two intended batteries
I. Place where Montcalm landed his artillery
K. Montcalm's camp
L. M. DeLevy's camp
M. M. De La Corne with Canadians and Indians
N. English encampment before retrenchments were made
O. Bridge over morass
P. English retrenchment

MONTCALM'S ATTACK

A. Artillery cove
B. Road to trench
C. First battery—length, 70 yd.;
   width, 20 ft.; height, 7 ft.;
   embrasures, 9 ft.
C. to D.—Line of trenches, 578 yd.
D. Second Battery—length, 74 yd.;
   width, 26 ft.; height, 8 ft.;
   embrasures, 10 ft.
E. to G.—Line of approach, 890 yd.

F. Third battery—not opened
H. Line up the hill and at the crest of
   the Garden
I. Garden
K. Fort William Henry
L. Morass
M. La Corne and Canadians
N. Fort George
P. Docks
Q. [Fort William Henry Hotel]
R. [Lake House]

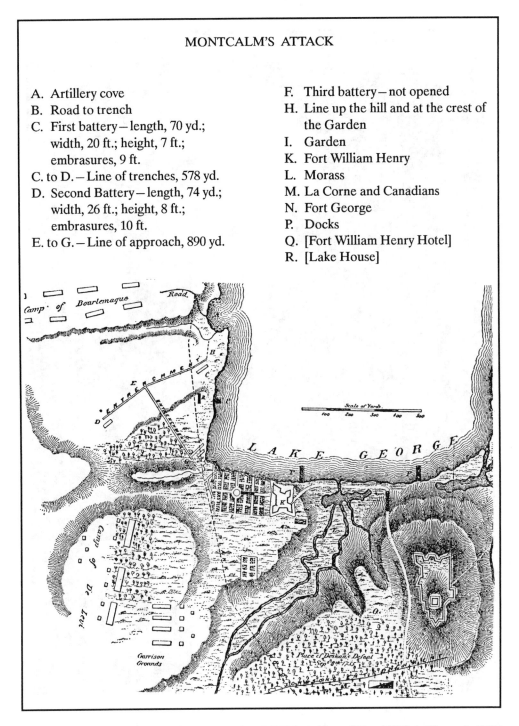

ABOVE. Map of the siege of August 1757. LEFT. A plan of Fort William Henry in 1757 and the English and French camps. (*History of Lake Champlain* by Peter Palmer)

Marquis de Montcalm.
(National Archives)

for 18 months, all French prisoners would be exchanged for an equal number of British upon delivery at Fort Carillon within three months, all sick and wounded were to be transported under French protection to Fort Edward, and "the Marquis de Montcalm, being willing to show Colonel Monro and the garrison under his command, marks of esteem, on account of their honorable defence, gives them one piece of cannon, or six pounder."[47]

Aware of the Indians' desire for plunder, Montcalm postponed signing the agreement until he assembled a council of chiefs of all the Indian nations to inform them of the articles of the capitulation and motives behind his actions. Montcalm had gone to great lengths during the expedition to consult with the Indians and treat them respectfully. He "asked their consent and their promise that their young men would not commit any disorder. The chiefs agreed to everything and promised to restrain their young men," noted Bougainville, an eyewitness to the meeting.[48] At noon the fort was turned over to the French, whereupon the British forces were brought to the entrenched camp. The Indians promptly entered the fort to pillage. The sick and wounded men who could not be moved were immediately butchered. Father Roubaud again witnessed atrocities: "I saw one of these barbarians come out of the casemates. . .[with] a human head, from which trickled streams of blood, and which he displayed as the most splendid prize that he could have secured."[49]

Not finding much plunder in the fort, the Indians and some Canadians could not be stopped from entering the entrenched camp and pillaging the British prisoners even though Montcalm had assigned guards. The Indians roamed the camp and assaulted some of the men for personal belongings while the women and children were frozen with horror. Montcalm and his officers personally went to the entrenched camp to prevent a massacre. It took until nine o'clock that evening to bring order to the British camp. Bougainville advised the British officers and troops to throw away all wine, brandy, and any other intoxicating liquor since the French had observed the consequences of the Indians during drunken escapades. The French officers, after learning that a large number of the Indians were lying in ambush along the road to Fort Edward, warned Colonel Monro not to leave during the night as originally planned. The Indians, although agreeing to the terms of surrender, were unhappy since they had been promised plunder by Montcalm before embarking on the expedition.

The next day on August 10 the British were to march to Fort Edward under French escort. One of the main reasons that the French didn't keep the more than 2,000 British and provincial troops as prisoners was the lack of supplies to feed such large numbers. By five o'clock in the morning the Indians, still seeking trophies and pillage, entered the huts and tents of the wounded, dragged 17 men out, and tomahawked and scalped them while Miles Whitworth, a Massachusetts surgeon, watched helplessly. By now panic had seized the British camp. According to the French account, the terror-striken British began their march to Fort Edward before the French escort had fully assembled. The British records, however, do not seem to indicate any absence of the French during the aborted march. The march had barely begun when the Indians began menacing the captives. Although Colonel Monro complained to the French officers, no action was taken. Joseph Frye of Massachusetts recalled that "the french officers however told us that if we would give up the baggage of its officers and men, to the Indians, they thought it would make them easy."[50] In an attempt to pacify the Indians, the British and provincial soldiers turned over their packs.

Within a short period of time, the frenzy became general with the Indians stripping the soldiers of their hats, swords, guns, and clothing. Although with the honors of war, the

French had allowed the British to retain their guns, they had no ammunition. Soon the massacre began at the rear of the column with men, women, and even children butchered. The troops were nearly stripped naked as the Indians literally tore their belongings from them; hundreds fled terrified into the woods. The British desperately appealed to the officers of the French escort, but they did not intercede in the chaos. Frye recorded that the French officers refused protection and "told them they must take to the woods and shift for themselves."[51] Hundreds more were taken captive by the Indians. The reason for the actions of the Indians was the denial of the spoils of war by the French that had been expected and promised when the campaign began. The European tradition of the honors of war meant nothing to the Indians who regarded the captured troops as enemies.

Upon hearing the cries and commotion, Montcalm and his officers ran to the scene and immersed themselves among the Indians in an attempt to stop the carnage. "Kill me, but spare the English who are under my protection," Montcalm reportedly demanded.[52] A few of the French officers were wounded in the melee. Montcalm arrived, however, after most of the butchery had been completed. Finally, the French restored order and retrieved a large number of captives from the Indians. The French and British officers then divided the few spare clothes remaining among the half-naked troops. Many of the men who escaped into the woods staggered piecemeal, disoriented, and hungry into Fort Edward on August 10 and over the next several days. Colonel Frye, who had fled into the wilderness, arrived at Fort Edward on August 12.

Some of the western Indians, after the massacre, dug up the fresh graves of the British and scalped them. Unbeknownst to the Indians, many of the British had died of smallpox. The disease later decimated their tribes at home. Most of the Indians, loaded with the prizes of war, left that day; others departed the following morning. One unfortunate Ranger, John McKeen from New Hampshire, was tied to a tree by the Indians the night after the massacre and used for target practice with knives and tomahawks, then set afire. Several hundred British prisoners that the French could not immediately retrieve were taken to Montreal by the Indians. After lengthy negotiations at Montreal and threats from August 19 through early September, the French were finally able to ransom most of the prisoners from the Indians. How many were killed and whether it involved the women and children has been the subject of debate and speculation. Father Roubaud did see "the son torn from the arms of the father, the daughter snatched from the bosom of the mother" and had successfully negotiated an exchange of a baby held by a Huron for a scalp acquired from a Christian Abnaki Indian.[53]

The remaining body of British were brought back to the entrenched camp at Lake George where they remained until August 15. On that morning Montcalm sent "an escort of three hundred men four hundred English ransomed from the Indians."[54] Halfway to Fort Edward a British detachment met the French and escorted the survivors with Lieutenant Colonel Monro the rest of the way. If there were only 400 left, most of the survivors would have had to reach Fort Edward on their own after fleeing the Indians on August 10.[55]

The actual losses of British and provincials during the siege and massacre, estimated at 200-300, are somewhat uncertain. Approximately 300 troops, over half from the provincial ranks, were still missing or held captive at the end of 1757. The losses of the French initially reported by the British as "twelve hundred men" were greatly exaggerated.[56] The French listed their losses on August 22 as only 17 killed and 40 wounded of the regulars, Canadians, and Indians.

The French immediately began a demolition of Fort William Henry which lasted for three days. The fort, with its crib-like structure for ramparts with earthern layers, proved difficult to break up and burn. According to the official French journal of the expedition, the vessels at Fort William Henry included "two sloops in the harbor, two on stocks, 4 large flat bateaux and eight barges."[57] British engineer Colonel James Montresor, however, listed "2 Galliots [galleys], 2 Scows, 5 whaleboats, 3 Batos, 2 Sloops" at Fort William Henry in his journal on July 27.[58] The French used the captured vessels to transport a tremendous amount of provisions, including 1,237 barrels of salt pork and 1,737 quarters of flour to Ticonderoga. In December of 1757 Rogers and a Ranger detachment found the British vessels underwater at the northern end of Lake George. Although the British reported that they were down to only seven small cannon when the fort surrendered, the French transported 23 cannon (8 bronze), 1 howitzer, 2 mortars, 17 swivels, 38,835 pounds of powder, 2,522 shot and other munitions back to Fort Carillon.[59] They also recovered six chests of "fireworks" from the fort. Satisfied with their accomplishment, the French departed on August 16, never to return again in force.

The following winter, Robert Rogers and his Rangers, after their return from the aborted Louisbourg expedition, walked the broken ruins of Fort William Henry. His brother Richard, who had died of smallpox just before the French siege, was one of the bodies that had been dug up and scalped by the Indians. The undisturbed earthern mounds of Fort William Henry could still be seen more than 100 years later on the edge of the lake. The area remained relatively undisturbed until archaeological work began on the site during the reconstruction of the fort in the early 1950s.

Robert Rogers and his Rangers examine the ruins of Fort William Henry in December 1757. Drawing by Gary Zaboly. (Lake George Historical Association)

Gravesite of Duncan Campbell, Hudson Falls, New York.
Photo by the author

4. Debacle: Abercromby Expedition

On A TYPICAL JULY EVENING, tourists leisurely stroll down to the tranquil waters of Lake George, but few realize that an epic struggle for a continent occurred in this valley more than 230 years earlier. Yet here, a flotilla exceeding 1,000 vessels conveyed the largest military expedition of the French and Indian War to their doom. As the boats weaved through the islands, the regimental flags fluttered in the breeze with the blare of fifes and trumpets accompanied by the shrill of bagpipes piercing the silence of the wilderness. Who among the 15,000 men of that expedition could foresee that the exuberance and camaraderie in anticipation of an easy victory would turn into terror and despair a few days later?

As the battle for North America continued between Britain and France, the 1758 British campaign called for the capture of Fort Carillon, constructed on a rocky promontory called Ticonderoga overlooking Lake Champlain, and then a push northward into Canada. Carillon by 1758 superseded Fort St. Frédéric as the largest French fortress on Champlain. The French had experienced considerable success in their control of the lake valleys during the campaign of 1757, with forts at Crown Point and Ticonderoga on Lake Champlain, the destruction of Fort William Henry on Lake George, and the defeat of the famed Rogers' Rangers in the "Battle of the Snowshoes" in March 1758. In the latter engagement 180 Rangers were nearly annihilated by a force of French and Indians in the vicinity of Trout Brook in Ticonderoga.*

William Pitt, the reinstated secretary of state, early in 1758 recalled Lord Loudoun for political reasons as well as for the military setbacks during 1757 at Oswego, Fort William Henry, and the abandoned Louisbourg expedition. Pitt indicated to provincial legislatures that the commander-in-chief position would be reduced to a military head only, thus ending the interference with colonial governors and assemblies. Legislatures would have more autonomy and direct financial assistance from England, which guaranteed renewed support for military expeditions.

* The subject of a surviving legend, Rogers' daring escape was supposedly made by deceiving his Indian pursurers into thinking that he had slid down the 500-foot cliff of Bald Mountain. Although Rogers did not mention the incident in his journal, by the time of the Revolutionary War the mountain was known as Rogers Rock.[1]

Although faced with hostilities in Europe, Pitt focused a good deal of his attention on the American war in 1758. The three-pronged strategy not only included the planned Carillon attack, but renewed expeditions against Louisbourg and Fort Duquesne. Pitt recalled Colonel Jeffery Amherst, a cautious but resolute and energetic officer from the German theater of the Seven Years' War. The seizure of Louisbourg, the strongest fortification in North America, would be a first step toward the capture of Quebec. Promoted to major general and assigned leadership of the Louisbourg campaign, Amherst caught up to the British armada at sea, under Admiral Edward Boscawen, before the fleet reached Cape Breton Island (Nova Scotia). After four attempted landings were prevented by severe weather, the troops finally disembarked on the craggy shore on June 8. Among the three brigadier generals with Amherst was 31-year-old James Wolfe, a gallant field officer who would later lead the attack on Quebec. In an effort to block the harbor to the fort, the French sank six of their large vessels at its entrance. The French efforts were to no avail; the garrison was forced to capitulate by the end of July. Several hundred cannon and 5,637 prisoners were taken by Amherst upon surrender of the fort.

The new commander-in-chief of British forces in North America, General James Abercromby, was given the assignment of the Ticonderoga operation. Abercromby's position, like many British officers of the eighteenth century, was achieved with the aid of political influence. Although he had been in the army all his life, he still had little in the way of a definitive combat record that would indicate his incompetence; most of his career as an officer had been spent in staff positions. At 52 and in imperfect health, he had a reputation as an inactive and uninspiring commander. A young recruit from Massachusetts noted in his journal that Abercromby was "an aged gentleman, and infirm in body and mind."[2] Rufus Putnam, a youthful, provincial soldier who would later serve as a general in

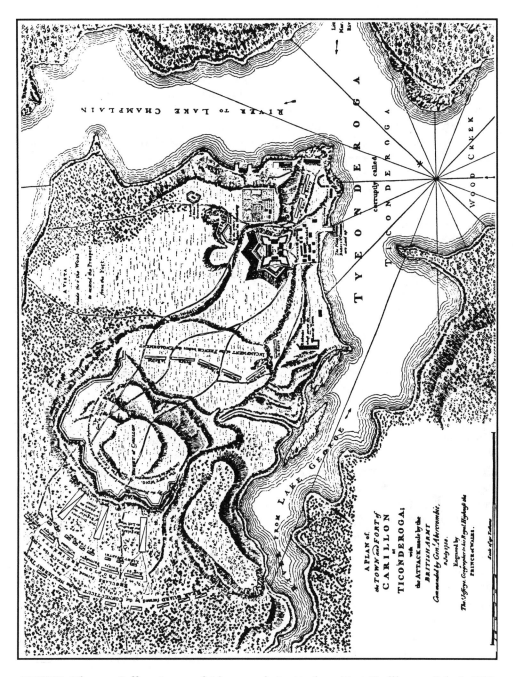

ABOVE. Thomas Jeffreys' map of Abercromby's attack on Fort Carillon on July 8, 1758. (*History of Lake Champlain* by Peter Palmer)

LEFT. Departure of Abercromby expedition on July 5, 1758. Painting by F. C. Yohn, The Glens Falls Collection, Continental Insurance Corporation. (*The Summer Paradise in History* by Warwick Stevens Carpenter, 1914) the American Revolution, noted that Abercromby was "an old man and frequently called granny."[3]

William Pitt had let Abercromby know that the intended field commander was 34-year-old George Viscount Howe with the rank of brigadier general in North America. The young nobleman breathed life into the body and soul of the army. While many British officers looked down on the provincial troops, Howe was extremely popular and on very close terms with both colonial officers and their troops. He scrapped tradition to suit the needs of warfare in the wilderness. To understand fighting in the wilds of America, he accompanied Robert Rogers and his Rangers in scouting forays, carrying his own blanket and bearskin. As a result of these experiences, he had his men cut their hair and the tails on their redcoats, brown their musket barrels to eliminate glare, discard wigs and other unwieldy baggage, and wear leggings as protection from briars. Howe ordered that no women accompany the troops to wash the soldiers' clothing. He instead set the example by going to a brook and washing his own clothes. The eighteenth-century armies typically provided a separation between men and officers, but Howe, scorning the trappings of rank, purposely became familiar with the common troops which endeared him to the army.

In late June Major General Abercromby declared the 1757 capitulation agreement of Fort William Henry "null and void" since the French had immediately broken it. He called upon the officers and soldiers of the 1757 garrison who, by the surrender terms, would have been prohibited within 18 months, to "serve in the same manner."[4] Abercromby notified the governor of Canada, the Marquis de Vaudreuil, of his decision. The French, however, knew that something was impending by early June when prisoners, taken by French Indians, divulged that the British army was assembling at Lake George. By June 19 the French discerned that the attack was to be on Carillon; by the end of the month they anticipated twenty to twenty-five thousand men in the assault on the fort. General Marquis de Montcalm, the highly energetic and very successful commander of the French army in North America, listened to the conflicting advice of his officers. Some felt a retreat north on Lake Champlain was prudent while others recommended making a stand against the overwhelming British force. Montcalm, the victor at Fort William Henry a year earlier, decided to oppose the British army. In Montcalm, the French had a career officer with nearly the opposite temperament of Abercromby.

By early July, Montcalm still had slightly fewer than 3,000 troops at Carillon, although reinforcements were expected. Governor Vaudreuil had decided to assemble 5,000 men at Carillon in mid-June, but political and personal rivalry with Montcalm delayed reinforcements to the fort. Vaudreuil, the Canadian-born son of a former governor of New France, was an ambitious but ill-informed leader with little military experience to serve as a guide. He never believed that the British would attack at Carillon and continued plans for an offensive expedition further down the Mohawk Valley. It was only at the last moment that troops were diverted to reinforce Montcalm. Even then the largest group showed up three days after the battle.

In early July 1758, an army of 6,367 British regulars and 9,024 provincial troops had gathered at the ruins of Fort William Henry on the southern shore of Lake George.[5] Many of the provincial regiments, hurriedly called up, had little training. Two days before embarkation, the Massachusetts non-commissioned officers were yet uncertain how to execute commands while the troops from Connecticut were attempting to learn how to change from a column to a line. A few men had never fired a musket. The provincial

Major Robert Rogers.
(National Archives)

regiment of Private Amos Richardson had just a single day of training the day before leaving for Ticonderoga. Richardson noted a "fine firing" of the muskets during the afternoon but recorded that "some of our men did shoot one of the regulars through the head, which killed him dead."[6] The following day Richardson's regiment was left behind at Lake George.

Provincial troops were raised through militia officers who ordered musters for their units, whereby lower-ranked officers would solicit volunteers. Unlike the regular army, many of the men and officers were related by blood or neighborhoods. If not enough men were enlisted, conscription of idle men in the town would occur. A conscripted man, nevertheless, could hire a substitute to take his place by paying a small fine to the colonial government and a larger payment to his replacement. As the war dragged on, the payment increased.

On the clear summer morning of July 5, the largest army ever assembled at that time in North America departed on approximately "900 bateaux and 135 Whale Boats, the Artillery. . .being mounted on Rafts," according to Abercromby.[7] Other vessels were also present with the fleet. Shipwright William Sweat in late June noted that "they are making a floating Batery."[8] Similarly, James Searing, a young New York regimental surgeon, observed that "three redeaus or floating batteries were prepared, two upon batteaux."[9] The floating batteries and rafts were hastily constructed at Lake George while most of the bateaux were built in Albany under Colonel John Bradstreet, commander of the "Battoe Service."

When the vessels were three miles from the departure point, an eyewitness reported that the entire surface of the lake was completely obscured by the fleet.[10] The sun gleamed down on the crystal clear water of the lake as the flotilla stretched for six miles, slowly moving on its way northward through the Narrows. The scene must have been spectacular, with the red-coated regulars along with the regal kilts of the Scottish 42nd Black Watch regiment in the middle and the blue uniforms and homespun browns of the provincial soldiers on both flanks against the lush green mountains overlooking the lake. Major Robert Rogers called the scene "a splendid military show."[11] The men were filled with optimism as the vessels made their way along the lake to the intermittent tune of the musical instruments of each corps—bagpipes, drums, fifes, and trumpets. Two weeks later a wounded officer recalled that "I never beheld so delightful a prospect."[12] It would seem that this force would be truly invincible compared to the French force at Fort Carillon with only a quarter as many men. By two o'clock in the afternoon, the French had received a signal that British bateaux were sighted on the lake.

By five o'clock in the evening, the expedition landed at Sabbath Day Point about two-thirds of the way up the lake. The expedition had supper there and waited for the artillery and provisions on the barges to catch up. Several fires were made to confuse the French about their plans for the night. By eleven o'clock in the evening the army renewed its voyage to the north. At five o'clock in the morning of July 6, the vanguard of the fleet reached the northern end of Lake George, disembarking at a point on the west shore later referred to as Howe's Cove or Landing.

At daylight the French observed their signal flag being raised and lowered on the mountain side indicating the British bateaux landings. Captain de Germain, with an advance party of French at the lakeside, fired on the British vessels before fleeing to the French camp. The British and provincial troops quickly plundered the belongings left by the French soldiers. A scouting detachment of 350 troops under Captain de Trepezec and Ensign de Langy, which had been sent the day earlier to a post between Bald Mountain (later Rogers

Langy and Trepezec at Bald Mountain (Rogers Rock) observing the approach of Abercromby's army on July 6, 1758. The armada consisted of three columns of 900 bateaux, 135 whaleboats, rafts, and three small radeaux, two of which were built from bateaux.
Drawing by Gary Zaboly.

Rock) and the lake, were now cut off by the British and provincial troops. The detachment was forced to try to reach the French camp via the thickly wooded area near Trout Brook in present-day Ticonderoga.

Abandoned by the few Indian guides who accompanied the detachment, the French soldiers became hopelessly lost in the dense forest. Meanwhile, the advance units of provincials under Major Robert Rogers, regulars led by Lord Howe, and Rangers with

View of Baldwin from Rogers Rock. Photo by the author.

Israel Putnam that had set out from the landing site accidentally stumbled upon the French party led by Trepezec about four o'clock in the afternoon. "Qui vive?" (Who goes there!) "Francais," replied the British, but the French were not deceived.[13] Suddenly, shots rang out and musket balls pierced the green foliage. The young general, Lord Howe, was killed instantly at the first volley by a ball that penetrated both his heart and lungs. Rogers recalled that Howe with his detachment "had broke the enemy, and hemmed them in on every side; but advancing himself with great eagerness and intrepidity upon them, was unfortunately shot and died immediately."[14] Sixteen-year-old David Perry, who had marched to Lake George with his militia from eastern Massachusetts, experienced his first action with the detachment: "[The] whistling of balls and roar of musquetry terrified me not a little."[15]

The British units decisively overwhelmed the French who suffered substantial losses, including 148 captured. Trepezec made it back to the French camp but later succumbed to his wounds. The day after the skirmish, Joseph Nichols, a hired replacement in the Massachusetts militia, "Observ'd in the Woods Many Slain men, An Awful Sight to

Behold."[16] The prisoners were held on Mutton Island (later renamed Prisoners Island) and sent to southern Lake George two days after the skirmish (July 8).

The death of Howe, the idol of the army, paralyzed the expedition. The stunned army floundered the rest of the day. As the body was brought into the camp, Howe's aide, Captain Alexander Monypenny, remarked that "scarce an eye was free from tears."[17] Robert Rogers, leader of the Rangers, observed that his death "seemed to produce an almost general consternation and languor through the whole [army]."[18] Abercromby, realizing that the field strategy would now rest on his shoulders, vacillated on the following day (July 7), finally ordering the army back to the original landing site on Lake George. The troops being "greatly fatigued" was the explanation that Abercromby provided in his report to William Pitt for the return of the army to the landing site at Lake George.[19] At 11 o'clock on July 7, Colonel John Bradstreet, an American-born regular officer who commanded the "Battoe Service," was sent by Abercromby north to the outlet of Lake George to capture the French sawmill and rebuild the bridges.

The hesitation of the British army provided valuable time for the French to fortify their position. At dawn on the 7th, the whole French army—officers and men alike—were busy building an entrenchment about a half-mile in front of the fort. The "Heights of Carillon," the highest part of the ridge before one reaches the fort, was chosen as the site of a defensive breastwork of logs. Montcalm and Dupont LeRoy, an accomplished engineer, designed the breastwork about one-third of a mile long which followed the sinuosity of the land with sections of the works flanking one another. According to Montcalm's report, the log wall "was formed by falling trunks of trees one upon the other and others felled in front, their branches cut and sharpened produced the effect of a chevaux-de-frise [projecting spikes]."[20] The wall, consisting of logs as large as three feet in diameter, was eight to nine feet high with a crude firing platform inside.

A number of cannon from the fort were brought to the breastwork. The forest was cleared a short distance in front of the breastwork and the ground covered with sharpened branches. While it may not have appeared to be much viewed from a distance, it would prove to be a fatal trap for the British. By the evening of the 7th the treacherous abattis was completed. Later that night Brigadier General Chevalier de Lévis finally arrived with his small reinforcements which enlarged the total French army to approximately 3,500. Not all the French were occupied making preparations to defend the fort. Sieur de Lotbinière, the fort's engineer and canteen franchisee, was busy putting his cash box in order with a bateau ready to sail if the engagement went badly. Just before the battle the price of a drink of brandy in the canteen fell but increased five times after the engagement.

While the French were busy building their snare, Abercromby's army had moved only a short distance to the abandoned French sawmill but had left the 40 pieces of artillery and other provisions at the landing site. Some of the provincial troops were engaged in building a breastwork adjacent to the outlet from Lake George. Thus far the British operations had obviously been very slow, but at this point Abercromby panicked, deciding suddenly to begin action since the French prisoners had reported that Montcalm had 6,000 men with the expectation of 3,000 reinforcements. However, British spies correctly reported to him that Montcalm had fewer than 4,000 troops.

After learning of the French breastwork, Abercromby chose to send Lieutenant Matthew Clark to reconnoiter the site in the early morning of July 8. Abercromby termed Clark "the Engineer," despite the fact that he was only a "commissioned sub-engineer" with only six months' service.[21] Although Clark has been characterized as a sub-engineer by many historians, Colonel James Montresor, an engineer himself, had referred to Clark as an "Engineer" in his journal four months earlier.[22] The decision to send Clark was based on the fact that Montresor was ill at the time and Abercromby had had a dispute with Lieutenant Colonel William Eyre, a more experienced and competent engineering officer. Lieutenant John Stark from the Rangers and some other British officers also climbed Rattlesnake Hill (later called Mount Defiance) to view the breastwork. Stark and others reported that it was indeed a strong defense. Despite the disagreement over the strength of the breastwork, Abercromby decided to follow Clark's advice that the wall was of flimsy construction and could be pushed down by the shoulders of the troops. The young Clark became a victim of his own faulty appraisal and was killed the very same day. Captain Charles Lee of the 44th Regiment of Foot, who would become a controversial major general in the American army during the Revolutionary War, later mused that cannon drawn up Rattlesnake Hill would command the French position. It was not until the Burgoyne invasion of 1777 that the mountain would actually be fortified.

Many of the provincial and British officers who fought side by side at Ticonderoga would find themselves on opposite sides at the Battle of Bunker Hill in 1775. General Thomas Gage, appointed second-in-command by Abercromby after Howe's death, 17 years later ordered the British assault on Bunker Hill in the American Revolution. Captain James Abercromby, nephew of the general, who served on this expedition and Amherst's the next year against Ticonderoga, was killed in the Battle of Bunker Hill. John Stark of the Rangers, who disagreed with Clark's assessment of the breastwork, went on to fight on the side of the colonists at Bunker Hill, later becoming a noteworthy general in the Continental army. Major Israel Putnam, who served with the Rangers at the Ticonderoga battle, commanded the Connecticut troops as a militia brigadier general at the Battle of Bunker Hill.

Actually, the French were in a rather precarious situation with their backs to Lake Champlain and provisions that would last only a week. Abercromby could have starved the French out or laid siege to the entrenchment and fort from the higher ground of Rattlesnake Hill. But on the morning of the 8th, Abercromby stunned many of his field officers by ordering a frontal attack on the breastwork with muskets and bayonets alone. He feared huge French reinforcements and thus decided not to wait to bring the cannon to the battlefield. As the army made preparations for the attack, Sir William Johnson with 440 Indians arrived late in the morning, taking a position on Rattlesnake Hill. Johnson, the victorious general at the Battle of Lake George in 1755, after viewing the overwhelming numbers of British, remained on the hillside while his Indians fired toward the fort.

Between nine and ten o'clock in the morning, Abercromby's army began an attack on the advanced breastworks of the French. About noon the line of march against the main entrenchment began, with Rangers, bateau men, and the provincial troops followed by the British regulars. By half past twelve in the afternoon under a hot July sun, the regulars with their bayonets fixed, in steady formal columns, rushed the French lines. The 42nd Highlanders, the Scottish Black Watch, advanced on the right-hand side of the French wall. As the drums rolled and the bagpipes screamed their challenge, the tight red ranks of the regulars trudged forward to their death. The stern regularity of the march broke down as soon as they tried to traverse the logs whose branches had been sharpened to points. A fatally wounded bagpiper propped himself against a fresh stump and continued to play a haunting call until death overcame his dedication. The men struggled up the wall only to be shot or impaled on the spiked branches — a mass of courageous red-coated and kilt-clad souls was left dangling in front of the entrenchment as the first attack was repulsed by the French. Young Abel Spicer, serving in a provincial regiment from Connecticut, observed that the regulars marched ten deep to the French breastwork and fired volleys point blank but "fell like pigeons."[23] Private David Perry's provincial regiment had simple instructions to run to the breastwork, but the men were killed so quickly that his regiment sought cover behind trees and logs: "the ground was strewed with the dead and dying. . .I could hear the men screaming and see them dying all around me."[24]

While the slaughter was taking place, Abercromby was two miles away, safe at the sawmill. When his men returned with the conclusion that the French wall was invulnerable to a musket attack alone — that artillery was needed — Abercromby imprudently ordered a second attack without artillery on the French lines. Prior to the first assault, Abercromby had ordered two floating batteries built for the LaChute River to bring a flanking fire on the French. According to Rufus Putnam, the vessels were hastily constructed scows: "There were also some Field pieces went down the River toward the Fort, on Floating Batteries which our men builded below the Falls."[25] The two vessels were quickly driven back by cannon from the fort.

As a fresh attack began, the red-coated soldiers charged up the log wall only to be repulsed again and again. The efforts to storm the breastwork were to no purpose reported one unidentified British officer, "for we were so intangled in the branches of the felled trees."[26] The abattis caught fire several times during the engagement, but the French troops quickly put out the flames. Uninjured soldiers under cover from the fire of the Rangers would move in to try to collect the wounded. Abel Spicer reported a trick by the French that became standard fare in Western movies two centuries later: "the french set their hats just above the top of the breast work for to deceive the soldiers" who would shoot their hats to pieces.[27] In another incident, M. de Bassignac, a captain in the French Royal-Roussillon, amused himself by placing a red flag on the end of his musket. The British, interpreting it as a flag of truce, moved forward to accept their surrender. The French soldiers, on the other hand, thought the British were surrendering and allowed them to approach the breastwork. When another officer, Captain Pierre Pouchot, saw the British advance, he ordered his troops to fire, "which laid two or three hundred upon the ground."[28] In all there were seven frontal assaults that day, but each time the British were thrown back, leaving the clearing before the wall more densely cluttered with the dead and wounded than before.

Montcalm, casting his coat off in the blazing heat of the summer, scampered over his lines, encouraging his troops by word and deed. The French had formed themselves into three lines behind the breastworks — each line taking its turn of fire at the vulnerable, but dauntless crusaders. Of their British adversaries, the French later wrote, "We must do them justice in saying that they attacked us with the most ardent tenacity."[29] Montcalm reported that the "English grenadiers and Scotch highlanders, continued charging for 3 hours without retreating or breaking, and several were killed within fifteen paces of our abbatis."[30]

There is no historical evidence that Abercromby had ever moved beyond the sawmill; had he gone to the battle site he surely would have seen the folly of his orders. At five o'clock in the afternoon, the start of another frenzied attack on the impenetrable log barrier occurred. A column of British regulars stormed the center of the wall while provincial troops at the French left flank provided a diversionary effort. This was followed swiftly by a massive attack by the 42nd Black Watch, led by Major Duncan Campbell of Inverawe,

Scotland.* As they approached the wall, the Canadian militiamen climbed the nearby trees to rain a deadly fire down upon the British. It was a blazing spark of desperation that drove the Black Watch and regulars forward, only to be repelled by French musket fire. Colonel Bougainville noted that the grenadiers and the Scotch Highlanders "returned unceasingly to the attack, without becoming discouraged or broken."[32] At six o'clock the British troops made their last attempt to charge the log wall. The utter hopelessness of the strategy was obvious as the slaughter continued, leaving the bodies of the fallen warriors piled at the foot of the wall or hanging from the sharpened stakes. At one point the panic and disorder caused the British to fire on their own troops.

By seven o'clock the defeat of the British was apparent to everyone. Major Duncan Campbell lay wounded, as did many of his 1,000 Highlanders who had suffered the most casualties in the battle. Finally, orders were given to stop the senseless massacre, although in the confusion many soldiers actually never heard them. After more than six hours of bloody slaughter, Abercromby decided that his brave troops "sustained so considerable a Loss, without any Prospect of better Success, that it was no longer prudent to remain before it."[33] Private David Perry later recalled that "We lay there till near sunset and, not receiving orders from any officer, the men crept off, leaving all the dead, and most of the wounded... We started back to our boats without any orders and pushed out on the Lake for the night."[34] The unit of Lieutenant Archelaus Fuller, a provincial officer, retired at sunset to a position in the rear where they were to hold their ground. However, many of the soldiers fell asleep, including Fuller, who awakened to find "that the army was chiefly gon."[35] Fuller's unit did not take to their bateaux until daybreak the next morning (July 9).

Most of the broken army moved back to the camp at the lake on the night of July 8. The trails leading back to the landing site were so clogged with the dead and wounded that one "could hardly walk without treading on them."[36] The movement of the regulars and provincials was reduced to a panic as the vanquished army degenerated into an uncontrollable mob. At the sawmill some order was restored to the paralyzed army, but the order from General Abercromby to return to the landing place on Lake George repeated the irresistible panic as the soldiers rushed in terror to the boats, convinced that they were being pursued by the French. Colonel Bradstreet took charge of the army, preventing the men from leaving in wild fright and confusion in the darkness. Joseph Nichols of the Massachusetts militia, while retreating that evening, heard that "the Enemy was coming to fall upon us," which created a frenzy over the bateaux that were lined fifteen deep on the shore; "The Cry of Enemy made our People Cry out & make Sad Lamentations."[37] Much of Nichols' unit apparently left in their bateaux that night. Similarly, the Connecticut unit of Lemuel Lyon departed in a panic at night after smashing "200 Barrels of Flour."[38] For most of the soldiers the retreat was confusing. Rufus Putnam was amazed at the sight of the "floating Batteries Rowing back"; when his unit was ordered to march at midnight, he assumed it was "to take Post on the hill East of Ticonderoga," but the men were directed back to the bateaux.[39]

---

*The legend of Duncan Campbell of Inverawe, Scotland, inspired many published versions including Robert Louis Stevenson's poem "Ticonderoga" published in 1891. According to the story, Campbell was warned by the ghost of his slain cousin that they would meet again at Ticonderoga. Unknown to Major Campbell was the fact that Fort Carillon was situated at a point that the Indians had named Ticonderoga. Actually, Ticonderoaga had been known by that name by provincial and British troops for years. The ghost reappeared in Campbell's tent the night before the attack. Campbell died from his wound at Ticonderoga and his gravesite today lies in the Union Cemetery between Hudson Falls and Fort Edward.[31]

Abercromby and his main force did not embark until the morning of July 9. In contrast to the gallant spirit of confidence on the trip to Ticonderoga, the British army abandoned provisions in their frenzied course to the southern end of the lake which they reached by the night of July 9. The disembarkation surprised and disheartened the army. John Cleaveland, a chaplain with a Massachusetts provincial regiment, declared that "this morning, to the general surprise of the whole army we were ordered to embark in the battoes, to leave the ground we had possessed. . .all dejected, partly on account of our returning, and partly on account of our being without much Food for Three Days."[40] Prior

"The Marquis de Montcalm congratuating his Troops after the Battle of Carillon, 8 July 1758." by Harry A. Ogden, watercolor on board, 1930. (Fort Ticonderoga Museum)

to reaching the Lake George camp, Abercromby "directed to forward all the heavy artillery back to New York," but the order was apparently never carried out.[41]

While some of the eyewitnesses placed the British loss at 5,000 killed or wounded, the actual number from Abercromby's official report was still a devastating 1,944 killed or wounded.[42] By contrast, the French losses were given between 375-444 men.[43] Although the British and provincial units tried to evacuate their wounded in the pandemonium, apparently many were left behind. "We got away the wounded of our company; but left a great many crying for help, which we were unable to afford them . . .none of those that we left behind were ever heard of afterwards," wrote young Perry of the provincial forces.[44] In rare instances there were a few survivors. After being badly wounded during the attack on the French breastwork, Jacob Towne, a provincial recruit from Topsfield, Massachusetts, was covered with a severed tree top by a comrade. Four days later he was discovered under the tree by the French and eventually recovered from his wounds.[45] Seventeen days after the battle, French scouts discovered "a great number of corpses on litters," the remnants of the wounded that were left by the British during the chaotic retreat.[46]

On the evening of July 8, with expectation of a renewed attack, the French worked with feverish resolve to repair their breastwork and finish their batteries on the right and left flanks. The next day Montcalm's forces spent the day burying the French and British dead on the field of battle. A company of volunteers sent to reconnoiter the British position later in the day found to their surprise that they had gone. The following morning Montcalm detached General de Lévis with eight grenadier companies along with some Canadians and volunteers to find the British. The French retraced the steps of the British army, finding many soldiers in the woods who were lost and 700 quarters of partially destroyed meal. "We found in the mud, on the road to the Falls, more than five hundred pairs of shoes with buckles."[47] Wounded men, provisions, 200 barrels of flour, and abandoned equipment were discovered in addition to the "remains of barges and burned pontoons."[48]

On July 11, M. Rigaud de Vaudreuil, brother of the governor and veteran of the two assaults on Fort William Henry in 1757, finally arrived with the long-awaited reinforcements, consisting mainly of Canadians and Indians. The 3,143 reinforcements brought troop strength to 6,669, still less than half of Abercromby's army. The following day Montcalm reviewed his army, which had been formed into a square on the battlefield. The victorious general made a speech thanking the soldiers in the name of the king and had a priest say a mass. Montcalm later dedicated a roughly hewn cross, painted red, at the French lines. A replica of that cross still stands on the access road to the fort. This was the last significant victory for the French in the war. It was also one of the largest and bloodiest battles in North America until the U.S. Civil War.

After two centuries, the lingering question remains. How could James Abercromby, a career officer, make such a tragic blunder in his conduct of the offensive against the French lines? In the first place, Abercromby had intended that Howe provide the field command while his role would be more of a logistical manager. When Howe was killed, he hesitated as the army faltered for a day and a half which gave the French precious time for building the log wall and for bringing in reinforcements.

Why hadn't the artillery been brought from the lake to smash the log wall, especially when there was some dispute among his officers as to the strength of the barricade? Abercromby's fear of immediate French reinforcements had some justification since de Rigaud's troops did reach Carillon within days of the engagement. However, Abercromby would still have had twice the troops of the French.

Abercromby, however, had little faith in the 9,000 provincial troops that were part of the expedition. Throughout the French and Indian War, British officers looked down upon the provincial troops with undisguised contempt, despite evidence to the contrary. British opinion on provincial military effectiveness stemmed partly from the background of political freedom and flexibility in military service of the provincial troops. The provincials were simply not willing to provide the blind allegiance and discipline required by the professional officers of the British army. A royal order in 1756 relegated colonial officers, regardless of rank, as captains with the least seniority during operations with British troops. This further intensified the division between British and provincial officers. A young Massachusetts officer resentfully suggested that British officers treated Americans like "Orderly Serjeants."[49] Abercromby used the regulars for the frontal assaults and treated the provincial troops as scapegoats for his defeat at Ticonderoga. "It is with concern that I tell you that from every circumstance that I have seen and which has happened, no real dependence is to be had upon the bulk of the provincials. . . Their officers with a very few exceptions are worse than their men."[50] Abercromby argued that more than two-thirds of the provincials retreated in haste to the landing site on Lake George on July 8, requiring him to post a guard at the bridge to stop them. A letter, however, by Captain Joshua Loring reported that "General Lyman's Connecticut line stood their ground and wanted to entrench after the defeat and carry on with the siege."[51] Another British officer, James Wolfe, who died in 1759 during the successful assault on Quebec, reflected on Abercromby's provincial troops. "The Americans are in general the dirtiest, most contemptible, cowardly dogs that you can conceive. . . . Such rascals as those are rather an encumbrance than any real strength to an army."[52]

The provincials, at the same time, reflected negatively on Abercromby's command of the Ticonderoga expedition. Colonel William Williams, who commanded a provincial regiment at Ticonderoga, wrote three days later to his uncle in Deerfield, Massachusetts, that "leaving the place we went to capture, the best part of the army is unhinged. I have told you enough to make you sick, if the relation acts on you as the facts have on me."[53] John Cleaveland at the time of the attack mused that "the conduct is thought to be marvellous strange, to order the entrenchment to be forced with small arms, when they had cannon not far off."[54] Rufus Putnam in his memoirs reflected on Abercromby's leadership: "I considered it the most injudicious and wanton sacrifice of men that ever came within my knowledge or reading."[55]

Ironically, the experience of the Abercromby expedition and other battles in the French and Indian War would set the stage for the next confrontation in North America. At the beginning of the American Revolution, the British were totally convinced that they could easily annihilate an inept American army. Captain Charles Lee scoffed at the British derision of American troops. He noted that the parade maneuvers and formal training of the regulars were of little military value in the American wilderness. His presence at Abercromby's defeat had an obvious impact on the myth of the invincibility of the British military. The American experience during the French and Indian War made them less apprehensive in the face of British threats after the war and more confident in their ideals and military ability.

While the Abercromby expedition to Carillon was a major failure in 1758, the British did achieve success in other campaigns during the year. Amherst's capture of Louisbourg was only one of three effective operations. Lieutenant Colonel John Bradstreet, head of the bateau service and participant in the Abercromby expedition, was finally granted permission at a council of war in mid-July at Lake George for a campaign against Fort Frontenac on Lake Ontario. Bradstreet moved quickly along the Mohawk River with his army to present-day Rome, New York, where construction of Fort Stanwix was to begin. Moving forward on August 12 with 2,600 troops and 300 bateau men, Bradstreet, with considerable secrecy, moved his artillery, supplies, and troops in 123 bateaux and 95 whaleboats toward Lake Ontario. On August 27 the undermanned Fort Frontenac, at present-day Kingston,

Ontario, fell to Bradstreet's army. The lightning raid, by eighteenth-century standards, was a logistical triumph which yielded an immense quantity of French provisions, artillery, furs, and vessels. After destroying much of the fort and war material, Bradstreet returned to Oswego with some of the provisions in the two largest warships. The two vessels were burned before Bradstreet's army embarked for Albany.

The Fort Duquesne expedition, renewed in 1758, was commanded by 48-year-old Brigadier General John Forbes, a Scottish veteran who had earlier served on Lord Loudoun's senior staff. Forbes decided to forge a new direct route through the Allegheny Mountains in Pennsylvania rather than use the existing road where Braddock had been annihilated three years earlier. Although Colonel George Washington and other Virginians opposed the plan, Forbes proceeded on his arduous expedition by mid- July. Most Virginians favored the old road through Virginia mainly for economic reasons. The ailing Forbes, often carried on a litter, established a number of staging areas, or supply depots, as the army cut its way through the primeval forest. On November 24, as the British army approached Fort Duquesne, the French blew up the fort and retreated. The French garrison had little choice but to evacuate since provisions were insufficient to withstand a siege due to the cutting of supply lines with the fall of Frontenac at the hands of Bradstreet. With his health failing, Forbes was carried back through snowstorms to Philadelphia where he died in March 1759.

During the rest of the 1758 summer at Lake George, Abercromby and his army remained relatively idle at the southern end of the lake. The Rangers were actively engaged in warding off French raiding parties while the rest of the troops built breastworks and ships and tried to avoid camp diseases that spread through the idle army. The French likewise had a relatively uneventful season after the July battle. On July 24 a detachment of 600 Indians and Canadians departed from Fort Carillon. They were to leave sooner, but games of lacrosse between the Iroquois and Abnaki Indians, where 1,000 crowns of belts and strings of wampum were at stake, delayed their departure.

Canadian Governor Vaudreuil, during the remaining season, pressed Montcalm to attack the British at Lake George. Because of the lack of provisions at Carillon for a major military expedition and recognizing the lack of any real military target at Lake George, Montcalm, for the most part, simply ignored Vaudreuil. The British wagon convoys at the time were mainly carrying wine, spirits, and other provisions of sutlers (private merchants) to the garrison at Lake George and were not worthy of attack by the whole French army.

Although the main French army was not engaged during the remaining months of 1758, their raiding parties still roamed the countryside. M. de St. Luc, a Canadian captain with a party of 300 Indians and 200 Canadians, attacked a convoy of 40 to 50 wagons between Fort Edward and Half-Way Brook (north of Fort Edward). One hundred sixteen English were reportedly killed, including 16 Rangers. Several women, children, and sutlers were killed or captured in the ambush. The French and Indians returned to Fort Carillon with 60 prisoners, 110 scalps, and some of the provisions and equipment pillaged from the wagons. Major Robert Rogers, with a force of 700, was dispatched after the French. The French and Indians, however, eluded the detachment. On August 8, after camping near Fort Anne, the remaining 530 troops with the detachment encountered a slightly smaller French party under M. Marin, a Canadian captain. Major Israel Putnam, marching at the head of the provincials, was captured along with a lieutenant and two others. After an hour of intense musketry, the French retreated with their prisoners. Rogers reported "the enemy's loss was

199 killed on the spot, several of which were Indians"; but Bougainville noted only 13 French and Indians killed on the field of battle.[56]

Major Putnam's ordeal after his capture is one of the extraordinary tales of the war. The Indians hauled the major to the rear, lashing him tightly to a tree. One young Indian entertained himself by throwing his tomahawk as close to the head of Putnam as possible without hitting him. Then a French or Canadian officer pressed his musket to his chest and squeezed the trigger. The flint struck, but the musket did not fire. The officer turned the weapon around and smashed Putnam in the face with its butt. Whether the musket misfired or the officer was just trying to frighten him further is unknown. At this point, Putnam may have been caught in a crossfire between the French and British. He was untied, stripped of his coat, shoes, and stockings and forced to carry many of the French knapsacks. Upon arriving at the encampment for the night, the Indians again lashed him to a tree, stripped him and heaped brush around him. As the flames leaped upward, a sudden shower doused the fire. When it ended, the Indians repeated the preparations and soon relighted the fresh brush. At this point Captain Marin, realizing what was occurring, broke through the crowd of Indians, kicked the brush aside, and cut Putnam down.[57] The 40-year-old Putnam was later exchanged for French prisoners and continued in military service to the end of the war. In 1762 he again cheated death as one of the few survivors of a shipwreck off Cuba during the ill-fated Havana expedition. Putnam at 57 commanded the Connecticut troops at the Battle of Bunker Hill in 1775 and two days later was appointed a major general in the Continental army. The energetic, persevering Putnam became the subject of many legends that continue to be debated by historians today.

A major shipbuilding effort at Lake George began in the summer and fall of 1758. When Colonel John Bradstreet, head of the bateau service, was sent to capture Fort Frontenac on the St. Lawrence, the command of the vessels on the lake went to Captain Joshua Loring of Hingham, Massachusetts. Loring, a former privateer and captain in the Royal Navy, was the first experienced seaman in charge of the naval activity on the lakes. He was also familiar with inland water with his command of a brig on Lake Ontario in 1756.

Some of the most closely recorded notes on the vessels constructed on Lake George during 1758 come from the journal of Captain Samuel Cobb, who commanded a company from the Massachusetts regiment during the attack on Carillon. The 39-year-old captain was a well-known shipwright from Maine (then a part of Massachusetts) who built more than 150 vessels during his lifetime. On July 19, barely a week after the disaster at Ticonderoga, Cobb noted in his journal that he "Began to Work on a Sloop to Draft and Mould her."[58] The sloop and other vessels were built at the southeast end of Lake George. Colonel Henry Champion with the provincial troops from Connecticut noted on July 25 that the army was "building a shipyard at ye southeast corner of ye Lake, building a breast work round it, building saw-pit in it, sawing ship plank and getting ship timber."[59] The Lake George camp in July consisted of a "Piqueted Fort where W. H. stood another opposite on East side of ye Swamp," a hospital, cabins for the wounded, and another breastwork located on Diamond Island.[60] The picketed forts, begun in late June, were probably little more than breastworks.

Pressured by Loring, Cobb and his carpenters worked on the sloop every day despite filthy living conditions and illness that plagued the camp. The sloop became stuck in her ways during an attempted launch on August 9 but was successfully launched on the following morning. Abercromby's purpose in building the sloop was "not only for Protection and

Security. . . but also. . .Cruising to and fro, up the Lake to watch and discover the Motions of the Enemy."[61] A contemporary newspaper described "the Earl of Halifax, 51 Feet Keel, about 100 Tons Burthen. . .to carry 18 6 & 4 pounders, 20 Swivels, 50 Sailors, and a Company of Marines," but an eyewitness suggested an armament consisting of "ten four pounders carried aboard, and there was two more for to be carried and twelve swivels."[62] During the course of the remaining season, the *Halifax* would complete six cruises on Lake George. The French, after receiving reports from scouts, called the *Halifax* "a bark carrying twelve four-pounders" and worried that the activity at Lake George was in preparation for a siege of Carillon in October.[63] The *Halifax*, used by the British in 1758 and 1759, was depicted

The sloop *Halifax*, built at Lake George in August 1758, was sunk in the lake for winter storage and raised the following year. Drawing by Montserrat Centeno.

in a "View of Lake George, 1759" by Thomas Davies while he was with Amherst's army (the original painting is now in the Fort Ticonderoga Museum).

By the end of August, Cobb and ten carpenters began work on "a Row Gally of 40 feet long 15 feet wide 5 feet deep to carry 12 pounders in the stern and 5 Swivels on a Side to go with 24 Oars."[64] The journal of Dr. Caleb Rea on September 14 reveals the readiness of the two row galleys; "the Row Gallys mounted with Guns & tryed by fireing their Canon."[65] These stubby vessels were the forerunners of the gunboats and galleys that the Americans would construct on Lake Champlain in 1776.

In late September Reverend John Cleaveland, still with the Massachusetts provincial soldiers, described a rare delineation of the construction of Indian canoes in his journal.

After dinner one night he walked down to the shore of Lake George to view two captured birch bark canoes, the largest of which was 35 feet in length, five feet wide, and carried 20 men. The inside was made "with Cedar Clap-Boards thin as brown paper and laid lengthways of ye Canoe upon which crossways of ye Canoe is another laying of Cedar."[66]

On September 18 Cobb and his carpenters were reassigned to Captain Thomas Ord, a British officer in charge of the artillery who had been supervising the building of a large radeau. The radeau, designed as a floating fort, was an idea that had surfaced earlier as evidenced by the detailed instructions sent to William Johnson at Lake George in 1755 by John Dies (chapter 2). In 1756 William Shirley had recommended to James Abercromby the capture of Ticonderoga or Crown Point "by attacking it with a floating Battery from the Lake at the same time, that it is attacked by Land."[67] "Radeau," meaning "raft" in French, denoted the flat-bottomed nature of the ship. The lower sides of a radeau inclined slightly outward while the upper sides or bulwarks curved inward at a steep angle over the interior of the vessel. The upper sides, fitted with cannon ports, fully enclosed and protected "ye men's Bodys & Heads" and "contriv'd so that tis impossible for the Enemy to board her."[68] The radeau was equipped with a large number of sweeps (oars) with a design for one or two masts and square sails.

Cobb's journal entries for each succeeding day mentioned working on the "Raddow." Only Sundays and days that he was incapacitated by the "Bloody flux" or dysentery did Cobb fail to labor on the radeau. Colonel Henry Champion, a provincial officer from Colchester, Connecticut, became an interested observer of the radeau construction. On October 7 Champion drew a sketch of the radeau in his journal with notation that "it is 51 feet in length, about 16 or 18 wide, straight flat bottom, flaring waist about 5 feet high, then turns with an elbow. . . The name of this creature is Tail and End, or Land Tortoise."[69] Dr. Rea also walked to the lakeside shipyard on October 7 to examine the new vessels under construction and drew a sketch in his journal of a type of vessel that he had never seen before. "One," according to Rea, "is very odd, being seven squared sided like this figure, besides she Tumbles in & makes seven squares more, so that she is truly fourteen square besides her bottom & top."[70] Christopher Comstock from a Connecticut regiment likewise made a drawing of the radeau which he labeled "Tail and End" and tried to explain the strange configuration as "Something Like a gambrel Roof house."[71]

With winter approaching the desolate region, the men strained to finish the vessels at Lake George. By mid-October, artillery and some of the bateaux had been hauled southward. The two row galleys were sunk in the lake on October 16 for safekeeping over the winter.[72] Finally, on October 20 Cobb reported that "we launched 2 Raddows," one measured 50 feet with a 19-foot width and 6-foot depth while the second was only 30 feet by 7 feet.[73] "We tryed the Raddows and Rowed well they went with 26 Oars," Cobb noted on October 21.[74] Snow in the air provided a new incentive for the troops to begin their long march homeward. On Sunday, October 22, only two days after their launching, Cobb related "Working on the Raddows Sinking them in the lake."[75] By then, some of the provincials had begun to refer to the strange-looking *Land Tortoise* as the "ark" or "Ord's Ark" while one New Hampshire soldier called it "the most odd vessel" at the lake.[76]

The sloop *Halifax, Land Tortoise*, row galleys, and other vessels at the lake, including 260 bateaux, were sunk in the depths of Lake George for protection. Because Fort William Henry had been destroyed by the French in the summer of 1757, the ships could not be safeguarded by a garrisoned fort over the winter. Leaving the vessels exposed would certainly result in their destruction as had occurred during a French raid across the ice in March 1757. Placing them in cold storage at the bottom of the lake with retrieval planned for the spring of 1759 was the only option available.

Given the state of the eighteenth-century technology, how were these large vessels sunk? One clue comes from Henry Champion, who noted that stone-filled cribs had been attached to the *Halifax* and *Land Tortoise* to sink them.[77] The rigging and cannon were removed from the *Halifax* before her sinking and buried onshore. The buildings were dismantled and boards buried or burned. On October 23 Cobb's regiment began their long, cold march home; three days later Champion and his regiment departed.

The French, later scouting Lake George, were taken by surprise when they found the camp completely abandoned with defensive works, storehouses (which were reportedly 350 feet long), and huts burned. Bougainville reported that the English had "buried bombs and shot and sunk their bark and part of their barges."[78] Montcalm immediately sent out a detachment with some "specialists" to try to dig up the shot and haul out the "bark" (*Halifax*) and "barges" (bateaux). "This detachment found twenty quarters of salt pork, two hundred barrels of lime, the location of the bark, fifty sunken barges, and several other caches in a neighboring swamp."[79] The French apparently did not raise any of the vessels; the *Halifax* was hoisted out the following spring with some difficulty by the British. Colonel Bougainville concluded that the decision by Montcalm not to attack the English at Lake George, as Vaudreuil had pressed for, was the correct one since they had burned their own entrenchment and departed.

Although Colonel Israel Williams of Massachusetts and others had called for a second attempt on Fort Carillon, no other expedition was formed for that purpose in 1758. Following a new proposal in late August by Colonels James Prevost and Thomas Gage to attack Carillon and subsequent news that six of General Amherst's battalions were to be sent to Lake George, Abercromby decided to make a second expedition to capture the French fort. Following a council of war in early October which included Amherst, Abercromby, and Gage, the plan for the renewed attack was shelved due mainly to the lateness of the season and the strengthening of the outer works at Carillon by the French.[80] Abercromby soon received his letter of recall from Pitt. The beleaguered general returned to Britain where his dubious record was acknowledged with a promotion to lieutenant general, but he never saw active service again. Amherst replaced Abercromby as the commander in North America. A year after the fateful expedition of 1758, an army nearly the size and composition of Abercromby's advanced again on Fort Carillon. This time, with a more cautious commander, the results were dramatically different.

Archaeological Discoveries

The vessels from the French and Indian War lay unnoticed at the bottom of the lake for many years. The first vessel to attract attention was a sunken hull in 15 feet of water near the steamboat dock at Lake George Village. The hull was described in many guidebooks during the late nineteenth century. The vessel, built of black oak, was 44 feet long, 14 feet wide, and 7 feet deep.[81] The sloop-like vessel, raised on July 2, 1903, yielded old military buttons and buckles, pewter spoons, pipes, grapeshot, and a 1743 Spanish coin. Historians speculated that it was one of the sloops destroyed by Vaudreuil in the March 1757 raid, but it is certainly possible that it was one of the vessels constructed later at the lake. Unfortunately, the vessel was cut up for souvenirs. Several frames, apparently from this vessel, were donated to the Lake George Historical Association in 1990.

Another vessel that has fascinated Lake George history buffs lay in the waters off Floating Battery Island, north of Black Mountain Point in the Narrows. Although there are several versions of how the island was named, the dominant story relates to the abandonment of one of the floating batteries used by Abercromby in the ill-fated 1758 expedition. In 1888 Charles Posson's guide to Lake George suggested that on the south side of the "Southernmost Island are the remains of two floating batteries built to accompany Abercrombie."[82] The daughter of the first forest ranger on the lake recalled seeing the vessel with all its ribs in place during the 1920s. In the 1950s Colonel Lorenzo Hagglund, the New York salvage engineer who raised the Revolutionary War schooner *Royal Savage* and the gondola *Philadelphia* from Lake Champlain in the 1930s, searched for a gunboat or floating battery around the island. After searching the south side of the island in the 1970s, I finally discovered remnants of the vessel. By then it was totally broken up with a few pieces scattered around a wide area. The remaining parts definitely appear to be of the hand hewn construction characteristic of the period. A keel, strakes (side boards), and a large bateau-type rib are identical to vessels of the eighteenth century. A larger frame (rib) from the vessel is presently in the Fort Ticonderoga Museum.

In July 1960 two divers discovered a 28-foot vessel from the French and Indian War with approximately 40 large, 13-inch mortar bombs off the southern shore of Lake George.[83] The vessel may have been two bateaux rigged as a pontoon or one of the small radeaux built from a bateau for the Abercromby Expedition. The 150-pound mortar bombs were subsequently raised and are presently displayed at Fort William Henry, Fort Ticonderoga, the Adirondack Museum, the Skenesborough Museum, and the Smithsonian Institution.

The most extensive archaeological discoveries in Lake George have been bateaux. Published reports on locations of sunken bateaux appeared as early as 1893.[84] In the late 1930s an amateur diver using a homemade apparatus observed a group of bateaux on the southeast shore of the lake. It was not until July 1960, however, that two teenage scuba divers rediscovered the bateaux.[85] In total, about 14 bateaux were located that summer. The archaeological work that ensued drew widespread attention involving the staff of the Adirondack Museum, a team of divers from the Smithsonian, and U.S. Navy divers from Washington, D.C. Three bateaux were eventually raised and preserved under the supervision of Robert Inverarity, then director of the Adirondack Museum. The sunken vessels were part of the "wet storage" ordered by General Abercromby in October 1758. Colonel John Bradstreet's report on the "State of the Battoes" on December 31, 1758, to the new commander-in-chief, General Jeffery Amherst, noted: "Sunk in Lake George—260" and "hid in the woods near Lake George—30."[86]

The 1960 bateaux were found on the bottom of the lake in orderly rows, indicating that they were probably sunk purposely. The recovered bateaux had a 32-foot bottom length and a 34-foot overall length, making them larger than those commonly used in rivers or streams where portaging would be a problem.[87] The examination of the curved ribs of the bateaux also indicated that the whaleboat influenced the design of the Lake George bateaux. During the summers of 1963 and 1964 the Adirondack Museum sponsored "Operation Bateaux" directed by Dr. Inverarity. Terry Crandall was charged with the search

the Name of thy
Creature is tail an End
or land tortoys

LEFT ABOVE. A 44-foot sloop raised from Lake George near the site of Fort William Henry in 1903. (Lake George Historical Association)

LEFT. Bateau from Lake George on display at the Adirondack Museum. Raised in the early 1960s, the vessel has a bottom length of 32 feet with an overall length of 34 feet. Photo by the author.

ABOVE. Original drawing of radeau *Land Tortoise* by Henry Champion. (Connecticut State Archives)

RIGHT. This Klein side-scan sonar record shows the 18th century radeau shipwreck *Land Tortoise* found in Lake George, N.Y. on June 26, 1990 by the LGBRRT.
(Copyright 1990 by Joseph W. Zarzynski, Klein Assoc., Inc.)

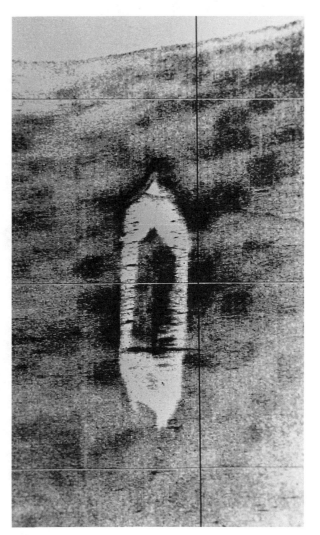

Bow showing mooring rings.

THE RADEAU

AND TORTOISE

1. Mooring ring and sweep port on the stern port section. 2. Open gunport. 3. Port side bow. 4. Inside of starboard section showing frames and sweep port holes. 5. Gunport lid on starboard side. Photos by the author.

1.

2.

3.

4.

5.

and underwater processing of the archaeological sites in Lake George for the museum. His extensive examination of over two dozen sites in the lake was a significant early archaeological study of French and Indian War vessels.

In July of 1965 the state police, with 15 qualified scuba divers and 17 trooper candidates, held a training exercise on several bateau sites. While the acting state historian identified the remains of the vessels, hundreds of relics including ribs, planking, and musket balls were taken from the bateaux piece by piece.[88] In retrospect this, unfortunately, was not a desirable archaeological project since the vessels were not measured, relics were mixed up, and the sites were disturbed for future research.

Twenty-seven years after their discovery in 1960, an archaeological workshop at Lake George held under the auspices of the Atlantic Alliance for Maritime Heritage Conservation would focus once again on one of the main bateau sites. The workshop at Lake George was organized by Joseph Zarzynski, author and lecturer, and taught by R. Duncan Mathewson, then chairman of the Atlantic Alliance and chief marine archaeologist for the seventeenth-century shipwreck *Atocha*. After classroom and pool instruction in the fundamentals of proper underwater archaeology including the use of a grid system, 21 sport divers with state notification began a thorough study of some of the remaining bateau wrecks. Philip Lord, Jr., senior scientist, Office of Archaeology, New York, was able to observe the survey through a monitor connected to a Remotely-Operated-Vehicle (ROV), a tethered underwater robot with a video camera. At the same time, the Lake Champlain Maritime Museum at Basin Harbor built an exact reproduction of the Lake George bateau that had been recovered in 1960.

Other bateau clusters have been found in recent years on the southwestern shore of the lake. Further study of these sites may determine how these vessels were sunk and retrieved, the use of sails, whether they were rowed by standing or sitting and whether the vessels were tied together when they were sunk. Unfortunately, with the expansion of scuba diving, many wreck sites were dismantled piece by piece for souvenirs. Although a 1958 New York law prohibited disturbing any archaeological or historic site, many of the sunken bateaux were systematically stripped of everything but their bottom boards. A new era which recognizes that our historic underwater wreck sites are finite resources is slowly dawning.

In June 1990, 232 years after her sinking, the ghostly outline of the *Land Tortoise* appeared on the printer of a side-scan sonar unit. Led by Joseph Zarzynski, the Lake George Bateaux Research Team, which had been awarded an Explorers Club flag to search for French and Indian war vessels, discovered the radeau. The *Land Tortoise* had been sitting perfectly upright for more than two centuries, last observed by provincial soldiers in 1758. The group had discovered the oldest completely intact warship ever found in the Western Hemisphere and the only radeau known to exist. Over the next two months, an archaeological survey was initiated that included the use of an underwater robot (ROV), photography, and physical measurements by divers. The group's work to nominate bateaux to the National Register of Historic Places now included documentation of the radeau for a similar nomination. I served as the historian on the project and the underwater still-photographer.

The archaeological survey of the *Land Tortoise* revealed a number of features that had not been disclosed in the wartime journals. The seven gunports, three on the starboard side and four on the port side, were designed asymmetrically to avoid interference between gun crews during the recoil and loading of the cannon. One gunport in the bow and another in the stern section allowed firepower from all sides of the radeau. Sweep ports on six sections of the *Land Tortoise* permitted complete maneuverability of the vessel, while two mast steps found in the hull floor indicated that the ship was intended for sail on the open lake. The upper-bow sections have a view hole on each side that would have allowed an observer to scrutinize a military engagement or the forward progress of the radeau without raising his head above the protective structure. The measurements taken in 1990, approximately 52 feet in length and 18 feet wide, are virtually identical to those given in the Cobb and Champion journals. The 26 sweep ports found on the vessel coincide with Cobb's description, while the configurations drawn by Champion, Comstock, and Rea parallel the outline of the radeau.

During 1991 the team continued their documentation of the radeau site under a permit from the state of New York. Prior to the 1991 archaeological survey, the state provided plastic permit signs to the team that warned other divers of the on-going archaeological study of the vessel. The free-standing signs encircled the radeau on the floor of the lake. Divers, working under the direction of archaeologists Robert Cembrola and D. K. Abbass, measured all frames, planks, and stanchions on the vessel including their exact location and spacing. Each stanchion was assigned a small numbered flag to aid the divers in the recording process. Each side of the vessel has 16 hardwood frames with an adjacent knee that serves as a stanchion for the upper sides. The vessel appears to be constructed of a combination of oak and pine which is consistent with historical records.[89]

Diary and journal records indicate that the *Land Tortoise* was never raised during the following campaign of 1759. Our group struggled with the mystery of the depth of the radeau at 107 feet given its planned retrieval. The mystery was largely solved by the diary of William Sweat who related the difficulty in sinking the flat-bottomed vessel which ended in the loss of the radeau during a haphazard operation after dark: "Sunday 22 Day, I was forced to go to work, a sinking our Radow, which wee got Ready at the Sun sect [set], & we Sunk her once; But one side Rise again, so that we were forced to work the chief of the night, Before we could keep her Down."[90]

Although there is no definitive answer as to how best to protect the *Land Tortoise* for future generations, all agree that the completely intact radeau is a national treasure.

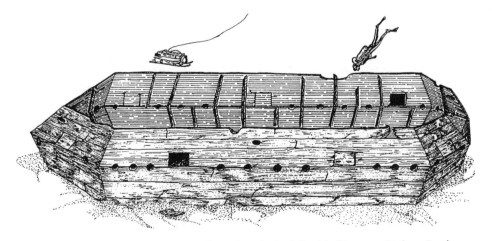

Drawing of radeau *Land Tortoise* by Linda Schmidt (Bateaux Below, Inc.)

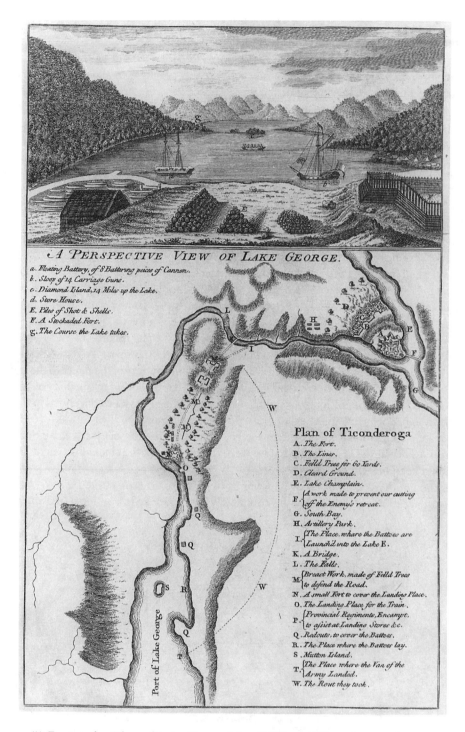

A PERSPECTIVE VIEW OF LAKE GEORGE.

a. *Floating Battery, of 8 Battering peices of Cannon.*
b. *Sloop of 14 Carriage Guns.*
c. *Diamond Island, 14 Miles up the Lake.*
d. *Store House.*
E. *Piles of Shot & Shells.*
F. *A Stockaded Fort.*
g. *The Course the Lake takes.*

Plan of Ticonderoga

A. *The Fort.*
B. *The Lines.*
C. *Felld Trees for 60 Yards.*
D. *Cleard Ground.*
E. *Lake Champlain.*
F. *A work made to prevent our cutting off the Enemy's retreat.*
G. *South Bay.*
H. *Artillery Park.*
I. *The Place, where the Battoes are Launch'd into the Lake E.*
K. *A Bridge.*
L. *The Falls.*
M. *Breast Work, made of Felld Trees to defend the Road.*
N. *A small Fort to cover the Landing Place.*
O. *The Landing Place for the Train.*
P. *Provincial Regiments, Encampt. to assist at Landing Stores &c.*
Q. *Redouts, to cover the Battoes.*
R. *The Place where the Battoes lay.*
S. *Mutton Island.*
T. *The Place where the Van of the Army Landed.*
W. *The Rout they took.*

Port of Lake George

"A Perspective View of Lake George" [and] "Plan of Ticonderoga" in 1759 by Henry Skinner with the radeau *Invincible* and sloop *Halifax*. First published in *The Universal Magazine*, London, 1759. (Fort Ticonderoga Museum)

5. Amherst Sweeps the Lakes

WILLIAM PITT'S OVERALL PLAN FOR 1759 not only included Jeffery Amherst's primary campaign to take the French forts on Lake Champlain and move into Canada, but also involved expeditions against Fort Niagara on Lake Ontario and Quebec City. In the early summer Brigadier General John Prideaux and Sir William Johnson were sent to re-establish the British base at Oswego and then move to capture Fort Niagara, the vital French outpost linked to other western posts. Leaving about 1,000 troops at Oswego under Lieutenant Colonel Frederick Haldimand, Prideaux and Johnson advanced to Niagara with over 2,000 troops and 900 Indians. A week after the siege had begun, Prideaux was accidently killed by a mortar discharged from his own lines. On July 25, following the defeat of a French relief force, Pierre Pouchot, a captain in the French regulars, surrendered his outnumbered force to Johnson.

In June, 22 British warships and a larger number of transport vessels, carrying an army of 9,000 men under Brigadier General James Wolfe, arrived at Quebec City. The British army, however, soon became stalemated in their attempt to establish a foothold in the city. The French, meanwhile, sent fireships (vessels set ablaze, loaded with munitions) against the British armada in the St. Lawrence River. Wolfe, wracked by illness during the summer, launched a successful assault in September on the Heights of Abraham above Quebec. The dramatic British victory came after more than 4,000 troops scaled the rocky ledges in the early morning hours of September 13. Wolfe, at the front with his men, pressed General Marquis de Montcalm, the successful commander at Carillon in 1758, into an immediate pitched battle. Without waiting for Colonel Louis de Bougainville's 3,000 reinforcements, Montcalm's army, which approximated Wolfe's force in size, marched straight into the muskets of the British line. Firing too soon, the French ranks were overwhelmed by the deadly British fire, which came at a closer range. Both Montcalm and Wolfe died on the field of battle. The governor of New France, Marquis de Vaudreuil, fled to Montreal as did Bougainville and his army.

The late spring of 1759 saw the gathering of a British and provincial army at Lake George for the fifth consecutive year. Once again the objective would be to drive the French from their fortifications on Lake Champlain. The leadership of Britain's main campaign for 1759 rested with the army's 42-year-old commander-in-chief, Major General Jeffery Amherst. Although Amherst had little command experience before coming to North America, his successful direction of the Louisbourg expedition in 1758 instilled confidence in his leadership. Amherst was essentially a careful military manager and firm disciplinarian who took few risks and planned for all eventualities. While the cannon and musket were the essential tools of his trade, he was also partial to the shovel and hammer. He would leave his mark on Lake George and Lake Champlain with three forts that still stand and the building of the first British fleet on Lake Champlain.

The campaign of 1759 ushered in a new military era in the history of Lake Champlain that would not end until the close of 1814. The age of major naval fleets forever changed the landscape in the struggle for the continent. As Colonel Louis de Bougainville, the erudite French journal keeper, observed in 1758, "the only way to assure ourselves the possession of Lake Champlain and St. Frederic River is by a strong naval force."[1] A race to build armed schooners, sloops, and radeaux would now determine the control of the two lakes.

By early June the British army began its trek to Lake George. Amherst himself reached Fort Edward by June 6. Preparations for the renewed campaign included moving provisions, artillery, ammunition, and bateaux to Lake George. Many officers who were with the ill-fated Abercromby expedition were back to try again. Veteran officers of the Lake George and Ticonderoga campaigns included General Phineas Lyman, Lieutenant Colonel William Eyre, Colonel John Bradstreet, Major Robert Rogers, and Captain John Stark, among others. At Fort Edward on the evening of June 17, a Canadian major and four men under a flag of truce arrived with letters from the French generals, Montcalm and Bourlamaque, concerning the exchange of prisoners. Amherst had expected the French flag of truce as a way of observing the preparations of the British army. The French at the time had a force of 3,000 regulars and Canadian militia under Bourlamaque at Fort Carillon. The French by June were nervously awaiting Amherst's army, which was erroneously estimated at 25,000. Meanwhile, Amherst's army was rebuilding the Fort Edward-Lake George road and brewing spruce beer, a preventative for scurvy made by boiling the cuttings from the tops of spruce trees in water. The Fort Edward camp was a major assembly point for the troops who arrived almost daily from distant colonies. On June 21 the drums beat a half hour before daybreak, signaling the start of the army's move to Lake George. Just before the march, the total army that Amherst commanded at Fort Edward included 6,537 regulars and 4,839 provincial troops. Amherst ordered intricate precautions against an ambush, but the march to Lake George was uneventful. By nine at night the rear guard had finally arrived at Lake George. A total of 6,236 troops was now at the lake.

The very next day Amherst met with his chief engineer, Colonel James Montresor, to plan the location for a new fort at Lake George. The site of the fort was the high ground used as the entrenched camp during the siege of Fort William Henry in 1757. Within three weeks "about 2 or 3 acres of foundation" were laid, a month later a provincial officer noted "the Walls [are] about 14 Feet thick Built of Stone & Lime."[2] Named Fort George, the fortification would encompass barracks and a hospital but was never completely finished; the remnants of the fort still stand in the Lake George Battlefield Park.*

---

* A visitor to the lake in 1767 described Fort George as a "redoubt amounting to 12 guns, about 200 yards from shore, and some barracks."[3] Additional work on the fortification occurred during the Revolutionary War. An ambitious reconstruction of the fort began in 1921 but was never completed.

General Jeffery Amherst.
(National Gallery of Canada)

One of the biggest tasks for the army was retrieving their sunken vessels from 1758 and building new ones. By June 25 Captain Joshua Loring, the commander of the naval forces, was busy trying to bring the sloop *Halifax* to the surface. Amherst noted the next day that "Capt. Loring can't get his sloop up which was to have come up very easily."[4] On July 4, after ten days of labor, the *Halifax* was brought slightly above water and hauled to one of the docks on the southern shore of Lake George. It took several more days to get all the

"A View of the Lines at Lake George, 1759" by Thomas Davies shows Amherst's Lake George camp with the radeau *Invincible* and sloop *Halifax*. (Fort Ticonderoga Museum)

water out before repairs could be made and a new mast cut. The cannon from the vessel that had been buried the previous fall were also successfully retrieved. Similarly, "a Row galley that had been sunk Last fall was found and got up to shoer,"according to Lemuel Wood, a 17-year-old provincial from Massachusetts.[5] Henry Skinner, a Captain-Lieutenant in the Royal Artillery, recorded the depth of the vessel at "40 feet water."[6] What remains to be understood is just how the seemingly Herculean task of raising these ships in the wilderness of North America was actually accomplished. There is evidence, however, that free divers were used to retrieve objects from the bottom of the lake in 1759.[7]

Apparently the army at Lake George mistakenly believed that the French had raised the radeau *Land Tortoise* since Skinner noted that "the only thing of any consequence that they have found is a floating battery."[8] Without the recovery of the *Land Tortoise*, another large radeau was constructed under the supervision of Major Thomas Ord, the commander of the artillery train. Although slightly behind schedule, the radeau *Invincible* was built in less than two weeks. On July 16 Ord's radeau splashed into Lake George at five o'clock in the evening. With the record construction time, Amherst found one problem, "a little mistake in the height of the Port Holes of the Radeau, but she will do."[9] A 1759 painting by Captain Thomas Davies, presently at the Fort Ticonderoga Museum, depicts a single-masted *Invincible* similar in design to the *Land Tortoise*, but a second contemporary drawing by Skinner shows the *Invincible* with two masts.[10] When completed the radeau *Invincible* was armed with "four 24 pounders, and four 12 pounders."[11]

Other vessels that were built as part of the 1759 navy on Lake George included 15 rafts or barges that carried provisions, horses, and artillery. The rafts "were made by building a stage on three battoes."[12] One huge barge in use during the summer of 1759 was described as the "great Scow" and the "great boat with 70 horses."[13] This was the vessel *Snow Shoe* launched on July 5.[14] The provincials also constructed another narrow row galley described as a "proe [sailing boat]" with "An iron eighteen-pounder" mounted in the stern.[15] This row galley with an 18-pound cannon was used in one action against the French on July 12 near the Narrows, but the French and Indians escaped in 20 canoes. Another vessel in use with one small cannon was probably a gondola; "50 of Gages went in the English flat-bottomed boat with a three-Pounder in her mounted as a swivel."[16]

Finally, when all the vessels were completed and loaded, the British and provincial army would again make an attempt on Carillon after four years of preparation and disappointment at Lake George. At two o'clock in the morning of July 21, the drums beat for the army to assemble. By six o'clock the vessels began to depart. By nine o'clock in the morning the rear of the armada got under way. Once more the lake witnessed the majestic pageant of an optimistic army with its banners fluttering and the various colors of the regular regiments and provincials against the steep green mountains. The expedition consisted of 5,854 regulars and 5,279 provincials divided into four columns as it traversed Lake George.

The advance guard of General Gage's light infantry had the English flat-bottomed boat at the head of 43 whaleboats.* The first column of Rangers, light infantry, and grenadiers rowed in whaleboats and a row galley with one 12-pound cannon; the second column had regulars rowing bateaux; the third column with the radeau *Invincible* was followed by 13 rafts carrying artillery on their carriages and bateaux holding the tools, hospital, sutlers, engineers, carpenters, and the *Snow Shoe* with provisions and two additional rafts with horses; and the fourth column of provincials with a row galley with one 18-pounder was followed by the bateaux two abreast.[18] The sloop *Halifax* cruised the rear of the fleet. Signals, consisting of colored flags, were to be made from the *Invincible* and *Halifax*. The men were ordered to row in turns and slowly to avoid fatigue; those not rowing were to sleep. Amherst was a careful leader who considered all the circumstances and details.

Whenever the wind favored the fleet, the soldiers put up blanket sails on their bateaux. Each bateau, carrying nine barrels of pork or twelve of flour with approximately 20 men,

---

* Amherst described the whaleboats in 1759 as "20 feet in the Keel, 5 feet 2 inches broad, 25 Inches Deep, 34 feet from stem to Stern. . .with Seven Oars besides the Stearing Oar."[17]

was marked and numbered to aid in organizing the fleet. Rain, however, during the day hampered the efforts to keep the columns of vessels straight. While there was still some daylight, the fleet came to anchor in present-day Hague. The radeau *Invincible* anchored with the supply rafts moored alongside. At the break of light on July 22, the fleet renewed its voyage northward. Between nine and eleven o'clock in the morning the army landed on the east side just below present-day Black Point in Ticonderoga at Weeds Bay. The advance guard of light infantry proceeded toward the sawmill where they met the French posted in three positions.

Brigadier General Chevalier de Bourlamaque, who was wounded during the defeat of Abercromby in 1758, was now in command of Carillon. While the French had troops at Carillon nearly equal to the numbers that Montcalm had mustered a year earlier, rations were short and disease raged inside the fort. Bourlamaque himself led 300 Indians and some grenadiers in a skirmish with the invading troops. The French commander did little to stop the British from reaching the high ground at Ticonderoga: "twas impossible for me to induce the Indians to march against the enemy. . .and I was obliged, after having got the other light troops to fire for some time, to make them fall back within the entrenchments of Carillon."[19]

Amherst's management style involved a calm, precise and methodical movement of troops toward an objective. Eli Forbush, a Massachusetts soldier, suggested that the march to Ticonderoga "was performed with ye greatest regularity, ye least noise, a noble calmness and intrepid resolution, ye whole army seemed to pertake of ye very soul of ye commander."[20] That night Amherst set up posts at the high ground, sawmill, and landing place. He had done his homework on Carillon and was sure of every move. The previous winter Rogers and his Rangers had been sent with Lieutenant Diedrick Brehm, an engineering officer, to reconnoiter the fort and entrenchments. The engineer stalked the snow-covered landscape at midnight, producing a detailed report on the fortifications.

The next morning, July 23, Amherst received reports that the French had taken their tents down and had gone off in three sloops and bateaux. The British and provincial troops proceeded to the high ground of the French entrenchment that had been used so effectively against Abercromby in 1758. A cannonade from the fort caused the soldiers to entrench themselves behind the French breastworks. In the past year the French had greatly strengthened the earthen and log entrenchment. Ironically, the French breastworks, where so many British had died a year earlier, now protected them. Actually, only about 400 soldiers were inside Carillon under Captain de Hebecourt. Bourlamaque, according to a prearranged plan and orders from Governor Vaudreuil, had abandoned the fort for Crown Point, taking with him about 2,600 regulars and Canadian militia and 400 Indians. In the meantime the British and provincial army erected a redoubt to defend the landing site and a breastwork along the road from the landing area to the sawmill. By the afternoon more cannon were brought up. Major Ord's total artillery train consisted of 38 cannon, 11 howitzers, and 5 mortars.

The cannonading from the fort lasted all day as the British and provincial troops dug in behind the wall. The garrison at Carillon fired a large number of huge 13-inch mortar bombs into the British lines. Although the cast iron shells made a frightening noise, they landed in the dirt before exploding. The following day, on July 24, the British troops continued their digging closer to the fort while Amherst ordered the "artillery to be got up as fast as possible."[21] Amherst's orders for the troops were to hold their fire until all the batteries were in place. The British flat-bottomed boat with the three-pound brass swivel in the bow was ordered to be drawn on a carriage from Lake George to the outlet below the falls on Lake Champlain. The road to Lake Champlain had been improved to facilitate moving some of the whaleboats and bateaux to the new launching area on the lower lake.

Late that night an accident occurred in the British entrenchment. Amherst had ordered the troops never to fire at night but instead wait for the enemy with fixed bayonets. After some of the troops became alarmed that the French were making a raid on their lines, the British troops began firing on one another leaving two killed and 12 wounded. As a result of the incident, different passwords including "Boston" and "London" were used each night

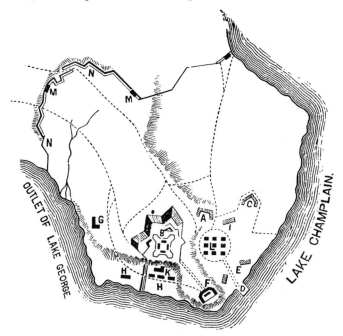

Plan of Fort Carillon, 1759.

A. Stone battery
B. The fort
C. Earth battery
D. Wharf
E. Stone houses for
   naval stores

F. Redoubt
G. Battery
H. Stone houses
   for prisoners
I. Lime kilns
K. Nine ovens

L. Gardens
M. Batteries in the lines
N. French lines

(*History of Lake Champlain* by Peter Palmer)

in the trenches. During the day of the 25th, the flat-bottomed boat and 50 whaleboats were launched in Lake Champlain. Robert Webster, a soldier with the Connecticut provincials, reported that "This day we got the General's boat over in to Lake Champlain and three or four whale boats."[22] Some of the 24-pound cannon and the 13-inch mortar were brought up to the entrenchment. The troops by then had dug within 600 yards of the fort while the French kept a continual 24-hour fire on their position. Colonel Roger Townshend, a personal friend of Amherst, was killed by a cannonball that fell in the trenches as the British troops became more vulnerable in their advance toward the fort.

By the evening of the 26th, much of the artillery was in place, with Amherst preparing to open fire at daybreak with a battery of six 24-pounders and another of mortars. However, before any of the batteries were ever used, several deserters appeared in the British trenches with news that the French had abandoned the fort, setting the wooden sections on fire and lighting a delayed fuse to blow up the magazine and all the guns which had been loaded up to their muzzles with powder. Amherst, by one contemporary account, offered 100 guineas to the deserters if they would go into the fort and cut the fuses. Not knowing if they would survive to collect the money, the deserters insisted that they didn't know where the fuses were.[23] Shortly thereafter, a tremendous explosion in the fort sent flames leaping into the summer sky. Fifty horses stabled above the fort's magazine were killed instantly in the explosion. The heat, flames, and secondary explosions made it impossible to approach the fort for most of the night. Amherst sent Colonel Haviland with the light infantry and Major Rogers with his Rangers in the English flat-bottomed boat and whaleboats to attack the rear of the fleeing French troops. Several French bateaux were found adrift loaded with powder; other bateaux had sunk. In all, 16 prisoners were taken, some of whom were from a French scouting party that returned to Carillon expecting to find their own army but instead became captives of the British.

Although the fort was still in flames, at six o'clock in the morning a sergeant from a regular regiment volunteered to go into the fort to pull down the French flag and hoist the Union Jack of Great Britain. By eight o'clock in the morning the British and provincial troops entered the fort to attempt to extinguish the fires and unload the artillery that had not been reached by the fire. Later that day Amherst totaled up 30 pieces of cannon, mortars, and a howitzer from the fort, and ordered up the sunken French vessels to be rebuilt to carry 24-pounders. Eli Forbush was quite impressed by the size and construction of Carillon. "The strength of ye Fort exceeds ye most sanguine imagination, nature and art are joind to render it impregnable, and had not ye enemy behaved like cowards and traitors they might have held out a long siege."[24] Young Lemuel Wood wrote a long, detailed description of the fort in his 1759 journal. Fort Carillon impressed Wood as the strongest fortress in North America; his observations included stone walls 24 feet high on the west and northwest sides with rooms beneath for soldiers and "Dark Prisons," a neatly arched room housing two large ovens in the northeast section of the fort, a two-story stone barracks spanning the fort's length, redoubts, and a breastwork to the west of the fort that crossed the entire Ticonderoga peninsula.[25]

The total casualties reported by Amherst in taking Carillon included 16 men killed, 51 wounded, and one missing.[26] While other accounts have slightly higher casualty figures, the operation was a far cry from the devastating losses of a year earlier. Amherst issued a public thanks at the head of each unit for the conquest of the fort.

The fire inside the fort reignited from time to time until July 30. Only one bastion and two walls had been demolished; the walls of the barracks, artillery casemates, the covered way, and 11 ovens were essentially untouched. Amherst ordered the rebuilding of the fort under Colonel William Erye along the same lines that the French had originally constructed it. By using the same plan, he could minimize the labor involved and save the new engineering for a fortification at Crown Point. Construction of a new barracks for the garrison, however, was part of the rebuilding effort at the fort, as was completing the French redoubt closer to the lake.

At this point the immediate push to Crown Point appeared to be hampered by a small French naval fleet on Lake Champlain. While Carillon was still burning, Amherst had scouting reports from Crown Point that "the two sloops and a Schooner are there to cover their boats."[27] The 10-gun schooner, rigged with topsails, was the *Vigilante*, constructed at St. Jean, Quebec, in the fall of 1757. Joseph Payant St. Onge, who had earlier piloted a 45-ton sloop built by the French at Crown Point in 1742, now commanded the "King's bark" *La Vigilante*. Payant's long naval career on Lake Champlain earned him the unofficial title of "Admiral of Lake Champlain."[28] The French also had three "xebecs" on the lake that were sloop rigged with overhanging sterns. The three sloops or "xebecs" — *La Musquelongy* (The Muskellunge), *La Brochette* (The Pike), and *L'Esturgeon* (The Sturgeon), constructed by Nicolas-René Levasseur at St. Jean in the fall of 1758 and spring of 1759 — carried eight guns each with a crew of 40-50. M. de Laubaras, an experienced naval officer, was appointed by the Marquis de Montcalm as the fleet commander on Lake Champlain in the spring of 1759.

On July 27, the morning after the fort had been abandoned, Amherst had instructed Captain Joshua Loring to repair the sawmill in order to begin construction of a brig for Lake Champlain to be completed as soon as possible.[29] The previous morning "3 Rogaleys [were] Drawn out of Lake george" and relaunched in Lake Champlain.[30] The sunken French bateaux were also to be raised and the British bateaux and whaleboats drawn from Lake George to Lake Champlain. Two small radeaux were also hurriedly constructed according to Eli Forbush. Forbush described the British vessels on Lake Champlain just before the departure for Crown Point: "We have two rydaus [radeaux] that carry Six 12 pounders in yr sides and one 24 in ye bowes. four roe [row] galleys yt carry one 18 in each of yr bowes one flat boat and one six pounder and four bayboats with swivals and a brig in great forwardness."[31]

At noon on August 1, a scouting party returned with the news that the French had abandoned Crown Point. The work continued in preparation for the British advance to that fortress. On August 4, at two o'clock in the morning, the drums beat assembly once again for a renewed voyage northward. The army in bateaux and whaleboats again formed in columns for the journey, but a strong north wind delayed the landing at Crown Point until the evening.

Upon reaching the French fortress, Amherst was ready with his building ideas. "I ordered the Engineers to reconnoitre the best place for erecting a Fort that I may set about it as soon as possible."[32] Fort St. Frédéric, named for the minister of the Department de la Marine, had taken its basic shape by 1737 but would be improved in the early 1740s. Nearly square in shape with four large bastions with sentry huts at each angle, St. Frédéric had a medieval castle or citadel standing four stories high with ten-foot thick limestone walls. The self-contained citadel was a fort within a fort, entered by a drawbridge over a ditch. The four-story structure contained all the essential facilities to withstand a siege, including 20 cannon. Inside the 24-foot outer walls were barracks, an additional magazine, storage buildings, and the chapel. Outside the walls were numerous structures, including the hospital, windmill, redoubts, and a small village southwest of the fort. Fort St. Frédéric was blown up when the French evacuated the fortress on July 31. When the provincial troops finally viewed St. Frédéric there was little left to impress them: "They have destroyed all their Buildings of value. They Blew up their Ciadell or Magazeen it is a very Large heap of Stones."[33] After the destruction of St. Frédéric, General Bourlamaque moved his army to

Views by Captain Thomas Davies, Royal Regiment of Artillery, 1759.

ABOVE. "A South View of the New Fortress at Crown Point." showing the radeau *Ligonier*, sloop *Boscawen*, and brig *Duke of Cumberland*. (Winterthur Museum)

BELOW. "South East View of Crown Point." (National Archives of Canada)

ABOVE RIGHT. "A South West View of the Lines and Fort of Tyconderoga." (National Archives of Canada)

RIGHT. Detail of "A North View of Crown Point" which shows the 84-foot radeau *Ligonier* built on Lake Champlain under the supervision of Major Thomas Ord who had also supervised construction of the *Land Tortoise*. (Library of Congress)

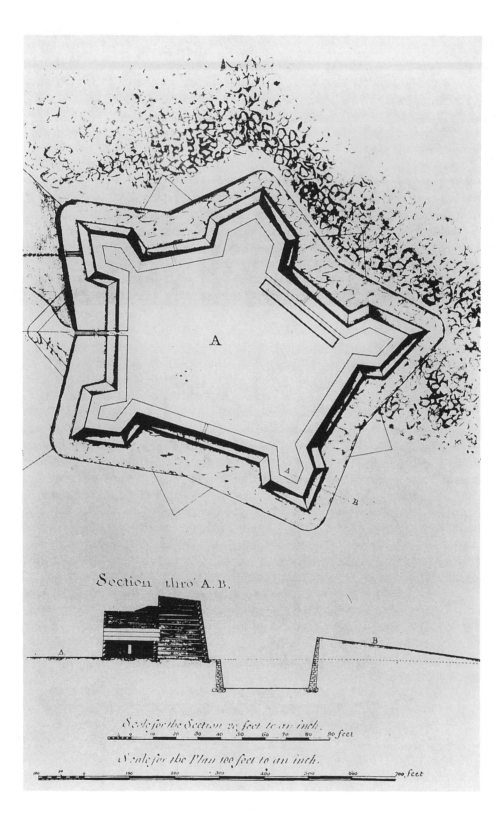

Section thro' A.B.

Scale for the Section 20 feet to an inch.
Scale for the Plan 100 feet to an inch.

the southern end of the Isle-aux-Noix in the Richelieu River (north of Lake Champlain) where the French army entrenched itself with 3,040 men and 100 cannon.

At Crown Point Amherst ordered 100 Rangers to open a road to Ticonderoga, 200 Rangers to cut a road across present-day Vermont to the Connecticut River, and troops to build several redoubts or small forts; he sent scouting parties to explore the source of the Hudson River and creeks in Vermont. Two days after landing at Crown Point, Amherst marked the ground out for the new fort. Within a few more days 400 men were at work on it, and by August 13 Amherst had assigned 1,500 men to the project. Although he had assured Pitt that he would move to Canada with the "utmost vigor and despatch," the varied construction projects slowed the progress.[34] Captain Loring had been left at Ticonderoga to build a brig, but the sawmill there was constantly breaking down due to the increased demand for sawed lumber for the new fort at Crown Point. In addition, many rainy days delayed much of the work.

On August 16 a deserter from the French squadron that had been anchored below Four Brothers Islands accurately reported the numbers, names, armaments, and officers of the French fleet to the British. Amherst immediately summoned Loring from Ticonderoga to reassess the need for a larger British fleet. Loring, upon learning of the size of the French fleet, suggested that the brig under construction would not be sufficient for control of the

LEFT. Plans for the fort constructed under Jeffery Amherst in 1759 at Crown Point. (National Archives of Canada) ABOVE. Crown Point showing remains of British fort (left) and Fort St. Frédéric (right). Photo by the author.

lake. After a meeting on the problem, Loring and Ord agreed that the fastest solution would involve building a radeau to carry six 24-pound cannon. The vessel, to be built in ten days, was very similiar to the radeaux *Land Tortoise* and *Invincible* that Ord had built at Lake George. On the first of September, a scouting party returned with news that a new sloop with 16-gunports had been launched by the French. Amherst immediately embarked on two courses of action. He ordered Ord to prepare "fire darts" (a type of incendiary device) and hand grenades to use to burn the new French sloop. More significantly, he ordered Loring to build a sloop when the brig was finished. Amherst and Loring decided on a sloop of 16 guns which further delayed the movement to Canada.

Two weeks later the scouting party that had been sent against the French sloop was back after failing to burn the vessel. The men had boarded the sloop with the combustible materials but were discovered by guards. The guards and troops in the French camp fired on the saboteurs, who luckily escaped unharmed. Amherst was unhappy with the raid since his orders were to try to burn the vessel at two o'clock in the morning; the men instead tried it at ten o'clock in the evening.[35]

While awaiting the completion of the vessels during September, Amherst dispatched Rogers and 220 men on a long expedition into Canada to destroy the Indian village of St. Francis on a tributary of the St. Lawrence River. The daring raid was in retaliation for the holding of Captain Kennedy and his party, whom Amherst had earlier sent to the village with a peace offer under a flag of truce. The onerous journey became the subject of Kenneth Robert's book *Northwest Passage*.

In mid-September at Ticonderoga the provincials raised two "Large flat bottomed Boats yT was taken when fort William Henry was and Sunk at ye Landing."[36] In the meantime, breakdowns at the sawmill extended the planned time for the three vessels under construction. However, the radeau *Ligonier* built at Crown Point was finished in the time promised with the launching on September 29. "She is 84 feet long & 20 feet broad on the Platform, where the Guns run out she is 23 feet & to carry six 24-Pounders."[37] The *Ligonier* had two masts, with the lower hull angling outward and the upper sides angling inward with gunports, according to a contemporary sketch (1759), "A North View of Crown Point" by Thomas Davies. When Major Ord tried the *Ligonier* against the wind in early October, the vessel apparently did not sail well.

After many disagreements over supplies, logs, and the sawmill operation among the principal officers, the brig and sloop finally arrived at Crown Point on October 10 and 11. Although the brig, christened the *Duke of Cumberland*, had been launched more than a month earlier, Loring constructed the quarter deck and fitted out the rest of the brig in the water.[38] The 155-ton brig was rigged with two masts and carried 20 cannon consisting of both 6-pounders and 4-pounders and 20 small swivel cannon. Crews with experience were hard to come by. Eventually 70 crew members and 60 troops to be used as marines were assigned to the vessel. The morning after the brig arrived at Crown Point, Lieutenant Alexander Grant, with the new 16-gun sloop, joined the fleet. The new sloop, *Boscawen*, mounting 6-pounders, 4-pounders, and 22 swivels carried a crew of 60 seamen and 50 marines. The 115-ton *Boscawen* was built of oak with a length of 80 feet and a 24-foot width. At one point in September, Amherst had been so anxious to get underway that he considered advancing against the French "with the Brig [and] Radeaux boats without waiting for the Sloop" but in the end decided to wait for the *Boscawen*.[39]

In the meantime, General Bourlamaque kept his four vessels cruising the lake with scouts observing the British position. Bourlamaque noted that Amherst "employed his army in erecting at St. Frédéric a fort much larger and stronger than that I had destroyed, until he should have a navy built superior to that we had on the lake."[40] In late August and early September, in two letters to Governor Vaudreuil, Bourlamaque calculated that Amherst would not attack in 1759. "Wise people believe they will defer to next spring. . .the odds are that Mr. Amherst has no intention to come here this year, and that he is satisfied with the building of a large fort at St. Frédéric."[41] However, as soon as the sloop had arrived, Amherst wasted no time in his advance on Bourlamaque's navy. Loring did not think that the *Duke of Cumberland* and *Boscawen* were strong enough to engage the four vessels of the French fleet, but Amherst, undeterred, gave orders to sail past the French, unobserved if possible, and cut them off from their base at Isle-aux-Noix. "You will at all Events do Your utmost to Come up and Attack them."[42]

During the afternoon of October 11, Amherst and his troops departed from Crown Point. According to one provincial officer at Crown Point, Amherst's fleet not only consisted of the 20-gun *Duke of Cumberland*, 16-gun *Boscawen*, 6-gun *Ligonier* (with one large mortar), but included "two arke" or small radeaux with a 24-pounder each and mortars, three row galleys mounting one 18-pounder each as well as an assortment of other artillery.[43] The fleet of bateaux was divided into four columns with the radeau *Ligonier* placed in advance of the center columns with Amherst aboard. Ranger Captain James Tute's method of rigging blanket sails which had been tested earlier was adopted with each bateau rigged with two blankets.[44] At four o'clock the *Duke of Cumberland* and *Boscawen* set sail with a fair wind and easily outdistanced the main fleet later that day.

The fleet rowed all night, following a lantern hung on Amherst's radeau. During the night an error occurred when troops under Major Reid from the Highlander Regiment in their bateaux followed "the light in the Brig for the one in the Raddeau [*Ligonier*]."[45] At daybreak the errant detachment found themselves among the French sloops south of Four Brothers Islands. Ensign MacKay and 11-20 men were taken prisoner. "I made all the sail with the Radeau I could," recorded Amherst after hearing the firing from the north.[46] Shortly thereafter, returning Highlanders reported the skirmish with the French. With the wind blowing hard against them, the radeau, row galleys, and the fleet of bateaux continued their advance until it was nearly dark when Colonel Peter Schuyler of New Jersey recommended going into a bay. The area was described as a large spacious bay on the western shore with a contiguous island where the Rangers were put ashore (Corlaer Bay and Schuyler Island).

On the first night, Loring with the brig and sloop had sailed past the French naval commander, M. de Laubaras, at Four Brothers Islands with his three sloops. The schooner *La Vigilante*, commanded by Joseph Payant St. Onge, was stationed further north on the lake near Grand Isle. At daybreak on October 12, Loring observed the schooner which appeared to be moving toward the two British ships. The *Vigilante* fired and the *Cumberland* and *Boscawen* gave chase whereupon the French schooner maneuvered into shallow water between the Sister Islands (Bixby and Young Island) on the west side of South Hero Island. The experienced French pilot drew the British vessels into a trap, with both British ships running aground. The *Boscawen* got off the shoal easily, but the *Cumberland* was forced to take eight cannon and all the troops off to lighten the vessel. By the time the British were free of the shoal, the *Vigilante* was long gone. After a time the British noticed the sails of the three sloops beating against the strong wind as they tried to reach Isle-aux-Noix. Instinctively, Loring dropped his sails and began a pursuit of the French fleet. Laubaras turned his vessels in a desperate attempt to elude the larger British ships. The French vessels, sailing into a setting sun, entered Cumberland Bay. They moved into a position off the western shore near present-day Cliff Haven, west of Crab Island. Loring, with the *Duke of Cumberland* and the *Boscawen*, followed the three sloops and anchored in a position that would block their escape.

Laubaras called a conference aboard *La Musquelongy* at which the French officers decided to scuttle their ships and walk back to Isle-aux-Noix. Onshore in the darkness, two scouting parties that had been sent by Amherst heard banging and hammering from the French sloops. Two long boats, however, escaped to Isle-aux-Noix to inform the garrison of Amherst's advance. The crews cut the masts and dumped some of the cannon, swivel guns, and muskets overboard. The next morning the crews of the British vessels were surprised to find the *Musquelongy* abandoned with guns spiked and the mast cut and the two other sloops sunk in five fathoms of water. The beleaguered French crews took nine days to reach Isle-aux-Noix overland. One last crew member wasn't picked up by the British until October 24. *La Vigilante*, at the same time, had hidden in the lee of Isle La Motte. The old lake pilot brought his vessel into Bourlamaque's headquarters on October 16 to the wonder of the garrison, whose men had thought the ship had been captured. Bourlamaque was infuriated, nevertheless, over the scuttling of the rest of the French squadron without a fight. Amherst's report to Lieutenant Governor James DeLancey of New York suggested a reason for the French sinkings. After an "officer" of the captured Highlanders had "greatly magnif[ied] our naval strength," the French had scuttled their vessels "in Such a Manner that they might easily get them off or up again."[47]

On October 13 Loring took the *Cumberland* to search for the French schooner, leaving Lieutenant Grant and the crew of the *Boscawen* to retrieve the *Musquelongy* and some of the sunken war materials from the two other sloops. Amherst and his army were grounded in the same bay for five days due to severe wind and stormy conditions. The temperature continued to drop each night with hard frosts on the last two nights. Two whaleboats dispatched to Captain Loring on October 13 returned on the evening of the 17th without getting through, but the crews were happy to be back since the waves were so high they feared that they would drown.

At last on the 18th of October the weather calmed down and Amherst received letters with the news that Quebec had been taken by the British. Surmising that the whole French army would now move to Montreal, Amherst decided to suspend the expedition and move back to Crown Point to finish the fort. Several days and nights of cold, blustery October weather also influenced Amherst's decision to call it a season. Amherst did sail to the site of the scuttling of the French sloops, landing his troops on Crab Island. The *Musquelongy* by now had been repaired and was ready to join the British fleet. Amherst ordered a contingent of Gage's Light Infantry and Rangers in whaleboats to help Loring, aboard the *Duke of Cumberland*, search for the missing French schooner. The next day the wind picked up from the north again; Amherst noted "an appearance of winter" and mused that it would take ten days to get to Isle-aux-Noix. "I ordered the Troops back to Crown Point to finish the works there as much as possible."[48]

By October 21 Amherst had returned to Crown Point and ordered the troops to work on the fort. Five days later the brig and sloop along with the French prize arrived at Crown

Point. After Loring reported that it was possible to raise the *La Brochette* and *L'Esturgeon* sloops, Lieutenant Grant was sent on October 27 with the *Boscawen*, the *La Musquelongy* (renamed the *Amherst*), and the two small radeaux with 200 men and equipment to raise the sloops.[49] By November 1 some of the provincials had mutinied and threatened to go home, but Amherst marched out troops to stop them. Four days later 100 deserters were captured but were pardoned by Amherst. On November 10, to observe the king's birthday, the garrison at Crown Point held a celebration. The next day more provincials began deserting, finally leading to a general march home of several regiments in the following days. During the morning of November 16, Grant brought the two French sloops that he had raised to Crown Point. The next day all the sloops sailed for Ticonderoga to be laid up for the winter at the King's Dock just north of the Grenadiers Redoubt.

"His Majesty's Fort of Crown Point" by mid-November had taken substantial shape as the last chimney was completed and the shingles set on the barracks roof. The fort, three or four times bigger than Fort St. Frédéric, would eventually be the largest British fortress in colonial America. Fort Crown Point would be formed into a pentagon with five bastions and three Georgian-style barracks which enclosed a parade ground of six acres. Redoubts, blockhouses, storehouses, and a village outside the walls would be completed over the years. Amherst also concluded construction for the season at Ticonderoga with completion of the barracks in November. Despite the priority construction at Crown Point, the Ticonderoga fort underwent substantial reconstruction as evidenced by Ensign Ebenezer Dibble's journal which listed a 90-foot stone barracks, a framed 173-foot barracks, a 209-foot magazine with casements, and another 190-foot stone structure.[50]

After discussion of building a blockhouse to defend the vessels in their winter berths at Ticonderoga, Amherst and his officers agreed on a wooden palisade or pickets adjacent to the wharfs and guards to be stationed on the vessels. Another method to protect vessels over the winter was apparently tried unsuccessfully with the *Ligonier*. Major John Campbell, in command at Ticonderoga, wrote Amherst in December that he "could not by any means get the Radau Sunk."[51]

With the winter fast approaching, Amherst with some of his troops headed south on Lake George in late November, then to New York City. Because of bad weather and ice on the Hudson, Amherst did not use the sloops on the river but was forced to walk a good part of the way to New York. Undaunted in his walk, he envisioned new construction projects; "A bridge might be built there at a small expense & would be a vast advantage to the Road."[52]

The campaign of 1760 would bring the final collapse of the French empire in North America. The strategy involved a three-pronged attack on the French forces in Canada which would ultimately converge on Montreal for the final blow. Brigadier General James Murray, in command of Quebec after Wolfe's successful battle for the city in September 1759, would move west on the St. Lawrence River toward Montreal. Amherst, leading the main army on the most difficult route, would move east on the St. Lawrence from Lake Ontario while Colonel William Haviland, in command of Crown Point in 1760, would move north on the lake, capturing Isle-aux-Noix before pushing to Montreal. The easiest passage to Montreal would have been through Lake Champlain, but a pincer attack from the east and west on the St. Lawrence would prevent the French from escaping and delaying the end of the war.

Colonel William Haviland at 42 years old had extensive experience in the Lake George and Lake Champlain theater during the French and Indian War. In 1757 Haviland led his regiment to America where he commanded Fort Edward in the winter of 1757-58 and fought under Abercromby in the aborted attack on Carillon in 1758. In 1759 he served with Amherst and commanded Crown Point during the following winter. During the spring of 1760 Haviland would be delegated a major role in the last campaign of the war in North America.

Before all provincial troops had arrived at Crown Point, Amherst on May 25 ordered Major Robert Rogers to raid the port of St. Jean on the upper Richelieu River and destroy the French vessels, provisions, and other war material that could be utilized at Isle-aux-Noix. He was then to raid Fort Chambly. Rogers with his 213-man raiding party successfully defeated a larger French detachment in a battle on the Point au Fer peninsula. The daring operation, however, was unsuccessful in destroying any of the French vessels, but the raid was a well-coordinated amphibious operation utilizing the *Duke of Cumberland*, commanded by Lieutenant Grant, and the four sloops in the British fleet. The larger ships acted as floating bases for the whaleboats and bateaux which had been carried to the northern waters on the decks of the brig and sloops.

During June and early July the army slowly mobilized as the provincal troops reached Crown Point. Lieutenant Thomas Moody from York, Maine, upon arriving after a march of six weeks, was impressed by the fortress on Lake Champlain. "Crown Point, Far surpasses the Idea that I conceived of it."[53] Reverend Samuel MacClintock, a chaplain with a New Hampshire regiment, was similarly impressed: "It is a pentagon with 5 bastions & 5 redoubts—the wall 40 foot thick, made of timbers and earth—a Casemt is round ye inside 18 foot deep, bomb proff."[54] While some troops were engaged in various construction projects, others target practiced, unloaded bateaux, and sweltered in extremely hot July weather. During the idle days before the expedition was to proceed northward, the troops entertained themselves with whaleboat races on the lake.

Following several days of feverish activity, the army at Crown Point embarked at ten o'clock in the morning of August 11. The diverse fleet included the *Duke of Cumberland*, the sloop *Boscawen*, the three captured French sloops (*Brochette, Esturgeon, Musquelongy*), the radeau *Ligonier* and two other small radeaux, three row galleys or "prows" with one cannon each, two long boats, 263 bateaux, 12 canoes, and 41 whaleboats.[55] Although the weather was clear the first day, the wind blew strongly against the vessels. The army of 3,300 men only moved approximately five or six miles in the wind, landing on a rocky area on the western shore for the night. The next day the adverse wind again handicapped their progress, requiring a tow of the radeau *Ligonier* "with 6 Battoes."[56]

After camping at Button Bay, the fleet renewed its voyage. The wind out of the north, however, continued and the army once more covered but a short distance. On August 14 the army was propelled to Schuyler Island by south winds with heavy seas and rain. One whaleboat split open and ten Rangers drowned. Seven bateaux were also sunk in the rough water. On the following day the favorable winds pushed the armada to Isle la Motte. On that same day the army finally reached Isle-aux-Noix, disembarking on the eastern shore of the Richelieu River. To protect the troops during the landing, the radeau *Ligonier* and row galleys maintained a fire on the French fort and vessels. The army began construction of a breastwork nearly a mile long on the eastern shoreline of the mainland, eventually erecting three batteries of cannon and one of mortars.

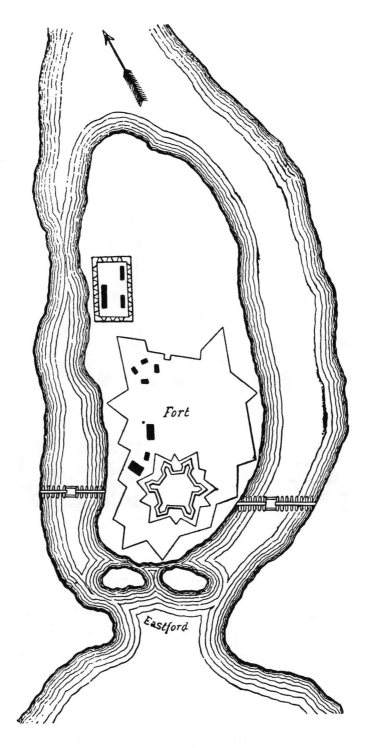

Fortifications at Isle-aux-Noix in 1760.
(*History of Lake Champlain* by Peter Palmer)

Plan, Elevation and *Section* of a Gallist to Row with 22 Oars besides Main-sail and Fore-sail on Occasion, to be Mounted with one 18 or 12 Pounders for a Chase two 6 or 4 Pounders 16 Wall Peices or Swivels and 250 Men, This Vessel in its Construction will partake of the Advantages of a galley or Xebeque in its Agility, and of a Sloop in its Sailing and defence with the Addition of a Prow for Boarding for Landing

Davies fecit 1759

Plan for a typical English row galley in 1759. (National Archives of Canada)

The following morning a bloody encounter occurred on one of the "row gallies" or small radeaux, when a cannonball from a French 18-pounder struck six men sitting on the deck of the vessel.[57] One or both legs of all six men were blown off. The survivors were moved to a small island just to the south, since named Hospital Island.

For several more days the British and provincial army worked on their breastwork; by the 20th of August the French began bombarding the British entrenchment with their artillery. The British at four o'clock on August 23 opened their batteries of cannon and mortars. The cannon duel resulted in severe injuries on both sides. In a bold move, Colonel John Darby, with two regular companies and Rogers with four of his Ranger companies, sought to break the siege on August 25 by dragging two howitzers and a cannon through the forest to the river bank on Isle-aux-Noix just below the fort and boom that the French had laid across the channel. At this point the British battery separated the French fort from their vessels. The French vessels included the schooner *La Vigilante*, the 65-ton sloop *Waggon*, one or two radeaux or "tartans," and several row galleys. The first shot cut the cable holding the radeau *Grand Diable* (also called a row galley) while another shot severed the head of its captain. The vessel drifted onto the shore where it was easily captured. The other vessels weighed anchor, with their crews pulling furiously on the long oars to evade the dreaded Rangers. Rogers and his men crossed the river and scurried along its shore through the dense foliage to head the French vessels off before they escaped into the open water. Rogers beat the vessels to the end of the channel and fired upon the lead vessel that soon ran aground on a muddy shoal. The Rangers swam to the vessel, capturing the crew with their menacing tomahawks. The schooner *La Vigilante* piloted by 60-year-old Joseph Payant St. Onge, who had outmaneuvered Loring the year before, was now finally captured. The other French vessels met with the same fate in the shallow channel and were seized. The three vessels taken in the action were listed as "one Rideau one Topsail Schooner & a Sloop" by Sergeant David Holden from Groton, Massachusetts.[58] The row galleys were apparently captured later.

The British and provincial troops opened new batteries closer to the French fort on August 26 but not without a cost. On the following day one French shot caused the explosion of a British magazine sending a provincial soldier 40 feet into the air. The troops on Isle-aux-Noix were now in a precarious position without ships to evacuate. The French had only about 1,700 troops at the island under Colonel Louis Antoine de Bougainville, the bright young officer who had served as an aide to Montcalm during the siege of Fort William Henry and the Abercromby defeat the following year. While Bougainville had much to report in his journal in the years of French victories, by 1760 his chronicle became notably brief. After midnight on August 28, Bougainville and his men deserted their fortress by an order of Canadian Governor Marquis de Vandreuil and withdrew to Montreal. The French army crossed to the western shore, probably in bateaux, and marched 12 miles through the dense forest to St. Jean. When the British and provincials entered the fort at Isle-aux-Noix the following morning, they "found one Capt. and 30 Privates together with a great many that were sick & Wounded."[59] Rogers and his men were sent by Haviland to follow the fleeing French army. By the time Rogers had reached St. Jean in his boats, Bougainville had set the port village on fire and was halfway to Montreal. Rogers pursued the French army, which he estimated at 1,500, until he caught up with the rear guard who fled under the Rangers' attack. Rogers' small force, however, did not engage Bouganville's main army but awaited Haviland's arrival at St. Jean.

By September 6 the French armies, pursued from the east and west, had converged on Montreal. Bougainville, deserted by the militia, entered Montreal from the south with a few regulars. The three armies of Amherst, Haviland, and Murray had now surrounded Montreal with 17,000 troops. Inside Montreal were the remnants of the entire French force in Canada, only 2,200 troops and several hundred soldiers from French colonies other than America. That night Governor Vaudreuil called a council of war with his officers who unanimously accepted his proposal for surrender. Ironically, Colonel Bougainville, who had formulated the terms of capitulation for the surrender of the British at Fort William Henry in 1757, now carried the surrender terms of the French. Amherst, recalling the atrocities of the war, demanded complete surrender of the French army with the conditon of not serving again during the war. Bougainville and some other officers presented a letter to Governor Vaudreuil "containing sharp protests against these humiliating conditions and the offer to attack the enemy at once."[60] But the next morning on September 8, 1760, Vaudreuil, with little real choice, signed the 55 articles of surrender.

French military officers and high civil officials were sent back to France in British ships. Many accusations of corruption and incompetence would be made as the result of the fall of France in America. Bougainville joined the French navy in 1763 making a two-year scientific voyage around the world and later became a commodore serving with the French fleet fighting for the Americans during the Revolution.

After the victory, Amherst returned to New York City by way of Lake Champlain, inspecting Isle-aux-Noix and Hospital Island. He arrived at Crown Point on October 15, noting his displeasure at the progress on the fortress. Amherst immediately set the men to work again. His interest in building even extended to a beaver dam which he dismantled on October 21 to see how it was constructed. On his trip to New York, Amherst inspected the fortification at Lake George. "The bastion enclosed at Fort George is very neat, mounts 15 Guns, is very small and a bad defence, but 'twas the shortest, cheapest & best method of finishing what was begun of the Fort."[61] Amherst was treated as a hero upon his arrival in New York City. The British government appointed Amherst the governor of Virginia, a largely perfunctory role with a substantial income, and governor-general of British North America. He returned to England in late 1763 but was urged to return by the king as the commander-in-chief in America at the beginning of the Revolutionary War. Amherst, however, declined the request despite many efforts to convince him.

In the fall of 1760, while the colonies were rejoicing with parades at the final defeat of the French, most of the provincial soldiers were still stationed at Crown Point and Ticonderoga where they were ravaged by many serious illnesses. As late as November 9, Thomas Moody noted "extreme Cold lying in open tents" at Crown Point.[62] Finally on November 19, Moody's provincial regiment began its long march home, battling the cold and snow squalls along the rough road (Number 4) built in 1759 through the wilderness of Vermont and New Hampshire.

Most of the vessels were brought to Ticonderoga at the end of the 1760 operations and remained under the direction of Lieutenant Alexander Grant through 1763. The most dramatic incident in Lieutenant Grant's tenure occurred during a storm on October 22, 1761, when the *Grand Diable*'s "row Ports fill'd in few minutes & Sunk" while delivering 150 barrels of provisions at Crown Point.[63] Several attempts were made to "weigh her but to little or no Purpose," but the provisions and some planks were recovered from the vessel.[64]

The forts on Lake Champlain were not shuttered after the last campaign of 1760. As late as 1762 several thousand troops were stationed at Crown Point with work continuing on the fort and redoubts.[65] After the peace treaty of 1763, however, the British maintained only small garrisons at Crown Point and Ticonderoga. Frances Grant, a visitor at Crown Point during the summer of 1767, noted that the "barracks on the inside. . .not finished" and the fort was "now going fast to decay, and it is said will be abandoned."[66] At Ticonderoga Grant was most impressed by the size and condition of Montcalm's breastwork that had stopped Abercromby.* Grant described the war fleet "laid up here, consisting of a large Brigantine which mounted 20 guns, two Schooners, two sloops, and some small craft; also a sloop constantly employed in the summer season between this place and St John's."[68] In all likelihood, the last official accounting by the British of the rival fleets from the French and Indian War was made on July 30, 1778. The brig *Duke of Cumberland* and sloop *Boscawen* were noted as "Lay'd up And Decay'd," the sloops *Brochette, Esturgeon*, and *Musquelongy* listed as "taken in 1759" were "In Service till Decay'd," while the "Schooner Vigelant," "Sloop Waggon," "Row Gally Grand Diable," and "Row Gally Petite Diable" were recorded as "Taken in 1760. . .Lay'd up till Decay'd."[69] Obviously, it was not a completely accurate report since the *Grand Diable* was still listed.

Fort George also remained active during the 1760s. In June 1761 the radeau *Invincible*, which had been at the northern landing on Lake George for about two years mired "in Mud," was blown by a squall "out of her bed and Carryed Almost to the Little falls."[70] The vessel was repaired and used the following month to move artillery stores to Fort George. The vessel used most often in this period to transport troops and provisions on Lake George was the *Snow Shoe*.[71] Exactly where these two vessels ended their careers at Lake George is unclear at this time. Although it is not known with certainty what happened to the *Halifax* sloop, the 1778 British return of the "Provincial Navy" which listed vessels from the French and Indian War included a sloop built at Lake George in 1758 that had been "Lay'd up And Decay'd."[72]

Archaeological Discoveries

A decade after the last battle, many of the vessels used by the British and French on Lake Champlain during 1759 and 1760 were still tied up to the military dock or "King's Shipyard" at Fort Ticonderoga north of the old grenadier battery. The vessels, with cannon and rigging removed, eventually sank in the shallow water of the wharf area. During the Tercentenary Celebration of Lake Champlain, plans were made to salvage the hull of a vessel reported to be that of Arnold's 1776 schooner "*Revenge*" which had sunk near the old military dock at Fort Ticonderoga. A vessel "about ninety feet long and twenty-two feet wide" was raised in January 1909 and subsequently displayed as the "*Revenge*" near the shoreline for many years.[73] The remains of the "*Revenge*" were shown in various publications including Max W. Reid's *Lake George and Lake Champlain* published in 1910. In the spring of 1948, a roof collapsed on the vessel causing major damage to the hull. However,

---

* Nine years later Ammi Robbins, a chaplain with the American army of 1776, observed the mass graves at the site of the Abercromby defeat where "numbers of bones, — thigh, arms, etc. — above ground."[67]

ABOVE. Salvage of the 90-foot brig *Duke of Cumberland* at Ticonderoga in 1909. (New York Lake Champlain Tercentenary Commission). BELOW. *Duke of Cumberland*, built in 1759, raised in 1909, mistakenly identified as *Revenge*. (Postcard, collection of the author) ABOVE RIGHT. Wreck of vessel raised around 1900 at Crown Point, destroyed by a fire on the parade ground during the 1940s. (Lester Fleming Collection) BELOW RIGHT. Remains of the *Duke of Cumberland* in 1984. Photo by the author.

as late as 1954 the Fort Ticondergoa Museum reported that it was planning to move the vessel and display it adjacent to the fort.

During the early 1950s the museum began exploratory diving on two wrecks that they had surmised dated to the Revolution. "We commenced exploratory diving last summer to determine the best possible means to raise the *Enterprise* and *Trumbull* lying in the mud off the shore at the Fort."[74] These conclusions were surprising because historical evidence did not indicate that these two vessels had sunk at the fort. One of these vessels, claimed to be the *Trumbull*, was raised in 1954, but the 75-foot vessel was probably not a war vessel and was burned in 1959.[75] Although one researcher in 1964 speculated that the *"Revenge"* hull was actually the *Duke of Cumberland*, the identification of these vessels at the Fort Ticonderoga dock remained a mystery until 1982.[76] During a survey of the area by the Champlain Maritime Society in cooperation with Fort Ticonderoga, the badly deteriorated hull of the *"Revenge"* was examined. Based on the remaining dimensions, construction, and historical data, the ship has been identified as the 1759 brig *Duke of Cumberland*. Three additional wrecks were discovered sunk in the mud at the old fort dock, including the sloop *Boscawen*, one of the French sloops, and a bateau.

A major underwater archaeological project was undertaken in 1983 by the Champlain Maritime Society and the Fort Ticonderoga Museum to study the wreck of the *Boscawen* and recover artifacts. The project, directed by Arthur B. Cohn with Kevin Crisman as the project archaeologist, was successful in anaylzing the construction of the vessel, obtaining accurate dimensions, and recovering 600 artifacts for conservation. Using a water dredge, archaeologist William Bayreuther and other divers were able to clear the mud from the vessel to obtain precise calculations of the remaining hull. A grid system of pipe was placed over the wreck that created five-foot-square excavation units to properly identify areas of study and artifact removal. The artifacts that were removed were immediately subjected to a preservation process using techniques developed for Texas A&M's study of the Revolutionary War brig *Defense* in Castine, Maine. The archaeological finds, preserved under the direction of conservator Heidi Miksh, included tools, grapeshot, cannonballs, gunlocks, a flask, buttons, buckles, clay pipes, eating utensils, coins, keys, blocks, and deadeyes. The excavation of the *Boscawen* over two summers represented the first state-of-the-art archaeological study and conservation of an eighteenth-century shipwreck in Lake Champlain.[77]

Other French and Indian War vessels have not fared as well. The *Duke of Cumberland*'s rotting frames remain at this date (1991) exposed to the elements at Fort Ticonderoga. A vessel salvaged in the waters off Crown Point in the early 1900s was displayed on the parade grounds of the fort for many years until a grass fire in the 1940s destroyed it. The existing photographs of the vessel indicate that it could be an eighteenth-century warship. This vessel could have been the *Grand Diable* or another vessel from the period.

Much of the armament that the French tossed overboard when they abandoned the *La Musquelongy* and scuttled the *La Brochette* and *L'Esturgeon* have been discovered near Cliff Haven in Plattsburgh. When the British brought the French sloops to Crown Point in 1759, they had their rigging and guns "except two brass 12 pounders, that Monsr. de L'oberatz threw over board, while Lt.' McKoy was there."[78] Mackay had earlier been captured by the French near Four Brothers Islands. The two cannon were among the British armament that the French took back to Carillon after their victory at Fort William Henry. Upon the evacuation of Carillon in 1759, they were placed on the French sloop *La Musquelongy*, then dumped into Lake Champlain.

The two sunken cannon remained undiscovered for 209 years until three young scuba divers in September 1968 found the cannon and a large anchor.[79] In subsequent dives, a swivel deck gun, muskets, a saber, and more anchors were discovered. The swivel gun was placed in the Clinton County Historical Museum in Plattsburgh. Unfortunately, the muskets and the saber blade fell apart without proper archaeological preservation. The remaining portion of the officer's bronze sword and musket were given to the museum by a diver in 1987.

The two elegantly engraved brass cannon, however, had a longer story. Although New York State authorities indicated that the cannon belonged to the state, little was done about it in subsequent years. In May 1982 the two cannon, offered at public auction by Sotheby Parke Bernet of New York City, were purchased on a conditional sale for $68,000 by the Fort Ticonderoga Museum. Spurred into action by the sale, the state was subsequently awarded the cannon in a court decision. One cannon was temporarily displayed at the Crown Point Museum and the other at the Clinton County Historical Museum. A ruling by the Court of Claims in 1987 awarded $45,500 for expenses and storage to the two original finders of the cannon.[80]

The search for vessels from the French and Indian War period has also continued in the Richelieu River. During 1978 and 1979, the Committee of Underwater Archaeology and History of Quebec conducted an extensive underwater survey of the Richelieu River in the vicinity of Isle-aux-Noix.[81] Thirteen archaeological sites were found in the search. One wreck site has been identified as a French bateau based upon the construction of the vessel which differed from British methods. The last decade has ushered in serious archaeological work which has attempted to study wrecks without disturbing or compromising the historic site for future researchers.

Remains of Fort George. Photo by the author.

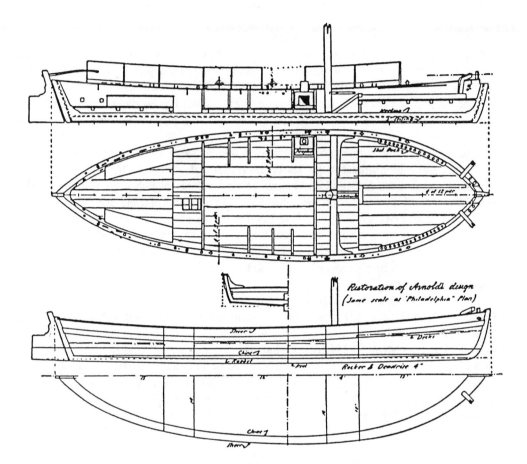

Benedict Arnold's gondola design at Chambly, Canada in 1776. The design was nearly identical to the gondolas later built at Skenesborough. (Smithsonian Institution)

6. From Champlain to Canada

ASIDE FROM THE LIGHTLY GARRISONED military outposts that were beginning to crumble in the lake valleys, the solitude of the wilderness returned when hostilities ended following the French and Indian War. For a short time, the tranquil, blue waters and lush green mountainsides witnessed only the occasional traveler. The years of peace, at the same time, saw the beginnings of a few settlements along the two lakes. Among the new migrants were the Stoughton brothers, John, Joseph, and Nathaniel from Connecticut, who had all served with the provincials and British during the war. In a partnership with Samuel Deall from New York City, the Stoughtons established a lumber business with a grant of 2,000 acres at the northern end of Lake George (Ticonderoga). Twenty-five thousand acres along the southern end of Lake Champlain were granted by the British Crown in 1765 to Major Philip Skene, who had accompanied the Abercromby and Amherst expeditions in 1758 and 1759. Skenesborough (Whitehall, N.Y.) soon flourished with tenants, mills, and a fine manor house. Similarly, William Gilliland, who served with the British army in America until 1758, bought soldiers' land claims near Willsboro and began a settlement along the Bouquet River in 1765. The following year, Captain Charles de Fredenburgh started a community at the outlet of the Saranac River (present-day Plattsburgh) and thereafter acquired 30,000 acres from the Crown.

As former soldiers, many settlers received land grants from the king of England in amounts based on their military rank; others simply purchased huge amounts of land at low prices. Before the Revolutionary War, settlers partially occupied areas on Lake Champlain that included Crown Point, Port Henry, Panton, and Sabbath Day Point on Lake George. Some of the biggest land speculators included Ethan Allen and his brother Ira who initially obtained New Hampshire land titles to 12,000 acres in present-day Vermont and expanded their holdings under the Onion River Land Company to 60,000 acres including land along Lake Champlain.

By 1775 events in distant parts of the colonies would engulf Lake George and Lake Champlain once more in turmoil, eventually transforming the idyllic setting into one of violence and bloodshed. The burgeoning national debt of Britain, largely caused by the Seven Years' War, combined with the prospect of supporting thousands of British troops in North America, resulted in proposals to raise revenue through taxation in America. Although the tax burden on the colonists was actually only a fraction of that placed on British citizens and per capita income was substantially higher in America, the colonists were in no mood for new demands on their economy. The need for revenue came at a time when the colonists no longer needed Britain and their army for protection from the French. As the colonists began nurturing their own identity, the prospects of greater control by Britain in the political and economic arena would prove divisive. Step by step, opposition to arbitrary British policies escalated into an inevitable clash and revolution.

Even before the first shots of the Revolution were fired on April 19, 1775, in Lexington, Massachusetts, military plans were proposed by the Americans for the Champlain Valley. John Brown, an attorney from Pittsfield, Massachusetts, was sent by the Massachusetts Committee of Correspondence on a covert mission to Montreal in February 1775 to deliver letters to sympathizers and to evaluate the Canadian position in the event of altercations with the British in the 13 colonies. After a rigorous journey to Canada through the broken ice of Lake Champlain which had frozen his boat to an island for two days, Brown penned a letter from Montreal to the Massachusetts Committee in Boston which detailed his findings and urged "the Fort at Tyconderoga must be seised as soon as possible should hostilities be committed by the Kings Troops."[1]

When hostilities erupted in Massachusetts, colonial forces quickly acted to take the fort. After news of the Lexington battle reached Connecticut, Benedict Arnold, a captain in the militia at New Haven, immediately pressed for action. Arnold, a muscular and energetic man of medium height, was an experienced sailor and merchant at the age of 34. His vigor, physical strength, and daring would make Arnold one of the most forceful characters of the American Revolution. Failing to make substantive headway with the more conservative New Haven militia, Arnold marched with some volunteers to Cambridge, Massachusetts, with a proposal to capture Ticonderoga. Within a few days, Arnold received an appointment from the Massachusetts Committee of Safety as "Colonel and Commander-in-Chief over a body of men. . .to march to the Fort at Ticonderoga, and use your best endeavours to reduce the same."[2] At the same time, a group from Hartford, Connecticut, accompanied by several more militia officers from Pittsfield, Massachusetts, with attorney John Brown, marched to Vermont to join Colonel Ethan Allen and his Green Mountain Boys to take the fortress at Ticonderoga.

The Green Mountain Boys were essentially a group of unruly patriots with no official militia standing who spent the period before the war harassing New York land claimants and settlers on the eastern side of Lake Champlain. Allen, as part owner of the Onion River Land Company, with his Green Mountain Boys roamed much of present-day Vermont forcefully ejecting any potential challengers to his land claims. In 1775 New York had offered rewards for the arrest of Allen and his cohorts for their activity against settlers. Allen himself had a reputation for his assertive personality and self-expression that was both vehement and oratorical. He was said to be able to throw bushel bags of salt with his teeth over his head as fast as two men could bring them to him.

Predictably, a disagreement between the two strong-willed leaders, Arnold and Allen, over command of the Ticonderoga expedition occurred. When Arnold arrived with his troops, the forces preparing to capture the fort were happy with the commitment of Massachusetts to the expedition, "but were shockingly surprised when Colonel Arnold presumed to contend for the command of these forces that we had raised."[3] Allen's men, however, insisted that they would serve only under their own officers. The expedition went forward and "[Arnold] entered the fortress with me side by side," according to Allen.[4] Before the raid, Captain Noah Phelps of Connecticut reconnoitered the fort on a spy mission and learned that the gunpowder in the fort had been damaged.[5] Although approximately 150 men assembled on the eastern shore of Lake Champlain on the evening of May 9, only about 83 actually captured the fort due to a shortage of boats to ferry them across the lake. At the same time, another detachment of 30 men led by Captain Samuel Herrick was sent to take Skenesborough where the son of Loyalist Philip Skene was captured along with Skene's trading schooner (called the *Catherine* or *Katherine*). Near daybreak on May 10, some of the American raiders at the fort entered through a wicket gate in the south wall while others scaled the wall on both sides of the gate. The Americans then rushed onto the parade ground and then on to the barracks. Allen along with Arnold climbed the stairs to the second floor of the west barracks and ordered the fort's commander, Captain William Delaplace, to surrender. The lightly garrisoned fortress (fewer than 50 men) surrendered without a fight. The capitulation of the fort yielded 86 cannon to the Americans.

Colonel Seth Warner of the Green Mountain Boys was later dispatched to capture Crown Point. Crown Point, which had fallen into substantial disrepair after a fire in 1773, held an assortment of 111 cannon including mortars and howitzers, but many were not workable.* The garrison of less than a dozen men quickly surrendered to the Americans. At the same time, Captain Bernard Romans, whose own orders from Connecticut to capture Ticonderoga had been ignored by the invaders, "captured" Fort George from its 65-year-old caretaker commander, Captain John Nordberg.

The capture of Ticonderoga renewed the dispute between Allen and Arnold over the command of the colonial forces. When Arnold tried to take command of the garrison, the Committee of War at Ticonderoga gave new orders in writing to Allen as commander. Arnold had forbidden looting of the fort, but the troops continued "in the greatest confusion and anarchy, destroying and plundering private property, committing every enormity, and paying no attention to the public service."[7] The gallons of rum in the fort also contributed to the lack of military discipline.

The confrontation ended when Skene's 41-foot schooner, renamed the *Liberty*, landed at Fort Ticonderoga on May 14. The following day Arnold took command of the *Liberty* along with two bateaux and sailed north to St. Jean, Canada (called St. Johns in American journals), with 50 men from his regiment who had finally reached Ticonderoga. Allen was undoubtedly glad to be rid of Arnold and the latter was happy to have a command. When the schooner became becalmed 30 miles south of St. Jean at eight o'clock in the evening on May 17, Arnold ordered 35 men in the bateaux to oar the larger vessel northward. At six o'clock the next morning the expedition arrived at St. Jean and "surprized & took a Sargeant & his party of 12 Men, the King's Sloop of about 70 tons, with two brass 6-pounders & 7 men, without any Loss on either Side."[8] Arnold and his men stayed two hours loading provisions into the sloop and into four captured bateaux while burning five other British bateaux before departing for Crown Point. Arnold had been lucky since a large British

---

* Most sources indicate that Crown Point was in a dilapidated condition in 1775. Aaron Barlow found "the Barracks within it are very beautiful, three in number, three stories high. The wooden work is consumed by fire. The stone work is all good and strong."[6] The forts at Crown Point passed through a series of private owners in the nineteenth and early twentieth centuries, but by 1910 the property had been deeded to the state of New York by the Witherbee, Sherman and Co. of Port Henry.

detachment from Montreal with more cannon for the sloop had been expected at any moment. Although the British apparently named the sloop, built in 1771, the *"Betsey,"* original sources simply called it the "King's Sloop" or "the armed Sloop of George the Third."[9] The sloop, in any event, was renamed the *Enterprise* and later fitted out with "Six Carriage and Twelve Swivel Guns" while the *Liberty* held "Four Carriages & Eight Swivels."[10]

Following the capture of the sloop, Arnold, with the only large vessels on the lake, sailed triumphantly southward where he soon met Ethan Allen about six miles south of St. Jean. Allen with four bateaux and approximately 100 men was determined to occupy St. Jean. Allen, however, had left Crown Point in such a hurry that he failed to bring enough food and supplies to sustain the expedition. Arnold, who tried to dissuade Allen from proceeding, "supplied him with Provisions, his Men being in a starving Condition.- He informed me of his Intention of proceeding on to St. Jean with 80 or 100 Men, & keeping Possession there."[11] Allen camped on the shore across from St. Jean but was attacked by 200 British regulars the next morning forcing his retreat back to Crown Point.

ABOVE. Traditional view of the capture of Fort Ticonderoga on May 10, 1775, by Ethan Allen without Benedict Arnold, engraving from a painting by Alonzo Chappel. (National Archives)
RIGHT. Benedict Arnold, mezzotint by R. Purcell. (Library of Congress)

Upon returning to Crown Point, Ethan Allen's Green Mountain Boys departed for home, leaving Benedict Arnold with his 150 enlistees as the de facto commodore of the lake and commander of the American forces at Ticonderoga and Crown Point. Arnold, however, had another run-in with Allen's officers in June. After an insult by Colonel James Easton, Arnold "took the Liberty of Breaking his head."[12] The incident would have lasting consequences for Arnold.

In the meanwhile, orders arrived from the Continental Congress to inventory the cannon at Crown Point and Ticonderoga and move them to the south end of Lake George. The thought of abandoning the forts on Lake Champlain, however, drew a loud outcry from Massachusetts, the Committee of the City of Albany, Allen, Arnold, and others in the northern colonies who saw the lake outposts as vital to the defense of the colonies. On May 29 Governor Jonathan Trumbull of Connecticut informed Massachusetts that the colony had ordered 1,000 men under Benjamin Hinman to march to Ticonderoga and Crown Point to defend the fortresses. The Continental Congress on May 31 officially reversed its earlier decision by requesting the governor of Connecticut to reinforce the forts on Lake Champlain and retain the cannon necessary for their defense.

Ethan Allen, in the interlude, had written a long letter on May 29 to Congress advocating an advance into Canada. Arnold made the same suggestion two weeks later. Allen and Seth Warner successfully lobbied the Continental Congress in June for authorization to raise an official, paid regiment of the Green Mountain Boys to serve in the northern theater. Allen's accomplishment in Philadelphia, however, later turned into disappointment when the Green Mountain Boys elected Seth Warner as their commander over the impetuous Allen. Arnold, at the same time, did not fare any better with his own command. On May 31 Colonel Joseph Henshaw was given instructions from Massachusetts for Arnold to give up his command at Ticonderoga to the Connecticut troops and return to Watertown, Massachusetts, to settle his accounts. The instructions, however, were never given to Arnold and new instructions on June 1 from the Provincial Congress of Massachusetts requested that he stay at his post to command the Massachusetts troops, at least until the Connecticut troops or New York militia assumed control of the garrison. When the Connecticut troops arrived, Arnold disputed the command of the fort. In response, Massachusetts appointed a committee to examine the conduct of Arnold, which brought a bitter reply from him. The chairman of the committee, Walter Spooner, in a letter to Governor Trumbull related Arnold's refusal to serve under the new appointee whereupon he "disbanded his Forces and resigned his Commission."[13]

Arnold soon left the lake and returned to his Connecticut home in July where his wife had died in his absence. Later that summer he traveled to Massachusetts to settle his accounts and collect his expenses for the Ticonderoga expedition. After receiving only half of what he had spent from his own funds, he resubmitted the bill to the Continental Congress and was eventually granted the remainder of the money.

By now the Revolution had taken a more ominous shape. Following the Battle of Bunker Hill in June 1775, the Second Continental Congress appointed George Washington as commander-in-chief of the American forces. Washington hastened to Boston where he commanded the troops until the British siege of the city was broken the following year with help from the cannon captured at Fort Ticonderoga.

During its June 1775 organization of the American army, the Continental Congress appointed Philip Schuyler as a major general and commander of the Northern Department.

The 41-year-old Schuyler, from the fourth generation of a Dutch family well-known in New York history, had served as an officer during the Battle of Lake George and with the unsuccessful Abercromby Expedition in 1758. Following quartermaster duty with John Bradstreet, Schuyler spent the last years of the war in private business that involved supplying provisions to Amherst's army which enhanced his knowledge of military logistics and his own personal finances. Soon after his appointment in 1775, Schuyler received orders to "exert his utmost power to destroy or take all vessels, boats, or floating batteries, preparing by sd Govr [Governor Guy Carleton of Canada] or by his order, on or near the waters of the lakes."[14] By the end of the month Congress had decided on an aggressive policy which included "making an Impression into Canada" and provided directions for the invasion to Schuyler.[15]

By July 17 Schuyler arrived at Fort George at the southern end of Lake George where he found the 334-man garrison in a filthy, undisciplined state. He immediately established work schedules, limits on drinking, orders on cleanliness and on the misuse of military supplies before departing for the northern landing on Lake George. When he reached the 102-man contingent at the blockhouse on northern Lake George at ten o'clock at night, Schuyler was annoyed to find the guards asleep at their posts. Proceeding to Ticonderoga the next morning, the new general found an inactive army of 335 men under Colonel Benjamin Hinman and the fort in poor shape. Soon a stream of orders to the men and requests for supplies and equipment for the invasion of Canada invigorated the garrisons at Fort George and the two Lake Champlain fortresses.

One of the most formidable tasks facing Schuyler was the construction of vessels that would carry the invaders into Canada. Lake George soon became a center for boat building with 30 bateaux completed by the end of July. In addition, two flat-bottomed boats measuring 40 feet by 12 feet were also built at Lake George. With intelligence that the British at St. Jean were rebuilding their fleet, Schuyler pressed to obtain carpenters and naval supplies to build and outfit an American fleet. The mills of William Gilliland at Willsboro had provided 5,000 board feet of lumber by early August with a pledge to double or triple that amount for Schuyler's navy. In a letter written on August 23 to Benjamin Franklin, Schuyler reported that he had enough vessels on Lake Champlain to move 1,300 men with 20 days of provisions and two large, sloop-rigged gondolas that had been built on the lake; "I have two flatt-bottomed Vessels amongst those we have Built they are Sixty Feet long and capable of carrying five twelve Pounders each, but I can unfortunately mount only one, as I have no Carriages."[16] The two gondolas, named *Hancock* and *Schuyler*, eventually sailed into Canada in late August.[17]

By mid-August the American navy on Lake Champlain consisted of the schooner *Liberty*, sloop *Enterprise*, gondolas *Hancock* and *Schuyler*, and two large bateaux armed with small swivel cannon. Other bateaux and large flat-bottomed vessels or scows were also being used on Lake Champlain at this time. Included among these was one formerly owned by Philip Skene that had been taken by Allen's men to ferry his troops across the lake during the May 1775 capture of Fort Ticonderoga.

Brigadier General Richard Montgomery, Schuyler's second-in-command, after mustering troops and aiding his commander's efforts to organize supplies for the Canadian invasion, reached Lake Champlain in August. Montgomery, with an impressive stature and likable personality, was later described by a soldier on the expedition. "His air and manner designated the real soldier."[18] Richard Montgomery at 37 years old had spent nearly half of his life as an officer in the British army. After graduating from Trinity College in Dublin, he began his military career as an ensign in 1756, subsequently serving during the French and Indian War with Amherst at Louisbourg, Crown Point, Ticonderoga, and Montreal. As a captain in the 17th Regiment of Foot, he sold his commission in 1772 in an apparent dispute over a promotion and sailed for America. Following three years of marriage and farming in New York, Montgomery reluctantly accepted a commmission from the Continental Congress as a brigadier general.

By August some of Brigadier General David Wooster's troops, led by Colonel David Waterbury of Connecticut, had arrived at Ticonderoga. While the men and provisions filtered into Ticonderoga and Crown Point, Schuyler sent scouting parties to Canada to observe British preparations. Early in August Schuyler had word from several sources that two vessels were under construction by the British at St. Jean.[19] Major John Brown, who had earlier in the year reconnoitered Canada, again returned in the summer to procure new intelligence of British activities. Brown journeyed into Canada with a number of men including a young sergeant from Connecticut, Bayze Wells, who would later record the naval battles on the lake in 1776.

On August 28, fearing new British reinforcements and the completion of the two vessels at St. Jean, Montgomery embarked from Ticonderoga for the invasion of Canada with 1,200 men, leaving approximately 1,000 troops at the forts. There is ample evidence that Schuyler and Montgomery agreed on the mililary plans for Canada. Thus Montgomery was not usurping Schuyler's power when he departed with the army, but simply putting into motion a plan that had already been formulated by Schuyler. By August 30 the fleet of bateaux and larger vessels departed from Crown Point just as Schuyler arrived at Ticonderoga from Albany. Montgomery reached Isle La Motte on September 2; Schuyler, despite being sick, met the army on the island at noon on September 4. Schuyler immediately issued orders to re-embark which brought the army, by now reduced to 900-1,000 men due to illness, to Isle-aux-Noix at seven o'clock in the evening. Only 15 years earlier, the provincial troops with the British army had landed on the eastern shore of the Richelieu River to prepare an assault on the French at Isle-aux-Noix and St. Jean (chapter 5).

On September 6 the expedition advanced on the fort at St. Jean where they were met by a fiery cannonade. While marching forward on the western shore, an ambush by Indians and Canadians was encountered by the army who "charged them with great Spirit & Firmness."[20] The troops built a small breastwork, but soon withdrew after the fort's cannon fire reached the barricade. Another breastwork was hastily constructed about three-quarters of a mile further south. The next morning, Schuyler decided to retreat with the army back to Isle-aux-Noix because of the inadequate munitions and artillery. At Isle-aux-Noix a boom or "Chevaux-de-frise" was constructed across the main channel of the Richelieu River on the west side of the island to prevent passage of the British ships. Another attempt by the Americans was made without success on St. Jean on September 10. A detachment sent to sever the route between Chambly and St. Jean was dispersed by enemy fire. Fearful of the fire from a British schooner at St. Jean, the men refused to return toward Chambly. Court-martials at Isle-aux-Noix followed the mutiny. On September 14 orders called for volunteers to try to capture the British schooner. According to Dr. Benjamin Trumbull, who served as a chaplain and volunteer orderly with the 1775 army, the men publicly declined the call. Trumbull thought the volunteer call odd and mused that "He

[Montgomery] feared that much Blame would fall on him, and to shift this from himself and lay it on the troops."[21]

Schuyler and Montgomery, however, were handicapped by minimal artillery, sickness among the army, and troops who thus far had been reluctant in the face of the enemy fort and schooner. Schuyler later reported to John Hancock that more than 600 troops of the American army were sick at the time at Isle-aux-Noix. Although bedridden on the island himself, Schuyler continued to play a crucial role in the strategy to take St. Jean. Schuyler, suffering "from a Bilious Fever & violent rheumatic Pains," was carried on September 16 to a covered bateau and returned to Ticonderoga.[22] At Ticonderoga Schuyler carried on his management of supplies and reinforcements to Montgomery with a corresponding stream of letters to the Continental Congress, George Washington, and others. Although Schuyler anticipated returning to the troops in Canada, recurrent bouts of violent fluxes, sweats, and rheumatic gout never allowed him to rejoin the army.

Even though many troops were ill at Isle-aux-Noix, new reinforcements including the Green Mountain Boys had swelled the ranks of the army. When Colonel David Waterbury and Major William Douglas, the "Commodore" of the American fleet, renewed the call for volunteers to capture the British schooner, 320 men were eventually raised for the operation. With approximately 1,400 effective troops, Montgomery launched a third assault on St. Jean on Sunday morning, September 17. Although some artillery had now been put in place by the Americans, it proved inadequate to besiege the fort. Montgomery, leading 500 troops himself, established a position north of St. Jean, cutting the road to the fort at Chambly. For the next week the Americans constructed breastworks and batteries to siege the fort. By three o'clock in the afternoon of September 25, two batteries of cannon and one with a mortar finally began to fire on the fort at St. Jean. The next day, however, began a week of stormy, cold, and wet weather that bogged the discouraged troops down in their muddy camp.

Unfortunately, the discouragement went beyond the rain. Some of the Canadians who were fighting with the Americans grew fearful of the outcome and left the army. Colonel Ethan Allen, who no longer commanded the Green Mountain Boys, had set out on September 18 with a small group of followers to raise a regiment of Canadians. Collecting about 30 Americans and only 40 or 50 Canadians, he rashly decided to march on Montreal. A separate party commanded by Major John Brown was to meet with Allen's men near Montreal. On September 25 Allen's detachment, which never saw any of Brown's group, became encircled by British regulars, Canadians, and Indians about two miles from Montreal. Some of Allen's men fled the scene leaving "but fort-five men with me. . . The enemy kept closing round me. . .with vast unequal numbers" until Allen surrendered despite a futile attempt to retreat.[23] Upon surrender, two Indians tried to kill Allen, but the resourceful insurgent grabbed hold of an officer and spun him around as a shield until rescued by a regular with a fixed bayonet. Allen, clapped in irons, sailed for England, where he spent several years during the Revolutionary War in prison. "Colonel Allen's misfortune will, I hope," wrote Washington to Schuyler, "teach a lesson of prudence and subordination to others who may be too ambitious to outshine their general officers, and regardless of order and duty rush into enterprises which have unfavorable effects to the public and are destructive to themselves."[24]

On September 25 at St. Jean "the Row Galley was launc'd," according to a journal attributed to Lieutenant John André, a British officer at the fort who would later play a major role in the treason of Benedict Arnold.[25] The vessel, armed with one brass 24-pound bow cannon and carrying 12 oars, crossed the lake on October 4 and fired on the Canadians who had constructed breastworks on the east side. By this time the Americans had most of their vessels in the vicinity of Isle-aux-Noix: "The Force on the Lake consisted of the Schooner Liberty mounting 2, 4 Pounders and two 2 D° with 8 or 10 Swivels. The Sloop Enterprise mounting 2 Brass 6 Pounders and four 3 D° with 11 Swivels. The Gundalo Schuyler mounting one 12 Pounder in her Bow and twelve Swivels on her Sides. The Gundalo Hancock mounting the Same metal. Two Bataux with Swivels."[26]

By the fifth of October, a 13-inch mortar called the "old Sow" arrived from Ticonderoga and was placed on duty lobbing mortar shells into the fort the following day. Work had been progressing slowly on a battery on the southwest side of the fort when a council of war was held to discuss strategy. At a council of war, officers would voice their opinion in a hierarchy of rank with the highest ranking officers speaking last. Nearly all officers including David Waterbury, second-in-command, favored a battery on the east side of the river to destroy the British ships. Although contrary to his own view, Montgomery acceded to the demands in order to maintain harmony. The battery, opened on October 14, paid dividends in only two days with the sinking of the British schooner. The vessel, which had been used only sparingly by the British, had been employed a few times to send a raking fire of grapeshot against the Americans on the shoreline. The 70-ton schooner *Royal Savage* was described by Captain Henry Livingston as "very long and something flat bottom'd—elegantly built & finish'd off-mounts 14 brass 6 pounders besides a number of swivels. . .a very handsome elegant vessell."[27] The schooner had sunk in shallow water by her dock and could easily be raised.

The Americans had further success on October 18 when Major John Brown and Captain Henry Livingston with help from nearly 300 Canadians and 50 Americans forced the surrender of Fort Chambly on the banks of the Richelieu River. The Canadians had carried three cannon in bateaux to Chambly from Montgomery's camp at St. Jean for the assault on the northern fort. The capitulation of Chambly brought more artillery and provisions, and six tons of gunpowder to the invading Americans. Cut off from Chambly and Montreal, the besieged garrison at St. Jean was reaching the end of the line. Washington, upon hearing the news of the surrender at Chambly, wrote Schuyler "on the Success of your enterprize So far I Congratulate You, as the acquisition of Canada is of unmeasurable importance to the Cause we are engaged in."[28]

Meanwhile, Brigadier General David Wooster, with 335 reinforcements on his way to St. Jean, was delayed for three days at Ticonderoga by heavy rains and gale winds. David Wooster, a crusty 64-year-old veteran of King George's War and the French and Indian War including the Abercromby defeat in 1758, became second-in-command after his arrival at Montgomery's camp on October 26. With Wooster at the head of the Connecticut troops, Montgomery accelerated the placement of batteries on the west side of the Richelieu. Although General Guy Carleton in Montreal tried to break the siege at St. Jean with 800-1,000 regulars, Canadians, and Indians, his army was repulsed on October 30 by Colonel Seth Warner with 300-350 of the Green Mountain Boys after five hours of fighting at Longueil on the banks of the St. Lawrence River.[29]

On November 1, after six hours of bombardment, Montgomery sent a letter proposing terms of surrender to the garrison at St. Jean. The next day, two officers from the fort requested a cessation of hostilities for four days and if relief did not arrive by then, the garrison would surrender. The British officers from the fort expressed their doubt that Carleton's forces had been defeated. Montgomery provided a prisoner to verify the British defeat of the relief force on October 30 and allowed officers from the fort to examine other prisoners held on the sloop *Enterprise*. Following the examination of the British prisoners, the commanding officer, Major Charles Preston, signed six "Articles of Capitulation" at

The schooner *Royal Savage*, described by an American officer as "a very handsome elegant vessell," was captured from the British at St. Jean in 1775. Drawing by Montserrat Centeno.

nine o'clock at night. The following morning the garrison of 600 (28 officers, 425 regulars, 75 carpenters, sailors, and Canadians, 72 women and children) marched out of the fort with the "Honors of War." The surrender of Fort St. Jean was the biggest triumph to date for the American forces. The British, during the siege, had fired 2,500 cannon shot with an equal number of musket balls at the Americans but succeeded in killing only 20 men.

The victory at St. Jean yielded two more vessels for the American fleet on Lake Champlain. Dr. Trumbull's report on the captured naval stores included: "The Schooner, called by the regulars the Brave or Royal Savage, of about 70 Tuns full riged pierced for 14 Guns 6 and four Pounders. One Rowgally carrying in her Bow one Brass 24 Pounder, and pierced for 2 Six Pounders-Besides she would have carried 20 Swivels. . . . The victorious Americans named the Schooner The Yankee, and gave the Name of Douglas to the Row Gally in honor to Commodore Douglas."[30] The new names for the vessels, however, did not endure. The schooner, which was raised by Commodore William Douglas, soon reverted to its original British designation, *Royal Savage*. The row galley has a more elusive record. It had been referred to as a "Gundoloe" by Robert Barwick, who served with a New York company during the Canadian campaign of 1775-1776.[31] Nevertheless, the vessel was called a row galley by most of the other eyewitnesses, and its original name might have been the *Revenge*.[32] By the end of November both vessels had made the voyage from St. Jean through a bitter storm to Ticonderoga.

While the attack on Canada by the Lake Champlain route was taking place, a more dramatic episode in American history was occurring along the rugged back rivers of present-day Maine. After meeting with George Washington in Cambridge, Massachusetts, Colonel Benedict Arnold received approval for his bold plan to attack Quebec. Recognizing the energy and optimism of the Connecticut native, Washington gave Arnold his first independent command which he eagerly embraced.

The stalwart volunteers marched on September 13, 1775, for Newburyport, Massachusetts, where they embarked six days later, to the cheers of hundreds of spectators, upon 11 coastal sailing vessels for the trip to Maine. At Pittston, Maine, on the Kennebec River, over 1,100 men loaded 225 bateaux for a journey to Quebec that was expected to take three weeks. The army included militia, farmboys, several wives, and a black soldier. Among the troops was 19-year-old Aaron Burr, who later served as vice-president under Jefferson after missing the presidency himself by one vote. Burr, however, was perhaps best remembered as the man who killed Alexander Hamilton in a duel in 1804.

Arnold and his men were unfamiliar with the rough terrain of Maine which required lugging the poorly built 400-pound bateaux and 65 tons of supplies over numerous rapids along the Kennebec River and beyond. By October 13 Arnold wrote to Washington at the second portage, from the Kennebec to the Dead River, describing his difficulties: "we have had a very fatigueing time, the Men in general not understanding Batteaus have been obliged to wade & hall them more than half way up the River."[33] By then he was down to 25 days provisions and 950 effective men. The men slogged through knee-deep mud in heavy rains (undoubtedly, the same rains that mired Montgomery's forces down at St. Jean) and were pressed forward by the determined optimism of Arnold.

In the rear, Lieutenant Colonel Roger Enos, after holding a council of war without Arnold, decided to turn back with his three companies of 300 men. The remaining army, now running low on provisions, much of which had spoiled, were bitter when they received news of Enos's departure on October 27. Dr. Henry Dearborn, a 24-year-old militia captain and New Hampshire physician, noted that the news "disheartned and discouraged our men" since Enos's troops departed with more than their share of the provisions and ammunition: "Our Men made a General Prayer, that Colo: Enos and all his men, might die by the way."[34] Enos was later court-martialed but acquitted largely because his main would-be accusers were in Canada.

By the beginning of November the men were starving and reluctantly killed and ate Captain Dearborn's faithful Newfoundland dog. The dauntless invaders were finally reduced to eating their "shaving soap, pomatum, and even the lip salve, leather of their shoes, cartridge boxes, etc."[35] More than 70 miles from Quebec, some of the men were forced to march barefoot in the snowy weather after their moccasins had been worn to shreds. At the same time, Arnold had pushed ahead to buy food for the army at friendly Canadian homesteads. Soon French farmers were driving cattle to the famished troops.

Slightly more than 600 survivors made it to the St. Lawrence opposite Quebec on November 9, 1775, after a journey of 45 days. Later Washington, pleased with his unfaltering colonel, wrote to Arnold: "It is not in the power of any man to command success, but you have done more – you have deserved it."[36]

The ragtag army of gaunt survivors without artillery or boats and only about 400 usable muskets gazed across the river at fortress Quebec. A letter from Arnold seeking help from one of John Brown's contacts in Quebec had instead been delivered to the acting commandant of the city, who destroyed the boats on the south shore of the river before Arnold arrived. Undaunted, Arnold ordered the building of scaling ladders, procured 25-35 canoes, and slipped past two British warships (the *Hunter* and *Lizard*) to land with 500 men at four o'clock in the morning of November 13 on the Quebec side of the river. On the Plains of Abraham, where Wolfe and Montcalm fought and died in 1759, Arnold assembled his men. The following day, a messenger with a flag was sent forward by Arnold demanding the surrender of the garrison. The flag was immediately fired upon that day and the next. Without equipment, there was little Arnold could do but await the arrival of Montgomery's army.

Meanwhile, Montgomery's Champlain army, after the surrender of the British fort at St. Jean, pushed immediately toward Montreal, with the first troops departing on November 5 and 6. Over the next several days some of the cannon were loaded on bateaux and moved to Chambly to be used in the siege of Montreal. Heavy rains, however, caused wagons, loaded with baggage, to sink in mud up to their hubs. As the Americans approached Montreal, Governor Guy Carleton evacuated his army and ships toward Quebec. The retreat apparently left the families of the British soldiers to fend for themselves. On a cold and wet November 10, Dr. Trumbull lamented the "miserable" condition of the British refugees from Montreal consisting of the wives and children of regulars, "women badly clothed, children bare foot. . .covered with Mud and Water" who had to travel by foot to New England.[37] On November 13 the American army marched into the undefended city of Montreal. The remaining inhabitants proposed terms of surrender to the Americans, but none were negotiated since the city had no army or military equipment to surrender at that point.

Before Carleton left on the evening of November 11, his men destroyed the remaining cannon at Montreal, most of the bateaux, and fled downriver in an assortment of 11 vessels. The Americans attempted to intercept Carleton and his fleet by racing to Sorel about 40 miles distant. Near the mouth of the Richelieu River, three batteries of artillery and "the Gondola mounting one double fortified 12 Pounder and carrying a large Number of Swivel Guns was also got down."[38] Apparently, the Americans were able to get the two gondolas, the *Hancock* and *Schuyler*, over the rapids at Chambly and eventually into the St. Lawrence River. Montgomery, in his November 17 report to Schuyler, disclosed that "Colo: Easton has 6 Guns mounted on shore 3.12 Pounders 1 Nine, do & two sixes at the Sorel & the two Row Gallies."[39]

Carleton's forces tried to by-pass the American batteries but were repulsed and bluffed into believing the Americans had heavy batteries in place on the shore. After the British threw powder and provisions in the river, eleven vessels including three schooners, two sloops, and a brig were surrendered by Brigadier General Richard Prescott to the Americans. Earlier, Carleton, disguised as a peasant, had escaped in the night by rowing through the American lines in a small vessel. Carleton, as a major general of British forces in Canada and governor of Quebec, took control of the defenses of the city of Quebec on November 20. In Carleton, the British had a shrewd politician as well as a military leader. Carleton had wisely pressed for passage of the Quebec Act of 1774 which he had a hand in drafting. The religious tolerance that the act provided brought support from the French Catholic clergy while other provisions favored the French propertied classes. Although Carleton misjudged the amount of support that the lower classes would give to defend British interests in Canada, the Americans also miscalculated when they counted on widespread help for the American attack on Canada. Once in Quebec, Carleton immediately issued a proclamation ordering all "useless, disloyal and treacherous persons. . .to quit the Town in four Days."[40]

On December 1 Montgomery with three schooners and artillery, provisions, and clothing reached the American forces besieging Quebec. At Quebec, the British still had the sloop *Hunter* with 32- and 24-pound cannon and the schooners *Lizard* and *Magdalen* and at least four other vessels. The *Hunter* continued to harass the Americans while the other vessels, whose cannon had been used to fortify the city, were laid up for the winter. Montgomery dispatched a letter to Carleton requesting the surrender of Quebec. Carleton, who regarded Montgomery with his 16 years of service in the British army as a traitor, had the letter tossed unopened into his burning fireplace. For the next two weeks the Americans organized their provisions and erected more batteries. Cannon and howitzers lobbed shells with little effect into the city, while Carleton's gunners poured fire back on the American batteries.

In the meantime, another saga in American history was unfolding at Fort Ticonderoga and Lake George where Henry Knox, dispatched by Washington, was to bring back artillery to relieve the siege of Boston. Knox reached Fort George on December 4 where he met one of the prisoners from St. Jean, Lieutenant John André, whose conspiratorial activity with Benedict Arnold was yet to transpire. Two days later at Ticonderoga, Knox noted that the troops were "Employ'd in getting the Cannon from the fort on board a Gundaloe in order to get them to the bridge [northern end of Lake George]."[41] This vessel may have been the row galley *Revenge* captured from the British at St. Jean that Robert Barwich had earlier described as a "Gundeloe." Other cannon were apparently hauled by cattle to the Lake George landing where they were loaded onto the "Scow, Pettiaugre [a double-ended vessel with double-mast rigging] & a Battoe."[42] Fifty-nine cannon and mortars weighing 119,000 pounds were taken from Fort Ticonderoga via Lake George. Knox sailed ahead on the "Pettiaugre" on December 9, but the scow carrying his 19-year-old brother William Knox hit a rock on the morning of December 10. The scow got free of the rock and reached Sabbath Day Point in the evening where the vessel sank. The scow was bailed out, repaired, and all the artillery reached the southern end of Lake George by December 15. With the help of Philip Schuyler, Knox employed enough men, oxen, and sleds (including 124 teams of horses) to begin the Herculean trek from Albany to Boston by early January.

By mid-December, two problems, in addition to the bitter weather, hindered the American army at Quebec: a lack of hard money and expiring enlistments of the troops. The local population in Canada would not accept Continental money. When the soldiers used it in Canada, they were forced to accept less than face value as it quickly depreciated. A second pressing issue involved the enlistments of many of the soldiers that were to end on January 1. If Montgomery didn't act by then, he might not have enough troops to take the Quebec garrison that winter. Montgomery also had to deal with the "Resentment against

Arnold" from some of the officers who would have been willing to stay on but under some other command than Arnold's.[43]

The capture of Quebec, however, was critical to the American cause since it would deny the British an essential base for their invasion into the 13 colonies via Lake Champlain. On December 23 Montgomery, in a display of democracy typical of many of the militia armies in America, called his troops together in a square and asked if they were willing to storm Quebec. With the support of the majority, he first called for an attack that night, then again on December 27, but both were canceled since the moon was too bright. The only hope for a successful attack on the city with so few troops was a surprise assault under the cover of darkness. In the middle of the night of December 31, in the midst of a fierce snowstorm, Montgomery and Arnold launched a dual offensive on the Lower Town with a strategy to break through the gates leading to the Upper Town. At two o'clock in the morning, the army began its march to the city walls. Arnold approached the Lower Town from the northeast and Montgomery moved close to the Lower Town from the southwest while Colonel James Livingston and the Canadian volunteers made a diversionary attack from the Plains of Abraham (above the Upper Town) near the St. John's Gate to the city.

As the two columns approached the Lower Town, suddenly sky rockets lit the sky green above the Plains of Abraham, an American signal that the diversion had begun. Unfortunately, the rockets that were also to signal the general attack were fired before the real invasion forces had reached their positions in the Lower Town. Montgomery's men hurriedly sawed the posts of a wooden stockade as the general drew his sword to enter the city. The men passed the barricade and began cutting through a second barricade below a blockhouse. Abruptly, a deadly burst of bright cannon fire punctured the darkness from the second floor of the blockhouse. The brave Montgomery was smashed by grapeshot and fell into the arms of Aaron Burr. Other officers and men were similarly cut down by the lethal fire from above. Colonel Donald Campbell, who now took over for Montgomery, ordered an immediate retreat although the firing had stopped, leaving the bodies of Montgomery and the other officers.

On the other side of the town, Arnold and his troops approached the first barricade to be crossed for entry into the Lower Town. As they attempted to force their way through the barricade, a langrage shot (nails, hunks of iron, etc.) and muskets spread flying metal into the troops, wounding Arnold in his lower left leg. Lieutenant John Starke of the British navy described the defenses of the city: "Some Guns judiciously placed in a house, formed a kind of masked Battery, which raked the Street which the Rebels occupied, and being loaded with grape Shot, they did effectual execution."[44] Arnold, although wounded, spurred his men on, now led by Captain Daniel Morgan. Morgan broke through the first wooden barrier and chased the British guards into a house where 50 soldiers surrendered followed by scores of local inhabitants who also gave themselves up to the Americans. By now the bells in the city were ringing their alarm. The Americans took the dry muskets from their captors and rushed to the second barrier. Finding the second barrier deserted by the defenders, Morgan was ready to rush through to the Upper Town, but other officers persuaded him to wait until Montgomery's force reached the planned rendezvous point (not realizing that Montgomery's forces had retreated). The moment was lost, however, since in a short period of time new British defenders arrived at the barricade. Morgan's men threw up their scaling ladders, but many were cut down by a hail of flying musket balls from the other side. "We got some of our ladders up," Captain Simeon Thayer from Providence, Rhode Island, noted, "but were obliged to retreat, our arms being wet, and scarcely one in ten would fire."[45] Carleton had now sent out several hundred soldiers to cut off the retreat of the Americans.

Captain Dearborn, whose contingent had gotten lost on the narrow streets in the blizzard, was now faced with British regulars who could not be distinguished from his own army: "I was at a Stand to know whether They were our men, or the enemy, as they were dress'd like us."[46] The reason for the confusion stemmed from the use of the British uniforms, brought by Montgomery from Montreal, that the Americans were forced to wear due to a lack of clothing. The Americans put small hemlock branches in their hats to

Death of General Richard Montgomery at Quebec City, January 1, 1776. Engraving
by W. Kelterlinus from a painting by John Trumbull. (National Archives)

distinguish themselves, but in the snowy darkness the branches were of little use. (Some of the Americans had slips of paper pinned to their caps with "Liberty or Death" written on them.) The British had the same problem and hailed Dearborn, asking who he was, "I answer'd a friend; he asked me who I was a friend to, I answer'd to liberty, he then reply'd God-damn you."[47] Outnumbered by six to one, Dearborn's detachment surrendered after their muskets failed to fire. Morgan, Thayer, and Colonel Greene with 130 prisoners did not retreat immediately "having been for upwards of 4 hours victorious in the Lower town," but were soon to become prisoners.[48] With 70 to 90 Americans lying dead or wounded (with total American casualties estimated as high as 221) on Quebec's streets, Morgan and his men fought from house to house in their retreat. The realization that they were totally surrounded forced a surrender between nine and ten in the morning.

In all, the British captured 426 men. Captain Thayer noted wryly that "were altogether imprisoned on the first of January, being a bad method to begin the new year."[49] It was, however, preferable to the fate of their fallen comrades, whose distorted bodies the prisoners observed in horse-drawn carts "heaped in monstrous piles. . .Many of our friends and acquaintances were apparent."[50]

General Montgomery was given a burial with honors in the city of Quebec by the British. The circumstances of his death left a bitterness toward Colonel Campbell by many of the soldiers. John Joseph Henry, a 16-year-old rifleman from Lancaster, Pennsylvania, later wrote a narrative on the "Death of General Montgomery" in which he called Campbell a "poltroon [coward]. . .The disgust caused among us, as to Campbell, was so great as to create the unchristian wish that he might be hanged."[51]

For the most part, the prisoners at Quebec were treated humanely by Carleton, although nearly a quarter of them who were of British birth were forced to join the Royal Highland Emigrant Regiment or be sent to England for trial as traitors. The others were eventually exchanged. Many American officers who fought at Quebec, including Aaron Burr, Henry Dearborn, Daniel Morgan, and Simeon Thayer, would fight many more battles during the Revolutionary War. Morgan was to play a decisive role on the Saratoga battlefield and as a brigadier general at the "Battle of Cowpens" in January 1781 that reversed American losses in the South, setting the stage for a final victory at Yorktown.

Arnold was promoted to brigadier general by the Continental Congress on January 10 for his role in the Canadian campaign . At the same time, however, he again planted seeds for his detractors who would later make accusations against his character. On February 1 Arnold wrote to John Hancock disputing a promotion to colonel for John Brown that had been promised by Montgomery, according to Brown. Arnold insisted that Montgomery felt that Easton and Brown were under a cloud, accused of "plundering the Officers, Baggage taken at Sorell, Contrary to Articles of Capitulation, and to the great scandal of the American Army."[52] Arnold would not support his promotion.

Following a recommendation from Schuyler, the Continental Congress on February 15 approved a committee to be sent to Canada to present American ideas about Canada's future, including an assurance of freedom for Canada, the need to establish an independent Canadian government, the possibility of Canada becoming a sister colony, and to seek cooperation in the struggle against Great Britain. The three-man committee, granted far-ranging powers by Congress, included Benjamin Franklin, Samuel Chase, and Charles Carroll. The committee did not reach Lake George until April 18, where they found Fort George in "ruinous" condition. The trip to Canada was unsuccessful, but Carroll's journey provided an interesting description of the two lakes in 1776. Franklin, Chase, Carroll, and Schuyler traversed Lake George in a bateau, described as "36 feet long and 8 feet wide. . .and carry 30 or 40 men . . . They are rowed. . .[and] have a mast fixed in them to which square sail or a blanket is fastened."[53] Carroll described Lake George as "a fine deer country and likely to remain so, for I think it never will be inhabited."[54] He was very interested in a "machine," devised by Schuyler for raising the boats at the northern end of Lake George and easing them onto four-wheel carriages to be drawn overland to Ticonderoga by six oxen.

An eighteenth-century description of the waters in parts of Lake George and Lake Champlain provides an insight into the condition of the lakes then and now. As Carroll reached the very northern end of "Lake George the water suddenly shallows from a great depth to 9 or ten feet or less. This change is immediately discoverable by the different colors of the water. The water is of deep bluish cast and the water of this river of whitish color" which he attributed to "white clay" along the banks.[55] The water in the southern basin of Lake Champlain along Crown Point and Ticonderoga has a distinctive milky cast today. John Trumbull, who served as the deputy adjutant general of the Northern Army at Ticonderoga in 1776, described the waters around Crown Point as "the filthy water of that peculiarly stagnant muddy lake."[56] Some eighteenth-century maps actually separated Lake Champlain into two sections, calling the southern part of the lake the St. Frédéric River.

At Ticonderoga, Carroll observed "3 schooners and one sloop. . .of these 3 schooners, two were taken from the enemy on the surrender of St. Jean."[57] The vessels were the sloop *Enterprise*, schooners *Liberty*, *Royal Savage*, and *Revenge*. Apparently, the *Revenge* which some earlier researchers thought had been built at Ticonderoga by Schuyler in 1776 was the captured row galley that was later re-rigged as a schooner. After Crown Point, Franklin, Chase, and Carroll next stopped at the home of Peter Ferris on Ferris Bay (now Arnold's Bay). The committee reached Montreal on April 29 where they proceeded no farther, realizing that they had arrived too late to influence the outcome of the American siege.

On May 11 Franklin left Montreal for the long trip back to Fort George and eventually to the Continental Congress. Samuel Chase and Charles Carroll stayed in Canada several more weeks penning a discouraging report to Congress on the state of military affairs. Although by then the tenuous military foothold in Canada was rapidly collapsing, they recommended that 6,000 men be sent immediately.

The siege of Quebec had continued in the spring of 1776 as supplies and reinforcements slowly arrived in Canada. In early April General David Wooster took command of the troops at Quebec, while Arnold, still suffering from his leg wound and a subsequent fall from a horse, moved back to Montreal. Wooster praised Arnold's siege in a letter to Washington: "General Arnold has, to his great honour, kept up the blockade with such a handful of men that the story, when told hereafter, will be scarcely credited."[58] By April Arnold had nearly 2,800 men but 800 were incapable of service due to illness (mainly smallpox). The problem of buying supplies with Continental currency had never been resolved, leaving Schuyler's supply lines from Albany overextended. A dozen bateaux loaded with provisions were required from Albany each day to supply the threadbare army in the north. Schuyler was successful in building large numbers of bateaux at the southern end of Lake George in the winter and spring of 1776. By March 22, 100 new bateaux were completed there, and Schuyler expected another 110 to be completed by May 10 with 50 more planned.

After three weeks in Albany, Major General John Thomas from Massachusetts reached Quebec on May 2, 1776, to become the senior commander replacing the ineffectual Wooster. Thomas was left with approximately 1,900 men due to enlistments running out and desertions. Of that number, 800-900 were estimated to be sick with smallpox. With news that large British reinforcements would be arriving soon, Thomas with Wooster at a council of war decided on a plan to retreat to a point south of Quebec. That evening reports came into the American camp that 15 British ships had been sighted 120 miles from Quebec. The very next day (May 6), however, the British fleet arrived sooner than expected, landing 1,800 troops immediately. General Thomas initially attempted to make a stand but could rally only 250 men. The Americans began a desperate retreat and "were obliged to leave all their baggage and bring nothing away but the cloaths upon their backs."[59] The American retreat was so sudden that the British troops found "the Commanding officers Dinner which he had left at the fire."[60] The Americans initially planned to hold Deschambault (25 miles south of Quebec), then Three Rivers, but eventually made their camp at Sorel about 100 miles south of Quebec on the St. Lawrence.

The Americans set fire to most of their ships before retreating from Quebec, but at least three schooners were recaptured by the British. The American army, nevertheless, still had vessels in Canada and were building more gondalos at Chambly on the Richelieu River. Benedict Arnold drafted a letter on May 8 in Montreal describing the American fleet on the St. Lawrence as two armed gondolas, a ten-gun schooner, and "four other Gondaloes are building at Chambly."[61]

The camp at Sorel was in miserable condition as smallpox swept the army. Many of the desperate soldiers, despite prohibitions, inoculated themselves against smallpox. Arnold devised a plan to inoculate all the soldiers on a rotating basis in Montreal. General Thomas, adamantly opposed to inoculation, reversed Arnold's orders insisting "that it should be death for any person to inoculate."[62] According to Dr. Lewis Beebe, a physician from Sheffield, Massachusetts,the very next day Thomas showed symptons of smallpox himself. When it was evident on May 21 that General Thomas had the disease, his command was relinguished to newly arrived Bridgadier General William Thompson, a 40-year-old Pennsylvania native who had a mixed record during the 1775 Boston siege. In less than two weeks General Thomas died of smallpox at Chambly. When the commissioners from Congress, Charles Carroll and Samuel Chase, reached Sorel, they discovered "little or no discipline among [the] troops. . .in want of the most neccessary articles. . .an army broken and disheartened."[63]

Although dismayed by the reports of the retreat from Quebec, Congress was still determined to make a stand in Canada. Brigadier General John Sullivan, a lawyer and militia veteran from New Hampshire, led several thousand fresh reinforcements by way of the lakes to hold Canada. By June 4 the confident Sullivan arrived at Sorel to take command of the disorganized, broken army. The news of 500 Americans captured two weeks earlier west of Montreal at "The Cedars" and expected offensives by the British army did not permit optimism, however.

Without proper information of the enemy forces, Sullivan quickly approved an earlier plan of Thompson's to stop the British advance at Three Rivers, seventy miles south of Quebec. Sullivan, with knowledge of 18 British ships but no more than 300 troops on land, dispatched General Thompson "with about two Thousand of our best Troops to attack them."[64] Thompson's estimate of the British strength the day before the engagement was uncertain, ranging from 500-1,500 men. The Americans crossed the St. Lawrence on the night of June 7 guided by a Canadian peasant who purposely led the invaders through 13 miles of deep swamp. Tired and disoriented, the men emerged from the swamp to find a much larger British force entrenched at Three Rivers along with shiploads of British troops offshore.[65] The Americans attacked the British advance guard at six in the morning, then with their drums beating, unsuccessfully assaulted the infantry at seven o'clock. The British, however, were not surprised since American drums beat to arms as early as three o'clock in the morning. After repeated attacks, British armed schooners continued a raking fire into the dense foliage. Eventually, the Americans retreated as the British troops tried to race them to their bateaux. Although some American versions of the story have Thompson and his officers surrounded by the British troops after wandering in the woods all through the following night, Lieutenant John Enys, an eyewitness with the British in the 29th Regiment of Foot, noted "About 7 or 8 in the Morning [June 9] great Numbers began to come in to us and give themselves up as prisoners, among whom was General Thomson who commanded."[66] Most of the Americans escaped, but 22-30 were killed while 300-500 were made prisoners.

Although Benedict Arnold suggested aggressive strategies in May 1776 for the holding of Canada including making a stand at Deschambault on the St. Lawrence, by June he became more pragmatic in view of the collapse of the American army. By June 6, even before Thompson's defeat, he proposed retreating to St. Jean and Isle-aux-Noix to make a stand. Four days later with no hope of American reinforcements, he pressed General Sullivan by letter not to lose one minute in securing a retreat from the superior British force. Arnold's letter, both rational and eloquent, obviously had an impact on the final decision to retreat. "Shall we sacrifice the few men we have by endeavouring to keep possession of a small part of the country which can be of little or no service to us?. . .These arguments are not urged by fear for my personal safety: I am content to be the last man who quits this country, and fall, so that my country [may] rise. But let us not fall all together."[67]

Arnold's resolute stewardship of his forces in Canada, however, still had detractors. Dr. Lewis Beebe, a brother-in-law of Ethan Allen and former Yale classmate of John Brown, in May described Arnold in his journal as an "infamous, villanous traitor," and later at Crown Point following Arnold's arrest of several officers, Beebe wished that "some person would try an experiment upon him, (viz) to make the sun shine thro' his head with an ounce ball; and then see whether the rays come in a Direct or oblique direction."[68]

Faced with overwhelming odds (about 13,000 British troops) and the devastating sickness that affected half the troops, General Sullivan retreated from Sorel, leaving only two cannon behind on June 14, 1776, hours before the British landed there. Arnold, after expropriating a variety of supplies from merchants in Montreal, evacuated his troops to St. Jean. When Arnold's 30 wagons of merchandise reached Chambly on their way to St. Jean, Colonel Moses Hazen (a former Ranger of Robert Rogers) interfered with the shipment, suspecting that it was plunder. The event would have some lasting consequences, including a charge of insubordination against Hazen by Arnold. Sullivan's army dragged the bateaux loaded with supplies and the sick up the rapids to Chambly. Once there "Genl Sullivan set fire to all the armed vessels, 3 Gundalows & fort at Chambly" and retreated to St. Jean.[69] With 3,000 men already sick at Isle-aux-Noix, Sullivan on June 18 moved the rest of his army to the island to await orders from Schuyler as the British approached St. Jean.

Again, the American army just missed the British. Lieutenant Enys later reported that "some of their Rear boats [American] were Still within Sight of St. Johns [Jean] when our people arrived at that Place."[70] At St. Jean the Americans had burned a schooner still on the stocks but were forced to leave 22 pieces of artillery behind. Arnold, however, was able to send the frames from a vessel being built at St. Jean to Lake Champlain. The Americans also had stripped the lead roofing, amounting to two and a half tons, from one of the houses in the fort to be reused as ammunition later. Arnold was the last man to leave St. Jean, pushing a canoe into the water himself. Without vessels at St. Jean, the British could not immediately follow the Americans on the Richelieu or Lake Champlain.

The scene at Isle-aux-Noix was horrible as smallpox and dysentary quickly spread to the rest of the army. Dr. Beebe vividly noted his impressions in his journal of the spectacle of a large barn filled with the sick, "many of which could not See, Speak, or walk. . .two had large maggots. . .Crawl out of their ears."[71]

In the last week of May, Schuyler had shipped 1,515 barrels of provisions to the army in Canada. A few weeks later he rushed empty bateaux from Lake George and Lake Champlain to rescue the 7,000-8,000-man army at Isle-aux-Noix. On June 20 Sullivan gave orders to transport the sick to Crown Point. From June 21 to the 27th, the sick men and their baggage were transported south with a temporary camp at Isle La Motte. With a shortfall in bateaux, many troops marched along the lake for 20 miles before being ferried to Isle La Motte. On June 28 the army reembarked for Crown Point from Isle La Motte in bateaux. The sloop *Enterprise* and the schooners were also used in the evacuation. After days of rain and intermittent thunderstorms, the troops reached Crown Point at midnight on July 2, 1776. The sick were sent across the lake to Chimney Point. Undoubtedly, Hospital Creek (north of the Chimney Point) derived its present name from that camp. Later the invalid soldiers were sent to the Fort George hospital where 2,000 sick were cared for.

Although the Americans felt that the Canadians did not give them enough support in their fight against the Crown, the view of British soldiers was quite different. "Many of the Canadians had taken a decided part in their favor, rendered them essential services" wrote one soldier while another maintained that "the peasantry of Canada are more friends to the Americans than to the British troops."[72] During the war two regiments of Canadians had been organized (1775-1776), but any real Canadian support for the colonies subsided after the American retreat from Canada in 1776. Although approved by Congress, a renewed invasion plan in 1778 was called off as impractical.

While the Canadian incursion was seemingly a total failure, in reality it forestalled the British invasion through Lake Champlain as a gateway into the colonies during 1776. In particular, Arnold's raid on St. Jean in May 1775 and Montgomery's capture of the fort in November deprived the British of a navy on Lake Champlain. By holding St. Jean until June 18, 1776, the British were not able to complete construction of a new fleet until late in the season of 1776 to challenge the American superiority on Lake Champlain. In the meantime, the Americans made major additions to their existing fleet of vessels that had been captured earlier. The assignment of additional British troops to Canada, caused by the American foothold in Quebec, diverted British resources from other strategic areas. This diversion ultimately delayed General William Howe's attack on New York which gave George Washington time to prepare for operations there.

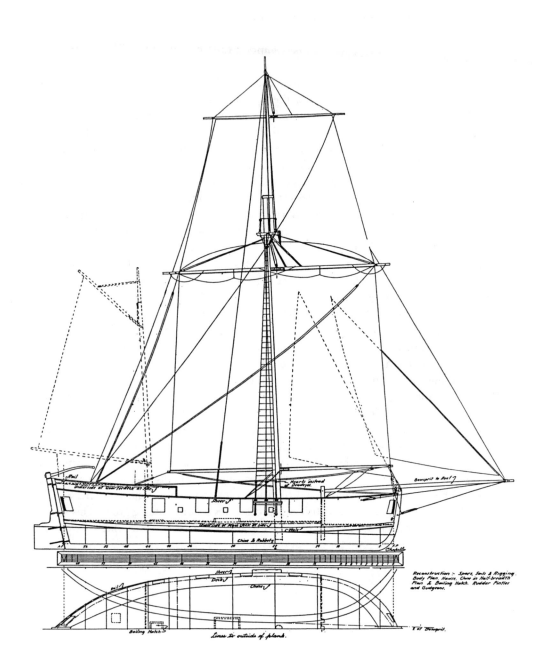

The 62-foot gondola *Loyal Convert* was captured on the St. Lawrence River by the
British during the American evacuation and dragged through the rapids at
Chambly to St. Jean. Reconstruction of an Admiralty drawing by H. I. Chapelle.
(Smithsonian Institution)

7. Battle of Valcour Island

As ONE APPROACHES THE CRAGGY SHORE of the southern tip of Valcour Island on Lake Champlain, it is hard to imagine that over two centuries ago this was the scene of a desperate struggle between 15 American warships and an overwhelmingly superior British fleet. The primitive island, with its tall, white spruce trees, evinces solitude as gentle waves break against the gray cliffs on its southern shore. Yet here cannon fire echoed from each shore; men were raked by devastating grapeshot, and vessels were smashed and sunk. Today's picturesque scene of blue water meeting the grays and greens of this detached bluff of land disguises the onslaught that sealed the fate of America's first naval fleet. Only a stone monument on the distant shore "Commemorating the Valor of American Forces Led by Benedict Arnold at the Battle of Valcour, October 11, 1776" signifies its stormy past.

To facilitate their invasion of the colonies, the British began a furious race to construct a naval fleet at St. Jean during the summer of 1776. The British strategy involved an invasion through Lake Champlain to the Hudson River with General John Burgoyne's army, while General William Howe's forces, after capturing New York City, would join with the northern army near Albany. These actions by the British army would effectively split the colonies in two, ending vital military, political, and economic links necessary to carry on the war. George Washington, following the British withdrawal from Boston in March, was engaged in defending southern New York from Howe's offensive during the summer and fall of 1776. Recognizing Lake Champlain and Lake George as the gateway in the north, the Americans made a major military commitment to stop the British advance on the lakes. This would involve building a fleet of ships on Lake Champlain to augment the existing four vessels in the American fleet (sloop *Enterprise* and schooners *Liberty*, *Revenge* and *Royal Savage*).

As the British army advanced southward on the Richelieu River in June 1776, Brigadier General John Sullivan with the American army at Isle-aux-Noix wrote to George Washington on the 24th suggesting the building of "Row-gallies to Command the Lakes."[1] The following day Benedict Arnold, with the knowledge that the British had brought the frames of vessels from England to be used on Lake Champlain, dispatched a similar request to

Washington urging that the lakes be immediately "secured by a large Number of (at least Twenty or thirty) Gundaloes Row Gallies & floating Batteries."[2] Arnold was involved in the construction of gondolas in Canada in 1776 and formulated a design for these vessels on the St. Lawrence that is quite similar to the vessels constructed later at Skenesborough, New York (Whitehall).

Although Arnold is often credited with much of the management and construction of the American fleet on Lake Champlain, several other officers had as much to do with its creation as Arnold. As early as May, General Philip Schuyler, the commander of the Northern Department, who had a large number of bateaux built in the spring of 1776, made preparations for the construction of gondolas in Skenesborough. Schuyler was in contact with Washington about materials for the gondolas a month before the letters proposing a fleet by Arnold and Sullivan had reached Washington. Skenesborough was chosen as the construction site for the fleet because of its iron forge and two sawmills. At a considerable distance from Ticonderoga, the Skenesborough location would separate the army from the highly-paid shipwrights and carpenters who were employed to build the fleet.

By June 24 Schuyler reported to Washington that "one gundalo is finished at Skenesborough and a second is already planking."[3] By then, Schuyler had plans for five more gondolas with a timetable of one constructed every six days. The Lake Champlain gondolas were flat-bottomed, sloop-rigged craft with a typical length of 53 feet over the posts and a 15-1/2 foot beam. The vessel had a square sail and topsail on its one mast but could be propelled by sweeps (oars). The gondolas were later fitted with one 12-pound cannon in the bow and two 9-pound cannon on the midship gun deck (one on each side) and a number of swivel guns mounted on brackets on the gunwales. Although gondolas and row galleys have achieved the most fame from the action on Lake Champlain, they were not unique to the lake, with John Adams and George Washington recommending the vessels during the same time period for use on the Delaware River and at New York City. Fifty carpenters from Philadelphia, reported one contemporary newspaper, were at Skenesborough "building Row Gallies, on the construction of those in the river Delaware."[4]

After the evacuation of Canada, the American army retreated as far as Crown Point in early July. Upon arriving at Crown Point, Colonel John Trumbull, the son of the governor of Connecticut, described the garrison: "at that place I found not an army, but a mob, the shattered remains of twelve or fifteen very fine battalions, ruined by sickness, fatigue and desertions."[5] With the death of General Thomas in May, Congress procrastinated until June 18 before naming Major General Horatio Gates as the commander of the American army in Canada. The 48-year-old Gates, noted for his offensive personality, was a veteran of the French and Indian War and a personal friend of George Washington. By the time Gates reached Albany on June 27, the American army under General John Sullivan had retreated from Canada. Since the Northern Army was no longer in Canada, a dispute over who was in charge of the army, Schuyler or Gates, arose in early July. In addition, General Sullivan, irritated by his replacement with Gates, later traveled to Philadelphia to tender his resignation to the Continental Congress but withdrew it before Congress acted. Congress on July 8, solved the Schuyler-Gates dilemma by placing Gates subordinate to Schuyler. While Schuyler remained commander of the Northern Army, Gates was its commander in the field.

Despite the dispute, on July 7 a council of war held at Crown Point with Generals Schuyler, Gates, Sullivan, Arnold and De Woedke agreed on a plan to abandon Crown

Point and move the army to Ticonderoga and the eastern shore opposite the fort, with the sick to be forwarded to Fort George. The council resolved to build gondolas, row galleys, and armed bateaux to attain superiority on Lake Champlain. Gates, in a letter to Governor Jonathan Trumbull of Connecticut, described the broken-down condition of Crown Point at the time: "The ramparts are tumbled down, the casemates are fallen in, the barracks burnt, and the whole a perfect ruin, that it would take five times the men of our army, for several summers, to put it in defensible repair."[6] Twenty-one field officers at Crown Point, nevertheless, petitioned Schuyler to reconsider the withdrawal to Ticonderoga. When the news of the abandonment of the famous fortress reached George Washington and his staff, it created a "general chagrin and consternation."[7] The criticism of the move was so widespread that Schuyler felt compelled to write a very long letter to John Hancock, president of the Continental Congress, spelling out in minute detail all of the rationale for the decision. Crown Point, in reality, was never totally abandoned since Colonel Thomas Hartley with a Pennsylvania regiment garrisoned the fort until the British ships arrived after the Valcour battle in October 1776.

By early June construction of a fleet at Skenesborough was well underway while Schuyler continued to press for much needed marine supplies and carpenters. The Marine Committee of the Continental Congress authorized a pay of 34-2/3 dollars per month with a month's pay in advance for shipwrights, a premium to attract skilled craftsman to the backwoods of New York. Although most of the workers were actually house carpenters, shipwrights from Connecticut, Maine, Massachusetts, Pennsylvania, and Rhode Island eventually formed a core of experienced marine craftsmen. In addition, blacksmiths, armorers, oarmakers, sailmakers, and other skilled workers arrived at Lake Champlain.

Becoming increasingly concerned with the progress of construction, Gates noted that the gondolas ordered by Schuyler "as he had no model to direct him, are in nothing but in name like those at Philadelphia."[8] Two of the gondolas had been finished by July 16 with two more expected to be completed within a week. While some of the vessels were at least partially rigged at Skenesborough, many of the later vessels were also rigged and armed at Mount Independence on the eastern shore of Lake Champlain directly across from Fort Ticonderoga. After several surveys by the engineers and officers in early July, the land at Mount Independence began to be cleared on July 18. The eastern shore, as a military camp, grew in scope in 1776 with extensive construction in the fall.

In the spring and early summer of 1776, the command of the four existing vessels of the American Champlain fleet, upon Schuyler's recommendation, was given to Captain Jacobus Wynkoop, a self-important officer who had previous experience with the American fleet on Lake Champlain. By July Gates became increasingly unhappy with Wynkoop whom he regarded as inefficient in command of the emerging fleet. With only a few gondolas completed by July 22, Arnold went to Skenesborough "to expedite the building of the gondolas."[9] As Gates' confidence in Arnold increased, he wrote John Hancock on July 29, 1776, that "General Arnold (who is perfectly skilled in maritime affairs) has most nobly undertaken to command our fleet upon the Lake."[10] Although Gates had not sought consultation on the appointment of Arnold, Washington and Schuyler both wholeheartedly approved of the selection. Jacobus Wynkoop, however, was not immediately informed of the change in command.

Arnold's boundless energy and enthusiasm were contagious among the workers at Skenesborough. This was in contrast to earlier reports received by Gates that the carpenters at Skenesborough had complained that the soldiers assigned to help them in the woods "would sit down by the trees instead of working."[11] Gates remarked that Arnold had gone to Skenesborough "to give life and spirit to our dock-yard."[12] At the end of July, Arnold informed Schuyler that he had left 200 carpenters at the Skenesborough shipyards with orders to "begin four Row Gallies, Nearly of the Constructions of those Built in Philadelphia."[13] The row galleys were to be 72 to 80 feet in length with a beam of 18 feet carrying two masts with lateen (triangular) sails. Galleys, like the gondolas, could be propelled by hand-pulled sweeps as well as by sail and were designed for operation in shallow water. Each galley carried 36 sweeps or oars.

Controversy again dogged Arnold at Ticonderoga in the summer of 1776. Arnold's charges against Colonel Moses Hazen for refusing to accept responsibility for goods seized in Montreal by Arnold during the Canadian evacuation resulted in a court-martial of Hazen in July. The goods, whose seizure was authorized by the Congressional Commissioners in Canada, were broken open, plundered, and stolen after Hazen failed to take charge of the goods delivered by Major Scott for Arnold. When the court of 13 field officers refused to hear testimony from Scott during the stormy court-martial and found Hazen not guilty, Arnold vigorously protested. The court took strong offense to Arnold's protest and demanded an apology, whereby Arnold refused, suggesting that when the war ended, "I will by no means withhold from any gentleman of the Court the satisfaction his nice honour may require."[14] With that challenge, the court turned to Gates with a demand for Arnold's arrest. After studying the situation, Gates dissolved the court and sent the records to Congress with the warning that "the United States must not be deprived of that excellent officer's service at this important moment...whatever is whispered against General Arnold as the foul stream of that poisonous fountain, detraction."[15] The incident would not be forgotten by Arnold's enemies. Although Arnold would be cleared of these accusations, the controversy would follow his American career until its conclusion.

Arnold's contribution to the naval fleet on Lake Champlain included his vigor in finding supplies, crews, and materials to fit out the new vessels. He dispatched work crews to the Onion River (Winooski River) and beyond for lumber, pressed for seamen to man the vessels, and even requested an experienced captain who had been convalescing at the Fort George hospital. Gates was similarly aggressive, as was Schuyler, who was away at Albany and German Flats meeting with Indian representatives of the Six Nations to obtain their neutrality. Schuyler demonstrated his ability to administer through correspondence.

The results of the renewed vigor in the construction process were evident by early August. By August 5, three gondolas had sailed: the *New Haven*, *Providence*, and *Boston*; the *Spitfire* was completed and nearly rigged; and another gondola (*Philadelphia*) was finished but not rigged. The names of the gondolas, for the most part, reflected the communities that the carpenters represented.

Another vessel, initially called a row galley, was sent to Ticonderoga on August 8 to be armed and rigged. This vessel, named the *Lee*, was built from frames belonging to a vessel that had been under construction at St. Jean when the Americans were forced to evacuate in June 1776. The frames, taken by Arnold, were numbered for easy reassembly later. The stubby *Lee*, with a length of only 43 feet, 9 inches, was called a row galley, cutter, sloop, and gondola by various contemporary sources because it apparently had characteristics common to all of these vessels.

As Arnold worked to put the fleet together, Captain Jacobus Wynkoop, aboard the schooner *Royal Savage*, continued to act as the commander of the naval forces despite the change of command. The pompous Wynkoop was deflated on August 10 when he mistook seagulls for the sails of the British fleet. After a "Large flock of White Gulls" appeared in his looking glass, Wynkoop ordered the boatswain to hail the American fleet with his trumpet.[16] Wynkoop called all the officers aboard his flagship for a council of war. Captain Seamon of the *Revenge*, however, after some time climbed the mast and identified the seagulls through his looking glass.

After scouts observed a signal fire on August 17 which could indicate the approach of the British, Arnold gave orders to Captains Seamon and Premier of the schooners *Revenge* and *Liberty* to proceed seven or eight miles north to scout for the enemy and cover troops sent under Colonel Thomas Hartley. When the vessels at Crown Point attempted to make sail, Wynkoop fired a swivel cannon from the *Royal Savage* halting their progress. The contradiction of Arnold's orders was based on Wynkoop's insistence that he was commander of the navy on Lake Champlain through his appointment by Philip Schuyler. Arnold boarded the *Royal Savage* and confronted Wynkoop and presented his appointment letter from Gates. While Wynkoop insisted that Arnold had not made clear his command earlier, Arnold, in an exchange of letters later that day, wrote that he was surprised by Wynkoop's attitude "as I acquainted you some time since that the Commander in chief had Appointed me to take command of the Navy on the Lakes."[17] Arnold warned Wynkoop that unless he followed his orders, he would have the disagreeable task of immediately arresting him. Wynkoop persisted in his belief that Schuyler's appointment gave him command of the fleet.

After his ordered arrest by Gates, Arnold noted that Wynkoop was sorry for his insubordination and pleaded to Gates that Wynkoop "may be permitted to return home without being cashiered."[18] Following Arnold's request, Gates sent Wynkoop with a pass without arrest to Schuyler in Albany but insisted that he not be returned to Ticonderoga. Wynkoop made an appeal to Congress, which was largely ignored, but he was never cashiered (discharged) from the service.

With reports that the British were building a fleet at St. Jean, the Americans pressed forward to deploy their fleet under Arnold in August. By August 18 Gates reported that he had nine vessels "fit for action" which included the *Enterprise, Royal Savage, Revenge, Liberty,* and the new gondolas *New Haven, Providence, Boston, Spitfire,* and *Philadelphia.* The first four vessels had been captured from the British in 1775. The *Revenge*, taken at St. Jean, had been referred to as a row galley by contemporary accounts of 1775 but was apparently re-rigged as a schooner at Ticonderoga.[19] The gondola *Jersey* and cutter *Lee* were not yet rigged. The other row galleys that Arnold had ordered were not finished as planned. The delay, Gates later reported to Congress, was caused by the "excessive sickness of that place [Skenesborough] [which] has greatly retarded the finishing of the galleys."[20]

Meanwhile, the British, knowing that the Americans were enlarging their fleet, were rushing to complete their own flotilla for Lake Champlain. Their strategy involved building some very large ships which would result in "our acquiring an absolute dominion over Lake Champlain."[21] To that end the British planned to bring vessels from the St. Lawrence into Lake Champlain via the Richelieu River and build additional ships at St. Jean. The 14-gun schooner *Maria*, named for General Guy Carleton's wife, had been captured by the Americans in November 1775 on the St. Lawrence. Recaptured by the British on May 6, 1776, with the American evacuation of Quebec, the 66-foot *Maria* was to be transported

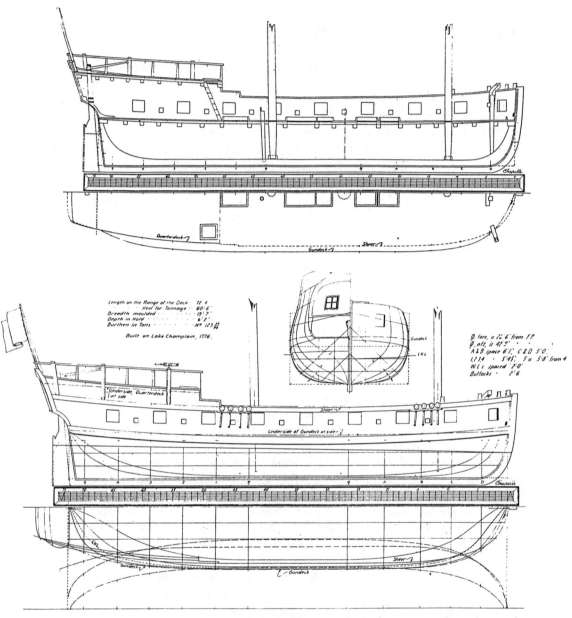

ABOVE. The galley *Washington* was built by the Americans in 1776 at Skenesborough. From Admiralty draughts by H. I. Chapelle, Chapelle Collection. (Smithsonian Institution)

RIGHT ABOVE. The gondola *Philadelphia* was built in 1776 at Skenesborough (Whitehall, N.Y.). Line drawing by H. I. Chapelle. (Smithsonian Institution)

RIGHT BELOW. "The *Philadelphia* sinking, assisted by the galley *Washington*, Battle of Valcour Island, Lake Champlain, October 11, 1776." Painting by Ernest Haas. (Lake Champlain Maritime Museum)

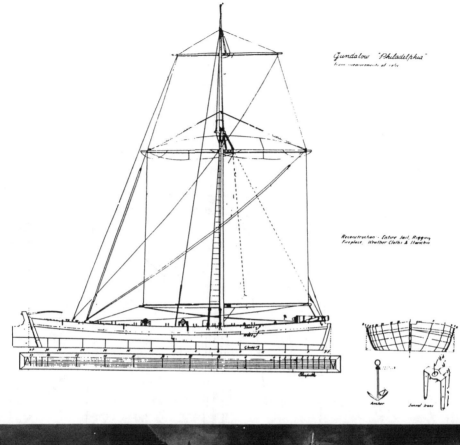

Gundalow "Philadelphia"
from measurements at site

Reconstruction - Entire Sail, Rigging
Fireplace, Weather Cloths & Stanchio

Anchor   Swivel brass

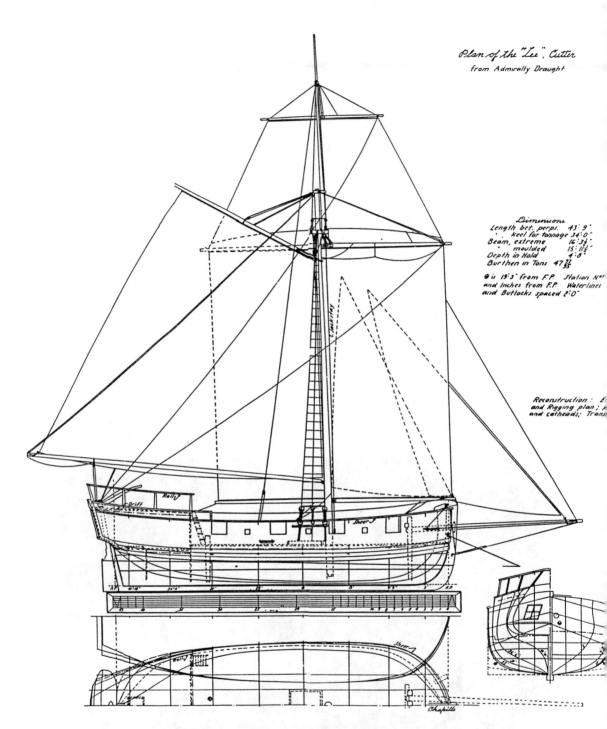

The cutter *Lee* was built from frames taken by Benedict Arnold during the
American evacuation of St. Jean in June 1776. Drawing by H. I. Chapelle
from Admiralty draught. (Smithsonian Institution)

overland on a newly-built road from Chambly to St. Jean. However, the road in July was found to be too loose to support the *Maria* or two other hulls that were to be moved overland. The *Maria* was subsequently taken apart and shipped by water to St. Jean where it was to be reassembled. The largest vessel, an 80-foot ship under construction at Quebec, later to be named the *Inflexible*, was likewise taken apart and transported in pieces in long boats to St. Jean for completion. The *Inflexible* would be finished at St. Jean in a remarkable 28 days. The 59-foot schooner *Carleton*, recaptured from the Americans at Quebec in May, was similarly dismantled and reconstructed at St. Jean.[22]

A 62-foot gondola, named the *Loyal Convert* by the British, was dragged through the rapids at Chambly to St. Jean. This vessel had also been taken from the Americans during the May 6 retreat from Quebec. The vessel was possibly one of the American gondolas, *Hancock* or *Schuyler*, built by Philip Schuyler on Lake Champlain in 1775, that had been dragged northward over the same rapids the previous November. The length is the approximate dimension given by Schuyler in 1775 for the gondolas.[23] The British also moved 30 long boats, many from their fleet on the St. Lawrence, over the Chambly rapids to St. Jean. The long boats, typically ranging from 20 to 40 feet in length, carried the frames and materials for the fleet to be constructed at St. Jean. In addition, some flat-bottomed boats and 400 bateaux were dragged over the rapids.

At St. Jean the British built "Twelve Gun Boats" from the frames brought from England and either built or dragged across the rapids "16 Canadian Built Boats."[24] Eventually, 20 to 28 of these gunboats would face the Americans in October 1776. The standard gunboat employed by the British was 37 feet long with a 12-foot beam carrying one mast and one cannon in the bow.

The most powerful vessel to be built by the British at St. Jean in 1776 was the large square-rigged, two-masted radeau *Thunderer* which would mount 2 howitzers, 6 twenty-four-pound cannon, and 8 twelve-pounders. One journal reported that the 91-foot *Thunderer* was "Built in a square of strong rafters, fitted however with masts, sails, wheel and a cabin like a ship."[25] Although the vessel was unwieldy to sail, if the wind was in the right direction the vessel sailed remarkably fast.

By the time the Americans were ready to sail, the British at St. Jean were still feverishly working on their vessels. On August 24 the American fleet, under the command of Benedict Arnold, departed from Crown Point with the *Royal Savage* and *Enterprise* in the lead, followed by the gondolas *New Haven, Boston, Providence, Spitfire, Philadelphia*, and *Connecticut* with the schooners *Revenge* and *Liberty* in the rear and a large number of bateaux. Gates' sailing orders, given over two weeks earlier, suggested that the "ultimate end" of Arnold's command would be to prevent the enemy invasion but warned that it was a defensive war and urged "no wanton risk or unnecessary display of the power of the fleet is at any time to influence your conduct."[26] The fleet was to be stationed in a narrow pass of the lake to thwart the British advance. If their fleet was stronger, Arnold was advised to retire to Ticonderoga after making every effort to retard its progress.

On the second night of the cruise, the American fleet was anchored off Willsboro when a violent gale from the northeast forced Arnold to sail to Buttonmould Bay (Button Bay, near present-day Panton, Vermont) for a safe harbor from the huge waves that the storm had set in motion. The American fleet renewed its voyage northward September 1. Three days later, Arnold moored the fleet across the narrow span of the lake at Windmill Point. At that time the cutter *Lee* and gondola *New Jersey* joined the American flotilla. September

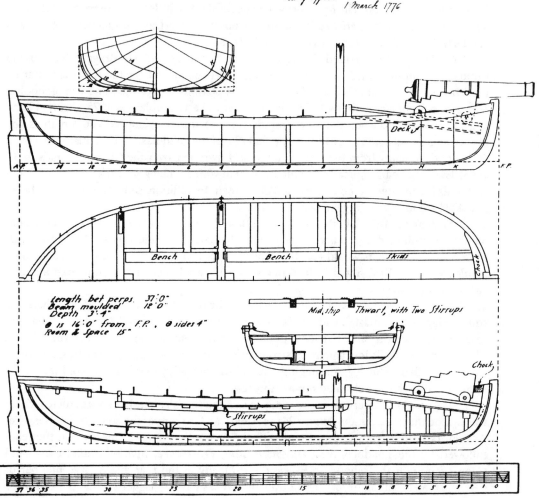

A Draught of a Boat to carry One Carriage Gun. Forward
Navy Office
1 March 1776

length bet perps. 37'0"
Beam moulded 12'0"
Depth 3'4"
Ø is 16'0" from F.P. , Ø sides 4"
Room & Space 15"

Bench   Bench   Skids

Mid.ship Thwart, with Two Stirrups

Deck

Chock

Chock

Stirrups

ABOVE. British gunboat of 1776 used at the Valcour engagement. Admiralty draught, Chapelle Collection. (Smithsonian Institution)

RIGHT TOP. Admiralty drawing of 66-foot schooner *Maria* which had been dismantled and rebuilt at St. Jean in 1776. (National Maritime Museum, Greenwich, England)

RIGHT. The radeau *Thunderer* employed by the British during the 1776 naval campaign. Reconstruction of Admiralty drawing by H. I. Chapelle. (Smithsonian Institution)

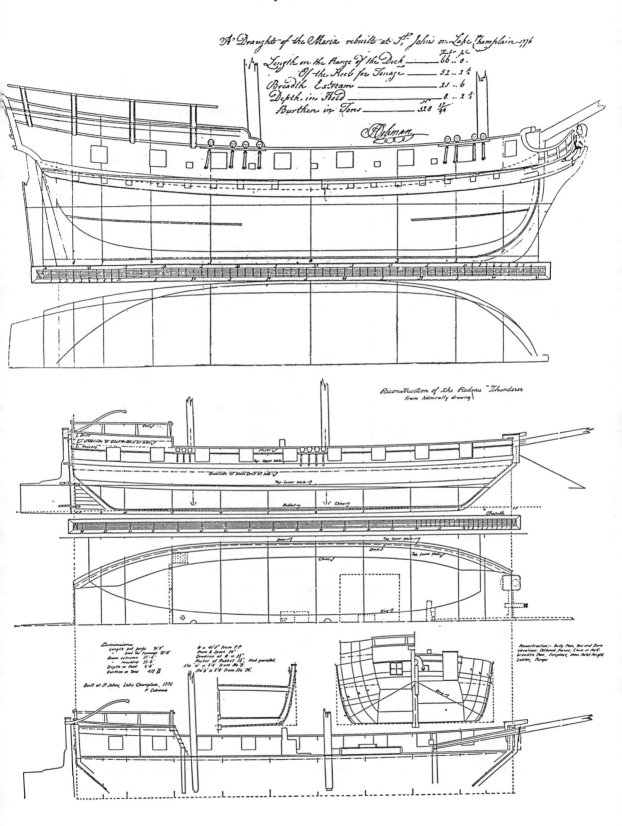

5 and 6 Arnold sent some of the crews to cut "Facines [branches] to fix on the Bows and Sides of the Gondolas to prevent the Enemies boarding and to keep off the small Shot."[27]

On the second day crew members of the *Boston* gondola were ambushed by Indians led by a British regular officer. The crews rushed back to the boat, but the melee resulted in the deaths of three men with six wounded. Believing the British were erecting batteries on the shoreline at Windmill Point, Arnold moved the fleet to a wider part of the lake at Isle La Motte on September 8.

At the northern anchorages, Arnold complained to Gates that his crews were "very indifferent Men, in general, great part of those who shipped for Seaman know very little of the Matter."[28] He pleaded with Gates for swivel cannon for the vessels, warm clothing for the crews, more seamen, and provisions while proposing arming bateaux with swivel guns at each end. At Isle La Motte, Arnold waited for the galleys that were far behind schedule. According to Colonel Jeduthan Baldwin, the first two row galleys did not reach Ticonderoga for rigging and arming until September 11 and 12. The galleys *Congress* and *Trumbull* would require more than two weeks to be fitted out. Although Arnold and others worried about the construction delays in the summer of 1776, in retrospect the building process was a remarkable achievement in itself given the circumstances. Building this fleet in a few months, including some of the gondolas in a matter of weeks largely with hand tools, was a feat of ingenuity and hard work.

The eighth and last gondola, *New York*, joined the fleet on September 11. With an anchorage at Isle La Motte that was less than satisfactory, Arnold sent scouts to find a new harbor. On September 18 after some intelligence about the British fleet at St. Jean, Arnold wrote to Gates of his intention to move to the bay east of Valcour Island (Plattsburgh, N.Y. today) "where is a good harbour, and where we shall have the advantage of attacking the enemy in the open Lake."[29] Three days later the American fleet anchored at Bay St. Armand, north of Cumberland Head. The *Liberty*, cruising near the western shore opposite Isle La Motte, was decoyed by a man dressed in French clothing. The man waded into the lake and requested the *Liberty* to come closer. Suspecting a trap, the captain sent a smaller boat near the shore. When the crew refused to be decoyed closer, 300-400 Indians, Canadians, and regulars rose up on the shore and fired on the vessel wounding several crew members. The boat "returned the fire with their swivels and small-arms" and the *Liberty* "fired several broadsides of grape" before returning to the fleet.[30]

The fleet sailed on September 24 for Valcour Bay. At Valcour, Arnold wrote Gates, reiterating his strategy "that few vessels can attack us at the same time, and those will be exposed to the fire of the whole fleet."[31] Although a few historians have criticized Arnold for not following Gates' original sailing instructions of not risking the fleet, Gates had plenty of time to order the fleet out of Valcour Bay. On September 21 Arnold again informed Gates of his intention to anchor at Valcour Bay but suggested moving if Gates did not approve: "I make no doubt you will approve of this measure; if not, I will return to any of my former stations."[32] Gates, however, never questioned Arnold's choice of anchorages and had full confidence in Arnold's leadership. Gates dispatched a letter to Arnold on October 12 (not having news of the previous day): "I. . .am pleased to find You, and your Armada, ride in Valcour Bay, in defiance of the power of our Foes in Canada."[33] Gates, for most of the time before the engagement, had been optimistic about the power of the American fleet. In mid-August, he confidently wrote that the naval force, after completion, would command Lake Champlain. Even in early October, after examining intelligence reports of British preparations, Gates was not entirely convinced that the British would engage the American fleet: "I am inclined to suspect they are rather Acting upon the Defensive."[34]

Scouts had continually observed the growth of the British fleet at St. Jean, but most reports underestimated the strength and size of the vessels. A September 20 report indicated the "sloop and schooners" were not finished, only two out of seven gondolas completed, and "no other vessels building" at St. Jean although timber was being cut.[35] Arnold felt the British would have a considerable naval force on the lake, but the intelligence that he received in mid-September of one ship on the stocks of 20 guns (*Inflexible*), several schooners, and some smaller craft at St. Jean still underestimated the fleet by omitting the large number of gunboats and the radeau *Thunderer*. Information from a Frenchman concerning the vessels at St. Jean, however, did mention a floating battery under construction, but Arnold thought the man a British spy and didn't believe the report. An undated intelligence report that more accurately portrayed the British squadron at St. Jean was not reflected in the letters of Gates or Arnold before the engagement at Valcour.[36] On the day before the engagement, Arnold had no recent intelligence because of the loss of the only two canoes with the fleet.

During the last two days of September and early October, the American fleet rode at anchor in Valcour Bay awaiting the British fleet. The weather was cold and windy as the crews practiced firing at marks and maneuvering their vessels. On September 30 the galley *Trumbull*, carrying 8 cannon and 16 swivels under the command of Captain Seth Warner, arrived at two o'clock in the afternoon. While the galley was a much needed addition to the fleet, Arnold complained that the vessel was only half-rigged, mounting cannon much smaller than he ordered. Cannon salutes pierced the wilderness six days later on October 6 when the galleys *Congress* and *Washington*, under the command of Captains Arnold and Thatcher respectively, finally joined the fleet. General David Waterbury, who had been working on the vessels at Skenesborough and Ticonderoga, arrived in the *Washington* galley to take his post as second-in-command of the fleet. The crews were glad to see the *Washington* since a barrel of rum for each gondola was among its cargo. Anxious to hear of news of the American army on Long Island, Arnold wrote to Gates on the following day. In his letter, he suggested moving the fleet back to Button Bay if the British did not appear by the middle of October, but the fleet was ready for action: "I make no doubt of giving a good account of them."[37] In early October, Arnold was still confident, believing the British "naval force, by the best accounts, near equal to ours."[38] As the American flotilla pitched and rolled in the stiff autumn gales of October 1776, the brave crews were unaware of the juggernaut coming their way.

With their largest vessel barely finished, General Guy Carleton, governor of Canada, and Captain Thomas Pringle, commander of the fleet, sailed with most of their ships on October 4 to Isle-aux-Noix, then to Point au Fer on the western shore of Lake Champlain. At Point au Fer, the British erected a blockhouse, assigning four companies to defend it. The British fleet remained at Point au Fer until October 10 while scouting parties searched for the American fleet and additional vessels were brought up. On the tenth of October Carleton received an erroneous report that the Americans had been seen in Cumberland Bay (or near Grand Isle). With that report, the second inaccurate sighting of the Americans, the British fleet sailed and came to anchor between Grand Isle and North Hero Island. The night before the battle, Captain Pringle was said to have received accurate information on the location of the American fleet, but other eyewitnesses noted that the American fleet was expected at Cumberland Bay.[39] The next morning, the British fleet, consisting of the ship *Inflexible*, schooners *Maria* and *Carleton*, radeau *Thunderer*, gondola *Loyal Convert*, 20 or more gunboats, long boats, bateaux, and canoes, made uneven progress as the cold, blue water lapped their hulls.*

ABOVE. The Battle of Valcour Island 1776 by Henry Gilder. (Windsor Castle, Royal Library, Her Majesty Queen Elizabeth II)

RIGHT TOP. "A View of New England Armed Vessels, on Valcure Bay on Lake Champlain, 11 October 1776" by Charles Randle. (National Archives of Canada)

RIGHT MIDDLE. "A View of His Majesty's Armed Vessels on Lake Champlain, 11 October 1776" by Charles Randle. (National Archives of Canada)

RIGHT BOTTOM. "God bless our Armes" depicts the American fleet at Valcour Bay on October 11, 1776. Watercolor by C. Randle, 1777. (Fort Ticonderoga Museum)

* Although most contemporary British sources do not name a sixth vessel in the British fleet, the contemporary painting of the Valcour battle by Henry Gilder in the Royal Collection, on display in Windsor Castle, depicts another sailing vessel with a bowsprit at the stern of the **Thunderer**. Likewise, the original drawing by Charles Randle in the National Archives of Canada shows what may be the same vessel labeled a long boat. Major General Friedrich Riedesel, a German commander with the British force on the lake, mentions six vessels in his memoirs.[40]

The sky was clear and a crisp northerly wind blew through the American fleet anchored in Valcour Bay on the morning of October 11. The Americans could see snow on the Adirondack Mountains to their west as the crews began their seventeenth day at the bay. The American fleet consisted of 15 vessels and some bateaux. The schooner *Liberty* had departed for another trip to Ticonderoga for provisions and the row galley *Gates* was still being outfitted at Ticonderoga. At eight o'clock in the morning, the guard boat of the American fleet fired an alarm as it brought the news of the approaching fleet. At half-past nine, Arnold ordered Colonel Edward Wigglesworth, third-in-command, out into a yawl to observe the motions of the British fleet. Arnold moved his flag to the galley *Congress* from the *Royal Savage*, probably because he believed that the row galleys would be better equipped for maneuvering during battle.

As the British fleet with its larger ships came into view, it must have stirred apprehension among the 500 green hands on their makeshift shoal vessels. General Waterbury immediately boarded Arnold's vessel to give his "opinion that the fleet ought immediately to come to sail, and fight them on a retreat in main Lake, as they were so much superior to us in number and strength."[41] But Arnold, undeterred by the size of the British fleet, ordered the American vessels in a line across the bay to receive the invading force. Arnold was probably correct since a haphazard retreat on the open lake against the faster British ships would have been a disaster, as the events of October 13 would later prove. To some extent the fleet had been built to be sacrificed to slow the British invasion; to save it and allow the British invasion to go forth unchecked was not a strategy Arnold would support.

The British fleet had almost twice the weight in cannon, more vessels, and more men who were trained sailors, and drew Royal Navy officers from the British fleet in the St. Lawrence. The fleet was accompanied by some bateaux, long boats, and canoes, but the main army consisting of 7,000 men in 300-400 bateaux did not depart until October 14 from Point au Fer. Fewer than 1,000 men in bateaux accompanied the fleet as boarding parties. The British ships sailed past Valcour on the stiff northerly wind and then, sighting the American vessels, had to sail upwind, as Arnold had anticipated, to attack them. The British gunboats, however, were successful in reaching a position, in a line from the southwestern tip of Valcour Island to the New York shore, which faced the American line to the north. Although many of the participants noted 20 gunboats in the British line, estimates ranged as high as 28 armed gunboats and longboats.[42]

After the Americans heard the news of the oncoming British fleet, Arnold "ordered the 2 schooners and 3 gallies under way immediately" to entice the ships into the bay.[43] Between ten-thirty and eleven o'clock the battle began. The *Royal Savage*, the only American craft in a class with the British warships, ran aground on the southwestern corner of Valcour Island after its masts and bowsprit were damaged and rigging shot away by three shots from the *Inflexible*. The gunboats then brought an incessant fire on the stranded *Royal Savage* as the *Loyal Convert* entered the bay. The crew of the *Royal Savage* abandoned the schooner, but not before Lieutenant Edward Longcroft, commander of the *Convert*, boarded the vessel and captured as many as 20 crew members before they could escape. Longcroft then turned the guns of the *Royal Savage* back on the Americans. When half of the boarding party were killed by return fire, Longcroft left the *Royal Savage* for his gondola.

For the next several hours the crews of the British gunboats and American vessels engaged in a savage duel as cannon burst solid shot, barshot, and grapeshot. Smoke from the American guns floated with the wind over the British boats as carriages recoiled back from each blast on both sides. Arnold, aboard the *Congress*, anchored in the hottest part of the crossfire, actually aimed the cannon himself on the open deck amid flying shot and splintering wood. Many of the American shots, however, missed their mark since "the G.Boats being low in the Water made the Shot go over their heads."[44] The British gunboats, on the other hand, were quite effective in lobbing shot upon the American vessels with

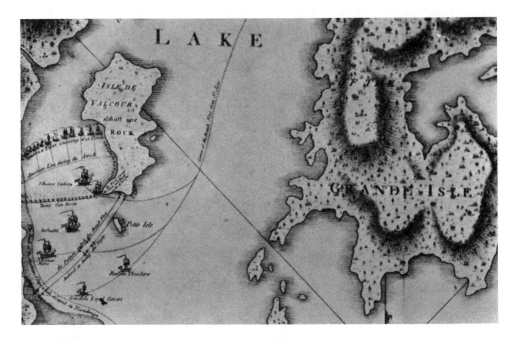

"The Attack and Defeat of the American Fleet under Benedict Arnold by King's Fleet Commanded by Captain Thomas Pringle, Upon Lake Champlain, the 11th of October, 1776" by William Faden, London, 1776. (Special Collections, Bailey/Howe Memorial Library, University of Vermont)

devastating results. According to Lieutenant James Hadden, "each Gun Boat carried 1 Gun in the Bow (or Howitzer) 7 Artillery Men, and 11 Seamen, the whole under an Artillery officer."[45] In the heat of battle, Captain George Pausch, chief of the Hesse-Hann artillery in the engagement, observed the gunboat of Lieutenant Dufais explode: "a chest went up into the air, and after the smoke had cleared away, I recognized the men by the cords around their hats."[46] Pausch rescued most of the crew (another gunboat, under Lt. Smith, took Dufais, the Bombadier, and an artillery man) which increased the number of men on his gunboat to 48, nearly sinking the vessel. The gunboat that exploded burned and sank in Valcour Bay.[47]

While the Americans were fighting the crews on the British gunboats, Indians led by Captain Christopher Carleton, nephew of Governor Guy Carleton, and Brigadier General Simon Fraser (local rank) with another group of Indians and Canadians fired ineffectively from both the shore and Valcour Island. The schooner *Carleton*, under the command of

Lieutenant James Dacres, by mid-afternoon had sailed into Valcour Bay to a position north of the British gunboats. The schooner was now exposed to the full force of the American line. The vessel became totally disabled as the American vessels concentrated their fire on the schooner. Lieutenant Dacres was wounded and knocked senseless, and the officer second-in-command, Robert Brown, lost his right arm. Nineteen-year-old Midshipman Edward Pellew took command of the *Carleton*, while Captain Pringle, lying far back in the schooner *Maria*, signaled recall to the *Carleton*. Pellew, who in later years would become one of Britain's most famous admirals, crawled out on the bowsprit amid flying shot to deploy a jib sail. When one of the tow ropes was cut by a shot, Pellew once more risked his life when no one else volunteered by again exposing himself on the bowsprit to secure the tow rope to the long boats of the *Inflexible*.[48] Eight men were killed and six wounded on the *Carleton* during the attack.

While the battle was raging, the 14-gun schooner *Maria*, reportedly the best sailing vessel in the fleet, remained far south of the action with her sails rolled up. Captain Thomas Pringle only vaguely directed the naval operations during the battle, while Governor-General Guy Carleton with his younger brother, Colonel Thomas Carleton, observed the engagement from the open decks. The next year, after learning of Pringle's account which failed to mention the effort of all the officers and vessels involved, Lieutenants John Schank (*Inflexible*), John Starke (*Maria*), and Edward Longcroft (*Loyal Convert*) wrote a scathing letter to Pringle, accusing him of mismanagement of the battle and making no attempt to use the *Maria* "while yourself in the Maria lay too with the topsails, and was the only person in the fleet who showed no inclination to fight."[49] Probably the only shots fired by the *Maria* were at the beginning of the engagement when the *Maria* "opened a lively cannonade" and "was replaced by the frigate 'Carleton;' and as she in turn retreated, the 'Inflexible' took her place only to retreat as others had done."[50] The *Inflexible* may have gotten into the action at the end of the clash since the vessel was said to have "sunk one of the rebel Gundalos."[51]

By five o'clock, the gunboats withdrew about 600-700 yards away but continued firing until dark. By then the American fleet, with three-fourths of its ammunition gone, had been badly damaged with the galley *Congress* receiving "Seven Shott between Wind & Water, was hulled a doz times, had her Main Mast Wounded in Two places & her Yard in One."[52] The *Washington*, likewise, had her hull pierced by shot, had her main mast shot away, and was leaking. The *Washington* also lost her first lieutenant and had her captain wounded. The gondola *New York* had lost all her officers except the captain. In total, approximately 60 men were killed or wounded during the engagement on the American side. At the end of the engagement the gondola *Philadelphia* sank from damage suffered in the cannonading. When the vessel was recovered in 1935, a 24-pound ball was found lodged in the outside planking at the bow. The shot that sank the *Philadelphia* probably came from a gunboat, some of which carried 24-pound cannon. Before dusk a British boarding party set the *Royal Savage* afire, resulting in an explosion of the remaining powder on the vessel. The fire burned all night before the hull settled into the water off the island. Benedict Arnold's personal papers and most of his clothes, which had not been transferred to the *Congress*, were aboard the *Royal Savage* when it burned and sank.

At dusk Arnold called a council of war in his cabin aboard the *Congress*. With little choice, Generals Arnold and Waterbury and the captains of the vessels agreed to retreat immediately to Crown Point with the crippled fleet. Some of the officers proposed sailing around the northern end of Valcour Island, but Arnold elected to take the fleet through the British line.* In the darkness, shrouded in a dense fog, the fleet inched its way along the western shoreline. With the galley *Trumbull* in the lead and a hooded lantern in the stern of each vessel to show only directly behind, the fleet carefully passed single file "with so much secrecy that we went through them entirely undiscovered."[54] Captain Pringle's letter to the secretary of the admiralty on October 15 stated that he "brought the whole fleet to anchor in a line as near as possible to the Rebels, that their retreat might be cut off."[55] Schank, Starke, and Longcroft, however, later disputed the report, suggesting that "the fleet was not brought to anchor as near as possible to the rebels. . .the rear of the British line was at least one mile from the western shore, and the van beyond the small island at the Southern end of Valcour."[56] The American fleet with the *Congress* and *Washington* in the rear made its way to Schuyler Island seven and a half miles to the south of Valcour.

At the break of dawn, the British peered at Valcour Bay, ready to finish the destruction of the American fleet. To their surprise the Americans were gone. According to General Riedesel, "General Carleton was in a rage" and sailed away to find the rebel fleet, but "forgot to leave instructions for the army on the land. . .the wind, however, being adverse, and nothing having been seen of the enemy, he returned" to Valcour Island.[57] Riedesel's story has been the most commonly accepted and repeated version of October 12, but Reidesel was not actually there. Lieutenant John Enys, aboard the radeau *Thunderer*, noted "at day light some of their fleet were Seen at a distance. Our fleet attempted to pursue them but the wind was so hard against us we were obliged [to] put back again."[58] Enys also reported that the *Thunderer* was in some danger when her lee boards caved in, causing the radeau to heel over enough to allow water to flood in through the gunports.

Early on the morning of October 12 the American fleet became widely separated. The *Trumbull* galley and some of the other vessels had only paused briefly at Schuyler Island while Arnold in the *Congress*, Waterbury in the *Washington*, and most of the gondolas eventually anchored at Schuyler to stop their leaks and mend the sails. Arnold wrote to Gates from Schuyler requesting a dozen bateaux to tow the vessels back to Crown Point in the event of southerly winds. The vessels came to anchor at Schuyler Island at markedly different times. The journal entry of Bayze Wells, aboard the *Providence*, "Arivd to Schilers Isleland and Came too the wind being hard against us" was made during the night of October 11-12.[59] Arnold's letter to George Washington on October 15 stated that the fleet only remained at Schuyler long enough to stop the leaks and mend the sails on the *Washington* when "at two o'clock, P.M., the 12th, weighed anchor with a fresh breeze to the southward."[60] Waterbury's account written on October 24 (and a later version on Feb. 26, 1777) suggested that the *Washington* was still under sail north of Schuyler Island on the morning of October 12: "The wind being against us, and my vessel so torn to pieces that it was almost impossible to keep her above water. . . I was obliged to come to anchor at twelve o'clock, to mend my sails. When we had completed that, we made sail, just at evening."[61]

---

* An interesting controversy arose in the late nineteenth century when some historians argued that Arnold had actually escaped with his fleet by sailing around the northern end of Valcour Island. As more journals were published, it became clear that this did not occur. The story is also linked to the tale of "Carleton's Prize," a solitary rock island three and a half miles east of Valcour, which was supposedly, mistakenly bombarded by the British fleet the next morning. The tale seemingly has no basis in fact although some have claimed to have found cannonballs there.[53]

By contrast, the galley *Trumbull* at dawn on October 12 had proceeded as far as Willsboro Point according to Private Pascal De Angelis, a 13-year-old recruit from Connecticut. The *Trumbull* remained anchored at Ligonier Point for repairs until "half after one at night, when 2 of the gundeloes came along and we hailed them; and they told that one of our gundeloes was taking water and the other sunk. Whereupon we gott underway and beat down the rest of the night."[62] A similar account was given by Colonel Edward Wigglesworth, a former shipmaster from Newburyport, Massachusetts, who was also aboard the galley *Trumbull*. On October 12 Wigglesworth noted "up with Schuyler Island and came to anchor under Ligoni's Point to wait for the fleet, stop our leaks, and secure our mainmast, which was split in two."[63]

Arnold's letter to Schuyler reported "two gondolas sunk at Schuyler's Island."[64] This statement has been the impetus for extensive searches around the island by the Smithsonian Institution, the National Geographic Society, the Woods Hole Oceanographic Institution and others (see chapter 9). The entry of Bayze Wells on October 12 noted the aborted British pursuit and related that the Americans had "to Leve three Gondolas and make the best of our way with boats two of which we Distroyd and one of them the Enemies made a Prise off."[65] Wells may have been counting the *Philadelphia* in the three gondolas since he failed to mention the vessel sinking in his October 11 journal entry. The vessel captured was the gondola *New Jersey* which the British recorded as taken on October 12.[66] The *New Jersey* was apparently one of the two gondolas that had been scuttled or abandoned by the Americans when discovered by the British.

The Memoirs of James Wilkinson, based on contemporary accounts but written years later, also place the *Trumbull* galley on the western shore five or six miles south of the rest of the fleet when a "breeze commenced, but several of the largest of the gun boats were struck by it, and driven into the lake, and two or three were forced on the eastern shore, where they were abandoned and destroyed."[67] The 1776 drawing by Charles Randle of the American fleet listed the gondola *Providence* as "Sunk 12 Octr in a Squall," but the captions, written after 1777, contained several errors regarding the gondolas.[68] Wilkinson's reference to the vessels on the eastern shore, however, has little substantiation.* Lieutenant John Enys, with the British fleet, described the discovery of "the Jersey on the opposite side of the Lake," but he seemed to imply the western shore of the lake as the location.[70]

The weary, half-starved American crews battled strong southerly headwinds on the evening of October 12. Whitecaps slapped against the bows of the leaking vessels and the crews shivered in the cold wind while futilely pulling on their long sweeps all through the night. The British, meanwhile, had also renewed their pursuit of the Americans during the evening of the 12th. As the wind moderated, Arnold's fleet made some progress: "at six o'clock next morning we were about off Willsborough. . . The enemy's fleet were very little way above Schuyler's Island."[71] At the same time, Captain Thomas Pringle on the *Maria* "saw eleven sail of their fleet" on the morning of October 13 (The *New Jersey*, *Royal Savage*, *Philadelphia*, and one missing gondola had been sunk or abandoned by then).[72] The chase began in earnest after the early sightings. With the wind from the north on October 13, the

---

* James Wilkinson accompanied Arnold to Quebec, served as his aide in 1776 at Lake Champlain, and was a brigade major at Ticonderoga before taking ill. Although not present at Valcour Island, Wilkinson described the October 11-13 lake battles in his memoirs based upon information from a friend who served as a sergeant on the **Congress** galley. Unfortunately, Wilkinson was regarded as a scoundrel with a long, checkered and controversial career and his memoirs are considered unreliable by some historians.[69]

ship *Inflexible* and schooners *Carleton* and *Maria* made better time on the lake than the shattered, leaky gondolas and galleys. The British gunboats and other vessels trailed the three lead vessels southward in a piecemeal fashion. After the rearmost vessels traveled only five miles from Willsboro, Lieutenant Wells noted that the British had sailed closer: "we being against the mouth of Gillilands Crick [Bouquet River] the Enemy hove in Sight and Persued us with all Speede."[73] The *Trumbull, Revenge, Enterprise,* and *New York* were well ahead of the two galleys, *Congress* and *Washington,* and the four gondolas as the three British ships closed in. The cutter *Lee* was "run into a bay" and abandoned by her crew sometime on October 13.[74] The vessels with Arnold desperately tried to escape the British, but "by the time we had reached Split-Rock, were alongside of us."[75] Just before Split Rock,

Engagement on Lake Champlain on October 13, 1776. Engraving printed in London for Robert Sayer and Jno. Bennett on December 22, 1776. (Special Collections, Bailey/Howe Memorial Library, University of Vermont)

Waterbury asked permission from Arnold to run his vessel onshore and blow it up, but Arnold refused, instructing Waterbury "to push forward to Split Rock, where he would draw the fleet in a line, and engage them again." When Waterbury reached Split Rock, he found the other vessels still fleeing "and left me in the rear, to fall into enemy's hands."[76] Arnold had sent orders via his yawl at nine o'clock for Wigglesworth "to lie by for the fleet, which I did, by stretching across the lake."[77] DeAngelis recalled that "we received orders from General Arnold to heave to and engage the British," but the vessels with Wigglesworth were apparently too far away from Arnold to regroup.[78]

The *Inflexible*, *Carleton*, and *Maria* immediately poured deadly broadsides into the two American galleys.* Although Captain Pringle aboard the *Maria* noted "the action began at twelve o'clock, and lasted two hours," Colonel Wigglesworth recorded "at ten, A.M., the enemy began to fire upon the two galleys in the rear."[80] Thirty miles away at Ticonderoga, Persifer Frazer reported that "the greater part of the forenoon we heard distinctly at this place an almost continual cannonading which ceased about 3 O'Clock."[81]

As the three British vessels surrounded the *Washington*, about "five Milds[miles] Belo Split Rock," the men left their oars "and after four or five shott the Washington galley strike without firing one gun."[82] At this point Colonel Wigglesworth, as third-in-command, with three other vessels nearby, "thought it my duty to make sail and endeavor to save the Trumbull galley if possible" by double-manning the oars, and throwing the ballast overboard to escape the British fleet.[83] Arnold on the *Congress*, following the eastern shore, now faced the full brunt of the large enemy warships as their fiery blasts pounded the already devastated galley. The rigging and sails were torn to pieces, and the first lieutenant and three others were killed in the cannon duel. Two vessels at the stern of the *Congress* and one alongside poured round after round of grapeshot and solid cannonballs into the striken vessel. On an open deck, Arnold directed his return cannon fire on the British vessels. The battle was a running engagement with a northerly wind during which the vessels sailed approximately nine miles from Split Rock to present-day Panton, Vermont.

Arnold, with no hope for escape, ran the *Congress* and four gondolas into a shallow bay, named for homesteader Peter Ferris, and beached the vessels on the northeastern shore: "I set her [*Congress*] on fire with four gondolas."[84] As the vessels were ignited, Arnold "ordered the colours not to be struck; and as they grounded, the marines were directed to jump overboard, with their arms and accoutrements, to ascend a bank about twenty-five feet elevation, and form a line for the defence of their vessels and flags against the enemy, Arnold being the last man who debarked."[85] Arnold might have escaped into the bay by initially passing by the inlet, then rowing his vessels through the British line, forcing the British ships to tack against the wind to reach the bay. The British fleet, which included seven vessels at that point, continued a cannonade from a distance. The house of Peter Ferris on the southeastern bank of the bay (which from that day has been known as Arnold's Bay) was struck by several cannonballs and grapeshot.

After observing from the *Maria* the firing and the explosion of the galley *Congress*, Dr. Robert Knox, the chief medical officer to the British army in Canada, noted that Arnold "remained on the beach till he set fire to them [vessels], burning the wounded and sick in them."[86] The story quickly circulated among other British officers and men as General Riedesel soon noted "a dreadful report was current, viz: that General Arnold. . . had also burned about thirty sick and wounded men who were on board."[87] Using Riedesel's journal, Von Eelking later embellished the story of the wounded, "their cries being heard above the crackling on the flames and the noise of the guns."[88] Among the American eyewitnesses to the events in the bay was fourteen-year-old Squire Ferris, son of Peter Ferris. Interviewed years later, Ferris told of only one wounded man accidentally left on the *Congress*.[89] Lieutenant Goldsmith, severely wounded by grapeshot, was lying helpless on the deck,

---

* While there is no apparent historical evidence that any part of the engagement began north of Split Rock, cannonballs discovered on the beach in Whallons Bay and Essex indicate that some action occurred in this area.[79] The cannonballs, however, may be related to a raid by a British flotilla under Daniel Pring in May 1814.

according to Ferris. Arnold ordered Goldsmith removed, but the gunner set fire to the galley ignoring the wounded officer's pleas: "He remained on deck at the explosion, and his body was seen when blown into the air.... To the credit of Arnold, he showed the greatest feeling upon the subject and threatened to run the gunner through on the spot."[90] From a distance, viewing a body blown into the air, Dr. Knox concluded that Arnold had consciously burned the wounded with the vessels.

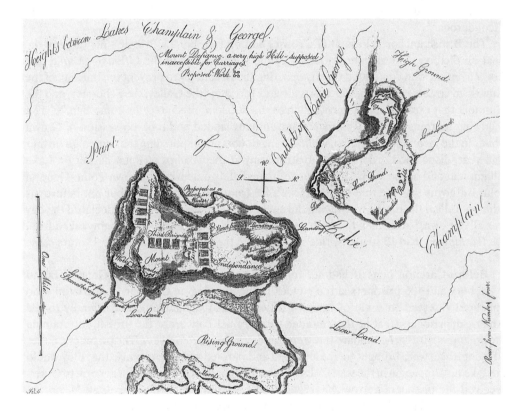

"Ticonderoga & its Dependencies August 1776."
From *Autobiography, Reminiscences and Letters* by John Trumbull, 1841.

Peter Ferris and his family accompanied Arnold and his men through the woods along the eastern shore of Lake Champlain, two hours ahead of the Indians dispatched by the British. The British destroyed the Ferris farm and shot all the cattle, horses, and hogs. "We travild by Land as far as against Putnam Point," wrote Bayze Wells "and thare met boats which took us on board we Arivd to Ticonderoga about Sun Set" on October 14.[91] After briefly stopping at Crown Point, Arnold had reached Ticonderoga at four o'clock in the morning on October 14 "exceedingly fatigued and unwell, having been without sleep or refreshment for near three days."[92]

Colonel Jeduthan Baldwin, the chief engineer at Ticonderoga, on October 13 recorded "about 3 o'Clock our Schooner [*Liberty*] came in Sight, Soon after a Sloop [*Enterprise*] & then another Schooner [*Revenge*], & then the Row Galley [*Trumbull*] & after a gundalow [*New York*], & they were followed by the Inhabitants from Crown point & from Panton."[93] The *Liberty*, on its way back to the fleet, promptly turned about and joined the urgent flight southward with the other four vessels. As early as eleven-thirty in the morning on October 13, Colonel Thomas Hartley's message to General Gates stated "I am told two sails are just in sight."[94] When the defeat of the Americans was known and the advance of the British imminent, Hartley's regiment at Crown Point burned the buildings and evacuated to Ticonderoga.

The British anchored in sight of Crown Point on October 13. Pringle's handling of the fleet on October 13 was later criticized by the commanders of the *Inflexible*, *Maria*, and *Loyal Convert*, who contended that by ordering the fleet to try to prevent the burning of the American vessels in Panton, which was already too late, "the Galley, the Schooner, and the Gondola that escaped, must inevitably have been taken, or shared the same fate."[95] The following morning the British rangers and Indians landed and took possession of Crown Point. In the meantime, Carleton, while having doubts about pursuing the campaign further that year, dispatched orders to the British army at their camps at Point au Fer on Lake Champlain and at the Richelieu River to immediately embark for Crown Point. General John Burgoyne was the first to depart with his troops at Point au Fer, but not before his adjutant rallied the troops by "waving the enemies colors, thirteen stripes, declared the day was all our own," according to Lieutenant William Digby.[96] The flag, probably taken from the *Washington*, had 13 stripes with a union jack in the left hand corner (the 13 stars came in 1777).

Before Carleton himself had set foot on Crown Point, he released General David Waterbury and 106 prisoners at ten o'clock in the morning on October 14. Carleton, who appeared reserved to some of his own officers, was magnanimous and friendly to the American prisoners treating the wounded with as much concern as the British, entertaining the prisoners with "grog" aboard the *Maria*, and praising their bravery. The prisoners, under a flag of truce, were brought to Ticonderoga and paroled with the promise that they would not take up arms again in the war. Colonel John Trumbull, deputy adjutant general to Gates, received the prisoners but quickly recognized Carleton's shrewd psychology. When the parolees related the "kindness" of their treatment, Trumbull ordered the men confined to the boats and advised Gates of the "danger" in permitting the men to speak to the troops at Ticonderoga: "accordingly they were ordered to proceed immediately to Skenesborough, on their way home, and they went forward that night, without being permitted to land."[97] The following day "Capt. Rew [Rice from the *Philadelphia*] came in through the woods with 16 men, they left Genl. Waterbury Just before he Struck. went into a battoe & went on Shore."[98] Ironically, the prisoners had an easier time than the crew that escaped through the rugged mountainside.

On board the *Maria* on the 14th, Carleton wrote the British secretary of state for the American colonies, Lord George Germain, summarizing the lake battles, listing the American vessels, and concluding that "the season is so far advanced that I cannot yet pretend to inform your Lordship whether any thing further can be done this year."[99] Carleton's list included the names of the *Jersey* and *Boston* gondolas and the cutter *Lee* which the British discovered in a bay.[100] Carleton had the *Boston* gondola confused with the *Philadelphia*, while Charles Randle's list noted that the *Providence* had sunk on the 12th, but other contemporary sources counted the vessel burnt on the 13th.[101] Undoubtedly, the British learned the names, with some errors, from the prisoners from the *Washington* (and the *Royal Savage*) before their release.

The Americans at Fort Ticonderoga and Mount Independence began increased fortifications in anticipation of a British attack. The loss of most of the fleet, while a disappointment, did not unnerve General Gates, who had the highest praise for Arnold's handling of the fleet. "It has pleased Providence to preserve General Arnold. Few men ever met with so many hairbreadth escapes in so short a space of time."[102] General Philip Schuyler called up more militia to bolster the 9,000-10,000 men already at Ticonderoga, but George Washington advised against the reinforcement: "Instead of calling up a number of useless hands and mouths, (for such I deem Militia in general), I would advise a collection of as much provision as could possibly be got together" which would be sufficient to keep the British at bay until the weather forced their retreat.[103] The troops were busy fortifying the old French lines from 1758 and strengthening Mt. Independence across the lake.

Between eleven and twelve o'clock on the evening of October 15, the edgy garrison was called to alarm "by 5 or 6 guns fired by the century [sentry]," recorded Dr. Lewis Beebe; "thro mistake the fire was at an ox, which was taken for one of the enemy, for not giving the Countersign when demanded."[104] Colonel Baldwin began supervision of a log boom across the lake on the 17th as rumors circulated that "Carleton said he would be in possession of Ticonderoga before Sunday & on his way to Albany where he was to have his Winter Quarters."[105] The men worked at a feverish pitch to complete the log boom across the lake by the 25th and began a floating foot bridge connecting Fort Ticonderoga to Mount Independence. Behind the boom was the remaining American fleet. Redoubts or gun batteries were built on both sides of the lake with a 20-gun battery on Mount Independence and another four-gun battery higher on the hill deployed in a half-moon. The bridge was completed on October 29 and four barracks raised in November as work progressed throughout the month.

On October 17 some of the British army that had departed from the upper reaches of Lake Champlain three days earlier had arrived at Crown Point. Battling "great swells," the bateaux carrying the rest of the troops did not reach Crown Point until October 20. Only a small part of the British army ever landed at Crown Point since there were not enough bateaux to bring them from St. Jean and Isle-aux-Noix. The British troops at Crown Point had erroneously estimated the American force at Ticonderoga as high as 20,000 men.

By October 20 Carleton had made up his mind to retreat back to Canada. Carleton's letter to Major General William Howe, fighting Washington's army in lower New York, disclosed "I fear the want of time (the severe season approaching very fast) to put. . . Crown Point in a state to quarter troops . . .will force us back to Canada."[106] Within two days, Carleton began making proposals for the navy on Lake Champlain for a renewed campaign in 1777, which would include building another ship the size of the *Inflexible*.

Strong southerly winds prevailed in October which seemed to prevent the British fleet from reaching Ticonderoga. By the 24th of October, the final decision to go into winter quarters in Canada was made, and General Burgoyne returned to Canada aboard the captured galley *Washington*. The troops, however, remained at Crown Point and made one advance toward Ticonderoga. Carleton had hoped that the Americans would evacuate Ticonderoga, but that was never considered by the garrison.

"Monday the 28th. . .in the morning our advanced boat made the signals that the enemy were approaching; alarm guns were fired from our different batteries & in a few minutes every person able to carry a musket was at his post," Persifer Frazer, of the Fourth Pennsylvania Regiment, wrote in a letter to his wife.[107] Three to five of the British gunboats followed by 13-15 other vessels appeared at Three Mile Point where a landing was made by the British troops. When one gunboat appeared within gunshot, the Jersey Redoubt, another battery east of the Jersey battery, and the galley *Trumbull* opened fire. The *Trumbull*'s fire hit the gunboat, killing one man and wounding another. Before long a rumor spread that 3,000 British troops had landed and were advancing on the American lines. The colors of the various regiments were mounted defiantly on top of the breastworks as a challenge to the British, wrote Frazier "to win them and wear them. – I never had greater satisfaction than to see the order with which our men were possessed."[108] By sunset, the British retreated to Crown Point. The Americans believed their resolute appearance helped to dissuade the British from attacking. "The number of our troops under arms on that day (principally however militia) exceeded thirteen thousand" observed Colonel Trumbull: "Our appearance was indeed formidable, and the season so far advanced . . .that the enemy withdrew without making any attack."[109]

The British troops disembarked from Crown Point on November 1st and 2nd for their winter quarters in Canada. The bateaux that departed on November 2 were forced to anchor in a "creek" due to severe weather. Lieutenant William Digby recorded that "our soldiers called this place Destruction Bay, and not unaptly, as there we saw the great execution the enemy suffered from the fire of our fleet in the engagement on the 11th and 13th of October. Some of their dead were then floating on the brink of the water, just as the surf threw them; these were ordered to be directly buried."[110] Although the bay was an estimated 17 miles from Crown Point according to Digby, the inlet was probably Arnold's Bay.

By the evening of November 3, the first scouting reports reached Ticonderoga that the British had departed from Crown Point. The militia at Ticonderoga was soon dismissed and most of the regular troops later sailed south on Lake George and the Hudson River with General Gates to join Washington's dwindling army that had retreated to New Jersey in the face of reverses at the hands of General Howe.

Colonel Anthony Wayne, who marched with General Thompson at the Three Rivers battle in Canada on June 1776, became commandant of Ticonderoga and Mount Independence for the winter. Wayne also supervised the remaining fleet from the Valcour engagement, which included the schooners *Liberty* and *Revenge*, sloop *Enterprise*, galley *Trumbull*, and the galley *Gates* which was completed following the battle. One surviving gondola, unnamed in almost all contemporary accounts, was the *New York*. The vessels were still manned in early winter when Wayne recorded in his orderly book that 26 men were to "go on board the New York Gundalow" on January 1, 1777.[111]

The praise for Arnold's courage and dedication during the Valcour engagement came from many quarters, including recognition by the British for his skill and boldness under fire. Gates noted the "gallant behavior and steady good conduct of that excellent officer" in a letter to Governor Trumbull of Connecticut, ten days after the engagement.[112] But Arnold had his immediate detractors. Colonel William Maxwell, who had served at Ticonderoga with Abercromby in 1758 and in Canada at Three Rivers in 1776, referred to Arnold as "our evil genius to the north, has, with a good deal of industry, got us clear of all our fine fleet" in a letter from Ticonderoga on October 20.[113] Richard Henry Lee, a member of the Continental Congress, wrote Thomas Jefferson criticizing Arnold as "fiery, hot, and impetuous, but without discretion" who failed to obtain proper intelligence and retire when faced with a superior force.[114]

Some historians argue that if Arnold had retreated to Crown Point with the fleet intact, the British would still have retired to Canada in 1776.[115] Any retreat on the open lake, once the British arrived, would have ended in a fiasco. Without the naval battle, Carleton could not have returned to Canada empty handed, not having engaged the Americans. The naval success was enough to allow Carleton to call off the northern invasion in 1776. Had the British taken and held Ticonderoga and Lake George in 1776, the fate of the United States, with a British base secured on Lake Champlain, might have been quite different in 1777. The delay at Valcour cost the British more than a week in a season of rapidly deteriorating weather. By the time Carleton had cleared the lake, sent for his troops at Point au Fer and the Richelieu, and had them row to Crown Point, it was October 20. The fleet was expendable in Arnold's view, but he manipulated it with great proficiency before it was lost.

The real value of the Valcour navy lay in its mere existence, which delayed the British advance until it was too late. General Riedesel, in reflecting on the termination of the British campaign, mused that "If we could have begun our last expedition four weeks earlier, I am satisfied that everything would have ended this year."[116] The completion of the *Inflexible* alone took four weeks and it was not finished until October. The year of delay that the Valcour fleet provided gave the Americans valuable time to organize a viable defense at Saratoga in 1777. That victory and French help turned the tide of the Revolution. As Admiral Alfred T. Mahan, the famous naval historian, so aptly concluded, "The little American navy on Champlain was wiped out; but never had any force, big or small, lived to better purpose or died more gloriously, for it had saved the Lake for that year."[117]

Monument overlooking Valcour Bay. Photo by the author.

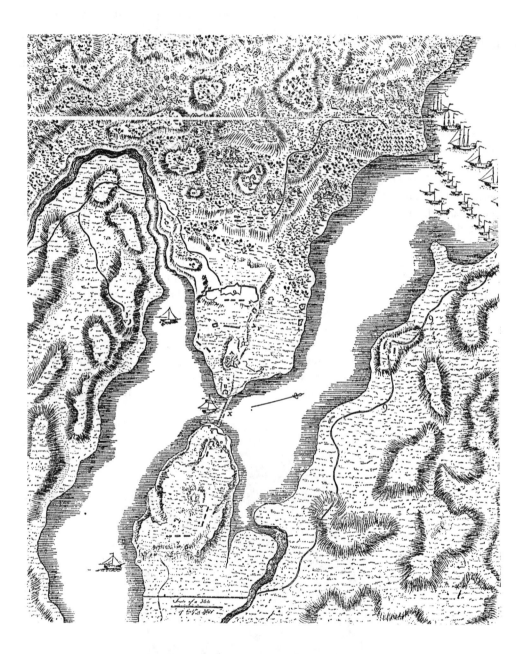

Map of American and British positions at Fort Ticonderoga and
Mount Independence in early July 1777.
(Collection of New-York Historical Society)

8. Invasion of the Lakes

IN LATE 1776, as the two opposing northern armies settled into their winter quarters, plans were already being formulated for a new round of naval construction on the lakes. On December 28, 1776, Congress authorized "two large floating batteries" for Lake Champlain based upon General Philip Schuyler's proposal to protect the bridge and boom connecting Mount Independence and Fort Ticonderoga.[1] Carleton had aleady recommended that a new vessel, the size of the ship *Inflexible*, be added to the existing British fleet on Lake Champlain. The British felt compelled to enlarge their navy especially after receiving a December 9 report which suggested "the rebels at Ticonderoga having put a 20 gun ship on the stocks . . .are making great preparations for another engagement on Lake Champlain next year."[2] The next month, an imprisoned British officer who had recently been exchanged disclosed that the Americans at Ticonderoga "had laid the keels of 26 boats, large and small."[3] The Americans, however, did not build another major vessel at the lake in 1777, but the British would complete their new 96-foot, 26-gun ship *Royal George*.

The garrison at Fort Ticonderoga was in no condition during the unusually bitter winter months of 1777 to build a 20-gun ship. The undermanned garrison was ill-clothed and fed. Colonel Joseph Wood, with his Pennsylvania troops, related that one-third of the men were barefoot at Ticonderoga. Following a visit to the makeshift hospital, Wood found "one man laying dead at the door, the inside two more laying dead, two living lying between."[4]

By the end of 1776, Washington's army had been pushed into New Jersey after military reversals in lower New York. Faced with expiring enlistments, Washington called on Congress and the forces at Ticonderoga for more reinforcements. When the prospects looked darkest for the patriot army, Washington and his men boldly crossed the Delaware River from Pennsylvania and successfully attacked the Hessian troops at Trenton the day after Christmas. Marshalling over 5,500 troops before daybreak of January 2, General Charles Cornwallis marched from Princeton to Trenton in hopes of trapping the rebel army. The British army, delayed by mud and skirmishes along the way, took ten hours to reach Trenton. The Americans repulsed a limited British and Hessian attack late that day, causing the British to retire for the evening in anticipation of wiping out the ragtag army the following day. Washington, however, outwitted Cornwallis by slipping out of the American encampment in the middle of the night to attack the rest of the British force at Princeton. Following two badly needed triumphs, the Continental Army marched to Morristown, New Jersey, for winter quarters.

In early 1777 orders to build a fort at Mount Independence were issued by General Schuyler in anticipation of a renewed invasion of Lake Champlain during the summer. Schuyler's instructions on February 13 to Colonel Jeduthan Baldwin, the chief engineer, included "Cassoons to be sunk in the Water at small Distances from one another and joined together by Stringpieces, so as at the same time to serve for a Bridge between the Fortifications."[5] The caissons at Ticonderoga were constructed of heavy logs formed into

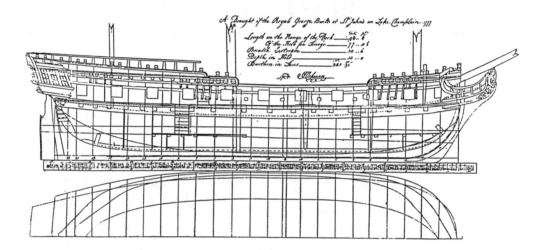

Admiralty drawing by P. Coleman of the 96-foot *Royal George*. The ship was constructed at St. Jean for the invasion through Lake Champlain in 1777. (National Maritime Museum, Greenwich, England)

cribs and filled with rocks. The log cribs were set on the ice, filled with rocks, and dropped to the bottom after the ice was sawed through. By the end of March 1777, most of the caissons or cribs had been put into place. In all, 22 of these piers were constructed to support the bridge and boom across the lake.* The finished bridge, as described by James Thacher, a surgeon with the American army, consisted of floats between the piers "each about fifty feet long and twelve wide, strongly fastened together with iron chains and rivets."[6]

Anticipating the British route of invasion through Lake George as well as Champlain, the Americans made a commitment to build vessels on the smaller lake. As early as February 21, the New York Committee of Safety authorized shipwrights to be sent to Lake George to build vessels. On March 24 Schuyler sent Captain Jacobus Wynkoop, the controversial commodore of the 1776 American fleet before Arnold assumed command, to Fort George to "employ the Carpenters in constructing two strong Schooners of Sixty feet Keel & twenty

* A 1983 archaeological survey by the Champlain Maritime Society found five of the the 1777 piers to be in remarkably good condition. A survey by the Lake Champlain Maritime Museum in 1992 discovered 21 caissons or cribs as well as a number of artifacts including a 10-foot cannon.

feet Beam. . .besides three other vessels are to be built without Deck's, These shou'd be so contrived as the Row fast and to carry a Cannon of twelve pounds shot in the Bow, and as many on each side as possible."[7] A week earlier, Schuyler had ordered his deputy quarter master general to overhaul the existing schooner on Lake George.

Progress, however, was very slow in building the new vessels. To some extent, Schuyler's absence during the spring of 1777 caused a slowdown in organizing resources for the Northern Department. In late March, following a long smoldering controversy over the command of the Northern Army, Congress directed General Horatio Gates to immediately go "to Ticonderoga, and take command of the army there."[8] Schuyler was absent from New York from late March until the first of June, engaged in dealings with Congress and on special assignment with the Pennsylvania forces. Following Schuyler's reinstatement as commander of the Northern Department, Gates departed from Albany (where he had remained since his appointment) rather than serve as Schuyler's deputy at Ticonderoga.

The British strategy of 1777 was quite similar to their aborted plans of the previous year. The British army with its German mercenaries was to invade through Lake Champlain under General John Burgoyne, nicknamed "Gentleman Johnny" for his flair and popularity. Governor Guy Carleton, the able commander of the invasion force in 1776, was replaced in 1777 by the over-confident Burgoyne, who boasted that he would be back in England, victorious within a year. Lieutenant Colonel Barry St. Leger, with the temporary rank of brigadier general, was to advance with a force of 2,000 Indians, Tories, and regulars through Lake Ontario to the Mohawk Valley. Eventually St. Leger's forces, which were meant to provide a diversion from the main invasion through Lake Champlain, would join with Burgoyne's army in Albany. Ultimately, General William Howe's army, in possession of New York City, would move northward to unite with Burgoyne's forces.

The plan to advance northward to meet Burgoyne, however, was not made clear in 1777 to Howe by Lord George Germain, the British secretary of state for the American colonies. The American plans for 1777 included blocking any British invasion at Fort Ticonderoga and Mount Independence. As early as January 30, 1777, Schuyler had written to Washington recommending at least 10,000 men for Ticonderoga to blunt the expected British incursion through Lake Champlain. However, both Congress and Washington incorrectly believed that many of the troops in Canada were destined for Howe's campaign in the south. Consequently, Ticonderoga remained drastically undermanned in the spring and early summer of 1777.

The British army and naval fleet made their final assembly at St. Jean on the Richelieu River in June. At St. Jean new fortifications had been erected, the ship *Royal George* constructed, and the frames of gunboats from England assembled. The latter gunboats, however, were not completed in time to depart with the invasion force. On June 5 advance units and some of the Indians, under the command of Brigadier General Simon Fraser, departed from their Richelieu River bases and arrived at the Bouquet River (north of today's Essex) on June 11. Four gunboats from the 1776 campaign accompanied the advanced corps to the Bouquet camp. Within a week of the Bouquet landings, General Burgoyne, characteristic of his theatrical style, set forth from St. Jean amid a grand spectacle of booming cannon and bands playing. Governor Guy Carleton and other dignitaries watched as Burgoyne boarded the schooner *Maria* while the flotilla maneuvered to begin its long journey of anticipated triumph.

The British had amassed nearly 8,000 men for the campaign. Nearly half, or 3,958 soldiers, were German mercenaries under the command of General Friedrich Riedesel, who had also headed the Hessian and Brunswick troops in 1776. It was common practice during the American Revolution for Britian to hire German troops. German princes profited from the arrangement while most of the troops signed up voluntarily, given the generous bounties and an eagerness for adventure in the New World.

The British fleet on Lake Champlain in 1777 consisted of the ships *Royal George* and *Inflexible*, schooners *Carleton* and *Maria*, radeau *Thunderer*, gondola *Loyal Convert* (also called *Royal Convert*), and the captured American vessels from 1776: row galley *Washington*, gondola *Jersey*, and cutter *Lee*. The guns of the *Loyal Convert*, *Washington*, and *Lee* were removed just before embarkation to make room for other artillery, stores, and provisions. Twenty-four to 28 gunboats, 25 bateaux for each regiment, and a dozen sloop-rigged long boats were part of the flotilla. A seven-gun vessel called the *Land Crab* was also used on Lake Champlain during the campaign. Other British vessels listed on "A General Return" at the end of 1778 may also have been on the lake in 1777.[9] The commander of the fleet appointed by Governor Guy Carleton in February 1777 was Captain Skeffington Lutwidge.

Thomas Anburey, a young lieutenant in the 29th Regiment of Foot, described the fleet as "one of the most pleasing spectacles I ever beheld. . [a] splendid regatta."[10] Burgoyne sailed with the fleet ahead of the main army which followed in the slower bateaux. By June 20 the fleet had landed at the Bouquet River, where General Fraser with some of the advanced corps and Indians had made a camp earlier. In an elaborate banquet at the camp, Burgoyne rallied the Indians but implored them to spare women, children, and prisoners from their hatchets. Burgoyne also issued a detailed proclamation which outlined the reasons for the invasion and encouraged loyal citizens to support his forces. The British army expected vital support from local inhabitants along the way, but the use of Indians actually galvanized the resistance against the invaders.

While Burgoyne celebrated with his Indian allies, Riedesel with the main army was forced to remain at Willsboro Bay due to violent weather. When his bateaux fleet made a second attempt to move south, an intense thunder and hail storm was followed "by a fog so dense that the drummers in the advance were obliged to beat their drums continually to keep the fleet together and indicate the course to be pursued."[11] After the fog, high winds and waves forced four of the boats onto Four Brothers Islands. Burgoyne's first brigade was similarly hit by high winds which turned a brig on her side and swamped two bateaux at Button Bay. Several days later Riedesel's army finally joined Burgoyne at Crown Point.

The small garrison at Ticonderoga was only vaguely aware of the juggernaut moving their way in June 1777. The command at Ticonderoga and Mount Independence on June 13 had been turned over to 40-year-old Major General Arthur St. Clair, a veteran of Amherst's campaign against Louisbourg and Wolfe's assault on Quebec during the French and Indian War. St. Clair had also served at the Three Rivers disaster in 1776 and the more recent actions at Trenton and Princeton. Less than a week into his command, he reported to Schuyler that scouts observed enemy vessels above Split Rock. By the 24th, St. Clair related a sighting of "three vessels under sail beating up, one at anchor about one mile above Split Rock, and the Thunderer behind it" to Schuyler.[12] At the time there were fewer than 2,500 effective men at the American fortifications.

During the spring of 1777, only a minimum had been accomplished to strengthen the fortifications and naval fleets on Lake Champlain. The bridge and boom across Lake

ABOVE. General Friedrich Riedesel and his troops were forced to remain in Willsboro Bay due to violent weather in 1777. Photo by the author.

BELOW. Watercolor of a British cutter and gunboat for Lake Champlain from journal of Simon Metcalfe, 1782. (Fort Ticonderoga Museum)

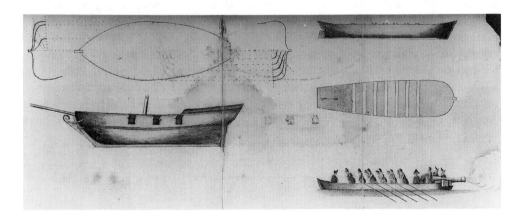

Champlain had finally been finished. The fort completed on Mount Independence was a "picketed" (log walls) structure that would hold 1,000 men.* Viewed by the British, the "star-shaped" fort which encompassed "a large square of barracks" was thought to require a full siege because of the abundance of heavy artillery.[13] Nearly 20 acres of timber had been cut around Mount Independence with three redoubts or gun batteries and a lakeside abbatis of pointed branches and logs constructed under the direction of Colonel Thaddeus Kosciuszko, an engineering officer from Poland. The Americans had also strengthened the entrenchments at the old French lines of Montcalm, held an outpost at Mount Hope overlooking the connection between the lakes, and maintained two block houses at the northern end of Lake George. Since Fort Ticonderoga itself was in poor condition in 1777, many of the Americans were spread out along breastworks and redoubts outside the fort.

The biggest addition to the American naval strength came on Lake George since the waterway was perceived as the obvious invasion route to reach Albany. Five large new vessels were to be built in the spring of 1777. The shipbuilding, however, which was to begin in March was considerably behind schedule. General Schuyler reported to Congress on June 25 that "one of the schooners at Lake George is launched: She is to carry fourteen guns. Another will be in the lake by the first of next month."[14] Although lumber had been cut for three row galleys, none were apparently completed. By early July Schuyler complained to Washington that he did not have enough cannon, "not a sufficient number even for the two small schooners on Lake George."[15]

By the end of June and early July, the British forces began their advance toward Ticonderoga and Mount Independence. The British strategy was to flank the American forts on land while moving their artillery into key positions. A full frontal assault with their fleet would draw deadly fire from the American batteries. Even before the British appeared in force, General St. Clair warned Schuyler on June 18 that it would be dangerous to give up Ticonderoga or Mount Independence "yet it is certain we cannot with our present numbers hold both."[16] His plan envisioned holding Ticonderoga as long as possible before retreating to Mount Independence. A week later, he again warned that there was no prospect of defending the forts unless the militia was called in.

On June 30 General Fraser's corps of advance troops camped at Three Mile Point. At five o'clock the next morning, troops in two divisions, under General William Phillips and General Riedesel, embarked from Crown Point in bateaux to the music of the different regiments. The corps under Phillips moved along the west side of the lake, while Riedesel's men pressed forward on the east shore. The British fleet, including the larger vessels and gunboats, sailed into a line spanning the lake at Three Mile Point on June 30. Despite the presence of the British fleet, St. Clair's letter to Schuyler on July 1 seemed to lack the urgency of the situation: "We have now two ships, eighteen gun boats, and three sloops, lying off the Three Mile Point, and they are forming a camp upon the point, and retrenching it. This does not look like their being strong."[17] From the British position, some of the armed vessels of the American fleet were observed behind the floating bridge. The vessels at the American outposts, all remnants of the 1776 fleet, included the galleys *Gates* and *Trumbull*, schooners *Liberty* and *Revenge*, sloop *Enterprise*, and gondola *New York*.

---

* During the summers of 1989 and 1990, University of Vermont archaeologist David Starbuck supervised a crew of 40 volunteers in a scientific dig for artifacts at Mount Independence. The state of Vermont had plans at this writing to open a visitor center on the site.

At noon on July 2 the American batteries opened fire on Fraser's advance troops, but without proper sighting the artillery barrage had little effect. Riedesel, with Colonel Heinrich Breymann and the German advance corps, moved forward to occupy a position to the north of Mount Independence. The fire resulted in a number of casualties on both sides during that day and the next. General Phillip's troops, which had advanced along the western shore, took Mount Hope without opposition, cutting off American communication with Lake George. By then one of the blockhouses on Lake George had been set afire and the sawmill abandoned. The cannonading along the lake continued as the radeau *Thunderer* was brought down to bombard the Americans. After the radeau proved too unwieldly to maneuver, her heavy guns were dismounted on July 4 to be used as siege artillery on land.

Nine hundred militia reinforcements arrived at the American forts from the east before the British could intercept them. As the siege continued, a 750-foot hill south of Fort Ticonderoga and across the Lake George outlet, called Sugar Hill (also Sugar Loaf Hill) or Mount Defiance, became the object of attention by the British. After reconnoitering the position, Lieutenant William Twiss, an engineer with the British, reported that the hill had command of both Ticonderoga and Mount Independence. Under the direction of General Phillips, "it was determined a battery should be raised on this post, for light twenty-four pounders, medium twelves, and eight inch howitzers."[18] Following the arduous task, accomplished in an amazingly short time period, the battery was ready late in the day of July 5. In his journal on July 5, Dr. James Thacher expressed "astonishment that we find the enemy have taken possession of an eminence called Sugar-loaf Hill" which he noted "is said ought long since to have been fortified by our army."[19] A year earlier, Colonel John Trumbull, deputy adjutant general to Gates, had recommended a battery for Mount Defiance and climbed the hill with Benedict Arnold and Anthony Wayne to prove that the summit was accessible. Likewise, Thaddeus Kosciuszko suggested that a cannon could be raised to the summit in May 1777, but the idea again fell on deaf ears.

Until then, General St. Clair still harbored hopes of defending the American position, but when a shot was discharged at the sloop *Enterprise* from the summit of Mount Defiance, St. Clair quickly changed his mind. Turning to Colonel James Wilkinson after the shot was fired, St. Clair observed "We must away from this, for our situation has become a desperate one."[20] At issue was the possibility that the battery could sever the line of retreat on the lake for the Americans in the face of an overwhelming British force.

In the early evening of July 5, St. Clair called a council of war with his other generals. The council of war, consisting of Generals Arthur St. Clair, Roche de Fermoy, Enoch Poor, John Patterson, and Colonel Pierse Long, unanimously decided to retreat as soon as possible. The orders to abandon, however, came piecemeal to the officers and troops. Lieutenant Colonel Stevens first heard the orders from St. Clair at seven o'clock, while Colonel Baldwin was told at nine o'clock that departure would be at two a.m. But the orders to strike their tents and load baggage was not given to the regiments until midnight. Most of the men were asleep when the orders were issued. Confusion soon overtook the surprised troops as they grappled in the darkness with heavy equipment and supplies. To avoid detection by the British, orders were given by St. Clair not to burn the buildings. At the same time, cannon from the Jersey battery were fired every seven minutes upon the British position to disguise the activity of several thousand men in retreat. The evacuation was aided by the fact that most of the large cannon and barrels of provisions had already been moved to Mount Independence in anticipation of making a stand there or retreating from that point. Many of the cannon that could not be loaded during the night of the retreat were spiked or disabled by the troops. At one o'clock in the morning of July 6, one participant later testified: "I saw the General [St. Clair] again on Mount Independence, who begged that we would make all the dispatch possible, and carry off all that we could in boats by day light."[21] While St. Clair's initial reaction to the advance of the British seemed restrained, his aide, Major Dunn, later indicated that "after they landed at Three Mile Point, . . . I do

Fort Ticonderoga. Photo by the author.

not believe he slept one hour in four and twenty, on an average, till the evacuation took place."[22]

Dr. Thacher, who had been awakened at midnight, tried to load the sick and wounded (about 100 men) and hospital supplies into bateaux as quickly as possible. Only four wounded men that could not be moved safely were left behind. Against St. Clair's orders, General Roche de Fermoy, a French volunteer in command of Mount Independence, burned his house there. The fire lit up the movement of the troops on the Mount and further lowered the spirits of the men.

At three o'clock in the morning most of those retreating by water departed, "Our fleet consisted of five armed gallies and two hundred batteaux and boats deeply laden with cannon, tents, provisions, invalids, and women" wrote Dr. Thacher.[23] Six hundred troops, under Colonel Pierse Long of New Hampshire, accompanied the vessels on their voyage to Skenesborough. In contrast to the bewilderment of the departure, the trip was nearly tranquil, according to Thacher: "The night was moon-light and pleasant, the sun burst forth in the morning with uncommon lustre, the day was fine, the water's surface serene and unruffled. . . . The drum and fife afforded us a favorite music; among the hospital stores we found many dozen bottles of choice wine, and, breaking off their necks, we cheered our hearts with the nectareous contents."[24]

"A View of Ticonderoga from a point on the Shore of Lake Champlain, 1777," by James Hunter which shows a British gunboat in the foreground and American vessels in the background. (National Archives of Canada)

The troops who remained at Mount Independence, preparing for their retreat on foot, however, did not have time to sample any wine. At sunrise the rest of the American army was still at Mount Independence. The main body of troops retreated early in the morning by an unfinished road through the wilderness to Castleton, Vermont. Open powder kegs in the fort and a trail of gunpowder were left outside to be touched off by four men after the retreat. Cannon on the east side of the lake, likewise, were to be touched off upon the advance of the British. The next day the British discovered the four men "dead drunk by a cask of Madeira" with the lighted matches close to the cannon.[25] Although the Americans tried to take as much as possible on their retreat, General Riedesel claimed that "Eighty large cannon, five thousand tons of flour, a great quantity of meat and provisions, fifteen thousand stand of arms, a large amount of ammunition, two hundred oxen, besides baggage and tents, were found in the camps of the enemy."[26]

Despite months of strenuous work, the great bridge and boom were broken through in a short time. Two British ships and the gunboats sailed to the south to cut off the retreat of the American vessels. Thacher reported that he had reached the Skenesborough wharf at three o'clock in the afternoon. The British fleet arrived in less than two hours. The *Royal George* and *Inflexible* did not sail into Skenesborough harbor, however; "the gun boats were engaged with the enemy's vessels; the well directed fire of which, obliged the crew of two of their ships to quit them, 3 other vessels were burnt, and blown up."[27] A British journal list of the vessels taken and destroyed at Skenesborough included: "1. – Turnbull [Trumbull] Galley – Taken, 2 – Liberty – schooner – loaden with Powder – Taken; 3 – Revenge – sloop – loaden with Powder – Blown up; – 4. – Gates Galley – Blown up; 5. – Enterprize Cutter – laden with provisions – Burnt." This is nearly identical to a *Connecticut Gazette* list published later in 1777.[28]

Many of the American and British diaries and journals describe five American vessels retreating to Skenesborough. The question of what happened to the sixth vessel, the gondola *New York*, remains a mystery. Lieutenant Hadden noted that the Americans, upon the appearance of the British at Skenesborough, abandoned their vessels "Five in Number, and one Skow with an Iron Howitzer, thus ended irrisistable Naval Armament Built last year."[29] The latter vessel may have been the *New York*.

At Skenesborough, the Americans fled under the attack of the British. Most ran through the woods to Fort Anne "so closely pressed by the pursuing enemy, that we frequently heard calls from the rear to 'march on, the Indians are at our heels.' "[30] The desperate refugees ran most of the night, reaching Fort Anne at five o'clock in the morning. Some of the bateaux with the sick and wounded escaped by way of Wood Creek, but nearly all of the provisions, baggage, and cannon fell into the hands of the British.

The troops under St. Clair, although their mood bordered on panic when they left Mount Independence, made good headway on their retreat toward Castleton. Burgoyne dispatched General Fraser and his advance corps early in the morning of July 6, followed by General Riedesel's troops, to pursue the Americans. The British marched swiftly until one in the afternoon before stopping on a hot, sultry July day. By then Fraser had learned from stragglers of the slower rear guard of the Americans. While Fraser's troops were resting, Riedesel with his force of grenadiers had caught up to the advance corps. Fraser and Riedesel decided to march a few more miles toward the Americans and camp until early the next morning.

The rear guard, under Colonel Seth Warner of the Green Mountain Boys with Colonel Ebenezer Francis and the Massachusetts regiments and Colonel Nathan Hale's New Hampshire regiments, was ordered by St. Clair to wait for the rearmost men then proceed to the main army in Castleton. Instead, they camped six miles from Castleton in present-day Hubbardton, Vermont. "At three in the morning our march was renewed," wrote Lieutenant Thomas Anburey with the British, and "about five we came up with the enemy, who were busily employed in cooking their provisions."[31] The 1,000 Americans rallied under the fierce attack. Riedesel's troops, who came after Fraser's initial attack singing their national hymns, marched headlong into the brisk fire of 400 American riflemen. At some length, the Americans, realizing that they were nearly surrounded, fled into the wilderness. The cost was high, with approximately 40 killed on each side, about 140 British wounded, and over

300 Americans taken prisoner. "After the action was over, a Colonel [Nathan Hale], with the remains of his regiment, to the amount of 230 [probably only 70], came and surrended himself prisoner," wrote Anburey.[32]

St. Clair's main force, rejoined by the remnants from the rear guard, proceeded on a circuitous route to Fort Edward, arriving there on July 12. Initially, St. Clair was to rendezvous with Colonel Long at Skenesborough, but Burgoyne's immediate attack there and the presence of British and German troops in eastern Vermont forced a long march, with dwindling provisions, around the British positions. The British chased the Americans to Fort Anne (about 11 miles below Skenesborough) where the Americans later counterattacked in several skirmishes. Although the British could have remained at Fort Anne, they chose to return to Skenesborough.

The British failure to occupy Fort Anne allowed General Philip Schuyler at Fort Edward to engage in a strategy to slow Burgoyne's advance by destroying the road connecting Skenesborough to Fort Edward. Schuyler sent Brigadier General John Nixon with a small army (1,100) of Continental soldiers and militia along with Colonel Samuel Herrick's Green Mountain Rangers to break up bridges, divert streams, cut trees into the roads and creeks, and place obstructions to block the passage of Burgoyne's army. Captain Rufus Lincoln's diary suggested that Burgoyne "had 40 Bridges to Construct one of two milds in length, besides others to repair and Some Skirmiging & firing on every Days march."[33] The failure to stop the Americans was the first error of many that led to Burgoyne's disaster at Saratoga. The retreat from Fort Anne by the British with the concomitant failure to prevent the destruction of the road might have been the crucial blunder of the Burgoyne campaign.

Why Burgoyne chose Wood Creek instead of Lake George for his passage south has been a question that has intrigued historians for decades. Upon arrival at Skenesborough, Burgoyne settled into Philip Skene's grand house to ponder his strategy. Philip Skene, who had been exchanged as a prisoner of war with the Americans, returned for a short period to England before sailing to Quebec with his son. From there Skene and his son joined Burgoyne at Crown Point. Skene, as a friend and advisor to Burgoyne, promised support and provisions from loyal families during the invasion. He was said to have convinced Burgoyne to make his way from Skenesborough to the Hudson River because Skene wanted a good road built that would enhance the value of his property (assuming the British would win the war).[34] Skene's interest in property values, ironically, might have changed the course of history.

Burgoyne later defended his decision not to move back to Ticonderoga and the northern end of Lake George by suggesting that the action would have created the impression of "a retrograde motion" on the minds of enemies and friends.[35] Burgoyne subsequently claimed that his push toward Fort Edward forced the abandonment of Fort George since the move cut the line of retreat for the Americans. Had Burgoyne gone back to Ticonderoga, it might have appeared that his army had given up the pursuit of a retreating army. Taking all of the troops, provisions, and cannon through the Lake George route with its 220-foot elevation above Ticonderoga would have created some of its own delays. In addition, moving the bateaux and other vessels from Lake George to Fort Edward probably would not have been achievable in a reasonable period of time. But the route through Wood Creek cost the British valuable time, taking 24 days to move less than 25 miles.

Burgoyne, however, decided to use Lake George to carry provisions, ammunition, and other military supplies to his advancing army. Once in control of Lake George, the British

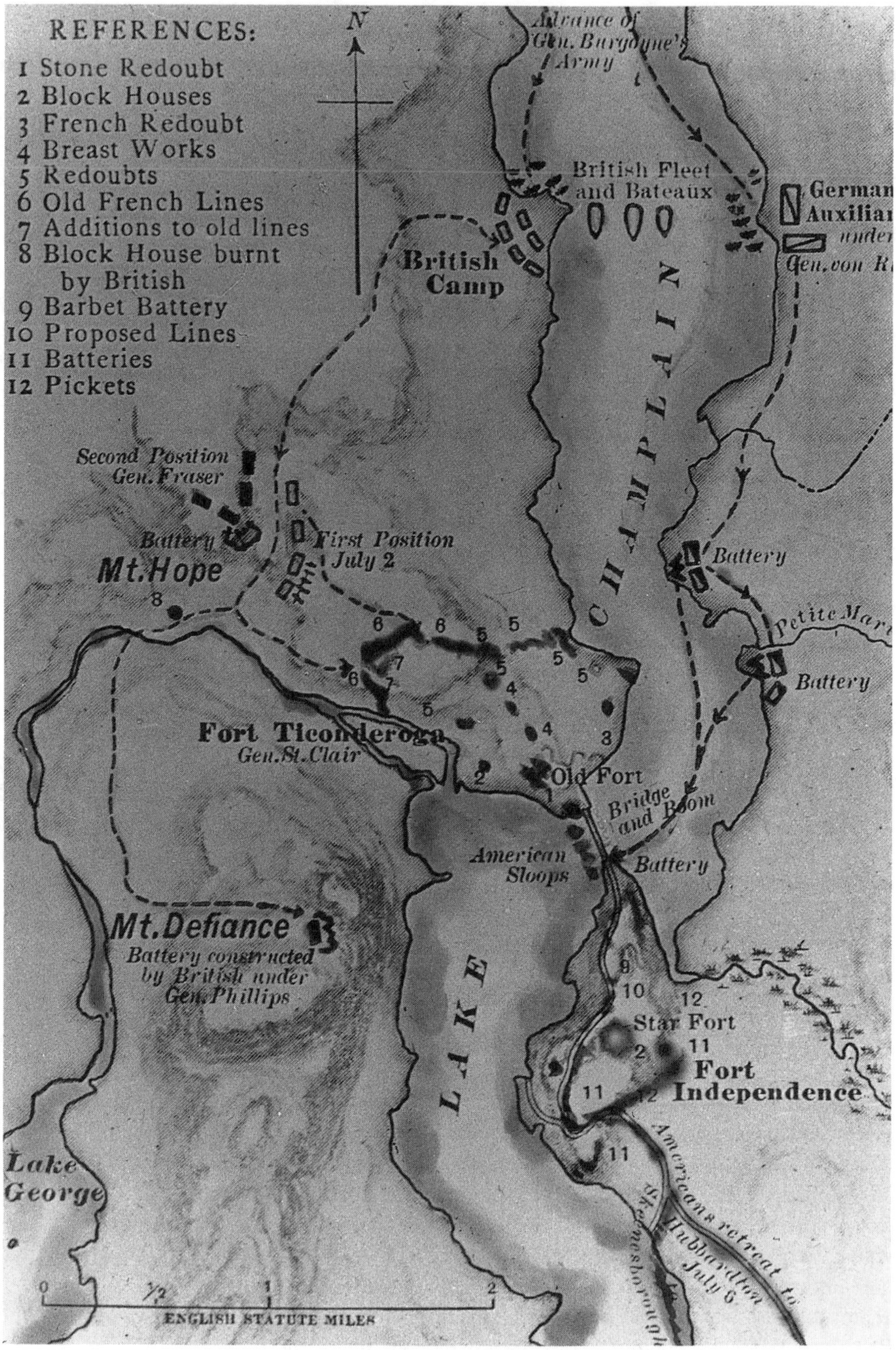
REFERENCES:
1 Stone Redoubt
2 Block Houses
3 French Redoubt
4 Breast Works
5 Redoubts
6 Old French Lines
7 Additions to old lines
8 Block House burnt by British
9 Barbet Battery
10 Proposed Lines
11 Batteries
12 Pickets
N
British Fleet and Bateaux
British Camp
CHAMPLAIN
Second Position Gen. Fraser
Battery
Mt. Hope
First Position July 2
Battery
Battery
Fort Ticonderoga Gen. St. Clair
Old Fort
Bridge and Boom
American Sloops
Battery
Mt. Defiance
Battery constructed by British under Gen. Phillips
LAKE
Star Fort
Fort Independence
Lake George
Americans retreat to Hubbardton July 6
ENGLISH STATUTE MILES

Map of Fort Ticonderoga, 1777. (National Archives)

planned to rebuild the road from Fort George to Fort Edward to carry the provisions. On July 11 Burgoyne wrote to Carleton of his plans: "My present purpose, Sir, is to get a sufficient number of Gunboats upon the Lake George to scour that Lake as expeditiously as possible, to support them with a proper force to attack Fort George."[36] On July 15, General Riedesel was ordered to Ticonderoga to supervise the transfer of vessels onto Lake George.

By late July Burgoyne had given directions to disarm all the larger vessels on Lake Champlain except the schooners *Maria* and *Carleton*, so that the fleet could be used to transport provisions for the advancing army. Only four armed "Tenders" would patrol Lake Champlain and four gunboats assigned to protect Fort Ticonderoga. "For Lake George and Hudson's River. Fourteen Armed Gun Boats at 7 Men each [and] Four Armed Gun Boats with 6 Pounders to cruize in Lake George" were hauled from Lake Champlain to Lake George.[37] The time that it had taken to bring the gunboats to Lake George further delayed Burgoyne's advance southward.

Schuyler had ordered the commander at Fort George, Major Christopher Yates, to move the ammunition to Fort Edward and abandon Lake George if the British arrived in strength. Yates set fire to the fort on July 16 and marched with 700 men to Fort Edward. In the days prior to the evacuation, the provisions, stores, and bateaux were removed to Fort Edward. The Americans at Fort George, noted Lieutenant Hadden on July 27, had "destroyed their Vessels (5 in number) including two on the Stocks."[38] Fort George, in

"A View of the old French fort, Redoubts and Batteries at Ticonderoga
on Lake Champlain and his Majesty's ship Inflexible" in 1777 from
Mount Independence by Henry Rudyerd. (Fort Ticonderoga Museum)

Hadden's 1777 description, was "a small square Fort faced with Masonry and contains Barracks for aboat a hundred Men secured from Cannon. . . The Rebels. . .blew up the Magazine on the side next the Water, which demolish'd that Face."[39] Riedesel, however, described the fort as having 12 cannon, barracks for 1,000 men east of the fort, and to the west of the magazine "where Fort William Henry formerly stood, is the large hospital, a building of great dimensions. . .surrounded by palisades, and to have a small redoubt on the hill south of it."[40] On the other hand, Schuyler portrayed the fort as only "an unfinished bastion of an intended fortification" with barracks that would hold only 30-50 men.[41]

Under the direction of General Philips, the British soon began building the road from Fort George to Fort Edward. Two companies of soldiers were assigned to Fort George and two more to Diamond Island with requisite gunboats for their defense. At Skenesborough Burgoyne had issued a proclamation to the inhabitants of the region to ally themselves with the British and save their property. Convinced of the dissension of the residents on the New Hampshire Grants, Burgoyne directed citizens, under threat of military action, to meet with Philip Skene, who would "communicate conditions upon which the person and property of the disobedient may yet be spared."[42] Only several hundred took the offer, contrary to Skene's more optimistic predictions, leaving the British without the support that earlier plans had anticipated. The death and scalping near Fort Edward on July 26 of young Jane McCrea, a local inhabitant betrothed to a Tory officer, at the hands of Burgoyne's Indians has long been thought to have coalesced opinion against the British. The impact of the event, however, has been minimized by modern researchers, although it is still subject to debate over two centuries later.[43]

Burgoyne finally advanced to Fort Edward by the end of July. Schuyler, meanwhile, continued retreating from posts but employed a scorched-earth policy to deny the British provisions. Schuyler's forces, however, at 4,400 men on July 20, began to increase as time passed. New officers also arrived including General Benedict Arnold on July 22. Nevertheless, Schuyler continued retreating, moving his headquarters between Moses Creek, where St. Clair's army had retreated, and Saratoga at the end of July. In early August Schuyler moved his army to Stillwater, about 11 miles below Saratoga.

On August 3 Burgoyne received the confounding news from General William Howe that his army would be in Pennsylvania rather than poised in New York to march north. After learning the news of the fall of Ticonderoga, Howe felt comfortable in departing with his armada southward. On August 16 Howe finally received instructions to "co-operate" with Burgoyne from Britain's American secretary, Lord George Germain, who was in charge of coordinating the military operations in America. According to one report, Germain was about to send a letter to Howe outlining the coordination of the two armies soon after approving Burgoyne's invasion plans but departed for a weekend in Sussex and forgot about the letter.[44] Subsequent letters to Howe also failed to spell out the strategy of support for Burgoyne until it was too late. The failure to communicate and coordinate the armies would prove fatal for Burgoyne's army.

Following the evacuation of Fort Ticonderoga and Mount Independence, there had been accusations of cowardice and treachery against St. Clair and Schuyler. James Wilkinson, an officer during the Ticonderoga retreat, found the daily rumors that the two generals were traitors to be without precedent. One outrageous rumor suggested that the two generals received "an immense treasure" from the British for their treachery when "silver balls, fired by Burgoyne into St. Clair's camp, and by his order [were] picked up and transmitted to Schuyler at Fort George."[45] The loss of Ticonderoga was a severe setback for the patriots, who considered the fortress akin to the Rock of Gibraltar. In retrospect, the retreat set the stage for the ultimate trap for Burgoyne's army. Congress, however, acted within a month to change the commander of the Northern Department. After Washington declined to name a replacement for Schuyler, Congress voted on August 4 to replace him as head of the Northern Army with their earlier choice, General Horatio Gates.

Schuyler and St. Clair were court-martialed the following year for the loss of Ticon-

Battle of Bennington, August 16, 1777, engraving from a painting by Alonzo Chappel.
(National Archives)

deroga. St. Clair, who had not received orders from Schuyler to evacuate Ticonderoga, was charged with neglect of duty, cowardice, and treachery. Officer after officer, however, testified that St. Clair was not a coward and had acted in a proper manner under the circumstances. The court unanimously found St. Clair not guilty with the highest honor. Similarly, Schuyler, charged with neglect of duty and incompetence, was unanimously found not guilty with the highest honor.[46]

Before Schuyler turned over his command, another battle in Vermont would add one more nail in the coffin of the British advance. In an attempt to obtain draught animals, cattle, and horses for the Brunswick dragoons, Lieutenant Colonel Friedrich Baum of the dragoons was to lead a combined force of 800 Germans, Canadians, Indians, Tories, and British regulars into Vermont. In addition, the raid was to be a diversion which might inhibit Arnold from leading a large force against St. Leger, who was then besieging Fort Stanwix on the Mohawk River. John Stark, a former Ranger with Rogers during the French and Indian War, had been commissioned a brigadier general of the New Hampshire militia. Leading 1,492 men and officers, Stark met Seth Warner at Manchester, Vermont. In Manchester, Stark turned back a request by General Benjamin Lincoln, appointed by the Continental Congress, to take command of the New Hampshire and Vermont troops.

Stark marched his troops to Bennington where he received intelligence from scouts that 200 Indians followed by 1,500 Germans and Tories had arrived at Cambridge, New York, about 14 miles northwest of Bennington. Stark immediately dispatched a message to Warner and his men to reinforce his New Hampshire militia at Bennington. The German dragoons, with their heavy boots, leather breeches, and unwieldy 12-pound swords, trudged toward Bennington where they halted late on August 14. Upon seeing the main body of the Americans, the German detachment entrenched themselves. Originally expecting easy pickings at Bennington, Baum now called for reinforcements from Burgoyne. Rain on August 15 delayed the battle and slowed reinforcements of approximately 600 men led by Lieutenant Colonal Heinrich Breymann. On the morning of the 16th, the Americans began their assault on the Germans entrenched on a sodded bluff. Colonel Baum first saw men in shirt sleeves moving forward which the "provincial" (probably Philip Skene) advised "were all loyalists and would make common cause with him."[47] The engagement began shortly in earnest as Stark's men attacked Baum's position from two sides. Just before the battle, Stark addressed his yeoman farmers turned soldiers: "There are your enemies the red coats, and Tories — We must have them in half an hour, or my wife sleeps a widow this night."[48] The Americans dislodged the Germans and British after heavy fighting, including hand-to-hand combat on the hill occupied by the Germans.

Baum had been fatally wounded and the first engagement over when at three o'clock in the afternoon Colonel Breymann was met by Philip Skene two miles from the battle site. As the fatigued troops began to advance, a force on a nearby hill was noticed. Skene assured Breymann that they were not rebels, but an immediate volley of muskets proved him wrong again. Fortunately for the Americans, Seth Warner's men arrived about the same time. After a renewed battle, Breymann himself was wounded and discovered five bullet holes through his clothing. The German drummers beat a call for a surrender meeting, but the Yankee militia unaware of its meaning, continued its fire. Finally, the remnants of the British and German army escaped into the woods in the darkness.

Stark reported 207 enemy killed at the battle and 750 prisoners with only 30 American killed and 40 wounded.[49] The Americans also seized muskets, ammunition wagons, swords, and four brass cannon. The cannon, originally captured from the French by Wolfe in 1759 at Quebec, were later used in the War of 1812. The Battle of Bennington was a memorable American victory over the best-trained European troops at the hands of rural militia, which had been earlier scoffed at by British officers. The event was a milestone in the northern campaign that brought new confidence and recruits to the American cause. Tied together, the Tory prisoners were paraded through Bennington. Ironically, the funds to pay the militia were drawn from the proceeds of the confiscation of Tory property.

Another event would further strengthen the American position against Burgoyne's army. Barry St. Leger with his force of regulars, Tories, and Indians had sieged Fort Stanwix (also called Fort Schuyler) at the head of navigation of the Mohawk River (present-day Rome, N.Y.) for three weeks in August. A relief force of militia under General Nicholas Herkimer was turned back in the bloody Battle of Oriskany on August 6. In reaction, Schuyler called for a new relief force for the beleagued garrison. Benedict Arnold volunteered for the command, departing with 800 men on the night of August 10. Just before they arrived at Fort Stanwix, a plan by one of Arnold's officers for releasing a prisoner (his brother remained as a hostage in one account) to exaggerate the size of Arnold's force among St. Leger's Indians was put into effect. At the time, St. Leger's army was within 150 yards of Fort Stanwix. Arnold forced marched his troops the last 10 miles but before arriving received a message from the fort that St. Leger had begun retreating. Whether the ruse had worked or the Indians were ready to abandon St. Leger, the result was the same. The second arm of the invasion from the north had been turned back. Now Burgoyne was alone in New York, deep in American territory with supply lines stretched to their limit.

On September 13 Burgoyne's army crossed the Hudson River and marched south along the western shore in Saratoga. On September 19 the two armies finally met in the first engagement of the Saratoga battles. The American army, with General Horatio Gates in command, had now grown to 7,000 men, entrenched at Bemis Heights in Saratoga. Bemis Heights, a rise of land named for a local tavern owner, was selected earlier for fortification by Thaddeus Kosciusko and Benedict Arnold. Burgoyne's forces advanced to the clearing of Freeman's Farm, about a mile north of Bemis Heights, on the morning of September 19. Gates initially planned to meet the British on the Heights, but Arnold vehemently argued for permission to lead an attack on the exposed flanks of the British army. Gates denied Arnold's request but dispatched riflemen and light infantry under Colonel Daniel Morgan and Major Henry Dearborn, both veterans of the Quebec assault in 1775. Although the Americans withdrew from the field late in the day, the victory was clearly theirs with about half the casualties compared to the British. Arnold and Gates, who once saw eye to eye at Ticonderoga in 1776, were now at odds over many issues. Arnold's arrogant demeanor, his alignment with former aides and friends of Philip Schuyler, and differences over strategy had worn an earlier friendly relationship thin.

As the first Battle of Saratoga was taking place, new engagements occurred on Lake Champlain and Lake George. General Benjamin Lincoln, who had over 2,000 militia at Pawlet, Vermont (south of Castleton), sent three detachments of 500 men each to Ticonderoga, Mount Independence, and Skenesborough. Lincoln's strategy was not designed to capture the posts, but to provide a diversion by moving on the rearward position of General Burgoyne: "this menace would oblige him to make heavy detachments and secure the several points necessary to cover his rear."[50] Lincoln's letter to Gates on September 14 also makes clear that the capture of Ticonderoga by John Brown was not the primary goal but "to release the prisoners & destroy the stores there [Lake George Landing]."[51] Thiry-three-year-old Lieutenant Colonel John Brown, who had accompanied Ethan Allen and Benedict Arnold on the 1775 capture of Ticonderoga, remained one of Arnold's strongest antagonists. At one point in late 1776, Brown passed out handbills against Arnold on the streets of Albany with the prophetic words "Money is this man's God and to get enough of it he would sacrifice his country."[52]

The three-pronged raid began without a snag as Brown advanced through the woods near Lake Champlain. Colonel Johnson who was to attack Mount Independence used the wilderness road from the Castleton-Hubbardton area, and Colonel Woodbridge with the third detachment marched to Skenesborough. Woodbridge, who met no resistance at Skenesborough, was joined by Lincoln's main force before both parties returned to Pawlet, Vermont. After marching all night, Brown, along with Colonel Samuel Herrick, reached the Ticonderoga area at dawn on September 18. At Ticonderoga Brown faced the 26-year veteran, Brigadier General Henry Watson Powell, with 1,000 troops, many of whom were scattered among several outposts around the fort. In short order, Captain Ebenezer Allen with 40 Vermont Rangers climbed the summit of Mount Defiance and overwhelmed the garrison at an unfinished blockhouse. At the same time, Brown and Herrick surrounded a British encampment east of Lake George (south of the LaChute River), taking many prisoners. The seizure of the sawmills brought additional prisoners.

Captain Lemuel Roberts with some of the Vermont Rangers then captured the boats at the outlet of Lake George before attacking a house on the eastern shore of the lake. A nearby barn was opened and 70-100 American prisoners, mostly from the Hubbardton battle who had been used by the British for work details, were released. The Americans also took possession of the old French lines and Mount Hope. Finally, the American raiders, equipped with one cannon, demanded the surrender of a blockhouse near the sawmills on the north side of the LaChute River from Lieutenant Lord of the 53rd Regiment. After the British officer from the blockhouse was allowed to observe the American forces from a hillside, he tearfully surrendered his garrison.

Brown demanded the surrender of Ticonderoga and Mount Independence suggesting to General Powell that "it will very soon be out of your power to stop the Mighty Army of the Continent surrounding you on every side."[53] Powell, however, regarded the demand as a bluff. In a letter to Carleton the next day, Powell related Brown's letter: "Mr. John Brown, who stiles himself Colonel Commandant summoned the Garrison to surrender... I returned for answer, I should defend the Garrison to the last."[54] Powell, nevertheless, sought reinforcements.

When the day was over, Brown wrote to Lincoln that he had 293 prisoners and "150 batteaus below the falls in Lake Champlain 50 above the falls including 17 gun boats and an armed sloop."[55] The gunboats on Lake George, most of which had been used in the Battle of Valcour Island in 1776, had been carried from Lake Champlain in late July. The captured sloop had been "armed with three 6 Prs., because she was found unfit for the transport service for which she was ordered," recorded John Starke of the schooner *Maria*.[56]

Brown and his men began a cannon fire from the old French lines onto Fort Ticonderoga, which was returned promptly by the fort's garrison. The British vessels at the forts, the *Carleton, Maria*, and two gunboats, were moved to a position north of the floating bridge to be out of range of the captured battery on Mount Defiance. After testing the defense at Mount Independence, Colonel Thomas Johnson's detachment of 500 men, under the command of Brigadier General Jonathan Warner of the Massachusetts militia, never made a serious attack on the fort although a surrender demand was made. Starke, aboard the *Maria*, noted that the "Mount was never attacked by the Rebels"; the only approach after September 18 was that of a stray cow during the night of September 21 which caused "a most thundering cannonade" from the fort and vessels which lasted until daybreak "when the lawless plunderer who had been so daring, was taken prisoner and carried into the garrison in triumph."[57]

The British fired from their vessels and batteries into the woods each night as a precaution against the Americans. Brown discharged some cannon shells into Fort Ticonderoga for four days but with no chance that Mount Independence could be taken, and fearing reinforcements under Sir John Johnson, he decided to withdraw. About 100 German troops arrived from Canada on the 21st followed by provision vessels and the *Loyal Convert* from Crown Point the next day, which may have hastened the decision by the Americans to leave. The 300 or more British prisoners with their American guards were sent to Skenesborough. Prior to departure, Brown also "destroyed four Gunboats at this end of Lake George, and two Gun Boats and some batteaux which lay about the bridge on this side of the Sawmill," according to General Powell.[58] Brown's plans now called for an attack on the British supply depot on Diamond Island in Lake George, a vital link to Burgoyne's army in Saratoga. Late in the afternoon of September 22, Brown departed with 420 troops aboard "20 Sail of Boats three of which were Armed Viz one Small Sloop mounting 8 Guns & 2 British Gun Boats."[59]

The fleet, battling heavy winds, came to anchor with great difficulty at Sabbath Day Point that night. A sutler (merchant) on the voyage, who had been dealing with the British and had been captured with his small boat at the northern landing by the Americans, escaped before reaching Sabbath Day Point. Brown had ordered the sutler "Terry & his Associates on board the Gun boats," but another officer ordered them off the boat to follow at the stern of Colonel Herrick's gunboat.[60] Upset over the disappearance of the sutler, who might alert the island's garrison, the officers deferred their attack the next morning and made camp on an island six miles to the north of Diamond Island.[61] The sutler did warn the British garrison, as Powell's contingent account recorded 30 pounds, 10 shillings paid "To Terry. . .for informing Captain Aubrey of the rebels' intention to attack Diamond Island."[62]

Forewarned, the two companies of the 47th Regiment under Captain Thomas Aubrey readied their cannon behind breastworks on the small island. The size of "Captain Aubrey's Detachment," Powell recorded, "on the Island and Fort George consisted of about two hundred men, half of them Germans."[63] At nine o'clock in the morning the sloop and gunboats advanced to cover an attempt to land troops in the 17 bateaux on the other side of the island. The booming cannon from the island batteries soon altered Brown's plans. For more than an hour, the armed ships and shore batteries kept up a heavy cannonade. The sloop, hit between "wind & Water," had to be towed off while "one of the Gun Boats [was] so damaged I was obliged to quit her."[64] Two Americans were killed, two others mortally wounded, and several more wounded in the engagement.

Brown ran the flotilla into a bay on the eastern shore (probably Dunhams Bay) and set it afire. After burning the vessels, the Americans donned packs weighing as much as 97 pounds and marched toward Skenesborough before the British had reached the eastern shore. Burgoyne later wrote that the gunboats from Diamond Island pursued the Americans to the east shore where they captured two of the principal vessels. However, Lieutenant George Irwine, commander at Fort George, noted that only one gunboat was retaken. Likewise General Powell's letter to Carleton a few days after the engagement suggested that the Americans "went into a Creek, not far from the Island. . .brought from thence a Gun Boat, with a twelve pounder on board."[65]

One lingering question regarding the battle concerns the location of the island and the bay where the vessels were burned. The small size of Diamond Island (erosion, however, accounts for some of its present size) makes it difficult to believe that it could hold two companies and supplies. Since the contemporary maps often did not label Diamond Island and erroneous mileage estimates are typical of the eighteenth century, some recent writers have proposed that the British used Dome Island with the vessels burned in Warner Bay rather than Dunhams Bay.[66] General Riedesel's 1777 journal noted, however, that Diamond Island was "seven miles from Fort George,"while at the same time General Burgoyne stated that the island was "three miles distant from the land" and, in a subsequent letter, "at the lower end of Lake George"; this coincides with Brown's estimate that Diamond Island "lies within 5 Miles Fort George."[67] The name of Diamond Island had been known at least as far back as the French and Indian War. The island received its name from the quartz crystals that were once easily found there (especially on the east side). In 1758 Amos Richardson, a soldier from Massachusetts, "went to Looking [for] Dimons in the Lake" while stationed on Diamond Island, which he indicated was located in the vicinity of Long Island.[68] Captain Alexander Monypenny's Orderly Book in the same year specifically mentions troops stationed on "the first island down the Lake."[69] The crystals found off Diamond Island were described in 1819 as "six-sided prism[s]" which "are hardly surpassed by any in the world for transparency and perfection of form."[70]

While nineteenth- and early twentieth-century writers agreed on Diamond Island as the location, there was a diversity of opinion regarding the bay where Brown abandoned his boats. One late nineteenth-century account suggested that "the remains of old boats may be seen in the water here [Dunhams Bay], which, it has been conjectured, were those of the plucky Brown," but another described Warner Bay "where the remains of these boats [Brown's] have been dug up from the shallow water near the shore."[71] Two weeks after the action on Lake George, the British and American armies met for their final, decisive confrontation on October 7. As Burgoyne readied his attack on Bemis Heights, he still held out hope for reinforcements from Sir Henry Clinton's army in New York City. Although Clinton moved northward on the Hudson capturing two forts, the diversion never helped Burgoyne's army, nor did Clinton try to reinforce Burgoyne. Clinton's message to Burgoyne, which disclosed that no reinforcements were to be expected, was intercepted on the lower Hudson River by the Americans. Upon capture, the messenger swallowed a small silver ball containing the message. The Americans gave the messenger a large dose of "tartar emetic" which brought forth the silver ball. Refusing to talk, the messenger was hanged.

By early October Burgoyne had a little over 5,000 troops, but the Americans had massed nearly triple that force at Saratoga. The wait for Clinton allowed American strength to grow steadily, nearly 1,000 a day toward the end. On the 7th Burgoyne led 1,500 regulars with 600 or more auxiliaries in three main divisions toward Bemis Heights. Much as in the first battle on September 19, Colonel Daniel Morgan's and Major Henry Dearborn's riflemen and light infantry were in the forefront of the advance. While the bloody battle raged, Arnold sat in his tent, stripped of his command by Gates as a result of heated altercations with the commander of the Northern Army. When Arnold had announced earlier that he would leave to join Washington's army, a petition was circulated among the general officers, including some previous antagonists, requesting Arnold to stay on. Arnold finally burst out of his tent on October 7, mounted his chestnut horse and galloped into history. Gates ordered an aide, Major John Armstrong, to bring Arnold back to headquarters. Taking charge of three regiments, Arnold turned the engagement into a major battle by breaking through the British lines and assaulting one of the British redoubts. After being drawn to a standstill, Arnold daringly galloped to the American left, riding within feet of blazing muskets, to lead four regiments against another British redoubt. As Arnold leaped over the redoubt's gate on his horse, a musket ball smashed the same leg that had been hit during the Quebec assault.

The British were finally decisively beaten on the 7th, losing four times as many men as the Americans and all their cannon that had been taken into the battle. General Simon Fraser and Sir Francis Clerke were mortally wounded in the clash, while Colonel Heinrich Breymann was shot and killed by one of his own men after using his sword on four of his soldiers to keep them in the battle. Burgoyne himself had shots pass through his hat and

British surrender at Saratoga, October 17, 1777.
Painting by John Trumbull. (National Archives)

waistcoat. While credit for the American success deservingly goes to other American officers, including Dearborn, Learned, Morgan, and Poor, Arnold's role was important to the outcome. Burgoyne, three weeks after the battle, credited his defeat to Arnold.

On October 8 Burgoyne's army began its retreat; the next day the sick and wounded of the British army fell into American hands. The British, in an attempt to retreat through Forts Edward and George, sent parties out to repair bridges on the northern route, but they were stopped by Americans who were in full control of the region. The American troops lined the east shore of the Hudson River and poured fire on the British troops in bateaux near the west shore. By the 13th, a council of war held by Burgoyne was unanimous in seeking a convention with the American army. With the uncertainty of Clinton's advance,

Gates consented to the easier terms of a convention rather than capitulation by Burgoyne. Burgoyne delayed the final surrender after hearing an optimistic but erroneous story from a Tory of Clinton's possible advance.

On October 17, as the American army assembled in "two lines, flags flying and fifes and drums shrilling 'Yankee Doodle,' while the enemy entered the meadow north of the Fishkill. . .to lay down their arms," the 13 articles of surrender were signed.[72] The British and German soldiers stacked their arms and passed by the American encampment. A German officer remarked that "not a man of them was regularly equipped. Each one had on clothes which he was accustomed to wear in the field, the tavern, the church, and in everyday life."[73] To the vanquished Germans, the Americans appeared erect, soldierly, and larger than life, or at least taller than Europeans.[74] The signed convention allowed free passage of the army back to Great Britain on condition of not serving again in North America. The surrender by any standard was a great victory, with the capture of seven generals, over 5,000 officers and men, and a considerable amount of arms. After the loss of Philadelphia, the success in the north was met with jubilation by Washington's army. In France Benjamin Franklin was able to use the victory to obtain open support from the French for the American cause. The American army finally seemed to turn the corner to eventual victory.

Several weeks after Burgoyne surrendered, General Powell at Ticonderoga destroyed some of the buildings, removed supplies and cannon, and burned the floating bridge to the water's edge before departing. The heavy supplies and cannon were loaded onto the British ships under Commodore Skeffington Lutwidge for shipment to St. Jean. Many of the troops marched north on the west side of Lake Champlain with cattle and some supplies during their retreat to Canada. Captain Ebenezer Allen and 50 Vermont Rangers followed Powell's withdrawal as far as the Bouquet River where the Americans captured cattle, supplies, and 59 men.

The lake valleys in the next several years did not return to peaceful solitude as a series of large scale raids by the British penetrated the interior of New York and Vermont. During those years, the British fleet sailed Lake Champlain freely under the command of Captains William Chambers and John Schank. Although the radeau *Thunderer* had sunk in late 1777, most of the fleet survived to the end of the war where it eventually sank at St. Jean. In 1778 the formidable British fleet included the *Royal George, Inflexible, Maria, Carleton, Washington, Lee, Loyal Convert, Jersey, Trumbull,* and *Liberty.* "A General Return of His Majesty's Arm'd Vessels on Lake Champlain" at the end of 1778 by Captain Schank also listed six 30-foot, sloop-rigged tenders: the *Spitfire, Spy, Lookout, Dispatch, Dilligence,* and *Nautilus* each armed with a few small cannon and swivel guns, five hoy-rigged (fore- and aft-rigged sloops) "Victuallers" or unarmed supply vessels included the 65-foot *Camel,* 56-foot *Commissary,* 42-foot *Ration,* 53-foot *Receipt,* and the 53-foot *Delivery.*[75] In addition, Schank recorded 12 gunboats, 16 long boats "From 20 to 30 feet long," 16 cutters "From 24 foot 5 Inch to 20 long," and two rowing barges with 10 oars and 12 oars.[76]

Following British raids into Vermont in March and July 1778, the British heeded reports from a spy in Saratoga that large amounts of supplies moving between Fort Edward and Saratoga were an indication of an impending invasion of Canada. Actually, the Americans had formulated plans to invade Canada with Lafayette as commander but that idea had been dropped. The new governor and commander of the army in Canada, General Frederick Haldimand, after hearing reports of invasion, was ready with a pre-emptive strike into the Champlain Valley. On October 24, 1778, Major Christopher Carleton, nephew of Sir Guy Carleton, departed from Isle-aux-Noix with 354 British and German troops and 100 Indians aboard a small fleet of vessels with orders "to destroy all the supplies, provisions, and animals which the rebels may have assembled on the shores of Lake Champlain, to take prisoner all the inhabitants. . .to destroy all the boats. . sawmills and grist mills."[77]

Carleton, who led Indians during the Valcour engagement in 1776, sent his raiders deep into Vermont, penetrating as far east as Middlebury. Using vessels from the original Valcour fleet, the schooners *Carleton* and *Maria*, cutter *Lee*, at least two gunboats, and bateaux, Carleton in three weeks assaulted and burned settlements along the bays, creeks, and shores of Lake Champlain. The total destruction included 47 houses, 48 barns, 103 stacks of wheat and hay, a blockhouse, sawmill, and gristmill. A large number of horses and hogs were killed and 100 head of cattle either killed or driven to Canada. Forty prisoners from both sides of the lake were taken aboard the ships to St. Jean and imprisoned later in Quebec.

Peter Ferris and his son Squire had their house burned on Arnold's Bay, the third time that the family had property destroyed by the British. The two Vermonters had helped the patriots several times, including Arnold's crews in 1776, and had also entertained the commissioners to Canada (Benjamin Franklin, among others) at their homestead. Captured while deer hunting below Crown Point, Ferris and his son spent several harrowing years in prison. In 1779 Ferris, then 54 years old, and his 15-year-old son escaped but were recaptured by Indians. After another escape attempt, the two were held separately in dungeons for 72 days. With their captivity above ground again, they and others escaped by digging under a wall. Lost in the wilderness for much of their 19 days of freedom, both were retaken and were not exchanged until 1782.[78]

Following raids in 1779 and early 1780, the British launched their biggest expedition (since Burgoyne's 1777 invasion) in the fall of 1780 against military targets in the lake valleys. On the 28th of September 1780, Major Christopher Carleton with an army of nearly 1,000 regulars, Loyalists, and some Indians (most of whom joined Carleton several days later) sailed first for Isle-aux-Noix. Because of additional Indians, a separate party under Lieutenant Richard Houghton (Haughton), a participant in the 1778 Vermont raids, was sent to the Onion River (present-day Winooski River). Houghton with his Indians and Loyalists also traveled on the White River and burned Royalton. At two o'clock in the morning of October 7, Carleton's fleet of eight vessels and 26 bateaux landed at Bulwagga Bay (between present-day Port Henry and Crown Point). There Carleton dispatched 100 men (rangers, Loyalists, and Indians) under Captain John Munro to march overland to join a second advance from Niagara by Sir John Johnson, son of Sir William Johnson from the Battle of Lake George in 1755.

Carleton pressed on with the main force, landing at South Bay in the darkness early on October 8. The vessels were sent back to Ticonderoga for a subsequent rendezvous and there 30 men were to portage two bateaux into Lake George. On the afternoon of the 8th, the army of 800 marched southward. The garrison at Fort Anne quickly surrendered; three officers and 72 privates were made prisoner. The Loyalists with Carleton were sent southward where they destroyed houses and barns in Queensbury, Fort Edward, and Stillwater. Captain Munro's party, which had traveled by way of the Schroon River, similarly plundered and burned houses in Ballston Spa.

By October 11 Carleton's army approached Fort George. After Carleton's Indians pursued a soldier from the fort, Captain John Chipman, in command of Fort George, sent about 50 of the militia after the Indians. The detachment of Americans under Captain Thomas Sill was quickly surrounded and defeated in a brief but bloody engagement. Carleton offered Chipman, with only a handful of troops left and short of ammunition, generous terms of capitulation, similar to those accepted by Fort Anne's garrison. With little choice, Chipman surrendered the fort. John Enys, a British officer who witnessed the Valcour battle, described the walls of Fort George as "Stone with a thick earth parrapet and good Bomb proofs for the Garrison" but the walls had been burned and in bad shape and the well unusable for the "filth" dumped into it.[79] Carleton ordered his men "to raise all the Boats belonging to the place which were Sunk in several different places."[80]

The next morning the recovered bateaux were loaded with a few captured cannon, supplies, and prisoners as the fort burned. Since there wasn't enough room in the boats for everyone, some of the party had to march along a crude trail on the west side of the lake called "Rogers's Road." On the morning of the 15th the party marched over "Roger's Rock, from the top of which we had a most beautyfull prospect of Lake George."[81]

On October 24 Captain Munro returned from his Ballston Spa raid and rejoined Carleton's fleet on the west shore above Crown Point. Carleton's raid had taken two forts, burned six sawmills, a gristmill, 38 houses, 33 barns, and 1,500 tons of hay. As the fleet got under way on its voyage back to Canada on October 26, an express boat arrived with a message from General Frederick Haldimand with orders for Carleton to stay on the lake. The purpose was to cover Captain Justus Sherwood, a Loyalist sent with a flag of truce to Vermont. Sherwood's mission was related to negotiations between Ethan Allen and the British, supposedly over prisoner exchanges, but actually concerning secretive dealings to have Vermont become a neutral state tied to British Canada.* With Congress's deaf ear on Vermont's plea for admission as a state, Allen, Governor Chittenden, and others were adamantly against Vermont land being split between New Hampshire and New York. Allen and his family, whose earlier controversial involvement over land with the Onion River Company was well known, still held large tracts of land in northern Vermont.

Major Carleton had written General Henry W. Powell on October 17 that "I am this moment informed that the despatches forwarded by the Commander in Chief [Haldimand] to Brigadier Allen of the State of Vermont was oblidged to be destroyed, the person who carrid them being pursued."[82] Allen required a cessation of hostilities in Vermont and New York while negotiations were taking place. As a brigadier general of the Vermont militia, Allen dismissed his army in late October. New Yorkers' suspicions, however, were raised by the dealings. Governor George Clinton of New York wrote to Washington that the Vermonters passed no information on when the British fleet sailed south on their way to raid New York; Philip Schuyler in a letter to Washington questioned whether Allen had turned traitor or was about to do so.[83]

Ira Allen, Ethan's brother, and Jonas Fay continued as the Vermont commissioners in 1781 during negotiations with the British which would make Vermont a Royal Province, neutral in the war and free to trade with Canada. General Haldimand, with the support of Lord Germain, was eager for the deal. The Vermont commissioners, however, stalled the agreement. In mid-October 1781, Colonel Barry St. Leger was sent with the British fleet and a force of 1,000 regulars and Loyalists to Ticonderoga by Haldimand as a show of presence to support the treaty. In an attempt to obtain a Vermonter as a messenger, St.

---

* After his release from British captivity, Allen was appointed a brigadier general in the Vermont militia in 1779.

Leger's men unwittingly shot a militia sergeant. A letter of apology, sent to Governor Chittenden by St. Leger, was opened by the courier, Simon Hathaway, who exposed its contents to everyone along the way. By the time Hathaway reached the Vermont Assembly, the citizens of the state were up in arms over the meaning of the letter.[84] At the same time news of the British surrender at Yorktown reached St. Leger at Ticonderoga; the army soon retreated back to Canada without orders from Haldimand.

Ira Allen later contended that the truce with the British held off their armies, preventing bloodshed in Vermont. Supporters of the conspirators also argued that the ploy was successful in eventually bringing Vermont to statehood. But the duplicity during a period of the nation's greatest need raised questions that are still being debated. Nearly a year after Yorktown, Ethan Allen, intransigent in his views, wrote to General Haldimand that "I shall do anything in my power to render the State a British Province."[85]

The two years after Yorktown brought a semblance of tranquillity to the lake valleys while military readiness continued as the peace treaty was finalized. During this period, George Washington established his headquarters at Newburgh on the Hudson River. With little to do, Washington embarked on inspection tours during 1782 and 1783. During late July 1783 Washington and his party moved north on Lake George in three boats, inspected Fort Ticonderoga and Crown Point, and returned south to the Mohawk River, where his inspection party traveled to Fort Stanwix (Schuyler). The peace treaty was finally signed in Paris on September 3, 1783. Although the British evacuated New York City several months later, they remained at their post at Point au Fer on Lake Champlain (south of Rouses Point, N.Y.) until June of 1796.

After the peace treaty, the settlers returned to the lake valleys to reestablish their communities and lives. Fort Ticonderoga and Crown Point became accessible quarries for new settlers to the region seeking foundation stones. Furniture from Ticonderoga, as well as floors, doors, and windows, were removed and reinstalled in farm houses. Even abandoned cannon, most spiked and unusable, were melted down to be reused for their iron. The only objects from the turbulent years of the Revolution that remained untouched were those that had fallen to the bottom of the lakes.

Ruins of Fort Ticonderoga by W. H. Bartlett. (Author's collection)

Raising of gondola *Philadelphia* at Valcour Island, 1935.
(Smithsonian Institution)

9. The Search for the Valcour Fleet

THE SEARCH FOR THE VESSELS of the Valcour fleet has been a history in itself, luring historians, divers, and the Lake Champlain citizenry into more than a century of tales about the sunken wrecks of Arnold's navy. All of the original 15 vessels that were present at the Valcour engagement (including two schooners, the *Revenge* and *Royal Savage*; one sloop, *Enterprise*; one cutter, *Lee*; three row galleys, the *Congress*, *Trumbull*, and *Washington*; and eight gondolas or gunboats, the *Boston*, *Connecticut*, *New Haven*, *New Jersey*, *New York*, *Philadelphia*, *Providence*, and *Spitfire*) eventually sank in Lake Champlain or the Richelieu River. Two other American vessels, the schooner *Liberty* and row galley *Gates*, were not present at the Valcour engagement, since the latter vessel was unfinished and the *Liberty* had sailed to Ticonderoga for provisions at the time of the battle. Both suffered the same fate as the rest of the fleet. The cold freshwater of the lake provides an ideal time capsule since the teredo worms that would ordinarily destroy submerged wood in salt water are absent in freshwater. Additionally, the only damage to iron objects has been simple corrosion rather than the more severe destruction of iron in salt water through electrolysis. However, some of the vessels were carelessly handled by salvagers, which has resulted in nearly total destruction.

Only one of the 15 vessels of the fleet remains on display for the American public at the Smithsonian Institution. Several of the ships were destroyed by souvenir hunters at the turn of the century; two have been raised and parts of one remain in storage; several were destroyed in canal construction, and at least one may still lie intact at the bottom of the lake. Presently, both New York and Vermont have laws to prevent the removal of historically significant artifacts from the lake. Unfortunately, the laws came too late to save some vessels that were recovered but subsequently were burned or allowed to deteriorate.

About half of the fleet sank along the north-south path of the running battle of October 11-13, 1776. Valcour Island in the north to Schuyler Island and on to Arnold's Bay in Vermont roughly traces the major areas of search for the vessels. At the very southern end of the lake at Whitehall several of the remaining vessels were scuttled in 1777. Corroborating information about specific events of the Valcour battle has been difficult because of a lack of detail in the few original American journals available and the insufficiency of direct observation of events recorded in many of the journals of British officers.

The flagship *Royal Savage*, the first vessel to sink in the battle after running aground on Valcour Island, had most of her guns salvaged by the British in November 1779. Until 1860 the schooner's hull remained undisturbed. At that time, the bow was pulled out of the water in an attempt to raise her, but she slipped back into deeper water.[1] In 1866 Peter Palmer in his *History of Lake Champlain* observed that "the hull of the schooner lies on the spot where she sunk, and her upper timbers can yet be seen during low water in the lake."[2] Local relic hunters soon stripped the exposed structure for souvenirs. The *Plattsburgh Republican* in 1868 reported that Captain George Conn anchored his vessel over the wreck and pulled up oak planking with a grappling iron. The oak pieces were later made into a cane, gavel, and rulers.[3]

In 1908 the *Glens Falls Daily Times* indicated that the *Royal Savage* was to be raised for the Champlain Tercentenary (1909) for display in Plattsburgh. After retrieving a rib and musket balls, a diver from Boston hired by the Tercentenary Committee, found "that about forty five feet of the hull is in a fair state of preservation and can be raised practically as it is."[4] The vessel was never raised since as late as the 1930s the *Royal Savage* could still be seen off the island. John Ferguson, as a teenager, searched for the wreck in 15-20 feet of water when he observed the vessel: "I realized that this was my chance to make history come alive, to grab a piece and hold it. I dove to the wreck several times grabbing anything within reach – wood, square nails, even grape shot that lay all around the hulk."[5]

In the summer of 1932 Colonel Lorenzo F. Hagglund, one of the top salvage engineers in the East, came to Plattsburgh during his vacation to search for the *Royal Savage*. He had originally heard of the vessel's history when he was in military training for overseas service in 1917 at Plattsburgh. Hagglund trudged along the bottom of the lake off Valcour Island with hardhat diving gear without luck, although he discovered cannonballs, bar shot, grapeshot, and other artifacts from the wreck. On the last day of his vacation, he rowed further out in the lake and caught the dim outline of the wreck from the surface in less than 20 feet of water. The position of the wreck was 150 feet offshore, just outside of the area he had covered with his diving gear.

After failing to interest either the federal or state governments, Hagglund returned in 1934 to salvage the vessel with his own resources. However, several weeks before Hagglund returned, another hardhat diver, Lieutenant Horace Mazet of the United States Navy, explored the wreck of the *Royal Savage*: "Walking slowly toward her, we were able to see her full length, picking out some 14 ribs still standing. . .Whitened musket balls of lead gleamed dully against dark oak timbers, and we were soon finding groups of rust-welded grape-shot oxidized to planks. . .cannon balls, coated with thick encrustations of rust, a bar-shot."[6] The surviving length, raised by Hagglund with 20 drums, was about 35 feet with a beam of 15 feet, which consisted of the keel, keelson, bottom planking, and most of the ribs. According to an article in the *U. S. Naval Institute Proceedings* in 1935, the timbers were dismembered and carefully marked and placed "aboard a box car and on their way to storage in the vicinity of New York City."[7] The wreck was apparently housed in several locations in New York State and has since been stored in a building near Lake Champlain.

Today, Colonel Hagglund's son is in possession of the *Royal Savage*. The remains form a length of approximately 27 feet, beam of 13-14 feet, and include 13 frames and over 100 individual artifacts. The relics are stored on Long Island, in Vermont, and upstate New

York. Other parts and artifacts of the *Royal Savage* that had been recovered earlier from the wreck site were displayed in the Hotel Champlain in Plattsburgh before their subsequent destruction by fire. Two decades after Colonel Hagglund had raised the vessel, Montreal divers found part of the vessel's 1,500 pound keel, a large anchor, and numerous cannonballs.[8] The anchor and a six-foot section of the stern holding a pin and ring (gudgeon) were displayed at the David M. Stewart Museum on St. Helene's Island in Montreal before being permanently loaned to the National Canadian War Museum in Ottawa. In the 1960s more relics were recovered by area divers off Valcour Island.

In the summer of 1935 Lorenzo F. Hagglund returned to Valcour Island with a crew of volunteers including J. Ruppert Schalk and his yacht *Linwood* to search for the gondola *Philadelphia*. By early August, using a sweep chain suspended from the *Linwood*, the *Philadelphia* was discovered intact and sitting upright mid-channel in Valcour Bay in 57 feet of water. Hagglund described her position on the bottom of the lake: "We advance towards it, and it takes shape. It is the hull of a vessel . . . . Now we are abreast of her mast. It is still standing upright."[9] The wreck was brought up in a cradle of ropes by a derrick on August 9, 1935. The recovered wreck included one of the most significant collections of early colonial artifacts ever discovered. Cannon, shot, tools, anchors, china cups, pewter spoons, buttons, shoes, a time glass, and even torn sails were retrieved — virtually everything aboard remained intact.

The *Philadelphia* was housed for the winter of 1936 at Shelburne Harbor, Vermont, with the intention of permanent exhibition on the campus of the University of Vermont. Funds for a building to house the ship were not forthcoming, however. The vessel was offered by Hagglund to the U.S. Navy, New York State, Vermont, and the Smithsonian Institution. All rejected the offer. Hagglund then began a tour with the *Philadelphia* on a barge around Lake Champlain. For the next decade it was exhibited along the Hudson River and Lake Champlain, spent summers at Crown Point and Fort Ticonderoga, and finally was exhibited in a barn in Willsboro, New York. In 1961, following the death of Colonel Hagglund, the vessel was acquired by the Smithsonian Institution and four years later, after preservation, was put on permanent display with constant humidity and temperature control in the Museum of History and Technology. The *Philadelphia* is the oldest intact warship presently on exhibit in North America.

At least one sister gondola remains at the bottom of Lake Champlain. Although Benedict Arnold's report of October 15, 1776, mentioned "two Gondolas sunk at Schuyler's Island," only one actually sank.[10] One of the two abandoned gondolas was the *New Jersey*, which was taken by the British on October 12. While some records suggest that the *New Jersey* was captured, the vessel was found abandoned. The British description which most closely matches the American records comes from a letter written by Captain Charles Douglass of the Royal Navy. It conveys the dispatches of Lieutenant James Dacres, commander of the schooner *Carleton*, and accurately accounts for the eight gondolas: "One taken the 12th; one sunk the 11th; four burnt the 13th; one escaped, and one missing."[11] Apparently, the *Jersey* was taken by the British after being scuttled by Arnold's forces.

There is no mention in the American documents of the crew of the *Jersey* surrendering to the British. General Waterbury's account of the surrender of the galley *Washington* makes no reference to another vessel being taken by the British. Likewise, Captain Thomas Pringle, aboard the British schooner *Maria*, writing about the events of the 13th, stated that "The Washington galley struck during the action, and the rest made their escape to

ABOVE. *Philadelphia* in Smithsonian Institution. (Smithsonian Institution)

BELOW. Raising the *Royal Savage* at Valcour Island, 1934. (Hudson Hagglund Collection)

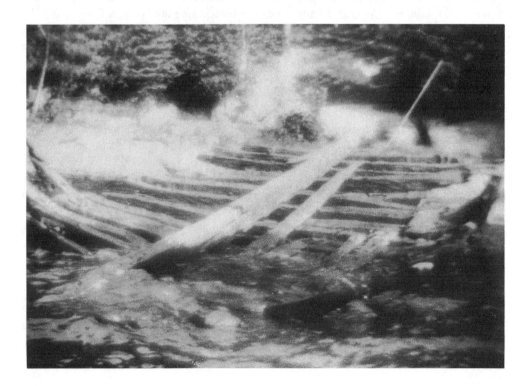

Ticonderoga."[12] General William Maxwell, writing to the governor of New Jersey from Ticonderoga on October 20, related that the fleet, under orders from Arnold, had separated to escape and subsequently was run on shore or destroyed: "but one row-galley fell into their hands."[13] Obviously, the Americans did not count the *Jersey* as captured. The *Jersey* was recorded as being "taken" by the British on October 12, a day when the American and British fleets were miles apart.[14]

Wreck of *Congress* at Arnold's Bay in 1890s.
(Lester Fleming Collection)

The most convincing evidence that the *Jersey* was found abandoned and had not surrendered comes from the journal of Lt. John Enys, a nineteen-year-old ensign in the British army, who witnessed the Valcour engagement from the *Thunderer*. After describing the action at Arnold's Bay in his journal, Enys recorded that "the Same day a party of Canadians found a Gondola Named the *Jersey* on the opposite Side of the lake and Soon after a Small Sloop Named the Lee was found."[15]

Part of the confusion over the location of the sinking of the other gondola stems from the fact that the fleet was not actually together during the retreat. Private Pascal DeAngelis, a 13-year-old boy from Connecticut, was aboard the galley *Trumbull* along the Willsboro shore while many of the vessels were at Schuyler Island. That night he learned from the retreating crews of two gondolas "that one of our gundeloes was taking water and the other sunk."[16] If the vessel that "sunk" was the *Jersey*, which was retrieved and taken by the British, then the gondola "taking water" may have sunk some distance from Schuyler Island. The following morning of October 13, the American fleet was spread over seven miles, according to General Waterbury: "Next Morning I Was a Bout half Way Between the Brothers and Split Rock and the Enemy to the South of the Brothers and General arnal a Bout two Milds a hed of me and the Rest of the fleet Scattered a Bout Seven milds in Lenth."[17] Nevertheless, the British spotted the whole fleet. Captain Pringle related that "Upon the 13th I again saw eleven sail of their fleet making off to Crown-Point, who, after a chace of seven hours, I came up with in the Maria."[18] The 11 vessels represented the American fleet minus the *Royal Savage, Philadelphia, New Jersey*, and one other sunk gondola.

Schuyler Island, site of Benedict Arnold's anchorage in 1776
and Robert Rogers' camp in 1759. Photo by the author.

The search for the last gondola began with Colonel Lorenzo Hagglund's exploratory diving at Schuyler Island and Ligonier Point from 1951-1953. Several gondola anchors were raised from the east side of Schuyler Island in the early 1960s and another from a reef near Basin Harbor, Vermont. One of the anchors is presently in the Colchester Lighthouse at the Shelburne Museum and a second in the Navy Memorial Museum in Washington, D.C.

In November 1967 New York State issued a permit to the Smithsonian Institution to explore the waters off Schuyler Island. After several days of diving operations in the frigid water, the search was temporarily halted. The following June the Smithsonian returned, aided by a grant from the National Geographic Society and side-scan sonar equipment from the Massachusetts Institute of Technology. A nine-day search, however, was repeatedly hampered by rough weather. The search parties and divers returned in late November of 1968 to continue their sonar probe. Although several targets were indicated on sonar and some wooden fragments found by divers, no shipwrecks were located. In a 1976 report, Dr. Philip Lundeberg, then Curator of Naval History at the Smithsonian, stated that he still hoped to return to Schuyler, concluding that "this Division looks forward to future opportunities to decipher the mystery of the Schuyler Island gondolas."[19]

The search for the missing gondola was renewed in the 1980s. A six-day side-scan/Loran/

Bow cannon protruding over the lead-lined stem of Benedict Arnold's
gunboat, discovered by the Lake Champlain Maritime Museum.
(Photo courtesy of the Lake Champlain Maritime Museum
with special thanks to Benthos, Inc.)

ROV (Remotely Operated Vehicle) survey of the Schuyler Island area in search of Arnold's lost gondola began in the summer of 1987. The group was led by Joseph Zarzynski, with Garry Kozak of Klein Associates, the manufacturers of sophisticated side-scan sonar equipment, and Vince Capone of Kaselaan & D'Angelo Associates of New Jersey, who provided the ROV. Kozak, manager of field operations for Klein Associates, had worked on National Geographic projects such as the 1843 *Breadalbane* wreck under the arctic ice and the War of 1812 wrecks of the schooners *Hamilton* and *Scourge* on the bottom of Lake Ontario. Unfortunately, the systematic search did not find the vessel, but it did relocate the wreck of the tugboat *William H. McAllister* which sank in 150 feet of water south of Schuyler Island.

In February 1988 an expedition of the National Geographic Society, directed by Emory Kristoff, which utilized sector-scanning sonar, Loran, and a ROV, searched the area off Schuyler Island. Kristoff worked with James Kennard, who had used side-scan sonar with Scott Hill earlier in the 1980s around Schuyler Island. The team searched the waters off the southern end of the island without success. If they had found the gondola, the plans were to leave it untouched. The vessel would have been historically documented, nominated for the National Historic Register, and perhaps incorporated into the National Oceanic and Atmospheric Administration Marine Sanctuary Program.[20] Kennard continued the search for the missing gondola with side-scan sonar in 1989.

The third group within a year to search near Schuyler Island was led by Arthur Cohn, director of the Lake Champlain Maritime Museum at Basin Harbor, with technicians and side-scan sonar equipment from the Woods Hole Oceanographic Institution and the research vessel from the University of Vermont Lake Studies Program. A three-day search off Schuyler Island in April 1988, unfortunately, did not turn up the gondola. The Woods Hole Oceanographic Institution in conjunction with the Lake Champlain Maritime Museum and the University of Vermont renewed the search for the missing gondola in 1989 with the most sophisticated equipment deployed to date in the Schuyler Island area.* The Lake Champlain Maritime Museum's team, under Cohn's supervision with lake historian Peter Barranco, continued the search effort in the 1990s with a multi-year, side-scan mapping of the lake bottom. In June 1997 Arnold's missing gunboat was finally discovered completely intact in the deep water off Schuyler Island with her mast standing and her 12-pound bow cannon still on the slide track carriage. After more than 220 years underwater, her cannon points eerily into the darkness, as if waiting for one more British warship to come into view.

Although the missing gondola has been called the *Providence*, original documents are somewhat conflicting on the name of the elusive vessel. A 1776 water color by Charles Randle in the National Archives of Canada entitled "A View of the New England Arm'd Vessels on Valcure Bay on Lake Champlain, 11 October 1776," identified the "Providence Sunk 12 Octr in a Squall."[21] While most of the captions are correct, Randle's list erroneously identified the "Philadelphia. . .Burnt 15 Octr" and the "Boston Sunk 11 Octr."[22] Another accounting of the American vessels, in an anonymous journal of a British officer lists the "Providence burnt 13th."[23] The list is virtually the same as that provided by Lieutenant William Digby in his journal, where under gondolas he recorded the "Providence – burnt. . . .13."[24] Both of these journals correctly indicate that the *Philadelphia* sank on October 11. Bayze Wells, serving on the *Providence*, did not mention in his journal the scuttling of his own gondola. That omission, however, certainly would not preclude the sinking of the *Providence* on October 12.

The five vessels (galley *Congress* and four gondolas) that Arnold burned and scuttled in what is known as Arnold's Bay in Panton, Vermont, have met with nearly total destruction. Surprisingly, some of the salvage occurred immediately after the battle. General Riedesel's journal on October 25, 1776, observed that "Part of the garrison were at this time engaged

*The side-scan sonar work in September 1989, supervised by David Gallo of Woods Hole and Arthur Cohn from the Lake Champlain Maritime Museum, discovered two nineteenth-century railroad cars, a ferry boat, and the completely intact wreck of the 73-foot schooner **Sara H. Ellen**, built at Isle La Motte in 1849. The 50-ton vessel with a molded bow and stern had departed from Ligonier Point for Burlington with a load of stone in December 1860 when the schooner foundered and sank in 300 feet of water during a winter storm.

ABOVE. American crews abandoning their battered vessels at Arnold's Bay,
October 13, 1776. Painting by Charles Waterhouse.
(Marine Corps Museum Art Collection)

BELOW. Aerial view of Arnold's Bay. Photo by the author.

at Buttonmole Bay [Arnold's Bay] in raising some of the sunken war material especially cannon."[25] When he had passed the bay in late October, approximately 20 cannon had been raised. One brass cannon was retrieved years later from the bay by the Ferris family and was reportedly used in the Battle of Plattsburgh during the War of 1812. An iron cannon raised from the bay in the 1930s is presently on display at the Lake Champlain Maritime Museum.

In 1842 Zadock Thompson mentioned that Arnold's fleet was still to be seen in the bay at low water.[26] Writing about Arnold's Bay in 1859, however, A. M. Hemenway suggested that "Of the 5 vessels sunk, 3 are known to have been raised, and 2 of them may still be seen in low water."[27] Philip Tucker, in his short essay "General Arnold and the Congress Galley" written in 1860, stated that "Edrick Adams, Esq., of Addison, who lived many years near Arnold's bay, informs me that he has seen the remains of three of them in the bay and knows their respective localities. . .near a point of this rock rest the remains of the Congress."[28] Mazet, after diving in the "opaque chalkiness" of Arnold's Bay in 1934, reported that "The wrecks of three of Arnold's vessels lie, stark and broken, held fast in the clay of the bottom, their few remaining ribs and timbers hardly recognizable as once having been boats."[29] Tradition has it that three of the gondolas were dragged out of the water with teams of horses during the nineteenth century and cut up for souvenirs. Eventually, the sparse remains of the vessels rotted away on neighboring farms with at least one of the vessels being burned on the shore of Arnold's Bay.

Near the turn of the twentieth century, a large section of Arnold's galley *Congress* was raised and remained on the nearby Adam's farm for several years as relic hunters carted away its dismembered parts. Some of its ten frames that have been handed down through several generations of families are still in existence. Canes and other souvenirs were fashioned from its timbers and frames. In 1901 a section of a knee (rib) from the *Congress* was displayed at the state fair (New York). In 1910 W. Max Reid's book *Lake George and Lake Champlain* reported that "All that is left of the *Congress* rests on the lawn back of Hotel St. Frederic at Chimney Point."[30] This was a section of the stern. Parts of the *Congress* were still to be seen in the late 1920s at Chimney Point. The last few frames of the vessel were acquired by Lorenzo Hagglund and are still in existence today. In 1990 two of the original frames were loaned to the Lake Champlain Maritime Museum by Hudson and Mary Hagglund.

The Champlain Maritime Society in 1984 began a side-scan sonar and diving survey of Arnold's Bay to determine if any portions of the historic vessels still remain in the bay. After examining a collection of artifacts recovered in 1960-61 by a New York diver, the Society subsequently discovered the ends of the frames of part of a vessel buried in the mud. A section of a gun carriage, beam, and frames were examined and determined to be from part of the bow area of the *Congress*.

What is considered the last gondola in Arnold's Bay was raised in 1952 by Lorenzo Hagglund, towed across the lake and sunk along the New York shore to prevent deterioration.[31] The vessel which had been deeply buried in the mud was in remarkable condition— much of the hull nearly as intact as the *Philadelphia*. The runners for the bow cannon were still present when the vessel was pulled out of the mud. The gondola was raised in October 1954 and set alongside the remains of the early nineteenth-century steamer *Vermont* near Ausable Chasm, New York, in what was to be a private naval museum owned by the Lake Champlain Associates. The group planned to build a huge masonry exhibition hall for the

"Museum of Naval History" with an issue of 300,000 shares of common stock. The museum backers intended to display the *Royal Savage*, the *Philadelphia*, the gondola from Arnold's Bay, the 1809 steamer *Vermont* and other artifacts.[32] Attempts to raise funds to preserve and display these relics never materialized.

In the 1960s Howard Chapelle, the noted naval historian, and Philip Lundeberg of the Smithsonian determined that the abandoned wreck in the woods near Ausable Chasm was indeed one of Arnold's gondolas. According to Dr. Lundeberg, the gunboat "revealed structural details virtually identical with those of the *Philadelphia*, including comparable over-all dimensions, flat-bottomed construction, similar frame and floor spacing, iron and treenail fastenings, and the characteristic keelson."[33] A stem piece of this gondola was given to the Navy Memorial Museum at the Navy Yard in Washington, D. C. After nearly 20 years of disintegration and dismemberment by souvenir hunters while it lay exposed in the woods, a few pieces of the gondola were removed in 1973 to make way for a campsite. Some of the frames from the gondola are presently stored in a barn in Willsboro, New York. The raising of historic shipwrecks without prearranged preservation facilities has often resulted in total destruction of the vessels. Many archaeologists now believe that building full-size replicas of historic ships may be preferable to raising fragile shipwrecks. The Lake Champlain Maritime Museum began construction in 1989 of a full-scale working reproduction of the gondola *Philadelphia* at an estimated cost of $430,000. Built from plans made available by the Smithsonian Institution, the replica *Philadelphia* is an exact copy of the original. The finished gondola was launched in 1991 as part of the Vermont Bicentennial and is slated for lake tours beginning in 1992.

What happened to the rest of the vessels? The galley *Washington* was captured on October 13 and remained in British service until 1784. The *Enterprise, Revenge, Trumbull,* and *New York* escaped the 1776 disaster and spent the following year in the area of Fort Ticonderoga. Most of them, however, sank to the bottom of the lake during the British invasion of 1777. When General John Burgoyne's forces approached Fort Ticonderoga on July 6, 1777, (the British fleet at that time included the captured *Jersey, Lee,* and *Washington*), the Americans evacuated the fort and fled to present-day Whitehall. The *Revenge* and *Gates* (a galley completed after the Valcour engagement) were set afire and blown up by their crews near Wood Creek Falls. The *Enterprise* burned and sank. During the construction on the Champlain Barge Canal from 1907-1912, several cannon, reportedly from the *Gates,* were salvaged and now rest on the lawn of the State Armory in Whitehall and in the Skenesborough Museum. According to one local newspaper account in late 1911, "two more large cannons, making a total of four, were taken from the bed of the harbor at Whitehall by the dipper dredge."[34] Parts salvaged from the other vessels found near Lock 12 are still in Whitehall, having been fashioned into checker boards, billiard cues, and canes.

What happened to the gondola *New York* still remains a mystery. Although a few secondary accounts suggest that the vessel was blown up before reaching Whitehall during the July 6, 1777, evacuation of Ticonderoga, the *New York* was probably scuttled in Whitehall.[35] The British record of the vessels taken and destroyed at Whitehall in July 1777, however, does not include the *New York*.[36] Some of the primary American sources also describe only the five larger vessels at Whitehall. Captain Rufus Lincoln with the Americans reported: "two of the galles were taken the other three Evacuated and blown up."[37]

In May 1782 Captain William Chambers of the Royal Navy reported the *Washington, Jersey,* and *Lee* still carrying provisions from St. Jean.[38] The "Return of His Majesty's Vessels on the Undermentioned Lakes" in 1784 listed only eight vessels in service on Lake Champlain which included the captured American vessels *Washington, Trumbull,* and *Liberty.*[39] The sloop *Liberty* was reported to be "old but repairable" as late as 1790.[40]

Nearly all the British vessels that sailed Lake Champlain during the Revolutionary War eventually settled to the bottom of the Richelieu River or were broken up in the vicinity of St. Jean. These included the *Inflexible, Carleton, Maria, Loyal Convert, Royal George,* and the captured American vessels *Jersey, Lee, Liberty, Trumbull,* and *Washington.* Some of the British gunboats used at Valcour, which had been transported to Lake George in 1777, are probably at the bottom of the lake. The radeau *Thunderer,* loaded with the sick and wounded from the Saratoga battles, sank in Lake Champlain after hitting a rock near Windmill Point in late 1777. A few of the British vessels, however, continued in military or commercial service for quite a few years before their demise. The armed schooner *Maria,* for example, was used for cargo inspection of trading vessels in 1787 at Point au Fer on Lake Champlain.[41] Two war schooners were acquired from the British in 1790 by Gideon King of Burlington for use as commercial vessels on Lake Champlain. Parts of the remaining vessels in the British fleet which had sunk at St. Jean were found when the Chambly Canal was constructed in the nineteenth century. An extensive side-scan sonar and underwater survey between 1978 and 1980 by Canadian archaeologists discovered numerous wreck sites in the Richelieu River. Although many wrecks were canal boats, artifacts recovered from the site of an old wharf near St. Jean date from the Revolutionary War.[42]

A schooner, identified as the *Revenge,* was raised off Fort Ticonderoga in 1909 and placed on display at the museum. The vessel deteriorated substantially after a shed collapsed on it in the spring of 1948. The wreck was not the *Revenge* since that vessel had been blown up in Whitehall in 1777. The Champlain Maritime Society examined the scant remains of the vessel in 1983. They tentatively identified the wreck as the brig *Duke of Cumberland* built under the command of General Jeffrey Amherst in 1759 for use in the naval campaign of the French and Indian War (see chapter 5). Another wreck was recovered from the waters off Crown Point at the turn of the century. From photographs the ship appeared to be an eighteenth century vessel. The vessel was displayed on the parade ground at Crown Point for many years, but a grass fire in the 1940s entirely destroyed the craft.

Another partial wreck was pulled out of East Bay in Whitehall in 1949 and rests at Fort Mount Hope in Ticonderoga. While an old sign over this vessel stated that it might be one of the gunboats from Arnold's fleet, an inspection of its construction suggests something else. On the half of the vessel that was dragged out of the bay in 1949 (the other half is still there) were found an 1812 Canadian coin in the step of the mizzen mast and a split 13-inch mortar that had been used at Fort Ticonderoga during the Revolution. After General Knox hauled cannon from Ticonderoga to Boston in the winter of 1775-1776, two mortars, among other munitions, found their way back to the fort in the spring of 1776. On August 1, 1776, one of the mortars was fired from a gondola and burst in half; the second mortar, fired the next day, also burst. The split mortars were used for ballast in the American row galleys. The galley *Trumbull* escaped the Valcour Island disaster in 1776 but was captured by the British near Whitehall in 1777 following a brief battle. After serving with the British navy, the vessel was probably broken up at the British shipyard at St. Jean. When the British built its fleet during the War of 1812 they apparently used the broken mortar as ballast.[43] The victorious American navy under Thomas Macdonough escorted its captured prizes to Whitehall in late 1814. Through research and actual measurements, the Champlain

Maritime Society identified the vessel in East Bay/Mount Hope as the 82-foot brig *Linnet*, built by the Royal Navy. This would explain the broken mortar and the 1812 Canadian coin on the same vessel. Nearly all of the 400 cannonballs, bar shot, and other relics found on the half of the vessel pulled out of East Bay were sold piece by piece to tourists over the last 30 years.

A new outlook on archaeological recovery may be necessary to preserve the invaluable artifacts in American waters. Additional measures are needed to discourage the piece-by-piece dismemberment of historic wrecks. Something could also be done to check the concealment and disintegration of existing relics. Philip Lundeberg of the Smithsonian has suggested a method that has been successful in the Scandinavian countries involving a partnership of the government with local sport divers. Amateur divers help excavate the wrecks, guard them from unauthorized dismemberment, and are given recognition in museums for their contributions.

The discovery of these priceless relics preserved in the cold waters of Lake Champlain has kept the story of Arnold's gallant 1776 fleet alive. The observation of a bit of history, untouched since it fell to its watery grave, creates a tangible link between the past and present. There is a certain degree of immortality attached to the surviving relics as they have been passed from generation to generation in the Champlain Valley. It is to be hoped that these artifacts will not be lost but at some point brought forth to be displayed in museums.

Gondola at Ausable Chasm in 1961, originally used at the Battle of Valcour Island, 1776. The vessel had been raised nearly intact from Arnold's Bay in 1952.
(Smithsonian Institution)

Master Commandant Thomas Macdonough by John Wesley.
(City of New York Art Commission)

10. War of 1812: Plattsburgh Bay

THE LAKE VALLEYS on the eve of the War of 1812 were no longer the wilderness that once dominated the region in the eighteenth century. While Lake George experienced a much slower rate of growth, by 1810 over 100,000 people lived in counties adjacent to Lake Champlain. Stimulated by trade with Canada to the north and commercial traffic to the south and east, communities grew rapidly along the lake. Burlington, Plattsburgh, Whitehall (formerly Skenesborough), and Vergennes, experiencing remarkable economic growth in the early nineteenth century, became dominant centers for commercial activity on Lake Champlain.

The clouds of war, however, were soon to engulf Lake Champlain once again in a rivalry with Britain over control of the strategic Champlain waterway. As a neutral party to the war between Great Britain and France, America experienced enormous growth in trade on the high seas by the turn of the century. The belligerents, Britain and France, soon began a series of actions that interfered with American ocean shipping. Although trouble with France on the Atlantic resulted in a virtual undeclared naval war for a few years, harassment by the British navy of American merchant vessels would have more lasting consequences. With the desertion of English sailors eager for the higher wages of the American merchant fleets, Britain stopped American ships and impressed seaman into the Royal Navy. The British, however, arrogantly forced many legitimate United States citizens (estimated at 6,000–9,000 men) into their navy. Provoked by the harassment, President Jefferson called for an embargo that essentially forbade all foreign trade. The disastrous effect of the embargo led to the passage of the Nonintercourse Act of 1809, which permitted trade with all nations except Britain and France. This legislation, upon expiration, was replaced by the Macon Bill of 1810, which reopened trade with the offending countries but promised reimposition of the nonintercourse on Britain or France if one should withdraw its restrictions on American shipping. Napoleon lifted his maritime restrictions on American shipping, prompting Madison's threatened renewal of the trade ban with Britain.

With no compromise on maritime restrictions by Britain, a 90-day embargo was signed into law in April 1812. Responding to increasing pressure as the altercations with Britain continued, Madison asked for a declaration of war in early June. Ironically, Britain had announced its intention to suspend the offending Orders in Council several days before the U.S. declaration, but without modern communication, America prepared for war. The reasons for war, however, were broader than simply Britain's maritime harassment. Support for the war was strongest from the West and South as frontiersmen were determined to defend and expand U.S. borders against Indians allied with Britain. Support of Indian claims by the British and weapons supplied to the Indians created a charged atmosphere on the frontier. The desire for annexation of Canada, an idea relatively dormant since the Revolution, became more prominent as expansionist motives flourished. The war, however, was not popular, especially in the New England states.

While British merchant ships were on their way to America with the good news of the end of the Orders in Council, Americans had begun planning their first inept advances into Canada. An immediate offer of peace by the British was rejected since it failed to make assurances that impressment of American seamen would end. Appointed brigadier general in April 1812, William Hull, a Revolutionary War officer and governor of the Michigan territory, advanced into Canada in July with more than 2,000 troops. Americans had thought that Canada could be taken easily, but unfolding events would soon dispel their optimism. After a series of defeats at the hands of a smaller force of British and Indians, Hull was forced back over the border resulting in the capture of Detroit by the British. Two subsequent invasion attempts by General Stephen Van Rensselaer and General Alexander Smyth at the Niagara River (near present-day Buffalo) were turned back, in part due to the refusal of the New York militia to cross the border and the incompetence of Smyth in the second attempt.

Sixty-two-year-old Major General Henry Dearborn, a veteran of Arnold's 1775 assault on Quebec and the Battle of Saratoga in 1777, was given the leadership of the army from Niagara to the east coast. In the fall of 1812 a large force of regular troops and militia was massed at Plattsburgh and Burlington, poised for an attack across the border. Dearborn had earlier accepted a proposed armistice from the governor-general of Canada, Sir George Prevost, based on the repeal of the Orders in Council, but the arrangement was denounced by Madison.[1]

At Plattsburgh, Dearborn met the new commander of the vessels on Lake Champlain, Lieutenant Thomas Macdonough. Macdonough, son of a Revolutionary War officer, entered the U.S. Navy as a midshipman at the age of 16. After distinguished service in a war with Tripoli and subsequent experience on navy frigates, Macdonough commanded a small flotilla of gunboats in Portland, Maine. In late September, Secretary of Navy Paul Hamilton ordered Macdonough to Lake Champlain to command the fleet there. After leaving Portland on October 5, the 28-year-old lieutenant arrived several days later in Burlington. The American plans for the war included control of the Great Lakes and Lake Champlain. Thus far in the war, the only success had been the remarkable naval victories on the high seas of the *Constitution*, *Wasp*, and *United States* over four British ships. The Americans hoped to duplicate these triumphs with competent, vigorous officers on the lakes.

The Champlain fleet was begun in 1809 with the construction of two small gunboats at Whitehall under the direction of navy Lieutenant Melancthon T. Woolsey, son of the New York Customs Collector. The 40-ton vessels, authorized by Jefferson in April 1808, were to check the smuggling with Canada along the Champlain route which remained rampant throughout the period despite the embargo.[2] When the war began, the two gunboats were at Basin Harbor in Vermont, one partially sunk. The two gunboats were placed under the command of Lieutenant Sidney Smith who managed to get the vessels back upon the lake. As the army mobilized on the northern frontier of the lake, six sloops were acquired by the War Department.[3] These vessels included the 65-foot *President*, 61-foot *Hunter*, and the 64-foot *Bull Dog* and three small sloops that remained as War Department transports after being found too old to carry guns.[4] The 75-ton *President*, built in Essex, New York, in 1812, was purchased from John Boynton while the smaller *Hunter*, built in 1809 in Burlington, was procured from Gideon King.[5]

The largest sloop, the *President*, was initially retained by Dearborn. The energetic Macdonough, however, soon sailed for Whitehall where he refitted the two sloops and gunboats. The *Hunter* was armed with two 12-pound cannon, four 6-pounders, and one 18-pounder on a pivot, while the *Bull Dog* had six 6-pounders and an 18-pounder on a pivot. Each gunboat carried one 12-pound cannon. Later, the *President* was given six 18-pound cannon and two 12-pounders after her hull was reinforced to support the heavier load. Sometime in late 1812, the *Hunter* was renamed the *Growler* and the *Bull Dog* the *Eagle* by Macdonough.[6]

Macdonough's fleet returned to the northern end of the lake in early November to escort the transports and bateaux, which were ferrying troops from Burlington to Plattsburgh, and to patrol the lake. After arriving back in Plattsburgh on November 10, General Dearborn began preparations for another invasion of Canada. An estimated 5,000–6,000 regulars and militia began their move toward the Canadian border on November 16. At the border, Dearborn finally assumed command of the army on November 19. At dawn, a detachment under Colonel Zebulon Pike (who had earlier discovered Pike's Peak) forded the Lacolle River about five miles from the border and besieged a blockhouse. Most of the Canadians and Indians in the blockhouse escaped, but a second American detachment mistakenly fired on Pike's men in a skirmish that lasted half an hour. Dispirited over the error and threatened by a British counterattack, the Americans, with their much larger army, hastily retreated to Plattsburgh.[7]

Macdonough sailed his fleet into Shelburne Bay for winter quarters and additional refitting but departed for a short time to marry Lucy Ann Shaler on December 12 in Middletown, Connecticut. Returning with his bride to Burlington, the young lieutenant skillfully began the task of refitting and enlarging the Champlain fleet. Fifteen carpenters arrived from New York in mid-February; supplies, carronades (short cannon firing heavy shot at close range), ammunition, and gun carriages arrived the following month. The *President* was fitted out with four more guns while the *Growler*, commanded by Lieutenant Sidney Smith, and the *Eagle*, under Sailing Master Jairus Loomis, had their quarter decks removed to increase their armament from seven to eleven guns.

Much of the military activity in 1813 focused on the Great Lakes region. The withdrawal of regular troops from Plattsburgh earlier in the year had left the defense of the border areas in the hands of militia. In one of the earliest actions of 1813, Brigadier General Zebulon Pike attacked and burned York (modern-day Toronto) but was killed in the raid when a magazine blew up. During the early part of 1813, a naval construction race occurred between the British and American navies which aimed at control of Lake Erie and Ontario. Commodore Isaac Chauncey had been sent to Sacketts Harbor, New York, in late 1812 to command the existing vessels and direct the building of a larger squadron. The Americans initially had relied on converted merchant schooners, as was the case on Lake Champlain, but the top-heavy vessels were no match for men-of-war. The Ontario schooners *Hamilton* and *Scourge* in Chauncey's fleet, for example, were blown over and quickly sank in a squall in 1813. At Kingston, Ontario, Captain James Lucas Yeo, who would later be the overall commander of the British fleet on Lake Champlain, engaged in a massive shipbuilding effort to gain absolute superiority over the American fleet. On Lake Erie, the navy sent Lieutenant Oliver Perry to present-day Erie, Pennsylvania, to command a fleet built by the New York shipwrights, Adam and Noah Brown.

On Lake Champlain in April 1813, the three largest vessels, the *President, Growler,* and *Eagle,* sailed for Plattsburgh. The American fleet at the time was far superior to the gunboats the British had stationed at Isle-aux-Noix on the Richelieu River, but in a surprisingly short time, the fleet would be lost. The flagship *President* was severely damaged when she ran aground at Plattsburgh, and the gunboats were temporarily taken out of service when one was blown over in a squall.

At the beginning of June, Macdonough ordered Lieutenant Smith with the *Growler* and Sailing Master Loomis of the *Eagle* to proceed north as far as the border to confine the British gunboats to the Canadian side of the boundary line. After a report that the British were planning to attack, Smith and Loomis were reinforced at one A.M. on June 3 by troops under Captain Oliver Herrick and Ensign Washington Dennison.[8] Deciding that their present position was unsafe, Smith at five A.M. ordered the two vessels further north across the border where he anchored below Hospital Island (about six miles from the border). Despite the assurances from Pilot Abraham Walters that the channel was wide enough, Smith immediately realized that his two sloops could no longer maneuver in the strong current and light south winds. Smith quickly ordered the vessels back to Lake Champlain. To their horror "At 15 minutes past six discovered four [actually three] of the enemy's gunboats in chase of us," Loomis later recorded in his report to Macdonough.[9]

The three British gunboats, which could readily maneuver upstream with oars, were sent by Major George Taylor from Isle-aux-Noix. At the same time, troops were landed on both banks of the Richelieu to complete the trap of the American vessels. By six-thirty A.M. the naval engagement began. The 24-pound cannon on the British gunboats soon began to inflict substantial damage to the sloops. The pilot of the *Eagle* was severely wounded early in the battle; a short time later, the guns of the *Eagle* were disabled temporarily due to damage to their breeching and ring bolts. While the vessels were engaged in their cannon duel, Taylor's troops onshore directed musket fire onto the open decks of the American sloops. A council of officers, hastily called by Smith, decided to retreat while still engaging the enemy gunboats, but the strategy was soon changed to a plan to board and capture the British gunboats. At eleven A.M., just before the attempt to board was to be made, a 24-pound ball smashed completely through the *Eagle's* hull exiting through three broken planks on the starboard side causing her to sink in shallow water. The British thereupon boarded and captured the *Eagle*. The *Growler* continued for 15 minutes longer, but with her ammunition nearly expended and her gaff boom (top spar) shot away, Smith had little choice but to surrender.

The *Growler* and *Eagle*, each with 11 guns, were brought to Isle-aux-Noix for repairs where they were subsequently renamed the *Broke* and *Shannon*. Despite the length of the battle, the casualties were light. Nearly 100 American officers and men were marched to Montreal and then sent to Quebec as prisoners. Some of the prisoners were later exchanged and returned to Lake Champlain. A court of inquiry held nearly two years later at Sackett's

Harbor found that the two vessels had been taken too far north of the border in a narrow channel where they could not maneuver. The court, however, ruled that Smith's general conduct on Lake Champlain was "correct and meritorious" and that the two sloops "were gallantly defended and that they were not surrendered until all further resistance had become vain."[10]

After the loss of the *Growler* and *Eagle*, Macdonough brought the *President* to Burlington on June 17. William Jones, Madison's new secretary of the navy, wrote to Macdonough with instructions to procure the necessary vessels, men, material, and munitions to regain control of the lake. Jones, a veteran of the Continental Navy during the Revolution with subsequent merchant shipping experience, was a successful and knowledgeable manager of navy resources, unlike his predecessor. The navy secretary authorized Macdonough "to purchase, arm, and equip in an effective manner two of the best sloops or other vessels to be procured on the lake."[11] He also gave Macdonough permission to build, if necessary, four or five barges or gunboats, 50 or 60 feet in length.

During the summer of 1813, Macdonough and his men were busy outfitting additional vessels at Burlington. The most significant purchase at the time was that of the 50-ton merchant sloop *Rising Sun* from Elijah Boynton, a vessel built in 1810 at Essex, New York, by Richard Eggleston.[12] The *Rising Sun* probably received its name from the widespread use of the rising sun symbol in early architectural designs on Essex buildings. The sloop was renamed *Preble* before she was ready for the open lake in late summer. Another sloop, the *Montgomery*, is presumed to have been purchased in the same period of time. Some historians, however, suggest that the *Montgomery* was one of the three transports retained by the army the previous fall and turned over to Macdonough in 1813.[13] Two smaller vessels, the *Francis* and *Wasp*, were rented and armed by Macdonough later in the summer of 1813. On July 24 the enterprising Macdonough was promoted to master commandant. Although referred to as "Commodore" Macdonough, that title was actually a courtesy and not a commissioned rank.

With the sudden increase in the size of the British navy at Isle-aux-Noix, requests for officers and seamen to man the new sloops were sent to the Royal Navy in Quebec. Following a letter from the governor-general of Canada, Sir George Prevost, that proposed a raid on public stores on Lake Champlain, Captain Thomas Everard of the sloop *Wasp*, volunteered for 14 days to lead the Lake Champlain raid with 50 of his crew and 30 crewman from transport vessels. Everard and his men soon proceeded to the Richlieu River aboard a steamboat. At the same time, Captain Daniel Pring was sent by Prevost from Kingston, Ontario, to command the fleet after Everard's departure. In late July Lieutenant Colonel John Murray, the commandant at St. Jean, was given instructions for the raid by the commander in lower Canada, Major General Roger Sheaffe: "The chief objective. . .will be to create a diversion" with the destruction of public buildings, military stores, and vessels, "but all private property. . .are to be respected."[14]

The expedition, led by Colonel Murray with 1,000 men aboard the *Broke*, *Shannon*, three gunboats, and more than 40 bateaux, departed on the morning of July 29 from Isle-aux-Noix. The naval command was temporarily under Captain Everard, the senior officer, while Captain Pring served as second-in-command. The British landed unopposed in Plattsburgh on the afternoon of July 31 since General Benjamin Mooers, head of the New York militia at Plattsburgh, had withdrawn with 300-350 men to a point three miles west of the town. Mooers, alerted on the 29th of the approach of the British fleet, called up the militia and futilely requested help from Major General Wade Hampton stationed at Burlington with army troops. After a contingent of prominent Plattsburgh residents pleaded "not to put up resistance, which could destroy the town," Mooers retreated because of an inadequate military force.[15] Before the British arrived, however, the Americans had removed supplies from the state arsenal.

With a map from a Canadian immigrant living in Plattsburgh, Murray's troops raided and burned the arsenal, a blockhouse, warehouses, and barracks. Despite Murray's orders not to plunder private property, houses were looted of their contents. On the morning of August 1, the British departed from Plattsburgh after taking a small commercial sloop, the *Burlington Packet*, and burning a storehouse on Cumberland Head. The expedition then split in two. Murray, with two gunboats and the bateaux, sailed north stopping at Point au Roche where more private property was compromised before reaching Maquam Bay, whereupon his troops marched to Swanton, Vermont. At Swanton, the British burned the barracks and hospital in addition to destroying bateaux and private property.

On August 2 "at half past two o'clock P.M. the two sloops [*Broke* and *Shannon*] and row galley. . .came within one and a half miles of the shore [Burlington] and commenced a cannonading which was returned by the vessels and battery and continued about twenty minutes," according to an eyewitness at Burlington.[16] The British vessels under Everard and Pring withdrew southward and Macdonough with several vessels later moved out of the harbor firing one gun in defiance. The British sailed for Shelburne Bay where they captured several small commercial vessels and at least one other vessel off Charlotte, Vermont. The biggest prize was the 50-ton sloop *Essex*, owned by Gideon King and Ezra Thurber, which was becalmed 15 miles south of Burlington following a delivery of 19 sailors to Macdonough. After being unable to tow the *Essex* back to the *Broke* and *Shannon*, the British boat crews burned the vessel.

Everard's report, written aboard the *Broke* on August 3, disclosed the observation of three sloops, two schooners, two one-gun scows, and a floating battery at Burlington: "Having captured and destroyed four Vessels, without any attempt on the part of the Enemy's armed Vessels to prevent it, and seeing no prospect of inducing him to quit his position, where it was impossible for us to attack him, I am now returning."[17]

On the morning of August 3, the British fleet was observed passing Cumberland Head with two captured sloops. At Chazy the fleet halted to plunder and expropriate stores and a schooner prior to withdrawing to Isle-aux-Noix. About the same time, a detachment from Murray's force marched to Champlain, New York, and burned two blockhouses, a storehouse, and barracks before returning to Isle-aux-Noix on August 4. The successful raid exposed the vulnerability of the towns along the upper lake, which in turn created incentives for a more substantial American fleet for the following year, as well as a need for more military cooperation between Vermont and New York.

With men borrowed from General Hampton's troops, Macdonough re-emerged on Lake Champlain in early September 1813 with the armed sloops *President*, *Preble*, *Montgomery*, *Francis*, *Wasp* and two gunboats. Two new 50-foot gunboats (presumably the *Alwyn* and *Ballard*) were launched a month later in October at Plattsburgh.[18] The four gunboats, mounting one long 18-pounder each, were named the *Ludlow*, *Wilmer*, *Alwyn*, and *Ballard*.[19] Macdonough now had the edge over the British fleet. When the American fleet approached the British squadron north of Plattsburgh in September, the latter retreated to the Richelieu River.

Further west on September 10, Commodore Oliver Perry, with a fleet superior to that of Captain Robert Barclay, decisively defeated the British in a bloody naval battle on Lake Erie. Perry's victory paved the way for General William Henry Harrison's defeat of the British at the Thames River battle in which the famous Indian leader Tecumseh was killed. The twin victories forced the British to evacuate Detroit. The military success, however, was not duplicated in the east. General James Wilkinson, veteran of the Champlain theater in the Revolution and implicated in the Aaron Burr conspiracy (1807), arrived at Sackett's Harbor in August to assume General Dearborn's command. Wilkinson's plans included a two-pronged attack from the east and west on Montreal. After a letter from Wilkinson, Secretary of War John Armstrong ordered General Hampton, then stationed at Burlington, to take Isle-aux-Noix and St. Jean in the Montreal operation. Subsequently, the Isle-aux-Noix plans were dropped when Macdonough, unwilling to risk his fleet again in the narrow channel of the Richelieu, declined Hampton's joint operation proposal. Macdonough, however, did agree to prevent the British fleet from entering Lake Champlain while Hampton's troops advanced northward.

After a rendezvous at Cumberland Head, Hampton's army proceeded west on the Great Chazy River in bateaux, arriving at the village of Champlain on September 20. In total, 4,000 troops, including cavalry and artillery, had reached Champlain by a land route. The army barely crossed the border when they turned back for lack of water. Hampton instead decided to try to reach Montreal by way of the Chateaugay River. Marching to present-day Chateaugay, New York, Hampton's army waited nearly a month for Wilkinson's advance from Sacket's Harbor. On October 21 Hampton's army finally moved toward Montreal. Hampton's regiments, however, were soon stopped by a much smaller force of French Canadian regulars, militia, and Indians on October 26 at a fortified position on the banks of the Chateaugay River. The Canadians successfully repelled the American army with heavy firing and repeated bugle charges in all directions, which duped Hampton into thinking the Canadians had a much larger force. The Americans retreated to Chateaugay and soon returned to Plattsburgh.

Wilkinson's force of 8,000 men similarly retreated on November 12, after a 2,000-man detachment was defeated along the St. Lawrence River by 800 British in a muddy field about 90 miles from Montreal (Battle of Chrysler Farm). Two American armies of more than 12,000 men had been turned back by fewer than 2,500 British and Canadian troops. The incompetent Wilkinson charged Hampton with the expedition's collapse ordering his arrest in Plattsburgh for "disobedience of orders."[20] Hampton escaped on the steamer *Vermont* to Whitehall and then to Washington, D.C. After an unauthorized advance into Canada that ended in another fiasco (Lacolle Mill) in early 1814, Wilkinson was himself called before a court of inquiry but exonerated in 1815.

On December 4, British vessels led by Captain Daniel Pring ventured as far as Cumberland Head where they burned an empty storehouse. Four American vessels under Lieutenant Stephen Cassin, second-in-command to Macdonough, unsuccessfully pursued Pring for three hours back to Canada. A little over two weeks later on December 21, Macdonough brought his fleet seven miles up Otter Creek to Vergennes for winter quarters.

Macdonough had chosen Vergennes for winter quarters in anticipation of a major shipbuilding program early in 1814. In addition to stands of oak and pine around Vergennes, the village's falls powered a host of industries, including eight forges, two furnaces, a wire factory, a rolling mill, and sawmills. Supplied by bog iron beds nearby, Vergennes had one of the most developed iron industries in the region. Vergennes not only had a secure lake access but was connected by roads to Burlington and Boston. Before moving to Vergennes, Macdonough had received instructions in December from Navy Secretary William Jones to make preparations for building 15 galleys on plans drawn of vessels under construction for Chesapeake Bay service: "The first class, 75 feet long and 15 wide, to carry a long 24 and a 42 pound carronade, row 40 oars."[21] On January 28 the navy secretary authorized Macdonough to build either 15 gunboats or a ship and three or four gunboats. Early in February Macdonough's suspicions were confirmed when an intelligence report suggested the British were building a large vessel of approximately 20 guns.

Macdonough decided upon a ship, whereupon the navy engaged Adam and Noah Brown of New York City, who had built Perry's successful fleet on Lake Erie the year before. Secretary Jones informed Macdonough on February 22 that a contract "to launch a Ship of 24 Guns, on Lake Champlain, in 60 days" had been signed with the firm on February 14.[22]

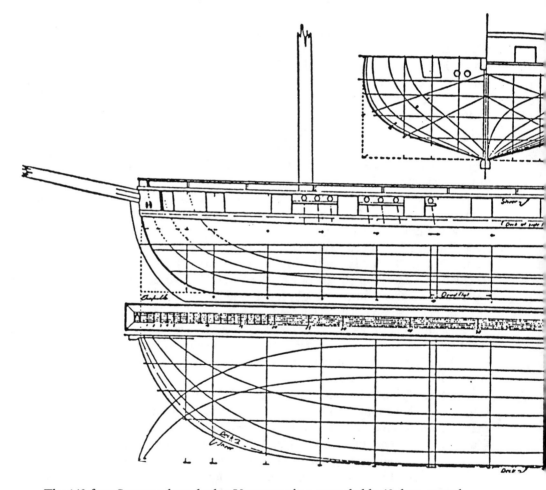

The 143-foot *Saratoga*, launched at Vergennes in a remarkable 40 days, served as the flagship of the American fleet at the Plattsburgh Bay engagement.

In addition, Jones wrote in the same letter that "Lt. Cassin says there is a New Boat 120 feet long, near Vergennes, intended for a Steam Boat; if she will answer, you are authorized to purchase her for use of the Navy."[23] By late February Noah Brown and his shipwrights had arrived in Vergennes and soon began cutting timber and constructing a makeshift shipyard. Early in March the keel of a 26-gun ship had been laid and the construction of five row galleys (also referred to as gunboats) had begun. In the end, six 70-ton row galleys with lengths of 75 feet and widths of 15 feet were built. The galleys, carrying two masts with triangular sails and 40 oars each, mounted one 24-pound cannon and one 18-pounder. The galleys, completed by late April, were named the *Allen, Burrows, Borer, Nettle, Viper,* and *Centipede.*[24]

In an amazing 40 days, the 26-gun ship with a length of 143 feet and width of 36 feet was launched at Vergennes on April 11. Originally, Macdonough named the vessel *Jones* but later changed it to the *Saratoga* upon learning that a new American brig on Lake Ontario

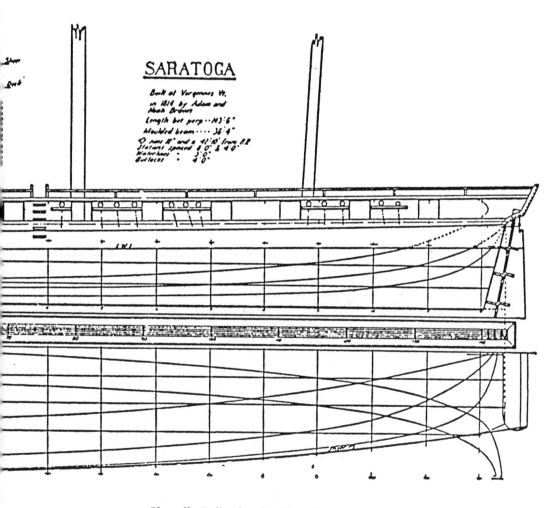

Chapelle Collection (Smithsonian Institution)

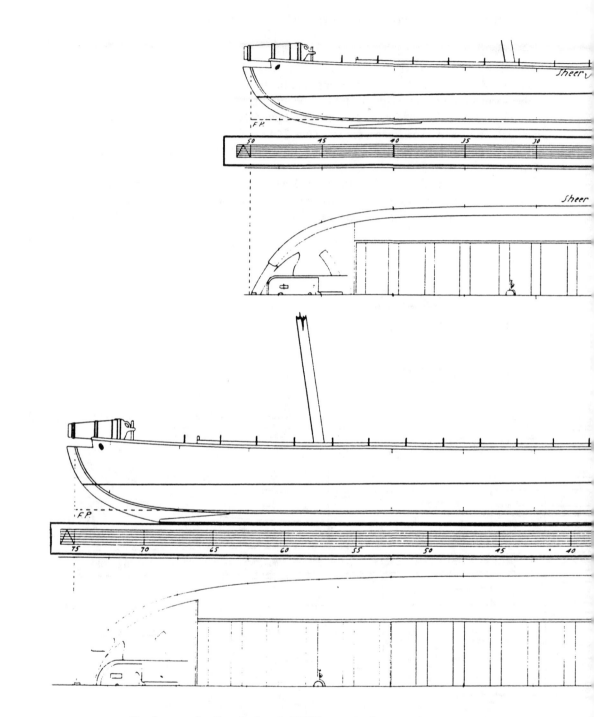

Gunboat and galley designs by William Doughty, naval contractor,
intended for use on Lake Champlain

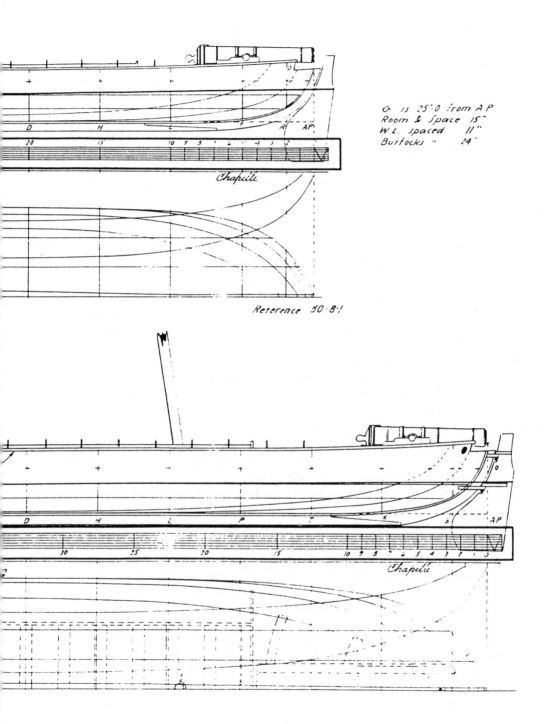

Chapelle Collection. (Smithsonian Institution)

had the same name.[25] After the launch of the *Jones/Saratoga*, Macdonough and Brown examined the hull of the unfinished steamboat owned by the Lake Champlain Steam-boat Company which Secretary Jones had suggested buying in his February 22 letter. Work had continued on the vessel by the steamboat company during the interim, but the company was apparently eager to sell the vessel. The governor of New York, after being informed of the company's desire to sell the vessel to the government, wrote a detailed letter to Secretary Jones recommending the purchase of the vessel at $15,000–$17,000 and its use as a steam-powered war vessel.[26] Noah Brown, however, appraised the empty hull at $5,000. Macdonough, who felt steamboat machinery was unreliable after observing the *Vermont* on Lake Champlain, decided with Brown to convert the vessel to a schooner. The company wanted $22,000 for the vessel and sent Jahaziel Sherman, who had supervised the building of the hull as the steamer's future captain, to Washington, D.C., where he negotiated a price of $12,000 with Secretary Jones.[27]

The new schooner, named *Ticonderoga* by Macdonough, was launched on May 12. The 120-foot vessel with a beam of approximately 26 feet was soon fitted, rigged, and mounted with 17 guns. The guns were taken from the two small sloops, *Francis* and *Wasp*, and the vessels were used for transports before being returned to their owners. For use on the *Ticonderoga*, Macdonough also removed guns, at least temporarily, from "the four old Gallies; two of which are very rotten, as they were build in 1808 [1809]."[28] Macdonough's entry "four old Gallies" is somewhat puzzling since two of the smaller galleys were supposedly constructed in 1813.

On May 9, 1814, Captain Daniel Pring, aboard the new 16-gun, 82-foot brig *Linnet*, "with the *Chubb* and *Finch* [previously the sloops *Broke* and *Shannon*, renamed for the fourth time], [sloop] Canada, the Flotilla of Gun Boats, a Tender. . .two merchant vessels," was dispatched to attack the American fleet at Otter Creek or block the channel.[29] The flotilla of gunboats consisted of seven or eight row galleys; one of the merchant sloops included the *Icicle*. While the purpose of the raid was to attack the American fleet before it could be completed, the chief benefit was to gain detailed information on the American vessels from two prisoners captured in a small boat on the open lake.

Hampered by southerly winds, Pring's flotilla did not appear at the mouth of Otter Creek until daybreak of May 14. Several days earlier, Major General George Izard at Plattsburgh had informed Brigadier General Alexander Macomb, stationed in Burlington, of the British approach. Fifty light artillery troops were sent under Captain Arthur Thornton from Burlington to man a battery, consisting of seven 12-pound cannon on ship carriages, mounted behind earthworks at the mouth of Otter Creek. Lieutenant Stephen Cassin with a detachment of sailors was also dispatched to assist Thornton's troops.

The engagement on May 14 lasted less than two hours causing little damage to either side. Without a sufficient landing force, Pring withdrew his forces from the mouth of Otter Creek. Macdonough brought almost all of the vessels to the mouth of the creek including the *Saratoga*, but the ships reached the site of the engagement after the British had departed. Macdonough reported the action immediately to the secretary of war, describing an attack of "One hour & a half" on the battery by eight galleys and a "Bomb" vessel along with the "new Brig, with several other Gallies, & four Sloops, were within 2-1/2 miles of the Point."[30] Three of the British galleys ascended the Bouquet River after the Otter Creek engagement to raid government flour stored in a gristmill at the falls (One galley had also chased a small boat up the Bouquet before the Otter Creek battle). Brigadier General Daniel Wright described the militia's fire from the banks of the Bouquet upon one of the galleys which was "so disabled as to oblige them to hoist a flag of distress when a sloop came to their assistance and towed her off."[31] The result of Pring's raid was another escalation of the naval race on Lake Champlain. With the detailed information on the entire American fleet, including the specifics on the 26-gun *Saratoga* from the two prisoners, Britain would later make plans for the largest warship to ever sail Lake Champlain.

Fort Cassin at the mouth of Otter Creek was the site of the May 14, 1814, battle with the British fleet under Captain Daniel Pring. Photo by the author.

The American fleet finally left Otter Creek on May 26. Macdonough's vessels now included the *Saratoga*, *Ticonderoga*, *Preble*, *President*, and *Montgomery*, and the six new galleys: *Allen*, *Borer*, *Burrows*, *Centipede*, *Nettle*, and *Viper*. The four smaller gunboats, temporarily disarmed, would wait until more crews and cannon were procured. The problem of recruiting had delayed the embarkation of the fleet and would continue to hamper the American navy on Lake Champlain throughout the summer of 1814. Lake service was disdained by most trained seamen, forcing Macdonough to request army troops. Several hundred soldiers, after repeated requests, were finally sent to Vergennes, which allowed the fleet to achieve enough manpower to patrol the lake by the end of May.

Macdonough reached Plattsburgh on May 29, whereupon he reported to the navy secretary that the *Saratoga* was a "fine ship" as was the *Ticonderoga* and the galleys were "also remarkably fine vessels."[32] The American fleet spent the next few days escorting transports and bateaux loaded with troops from Burlington.* The American fleet later moved northward to Point au Fer, which forced the British squadron a mile into the Richelieu River to a position near Ash Island. Early in June, Macdonough reported to Navy Secretary Jones that the British had laid the keel for a ship bigger than the *Saratoga*. A string of letters ensued from the Champlain commandant pleading for orders from Jones to build a new 18-gun brig. The navy secretary, having trouble meeting the debts incurred for the *Saratoga, Ticonderoga*, and galleys, failed to respond to Macdonough's requests for the new ship. President James Madison, not willing to chance the loss of Lake Champlain, overruled Jones' decision in late June for the only time during the war. In early July, Jones authorized Adam and Noah Brown to build a brig of 18 guns immediately at Lake Champlain. Macdonough, however, first learned of the decision to build the brig when Adam Brown arrived at the *Saratoga* on July 18 at Point au Fer to discuss the plans for the vessel.[34]

While the shipbuilding race proceeded at Isle-aux-Noix and Vergennes, the problem of smuggling along the Lake Champlain corridor to Canada continued. From the Jefferson administration through Madison's war years, commercial relations with Canada along Lake Champlain continued despite prohibitions. Even Gideon King, who sold vessels to the American forces, had been characterized as a "notorious smuggler" from Burlington.[35] Since the British paid more for cattle, Americans simply drove cattle (in one case 130 yoke of oxen were used to haul British military stores) across the border.[36] On July 31 General George Izard reported to Secretary of War Armstrong that revenue officers were unable to stop the outrageous smuggling: "on the eastern side of Lake Champlain. . .supplies of cattle...are pouring into Canada. Like herds of buffaloes they press through the forest, making paths for themselves."[37]

Governor-General Prevost had plans in August 1814 for the northern invasion of Lake Champlain but resolved not to take offensive action on the Vermont side of the lake. Prevost was well aware of the mixed political role that Vermont had played in the last war. As late as 1813, Governor Martin Chittenden prohibited Vermont militia from serving on the New York side of Lake Champlain. In his August 5 letter to the British colonial secretary of state, Lord Bathurst, Prevost suggested that Vermont displayed "a decided opposition to the war. . .I mean for the present to confine myself in any offensive Operations which may take place to the west side of Lake Champlain."[38] Three weeks later on August 27, Prevost's letter to Bathurst disclosed that "Two thirds of the army are supplied wih beef by American contractors, principally of Vermont and New York."[39]

Americans were even smuggling naval supplies to the British shipyards at Isle-aux-Noix. Sailing Master Elie Vallette in the galley *Burrows* destroyed two spars, 80 and 85 feet long, being towed to the border. A little more than a week later Midshipman Joel Abbot in a covert operation destroyed four more spars, resembling a mainmast and three topmasts, four miles over the border. The smugglers never gave up; on July 23 two American galleys intercepted a large raft loaded with planks, spars, and 27 barrels of tar a mile from the border.[40]

Although bottled up in the Richelieu River, the British worked furiously to finish a fleet they hoped would command the lake. In anticipation of the larger fleet, Captain Peter Fisher had been appointed commander of the British naval fleet on Lake Champlain in June. Pring,

---

* Richard Eggleston, a shipbuilder at Essex, New York, built over 250 bateaux for the American army during the war.[33]

however, remained commander of the brig *Linnet*. The fleet consisted of the 60-foot sloop *Chubb* with 11 guns, the 58-foot sloop *Finch* also with 11 guns, and 12 galleys or gunboats, mounting either one or two cannon ranging from 18 to 32 pounds, named *Sir James Yeo, Sir George Prevost, Sir Sidney Beckwith, Brock, Murray, Wellington, Tecumseh, Drummond, Simcoe, Marshal Beresford, Popham,* and *Blucher*.[41]

The British pinned their hopes for naval supremacy on one huge ship. The vessel, hastily built under the direction of William Simons at Isle-aux-Noix, would mount 36 guns. The 831-ton, squared-rigged, three-masted ship with a length of 146 feet on the gundeck and a 36-foot beam with two gun decks in the bow and stern was the largest fighting vessel ever used on the lake.[42] Launched on August 25, the frigate would be named *Confiance* after a French ship which Commodore Sir James Lucas Yeo had captured and commanded early in his naval career.[43] Yeo had overall naval command on the Great Lakes and Lake Champlain. Short of men and fittings since Yeo had channeled much of the naval stores to Kingston on Lake Ontario for his own shipbuilding needs, the *Confiance* would require another 17 days to complete.

At the American shipyard at Vergennes, Adam Brown and his carpenters launched the new brig on August 11 in a record 19 days following the laying of her keel. It would take another two weeks, however, to finish the 120-foot brig. Just before the vessel's completion, Master Commandant Robert Henley, an ambitious officer with previous experience on the *Constellation* during the undeclared naval war with France, arrived with an appointment from Secretary Jones to command the new brig. Henley had commanded a gunboat division only briefly during an engagement in 1813 and was anxious to distinguish himself in the war. The independent and self-important 31-year-old officer immediately wrote directly to the secretary of navy with his name for the brig, the *Surprise*.[44] Macdonough, however, had written to Secretary Jones in early August asking his suggestion for a name "for the Brig or may I call her the Eagle."[45] On the morning of August 27, fresh southerly breezes snapped the new white sails of the *Surprise* as the brig reached Macdonough's anchorage near the Canadian border. The American fleet was now complete mounting 92 cannon, which included six on the sloop *Montgomery* and one gun each on the four older gunboats. The sloops *President* and *Montgomery*, former merchant sloops, were converted to transports and were no longer part of the war squadron.

The American fleet began training with the expectation of a strong naval force leading an invasion of British troops into the Champlain Valley. In late July and early August, General Prevost noted the arrival of brigades from the Duke of Wellington's army, which had just defeated Napoleon's best troops in the Peninsular War (1809-1814). Two huge naval convoys of 60 transports, loaded with Europe's best troops, sailed directly from France to Canada. At the end of August, more than 13,000 troops had been transferred from Europe. This was in addition to the thousands of regulars and militia already in Canada.

The traditional interpretation of the British strategy, still reflected in some modern histories of the war, suggested that the British planned to move through Lake Champlain and advance south along the Hudson River, thus severing the New England states from the rest of the country.[46] Soon after the battle at Plattsburgh, Governor Daniel Tompkins presented this interpretation to the New York legislature: "One great object...was to penetrate. . .Lake Champlain and the Hudson, and, by a simultaneous attack with his maritime force on New York, to form a junction which should sever the communication of the states."[47] Prevost's instructions from Lord Bathurst on June 3, however, were only to establish a foothold at Lake Champlain: "any advanced position on that part of your frontier which extends towards Lake Champlain, the occupation of which would materially tend to the security of the Province," but not to risk "being cut off by too extended a line of advance."[48] A dispatch on August 5 by Prevost lamented the lack of progress of the fleets which were to cooperate with "the occupation of Plattsburg."[49] After the battle Prevost described his intentions "to establish the Army at Plattsburg and to detach from thence a Brigade for the destruction of Vergennes & its Naval establishment."[50]

In early August of 1814, commissioners from Great Britain and the United States met at Ghent, Belgium, to negotiate an end to the war. The initial claims were unrealistic in light of the final settlement, but at the time at least some were plausible given the military build-up. The British demanded land cessions in the upper part of Maine, west of the Great Lakes, the Champlain Valley, and land between the Ohio River and the Great Lakes. The Americans, not to be outdone, wanted the cession of Canada along with solutions to issues surrounding violations of American rights on the high seas. For the British to support their land claims, there would be a need to occupy some of the regions demanded.

The American operations in 1814 were generally more successful with more competent generals, but the news was not all good. In early July tough American troops under Generals Jacob Brown and Winfield Scott were successful in several fierce battles on the Niagara frontier but withdrew to Fort Erie. As the main army was unloading in Canada, a British diversionary force under Vice Admiral Alexander Cochrane and Rear Admiral George Cockburn roamed the American seaboard with troops of General Robert Ross to destroy any vulnerable cities on the coast. After a brief skirmish, the militia protecting Washington, D.C., ran in the face of Ross's experienced regulars. The British burned the city and withdrew with plans to raid Baltimore.

In the northern theater, the continuing naval construction race on Lake Ontario between Commodores Yeo at Kingston and Chauncey at Sackett's Harbor left the main British thrust into America at Lake Champlain. Major General George Izard, a competent officer who had served the year earlier under Hampton, was assigned the main command of the American army at Plattsburgh. Brigadier General Alexander Macomb, a 32-year-old professional soldier who had graduated from West Point, was assigned by Izard to Burlington to head several regiments. In August Izard commanded a force of 5,100 men, including Macomb's regiments brought from Burlington. Six hundred troops were assigned to the construction of forts at Plattsburgh and Cumberland Head, while 4,500 were camped at Chazy and Champlain. On July 19, thinking the action would be on the Niagara frontier, Izard asked for a transfer to the west. Once aware of Prevost's troop increases, Izard wrote back to Secretary of War Armstrong to rescind his request. By then, however, Armstrong had already made the decision that it would be good policy to "carry the war as far westward as possible while we have ascendency on the Lakes."[51] Izard warned Armstrong that he would go, "but I shall do. . .with the certainty that everything in this vicinity. . .will in less than three days after my departure be in the possession of the enemy."[52] Izard departed with several thousand troops at the end of August remaining at Lake George for two days hoping for a change of orders. His march to the Lake Ontario frontier was largely a wasted effort. Armstrong, after the burning of Washington, was forced to resign on September 3.

After the last of Izard's troops left on August 29, Macomb had approximately 1,500 effective regular troops left with another 900 sick from dysentery and typhus. Two days after Izard's main army had departed, the first elements of the British invasion crossed the border into New York. Macomb immediately called on Major General Benjamin Mooers of the New York militia and Governor Chittenden of Vermont for militia. Mooers, on his own authority, called out the militia from the counties of Clinton, Essex, and Franklin while Chittenden, following the earlier precept that Vermont militia would not serve outside her borders, appealed for volunteers. About 700 New York militia from the three counties marched immediately to Plattsburgh while the residents fled in panic with word of the British approach. Just before Prevost's army reached Plattsburgh, Macomb had assembled only 3,400 troops, but 1,400 were sick and 250 were serving on Macdonough's fleet; his orders to the troops declared "The eyes of America are on us. . .Fortune always follows the brave."[53] By the time the battle began on September 11, 2,500 Vermont volunteers under General Samuel Strong had arrived in New York from towns across Vermont. Luckily for the Americans, the delay in bringing the British fleet to Plattsburgh caused Prevost to postpone his attack on the American position. Three redoubts or forts in Plattsburgh — Fort Scott, Fort Brown, and Fort Moreau — were strengthened in the meantime.

Prevost's army, consisting of thousands of veterans of the Napoleonic Wars, did not reach the Plattsburgh area until September 6. While contemporary reports and subsequent writers put the size of Prevost's army at Plattsburgh as high as 14,000 men, only 8,200 reached Plattsburgh with 2,100 troops at outposts between the town and the Canadian border.[54] When the British troops reached Dead Creek in Plattsburgh on the morning of the 6th, the American galleys, which had been stationed there the day before, opened fire on the invaders. The British soon brought up some of their artillery to bear on the American vessels. Macdonough dispatched Lieutenant Silas Duncan in the *Saratoga*'s gig (launch) to order the galleys back. The unfortunate Duncan was severely wounded (later losing his right arm) but still delivered his orders. Most of the town fell to the British in one day, but the Americans sabotaged roads and removed planks from the bridges across the Saranac River. Macomb, whose men occupied the three forts south of the Saranac River, conspicuously paraded his troops to exaggerate his numbers and planted false information of additional troops nearby for British consumption.[55] With fewer than one-third the troops (over 700 American sick had been sent to Crab Island), Macomb faced the best European army.

Oftentimes, the chronicle of the battle of Plattsburgh neglects the vital role played by General Alexander Macomb. Had he accepted the counsel of some of his officers to abandon the forts and retreat southward in the face of an overwhelming British army, the outcome of the naval engagement may have been different. With British control of the cannon at the forts, Macdonough's strategy based on an anchorage in Plattsburgh Bay could have been compromised. But Macomb was unequivocal in making a stand at the forts.

On September 1, after receiving an intelligence report and a suggestion from General Macomb, Macdonough moved his fleet from a position north of Cumberland Head to Plattsburgh Bay. Macdonough's strategy for engaging the British had striking similarities to that of Benedict Arnold at Valcour Bay in 1776. A northern wind that would carry the British to Plattsburgh would also make it difficult for the enemy fleet to position itself in the bay. A close-range battle in the bay would permit the American fleet to use its carronades, more effective at shorter distances, than would a more distant battle on the open lake where the British had superiority in long-range guns. By September both sides had fairly accurate intelligence of the composition of each other's fleets. Macdonough moved his fleet to a position, presumably out of range of the shore batteries, about 100 yards off Cumberland Head where the vessels, in a north-south line, were set in an intricate anchoring system with spring lines. With two anchors dropped on each side of the bow and the stern anchored, the vessels could be turned end to end to bring the fresh guns from the opposite side of the ship to bear on the enemy should the guns on the original side become disabled.

Macdonough's fleet included the *Saratoga*, *Ticonderoga*, *Surprise*, *Preble* and ten galleys/gunboats. The sloops *President* and *Montgomery* had been assigned to transport duty with the latter vessel transferring some of its crew to the undermanned brig on September 2. Four days later, the brig *Surprise* (a name that Macdonough personally had never used) was redesignated the *Eagle*.[56] In all probability, Macdonough made the decision himself to change the name from Master Commandant Henley's designation to his original selection. Joseph Smith, the first lieutenant of the short-handed *Eagle*, approached General Macomb on September 7 with a note from Macdonough requesting more troops. When Macomb refused, the enterprising lieutenant asked for Macomb's prisoners. Forty prisoners (all soldiers) in ball and chain were freed and taken aboard the *Eagle* for a regimen of gun training. A few days later, six musicians in the army band (one brought along his wife) were recruited as crew members aboard the *Eagle*. From September 7 through 11, the two armies and Macdonough's navy awaited the arrival of the British fleet at Plattsburgh Bay.

The flagship of the British fleet, the 36-gun *Confiance*, was still being completed in early September when Commodore Yeo sent Captain George Downie from Lake Ontario to command the ship and the British fleet. Downie, unfamiliar with Lake Champlain and his new crews, arrived at the Isle-aux-Noix shipyard on September 1 but did not assume command until the 3rd.[57] On the same day, Captain Daniel Pring with the *Linnet* sailed with the galleys to protect the advancing British army on the New York shore. Pring remained at Isle La Motte until the rest of the fleet was ready to sail. With pressure from Prevost to sail, Downie departed from Isle-aux-Noix with the *Confiance* unfinished on September 7. After temporarily grounding the vessel in the river, Downie moved as far as Ash Island where he was joined by Pring with the *Linnet*.

On the 8th at Point au Fer, Downie indignantly answered Prevost's letter, written earlier in the day, which had again pressed for the arrival of the *Confiance*: "I stated to you that this Ship was not ready. She is not ready now, and, until she is ready, it is my duty not to hazard the Squadron before an Enemy who will be superior in Force."[58] Downie anchored off the Little Chazy River opposite Isle La Motte where finishing work continued and crews had their first chance at gun practice. Downie informed Prevost of his intention to depart at midnight on September 10, but unfavorable winds delayed the departure until the early morning hours of the 11th.

The artificers and riggers left the vessel only a few hours before the battle. Prevost and Downie agreed upon a scaling of guns (shooting cannon without a ball) as a signal to prepare for a joint land and naval assault on the American positions. At quarter past five in the morning, the British fleet fired their blank shots just north of Cumberland Head.[59] All the commanding officers were shortly called by Downie aboard the *Confiance* for directions as to which American vessels they would each engage. "Having approached within a League of Cumberland Head the Enemys Mast Heads were seen over the Land," recounted First Lieutenant James Robertson of the *Confiance*, "Captain Downie accompanied by the Master went in his Gig [small boat] to reconnoitre their position."[60] After inspecting the American position, Downie returned in his boat to the fleet with final instructions for the officers and crews. The *Linnet*, supported by the *Chubb*, was to attack the *Eagle*; the

Confiance would fire her starboard guns into the *Eagle* and her port battery into the *Saratoga*; the galleys were to fire and board the *Ticonderoga*; and the *Finch* would support the galleys and later engage the *Preble*. The supply sloop *Icicle* would remain in the distance.

The British fleet moved into Plattsburgh Bay after eight o'clock on the morning of the 11th (there are slight differences in the recorded time of the battle by original participants).[61] The two fleets were nearly evenly matched although the British vessels, primarily the *Confiance*, had greater weight in long-distance cannon. Both fleets had a hodgepodge of crews consisting of trained seamen and inexperienced land troops. None of the crews, however, were prepared for the devastating savagery of the ensuing battle. The British commander decided to engage Macdonough on the latter's pre-arranged position in the bay rather than try to fight at a distance on the open lake. Although pressure from Prevost played a role in Downie's decision to immediately engage, the British naval commander was overconfident of his frigate's ability to destroy the American fleet. Two days before the engagement, Prevost had reported to Downie that the American fleet was "insufficiently manned" and had staffed the new brig *Eagle* with prisoners. Downie was said to have felt that the *Confiance* alone was a match for the whole American fleet.[62]

When the British sailed closer, the American fleet was in a line from north to south with the *Eagle* the farthest north, adjacent to the *Saratoga*, *Ticonderoga*, and the *Preble*. The six larger American galleys and four smaller gunboats were stationed in four divisions west of the larger ships (one division of three galleys was northwest of the *Eagle*'s position). On the shores of Cumberland Head, anxious residents viewed the scene as history was about to unfold. Similarly, British and Canadian civilians including women watched the battle from a small vessel at a safe distance, confident of a British victory.[63] Meanwhile, the prearranged, coordinated attack on land got off to a late start. The British troops were ordered by Prevost to make breakfast as the British fleet approached Plattsburgh Bay.[64] Although the British batteries opened on the American forts as the naval engagement commenced around nine o'clock, the orders to the British army to ford the Saranac River did not come until an hour later.

The British fleet, tacking against the light northerly breeze, had difficulty reaching its planned positions in the bay. Macdonough and his men, amid the anxiety and grim expectations, knelt on the deck of the *Saratoga* for a brief prayer before the onslaught began. As the *Confiance* maneuvered into position, Master Commandant Robert Henley directed a hasty broadside from his long 18-pound cannon, but the shots fell short of the British flagship. When the *Linnet* sailed past the *Saratoga* on her way to a position to engage the *Eagle*, a broadside aimed at Macdonough's ship fell short, except for a shot that struck a hen coop aboard the American flagship. The bird, a gamecock kept by the seamen, jumped on a gun-slide, flapped his wings and crowed lustily and defiantly, according to eyewitnesses.[65] The *Saratoga*'s crew sent up a cheer, regarding the incident as a good omen. Soon afterward, Macdonough fired a single gun from the *Saratoga* as a signal to his fleet to begin fire on the enemy. The *Confiance* was immediately hit with a piercing fire that shot away two anchors on her port bow. Without firing a shot, Downie continued his maneuvering but prematurely anchored his vessel at a distance from Macdonough's flagship. Once in place, a double-shotted broadside from the *Confiance* ripped through the decks of the *Saratoga* instantly killing or wounding 40 of her crew. The blast shook the *Saratoga* so violently that half the crew was flattened.

ABOVE. "The Plight of the English Flagship" *Confiance* from *Naval Action of the War of 1812* by James Barnes, 1896.

BELOW. "MacDonough's Victory on Lake Champlain," painting by H. Reinagle, engraved by Benjamin Tanner. E. Newbold Smith Collection. (Philadelphia Maritime Museum)

RIGHT. Plattsburgh Bay from the *Dedication of the Thomas Macdonough Memorial*, 1926.

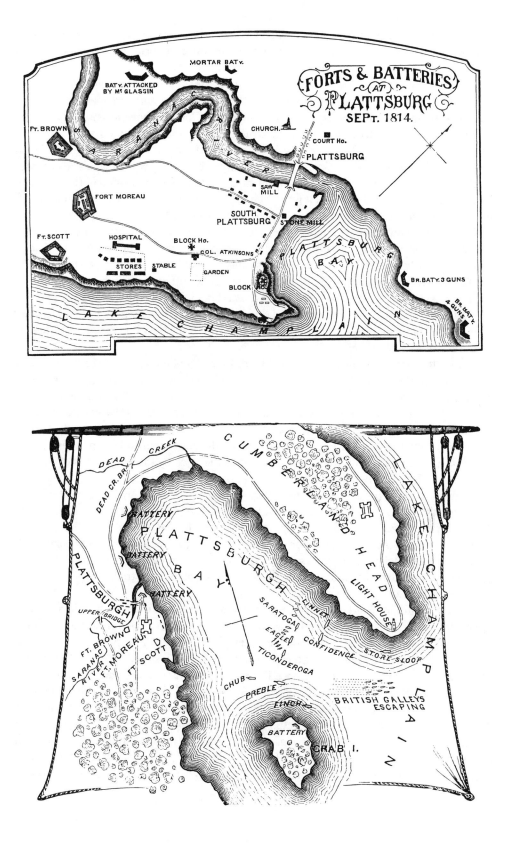

By now nearly all the vessels were engaged in the battle. The *Linnet,* just to the northeast of the *Eagle,* emitted a raking fire upon the bow of the American brig while the sloop *Chubb* fired on the *Eagle's* stern. Four British galleys and the *Finch* engaged the *Preble* and *Ticonderoga.* The six American galleys and four gunboats supported the *Eagle* and *Saratoga* on the northern end of the American line and the *Ticonderoga* and *Preble* at the southern end. Fifteen minutes after the action had commenced, Captain Downie was killed almost instantly when a shot from the *Saratoga* struck a 24-pound cannon on the *Confiance,* throwing it completely off its carriage into the British commander's groin. The fallen commander had no part of his skin broken; the only visible injury was a black streak across his chest. His watch had been flattened upon impact with its hands pointed to the hour and minute when he received the fatal injury.[66] The cannon that killed Downie remains (1989) at the U.S. Naval Academy at Annapolis on the lawn next to Macdonough Hall.

Only 15-20 minutes into the action, the cutter *Chubb,* commanded by Lieutenant James McGhie, had her cables, bowsprit, sails, yards, and main boom shot away. The *Chubb* drifted helplessly through the American lines while most of her crew remained below deck. Lieutenant McGhie, after two of his finger tips were shot off and receiving a wound to his thigh from a splinter, went below deck where he was later joined by ten soldiers and marines who left their stations. With five dead and three times that number wounded, only six men were left on the deck of the vessel when McGhie ordered Midshipman James Bodell to strike the colors and surrender.[67]

From a vantage point on Cumberland Head, Julius Hubbell observed the thunder and destruction on the water: "The firing was terrific, fairly shaking the ground, and so rapid that it seemed to be one continuous roar, intermingled with spiteful flashing from the mouths of the guns, and dense clouds of smoke soon hung over the two fleets."[68] Macdonough, while sighting cannon on the *Saratoga,* was knocked senseless onto the deck when a cannonball cut the spanker boom in two, causing the heavy spar to fall upon him. As he regained his composure, he was again knocked to the deck by the flying head of his own gun captain which had been severed by a cannonball.[69]

At the southern end of the line, the sloop *Preble,* commanded by Lieutenant Charles Budd, and the schooner *Ticonderoga,* under Lieutenant Stephen Cassin, were engaged with the British cutter *Finch* and four galleys. Actually, only four British galleys, the *Marshall Beresford, Murray, Popham,* and perhaps the *Blucher* (or *Wellington*) were vigorously engaged in the attack at the southern end of the line.[70] Most of the galleys, largely manned by French Canadian militia who spoke no English, were out of range to the leeward off Crab Island during much of the engagement.[71]

The *Finch* initially fired on the *Ticonderoga,* but soon acting Lieutenant William Hicks turned the cutter's guns on the *Preble* as did some of the galleys. After an hour into the battle, to the cheer of the British crew, "the Enemy's Sloop [*Preble*] slip her cable and haul down her Colours to me."[72] Lieutenant Budd moved the sloop to the safety of the Plattsburgh shoreline. Lieutenant James Robertson, who assumed command of the *Confiance* when Captain Downie was killed, also observed the *Preble* "retire in shore with her colours struck, where however she afterwards rehoisted them."[73] After the *Preble* left, the fire of the galleys and *Finch* was directed at the *Ticonderoga.* Although the British galley crews had hoped to board the *Ticonderoga,* the schooner successfully fought off their attackers but suffered six men killed and six wounded. Most of the crews of the American galleys and gunboats, similar to their British counterparts, were reluctant to play an aggressive role during the battle. The 75-foot American galley *Borer*, commanded by Midshipman Conover, advanced to the bow of the *Ticonderoga* but was hit directly, killing three crew members and wounding one. Seven of the ten American vessels had no casualties at all, while the *Centipede* and the smaller *Wilmer* suffered one injured crew member each. The low casualties were also the result of the vessels' small size and height, which made them less important targets at the northern end of the line where the fire of *Linnet* and *Confiance* focused on the *Eagle* and *Saratoga*.

"Battle of Plattsburgh Bay," lithograph, *American Naval Broadsides*,
E. Newbold Smith Collection. (Philadelphia Maritime Museum)

Following a crippling broadside from the *Ticonderoga*, the *Finch*, with three and a half feet of water in her hold and the main boom, mast, and rigging severely damaged, drifted out of control toward Crab Island. The *Finch* ran aground on a reef on the northeast side of the island whereupon two cannon, manned by convalescing soldiers, fired on the striken cutter. The *Finch* returned the fire, forcing the gunners to seek cover. Hicks "then order'd four Eighteen Pound Carronades to be hove overboard but without any Effect to her."[74] The vessel could not be refloated but did not strike her colors until the *Confiance* surrendered and the galleys had fled.[75]

In the heat of the battle between the *Saratoga* and *Confiance*, confusion reigned as the men struggled in the heat and blood to cripple each other's flagships. The Americans overloaded cannonades, often cramming them with shot as far as the muzzle. The confusion may have been worse on board the *Confiance*. After the battle, one cannon was found to have been loaded with two balls but no powder; another had been loaded without shot, and a third had the wad and cartridge loaded in reverse order. The inexperienced crew on the British frigate often failed to push in the quoin or gun-wedge under the rear of the cannon which loosened after each shot. The muzzle of the gun would thus be raised higher and higher causing the shots to fly over the heads of the crew on the *Saratoga* and into the lower rigging and hammocks.

At 10:30 the brig *Eagle* had her starboard anchor spring shot away causing the vessel to turn in a direction so that her remaining guns were no longer effective. By then the dead on her deck included two of the musicians recruited at the last minute for the engagement. When the wife of one of the army musicians replaced the powder boy who had been killed, she had to step over the dead on the bloody deck, one of whom she recognized as her husband.[76]

With the guns of the *Eagle* serving no purpose, Henley promptly made the decision to leave his station: "I ordered the cable cut and cast the brig, taking an advantageous position a little south of the *Saratoga*."[77] The *Eagle* anchored between the *Saratoga* and *Ticonderoga*, leaving the flagship endangered by the *Linnet*'s guns. Although Macdonough was restrained in his criticism of Henley, he noted in his report two days later to Navy Secretary Jones that the move left him "exposed to a galling fire from the Enemy's brig [*Linnet*]."[78]

Late in the battle, Macdonough's starboard guns were nearly all unusable or dismounted. By the prearranged plan, the stern anchor was disengaged and the bow cable cut, allowing the *Saratoga* to be turned end to end. The American flagship could now bring fresh guns to bear on the *Confiance*. By then the British flagship was torn to pieces with mangled bodies strewn across her decks. Many of the dead had been thrown overboard while "the numerous wounded below were frequently moved from place to place to prevent their being drowned" as water poured into the shattered hull.[79] Lieutenant Robertson sought to duplicate the *Saratoga*'s maneuver, but in the middle of the turn, the *Confiance* became stranded with her bow facing the *Saratoga*. By then the British crew had enough: "the Ship's Company declared they would stand no longer to their Quarters, nor could the Officers with their utmost exertions rally them," Robertson later testified.[80] Desperate to save his ship, Robertson tried to signal the galleys in the far distance for assistance, but "the Signal book, in consequence of the Captain's Death, had been mislaid."[81] Reluctantly, Robertson called the surviving officers together for a council, which decided upon surrender since "keeping up the Colours any longer would be a Wanton and useless waste of human blood."[82]

The *Saratoga*'s fire was now directed on the brig *Linnet*, whose masts, sails, and rigging had been shot away, making escape impossible. With a foot of water above the lower deck and no chance of being towed away by the elusive galleys, Pring surrendered his brig about 15 minutes after the *Confiance* had given up. Macdonough initially ordered the American galleys to pursue the 12 fleeing British galleys but quickly rescinded the command in order to use the vessels and their crews to save the sinking ships. While Macdonough's official report to the secretary of navy mentioned that "Three of their Gallies are said to be sunk," no British galleys sank in the engagement.[83] Macdonough also recorded 13 galleys with the British fleet but evidence suggests that 12 or perhaps only 11 were present.[84] Macdonough probably mistook the supply sloop *Icicle* for a galley which was among the galleys that had retreated from the main action. The galleys regrouped and hastily retreated north, passing a house near the ferry landing on Cumberland Head. The escaping galleys were serenaded by the residents with tin pans, bells, and horns, but the chorus was silenced by a cannon shot fired into the house.[85]

The battle, which ended about 11:20 A.M., had raged for two hours and 20 minutes, with deafening cannon booms accompanied by musket fire, hissing rockets, and artillery fire on shore. Midshipman William Lee aboard the *Confiance* at the end of the engagement found his clothes "literally torn all to rags with shot and splinters; the upper part of my hat was also shot away. There is one of the marines who was in Trafalgar action with Lord Nelson, who says it was a mere fleabite in comparison with this."[86] The rigging, masts, spars, and sails on the *Confiance* and *Linnet* were virtually all shot away. There were 250-300 rounds shot in the hull of the *Confiance* (Macdonough's original report had 105), 55 in the *Saratoga*'s hull, 39 in the *Eagle*, and 30 to 50 shot holes in the *Linnet*.[87] Macdonough also recorded that "the *Saratoga* was twice set on fire by hot Shot from the Enemy's Ship," but British officers denied the use of hot shot by the fleet in subsequent court-martial testimony.[88] The casualties were high on both sides: 52 American dead and 58 wounded with estimates of 54 to 57 British killed and 116 wounded (Lieutenant James Robertson reported the *Confiance* alone had 40 killed and 83 wounded).[89] Many of the dead on the *Confiance* had been thrown overboard during the engagement; some of their bodies continued to float to the surface days after the battle.

When the battle on the lake began, Prevost's batteries began a barrage of shells, balls, and congreve rockets which fell as thick as "hailstones" on the American forts and land positions. Prevost, however, did not dispatch troops to ford the Saranac River and attack the American positions until ten o'clock, halfway through the naval battle. At three different points the British army attempted to cross the river. After initially getting lost, the British managed to reach the upper ford on the Saranac where they were eventually successful in dispersing a spirited detachment of American militia and volunteers. The British who

The land battle at the Saranac River crossing with the fleets in the background from an 1816 engraving. (Schaffer Library, Union College)

attempted crossings at the two lower fords located at the bridges were repulsed by American regulars. By the time British troops had crossed at the upper ford, Prevost "had the extreme Mortification" to hear shouts of victory from the Americans over the *Confiance*'s surrender: "This unlooked for event Depriving me of the cooperation of the Fleet without which the further prosecution of the service was become impracticable, I did not hesitate to arrest the course of the Troops advancing to the attack."[90]

Late in the day the British ceased their bombardment and then withdrew their artillery at dusk. At sundown the American forts fired one last salute with their guns accompanied by the tune "Yankee Doodle." "At two the next morning," General Macomb later reported to the secretary of war that "the whole army precipitately retreated, leaving the sick and wounded to our generosity."[91] During the hasty flight, large amounts of provisions, cannon-balls, shells, and tents were abandoned, some dumped in ponds, creeks and Lake Champlain. John Suth Sinclair, commander of the artillery, later disclosed "that a Sloop laden with Stores (partly Ordnance Stores) unfortunately sank off Isle la Mothe [Motte] and fell into the hands of the Enemy."[92] On November 6 Macdonough reported "A Transport Sloop has recently been raised at Isle la Motte, which was Sunk by the Enemy loaded with their Naval Stores, and various Instruments of War."[93] In addition, about six tons of shells hidden in the waters off Chazy were also recovered.

Within half an hour of the conclusion of the naval engagement on September 11, Macdonough wrote a simple message to Navy Secretary Jones: "The Almighty has been pleased to grant us a signal victory on Lake Champlain in the capture of one frigate, one brig, and two sloops of war of the enemy."[94] After a short period of time, Captain Pring and Lieutenants Robertson, McGhie and Hicks boarded the *Saratoga* and presented their swords to Macdonough. The American commander, in a magnanimous gesture, bowed and declared, "Gentlemen, return your swords into your scabbards and wear them. You are worthy of them."[95] The wounded men from both sides were treated at the hospital on Crab Island; 47 of the most seriously wounded were paroled to Isle-aux-Noix by Macdonough. The British and American dead were buried side by side in unmarked graves on the north end of the island. The bodies of the dead officers, including Captain Downie, however, were covered with flags and buried on the shore in a formal funeral ceremony on September 14. The next day many of the 367 prisoners, well enough to travel, departed on the steamer *Vermont* for their journey to prisons further south. The officers of the *Linnet* wrote a letter on the steamer just before departure, expressing their gratitude for the "honorable treat-ment" by Macdonough. Similarly, Lieutenant Robertson, at the request of the surviving officers of the *Confiance*, conveyed a feeling of debt to Macdonough for the "unbounded liberality and humane attention not only extended to themselves but to the unfortunate wounded seamen and marines."[96]

Macdonough, of course, was honored for his part in the victory, including public dinners in Plattsburgh and Burlington, gifts of land by Vermont and New York, a gold medal from Congress, and promotion by the navy. Most of the troops who served in Plattsburgh went unpaid during 1814, as did Henry Delord and William Bailey who granted $20,000 in credit to officers and soldiers at their store in Plattsburgh. The partners eventually went bankrupt, with unsuccessful appeals to Washington for repayment made as late as 1841 by Bailey and Delord's widow.

In the following year of 1815, the Royal Navy held a court-martial for Captain Pring and the other officers who participated in the Plattsburgh naval engagement. The hearings, held aboard the *H.M.S. Gladiator* in Portsmouth Harbor, England, from August 18 to 21, 1815, honorably acquitted the naval officers except Lieutenant James McGhie of the sloop *Chubb*, who did not appear at the trial, and Lieutenant Rayham, the commander of the galleys, who had been cashiered from the service earlier. The blame for the naval failure was placed on General Prevost who had urged the *Confiance* "into Battle previous to its being in a proper state to meet its Enemy by a promised Cooperation of the Land Forces, which was not carried into Effect."[97] The court also "agreed that the Attack would have been more effectual if part of the Gun Boats had not failed in their Duty."[98] Although obviously conjecture, some officers contended that Prevost's shore batteries could have driven Macdonough from the bay before the battle. With this viewpoint, Prevost could have prevented the defeated British squadron from falling into American hands by providing a covering fire had the British army stormed Macomb's positions. Broken by the negative publicity of the naval court-martial which impugned his reputation, Sir George Prevost died in early January 1816, a month before he had a chance to present his side of the story in a court-martial hearing.

Although the British army and navy had made inroads in Maine and Commodore Yeo in late 1814 had blockaded the American fleet at Sackett's Harbor, the British had been turned back at Baltimore and decisively defeated in Plattsburgh Bay. When London newspapers published the outrageous demands of the British peace delegation at Ghent, the body politic and populace indicated increased disfavor with the war. Similarly, the Hartford Convention, which did not actually meet until December 15, manifested the disagreement over the war by some of the New England states. With the failure to strike a foothold in Lake Champlain at Plattsburgh and due to public pressure, the British dropped their territorial claims. The American delegation correspondingly jettisoned the maritime demands that the war had originally been undertaken to end. The result was the Treaty of Ghent, signed on Christmas Eve of 1814, which preserved the status quo on all boundaries. While this was certainly not a victory for America, the young nation proved its resilience against Europe's greatest power and emerged with an enhanced realization of national identity. Ironically, one of the most notable battles of the war, Andrew Jackson's successful defense of New Orleans, occurred several weeks after the signing of the peace treaty without the participants knowing of the settlement due to the slow communications of the day. But Jackson's victory insured ratification of the treaty and put an end to British plans for Louisiana.

The engagement at Plattsburgh Bay was the turning point of the war. "The battle of Lake Champlain, more nearly than any other incident of the War of 1812 merits the epithet 'decisive' " wrote the noted American naval historian, Captain A. T. Mahan (later Admiral) in 1905.[99] Theodore Roosevelt's earlier volume, *The Naval War of 1812*, credits Macdonough's foresight and resource with the victory by forcing "the British to engage at a disadvantage . . . . His skill, seamanship, quick eye, readiness of resource, and indomitable pluck, are beyond all praise."[100]

The American naval squadron remained at Plattsburgh Bay in the fall of 1814, making repairs to the devastated vessels. In early October Macdonough transferred to the *Eagle* while sending the *Saratoga, Confiance, Linnet*, and *Ticonderoga* to winter quarters in Whitehall. He retained the ten galleys, sloops *Preble, Montgomery, Finch*, and *Chubb*. At the end of the fall, the vessels were put into winter quarters at Whitehall under Lieutenant Charles Budd. In the meanwhile, Macdonough journeyed to New York City to command the first steamship of war, the 150-foot *Fulton First*, built by Adam and Noah Brown. Orders issued on December 27, 1814, by the new navy secretary, Benjamin Homans, recalled Macdonough to Whitehall to take measures "to repell an expected attempt of the enemy to destroy the fleet."[101] Although there was no raid, Macdonough did obtain intelligence that the British were building more vessels at Isle-aux-Noix. With the news that the Treaty of Ghent had been signed and the possibility of renewed hostilities remote, the American fleet and captured British vessels were laid up in "ordinary" with a dismantling and storing of the guns, sails, and naval stores in early March 1815.

Macdonough soon left Lake Champlain, spending most of the next ten years commanding American navy frigates. In August 1825, after news of his wife's death reached Macdonough, then in command of the Mediterranean fleet aboard the *Constitution*, the ailing commodore decided to return home with his four-year-old son. Six hundred miles from America, the hero of Lake Champlain died aboard the merchant brig *Edwin*.

In May 1815 the fleet at Whitehall was placed under the command of Captain James Leonard, an officer court-martialed during the war and relegated to secondary duty. Following an authorization for a public sale by the navy, the sloops *Preble*, *Montgomery*, *President*, *Chubb*, and *Finch* were sold with prices ranging from $805 to $2,430. The four oldest gunboats, *Ludlow*, *Wilmer*, *Alwyn*, and *Ballard*, were sold for less than $100, but the sale of the six 75-foot galleys was canceled since bids were too low. The larger vessels remained moored end to end at the "Elbow" north of the center of Whitehall, while the six galleys were sunk for preservation in 1815. The following year, the galley *Allen* was raised and used for survey work on the lake.[102] In later years, the vessel was used for patrol duty.

In the fall of 1819, Professor Benjamin Silliman, aboard the steamboat *Congress*, viewed the mothballed fleet at Whitehall: "As we passed rapidly by, a few seamen showed their heads through the grim port-holes. . . . Spareless, black and frowning, these now dismantled ships, look like the coffins of the brave."[103] In January 1820 the rotting *Confiance* settled on the bottom in six feet of water. During the following summer, Captain Leonard brought the *Eagle*, *Linnet*, and *Ticonderoga* to new moorings along the banks of the Poultney River (East Bay). Late that year, the *Saratoga* and the *Confiance*, after being temporarily pumped out, were likewise brought into the East Bay. When Professor Silliman again passed Whitehall "in June 1821, these vessels were lying a little way down the lake, mere wrecks, sunken, neglected and in ruins."[104]

The *Saratoga* settled in shallow water in 1821 with her upper works, which had been modified as barracks, above water. At least for some of the time, the abandoned vessels were used by local squatters as dwellings. Large sections of the *Confiance* were broken up as a navigation hazard in 1824 after the vessel washed into the lake channel. Following an unsuccessful auction in June 1825, which required the removal of the vessels, the remaining fleet was sold to salvagers who were not required to remove the hulks. Over the years, salvagers removed all of the exposed wood and iron on the vessels. The *Eagle*, however, sank on her port side before wrecking crews could rip her apart.[105] A portion of the hull of the *Confiance* apparently swung out from the Poultney River again during the high waters in 1869 (There is some suggestion that this vessel might have actually been the *Saratoga*). Several years later the vessel was blown up and 300 pounds of copper salvaged from the hull.[106] The famous vessels that had changed the course of history thus ended their careers ingloriously as junk.

ABOVE. Remains of British brig *Linnet*, used at "Battle of Plattsburgh Bay" in 1814, at Fort Mount Hope. Raised from East Bay in 1949. Photo by the author.

BELOW. Remains of *U.S.S. Ticonderoga* raised in 1958 at Whitehall.
Photo by the author.

Following the War of 1812, peace finally became a permanent state of affairs along the Lake Champlain corridor but not without new fortifications. In 1816 construction of an American fort began on a site north of Rouses Point. Despite problems with the inadequate foundation built on quicksand, work continued on the fort through 1818. A new land survey under the Treaty of Ghent disclosed in January 1819 that the fort's location was partially on Canadian soil. The fort resembled a "great stone castle" when observed by Professor Silliman in 1819.[107] Thereafter, the abandoned fortification became known as Fort Blunder by residents who subsequently carted away materials for local buildings. Years later in 1842, the Webster-Ashburton Treaty re-established the fort area on American territory. In 1844, construction of a new fort, named Fort Montgomery for the hero of Quebec in 1775, finally began. The immense stone fort with five bastions was surrounded by water and connected by a drawbridge over a moat to the mainland. Nearly completed, Fort Montgomery's construction was suspended in 1870 and the fort abandoned in 1908 with the cannon given to cities and towns. Although designed for an 800-man garrison, apparently only one sergeant and an engineer ever occupied the outpost. Some of the fort's walls were used as foundation material during the construction of the Rouses Point Bridge in the 1930s. Today the crumbling fort, owned by a Canadian developer, stands in silent vigil over the calm waters of the Richelieu and Lake Champlain. The ruins of Fort Montgomery are in stark contrast to the excellently preserved fortification on Isle-aux-Noix. Fort Lennox, built by the British between 1819 and 1829 to guard the Canadian frontier from the Americans, was constructed on the original ruins of the 1759 French fort. Today, the massive stone fort is a Canadian National Historic Park and military museum.

Archaeological Discoveries

The wrecks of the *Ticonderoga, Linnet, Eagle*, and galley *Allen* remained relatively undisturbed near the first major bend in the Poultney River until the mid-twentieth century. The *Linnet*, then an unnamed wreck, was broken into two pieces by cables in a clumsy salvage attempt in 1949.[108] The retrieved section of the vessel was then displayed at Fort Mount Hope in Ticonderoga with an erroneous sign identifying the vessel as one of Arnold's gondolas of 1776. Cannonballs and pieces of the wreck were sold for years at a Route 9 antique shop in Ticonderoga. A second vessel, the schooner *Ticonderoga*, was raised in 1958 and is now on display under a shed at the Skenesborough Museum in Whitehall. Since the locations of the wrecks have been well known for years, divers in the 1950s and 1960s removed hundreds of valuable artifacts.[109]

When I first observed the frames of what later was identified as the brig *Linnet* protruding from the water in 1970, it seemed incredible that even part of the vessel could still exist, partially out of the water, 156 years after entering Lake Champlain. Using information from a local resident, I crossed East Bay with my scuba equipment to another wreck where I literally crawled hand over hand inside the vessel in five-inch visibility.[110] This relatively intact vessel was identified as the brig *Eagle* over a decade later by the Champlain Maritime Society in its comprehensive study of the vessel. The 1981-83 study was sponsored by the Vermont Division for Historic Preservation with federal grant funds and a grant from the Vermont Historical Society. One hundred fifteen feet of the *Eagle* was still intact in the bay with ten of the original 24 gunports still in existence. The results of the study also indicated that the *Eagle* had a very shallow draft (seven feet three inches in the hold), which would contradict early depictions of the battle that showed vessels similar in hull design to ocean warships. In addition to the thorough measurements of the structure and the determination of the original dimensions of the vessel, divers discovered shot garlands, iron fittings, two bottles, a few tools and shot on the wreck.[111] The study also identified the 56-foot section of the partially sunk vessel as the remains of the *Linnet* and discovered the 75-foot galley *Allen*.

The motivation for divers sometimes working in zero visibility is the chance to literally touch history. Archaeological work provides a means of enhancing one's historical perspective as a participant rather than as a mere observer of historic relics.

Fort Montgomery.
(Special Collections, Benjamin F. Feinberg Library at SUNY, Plattsburgh)

Canal schooner near Vergennes in the 1880s.
(Special Collections, Bailey/Howe Memorial Library,
University of Vermont)

11. Champlain Canal Boats

With THE END OF THE WAR OF 1812, trading schooners and sloops once again plied the water highway of Lake Champlain in peace. Soon a new type of vessel, the canal boat, would appear on the lake and eventually supersede the traditional commercial sailboat. "I've seen the water down there solid with canal boats," an old-timer nostalgically remarked earlier this century.[1] In the heyday of business traffic on the lake there was a "forest of masts" from canal schooners and other commercial vessels in the lake harbors. Once men and women toiled on the large canalers carrying cargoes of lumber, pulpwood, iron ore, marble, granite, and coal to supply the needs of a growing nation. Before trains and trucks, these vessels were the chief means of inland transportation of bulk cargo in the eastern United States. On the bottom of the lake today the ghostly images of many of these vessels remind scuba divers of the once thriving commercial traffic on the lake.

In 1761 Philip Schuyler of Albany, veteran of the French and Indian War and later a general in Washington's army, visited England where he viewed the operation of the Bridgewater Canal. After returning to the colonies, he recommended the construction of canals in America. Charles Carroll, one of the Congressional Commissioners sent to Canada in 1776, noted in his journal that Philip Schuyler suggested a water route between New York and Quebec via "locks and a small canal cut from a branch that runs into Wood Creek, and the head of a branch which falls into the Hudson's River."[2]

By 1785 Elkanah Watson, who had earlier been sent with dispatches to Benjamin Franklin in Paris, returned to America with ideas about canals based upon European observations. After a two-day visit to Mount Vernon in which George Washington, as president of the "Potomac Company," described plans for a canal between the Ohio and Potomac rivers, Watson became a strong advocate of canals in New York State. Watson's ideas found fertile ground with Philip Schuyler, who had strong political influence and a predisposition to canals. In 1792 legislation incorporating two private canal companies, the Western Inland Lock Navigation Company and the Northern Inland Lock Navigation Company, was passed by the New York legislature. Schuyler was elected president of both companies and Watson a director. Although not a financial success, the Western Company did complete a canal that would be a forerunner of the Erie Canal. The Northern Company, which was to connect the Hudson River to Lake Champlain, spent $100,000 in an unsuccessful attempt to build a waterway through Wood Creek.[3] While the Northern Company was a failure, the project provided a background of experience for the builders of the Champlain Canal.

In 1807 the U.S. Senate instructed the secretary of treasury, Albert Gallatin, to prepare "a plan for the application of such means as are within the power of Congress, to the purposes of opening roads and making canals."[4] The far-sighted plan of federal outlays to improve transportation was aimed at stimulating economic growth. Included in his plan for northern water linkages was a canal from the Hudson River to Lake Champlain. Although federal help was not forthcoming, the state senate in 1812 appointed commissioners to study New York canal routes. Their report found that "a canal, between Lake Champlain and Hudson's river, is one of those things which are deemed of national importance."[5] Following subsequent reports delineating the economic benefits and cost estimates, the state legislature on April 15, 1817, authorized work to begin on both the Erie and Champlain canals.[6] Support for the building of the canal included the lumber business along the lake, the iron mining industry on the New York shore, and the Vermont marble cutters.

By the end of 1819 the Champlain Canal had been completed from Whitehall to Fort Edward. The size of the Champlain Canal was the same as the Erie, 40 feet wide at the top, 28 feet wide at the bottom, and four feet deep with locks 90 feet in length and 15 feet wide. The original locks were made of wood but were replaced by masonry. After six years of work, the Champlain Canal opened for traffic in 1823. On October 8, 1823, the *Gleaner*, a sailing canal boat built in St. Albans, Vermont, became the first boat through the waterway. The success of New York canals was immediate. Tolls collected on the Erie Canal for its first nine years exceeded the entire initial cost and maintenance of the canal. The chief advantage of canals was a matter of physics as well as economics. A horse or mule could drag a load fifty times heavier through water than on land.

Upon completion of the canal, Lake Champlain took on a renewed importance as a wave of enterprise emerged in the port towns along the lake. By 1833 there were 232 canal boats registered at the ports of Lake Champlain or along the Champlain Canal in addition to other sailing, steam, and horse-powered vessels that were on the lake.* Ten years later the number of canal boats doubled to an estimated 450. Following the opening of the Chambly Canal in 1843, which connected Lake Champlain to the St. Lawrence, trade in the region further accelerated. The proposal for a St. Lawrence–Lake Champlain ship canal first came in 1785 from Ira Allen, a Vermont merchant and Ethan Allen's brother. The same British engineer (Twiss) who helped fortify Mount Defiance in 1777, positively evaluated the possibility of a Canadian canal to Lake Champlain in 1785.

Two basic types of canal boats were on the lake. One was strictly a canal boat that had to be towed on the open lake while the other was a new class of boats that adapted to both lake and canal navigation. These latter vessels, developed by shipbuilders at the lake, were half sloop or schooner and half canal boat. The maximum size of these vessels was dictated by the smallest lock in the canal network. The masts would be taken down when the vessel entered the canal in order to pass under low bridges. Along the canal the boat would be

---

* Traditional schooners and sloops continued to ply the lake during the canal boat era including the **Billow, D. A. Smith, Daniel Webster, General Scott, Glass Maker, Henry Clay, Hercules, Jenny Lind, J. W. Holcomb, Lafayette, Montgomery, Sarah Ellen, Waterlou,** and **Water Witch** (converted steamer).

pulled by mules or horses, but out of the canal it would sail on the open lake. This convertible vessel would save three or four days for shippers at Whitehall, the entry point for the canal when going south. Steamers and traditional schooners would have their cargoes reloaded on canal boats, whereas the canal schooner simply dropped its masts and continued on.

The towed canal boats upon reaching Lake Champlain were often formed into a tremendous tow of 30 or 40 boats. Since the tolls were lower on the Chambly–Champlain route, cargo from Canada was often routed along the Champlain corridor rather than the more expensive Erie Canal route. Guides to Lake Champlain in the nineteenth century noted "large fleets of canal boats discharging their coal from Pennsylvania, and receiving return cargoes of iron ore" in communities such as Port Henry, New York.[7] The construction of the canal boat was often dictated by the types of cargo to be carried. Many of the boats that carried ore and coal were slab-sided with much of their deck open to the cargo hold of the vessel. In 1862 the state of New York legislated rounded bows for canal boats since accidents had increased significantly. When a squared-bow canal boat collided with another vessel, it could sheer off the whole side of the boat, spilling its contents into the canal.

The average life of a wooden canal boat used on freshwater was approximately 20 years unless it was rebuilt. The boats often leaked requiring hours of pumping. If the leak was located, a "Medicine Spoon" was used to plug the hole without taking the vessel out of the water. A long-handled wooden box with dry horse manure or sawdust would be pushed under the bottom of the boat, and the incoming water would draw the manure into the leaky seams. Similarly, an open potato sack filled with the same ingredients would be hauled back and forth over the bottom of the boat to seal a leak.[8]

The dimensions of the sailing canal vessels and the towed canal boats were quite similar. Their length and width were determined by the size of the existing locks. The earlier canal vessels were usually 77 to 79-1/2 feet long and about 13-1/2 feet wide and were sloop-rigged (one mast). After some enlargement of the canal in the 1860s, the boats became slightly larger with a typical length of 88 feet and a width of 14-1/2 feet. The added length allowed the vessel to be schooner-rigged with two masts.

A hodge podge of legislation over the years led to an enlargement of the Champlain locks and prism (surface width, bottom width, and depth of canal). In 1860 a prism of 50' x 35' x 5' was authorized; by 1870 authorization of a 58' x 44' x 7' prism was achieved. However, much of the construction took years to complete. In a speech to the New York Assembly on April 5, 1864, Andrew Meiklejohn pleaded for further improvements in the canal. While many of the locks matched those of Erie, Meiklejohn suggested that the Champlain Canal was not large enough causing "one-third of our time. . . lost in the effort to navigate the canal."[9] It wasn't until 1877 that all locks on the canal matched the 110' x 18' dimensions of the Erie Canal. By 1890 only 20 miles of the enlarged prism had been completed.

Both the sailing canal boat and the towed canal boat were cargo carriers as well as houses. Lake ports before 1875 resembled small floating villages where one would have to cross 40 or 50 boats to reach a wharf. The acre of vessels would also provide a handy marketplace for local merchants serving the needs of the crews living on the boats. The stern section of canal boats contained a cabin for living space, some with only the minimum essentials, while others were slightly more elaborate. Lighting was provided by kerosene lamps and meals were prepared on a wood or coal stove. Typically, the stern had four windows; the top of the cabin which extended a few feet above the deck usually had two or

ABOVE. Essex, NY—site of extensive canal boat construction. Photo by the author.
BELOW. Canal sloops at Burlington wharf in 1905.
(Special Collections, Bailey/Howe Memorial Library, UVM)

ABOVE. Burlington, VT. Photo by the author.
BELOW. Canal schooner *P. E. Havens* built in Essex, NY in 1865. Abandoned in 1903.
(Special Collections, Bailey/Howe Memorial Library, UVM)

three windows on each side. Cabin windows were often not screened, causing flies and mosquitoes to inundate living quarters. Shelves, chests of drawers, tables, chairs, and cupboards were added to cabins. The best cabins had side berths as bedrooms with sliding doors; others had curtains for privacy. The vessels had no toilet facilities and used wash water from the canal or Lake Champlain. In a 1921 survey of canal families, it was found that drinking water which was said to be very clear came directly from Lake Champlain.[10] The better cabins had fixed basins with gravity-fed water from a tank on the deck; others simply had a barrel of water on the deck or in the cabin. The 1921 survey also found that approximately half of the families did not have sleeping space for every member of the family. During the warmer months, some of the family members would have to sleep under an awning on the deck. On the open lake, independent owners could sail or tow their canal boats 24 hours a day, but work hours were eventually restricted to 10-12 hours on the Champlain Canal.

Despite these hardships, children living aboard canal boats were fairly common. At the age of seven, Martha Robbins lived on a Whitehall-built canal boat with her mother and uncle. During the years 1897–1907, her trips included those to Canada through Lake Champlain and to New York City. "The cargo from the North might be lumber, hay, or spruce pulpwood from Three Rivers [Canada] cut in two foot lengths and you had real spruce gum to chew! If the cargo was pulpwood, you might drop off from the tow at Ticonderoga but usually Fort Edward."[11] When the lake turned rough, the tows would pull into harbors such as Snake Den or Burlington. Upon reaching Whitehall, the families would usually stock up on groceries to last through Albany or further. Martha recalled: "At that age my one big ambition was to ride one of the mules while towing." After a few years, her uncle finally let her ride on the mule one day, but the towline snapped sending Martha flying onto the towpath. "That ended my mule riding career."[12]

Wash flapping in the breeze usually indicated the presence of a family on the canal boat. In the summer when it was very hot, whole families essentially lived on deck under awnings. The gypsy life was either loved or hated by family members. Life for the children was not easy with many accidents reported, irregular school attendance, lack of recreation, and illness. Young children were often tied to the towing post or deck to prevent them from falling into the canal or lake. Boys worked with their fathers until they were old enough to operate their own boat. The job of a canal boat captain became an occupation handed down from father to son. One mother explained the family tradition in canal boating this way: "The children are brought up on the boat and don't know nothin' else, and that is the only reason they take up 'boating'."[13] One youngster with boating experience, who used his inheritance from his deceased mother to buy his own boat and a team of mules, became a captain at 14 years old. He had virtually no formal education and never learned to read or write. Several of his sons also became boatmen, and a 16-year-old grandson was working with the captain when he was still boating at 68 years old.[14]

In the cold months, if an unforseen cold snap closed the navigation for the season, the canalers would be forced to stay in ports such as Ottawa, New York City, or other points away from their winter residences. In that case the whole family spent the winter on the boat. In larger cities the children of canal boat families, trapped by the winter ice, would sometimes attend local schools. One winter, Martha Robbin's family from Whitehall failed to make it back to the lake and spent the winter aboard the boat in Brooklyn.

ABOVE. Canal boats engaged in the pulpwood trade at Ticonderoga.
(Ticonderoga Historical Society)
BELOW. Canal boat *W. N. Sweet* launched in 1902.
(Special Collections, Bailey/Howe Memorial Library, UVM)

The packet canal boat, as another distinct class of canal vessels, dominated passenger traffic in the first three decades of the Champlain Canal. Until the arrival of railroads, packet boats nearly monopolized passenger traffic to New York City and immigrant transportation to Buffalo from the Champlain Valley. The difference between a freight canal boat and a packet involved the cabin, which extended nearly the entire length of the packet vessel with only narrow walkways along the gunwales. Behind the cabin was a small landing for standing and the steering mechanism. One could also stand or sit on the roof of the cabin but had to duck for low bridges. If a passenger on the roof fell asleep and failed to hear the call "low bridge" from the crew, their nap would have a rather rude awakening. Inside the cabin were long benches or seats at each side, a long table for dining, and a little stove for cold weather trips.

At night the cabin was oftentimes divided with one-third of the forward section for the women separated for privacy by curtains. Some of the bedding was spread across the seats while others were hung by cords from the ceilings in a berth/hammock arrangement. Nineteenth-century historian Benson Lossing compared the cabin to a "Turkish bath" after a night on a Champlain canal packet.[15] Other passengers on packets complained that sleeping was out of the question with the nightlong serenade of children crying in the women's section of the cabin. Charles Dickens likened the rows of bunks in the canal packet to bookshelves and the passengers to large folio volumes that, once placed, could not be moved. In the morning, Dickens found the odors of breakfast mixed with bar smells of gin, whiskey, brandy, rum and "a decided seasoning of stale tobacco."[16] No wonder Dickens later referred to the luxurious Lake Champlain steamers as "floating palaces."[17]

Canal packets utilized the fastest horses along the towpath; when a horse slowed down with age it was relegated to towing freight boats. The packets had the right-of-way over the freight canalers because of passengers, the larger size crew, and physical dimension of the vessel. Packets usually employed one man on the crew with a reputation as a fighter to serve as the "bouncer." His job was to quell any disorderly or rowdy conduct on the vessel, which typically meant throwing the culprit into the canal.

The 1830s and 1840s witnessed the expansion of lake and canal traffic due to the increase in immigrants from Canada on their way west. Nearly every lake port had a line of boats that traveled between the lake and Buffalo. The Vergennes-Troy Line, the Albany-Vergennes Line, and the Westport and Buffalo Line carried many immigrants heading westward with departures once or twice a week. Small steamers such as the *Washington* were used to tow the packet vessels on the waters of Lake Champlain. Once the steamer reached Whitehall, the packet would be towed through the canal, day and night, by relays of horses. At the junction of the Erie Canal passengers could transfer to a line of western boats. At the southern end of Lake Champlain, the Emigrants' Line and the Western Line in Whitehall competed for European immigrants that arrived in Canada and passed through Lake Champlain. Many Irish immigrants, after landing in Montreal, made their way to St. Jean on the Richelieu River where they boarded a Lake Champlain steamer to Whitehall. The Emigrants' Line advertised in 1846 that their boats "are all new, and fitted up in the best style for comfort, convenience and accommodation of the traveling public."[18] Apparently, Dickens missed these boats on his trip to Lake Champlain. To reassure passengers, ads also boasted that "the boats of this line will be commanded by experienced and sober men."[19] The advertisements for the Western Line stressed that "Capts. of Line boats are worthy and trusty."[20] Both lines were also towed by relays of fresh horses stationed at points along the canal tow path rather than the old method of carrying fresh horses on the boat, which passengers found offensive. Usually six or seven days were required to reach Buffalo from Whitehall. In 1848 over 4,000 immigrants, mostly Irish, passed through Lake Champlain and the canals of New York.

Some of the immigrants, upon arrival at Whitehall, would be solicited for passage on freight canal boats by unscrupulous agents. They would be shown the main cabin of the vessel with adequate berths, a cookstove, and other reasonable amenities. After they paid their fare and the boat had departed from the wharf, the captain, in no uncertain terms, would inform them that if they set foot in that cabin they would be thrown in the "drink." Thus many of the immigrants ended up huddled in the recesses between the piles of lumber carried by the canal boats. Day or night, rain or shine, men, women, and children sat out in the elements as the canal boats moved at two or three miles per hour.

There were many freight line canal boat companies in the Champlain Valley over the years. The firm of Mayo & Follett located in Burlington entered the freight forwarding business with their first canal boat *Vermont* in 1823. The Merchants' Line, established in 1841 by Follett and Bradley of Burlington, used a standarized fleet of 20 or more sloop-rigged sailing canal boats. The New York and Canada Line, begun by W. H. Wilkins of Burlington, conducted business between Quebec, Montreal, and New York City in 1854. By 1859 the New York and Canada Line merged with the Copeland Line founded by C. Copeland in 1856. Together the new company had 31 boats operating in the canals, Lake Champlain, and Canadian rivers. H. G. Burleigh was the force behind the founding of Burleigh and Marshall in Whitehall in 1859, which was succeeded by the firm of Burleigh Brothers. In the 1880s this firm was consolidated with Robert Cook and the Whitehall Transportation Company to form the New York and Lake Champlain Transportation Company. Shortly thereafter, Burleigh and Cook began separate lines which were again consolidated into the Lake Champlain Transportation Company after Burleigh's death in 1900. The new company operated with six tugs and a fleet of canal boats and barges before being absorbed by the Murray Transportation Company of New York.

After years of financial maneuvering, the Northern Transportation Line of Whitehall became the dominant canal and freight line on Lake Champlain. Asa Eddy began one of the earliest lines of canal boats on the lake in Whitehall when the canal opened in 1823. By 1831 he sold his operation to Peter Comstock who had a small line of boats at the time. Comstock is one of the famous characters of Champlain history who was noted for driving a team of horses with provisions to Plattsburgh during the 1814 battle, canal boat races, deal making, and his steamboat rivalry with the Champlain Transportation Company of Burlington. Comstock's company changed hands several times; by 1856 a consolidation of canal lines including the Northern Transportation Line (formerly the Six Day Line), the Northern Lake Line, Stark and Company's Northern Line, and the N. T. Jellson Line created the Northern Transportation Line. The NTL owned canal boats as well as freight and tow steamboats on Lake Champlain which included the steamers *Oliver Bascom*, *Ethan Allen*, *William Birkbeck*, *Boston*, and *J. H. Hooker*.

When the Copeland Line and the New York and Canada Line merged in 1859 to compete more effectively with the Northern Transportation Line, the latter firm offered higher salaries and commissions to shipping agents. Shortly thereafter, the NTL began a rate war. After a few years the Copeland–New York and Canada Line was forced into a consolidation with the Northern Transportation Line . Although the NTL was successful in eliminating much of the competition on the lake, there was one source of competition that would eventually win out — the railroad. The support for railroads included the mining and lumber interests on Lake Champlain who wanted transportation all-year round. In an effort to protect its investment in canals, the state legislated that railroads could only carry passengers and baggage. Later the state allowed railroad freight traffic but required tolls paid equal to the cost of using the Champlain Canal. Eventually this requirement ended, and by 1875 the Delaware and Hudson Railroad completed a line from Whitehall to the Canadian border.

Canadian sailing canal boats on the Richelieu River at the turn of the century.
(Postcard, author's collection)

Canal towns such as Whitehall have been compared to those of the Wild West, especially on payday. It was standard practice to withhold the canal laborers' pay for the last two months of the season until the last day of navigation on the canal. A drinking, gambling, and fighting spree usually resulted with some workers losing their wages. The hapless crew members who lost their money often spent the winter at the "poor farm" near Whitehall awaiting the opening of the next canal season.

The lumber industry along Lake George and Lake Champlain was stimulated by the opening of the Champlain Canal. Essex County, New York, saw new docks and an improvement in existing facilities at Ticonderoga, Crown Point, Port Henry, Essex, and Port Kent. These ports were jammed with canal boats, schooners, and sloops as lumber fever encompassed the region. Unfortunately, it initially meant the denuding of many of the lake and river shores in the valley. During the first half of the nineteenth century, the village of Ticonderoga overflowed with lumber activity as the outlet for the huge Lake George lumber region. In Ticonderoga two-thirds of the lumber business was attributed to Joseph Weed, who shipped 340 boatloads of lumber in one year alone. Weed's canal boats included the *Black Mountain, Bolton, Lyon*, and *Swallow*. Boats at one time were able to navigate all the way into the basin at the "Lower Falls" in Ticonderoga before the waste from the paper mills filled in the waterway. By 1852 Ticonderoga exported 600,000 pieces of lumber and Port Douglas 200,000 pieces, and 1,625,000 board feet were shipped from Port Kent.[21]

The opening of the Champlain Canal touched off a huge import market of Canadian lumber. In 1849 alone, over 15 million board feet of lumber came through the Champlain Canal from Canada destined for Troy and New York City. Part of the trade resulted from lumber that was bound for New York City from Lake Ontario. Hundreds of miles shorter, the natural route through the Erie Canal involved 136 miles of tolls. Lumber diverted to the longer Lake Champlain route saved substantially on tolls with the shorter canal mileage of the Champlain Canal. By 1850 roughly twice the amount of lumber reached New York City by the Champlain Canal compared to the Erie.

By the 1880s and 1890s, 400 canal boats and steamers as well as hundreds of Canadian vessels were involved in the lumber trade. Since international regulations did not allow Canadian vessels to pass out of the lake, larger canal boats were built that carried 250,000 board feet of lumber. These vessels would still fit the larger Canadian canals. The Canadian vessels were most often unloaded in Burlington where the lumber would be transferred to American canal boats for the trip south or to railroad cars destined for Boston. Burlington, as one of the first markets to import Canadian lumber, became the location of numerous lumber forwarding companies and manufacturing enterprises. Often stockpiles of lumber adjacent to the wharves covered 30 or 40 acres. The direct connection of Burlington to some eastern cities by railroads made it a natural center for the lumber business. The volume increased so rapidly that the construction of a breakwater was needed to offer protection for boats that had to wait to be unloaded or cleared by Customs. Canadian imports into Burlington amounted to 175 million board feet of lumber each year by 1871.

As time passed, the railroads took a larger share of the lumber market away from canal boats. However, canal boats continued in some areas for many decades. The Diamond Match Line utilized boats to import thousands of feet of match blocks. The International Paper Line at Fort Edward and Fort Miller Pulp and Paper Line brought in most of their pulpwood by canal boat right into the twentieth century.

The canal era stimulated the shipbuilding industry in many communities along the lake. In 1846, 14 boats were launched in Ticonderoga with an average of a dozen a year continuing for another decade. Essex, New York, famous for its early shipbuilding, built 53 documented vessels between 1814 and 1870. Many were the sloop-and-schooner-rigged canal boats that sailed the lake until the turn of the century. One Essex yard, the Hoskins, Ross and Co., accounted for a major share of the canal boats built in this era. Although records for Willsboro are very incomplete, shipbuilding extended from approximately 1835 to 1865 with the documentation of the names and dimensions of seven sloop-rigged canal boats and scows. Canal boats were also built in Chazy, Peru, Plattsburgh, and Whitehall, New York and in Burlington, Colchester, Isle La Motte, Milton, Swanton, and Vergennes, Vermont.

The mining industry in the Adirondacks and the marble quarries of Vermont were some of the biggest users of canal boats on the lake. The iron companies of Crown Point, Moriah,

Port Henry, and the Westport area were net importers and exporters of raw materials and finished goods. Several mines along the lake at Split Rock Mountain included a granite quarry at Barn Rock Harbor, a graphite mine near the Split Rock Lighthouse, and iron mines at Ore Bed Point and Grog Harbor. These, as well as others, were directly serviced from the lake with canal boats and schooners. By the 1890s the iron ore veins ran out at Split Rock Mountain and the mines were closed. The larger mines, however, near Mineville, Moriah, and Port Henry were a major industry in the Champlain Valley for more than a century. Andrew Meiklejohn, in his plea for a larger canal in 1864, cited the growth of output from Port Henry as evidence: "The iron ore shipped over this canal from Port Henry alone was 7,000 tons in 1850, while last year [1863] it had mounted up to 145,000 tons."[22] Anthracite coal from Pennsylvania was also shipped to the western shore of Lake Champlain for the iron industry. Granite for buildings, breakwaters, and road edging from the North Country was carried for years on the canal boats. Marble, especially the black and grey marble from Isle La Motte, was used in many of the public buildings throughout the United States via Champlain canal boats.

According to Captain Frank Godfrey, a veteran of the New York canals, the later years of the ore trade on Lake Champlain used three types of canal boats. The biggest were strong, heavy canal boats with nine-foot sides and a full deck. These vessels were loaded with 250–255 tons of ore, 110 tons on the deck and 145 tons inside. At Troy the deck ore would be transferred to vessels going to Wilmington, Delaware. On the return trip, the vessel was so high that it would not fit under the low bridges unless it was reloaded (usually with coal). The second type were first-class, dry-cargo boats with a full deck and eight-foot sides that would take ore from Port Henry to the Rome Iron Works in Rome, New York, and return with salt or shipments from canning factories for the Spaulding Kimball Line or the O. J. Walker Company in Burlington. The third type were old worn-out, open-deck boats that were kept afloat by "Medicine Spoons" and pumps. Godfrey knew one owner with three of these old boats who suggested that "The only thing I don't like about the ore is to get up in the morning with two, or three feet of water in the hold."[23]

Between 1870 and 1915 approximately 1,500–1,800 canal boats worked the Champlain route. Gradually, however, the days of the canaler began to decline in the Champlain Valley despite the fact that tolls were eliminated in 1882. In 1890 the volume of commerce on the Champlain Canal reached a peak of a million and a half tons. However, by 1907 it had dropped to less than half that amount. The reduced volume had several causes which obviously included the increased railroad traffic. By the turn of the century the fleets of sloop and schooner-rigged canal boats had largely disappeared from the lake. Part of the change resulted from the gradual reduction of trade through New York City. Differential rail freight rates often favored other Atlantic ports including Boston, Baltimore, Philadelphia, Norfolk, and Newport News instead of New York City. By 1902 iron ore traffic had ceased between Port Henry and Wilmington, Delaware, via the Champlain Canal. In spite of the railroads, some canalers continued to ply the lake and canal. Pulpwood for the region's paper mills continued to be carried by canal boats as late as the 1920s.

Efforts were made to make the canal more competitive by enlarging it again. The new Champlain Barge Canal opened in 1916 with locks similar in construction and operation to that of the Panama Canal. The Whitehall lock was 310 feet long, 45 feet wide, and could handle vessels with 12-foot drafts. After the opening of the new barge canal, tonnage began to increase for a number of years. However, the single canal boat towed by mules was eventually replaced by fleets of barges propelled by steam tugs. Some new vessels were purchased for the ore trade by the Witherbee-Sherman Company of Port Henry for use on Lake Champlain in the twentieth century. A fleet consisting of one barge canal-size-steamer, four Erie steam canal boats, a steam tug, and other canal boats were used at Port Henry until the mines were leased to the Republic Steel Corporation in the fall of 1923.

Today, one occasionally sees a modern 200-foot tanker barge on the lake. Gone is the graceful canal schooner and with it the hustle and bustle of the lake ports, replaced by the giant, square steel tanker which appears nondescript as it navigates the lake.

Archaeological Discoveries

Many canal boats ended up at the bottom of the lake for a number of reasons. Storms on Lake Champlain could be treacherous especially when a vessel was overloaded with iron ore or marble and using too much sail. When the lake became turbulent during storms, vessels would try to navigate into protected harbors. Some vessels never reached the safety of sheltered inlets, however. During a storm, steamboat tow captains would often cut loose the tow of canal boats to save the tow vessel. As the boats were blown cross wind, the crews would desperately struggle to cut loose the other vessels. Without engines and enough anchor line to reach bottom in deeper waters, the boats were at the mercy of the waves and often sank. Others sank because of human error or were abandoned when they outlived their usefulness.

When a boat sank in a canal it was either brought up or destroyed to clear the waterway. The canal boats that sank in Lake Champlain, however, are still there. In the last ten years a number of perfectly intact sailing canal boats have been located by side-scan sonar and divers. Spearheaded by the Champlain Maritime Society, a non-profit organization dedicated to the preservation of the maritime heritage of Lake Champlain, a whir of publicity surrounding the discovery, identification, and conservation of shipwrecks occurred in the 1980s. Two of the many canal boats in the lake are today protected in Underwater Historic Preserves by the state of Vermont. Art Cohn, then Vice-Chairman of the CMS, headed the Underwater Parks Committee which was successful in 1985 in starting the first preserve with the support and aid of Giovanna Peebles, Vermont's state archaeologist. The vessels in the preserves are identified by yellow buoys which are connected to cement pads and identification signs on the bottom. The mooring buoys protect the sunken vessels from accidental anchor damage while the signs outline safety procedures and warn divers that it is illegal to remove artifacts from the wrecks. Wooden deadeyes, cleats, and other historic objects have been purposely left on the ships for divers to see and photograph. It is an experimental program which has been an outstanding success and a model for New York to consider.

An Essex-built canal schooner is one of the most popular and interesting wrecks in Lake Champlain today. The 88-foot *General Butler*, built in the shipyard of Hoskins and Ross in 1862, was named after the Civil War general, Benjamin F. Butler. On December 9, 1876, battling ten-foot waves during a winter storm with a full load of Isle La Motte marble, the *Butler*'s steering gear cracked and the vessel drifted helplessly. In a desperate attempt to save the vessel, William Montgomery, an experienced captain on the lake, jury-rigged the

The canal schooner *O. J. Walker* was built in Burlington in 1862. Sunk in 1895, it remains intact today
on the bottom of Lake Champlain. Drawings by
Montserrat Centeno.

THE CANAL SCHOONE

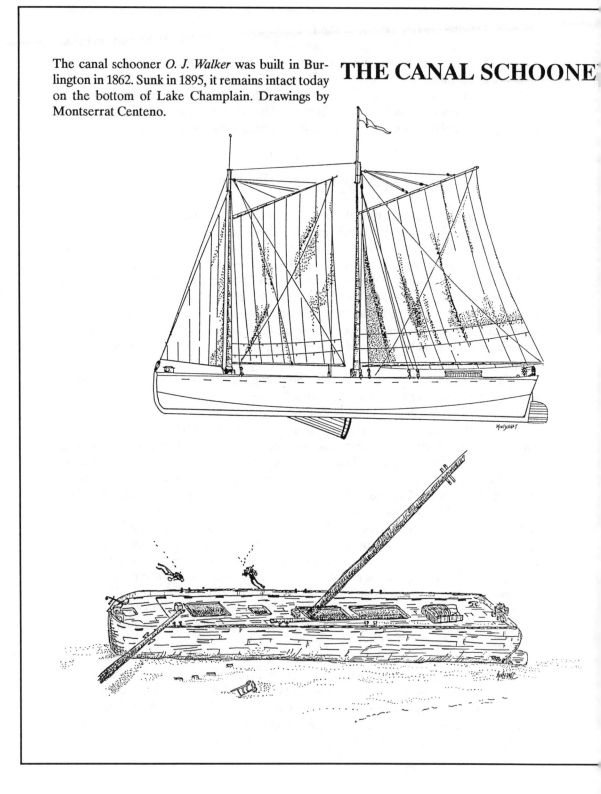

O. J. WALKER

The wreck of the *O. J. Walker*. Photographs by the author: 1. Mast. 2. Windlass and anchor. 3. Cabin on deck. 4. Side-scan sonar image (Joseph Zarzynski and Klein Associates, Inc.). 5. Bow with twin deadeyes and anchor. 6. Windlass and anchor.

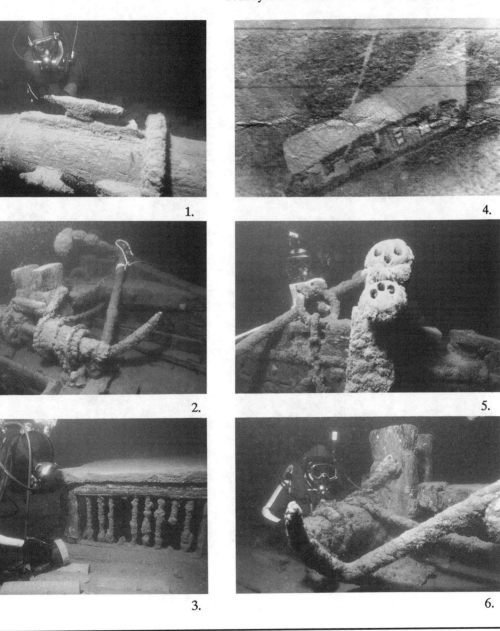

1.

4.

2.

5.

3.

6.

steering mechanism (chaining the rudder post to the tiller handle). The effort was fruitless as the vessel smashed into the Burlington breakwater. The passengers, crew, and captain leaped to safety, but the *Butler* sank within seconds only to be discovered 104 years later in 1980. The vessel was found by Dean Russell and Scott McDonald, using information provided by local Lake Champlain historians Peter Barranco and Merritt Carpenter. Today the schooner lies intact in 40 feet of water with two buoys attached to it. Presently, the vessel is complete with its entire hull, decking, hatches, cleats, deadeyes, windlass, mast supports, rudder, iron cookstove, and the jury-rigged tiller bar.[24] The vessel appears to be a Hollywood version of a shipwreck rather than the rows of broken ribs typical of many sunken vessels.

A second canal boat buoyed for the public at Proctor Shoal is the 90-foot *A. R. Noyes* that broke loose while being towed by the steam tug *Tisdale* on October 17, 1884. The relatively intact vessel, located with side-scan sonar in 1984 by veteran New York divers Jim Kennard and Scott Hill, lies in 65–75 foot depths. The cargo of coal is still in the *Noyes* as are two coal shovels with a mule harness nearby. The cabin is well preserved, but the bow section was damaged as the cargo of coal shifted when it went down. Artifacts have been intentionally left on the vessel to allow visitors to understand the history of the wreck and to demonstrate that these vulnerable artifacts are in the public trust to see. If we are to enjoy these wrecks, divers must recognize that souvenir hunting will destroy these historic resources that could be preserved for future generations.

The canal schooner *General Butler*.
ABOVE. Rudder.
LEFT. Windlass on the bow. Photos by the author.

The canal schooner *General Butler*: ABOVE. Tiller bar, jury-rigged during 1876 storm.
BELOW. Mast support or tabernacle.   Photos by the author.

Another fully intact canal boat was discovered in October 1978 by Canadian divers with side-scan sonar operated by Dr. Harold Edgerton of the Massachusetts Institute of Technology. At the time the Canadian team was searching for War of 1812 wrecks and identified the wreck only as a "merchant sloop of the early 19th century."[25] The vessel is a sloop-rigged canal boat which represents the earliest class of canal sloops appearing on the lake after 1823. The 79-foot sloop lies in 55 feet of water near Isle La Motte. The vessel's name is presently unknown, but she is somewhat similar in dimensions to a few Willsboro-built canal sloops. The vessel went down with a full load of marble which is still there, including a nine-foot block wedged near the windlass on the deck.[26]

Two other canal schooners, the *Cornelia* and *O. J. Walker*, foundered in the 1890s on separate occasions during gale winds as they tried to reach Burlington.[27] The schooner *Cornelia* was racing another vessel to be first at the dock for unloading, but too much sail for the gale wind caused the vessel to sink. The *Cornelia* has been located between Juniper Island and Burlington, but little is known about the condition of the vessel at this writing. The two-masted *O. J. Walker* sank on May 11, 1895, with a load of bricks and clay tiles (or chimney flues) after springing a leak during a severe gale. First discovered with side-scan sonar by James Kennard and Scott Hill, the vessel sits perfectly intact in 55–65 foot depths. The 87-foot *Walker*, built in Burlington in 1862, is entirely preserved with a cabin, windlass, anchor in the bow, bricks, tiles, wooden dollies, deadeyes, and a large wooden steering wheel in the stern. At the time that I photographed the vessel, it had not been archaeologically surveyed.

There are many other canal boat wrecks including several in the Whitehall area and one with a full load of coal in the channel that extends north of Whitehall. There are also sunken canal boats and barges off Port Henry, Westport, north of Potash Bay, Barn Rock Harbor, Diamond Island, Ligonier Point in Willsboro, Schuyler Island, Port Kent, and Shelburne Bay. Presently, there is a critical danger in New York State, both in Lake George and Lake Champlain, that historic vessels will be ripped apart by souvenir hunters. A wreck of a canal boat in Barn Rock Harbor illustrates the problem. The bow of the vessel once held a huge windlass attached by two beams running from the top of the inside bow to the bottom of the vessel. The windlass is a nautical apparatus with a wood or metal drum on each side which was used to hoist anchors or cargo aboard. In 1985 someone ripped the entire windlass out of this canal boat. This kind of unmindful souvenir hunting eventually destroys a vessel since it weakens the structure holding it together. Untreated artifacts in private hands often end up being thrown away. Today, some divers recognize that historic shipwrecks are finite resources to be left intact for others to see. However, it only takes a few to destroy these vessels.

New York needs to consider a change in public policy to offer protection for its shipwrecks. Perhaps the historic preserve program of Vermont could serve as a model for New York. At this time New York laws require a permit for exploration of an archaeological site and a second permit from the commissioner of education for the removal of any artifact. These laws were upheld in January 1984 by the New York Supreme Court in a case involving cannon that were taken from Lake Champlain in 1968. Unfortunately, current public policy in New York is not working in the majority of cases. Designation of underwater historic preserves with an emphasis on the education of the diving public might be an answer for some of the wreck sites.

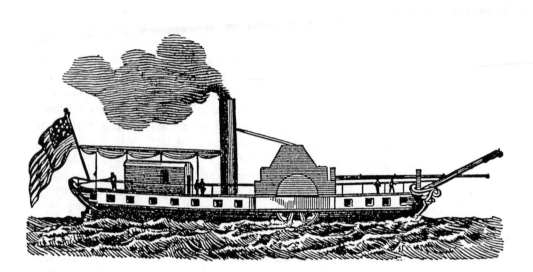

Two of the earliest steamers on Lake Champlain.
TOP. The *Phoenix*, launched in 1815.
BOTTOM. The *General Greene*, launched in 1825.

12. Steamboats of Lake Champlain

ALTHOUGH THE COMMERCIAL STEAMBOAT ERA began as early as 1809 on Lake Champlain, a viable network of trading schooners and sloops had existed for two decades on the lake. Following the migration to Vermont of Gideon King from New Lebanon, New York, and Benjamin Boardman, along with master shipbuilder Daniel Wilcox from Connecticut, shipbuilding and commerical traffic burgeoned on the lake. Gideon King with Job Boynton initiated the shipbuilding boom in the late 1780s with two small cutters for service to Burlington, Essex, and Plattsburgh. In 1790 the two entrepreneurs purchased two old warships in Canada to haul cargo between St. Jean and Burlington. That same year Boardman and Wilcox launched a 30-ton sloop, followed by two more vessels by King and Boynton in 1793. By the early part of the nineteenth century, Gideon King's son (with the same name) emerged as the owner of the largest fleet of vessels and became known as the "Admiral of the Lake."[1] As trade grew, the demand for new vessels mushroomed, encouraging new shipbuilders along the lake. Burlington, Essex, and Whitehall dominated the shipbuilding business, although a few vessels were built in other locations. When the first steamboat plied the lake, there were more than two dozen sailing vessels exceeding 30 tons in service (see Table).

While much of the technology of steam propulsion had existed for some time in the eighteenth century, it was not until the 1780s that definitive work on a steam-powered vessel occurred in America. In Bath, Virginia, George Washington was present in 1784 when James Rumsey's model boat, powered by a waterwheel with vertical poles, moved upstream. A year later, in a letter to Washington, Rumsey suggested that steam could power his planned vessel. Rumsey obtained monopoly rights for his proposed vessel in both Virginia and Maryland. After two unsuccessful vessels, Rumsey eventually succeeded with a steam-powered boat using an early form of jet propulsion. On December 3, 1787, General Horatio Gates of Revolutionary War fame was among the spectators who watched in astonishment as the vessel moved three miles an hour on the Potomac River. Following financial setbacks, Rumsey died of apoplexy in 1792 after addressing the Society of Arts in London on his ideas.

Rumsey's more successful rival, John Fitch, an ingenious jack-of-all-trades entrepreneur, built a model of a steamboat and petitioned Congress in 1785 for support. Although failing to gain Congressional backing, Fitch received monopoly rights for 14 years to operate steam-powered boats in New Jersey and three other states. Following mechanical setbacks and rocky financial dealings, Fitch achieved eight miles an hour with his 60-foot steamboat on the Delaware River in April 1790. The small boat ran several thousand miles during the summer of 1790 but was a financial loss due to low passenger use. Lower prices by Fitch with a resulting increase in passenger traffic might have changed the historical recording of the first successful steamboat in America.

Others experimented with steamboats in the early 1790s including Captain Samuel Morey of Vermont, who built a small steam-powered sidewheeler on the Connecticut River. In 1793 Morey's new steamboat, equipped with a stern wheel, traveled from Hartford to New York. His success drew the interest of Robert R. Livingston. Livingston was granted a monopoly in 1798 for boats moved by fire or steam on the waters of New York State, but his steamboat, built with his brother-in-law John Stevens, fell apart. While serving as minister to France (where he negotiated the Louisiana Purchase), Livingston sought out inventor Robert Fulton, then living in Paris, for a partnership in the building of a steamboat. After the development of an operational submarine, Fulton produced a 74-foot steamboat in 1803 which created a sensation as it crossed the River Seine four times at four and a half miles an hour. Fulton then traveled to England for a special order steam engine but lingered for two and a half years under contract to the British for his submarine ideas.

When his funding ended in Britain, Fulton returned to the United States in 1806 after a 20-year absence and began construction of a 146-foot passenger steamboat for service on the Hudson. With financial backing from his partner Robert Livingston, Fulton completed the well-built and appointed steamboat in eight weeks. Powered through side paddle wheels, the steamboat offered interior cabin room six and a half feet high and displayed an ornately decorated bow and stern. After a trial run around Manhattan, Fulton made a perfect 32-hour, 150-mile trip from New York City to Albany on August 17, 1807. He simply called the vessel *The Steamboat*. Fulton's steamboat apparently was never called the *Clermont* during his lifetime. Clermont was the name of Livingston's estate on the Hudson; the vessel, however, was later named the *North River Steamboat of Clermont*. Fulton had built the first large, mechanically flawless steamboat that achieved commercial success. He had hoped to build a steamboat empire with monopoly rights, but new competitors, lured by potential profits, dashed those dreams with legal challenges to his New York State monopoly. Attempts to gain a U.S. patent were similarly foiled by partial patent rights obtained by James Rumsey and John Fitch.[3]

John and James Winans, who had worked on the hull of Fulton's steamboat, moved to Burlington in 1808. With their previous boatbuilding experience (James had also been the pilot on Fulton's boat), the two brothers with the support of local businessmen proceeded to build a steamboat that same year. Completed in 1809, the 167-ton *Vermont* measured 125 feet with a 20-foot beam. The vessel had a flush deck, an 18 by 25-foot cabin below deck with side by side berths, and at least one mast and a 20-horsepower steam engine which powered open side paddlewheels.[4] The rules for passengers of the *Vermont* were similar to those of Fulton's steamboat. The back cabin of eight berths was reserved for women and children while the "great cabin of sixteen berths" was for use by the men: "cleanliness,

EARLY LAKE CHAMPLAIN COMMERICAL SAILING VESSELS [2]
(1793-1814)

Name	Tons	Year	Owner	Master Carpenter	Where Built
Dolphin	25-30	1793	Gideon King	Wilcox	Burlington
Burlington Packet	30	1793	J. Boynton	Wilcox	Burlington
Lady Washington	30	1795	Gideon King	Jones	Burlington
Maria	30	1796	Gideon King	Fittock	Burlington
Name Unknown	30	1800	Gideon King	Fittock	Burlington
Union	30	1800	J. Boynton	Fittock	Burlington
Elizabeth	40	1800	Daniel Rose	Eggleston	Essex, N.Y.
Jupiter	40	1802	Gideon King	Eggleston	Essex, N.Y.
Juno	40	1802	Gideon King	Wilcox	Essex, N.Y.
Unetta (*Euretta*)	30	1803	E. Boynton	Eggleston	Essex, N.Y.
Independence	35	1805	S. Boardman	Eggleston	Essex, N.Y.
Privateer	40	1807	Gideon King	Wilcox	Burlington
Hunter	50	1809	Gideon King	Wilcox	Burlington
Emperor	50	1810	H.& A. Ferris	Young	Westport
Rising Sun	50	1810	E. Boynton	Eggleston	Essex, N.Y.
Eagle	60	1810	S. Boardman	Eggleston	Whitehall
Essex	50	1810	Gideon King	Eggleston	Essex, N.Y.
Boston	30	1810	Gideon King	Wilcox	Burlington
Saucy Fox	50	1810	Gideon King	Eggleston	Essex, N.Y.
Gold Hunter	50	1811	E. Boynton	Young	Whitehall
President	75	1812	J. Boynton	Eggleston	Essex, N.Y.
Fair Trader	75	1812	J. Boynton	Eggleston	Essex, N.Y.
Morning Star	50	1812	S. Boardman	Eggleston	Whitehall
Jacob Bunker	65	1812	H. E. Chittenden	n.a.	Burlington
Richard	60	1812	Gideon King	Eggleston	Essex, N.Y.
Leopard	50	1813	J. Boynton	Eggleston	Essex, N.Y.
Boxer	50	1813	Gideon King	Eggleston	Essex, N.Y.
Paragon	75	1814	Gideon King	Eggleston	Burlington

*other sailing vessels on the lake with less documentation included the *Sally, Swallow, Greyhound, Nancy, Youth, Polly, Franklin, Elisa, Constellation, Liberty, Champlain, Mars,* and *Enterprise.*

neatness and order are necessary; . . . It is not permitted for any person to lie down in a berth with their boots or shoes on."[5]

Although the steamer *Phoenix*, built by John Stevens in 1808 for subsequent use on the Delaware River, preceded the *Vermont*, the latter steamboat is often credited with being the first regularly scheduled steamboat after Fulton's original vessel. The *Vermont* began regular service in June 1809 with trips from Whitehall to St. Jean, Canada, scheduled for

Stern section of steamer *Phoenix* in 110 feet of water near Colchester Shoal.
Photo by the author.

24 hours, but with frequent breakdowns the actual schedule was one round trip per week. The steamer was used during the War of 1812 to ferry troops and supplies along the lake and was nearly captured by the British in May 1814. Warned by an informant, Captain John Winans changed direction before being ambushed. Following the war, the *Vermont* re-established service to St. Jean from the United States. The demise of the steamboat occurred on October 15, 1815, when its connecting rod broke a hole through the hull, sinking the vessel near Bloody Island in the Richelieu River. The steamer lay on the bottom of the river until 1953 when the Lake Champlain Associates, Inc., which included Lorenzo Hagglund, the salvager of the *Royal Savage* and *Philadelphia*, raised the remaining hull with oil drums. The *Vermont* was hauled to a site on the Port Kent Road near Ausable Chasm, New York, to be displayed in a naval museum that never materialized.[6] The frames and timbers of the *Vermont* were still solid in the early 1970s as it lay abandoned in dense foliage 100 feet from

the road. The *Vermont* survived until 1973 when nearly all of the vessel was destroyed to clear the land for a campsite. Ironically, in an effort to save the vessel, the Lake Champlain Associates created the circumstances that led to its total destruction. The current philosophy among many preservationists is to leave the vessels underwater and protect the sites by the creation of historic preserves.

Before the sinking of the *Vermont*, a lawsuit against Elihu Bunker, owner of two Hudson River steamers, the *Hope* and *Perseverance*, claiming violation of the Fulton/Livingston monopoly rights, set the stage for future steamboat development on Lake Champlain. As part of the settlement, Bunker was to sell his Hudson River steamers but gained the right to operate steamboats on Lake Champlain and subsequently used the engine of the *Perseverance* for a new vessel on the lake. With the license to operate on Lake Champlain, Bunker's original investors from New York, along with new Vermont business interests, were given a charter from the New York legislature under the name of the Lake Champlain Steam-boat Company. The former captain of the *Perseverance*, Jahaziel Sherman, was sent to Vergennes to supervise the building of the new steamboat. While under construction in 1814, the vessel was sold to the navy for a profit, whereupon Thomas Macdonough converted the vessel into the war schooner *Ticonderoga*.

Within four months of the end of the War of 1812, a new steamer was launched at Vergennes by the Lake Champlain Steam-boat Company. The 336-ton *Phoenix*, propelled by a 45-horsepower engine, had a length of 146 feet and a beam of 27 feet with handsomely appointed cabins, a smoking room, barbershop, sitting room, small stateroom, baggage room, kitchen, and captain's office. The hull was rounded and deeper than the *Vermont* with enclosed side paddlewheels amidship, one forward mast with a large square sail, and a bowsprit. The flush main deck, circumscribed by a railing, was partially covered with a canvas awning. The *Phoenix* carried cargo and passengers between Whitehall and St. Jean on a regular schedule for four years. After a new engine was installed in 1817, the *Phoenix* achieved eight miles an hour on her regular runs. That same year the *Phoenix* transported President James Monroe to Plattsburgh and the following year carried the remains of General Richard Montgomery, who had been killed in the attack on Quebec in 1775, for reburial in the United States.

On the evening of September 4, 1819, the *Phoenix* departed from Burlington for Canada with 46 passengers and crew: "We left Burlington at 11:00 P.M. with everything in apparent good order about the vessel," Richard Sherman later recollected.[7] Richard Sherman, the 21-year-old son of Captain Jahaziel Sherman, commanded the *Phoenix* that fateful night since his father was confined to his bed in Vergennes suffering from a fever. About one in the morning near Providence Island, a fire was discovered on the vessel by a special messenger from the Bank of Burlington who had gone to check on the $8,500 in Montreal bills of exchange that he was carrying to Canada for collection. The passengers were awakened and two life boats launched, but the second boat departed for Providence Island with extra space available. When one passenger proposed turning back for the remaining people aboard the flaming vessel, the steamer's engineer on the lifeboat threatened "to knock the first man overboard with an oar" who should rise to make the first attempt to turn back.[8] Eleven people were left on board—tables, benches, and boards were subsequently thrown overboard to save the remaining passengers, but six, including a woman and a 12-year-old boy, were lost. The second lifeboat returned to the steamboat to rescue survivors from the blazing wreck or from the water, but by then it was too late for some of the passengers. Richard Sherman was later remembered as the hero of the disaster. After the last lifeboat departed, Sherman discovered the chambermaid unconscious under a settee. "Lashing her to the plank he had prepared for his own escape," Captain Sherman "sprung from the burning wreck as it was about to sink."[9]

The flames leaped into the black sky all night until the *Phoenix* burned to its waterline. The burning hull drifted in the wind until running aground on Colchester Shoal, north of Burlington. The cause of the fire was later attributed to a candle left burning in the pantry rather than any mechanical failure. In the confusion after the catastrophe, one passenger absconded with the $8,500 but was pursued to Grand Isle where he ultimately surrendered the money. Rumors that the commercial sailing interests on the lake might have sabotaged the steamboat were never substantiated.

After the engines were removed from the wreck of the *Phoenix*, it apparently began a slow descent down the steep northerly slope of the shoal. Although divers searched for the remains of the *Phoenix*, its location remained undiscovered until 1978 when dive instructor Don Mayland found the wreck accidentally while practicing a deep dive with a student. The vessel was lying in depths of 60 to 110 feet, untouched for 159 years. A 1983 archaeological survey by the Champlain Maritime Society recovered fragments of English china, pottery, wine bottles, kitchenware, buttons, and keys. In 1985 the *Phoenix* became one of the first wreck sites designated an Underwater Historic Preserve by the state of Vermont. Today, the vessel is accessible to all divers since a large mooring buoy floats over the wreck to which boats can tie up. The buoy is attached to an anchor pad with an underwater sign which briefly describes the wreck and warns divers that any removal of artifacts, wood, etc. is forbidden by law. The bow section, which stands about 15 feet from the bottom, lies at 60-foot depths; the stern lies in 110 feet of water. The frames, the rudder hardware at the stern, the iron rods that held the engine, the keel, etc., remain on the *Phoenix*.

Before the *Phoenix* burned, the Lake Champlain Steam-boat Company completed the 128-ton, 90-foot steamer *Champlain* in 1816, similar in design and appearance to the *Phoenix*. To deter the Winans brothers from building a new steamboat with the engine salvaged from the *Vermont*, the Lake Champlain Steam-boat Company contracted with John Winans for installation of the recovered engine and boilers into the *Champlain*. Although the Vermont legislature in 1815 granted the Lake Champlain Steam-boat Company monopoly privileges for 23 years, the company was inclined to check any potential competition before it began. The steamboat monopolies, however, would be declared unconstitutional in 1824. Following Daniel Webster's fervent arguments against steamboat monopolies in Gibbons V. Ogden, Chief Justice John Marshall ruled that steamboats "can no more be restrained from navigating waters and entering ports" than sailing vessels.[10] After this decision, the steamboat company would use the route of mergers and acquisition of rival vessels to dominate steamboat traffic on the lake.

The *Champlain*, commanded by Captain George Brush, was placed on the Whitehall-St. Jean run during 1816. Her four miles an hour speed was increased to six the following year when the engine was replaced with the original engine from the *Phoenix*. The original engine of the *Champlain* that had been salvaged from the *Vermont* was then used for Lake George's first steamboat. With only two seasons of service, the *Champlain* burned at her dock in September 1817 due to the faulty location of the boilers. The second engine and boilers on the *Champlain* that had originally come from the Hudson River steamer *Perseverance* were now placed in a new steamboat whose construction had begun at Vergennes in late 1817.

Completed in 1818, the *Congress* resembled the *Phoenix* in appearance and accommodations. The 108-foot *Congress*, described by Professor Benjamin Silliman in the fall of 1819 as "a neat and rapid boat," made three trips a week between Whitehall and St. Jean at eight miles an hour.[11] Unlike the first three steamboats on Lake Champlain, the *Congress* did not burn or sink in the lake but was retired without mishap in 1835.

With the destruction of the *Phoenix* in 1819, the steamboat company had only the *Congress* for regular service on the long Whitehall-St. Jean route. Before the end of 1819, the company began construction of the 150-foot *Phoenix II*, the last of the large steamers to be built at the Vergennes shipyard. Somewhat larger than the original *Phoenix*, the new vessel, completed in 1820, used the original engine salvaged from the wreck at Colchester Shoal. The *Phoenix II*, decorated elaborately in a patriotic fashion, carried the Marquis de Lafayette on his American tour in 1825; three years later the steamer was relegated to freight service with eventual retirement in 1837.

The *Congress* and *Phoenix II* were the first vessels to initiate "popular excursions" with an advertisement: "to view the remains of those ancient fortresses, Ticonderoga and Crown Point, and...the Battle Ground of Macdonough's Naval Engagement-Plattsburgh."[12] While stories of the early nineteenth-century steamboats conjure up romantic images of a period long past, many contemporary eyewitnesses were not as impressed. Captain Basil Hall of the British navy had only complaints about his 1827 trip aboard a crowded steamboat on Lake Champlain: "The machinery was unusually noisy, the boat weak and tremulous, and we stopped, backed, and went again, at no fewer than eleven different places, at each of which there was such a racket that it was impossible to get any rest."[13]

Beginning in the mid 1820s, Lake Champlain witnessed an expansion of steamboat services at several locations on the lake. Although sail ferries had existed at several points along the lake before the end of the eighteenth century, it was not until 1825 that a steam ferry was put into service. In 1824 the Vermont legislature chartered the Champlain Ferry Company to operate between Burlington and Port Kent. Completed at Shelburne Harbor, the 115-ton, 75-foot *General Greene* ran until 1833 when the vessel was converted to a sloop. The 136-foot *Winooski*, completed in 1832 by the Champlain Ferry Company, replaced the *Greene* on the Burlington-Port Kent-Plattsburgh route.

Another ferry service, chartered by the Vermont legislature in 1821 to operate between Charlotte and Essex, relied upon horse-powered vessels until 1827. One of their vessels utilized six horses on a treadmill connected to cog wheels which turned the side paddle wheels of the ferry. The earliest American horse-powered boat was built on the Delaware River in 1791 by John Fitch, the steamboat innovator. As many as 16 horse boat designs were filed with the U.S. Patent Office including one granted to Barnabas and Jonathan Langdon of Whitehall on June 5, 1819. The Langdons' design had one horse on each side, one facing the bow and the other the stern. Each horse or set of horses had to be carefully coordinated by a horse driver or the vessel would be difficult to steer. The firm of Henry Ross and Charles McNeil used the horse boat *Eclipse* as well as other horse boats for several decades on their Charlotte-Essex crossing. Other horse boats included the *Eagle* at the Westport-Basin Harbor crossing and the *Gypsy* which operated between Chimney Point-Crown Point-Port Henry. Horse boats, which existed well into the second half of the nineteenth century, were also used in other sections of the Northeast, including Lake Winnipesaukee, the Connecticut River, and the Hudson River. James Kennard and Scott Hill, working with the Champlain Maritime Society in 1983, discovered a nearly intact

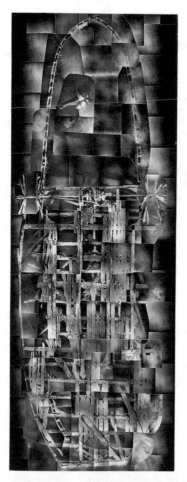

Horse ferry sunk in Burlington Harbor.

The vessel is one of Vermont's Underwater
Historic Preserves.

ABOVE.
Paddle wheels. Photo by author.

LEFT.
Photo mosaic by Scott Hill.
(Funded by National Park Service)

BELOW.
Gears for paddle wheels. Photo by author.

63-foot horse boat near Burlington using side-scan sonar. The vessel, which may be the *Eagle*, has a circular horizontal walking platform for the horses connected to two eight-foot diameter paddle wheels. On September 20, 1989, Vermont's Governor Madeleine M. Kunin dedicated the sunken horse ferry as the state's fourth Underwater Historic Preserve.

Following the collapse of one of Ross and McNeil's horse boats under a heavy load in 1827, the firm built the 92-foot steamer *Washington* at Essex for service between Charlotte and Essex. In addition to the Lake Champlain Steam-boat Company, the Champlain Ferry Company, and the Ross-McNeil line, two more competitors were soon to emerge on the lake: The Champlain Transportation Company and the St. Albans Steam Boat Company.

On October 26, 1826, the Champlain Transportation Company, which was to dominate steamboat commerce on the lake through the twentieth century, was chartered by the Vermont legislature with rights for "transporting by the aid of tow-boats or otherwise, passengers, goods, wares and merchandise...upon the said Lake Champlain."[14] With broad powers delineated in the company's charter, the founders decided to build the largest and most powerful steamboat to date on the lake. The 162-foot *Franklin*, built at St. Albans Bay, Vermont, was powered by a 75-horsepower engine which propelled the vessel at 10 miles per hour. Launched in July 1827, the *Franklin* was the first steamer with a covered main deck (promenade deck) and offered 84 berths, which were larger than those of any vessel on the lake. The *Franklin*, under Captain Jahaziel Sherman, immediately offered strong competition to the aging *Congress* and *Phoenix II* on the Whitehall-St. Jean run.

The St. Albans Steam Boat Company, chartered by the state of Vermont in 1826, two years later completed the 89-foot, 30-horsepower *MacDonough*, named after the victorious commander of 1814, for use between St. Albans and Plattsburgh. As a tow boat in the last years of her career, the 138-ton vessel "ran onto a reef opposite Barber's Point on the Vermont side and was wrecked there in a gale of wind," according to Captain Ell B. Rockwell, who spent over 80 years on the lake and had served as a cook on the schooner *Cynthia* in the early 1840s.[15] Other sources indicate that the *MacDonough* was trying to retrieve a canal boat that had broken loose from a tow during a gale on November 16, 1841, when it "was wrecked upon the reef of rocks in Panton Bay."[16] The engine was later taken out and the remaining "hull abandoned were it lay."[17] The Champlain Maritime Society sponsored an unsuccessful field search for the vessel in 1984.

With more competition developing on the lake, consolidation of steamboat interests began in 1828. The Lake Champlain Steam-boat Company leased the *Congress* and *Phoenix II* to Timothy Follett and C. P. VanNess, canal freight operators, who formed a pool or cartel arrangement with the Champlain Transportation Company whereby only one steamer would make the Whitehall-St. Jean run and profits would be equally divided. The *Franklin* and *Congress* alternated on that run while the *Phoenix II* was assigned freight service. In a similar move, the Champlain Transportation Company purchased the *Washington* in 1828 from Ross and McNeil and promptly restricted the vessel to towing. Facing continuing losses, the Lake Champlain Steam-boat Company was sold to Isaiah Townsend of Albany in 1830, who in turn sold the company's two vessels, the property at Shelburne Harbor, and all equipment to the Champlain Transportation Company in 1833. In both purchases, the Champlain Transportation Company financed the deals with the issuance of stock. The Champlain Ferry Company, the St. Albans Steam Boat Company, and a new steamer built for Jahaziel Sherman offered the only remaining competition for the Champlain Transportation Company.

The 90-foot *Water Witch* was built by Samuel Wood at Fort Cassin on Otter Creek for Captain Jahaziel Sherman in 1832. The steamer's narrow beam of 17 feet and relatively powerful 40-horsepower engine moved the vessel at eight miles per hour. Although the passenger accommodations were inferior to other steamers, the ability to carry freight made the independent steamer practical on the Vergennes-Whitehall run. Consistent with its monopoly strategy, the Champlain Transportation Company formed a collusive agreement on November 21, 1833, with Sherman whereby "at no time to permit his Steam Boat Water Witch to go North of Fort Cassin so as to interfere with the regular business. . .by the Champlain Transportation Company."[18]

The elegant steamer *Burlington* built in 1837 at Shelburne Harbor carried passengers such as the English novelist Charles Dickens and President Martin Van Buren. (Special Collections, Bailey/Howe Memorial Library, UVM)

On January 27, 1835, the Champlain Transportation Company completed its consolidation on the lake with the purchase (through stock sales) of the Champlain Ferry Company with the *Winooski*, the St. Albans Steam Boat Company with the *MacDonough*, and the *Water Witch* from Sherman.[19] The *Water Witch* was placed in towing service in 1835 by the company but the next year was converted into a two-masted schooner and sold. Captain Ell Rockwell remembered the vessel as a schooner: "her cabin was finely decorated as a steamer and never changed."[20] On April 26, 1866, the *Water Witch* was headed for Burlington loaded with iron ore from the Cheever Ore Bed in Port Henry when it foundered south of Diamond Island during a spring squall. According to the newspaper report on the following day, the vessel sank so quickly that the lifeboat was not deployed: "Capt. [Thomas]

Mock kept his wife and two children above water for nearly twenty minutes, until picked up by Capt. Eaton [sloop *Trader*]. An infant child of Capt. Mock's went down on board the schooner."[21]

The *Water Witch*, first discovered by Canadian diver Derek Grout in 1977 and relocated by James Kennard with side-scan sonar, lies completely intact in 75-80 feet of water. The vessel's primitive windlass, bowsprit, two anchors, wooden cleats, pulleys, deadeyes, tiller bar, and other parts remain undisturbed in eerie silence after 125 years underwater. The cabin, whose wooden panels with white trim have largely fallen into the silt, extends the width of the vessel and about 12 feet back from the entrance. One mast lies broken on the

Anchor on bow of *Water Witch*. Photo by the author.

deck, the other beside the schooner. About 30 feet astern of the vessel lies the small lifeboat that Captain Mock had tied to the stern. The *Water Witch*, which combined both the steam and sail era of the nineteenth century, may be the nation's oldest completely intact commercial vessel.

By 1835 the Champlain Transportation Company owned every steamboat on the lake. The steamboat company soon began a modernization program with the completion of the 190-foot steamer *Burlington* in 1837. The *Burlington* was to carry many famous passengers including President Martin VanBuren and Henry Clay in 1840 and Charles Dickens in 1842. Dickens found the *Burlington* "a perfectly exquisite achievement of neatness, elegance, and order."[22]

Although the walking-beam engine design had been on the lake earlier, the *Burlington*'s 200-horsepower engine was the largest and most powerful steam engine to date on Lake Champlain. The walking beam, resembling an oil field pump, was connected to the steam cylinder by a connecting link on one side and to the paddlewheels by a connecting rod on the opposite side. When the engine operated, the iron "walking beam," mounted high amidship, would tilt back and forth as it transmitted power to the paddlewheels. The construction of the early nineteenth-century steam engines was quite remarkable considering the lack of gas and electric arc welding, high-speed electric and pneumatic drills etc.

While the Champlain Transportation Company was building the *Burlington*, their brief monopoly was challenged by Peter Comstock, an industrious canal boat operator who had started construction of a large steamboat in Whitehall. As a director of the acquired Champlain Ferry Company, Comstock had been "well taken care of" in 1835 by the Champlain Transportation Company.[23] To protect its monopoly, the latter company bought the unfinished steamer from Comstock in 1836, made him a director, and paid him a salary for eight years as an agent of the company; in return he was "not to build or cause to be built during said term of eight years, any other Boat in opposition to this Company."[24] The Champlain Transportation Company enlarged Comstock's steamboat to a 215-foot length and added a 200-horsepower steam engine before completion in 1838. Although considered a sister ship, the *Whitehall* was not as elaborately finished or ever as famous as the *Burlington*.

In 1842 the Champlain Transportation Company replaced the steamer *Winooski* with the 166-foot *Saranac* built at Shelburne Harbor for the Burlington-Port Kent ferry service. The company's position seemed secure and profitable with $5.00 through-passage rates on the steamers *Burlington* and *Whitehall*, but opposition to rates led to an incipient steamboat company composed of New Yorkers. The new company was incorporated with a broad charter by the New York legislature on January 22, 1841, under "the name of the New-York and Champlain Steam Transportation Company, for the purpose of navigating Lake Champlain."[25] The New Yorkers decried the "complete monopoly" of the Champlain Transportation Company where "boat after boat has been purchased in and laid up, such has been the profits of the concern that...divide 50 per cent."[26] Once again, however, the Champlain Transportation Company bought out the potential stockholders but before any vessel was ever built. The CTC owners could not relax, however. Peter Comstock, with his agreement expiring, resigned as a director and began building another steamboat at Whitehall. After a policy of acquisition of all competitors, the Champlain Transportation Company abruptly changed its strategy and decided to compete with the new steamboat. Completed in 1844, Comstock's 185-foot steamer *Francis Saltus*, commanded by veteran sloop Captain H. G. Tisdale, offered strong competition for the *Burlington*.

The steamer *Saranac* was recalled from ferry service by the Champlain Transportation Company, refitted and lengthened to compete with the *Saltus*. The resulting rivalry led to an all-out contest of speed between the two vessels as passengers cheered on the captains and crews while placing side bets on the results. Stops were often skipped to make up time as the crews tossed pine pitch into the boilers to raise steam pressure and tied down safety valves. With Comstock's cabin fare cut to 50 cents and deck passage only 25 cents, the CTC cut fares to $3 on the *Burlington* and the *Whitehall* and 25 cents on the *Saranac*. With mounting financial problems due to low fares, Comstock's control of the *Saltus* was passed to the firm of Grant, Coffin and Church of Troy, New York.

When an agreement in the summer of 1846 to "divide the gross receipts" of the Champlain Transportation Company's steamers and the *Saltus* was not adhered to by the Troy owners, the CTC commenced building a larger steamboat to compete with the *Saltus*.[27] The steamer *United States*, with a length of 240 feet, beam of 28 feet, and displacement of 648 tons, was easily the biggest vessel to date on Lake Champlain. With elegant staterooms on the second deck and 250 horsepower that propelled the vessel at 19 miles per hour, the *United States* in 1847 far surpassed the performance and amenities of the *Saltus*. As passenger traffic on the *Saltus* declined in favor of the more contemporary steamer, the end for the Troy owners neared. On February 10, 1848, the Champlain Transportation Company acquired the *Saltus* and the *Montreal*, a 224-foot steamer hull under construction at Whitehall.

While the passenger steamer traffic was consolidated by the Champlain Transportation Company, the freight and towing service saw several competitors over the years. The Northern Transportation Line, controlled by Peter Comstock in the mid-nineteenth century, built the 136-foot, 50-horsepower steamer *James H. Hooker* in 1846 (converted to a barge in 1879). In 1847 the newly formed Steam Tow-Boat Company completed the 136-foot, 75-horsepower *Ethan Allen* for towing operations. A year later, Ross and McNeil finished the 80-foot horse boat *Boquet*, which was subsequently converted into a 30-horsepower steamer. Likewise, the 127-foot steamer *Boston*, built by the Champlain Transportation Company in 1851, was sold the following year to the Rutland and Burlington Railroad to be used for transfer of freight and passengers. The Northern Transportation Line also built the 136-foot *Oliver Bascom* in 1856 with 150 horsepower for towing service.[28] Some of the towing vessels changed ownership several times in their careers on the lake. The *Ethan Allen*, for example, was owned by the Steam Tow-Boat Company, the Vermont Central Railroad, the Champlain Transportation Company, and the Northern Transportation Line.

After a period of time the Northern Transportation Line consolidated much of the towing and freight operations on the lake. One of their 1870 handbills advertised "the New and Powerful Steamer, *L.J.N. Stark*, exclusively for freight. . .And will run the Steamers *Oliver Bascom, J. H. Hooker, Boston,* and *Ethan Allen* for Towing."[29] The *L. J. N. Stark*, built at Whitehall in 1869, had one of the shortest careers on Lake Champlain. The 185-foot vessel with a 26-foot beam was commanded by Captain Richard Arbuckle during her one-year stint on the lake. While carrying a load of hay in 1870, the sidewheeler caught fire and sank just south of the Point Au Roche light (north of Plattsburgh). The night watchman was the only person lost in the accident. The wreck lies south of the light in 10 to 18 feet of water.

The passenger business on the lake was stabilized in 1848 with control of all the large steamboats by the Champlain Transportation Company. In the following year, several local directors of the company sold their interest in the company to owners of the North River Steamers (a Hudson River line), who inaugurated the "North and South Through Line" whereby passengers could buy a single ticket for passage from New York City to Montreal via railroads and steamers.

New competition for the Champlain Transportation Company, however, appeared in 1852 with the opposition line of T. D. Chapman and Associates who put into service the 250-foot steamer *R. W. Sherman* built at Whitehall by Thomas Collyer in 1851. The builders of the *R. W. Sherman*, eyeing the competition, designed the vessel for the highest possible speeds. The vessel, at 19 miles per hour, set a record of 27 minutes from Port Kent to the northern end of the Burlington breakwater in 1852. In a move to turn an apparent quick profit, the Champlain Transportation Company sold all assets (except its charter) to the Rutland and Burlington Railroad on August 31, 1852. The following year, however, the Champlain Transportation Company bought the *R. W. Sherman* and another steamer, the *Canada*, nearing completion at Whitehall. In 1853 the *Sherman*, renamed the *America* by the company, and the 260-foot *Canada* were the most modern and efficient steamboats in Lake Champlain service. Following two years of disappointing operations, the Rutland and Burlington Railroad sold the steamers *United States, Burlington, Whitehall, Saranac*, the unfinished *Montreal*, and the Shelburne facilities back to the Champlain Transportation Company in 1854 for one-third their purchase price.

The steamer *United States* continued in service on the lake with the *America* and *Canada*, but the *Burlington, Saranac*, and *Whitehall* were sent to Shelburne Harbor to be broken up. The *Francis Saltus*, not included in the buy-back from the Rutland and Burlington Railroad, once again became the subject of controversy on the lake. After its sale to a director of the Plattsburgh and Montreal Railroad and a payment to lay-up the steamer in 1856, the vessel was seized by Captain Lot Chamberlain of the CTC on the basis of an unpaid lien for repairs. Following two court orders and another seizure, the steamer was brought to the CTC facilities at Shelburne where a standoff occurred at gunpoint when 100 men from Plattsburgh attempted to reclaim the steamer. The saga of the *Saltus* did not end until 1858 when the Champlain Transportation Company once again purchased the vessel. The following year the company finally ended the wild career of the *Saltus* by ordering her dismantled. The remnants of the old challenger lie today in the shallow water of Shelburne Harbor.

After the aging *Saranac* was dismantled in 1855, her engine was placed in the 224-foot steamer *Montreal*, which had been reacquired by the Champlain Transportation Company. The hull of the *Montreal* had been built in Whitehall in 1847, but the steamer wasn't completed until 1856 at Shelburne. The *Montreal* was placed in passenger service through 1868 when the steamer was converted for towing duties. Twelve years later, the *Montreal* burned in Maquam Bay.

During the Civil War, the Champlain Transportation Company moved a large number of volunteers and some of their horses from northern New York to Whitehall on their way to join the Union Army. Aside from the 1864 raid by 22 Confederate soldiers on St. Albans, Vermont, the Champlain Valley's role in the Civil War consisted largely of supplying men and materials. Before the end of the war, the CTC made plans for a new steamer to replace the *America*.

The Champlain Transportation Company, under the presidency of Colonel LeGrand Cannon (1864-1895), made substantive changes in the financial structure of the firm and

RIGHT. Lake Champlain Steamers.
TOP. The *Adirondack* built at Shelburne Harbor in 1867 and retired eight years later.
MIDDLE. The 260-foot *Canada* built at Whitehall in 1853.
BOTTOM. The 240-foot *United States* completed at Shelburne Harbor in 1847.
(Special Collections, Bailey/Howe Memorial Library, UVM)

services offered to passengers. Cannon's association with the Rensselaer and Saratoga Railroad (controlled by his brother-in-law) led to the purchase of the Champlain Transportation Company by the railroad. Following a purchase of the majority of stock in the Lake George Steam Boat Company on January 8, 1868, the Champlain Transportation Company assumed control of the Lake George operation. On May 1, 1871, the Rensselaer and Saratoga Railroad permanently leased all holdings to the Delaware and Hudson Canal Company; thus control of both steamboat companies fell under the Delaware and Hudson. The Delaware and Hudson soon coordinated its train schedules and lake steamer runs with the Hudson River Day and Night Lines to provide continuous service between New York City and Montreal.

In the spring of 1867, the 251-foot *Adirondack*, displacing 1,087 tons, finally reached completion at Shelburne Harbor. By the 1860s the Lake Champlain steamers had been converted from wood to coal burning. The steamer *United States* had been the first on the lake in 1858 to make the conversion to coal; the *Adirondack* was the first of the Champlain Transportation Company steamers originally designed for coal. The *Adirondack* was taken out of service in 1875 because of a vibration that could not be overcome by the builders and the reduced traffic due to railroad competition. The engines were sold for installation on a steamboat on the Hudson River and her elegant upper works, including cabin fixtures and furnishings, were sold for use on the steamer *City of Cleveland* on the Great Lakes. Today 222 feet of the *Adirondack* lies southwest of Colamers Island in 10-15 feet of water. The vessel is probably the most intact steamer hull in Shelburne Bay.

To replace the 18-year-old *Canada*, the Champlain Transportation Company in 1871 completed the most opulent and powerful steamboat built on Lake Champlain in the nineteenth century. The 1,500-horsepower, 262-foot *Vermont II* could achieve 19 miles per hour. The vessel offered 61 staterooms, a bridal room, barbershop, president's room, a walnut and chestnut stateroom hall 171 feet in length, and a dining room designed to seat 150 people at a time. Many distinguished travelers crossed the lake on the handsome steamer including U.S. Grant and General Philip Sheridan.

Several smaller steamers were also built in this period. In 1868 the St. Albans, Grand Isle, and Plattsburgh Ferry Company operated the steamer *River Queen* between St. Albans Bay, Maquam Bay, and Plattsburgh. The small steamer crashed onto a rock ledge at Hathaway's Point on the St. Albans shoreline on October 30, 1868, and sank. The *Grand Isle*, built as a passenger steamer in 1869 at Essex, was later sold to the Northern Transportation Line after failing to generate the expected profits. Lastly, the 132-foot *A. Williams*, built at Marks Bay in Burlington in 1870 by Andrew Williams of Plattsburgh and Warren Corbin of South Hero, Vermont, was sold to the Champlain Transportation Company in 1872. The vessel had a successful career of 23 years on the lake before retirement and dismantling at Shelburne Bay.

In 1873 the Champlain Transportation Company purchased a 258-foot steamer that had been used as a railroad ferry. Two years later, the steamer would become the most famous shipwreck in the long history of steamboat traffic on Lake Champlain. Originally named the *Oakes Ames* after a Massachusetts congressman and railroad financier, the steamboat was built in 1868 to haul loaded railroad cars across the lake. Two vertical walking-beam steam engines of 270 horsepower each allowed independent power for both paddlewheels while leaving an unobstructed main deck for a pair of railroad tracks. With an overall length of 258 feet, a beam of 35 feet, and an overall width of 61 feet, the *Oakes Ames* was among the biggest vessels ever used on the lake. The steamer was designed to carry 14 loaded railroad cars in addition to freight and passengers.

For five years the *Oakes Ames* made four round trips daily between Burlington and Plattsburgh carrying railroad cars. Nearing the expected completion in 1874 of a railroad line from Ticonderoga to Plattsburgh, there would be less need for the *Oakes Ames* as a portable railroad bridge. Thus in 1873 the *Oakes Ames* was sold to the Delaware and Hudson Railroad which had control of the Champlain Transportation Company at the time. The Delaware and Hudson subsequently sold the vessel to their subsidiary, the Champlain

The steamer *Oakes Ames*. Watercolor by James Bard, Museum of the City of New York. (Special Collections, Bailey/Howe Memorial Library, University of Vermont)

Transportation Company, for $85,000 to be refitted the next year as a passenger steamer. The Champlain Transportation Company changed the name of the vessel to the *Champlain* as "indicative of the geographical features of Lake Champlain and its neighborhood."[30] The actual reason for the name change probably had more to do with the notorious reputation Congressman Oakes Ames had acquired from involvement in the Crédit Mobilier financial scandals.

The remodeled vessel displayed thick imported carpeting from Brussels, fine butternut and black walnut wood panels, expensive black walnut furniture, 41 cabins, a post office, barbershop, 115-seat dining room, and a huge 162-foot main stateroom. The *Champlain* operated as a passenger liner during 1874 and 1875. To change a ship's name, however, was said to be an omen of bad luck. This magnificent steamer, unfortunately, would fulfill the ominous prophecy.

After mechanical trouble sidelined the steamer *Vermont II* in the summer of 1875, the *Champlain* was placed in regular service along the lake. On July 15, 1875, the *Champlain* left Ticonderoga at 9:30 in the evening for its northern run. At Westport, 23 passengers

ABOVE. Supports for paddle wheels on the steamer *Champlain* sunk north of Westport, New York in 1875. Photo by the author.
RIGHT. The wreck of the *Champlain*. (Special Collections, Bailey/Howe Memorial Library, UVM)

disembarked from the vessel leaving 53 adults and a number of children plus a crew of approximately 47. As the *Champlain* departed Westport a few minutes after midnight with "a bright moonlight and with no wind," the Senior Pilot John Eldredge, a veteran of 20 years on the lake, lit his pipe and took the wheel from Second Pilot Ell Rockwell.[31]

Fifteen minutes later at 12:20 A.M., the vessel traveling at 16 miles per hour crashed on the rock ledge at Steam Mill Point only four miles from Westport. Crewmen Walter Hedding and Edwin Rockwell, nephew of the second pilot, were seated at a table in the hold having a midnight snack when a big rock burst through the bottom of the ship along with a thundering crack and a surge of water. Amid splintered walls, buckled floors, and escaping steam, the crew and passengers scurried above, fearful that the steamboat was about to explode. Without vulnerable connecting pipes, the separate engines mounted on each side of the vessel were quickly shut down by the engineers, thus avoiding scalding injuries to the crew and passengers. Second Pilot Rockwell, who had just retired to his cabin for bed before the crash, was the first to reach the pilot house from his adjoining cabin. According to Rockwell, who delighted in retelling the story, Pilot Eldredge after the crash was still holding onto the steering wheel staring blankly at the mountainside. Eldredge "turned cooly" to the second pilot and asked, "Ell, can you account for my being on the mountain?" Rockwell replied, "Yes, Mr. Eldredge, you were asleep." Eldredge swore that he was steering the vessel on "her true course."[32]

Captain George Rushlow, who had been engrossed in a conversation with a passenger in his room on the main deck when the accident occurred, immediately sprang into action to stabilize the vessel and make accommodations for the passengers to get off the *Champlain*. The frightened passengers, many of whom were still in the "grand saloon," were calmed by the steady voice and directions of Captain Rushlow. Although there was some initial screaming after the crash with one person fainting, the most serious injury was the broken tooth of a female passenger. Not all the passengers were unsettled by the disaster, however. When the *Champlain* collided with the shoreline, Mrs. Smith Weed awoke with a shriek which sent her husband to the stateroom window. Observing the stillness outside, Weed concluded "They must have struck [the] Westport dock pretty hard" and the couple returned to bed.[33] Within eight minutes of the disaster, gangplanks were set up and passengers stood safely on the rocks examining the wreckage. The bow had been driven "sixty feet upon the rock" according to a contemporary newspaper account.[34] The boat began filling with water, breaking in "two where she was lying across the rock" soon after the passengers got off.[35] When the vessel broke, both ends settled with the stern sinking in water up to the promenade deck. By then most of the baggage in the stern had been retrieved.

Rushlow promptly dispatched Second Pilot Rockwell in a life boat to hail the steamer *Adirondack* that was in sight traveling from the north. The *Adirondack* came alongside the stricken vessel at two A.M. to collect the passengers and their baggage and return them to Ticonderoga. Rockwell was then towed to Young Bay where he awoke Captain Connor of the schooner *Mary D. Craig* to take valuables off the *Champlain*. Later the tugboat *J. G. Witherbee* was employed to retrieve freight from the wrecked steamer.

Pilot John Eldredge, in the meanwhile, sat in disbelief in the pilot house as the rest of the crew scrambled to clear out the vessel. Engineer Joseph Trombly saw Eldredge at the break of dawn "with his valise and coat on his arm" disappear over the mountain.[36] Following wild rumors by the public on the cause of the wreck, the U.S. Local Inspectors of Steam Vessels held formal hearings by the end of July on the disaster. Evidence, corroborated by several witnesses, found that Eldredge had been in the habit of buying morphine, which was widely available from druggists in the nineteenth century. One druggist from Burlington testified that Eldredge had bought two or three bottles of morphine several weeks before the disaster. Eldredge at 61 years old had a reputation as an excellent navigator of Lake Champlain and knew every inlet and reef on the lake, but he was stripped of his license. When the inspectors told him that his pilot's license had been revoked forever, he was said to reply; "Gentlemen, wait until I ask you for one."[37] The discredited pilot disappeared in the West without taking his last pay. Years later, he wrote the company for money from a home for the aged. The Champlain Transportation Company sent him a small check which was the last that anyone in the valley heard of him.

The other two officers, on the other hand, continued their careers on Lake Champlain. Captain George Rushlow who began his career in 1844 aboard the schooners *Hornet* and *Melvina* saw 60 years of service on Lake Champlain. The all time record, however, goes to the second pilot of the *Champlain*, Ell Rockwell. Rockwell, who started out as a cabin boy in 1844 on the schooner *Cynthia* on Lake Champlain, eventually became a captain for the Champlain Transportation Company serving until the age of 98 when he retired as captain of the steamer *Vermont III* in 1928.

The crash of the vessel was a night to remember for most of the crew and passengers but not for everyone. In the wee hours of the morning the captain sent a waiter through a small hole cut in the bulkhead to work his way to the dining room for food. The waiter came flying back with the report that a dead man was lying in a cabin. The hole was made bigger to allow Second Pilot Rockwell to enter the cabin. Sure enough, a man lay still on a bed with part of his mattress in the water. "About four feet of water was in the room and his shoes were floating in it," recounted Rockwell.[38] "About four feet from his head was the side which struck the mountain and timbers and planking were all broken right up to his head. I thought he was dead."[39] Rockwell shook him until he woke up. Evidently, the passenger was a law student who had passed the bar exam the day before and had consumed too much to drink.

To prevent the *Champlain* from slipping into the deep water at Steam Mill Point, the vessel was cabled to the trees onshore. During the following six weeks, the hull was stripped of her superstructure, boilers, and engine. One engine was used on the steamer *Horicon* built at Lake George in 1877. Souvenir hunters also descended on the vessel, stripping off the black walnut ornamental woodwork. A Plattsburgh newspaper account described the interior stripping which "necessitated a voyage through part of the steamer in a small boat . . .the most persistent and daring of this army were women."[40] The Champlain Transportation Company did not collect on its insurance policy which only covered destruction by fire. The company, however, did salvage all of the machinery and even ran tourist excursions for 50 cents aboard their smaller steamer *A. Williams* to the site of the wreck. After the salvaging effort, the cables were cut and most of the hull was scuttled in the adjacent water.

Today, 163 feet of the wreck remains a haven for tourists with modern scuba gear. The hull of the *Champlain* "was sunk in the deep water near the spot where she had crashed on the rock," according to early reports.[41] For years divers repeated the story that the wreck was in two sections with one undiscovered portion in 150 or more feet of water. In 1980, however, the New York search team of Joseph Zarzynski of Wilton and James Kennard and Scott Hill from Rochester, New York, after deploying side-scan sonar at the wreck site, found no other sections of the vessel. The bow section of the *Champlain* was apparently

Lake Champlain Steamers.

LEFT TOP. *Reindeer* at Burlington wharf.
LEFT MIDDLE. The 142-foot *Maquam*, 1881-1906.
LEFT BOTTOM. *A. Williams*, 1870-1893.
ABOVE. *Francis Saltus* at Whitehall, 1844.
BELOW. *Vermont II* in Shelburne Harbor.
(Special Collections, Bailey/Howe Memorial Library, UVM)

dismantled on the shore before the remaining hull was scuttled in the lake. The surviving section of the vessel lies in 15-35 feet of water about 100 feet south of Steam Mill Point.[42]

By 1875, following the completion of a railroad between Ticonderoga and Plattsburgh, a plateau of steamboat demand had been reached on the lake. The expansion of rail lines meant the abandonment of Whitehall as the southern terminus and Rouses Point in 1876 as the northern stop for the lake steamers. Ticonderoga's 1,550-foot semicircular railroad bridge at the base of Mount Defiance became the new southern depot, while Plattsburgh's rail terminal by the lake served as the northern end of the line for the lake steamers. For the first time, steamboats were no longer the vital link between New York City and Montreal. The first casualty of the new economic reality was the eight-year-old *Adirondack*, retired and dismantled at Shelburne Harbor in 1875. This reduced the Champlain Transportation Company's fleet to the *Vermont II* and the smaller *A. Williams*. To turn a profit, the company advertised the steamers to tourists for their access to the geography and history of the lake. The trip for tourists through Lake George and Lake Champlain was made more convenient after 1874 by the construction of a rail line by the Delaware and Hudson between the Baldwin Landing in northern Lake George and the Montcalm Landing at Ticonderoga on Lake Champlain. By 1882 the Delaware and Hudson expanded rail lines to the southern end of Lake George from Glens Falls.

In the early 1880s two passenger steamers were built on Lake Champlain, successfully taking advantage of the growing rail connections. The 142-foot *Maquam*, built in 1880 under master carpenter A. J. Cookson at Swanton, Vermont, began service the following year for the St. Johnsbury and Lake Champlain Railroad Company. In 1897 the steamer was purchased by the Champlain Transportation Company to run between Burlington and St. Albans and for special excursion trips. The *Maquam* was used to transport President William McKinley in the summer of 1897 while he vacationed at the Hotel Champlain (now Clinton County Community College), just south of Plattsburgh. The vessel had an unusual tendency to roll in the waves which often caused jokesters to run back and forth across the forward deck to exacerbate the rolling until the captain ordered the crew to interrupt the mischief makers. After 24 years of service, the *Maquam* was retired from service in 1905 and her hull cut up at Shelburne Harbor the following year. The second steamer launched in the 1880s was the 168-foot *Reindeer*, built at Alburgh, Vermont, under master carpenter Jermiah Faulks for the Grand Isle Steamboat Company. The *Reindeer*, which began passenger service in 1882 between Burlington and St. Albans, was one of the few steamers in the history of the lake never to operate under the ownership of the Champlain Transportation Company. After many years of excursion service, the steamer sank at the Central Vermont wharf in Burlington in 1902. The *Reindeer* was subsequently raised and taken to Whitehall for dismantling with her 800-horsepower engine cut up for scrap iron.

With the Champlain Transportation Company's two steamers, *Vermont II* and *A. Williams*, turning a profit in the 1880s, the company decided to build a larger vessel to replace the smaller of the two steamboats. In a departure from previous wood construction, the Champlain Transportation Company built the 1000-horsepower, 205-foot *Chateaugay* with an iron hull. The *Chateaugay*, a marvel of inland steamboat construction, began passenger and excursion service in 1888. The 1,200-passenger vessel operated until 1917 when it was temporarily laid-up due to a drop in tourism during World War I. She operated for a few years after the war but was out of service from 1922 to 1924. When the Champlain Transportation Company decided to remodel the *Chateaugay* as a car ferry, David Collins of the Steamboat Inspection Service was sent to Shelburne to assess the safety of changing the old steamer. Collins, who had served on Warren Harding's presidential yacht as an engineer, warned the company that "making changes in a boat that was built in 1888 is a waste of money and I can never O.K. it."[43] But after inspection he remarked, "if anybody had told me a vessel thirty-seven years old could be in the shape she is I wouldn't have believed them."[44] The superstructure on the forward and aft deck was cut down to allow automobile ferry service. By the end of the decade, the *Chateaugay* had carried over 48,000 cars between Port Kent and Burlington.

At the end of the Great Depression, the engineless *Chateaugay* was relegated to service as a clubhouse for the Burlington Yacht Club. Following a fire on December 22, 1939, that totally destroyed the old steamer *Mount Washington* on Lake Winnipesaukee, New Hampshire, the newly formed Mount Washington Steamship Corporation purchased the *Chateaugay* for $20,000. In the spring of 1940 the vessel's hull was cut into 20 sections at Shelburne and loaded on barges to be taken back to Burlington where eight railroad cars carried the old vessel to Lake Winnipesaukee. Launched in August 1940, the *Mt. Washington II* survives to this day on the lake. In the winter of 1982-1983, the renamed *M/S Mount Washington* was lengthened by 24 feet. If Inspector Collins could now examine the hull after more than 100 years of service, he surely would be impressed.

Following the success of the *Chateaugay* on Lake Champlain at the turn of the century, the Champlain Transportation Company launched the largest steamer ever built on Lake Champlain. The iron-hulled 262-foot *Vermont III*, completed in 1903, had a beam of 62 feet at the widest point and displaced 1,195 tons. The 1,800-horsepower engine propelled the vessel at speeds of 23 miles per hour. The *Vermont III* was a floating palace with mahogany furniture, red carpeting, a white and gold stateroom hall with an ornate staircase, and 50 staterooms with running water. The retirement of the *Vermont II* in 1902 and the *Maquam* in 1905 ended the era of wooden steamboats owned by the Champlain Transportation Company. The *Vermont II*, like the *Maquam* later, was hauled out of the lake at Shelburne Harbor and cut up in the summer of 1903. Although the *Vermont II* and *Maquam* were hauled out at Shelburne, most of the earlier wooden steamers, outliving their usefulness, were stripped of engines, the useful portions of their superstructure, and left to settle in the bay.

Shelburne Harbor became a graveyard for at least a dozen scuttled lake steamers of a bygone era. Just below the surface in five to ten feet of water, the massive timbers of these vessels unfold like gigantic brontosaurus skeletons. Although some are quite broken up, probably due to shipyard and marina construction as well as ice damage, at least a half dozen of the hulls are substantially together. In 1983 the Champlain Maritime Society examined and measured six of the hulls.[45] Most of the steamers have massive frames, engine mounts, keels, and keelsons that are quite solid, considering that almost all have been on the bottom for more than 100 years.

In addition to the 222 feet of the *Adirondack* lying southwest of Colamers Island, the most visible wrecks are located on the north side of Pine Point (just south of the present Shelburne Marina). The most intact wreckage in this area is the steamer *Burlington*, lying in a north-south direction with the bow area facing the shore in the shallow water. Dismantled in 1859 at Shelburne, 161 feet of her length and 25 feet of width include 83 frames, the stern post, and the rudder. Touching the port side of the *Burlington*'s bow area is another steamer lying in an east-west direction with an existing length of 210 feet and width of 27 feet. Although an old Shelburne Shipyard drawing placed the *Whitehall* (original length of 215 feet by 23) in this locality, the wreckage may be the *Canada* or perhaps the *United States*, both of which were also dismantled near this area. As many as 149 frames remain on the port side of the vessel as well as massive engine mounts about 59 feet from the stern. To the starboard side of the *Burlington* lies 125 feet of the wreckage of either the *Francis Saltus*, abandoned in this area in 1859, or possibly the *A. Williams*, dismantled in 1893. This vessel lies close to the shoreline in an east-west direction in five feet of water. Another steamer wreck, measuring 135 feet by 23 feet, also lies on the starboard side of the *Burlington* in an east-west direction. This fourth steamer on the north side of Pine Point is believed to be the *Franklin*, abandoned in the vicinity in 1838. On the south side of Pine Point are the scattered remains of the steamer thought to be the *United States*. The steamers *Saranac* and *Winooski* and sloop *Hann*, listed on the Shelburne drawing, were hauled further out in deeper water during construction of the present marina. The area north of the old shipyard on Shelburne Point has only scattered wreckage of the 81-foot steamer *Herald*, the 250-foot *America/Sherman*, tug *Pocahontas*, yacht *General Allen*, the 55-foot shipyard tender *Osceola*, and a scow.[46] In addition to the large passenger steamboats, there was a variety of smaller steam vessels such as the *Herald* on the lake during the late nineteenth century and early twentieth century.*

With the retirement of the *Maquam* in 1905, the Champlain Transportation Company decided to build a larger vessel as its third steamer on the lake to compliment the *Vermont III* and *Chateaugay*. The 220-foot, 1,500-horsepower *Ticonderoga* was completed at Shelburne Harbor in 1906. The steel hull plates were built by the T. S. Marvel Company in Newburgh, New York, and shipped to Shelburne for assembly and the building of the wooden superstructure. The huge engine, built by the W. and A. Fletcher Company of Hoboken, New Jersey, powered immense iron sidewheels. The superstructure contained a finely decorated main stateroom hall with fluted stanchions, newel posts and banisters of cherry, butternut-paneled stateroom doors, rich patterned carpeting, and gracefully curved timbers supporting a stenciled ceiling.

The *Ticonderoga* was given the Westport-Plattsburgh run while the *Chateaugay* was assigned the excursion trade, formerly the task of the *Maquam*. In 1909 during the Tercentenary Anniversary of the discovery of the lake by Samuel de Champlain, the *Ticonderoga* played an important role in transporting dignitaries, including President William Howard Taft. Although World War I slowed the tourist trade, the *Ticonderoga* continued to operate with special excursions for the officer trainees at Plattsburgh and Fort Ethan Allen in Burlington to the sites of the Valcour and Plattsburgh battles.

Returning to service in 1920 after a serious grounding in 1919, the *Ticonderoga* carried passengers throughout the decade, including such notables as General John J. Pershing, who made a tour of inspection of the Plattsburgh army post and Fort Ethan Allen in 1924. Unfortunately, the Great Depression caused large financial deficits and resulted in the Delaware and Hudson's sale of the Champlain Transportation Company to Horace W. Corbin of Burlington in 1937. Corbin, a World War I pilot and grandnephew of General George Custer, was no stranger to Lake Champlain transportation. He owned the Grand

---

* A partial list of smaller steamers on the lake in the late nineteenth century includes the 58-foot **Alexander**, 45-foot **Ausable**, 99-foot **Burleigh**, 80-foot **Curlew**, 85-foot **Defender**, 123-foot **Elfrieda**, 81-foot **Herald**, 94-foot **H. G. Tisdale**, 118-ton **J. G. Weatherbee**, 59-foot **Kestrel**, 48-foot **Lillian**, 54-foot **Mariquita**, 44-foot **Valcour**, 63-foot **Victor**, and 53-foot **Water Lily**.[47]

ABOVE. Old steamboat wrecks at Shelburne — steamer *Burlington* in foreground. (Special Collections, Benjamin F. Feinberg Library, SUNY Plattsburgh)
BELOW. Shelburne Shipyard, Vermont. Photo by the author.

Isle to Cumberland Head ferry and was the nephew of the builder of the steamer *A. Williams*. By the end of the 1930s only the *Ticonderoga* operated for occasional excursion parties. The engines of the *Vermont III* and *Chateaugay* were sold for scrap with the latter hull going to Lake Winnipesaukee in 1940 while the *Vermont III*'s hull was stripped for conversion to a diesel freight boat for duty on the South Atlantic coast after World War II. The Delaware and Hudson also ended its control of the Lake George steamboats during the Depression by first leasing the vessels and facilities and finally selling them in 1939.

During World War II, the *Ticonderoga* was brought to new life again as a freight, passenger, and excursion steamer since gasoline rationing did not impinge on the coal-burning steamer. The Shelburne Shipyard, leased to the Donovan Contracting Company of St. Paul, Minnesota, by Horace Corbin in 1941, began construction of war vessels, the first on the lake since the War of 1812. Sub-chasers, tugboats, and torpedo lighters were constructed by shipyard workers and taken through the Champlain Canal to ultimate ocean service for the U.S. Navy. The shipyard was sold by the Champlain Transportation Company in 1946 to the wartime yard superintendent, L. J. Aske and his brother Wendell Aske. The shipyard subsequently built ferries, pleasure craft, and 73 motor boats for the U.S. Navy between 1952-54.[48] Following the war, the Champlain Transportation Company itself was sold to Lewis P. Evans, Jr., Richard H. Wadhams, and James G. Wolcott, who moved the company into the modern but less exciting era of steel-hulled ferries. The history of ferry crossings on Lake Champlain is a chronicle in itself.[49]

By 1950 the *Ticonderoga*, which by then had been purchased by Captain Martin Fisher, was in deep financial trouble. Following a fund-raising campaign under the leadership of Ralph Nading Hill and the Burlington Junior Chamber of Commerce, the *Ticonderoga* was able to steam through the 1950 season. The interest-free loan to the Fisher Steamboat Company from the Junior Chamber, however, was not able to keep the company solvent. In late December of the same year, Electra H. and J. Watson Webb, then assembling a village museum at Shelburne, purchased the *Ticonderoga* for passenger service during the summer months. The Shelburne Steamboat Company operated the last sidewheeler as a marine museum and excursion boat for three more seasons. Although the revenue from the *Ticonderoga* covered her operating expenses every year (50,000 passengers in 1953), the lack of steam engineers, rising fuel prices, and the increasing age of the vessel induced the Webbs to transport the steamer two miles overland to the Shelburne Museum grounds. After the steamer was floated onto 16 railroad freight cars in a berthing basin dug for the maneuver, the *Ticonderoga* inched its way on a set of double tracks for 65 days and 20 hours before reaching its permanent retirement home in the museum on April 6, 1955. A National Historic Landmark since 1963, the *Ticonderoga* remains a star attraction at the Shelburne Museum. A million dollar donation in 1992 to renovate this last North American passenger sidewheeler has insured its continued display at the museum.

After a 23-year absence of tourist excursions on Lake Champlain, the 65-foot, twin-diesel *Juniper*, sailing from Plattsburgh, renewed the tradition of the cruise boat on the lake. The *Juniper* began her career in 1945 as the *Big Bottle*, a transport vessel for the Pepsi-Cola Company in the waters around New York City. Purchased by the Lake Champlain Transportation Company in 1952, the vessel was renamed the *Juniper* and spent the next 15 years on the ferry run between Essex and Charlotte. After retirement as a ferry and work vessel, the *Juniper* was acquired by Frank Pabst of Plattsburgh with local investors. Pabst, a colorful entrepreneur and marine history enthusiast, rebuilt the *Juniper* and began

The 220-foot *Ticonderoga* (1906-1953), presently on display at the Shelburne Museum. BELOW. Interior of the *Ticonderoga*. Photos by the author.

his nostalgic excursions into the history and adventure of Lake Champlain on June 26, 1976. Today, Captain Pabst continues his unique personal description of the Battle of Valcour Island, rumrunner hideouts during prohibition, the Garden Island treasure from the French and Indian War, and the tumultuous naval battle fought on Plattsburgh Bay.[50]

The 1980s witnessed the introduction of two additional excursion boats on Lake Champlain. The 65-foot, stern-wheel *Spirit of Ethan Allen*, owned by the Green Mountain Boats Lines, Ltd., began operations with scenic narrated cruises, dinner cruises, and sunset excursions in 1983. The 150-passenger vessel, originally built in Virginia in 1972, has been modeled as a Mississppi steamboat with two decks. The second new excursion boat, the 112-foot *Mount Independence*, which began cruises from its homeport of Whitehall in 1986, was one of the most ambitious but short-lived operations on the lake. The ex-submarine chaser (1943) was rebuilt as a 133-passenger tour boat offering a range of ten separate trips on Lake Champlain and the Champlain Canal, but operations were suspended after only two years. Shortly thereafter, the 60-foot *M/V Carillon*, owned by Mahlon and Gena Teachout, began tours in the area of Fort Ticonderoga and Mount Independence in 1990. Built by Scarano Boat Builders of Albany, the 49-passenger *Carillon* was designed to resemble a classic 1920s Thousand Island tour boat with a long mahogany-trimmed cabin and swing-up windows.

ABOVE. The steel-hulled *Chateaugay*, built in 1888 at Shelburne Harbor, continues in service as the M/S Mount Washington on Lake Winnipesaukee, New Hampshire. (Postcard, author's collection)
RIGHT ABOVE. The 262-foot steel-hulled *Vermont III* was built in 1903 and ended service on Lake Champlain during the Great Depression. (Special Collections, Bailey/Howe Memorial Library, UVM)
RIGHT . The ferry *Roosevelt II* was built in 1923 and scuttled in the lake in 1959. (Special Collections, Bailey/Howe Memorial Library, UVM)

In addition to the motorized excursion boats, windjamming schooners have also made their appearance on Lake Champlain in the past decade and a half. The 58-foot schooner *Richard Robbins*, built in 1902, began windjammer cruises on the lake in the summer of 1978. After the *Richard Robbins* departed from Lake Champlain, the equally breathtaking schooner *Homer W. Dixon* began sailing cruises on the lake in 1983. The roomy 77-foot *Homer W. Dixon* includes 12 double cabins, a spacious aft galley, and a lounge area in the bow.

The future of Lake Champlain for excursion tours, recreational boating, sightseeing, and scuba diving has been the subject of debate for more than 40 years. Lynn Watt's 1969 article "Is Champlain Doomed?" (*Vermont Life*) outlined the continuing deterioration of water quality due to municipal sewage, agricultural fertilizers, and industrial waste.[51] Although Vermont passed its first pollution control act in 1949, major pollution problems continued to plague Lake Champlain years later. On the New York side of the lake in 1969, 19 municipalities and industries were still discharging raw sewage and industrial waste into the lake. After the Federal Clean Water Act of 1972, both New York and Vermont made significant strides in preventing pollution. In August 1988 a cooperative agreement to chart a new course for Lake Champlain was signed on the tour boat *Juniper* by Governors Madeleine Kunin of Vermont and Mario Cuomo of New York and Quebec Premier Robert Bourassa. The "Memorandum of Understanding" encompassed plans to protect water quality and to regulate shore and lake development.

Under the leadership of the Lake Champlain Committee, founded in 1963, public awareness of the need to preserve the finite resources of the lake basin has been raised. Despite intense efforts, the problems facing the lake continue. Industrial pollution persists in several areas of the lake. Burlington's storm drain/sewage system continued to overflow into the lake during heavy rains during the 1970s and 1980s. The combined sewer overflows were still closing the city's beaches in 1988 and 1989. Each year an estimated 825,000 pounds of raw sewage are discharged into Burlington's harbor.[52] Ironically, the harbor area contains three of Vermont's Underwater Historic Preserves. Plans and funding are finally on their way to implement a solution to the city's sewage problem. In 1990 the Lake Champlain Special Designation Act committed federal funds over a five-year period to a major pollution control effort. Despite the ongoing water-quality problems, the heightened public awareness and government commitment to solve these problems has provided some optimism for the preservation of Lake Champlain.

Burlington, Vermont.
Photo by the author.

The 61-foot steamer *Lillie M. Price* at the Lake House dock.
(Lake George Historical Association)

13. Steamboats of Lake George

THE BEAUTY OF THE CLEAR, blue waters of Lake George, surrounded by steep mountains reaching heights of 2,500 feet, quickly became apparent to visitors and potential settlers in the late eighteenth century. Writing to his daughter in 1791, Thomas Jefferson observed: "Lake George is, without comparison, the most beautiful water I ever saw; formed by a contour of mountains. . .finely interspersed with islands, its water limpid as crystal."[1]

Early land patents included 500 acres granted to colonist Samuel Adams in 1766 at Sabbath Day Point and 1,595 acres at present-day Lake George Village conveyed to General James Caldwell from Albany in 1787. Large land tracts, owned by John Thurman of New York City, were incorporated in 1792 into the township of Thurman, covering much of present-day Warren County. From these land tracts and earlier grants, the towns of Bolton in 1799, Rochester in 1807 (changed to Hague in 1808), and Caldwell in 1810 (Lake George Village today) were carved out as the first permanent communities on Lake George. Although settled earlier, the town of Ticonderoga was not defined until 1804. Lumbering initially became one of the most important commercial endeavors, but the tourist trade eventually played a major role in life along the lake in the nineteenth century.

The Adams Tavern, established by 1765 at Sabbath Day Point, was the earliest tavern on the lake.[2] The first tavern at the southern end of the lake has been called the "Long House" and by some reports was a building remaining at the close of the Revolution. Although a British raiding party burned Fort George in 1780, Professor Benjamin Silliman from Connecticut, traveling in 1819, remarked "on the very shore, we observe one of the old barracks, formerly belonging to the fort, now exibiting a tavern sign, and, till within a few years, constituting the only place of accommodation to those who visited Lake George."[3] By 1821 the town of Caldwell, named for the original promoters of the settlement, James Caldwell and his son William, had 500-600 inhabitants.

Professor Silliman was one of the early writers proclaiming the beautiful scenery and clarity of Lake George to potential visitors: "Everyone has heard of the transparency of the waters of Lake George. . .in fishing even in twenty to twenty-five feet of water the angler may select his fish, by bringing the hook near the mouth of the one which he prefers."[4]

Another historical travel book, written in 1853 by Henry Marvin, suggested that "the water is so transparent that a white object may be seen at the depth of near forty feet."[5] The publication in 1826 of James Fenimore Cooper's most famous novel, *The Last of the Mohicans*, exposed readers of fiction to the vivid descriptions of the beauty of Lake George (called Horicon in the book) and the stirring adventures of his characters during the French and Indian War.* As the reputation of Lake George grew, more and more hotels were built in the nineteenth century.

On the heels of the experience with steam-powered vessels on Lake Champlain, the first steamboat was completed at Lake George in 1817. The Lake George steam boat company, with James Caldwell and John Winans among the directors, was chartered by the state legislature from April 15, 1817, to 1838.** The company's first steamboat was begun in 1816 by John Winans, who had also completed construction of Lake Champlain's first steamer, the *Vermont,* in 1809 at Burlington. The 80-foot, 20-horsepower *James Caldwell* used the engine and boilers that had been salvaged from the wreck of the *Vermont* and also used for one season in the steamer *Champlain.* The *James Caldwell* was reportedly built "at Ticonderoga, above the rapids" probably because of the accessibility in transporting the engine and boilers from Lake Champlain.[6] The vessel resembled the early Lake Champlain steamers but featured an odd brick smokestack. Traveling at only four miles per hour, the *James Caldwell* took a full day to traverse the length of the lake with a return trip the following day. Although once struck by lightning, the steamer survived three seasons before burning under mysterious circumstances at her Caldwell dock at the Lake House in 1819. Professor Benjamin Silliman's tour of the lake in 1819 included reference to the "wreck of a steam-boat, recently burnt to the waters edge, lay near the tavern" and suggested that renewed steamboat service would make the lake a "great" resort.[7]

Since the steamer *James Caldwell* "did not pay," according to a nineteenth-century newspaper account, it took until 1824 before the next steamboat was constructed at the lake.[8] The 102-foot *Mountaineer* was built at Caldwell by John Baird and Captain Jahaziel Sherman. At the time, Baird owned the Lake House Hotel on the present-day site of Shepard Park in Lake George Village, while Sherman was the builder and master of many early Lake Champlain steamboats. Nineteenth-century sources indicated that the vessel had a keelson but no frames with a hull "made of three tiers of inch oak plank, two of which ran fore and aft" with another course in the opposite direction fastened by cedar pins.[9] This unusual construction was said to cause the vessel to "weave and twist like rubber," according to Captain Elias S. Harris, whose "first ride on a steamboat was on her."[10] Captain Harris, however, was somewhat prone to exaggeration.

The steamer, painted red, white, and blue, operated for 13 seasons with a faster schedule than the *James Caldwell* due largely to Captain Lucius C. Larabee's practice of transferring passengers while underway from rowboats to the steamer's yawl that was towed astern. The yawl would then be pulled alongside the steamer for boarding. The practice was necessary since the only wharves were at the ends of the lake and one each in Bolton and Hague. Larabee, however, would always slow down to pick up female passengers. The *Mountaineer* ended service in 1836 and subsequently "rotted down" and sank above the "rapids at

---

* Cooper led an unsuccessful campaign to rename Lake George "Horicon."
** During the nineteenth century, the company had at least four names, each written differently: the Lake George steam boat company (1817), the Lake George Steam-Boat Company (1819), the Lake George Steam Boat Company (1854), and the Lake George Steamboat Company (1872).

Ticonderoga" in an area of Ticonderoga Creek called the "Boat Grave Yard" near the old lime and charcoal kilns.[11] The vessel's remains were still observed as late as the 1890s.

After the sale of Jahaziel Sherman's steamer *Water Witch* to the Champlain Transportation Company, the steamboat pioneer returned to Lake George to build a more up-to-date steamer. The Lake George Steam Boat Association filed a letter of intent for incorporation in New York on February 10, 1837, to build and operate a steamboat on the lake. However, the company apparently never obtained a state charter. While there are discrepancies in the reported dimensions of the new steamer, an early newspaper account

The steamer *William Caldwell* at Black Mountain, print by W. H. Bartlett, 1839.
(Collection of Betty Ahearn Buckell)

listed the *William Caldwell* as 110 feet in length with a 17-foot beam.[12] Begun in March 1837, the 150-ton steamer was completed for $18,000 in August at the Homelands Dock (one-half mile north of the present Baldwin Landing) on the Ticonderoga outlet. The vessel appears to have had two decks and twin smokestacks in a drawing on an 1844 poster. The drawing for the *William Caldwell* on the poster, however, is virtually identical to an 1834 poster advertising the steamer *Phoenix II* and the 1836 poster of the *Franklin*, both on Lake Champlain. The posters, printed by the same firm, used the same drawing for all three vessels. A more accurate drawing by W. H. Bartlett in 1839 shows the twin smokestacked *William Caldwell* with one deck and a bowsprit.

The *William Caldwell* initiated the first through service via land connections by carriage to Lake Champlain. The steamer departed the Lake House at eight o'clock in the morning and remained for three and a half hours at the northern landing to allow tourists time to visit the ruins of Fort Ticonderoga. Taverns at the northern outlet of Lake George also provided rooms and meals to travelers. The area known as Alexandria, named for English landowner Alexander Ellice at the turn of the nineteenth century, offered the Alexandria Hotel which was built before 1825 (and is still standing). After a time, the stagecoach line of Captain William G. Baldwin carried passengers to Lake Champlain from the Homelands

The steamer *John Jay* at Cooks Landing.
(Collection of Betty Ahearn Buckell)

Dock (also called Cooks Landing). The *William Caldwell* was retired in 1850 and eventually settled on the bottom of the lake after being abandoned in a cove north of the Lake House in Caldwell.

By 1848 the 142-foot steamer *John Jay* was completed in Ticonderoga by Ferris Collyer for John Jay Harris at a cost of $26,000. One steamer captain described the vessel as "about 145 feet in length, painted white, with a lower and upper deck, the latter being approximately fifteen feet above the guards. In 1855, the company added a wooden roof or canopy over the upper deck."[13] The 250-ton steamer, made entirely of oak, plied the lake at 13 miles per hour with a sturdy, wood-burning, 75-horsepower engine. The *John Jay* operated for several years under Captain Lucius C. Larabee before a new steamboat company was organized in 1854 at Caldwell to purchase and run the steamer. Although the steamers *William Caldwell* and *John Jay* had navigated Lake George for a total of 16 years without a state charter, a reincarnated Lake George Steam Boat Company was chartered in 1854 by the state legislature. The steamer *John Jay* was purchased with all her equipment from Harris for $18,000 by the new company in the spring of 1854.

The *John Jay* continued her successful but uneventful career until July 29, 1856, when the one and only fatal steamboat accident of the Lake George Steam Boat Company

The steamer *John Jay* at the Lake House (present site of Shepard Park,
Lake George Village) from *Gleason's Pictorial Drawing-Room Companion*, 1854.
(Author's collection)

destroyed the boat, taking six lives. The steamer had left Ticonderoga under Captain James Gale at six o'clock in the evening, a later departure than usual. According to the boat's pilot, Elias S. Harris, brother of the builder of the *John Jay*, the boat began "taking fire when passing Friends Point."[14] The steamer, with 80 passengers aboard, was then about five miles south of her Ticonderoga dock. According to Harris, a gale wind from a severe thunderstorm had stopped the draft in the smokestack causing high pressure to "burst open both doors of the furnace" spewing red-hot embers into a pile of nearby wood.[15] A newspaper account written a few days after the accident, however, suggested that the fire had been caused by burning "pitch-pine wood, which choked up the smoke-pipe, so as to drive the fire and smoke into the fireroom."[16] Pitch pine, although somewhat dangerous, was often used to coax extra speed from a steamer. The burning vessel continued past Waltonian Island as the crew attempted to land the boat on the Hague shore.

The hero of the disaster, at least by his account, was Pilot Elias Harris. Although blinded by the smoke and steam from the erupting boilers and the burning vessel, Harris felt his way to the stern where he attempted to jury-rig the tiller bar since the ropes connecting the steering wheel to the rudder had burned away. Harris, guessing at his course, somehow managed to steer the blazing vessel by hand into the shore just below Temple Knoll Island. The *Glens Falls Republican* on August 5, 1856, reported: "After striking the rocks she shot out into the Lake some thirty or forty rods. At this point the passengers became alarmed, and as the flames raged with fury, driving them from place to place, they jumped overboard and many saved themselves by clinging to chairs, trunks, life-preservers, tables, etc., that had been thrown overboard."[17] Pilot Harris later maintained that "jumping over the rail forward of the moving wheels was the cause of the most of the drowning" since the turning paddlewheels created a current which pulled the victims into deeper water.[18] Five of the bodies were recovered immediately after the wreck, but despite a company reward of $100, the body of a Connecticut woman was never found.

There were many heroic acts during the catastrophe. William George, a carpenter on the steamer, saved a "young lady" who had pleaded for him to save her life: "She threw both arms around his neck and as the boat struck, he jumped to the shore with the lady upon his back."[19] When George later discovered Captain Gale struggling in the lake, he scrambled into the water, despite an injury, and dragged him ashore by his hair. William Brunet, who worked at Garfield's Hotel (across from the present-day Hague Town Beach), also assisted many women to shore after the crash and recovered three bodies.

Richard Shear, known as "Old Dick" or the "rattlesnake man," was aboard the *John Jay* with his box of rattlesnakes which he displayed to tourists for a fee. In the confusion of the disaster, the box of rattlesnakes was thrown overboard. A little girl, the daughter of a Ticonderoga resident, was placed on the box and safely drifted to the shore, despite the elevated heads of the rattlers who had poked themselves through the top of the box to silently witness the calamity.

Not all the witnesses to the disaster, however, were as altruistic as the heroes who saved the passengers. "A young man living there threw off his outer clothing, saved six persons from the burning vessel, and while he was doing it some public spirited person stole his watch"[20] A *New York Herald* reporter noted the "land sharks" or "vultures" on the night of the disaster who "had a great pile of shawls, bunnets, bags, parasols, hats, canes, & c., which they were pulling over."[21]

The cause of the accident was never conclusively determined. Whether the engine was over stoked with pine pitch to make up for the late departure that evening is unknown. The rock that the *John Jay* hit that night has since been known as Calamity Rock. Today, the broken wreckage of the steamer is still there and visible from the surface. She lies south of Temple Knoll (Cooks Islands) and Buoy B5 in the shallow water directly in front of a private house. The stern section of the *John Jay* is still intact at a 10-foot depth with its white paint yet visible if you brush away the light silt with your hand. Frames (ribs), the keelson, keel, a section of the apron and inner stempost, and other scattered wreckage lie in the shallow water adjacent to Calamity Rock. Charred parts of the steamboat can be found 60 feet down an underwater bank near the site of the wreckage.

Twelve days after the tragedy in Hague, the directors of the steamboat company, meeting at the Fort William Henry Hotel, decided to build a new steamboat at a cost limited to $20,000. The engine, boilers, and machinery were to be salvaged from the wreckage of the *John Jay*. The keel of the new steamer was laid on November 7, 1856, on the west shore of Lake George at Caldwell. Thomas Collyer, who had earlier built the steamers *Francis Saltus* and *America* on Lake Champlain, was in charge of building the new 260-ton craft at Lake George. The 140-foot steamer with a beam of 22–24 feet was finished in a record six months at a cost of approximately $26,000. The *Minne-Ha-Ha*, denoting "Laughing Water" in Henry Wadsworth Longfellow's poem "Hiawatha," was launched on May 12, 1857,"amist the plaudits of the multitude [estimated at 1,500] who assembled to witness the spectacle."[22] The 400-passenger *Minne-Ha-Ha* had a single smokestack and two decks with the forward top deck open. The steamer was a financial success, but the disruption of the Civil War which drastically reduced the tourist trade cut revenues in half for the *Minne-Ha-Ha*. After the Civil War the steamer's business recovered and notable passengers such as Major General George B. McClellan, former commander-in-chief of the Union Army, traveled on the vessel.

By the late 1860s, expanding railroad lines and business consolidations, which had affected many sectors of the American economy, reached Lake George. As early as 1866, the Champlain Transportation Company, under the presidency of Colonel Le Grand Cannon, had purchased enough stock in the Lake George Steam Boat Company to replace the officers including the president. The new president, Colonel Le Grand Cannon himself, following an amendment to the charter of the Lake George Steam Boat Company, completed the full takeover of the company by the CTC in 1868. The Champlain Transportation Company was itself the target of a friendly takeover in 1868 by the Rensselaer and Saratoga Railroad whose president, George H. Cramer, was Cannon's brother-in-law. With the expiration of the Lake George Steam Boat Company's charter in 1869, the operation on Lake George was conducted under the name of the Champlain Transportation Company. On May 1, 1871, the Delaware and Hudson Canal Company (Colonel Cannon was also a member of the board of directors) leased in perpetuity all of the assets from the Rensselaer and Saratoga including the two steamboat lines. The coordination of the Delaware and Hudson's train schedules with the lake steamer runs was soon accomplished, which allowed continuous service between New York City and Montreal. Four years later, the Delaware and Hudson constructed a railroad line to the Montcalm Landing at Ticonderoga on Lake Champlain from the Baldwin Landing of northern Lake George. By 1882 the Delaware and Hudson had also connected its rail lines to Caldwell from Glens Falls.

With the infusion of new capital into the Lake George operation, Colonel Cannon and the board of the Champlain Transportation Company authorized funds to build a second steamer on Lake George. Elijah Root, the chief engineer of the CTC, was directed to supervise construction of the vessel. In the late spring of 1869, the firm of Neafie and Levy of Philadelphia completed the 64-foot *Ganouskie*, named for a bay today called Northwest Bay. The propeller-driven vessel had one main deck with only a pilot house and a larger observation cabin in the aft section of the upper deck. The sturdy little steamer was converted from a wood-burner to coal in 1877. The *Ganouskie*'s first captain, Arnold Hulett, had the habit of exaggerating his maritime experiences and knowledge of Lake George to curious passengers. "There is not a single rock or reef in the waters of Lake

George that I don't know," Hulett once boasted, only to have the steamer scrape over a rocky reef, to which he nimbly returned, "There's one of them now."[23]

In 1872 the board of directors of the Champlain Transportation Company decided to resurrect the steamboat company on Lake George as a separate corporation. The Champlain Transportation Company had always endeavored to monopolize the steamboat trade on Lake Champlain. With the expiration of the old Lake George Steam Boat Company's charter, the CTC may have sought a new charter for Lake George from New York State to forestall any potential competitors who might have solicited a charter in the future. The New York legislature in 1872 approved a charter of the Lake George Steamboat Company until 1887. The new president, Colonel Le Grand B. Cannon, had been the president of the last Lake George company and the president of the CTC at the time. The charter of the Lake George Steamboat Company was renewed in 1887, 1902, and 1916. The 1916 recharter was extended to 2417!

ABOVE. *Ganouskie* at Huletts Landing. (Lake George Historical Association)
RIGHT TOP. *Minne-Ha-Ha* at Caldwell dock, *Ganouskie* in background. (Special Collections, Bailey/Howe Memorial Library, UVM)
RIGHT MIDDLE. *Minne-Ha-Ha* as hotel at Black Mountain Point. (Lake George Historical Association)
RIGHT BOTTOM. *Minne-Ha-Ha* falling in ruin at Black Mountain Point in the 1890s. (Aaron Feigen Collection, courtesy of Betty Ahearn Buckell)

Following a "request" from the CTC, the Lake George Steamboat Company built the largest steamboat on the lake to date at Cooks Landing, Ticonderoga, during 1876-1877. The 643-ton, 195-foot *Horicon*, a name from James Fenimore Cooper's *Last of the Mohicans*, could achieve 14 miles per hour with her 270 horsepower. The engines and boiler for the new steamer were salvaged from the steamer *Champlain*, wrecked north of Westport on Lake Champlain in 1875. The 1,000-passenger *Horicon*, the first large steamer built under the Champlain Transportation Company umbrella, was elegantly furnished throughout with a main saloon on the promenade deck 108 feet in length and 27 feet wide finished in butternut and black walnut. According to Charles Posson's 1888 travel guide, the vessel also had three staterooms and an unheard of crew at the time of "three officers and twenty-four men."[24]

Lake George had changed by the 1880s with the addition of more hotels and boarding houses along the lake and in the picturesque Narrows. An enlarged Fort William Henry Hotel, the Kattskill House, Marion House, Algonquin, Sagamore, Kenesaw House, Pearl Point House, Hundred Island House, Hulett House, Phoenix House, Trout House, Island Harbor House, Rogers Rock Hotel and more than a dozen other hotels were part of the landscape as the flood of tourists reached Lake George via expanding rail connections.

With the operation of the *Horicon*, the Lake George Steamboat Company sold the old *Minne-Ha-Ha* to Cyrus Butler, owner of the Horicon Iron Company in Ticonderoga and a small hotel at Black Mountain Point in the Narrows. In 1877 Butler towed the engineless vessel to the small bay at Black Mountain adjacent to his hotel, the Horicon Pavilion. Butler had earlier attempted to construct a canal between Red Rock and Paradise bays with the intention of mooring the *Minne-Ha-Ha* as a hotel on the latter bay, but the project was abandoned as too costly. At Black Mountain Point the vessel was converted into a 25-room hotel and dining facility. Following a fire on April 21, 1889, that destroyed the Horicon Pavilion, the old *Minne-Ha-Ha* was abandoned in the bay. In July 1893 a local newspaper reported that "storms and ice are fast causing the craft to fall into ruin, and it will not be very many years before the boat totally disappears."[25] To clear the channel and avoid accidents by curious visitors, the upper portion of the old steamer was dismantled and the hull later dynamited. Today, the huge beams, keelson, and frames of the *Minne-Ha-Ha* can still be seen from the surface of the bay, just north of the public docks at Black Mountain Point.

As a period of prosperity unfolded in the 1880s for the steamboat line on Lake George, the company decided to build a larger steamboat to replace the *Ganouskie*. The financing of the new vessel was facilitated by the separation of the Lake George profits from the Champlain Transportation Company. The 172-foot *Ticonderoga*, the first passenger vessel to bear the famous name, was the last of the firm's large steamboats on the lake built completely of wood. Constructed by the company's carpenters at Cooks Landing, the last of the classic nineteenth-century designs exhibited hog-frames, masts, swinging oil lamps, and hand steering gear. The *Ticonderoga* was the last of the Lake George Steamboat Company's vessels launched at Cooks Landing. Today, one can still observe the remains of the old wooden landing in the shallow water on the western shore.

The two steamers, *Horicon* and *Ticonderoga*, operated during the heyday of nineteenth-century tourism. The company's 1885 slogan "The Most Delightful One Day Excursion on the American Continent" was echoed by many of the travelers of the day including General William T. Sherman of Civil War fame.[26] By the 1880s, travel/history guides of B. F. DeCosta,

Charles Possons, T. E. Roessle, Seneca Ray Stoddard, the R. S. Styles' Printing House, and others spread Lake George's reputation for beauty and historical lore. As the demand for day excursions increased, the steamboat line began picnic lunch stops on the grounds of various hotels along the lake. With complaints of litter at the hotels, the Lake George Steamboat Company purchased Fourteen Mile Island in 1888 at the entrance to the Narrows for their excursion stopovers. The acquisition included the 48-room Kenesaw House (later called the Fourteen Mile Island House) which was leased to a concessionaire.

Meteor at Black Mountain Point.
(Lake George Historical Association)

A shooting gallery and other attractions were built on the island, but the public eventually wearied of the same stop. The hotel closed in 1896 and the company sold the island in 1905.

The introduction of the *Ticonderoga* to Lake George in 1884 resulted in the retirement of the *Ganouskie* to Cooks Landing. Although the idea of transferring the vessel to Lake Champlain as a tug was considered, the *Ganouskie* was sold in 1886 to G. W. Howard, who towed the vessel to a mooring at Big Burnt Island in the Narrows. The engine and boiler had been removed from the vessel and sent to the Champlain Transportation Company's shipyard at Shelburne Harbor prior to her sale. The *Ganouskie* remained at Big Burnt Island for several years as a floating saloon. The business failed, however, after the novelty of the floating bar, which displayed a large glass box of rattlesnakes, wore off. Although one report suggests that the hull "was sunk in the deep waters east of Dome Island," the hull may have rotted in Ticonderoga Creek after the superstructure was dismantled and taken to Whitehall.[27]

In February 1895 the Lake George Steamboat Company purchased the 93-foot, propeller-driven steamer *Mohican* from Captain Everett Harrison of Glens Falls for $13,000. Harrison had built the *Mohican* to replace his 90-foot steamer *Island Queen* which had been destroyed by fire. The *Island Queen*, known as the *L.G.A.* (Lake George Assembly) during her first year of operation in 1890, was a 250-passenger propeller steamer "double-decked from stem to stern."[28] The *Island Queen* made two regular round-trips each day from Caldwell to Paradise Bay with stagecoach connections to Glens Falls. The *Island Queen* burned early in the morning of November 12, 1892, while tied up at Cedar Landing on Kattskill Bay.

The *Mohican*, begun by H. G. Burleigh and Everett Harrison in 1893, was designed as an excursion boat by Henry T. Marvin of Brooklyn, New York. The 350-horsepower engine for the *Mohican* was built in Glens Falls while the sturdy oak vessel was finished in Caldwell. The *Mohican* operated for only one year before her sale to the Lake George Steamboat Company. Although just prior to the purchase the Lake George Steamboat Company considered building a smaller steamer that could navigate Paradise Bay with excursion parties, the plans were reportedly dropped as too expensive. The company's decision to buy the *Mohican*, however, may well have been made to eliminate potential competition, a policy that had been used effectively throughout the nineteenth century by the Champlain Transportation Company. After remodeling to accommodate more passengers, the *Mohican* began local passenger service in the summer of 1895, making 32 stops on the lake during her daily runs.

By the end of the nineteenth century, smaller steamers accounted for a notable amount of traffic on Lake George. In her last year of operation in 1888, the 61-foot steamer *Lillie M. Price* made two excursions daily from the dock at Caldwell to the Narrows "making a complete tour of the famous Hundred Islands, and into Paradise Bay, touching at all hotels on the way, and affording an enchanting trip."[29] Other small nineteenth-century commercial steamers included the *Hiawatha, River Queen, Julia, E. D. Lewis, Meteor, Owl, Mamie, Locust, H. Colvin,* and *Mary Anderson.* Private steam yachts, charter steam launches, and naptha yachts also became familiar sights on the lake by the turn of the century.* The yachts became the main attraction at annual regattas, the first of which was held in Hague in 1888. One of the most unusual excursion boats of the period was the 80-foot *Ellide*, originally

RIGHT TOP.
Horicon, 1877–1911.
MIDDLE.
Ticonderoga .
BOTTOM.
Ticonderoga burning at Hawkeye Point, August 29, 1901.
(Lake George Historical Association)

* Partial lists of steam yachts published in the **Lake George Mirror** (1882–1899) included the **Latona, Nonowan-tuck, Minnette, Caprice, Danellia, Paragon, Cosey, Waterbelle, Eva B, Orient, Fanita, Crickett, Cyric, Pocahontas, Geneva, Wanda, Vagabond, Theta, Pampero, Pastime, Helen, Isolde, Gladys, Katrina, Nahma, Mirror, Marie Louise, Helen R, Camper, Ruth, Vanadis, Crusader, Majorie, Middy,** and **Echo**; charter steam yachts included the **Marion, Rover, Comus, Mamie, Olive, Kismet, Camera, Saranac,** and **Neptune**; the **Oneita, Marie Louise,** and **Saunterer** were listed as naptha yachts. The Hague-built, Sexton boats, not listed above, included the **Cecilia, Ella, Gypsy, Locust, Mohawk, Passaic,** and **Uncas.**[30]

built as a private steam yacht for E. Burgess Warren of Green Island. The 800-horsepower, mahogany steamer cut through the water at more than 40 miles per hour, breaking the world record for a steam launch. The *Ellide*, under Captain W. W. Burton, made three excursion trips daily in later years with more than 30 possible stops per trip for a one dollar ticket. As late as the 1920s, the "speed yacht" *Ellide* was listed in the *Lake George Mirror* under steamboat service available to the public for short trips.[31] The *Ellide* was eventually stored in a boathouse at Green Island, only to be broken up years later.

One of the smaller steamers was involved in an accident that claimed the greatest loss of life on Lake George during the steamboat era. On the night of August 3, 1893, the one-year-old steamer *Rachel* sank near the shore in the Narrows. Twenty-seven passengers, bound for a dance at the Hundred Island House on the eastern shore of the Narrows, departed at 8:45 P.M. from the Fourteen Mile Island Hotel in the 55-foot steamer. Claude Granger, a two-season employee of the hotel on Fourteen Mile Island, had taken temporary command of the vessel since the regular pilot became ill. In the darkness the vessel crashed into the submerged remains of an old pier south of the Hundred Island House. Granger blew the *Rachel*'s whistle in distress until the vessel sank. Tourists and employees from the Hundred Island House rushed to the lakeside with fluttering lanterns. Although the rescuers quickly launched rowboats, seven women and a mother and son lost their lives. Some of the victims had been trapped under the shade deck as the vessel sank "on her side with her port bow stove in and seven feet of water above her smoke stack."[32] In the aftermath, the newspapers called for legislation to require an examination and licensing of pilots and engineers on Lake George. The *Rachel*, which had been valued at $4,000, was raised four days later with the use of two scows.

Eight years after the disaster of the *Rachel*, the steamer *Ticonderoga* was totally destroyed by fire at the northern end of the lake. Following a moonlight excursion to Fourteen Mile Island on the evening of August 28, 1901, the *Ticonderoga* departed from her Baldwin dock without passengers at 7:20 the next morning for another trip to the southern end of the lake. Just before reaching her first stop at the Rogers Rock landing, a fire, apparently smouldering all night under the boiler-room floor, "burst from the engine room. Hurriedly the pumps were manned and the crew worked bravely to save the steamer. But instantly and almost mysteriously the entire steamer was enveloped in flames."[33] The elegant wooden steamer, remodeled and lengthened by 15 feet in 1896, was steered by Captain Frank G. White into the Rogers Rock dock. The crew frantically tied the *Ticonderoga* to the dock and cut holes through the deck in two or three places in order to pour streams of water on the flames. The blaze, however, soon set fire to the dock and burned the ropes away. Captain White and his crew escaped, but two women, employed in the kitchen in the aft section, narrowly eluded disaster when they were saved by one of the crew members in a small boat at the stern of the burning vessel. Engulfed in flames, the unmanned steamer drifted northward to Hawkeye Point. The *Ticonderoga* ran aground on the reef and burned completely to the waterline within two hours as horrified onlookers from the shore and steamer *Horicon* watched helplessly. The unsightly wreckage of the *Ticonderoga*, potentially discouraging to steamboat passengers, was removed from the lake during the winter of 1902.[34] Today, only a few broken dishes, spikes, and beams lie scattered at 5- to 30-foot depths on the southern side of the reef at Hawkeye Point.

Following the calamity of the *Ticonderoga*, the Lake George Steamboat Company made immediate arrangements to build the first modern steel-hulled sidewheeler on the lake. The keel of the steamer *Sagamore*, a name again drawn from Cooper's *Last of the Mohicans*, was laid at Caldwell on March 3, 1902. Launched by April in record time, the *Sagamore*, with an original length of 203 feet and width of 57-1/2 feet, was modeled after the steamer *Chateaugay*, built by the Champlain Transportation Company in 1888. The elegant 1,500-passenger boat had a dining hall on the main deck, a hurricane deck for sightseeing, lavish furnishings in the cherry-trimmed interior, electric lights, a barber shop, and a powerful searchlight for night trips. The silver and china were stamped with the *Sagamore* monogram, the interior halls completed with hazel wood and mirrors, ceilings decorated in gold leaf on white, and an upper-hall floor covered by a lavish red carpet with green plush rosewood chairs. Within a few weeks of operation, the *Sagamore* exhibited a top-heavy condition due to the extra headroom provided between decks. In September 1902 the vessel was withdrawn from service, cut in half amidship, and lengthened 20 feet to augment stability.

The *Sagamore* re-entered passenger service in 1903 with a length of 223 feet and a 1,125-ton displacement. The work was done on a parcel of land purchased in 1885 on the Baldwin shoreline (Hearts Bay today). Previously, steamers had been built and repaired at the rented Cooks Landing facility. The set of ways used on the *Sagamore*'s repair, still solid after nearly a century underwater, can be observed in the waters off the Baldwin shore. Another set of ways, built in 1910 and enlarged in 1927 with a marine railway, lies east of the original ways on Hearts Bay.

Because of a host of design and mechanical problems, the company decided to replace the 13-year-old *Mohican* with a new steel-hulled vessel. The building of the hull and engines of the new *Mohican* was contracted to the W. and A. Fletcher Company of New Jersey. The hull, subcontracted to the T. S. Marvel Shipbuilding Company, was built in sections at Newburgh, New York, and shipped to the Baldwin yard for re-assembly in 1907. Completed the following year, the 115-foot *Mohican II* utilized 550-horsepower engines with twin-screw propellers. The new vessel was very similar in design and appearance to the original *Mohican*. The first *Mohican* was brought to the Baldwin ways where the vessel was dismantled and cut up. The *Mohican II*, although rebuilt several times, survives today as the oldest vessel in service at Lake George. During the early decades of service, the *Mohican II* handled full-lake trips in the slack season while supplementing the larger steamers during the summer. In addition, the *Mohican II* offered regular Paradise Bay excursions.

An examination of the aging *Horicon* in the fall of 1908 revealed the need for expensive repairs on the hull and machinery. During the following year, the steamboat company made plans for the largest and most powerful steamboat ever used on Lake George. The W. and A. Fletcher Company again received the contract and once more engaged the T. S. Marvel Shipbuilding Company to build the hull. The hull, built in Newburgh, was re-assembled at Baldwin for a December 1, 1910, launching. The 230-1/2-foot *Horicon II* began service in late July 1911 (commissioned on August 20) by taking the *Sagamore*'s route; the latter steamer assumed the trek of the original *Horicon*. The huge $200,000 *Horicon II* had three levels: the main, saloon, and hurricane decks which originally were designed to accommodate 1,500–1,700 passengers. The vessel's accommodations included finely upholstered furniture, a 100-seat dining room, eight observation and overnight staterooms, and a closed sewage system with pump-out facilities at the Lake George dock. The luxurious interior was finished in natural wood with butternut and cherry trim. The 1,280-horsepower engines propelled the *Horicon*'s 22-1/2-foot paddle wheels at a speed of 21 miles per hour, one mile per hour faster than the *Sagamore*. The handsome new steamer was an immediate financial

TOP. Hull of *Horicon II* under construction, 1910.
ABOVE. *Horicon II*. (1911–1939)
RIGHT TOP. *Sagamore* under construction at Pine Point, 1902.
MIDDLE. *Sagamore* at Baldwin shipyard.
BOTTOM. Luxurious *Sagamore* (1902–1937).
(Lake George Historical Association)

success, carrying a large share of the 120,000 passengers who traveled on the company's three steamboats in 1911.

Just before the time of the launch of the new *Horicon*, the Lake George Steamboat Company began operation of its first regularly scheduled gasoline yachts. The company leased the 45-foot, 25-passenger *Mercury* in 1909 to service the southern end of the lake. In June 1910 the company purchased the 54-foot *Pampero* for $1,200 from Harrison B. Moore,

Pampero on shore of Lake George in 1990. Photo by the author.

a former commodore of the New York Yacht Club and summer resident of northern Lake George. The *Pampero*, built in 1876 and exhibited at the Philadelphia Centennial in that same year, was a finely finished steam yacht of teak and mahogany with stamped sheet metal frames (ribs). The long narrow vessel with a 36-foot canopy top was brought to Lake George in 1877. When the Lake George Steamboat Company acquired the vessel, the steam engine had already been replaced with a gasoline model. The boat was to be used to pick up passengers at small private docks which were either too small or shallow to handle the larger steamboats. The 20-passenger *Pampero* made four round trips daily in the southern basin, including Paradise Bay excursions, with occasional charters in the evening after her scheduled seven o'clock cruise.

Following two profitable seasons for the *Pampero*, the Lake George Steamboat Company decided to build a larger gasoline yacht for local service on the lake. The 70-foot *Mountaineer II*, named for the second steamboat on Lake George, was completed by yacht

TOP. *Mohican* and *Mountaineer* at Lake George docks.
(Special Collections, Bailey/Howe Memorial Library, UVM)
ABOVE. The tour boat *Roamer*, 1938.
(Lake George Historical Association)

builder Alexander McDonald in June 1912 at Mariners' Harbor, Staten Island, New York. The 75-passenger *Mountaineer II* with a 125-horsepower gasoline engine began service in July after being transported to Lake George Village from Staten Island. The vessel's hull was constructed with white oak, the deck of yellow pine, and an enclosed cabin, framed in mahogany with large glass windows, extended for 54 feet on the deck. The *Mountaineer II* made four scheduled trips daily, one hour apart from the departures of the *Pampero*. After two years of operation, it became clear that passengers preferred the comfort of the larger *Mountaineer II* to that of the *Pampero*. Consequently, the *Pampero* was retired at the end of the 1913 season and sold to James McCabe of Ticonderoga in 1916. A large, deteriorated vessel presently on the wooded shore of Lambshanty Bay on the east side of the lake has been identified as the old *Pampero*.[35] In the twilight of her career, the *Pampero* hauled logs and loggers to a sawmill located on the shore of the bay. Except for 1919, the *Mountaineer II* remained in commission through 1921. By the 1920s the *Mountaineer*'s six cylinder engine, no longer an up-to-date powerplant, consumed large quantities of gasoline and was incapable of moving the vessel at the higher speeds of more modern boats. In 1927 the *Mountaineer II* was sold for $500 and converted into a cruiser/houseboat.

The *Mountaineer II* was not the only yacht offering tour boat rides during the World War I era and the 1920s. The 75-foot steamer *Scioto*, which had been on the lake since the turn of the century, began regular service under owner Captain Frank Hamilton as the "Kattskill Bay Line" on the southern section of the lake on June 27, 1915.[36] The 50-passenger *Scioto* had a small enclosed cabin just aft of the mid-section with a canopied roof over much of the remaining length of the vessel. During the 1920s, Hamilton made summer and early fall trips to Paradise Bay with the *Scioto* in addition to regular summer evening cruises by searchlight (after 1924). Paul Goodness acquired the vessel from Hamilton and continued the Paradise Bay cruises during the 1930s. Although one published report stated that "the *Scioto* became unseaworthy and was deliberately sunk by its owners in the narrows," other veterans of lake history have identified the wreck on the southwest side of Canoe Island as the *Scioto*.[37] The wreck at Canoe Island has been observed by local residents at least since the early 1940s. After the *Scioto*, Paul Goodness reportedly purchased the *Mountaineer II*, rebuilt the superstructure in 1938, and operated the vessel briefly as the tour boat *Scioto II*. After a few more owners, the *Mountaineer II* ended her career awash on the rocks at the southern end of Warner Bay on the east side of the lake. Later the vessel was broken up.

During the era of the *Scioto* and *Mountaineer II*, two other vessels made their appearances as commerical tour boats. The mail yachts *Iroquois* and *Heron*, owned by Frank Colton and E. J. Burton, offered daily excursions of the entire lake. The 75-foot *Iroquois*, the more elegant of the two vessels, was built as a private yacht in 1902 with a large cabin finished in mahogany, a 175-horsepower triple expansion engine, a toilet, electricity, and schooner-rigging with a bowsprit. In the 1920s, the *Iroquois* became the steam yacht of the Silver Bay Association in Hague; the vessel operated in the 1930s and was broken up in the southern basin in the late 1940s.[38]

By the 1920s Lake George was undergoing yet another transformation caused by changes in transportation and the economy. The availability of the automobile to the general population opened the beauty of Lake George to thousands of short-term visitors. Old hotels and boarding houses were soon facing competition from cabins catering to the motoring public. In place of the families of the wealthy spending leisurely summers at the lake, tourists with only a week's vacation came to dominate the economy of the villages along the lake. Millionaires Row, a 10-mile stretch from Lake George Village to Bolton Landing consisting of palatial estates of prosperous financiers, publishers, statesmen, etc., was eventually supplanted by cabins and motels.

While the changes along the shoreline brought more intensive utilization, the islands and the shoreline in the Narrows have largely returned to a natural state. During the nineteenth century, New York State had leased or sold islands for private summer cottages, some for as low as ten dollars. The Narrows also encompassed five large summer hotels serviced by the steamboats. Portions of the mountainous shores were often denuded by the lumber industry earlier in the nineteenth century. By the 1880s the new forest commission (Department of Environmental Conservation today) took a more preservationist attitude toward state land at Lake George. Legislation and the "forever wild" constitutional amendment further solidified the movement toward conservation. Hotels and lumbering disappeared from the middle of the lake and after the turn of the century the state began taking back the islands, requiring removal of private bungalows. The state continued to acquire land in the twentieth century, including the 1941 purchase of much of the huge estate at Shelving Rock of George O. Knapp, co-founder of the Union Carbide Corporation.

The steamboat business continued with routine service until 1927 when a dramatic accident nearly resulted in disaster. The *Sagamore* had departed from Ticonderoga in dense fog about seven o'clock in the morning of July 1, 1927. After successfully negotiating the first landing at Rogers Rock, the first pilot was forced to navigate by compass while the second pilot counted the paddle wheel revolutions to measure distance. "With a blanket of fog so dense that the captain and pilot were unable to see the main deck from the pilot's house," the *Sagamore*, turning for the Glenburnie Landing, crashed head-on into the vertical rock ledges of Anthony's Nose shortly before nine o'clock.[39] The screeching of the steel hull against the immovable stone promontory echoed across the lake. The stricken vessel was backed away from the mountain by Captain John L. Washburn as frantic crew members pressed mattresses into the openings of the crumpled hull plates. The *Sagamore* steamed a half mile to the Glenburnie dock where the passengers and mail were safely unloaded. The vessel then settled in 18 feet of water north of the dock. Three weeks later, the *Sagamore* was raised and towed to the Baldwin shipyard for extensive repairs. To haul the *Sagamore* out of the water, a marine railroad was constructed at the site of the ways that were built in 1910 for the *Horicon II*. Before the use of the 540-foot marine railway, steamers had to be laboriously hauled out by seven teams of horses. The marine railway, built in the summer and fall of 1927, is still in operation at this writing. After repairs, the *Sagamore* returned to service during the first week of May in 1928.

The late 1920s and 1930s ushered in significant changes for steamboat activity on Lake George. While the automobile had been present for quite some time, it was not until the late 1920s that paved roads connected the entire western side of the lake from Lake George Village to Ticonderoga. In 1928, following the earlier completion of a paved road from Hague to Ticonderoga, the state completed a paved roadway over the sharp prominence of Tongue Mountain between Bolton and Hague. Combined with the significant drop in traffic due to the Great Depression, the Delaware and Hudson suffered a $200,000 deficit in their steamboat business on Lake George and Lake Champlain. The Lake George steamers carried only 50,000 passengers in 1932 compared to 110,000 in 1923. At the beginning of 1933, the board of directors of the Delaware and Hudson decided to discontinue steamer service on Lake George.

After considerable dialogue with area residents and the Delaware and Hudson, Frederick W. Kavanaugh, a former state senator, established the Lake George Transportation Corporation which subsequently leased the three steamers and marine facilities from the D and H. The new company immediately invested $25,000 in the transformation of the *Horicon II* into a showboat complete with dining accommodations, three cocktail lounges, and conversion of the second deck to a grand ballroom. Beginning on July 1, 1933, the 1,000-passenger steamer, under the command of Captain Alanson A. Fisher and Pilot Martin Fisher and a staff of 60, began moonlight cruises with big name bands every evening during the summer. The *Mohican II* continued to run daily round-trips over the length of the lake from the Baldwin Landing while the *Sagamore* completed similar trips from Lake George Village. During the following year, the *Mohican II* was operated by Captain George Stafford under a leasing arrangement.

After bankruptcy by Frederick Kavanaugh, the assets of the steamboat line reverted back to the D and H in late 1934. The profitless *Sagamore* was retired in 1934 to the Baldwin dock whereupon its wooden superstructure soon began to deteriorate. Beginning in late 1935, the once proud sidewheeler was slowly dismantled for scrap. The *Horicon II* Showboat, which operated through 1937 (except for 1935), was making two cruises each day with music and entertainment at ticket prices as low as one dollar but was idled by 1939. At that time, the Delaware and Hudson decided to liquidate its remaining assets at Lake George. George Stafford, a native of Plattsburgh who had operated the *Horicon II* Showboat in her last season and commanded the *Mohican II* in 1939, arranged for the purchase of the remaining property from the D and H. On July 28, 1939, local newspapers revealed the purchase of the Lake George Steamboat Company in the name of Concetta Stafford, wife of Captain George Stafford. The principal assets in 1939 included the steamers *Horicon II* and *Mohican II* as well as the Caldwell dock, the Baldwin shipyard, numerous buildings, eight acres, and 1,800 feet of lakeshore property.[40]

The *Horicon II*, built at a cost of $200,000 in 1911 and renovated in 1933 for $25,000, was sold to a scrap dealer in the fall of 1939 for $5,000. The last sidewheeler was gone forever from Lake George. During World War II, the sturdy *Mohican II* maintained her daily round-trips over the length of the lake. In this period, Stafford dispensed with much of the Baldwin property, selling shorefront lots for as little as $150 and new dishes from the steamers for ten cents each. The remaining assets were sold in November 1945 to Wilbur

RIGHT TOP.
The 75-foot *Scioto* had a 25-year career on Lake George as a
tour boat before being sunk near Canoe Island.
(Lake George Historical Association)
MIDDLE.
The 81-foot tour boat *Sayonara*.
Photo by Richard Dean.
BOTTOM.
The tour boat *Ranger* in the 1950s.
(Lake George Historical Association)

E. Dow, Jr., an admiralty lawyer with years of maritime experience. The new Lake George Steamboat Company under the energetic leadership of Dow was revived as a major tourist attraction at the southern end of the lake. The first changes occurred after the end of the 1946 season when the *Mohican's* Fletcher steam engines were replaced with four diesels and the wooden superstructure on the vessel was remodeled along more modern lines.

From the 1930s through the 1950s, the Lake George Steamboat Company was not the only tour boat business on the lake. Not only did the steam yacht *Scioto* operate in the early 1930s, but large sightseeing speedboats, including the *Empress* and *Sea Sled*, became popular with tourists. During this time, the 45-foot tour boat *Forward*, owned by Alden Shaw and Leonard Irish, burned and sank off Diamond Island. Originally built in 1906 for William Bixby, the vessel had a long, open cockpit with twin gasoline engines and propellers. While on a fishing outing near Diamond Island, the boat reportedly caught fire and sank. Rediscovered by divers, the *Forward* is partially intact today with little evidence of fire damage. On May 25, 1938, Alden Shaw and Walter Harris, son of Captain Elias S. Harris, made the maiden voyage in their new 48-foot tour boat *Roamer*. The *Roamer*, built by John E. Lindsey and son at a cost of $10,000 at Alexandria Bay on the St. Lawrence River, had arrived via truck in late November of 1937. The 60-passenger vessel, which began Paradise Bay tours in June 1938, had a long windowed cabin providing passenger seating for most of the boat's length.

By 1940 Paul Goodness had acquired the 81-foot yacht *Sayonara* from George O. Knapp. The vessel had once served as the private steam yacht for Knapp's palatial estate at Shelving Rock. After Knapp's 65-foot steam yacht *Vanadis* burned at her dock in the fall of 1909, he commissioned the *Sayonara* in the following year. The long, narrow vessel had an elongated glass enclosed cabin of East India mahogany with handcrafted panels and cabinets that extended for much of her length. After a brief stint as a tour boat under Paul Goodness, the *Sayonara* was purchased in the 1940s by Alden Shaw and Harmel Burton. The handsome tour boat *Sayonara* plied the lake for a few years beginning in 1946 before being placed in temporary storage in her old boathouse at Shelving Rock. During the 1940s, the firm of Alden Shaw and Doug and Harmel Burton, known as the Lake George Marine Industries, Inc., also owned a fleet of 10 large sightseeing runabouts known as the "Miss Lake George Speed Boats."

In 1946 the Lake George Marine Industries, Inc., purchased an 80-foot PT boat built during World War II for the navy by the Elco Boat Company of Bayonne, New Jersey. On May 31, 1947, the 40-ton *Ranger*, named for the Rogers' Rangers of French and Indian War fame, was launched at Lake George Village. The sleek *Ranger* had an enclosed 40-foot cabin with a permanent canopy that extended from the rear of the cabin to the stern of the boat. Much of the renovation was completed with African mahogany which had been used in the original construction of the vessel. The 150-passenger *Ranger* cruised at 20 knots with three 225-horsepower General Motors diesel engines driving three propellers. The vessel made two trips daily; one involved a complete cruise of the length of Lake George.[41] By the mid-1950s, the *Ranger* was retired, taken out of the lake and cut up due to hull deterioration. With the retirement of the *Ranger*, the yacht *Sayonara* returned to service by June 1956 after hull repairs and the installation of twin Chrysler marine engines. Lake George Marine Industries under Alden Shaw continued to run the *Roamer* cruise boat during the entire period.

As the popularity of Lake George increased as a vacation destination in the post-war era, the Lake George Steamboat Company decided to add another large vessel to its operation. Following the rejection of expensive bids on a brand new vessel, Wilbur Dow, Jr., purchased the 168-foot Landing Craft 1085 from the McAllister Lighterage Company for $11,000 in late 1949. Built by the DeFoe Shipbuilding Company of Michigan in 1944, the vessel had served in the Pacific during World War II. Decommissioned in August 1947, the 1085 served as the mother ship for a mothball fleet on the east coast. The vessel reached Lake Champlain via the Champlain Canal, whereupon the hull was cut into four sections and carried by truck to Lake George in early 1950. After receiving a new superstructure, decking, and interior, the 360-ton, 900-horsepower *Ticonderoga II* began her career as a cruise boat on Lake George. The vessel was further modified in the 1950s with the addition of a large dining room and an expanded cocktail lounge. The *Ticonderoga II*, the second vessel to bear this name on Lake George, renewed the steamboat company's round-trip service over the entire length of the lake. At the time of the introduction of the *Ticonderoga II*, the *Mohican II* was assigned to trips from the Baldwin dock. In 1961 the *Mohican II* returned to the Lake George Village dock as the demand for shorter sightseeing cruises increased on the southern part of the lake. Extensive remodeling of the *Mohican II* occurred during the fall of 1966 and the following spring when the entire wooden superstructure was supplanted with a fireproof steel structure and decking. Although the rebuilt *Mohican II* exhibits larger glass windows and painted steel, the vessel has a more classic shape with a tall smokestack and a more prominent pilot house reminiscent of the original *Mohican* configuration (1894, 1908).

Following World War II, the estates located between Lake George Village and Bolton Landing were largely subdivided into cabins and motels to accommodate the burgeoning tourist trade. The completion of Interstate 87, the Adirondack Northway, in the late 1960s made Lake George more accessible than ever by automobile. The Northway accelerated the movement toward more motel rooms as well as encouraging the development of second homes along the lake. The increase in the number of tourists led the Lake George Steamboat Company to add a third vessel to their fleet in order to provide vacationers with one-hour lake excursions. Concluding that the new vessel should be an attraction in itself, Wilbur Dow, Jr., decided on a steam-powered vessel. Since the contemplated vessel would have a length of only 100 feet, a Mississippi sternwheel riverboat was built rather than a sidewheeler which might have appeared stubby. Unfortunately, a sternwheeler was not historically indigenous to Lake George waters. The hull, built at the company's drydock in Baldwin, was launched in little more than two months in late 1968. Completed at Lake George Village in the spring of 1969, the 103-foot *Minne-Ha-Ha II*, named for the nineteenth-century steamer, utilized a 200-horsepower steam engine with 12-foot paddlewheels. The engine room was enclosed in glass to allow passengers to observe the marvels of the steam engine and bell signals between the engineer and pilot. On August 1, 1969, the *Minne-Ha-Ha II* began her daily schedule of six hourly trips. At seven miles per hour, however, the *Minne* never travels out of view of the steel pier on her hourly cruises. The boat, nevertheless, continues to be a captivating sight on the lake with her chugging steam engine and calliope reverberating along the shoreline.

Alden Shaw's tour boat operation, Lake George Marine Industries, was also an active business at Lake George during the 1960s. In the fall of 1965 Shaw purchased the 68-foot *Patricia*, then in operation near the Straits of Mackinac in Michigan. The one-year-old steel vessel, originally built in Erie, Pennsylvania, had her pilothouse raised slightly at Lake George, as was the case earlier with the *Sayonara* tour boat. The *Patricia* with twin 190-horsepower diesels operated from 1966 to 1970 when the business was sold to Peter and Donald Smith. The Smiths continued with the tour boats *Roamer*, *Sayonara*, and *Patricia* on Beach Road in Lake George Village. The Lake George Steamboat Company, also located on Beach Road, began litigation which would remove the competing boats of

The *Minnie-Ha-Ha*, *Mohican*, and *Ticonderoga* at Lake George Village steamboat dock. Photo by the author.

the Smith Brothers from dockage on the road. Based on the contention that a local government did not have the right to lease public land to private enterprise, the Lake George Steamboat Company eventually won the case after a series of court appeals against the Smiths. The Smiths subsequently moved the three tour boats to a dock on the western shoreline. With a less visible location, the profits from the *Roamer*, *Sayonara*, and *Patricia* dropped precipitously. In 1973 Alden Shaw who held the note on the three boats foreclosed on the Smiths. The Lake George Steamboat Company subsequently purchased all three vessels in the late summer of 1973, thereby eliminating any potential competition.

After operating briefly and unprofitably for the Lake George Steamboat Company from Bolton Landing, the *Roamer* was sold in 1981 and continued her long career on Skaneateles Lake, New York, as the tour boat *Barbara S. Wiles*. The *Patricia*, renamed the *Sunshine City*, was transferred by the steamboat company to Tampa, Florida, in the fall of 1973 where the vessel was eventually sold. The *Sayonara*, however, was not as lucky. The vessel was placed in her boathouse at Shelving Rock where she sat largely untouched for more than ten years. The vessel was later sold to George Owen Knapp II and Sarah Knapp Sprole by the steamboat company for $1. After an unsuccessful attempt to sell the vessel, a New Hampshire salvager removed much of the mahogany superstructure and plans were made to burn the rest of the vessel. After learning of the planned burning of the *Sayonara*, I initiated the "Save the *Sayonara* Committee." After a year-long effort to save the vessel by proposing the creation of an underwater historic preserve adjacent to state forest lands in the upper Narrows of Lake George, the committee's application was rejected by the state. On May 7, 1988, the *Sayonara*, along with her boathouse at Shelving Rock, was burned with a state fire permit. Although this was a special case involving the sinking of an historic vessel, there were precedents for such projects in other states.

In 1988 Congress passed the Abandoned Shipwreck Act whose purpose is "to promote cooperative efforts. . .to locate and protect abandoned historic shipwrecks on, in or under State submerged lands."[42] With encouragement from this legislation and Vermont's example, the state of New York began planning in 1991 for likely preserve sites in state waters. The Lake George Park Commission, supported by several state agencies, began an approval process in 1991 for the lake's first underwater preserve. The proposal for preserves was initiated by Bateaux Below, Inc., a non-profit archaeological group certified by the Education Department of the state of New York.

The removal from Lake George of the *Roamer*, *Sayonara*, and *Patricia* did not end the competition in sightseeing rides on the lake. By the summer of 1977, James Quirk, operator of the U-Drive Boat Rentals at Lake George, brought three 40-foot fiberglass cruise boats to Lake George from the Thames River in Connecticut. The 58-passenger boats, built in 1974 by Anchorage, Inc., of Warren, Rhode Island, were propelled by 150-horsepower diesels. The Lake George Boat Tours, located adjacent to Beach Road on the western shore, began a schedule of lake tours every half-hour during the summer of 1977. The three canopied boats, the *Ethan Allen*, *Algonquin*, and *De Champlain*, continue to offer one-hour cruises on the half-hour in season. Renamed Shoreline Cruises, the company purchased the double-deck, 65-foot *Defiance* in 1983 at New London, Connecticut. The 600-horsepower steel *Defiance* made one-hour trips, moonlight cruises, and daily lunch and supper cruises during the late 1980s. In 1987 Shoreline Cruises contracted with the Scarano Boat Building Company of Albany to build an 85-foot tour boat. The *Horicon*, the third tour boat with the same name on the lake, is a triple-deck boat made entirely of mahogany, teak, and yellow pine. The boat has an appearance somewhat similar to the original *Mohican* of the Lake George Steamboat Company. Powered by two 250-horsepower engines, the 300-passenger *Horicon* began offering Paradise Bay tours, dinner cruises, and late evening departures with live entertainment during the summer of 1988.

Another addition to the fleet of tour boats on the lake was built in late 1986 for the owners of the restored Sagamore Hotel on Green Island in Bolton Landing. The 72-foot *Morgan*, built by Bill Morgan of Silver Bay, utilized a wood frame encased in fiberglass. Morgan, the owner of the Hacker Craft Boat Company in Hague, fabricated the entire vessel with local craftsmen at the Sagamore Hotel site. Today, the 80-ton tour boat offers sightseeing and dinner cruises with seating for 100 hotel guests and area visitors.

During the years of expansion by the smaller rivals, the Lake George Steamboat Company was not idle. In the early 1970s Wilbur Dow, Jr., and his son William Dow inaugurated the New Orleans Steamboat Company as a subsidiary of the Lake George company with the eventual acquisition of five vessels. A significant step was taken by the company in August 1979 when the keel was laid for the largest ship on the lake since the departure of the *Horicon II* in 1939. The 190-foot *Lac du Saint Sacrement*, a name that Father Isaac Jogues had given to the lake in 1646, was to be a three-quarter scale replica of the classic Hudson River Day Line steamer *Peter Stuyvesant*. The *Saint* took ten years to be completed, over eight years being spent at the company's drydock in Baldwin. For much of the 1980s, curious onlookers flocked to the Baldwin shore to observe the mammoth hull under construction. The lengthy building process was due to the decision to rely on the company's Lake George profits each year to fund the purchase of parts and supplies. The total cost approximated $4.25 million dollars for the vessel. Nearly all the work was accomplished by skilled local workers, most of whom spent the whole decade on the boat as their sole occupation.

The 85-foot *Horicon,* built by the Scarano Boat Building Company
for Shoreline Cruises, began operating on Lake George in 1988.
Photo by the author.

Finished in June 1989, the 190-foot by 40-foot wide *Lac du Saint Sacrement* with four decks dwarfs her sister ships at the steel pier at Lake George Village. Powered by two 625-horsepower Caterpiller diesel engines with twin 66-inch propellers, the 500-ton vessel cruises at 14 miles per hour leaving only a minimal wake. The vessel carries an extensive array of electronic gear and radar in the wheel house with electric-hydraulic steering, bridge wings, a 200-horsepower bow thruster for docking maneuvers, and four lifeboats. Amenities such as the mirrored ceiling over the dance floor and a grand double staircase with brass railings are reminiscent of the heyday of luxurious steamers such as the *Horicon II.* The *Saint* assumed the *Ticonderoga*'s cruises; the latter vessel was dismantled at the Baldwin shipyard in 1993.

By 1991 one might wonder if all the new tour boats could survive financially. More importantly, could Lake George survive the intensity of use that had increased significantly over the last two decades? At the time of this writing, the controversy over the spreading milfoil beds and the deterioration of water clarity in the southern basin of the lake had led to widespread discussion of environmental issues. As a young boy from Connecticut in 1952, I was amazed by the clarity of Lake George. I could actually see my feet on the bottom of the lake at the "Million Dollar Beach"! The beauty of Lake George and the transparency of its water were often noted by eighteenth-century soldiers who had trudged to its shores during the French and Indian War. While it may be normal for some deterioration of water

The 190-foot *Lac du Saint Sacrement* completed at Lake George in 1989.
Photo by the author.

quality to occur over centuries, it is unnatural for the waters of a spring-fed lake to visibly degenerate during only one lifetime.

Rising coliform counts forced the temporary closing of public beaches in Lake George Village during the summer of 1988. With 300 acres of milfoil, condominiums sprouting like mushrooms, and 10,000 boats on the lake on the average summer weekend, Lake George as the "Queen of American Lakes" seemed to be headed downhill. The Task Force for the Future of the Lake George Park aptly recognized the risk that Lake George was in danger of being "loved to death."[43] The survival of the lake in the end will not only depend upon basin-wide planning but individual observance of environmentally safe practices including the maintenance of septic systems, avoidance of lawn fertilizers, use of sealed boat toilets, etc.

In less than two centuries, Lake George and Lake Champlain have gone from a totally primitive setting to the hustle and bustle of the twentieth century with its concomitant problems. The native Americans who once inhabited the two lakes had minimal impact on the environment but were quickly dislodged during the ensuing military rivalries. As "highways of empire," the two lakes witnessed the English and French and later the Americans and British vie for control of their strategic waters. Where men once anxiously awaited the onslaught of enemy soldiers in laboriously constructed forts, summer visitors today calmly examine the relics that once determined the very beginning of a nation. Where the thunder of cannon from war fleets once shattered the silence of the wilderness, modern sailboats leisurely glide over tranquil waters. Below the serene surface, however, lie fragments of history in quiet solitude as reminders of turbulent days long ago. Likewise, the schooners, steamers, and canal boats that rest on the bottom of the lakes are mute testimony to the once-thriving commercial era. As the sun slowly sinks to the edge of the rugged mountains on the western shores of each lake, glimmering sparkles dance across their surfaces in peaceful harmony, belying the once tempestuous past of each lake.

"Launch Party at Adirondack Camp" in Sexton-built *Gypsy*.
(1920 postcard, author's collection)

ABOVE.
Stern section of steamer *John Jay* sunk at Hague, N.Y., 1856. Photo by the author.
BELOW.
Wreckage of the tour boat *Scioto* sunk at southwest corner of Canoe Island.
Photo by the author.

Replica of the gunboat *Philadelphia* at launch in 1991.
Photo by the author.

Notes

Abbreviations

AAS	American Antiquarian Society, Worcester, Massachusetts
AA5	Peter Force, ed., *American Archives, Fifth Series*, 3 vols. (Washington, D.C.: M. St. Clair Clarke and Peter Force, 1848-53)
BFTM	*The Bulletin of the Fort Ticonderoga Museum*
Coll. Conn. HS	*Collections of the Connecticut Historical Society*
Coll. NYHS	*Collections of the New-York Historical Society*
CSL	Connecticut State Library, Archives Division, Hartford, Connecticut
EIHC	*The Essex Institute Historical Collections*
GFR	*Glens Falls Republican*
LGM	*Lake George Mirror*
MAH	*The Magazine of American History*
MASS HS	Massachusetts Historical Society, Boston
NAC	National Archives of Canada, Ottawa
NDAR	William Bell Clark and William James Morgan, eds., *Naval Documents of the American Revolution*, 9 vols. (Washington, D.C.: Naval History Division, Department of the Navy, 1964-86)
NEHGR	*New-England Historical and Genealogical Register*
NRCNA	Naval Records Collection, National Archives, Washington, D.C.
NYSL	New York State Library, Revolutionary War Manuscripts, Albany New York
NYCD	E. B. O'Callaghan, ed., *Documents Relative to the Colonial History of the State of New York,* 10 vols. (Albany: Weed, Parsons and Company, 1853-58)
NYD	E. B. O'Callaghan, ed., *The Documentary History of the State of New York, 4 vols.* (Albany: Weed, Parsons & Co.: Charles Van Benthuysen, Public Printer, 1849-51)
PRO	Public Record Office, London

1. Years of Conflict

1. Louis Antoine de Bougainville, *Adventure in the Wilderness: The American Journals of Louis Antoine de Bougainville 1756-1760*, trans. and ed. Edward P. Hamilton (Norman, OK: University of Oklahoma Press, 1964), 246.

2. Ibid.

3. For information on the history of the native population at Lake Champlain see William A. Haviland and Marjory W. Power, *The Original Vermonters* (Hanover, N.H.: University Press of New England, 1981), 31, 38, 54, 59, 95, 105, 148-55, 199, and John C. Huden, comp., *Archaeology in Vermont* (Rutland, VT.: Charles E. Tuttle Company, Inc., 1970, 3-6, 73-74, 100.

4. H. P. Biggar, ed., *The Works of Samuel De Champlain* (Toronto: The Champlain Society, 1925), Volume 2, 1608-1613, 91-92.

5. Joseph W. Zarzynski, *Champ—Beyond the Legend* (Port Henry, N.Y.: Bannister Publications, 1984), 82.

6. Biggar, 93.

7. Ibid., 96.

8. John Wagner, "Au Plaisir," *Adirondack Life*, January/February 1988, 55.

9. Biggar, 99.

10. Ibid., 101.

11. Guy Omeron Coolidge, *The French Occupation of the Champlain Valley from 1609 to 1759* (1938; reprint ed., Harrison, N.Y.: Harbor Hill Books, 1979), 17.

12. *NYD*,1: 69.

13. *NYD*, 1: 70; Coolidge, 36.

14. *NYCD*, 9: 423.

15. Coolidge, 59.

16. *NYCD*, 4: 193.

17. Ibid., 196.

18. Ibid.

19. For some details of the Phips expedition see *NYCD*, 9: 456-58.

20. Ibid., 76.

21. For more on the military career of Francis Nicholson see Stephens Saunders Webb, "The Strange Career of Francis Nicholson," *The William and Mary Quarterly* 23 (October 1966): 515-48.

22. *NYCD*, 9: 843.

23. Peter S. Palmer, *History of Lake Champlain*, 4th ed. (1886; reprint ed., Harrison, N.Y.: Harbor Hill Books, 1983), 56; See also "Rock Inscription at the Ruins of Old Fort St. Frederick at Crown Point," *Proceedings of the New York State Historical Association* 10 (1911): 107-13.

24. Coolidge, 97-98.

25. Ibid., 116-17.

26. Ibid., 122-23.

27. John C. Huden, "The Admiral of Lake Champlain," *Vermont History* 30 (January 1962): 67.

28. James Sullivan, ed., *The Papers of Sir William Johnson* (Albany: The University of the State of New York, 1922), Volume 2, 75.

29. Edward P. Hamilton, *The French and Indian Wars* (Garden City, N.Y.: Doubleday & Company, Inc., 1962), 123.

30. Coolidge, 147.

31. Adolph B. Benson, ed., *Peter Kalm's Travels in North America* (New York: Dover Publications, Inc., 1937), 391.

32. Coolidge, 150; "Rock Inscription," 112.

2. Battle of Lake George

1. Fred Anderson, *A People's Army — Massachusetts Soldiers and Society in the Seven Years' War* (New York: W. W. Norton & Company, 1985), 8.

2. Palmer, 56.

3. John W. Krueger, *A Most Memorable Day: The Battle of Lake George, September 8, 1755* (Saranac Lake, N.Y.: North Country Community College Press, 1980), 8; Anderson, 10.

4. Delphina L. H. Clark, *Phineas Lyman — Connecticut's General* (Springfield, MA.: Connecticut Valley Historical Museum, 1964), 16.

5. Sullivan, 1: 783.

6. Ibid., 1: 861.

7. *NYD*, 1: 69.

8. John Gardner, "Famous Boat Type in Transitional Stage," *National Fisherman*, May 1967, 28-A.

9. James Hill, "The Diary of a Private on the First Expedition to Crown Point," ed. by Edna V. Moffett, *The New England Quarterly* 5 (1932): 608; See also John Burk, "John Burk's Diary," in *History of the Town of Bernardston*, by Lucy Cutler Kellogg (Greenfield, MA.: Press of E. A. Hall & Co., 1902), 45.

10. Sullivan, 2: 10; There were continuing problems with the wagoners. Rev. Samuel Chandler noted on November 23, 1755, that "some of the waggoners who were hired to carry down the sick have turned them out in the woods & left them some of whom died." Samuel Chandler, "Extracts from the Diary of Rev. Samuel Chandler," *NEHGR* 17 (October 1863): 352.

11. Sullivan, 2: 10.

12. Ibid., 13.

13. Ibid., 19; Governor Vaudreuil, however, estimated the total force at 3,573, *NYCD*, 10: 319.

14. *NYCD*, 10: 344.

15. Ibid., 335 (The figures vary on the Dieskau Expedition, see Sullivan, 2: 26-27, 58, 72).

16. *NYCD*, 10: 342.

17. Krueger, *Most Memorable Day*, 13, 15.

18 *NYCD*, 10: 342; Sullivan, 2: 72-73; Krueger, *Most Memorable Day*, 28, 30; There are a variety of stories regarding the origin of the first shot, see Wyllis E. Wright, *Colonel Ephraim Williams: A Documentary Life* (Pittsfield, MA.: Berkshire County Historical Society, 1970), 136.

19. *NYCD*, 10: 318.

20. Charles Henry Lincoln, ed., *Correspondence of William Shirley* (New York: The Macmillan Company, 1912), Volume 2, 255; See also James Gilbert, "Journal Kept by James Gilbert" *Magazine of New England History* 3 (1893): 195 for other details on the battle.

21. M. Pouchot, *Memoir Upon the Late War in North America Between the French and English*, 1755-60, trans. and ed. Franklin B. Hough (Roxbury, MA.: W. Elliot Woodward, 1866), 47.

22. D. Clark, *Phineas Lyman*, 19.

23. There is some dispute as to the time when Johnson retired, see Milton W. Hamilton, *Sir William Johnson*, (Port Washington, N.Y.: Kennikat Press, 1976), 165, 173-74, 357; Krueger, *Most Memorable Day*, 37; C. Lincoln, *William Shirley*, 2: 260.

24. Thomas Williams, "Correspondence of Doctor Thomas Williams of Deerfield, Mass., A Surgeon in the Army," *The Historical Magazine* 7 (April 1870): 211-12.

25. D. Clark, *Phineas Lyman*, 19; M. W. Hamilton, *Sir William Johnson*, 164; Some of the booty was brought into the Lake George camp by troops from Fort Lyman, see Richard Godfrey, "A Journal of the March of Captain Richard Godfrey's Company, 1755," in *History of Taunton, Mass.*, by Samuel H. Emery (Syracuse, N.Y.: D. Mason, 1893), 423.

26. *NYCD*, 10: 343; See also Lawrence Henry Gipson, *The Great War for the Empire: The Years of Defeat, 1754-1757* (New York: Alfred A. Knopf, 1946), 6: 173.

27. *NYCD*, 10: 343.

28. Ibid.

29. Sullivan, 2: 45.

30. Ibid., 184.

31. C. Lincoln, *William Shirley*, 2: 257-58.

32. Allan W. Eckert, *Wilderness Empire* (Boston: Little, Brown and Company, 1969), 345; *NYCD*, 10: 336; Wright, 148.

33. Seth Pomeroy, *The Journals and Papers of Seth Pomeroy*, ed. by Louis Effingham De Forest (New York: Society of Colonial Wars in the State of New York, 1926), 115.

34. C. H. Lincoln, *William Shirley*, 2: 258.

35. Pomeroy, 116.

36. Sullivan, 2: 49.

37. Ibid., 214.

38. E. P. Hamilton, *French and Indian Wars*, 213.

39. Sullivan, 2: 9.

40. C. H. Lincoln, *William Shirley*, 2: 270.

41. Sullivan, 2: 40.

42. Ibid., 53, 150.

43. C. H. Lincoln, *William Shirley*, 2: 282.

44. Sullivan, 2: 193.

45. Ibid., 166, 169; See also M. W. Hamilton, *Sir William Johnson*, 174.

46. J. Hill, "Diary," 608; Burk, 45.

47. Sullivan, 1: 863, 875.

48. Sullivan, 2: 160.

49. Ibid., 305.

50. Ibid., 319.

51. Nathaniel Dwight, "The Journal of Capt. Nathaniel Dwight of Belchertown, Mass., During the Crown Point Expedition, 1755," *The New York Geneological and Biographical Record* 33 (April 1902): 65-66.

52. Lyman's role in the engagement had immediately raised a storm of controversy after the publication of his letter in newspapers which gave much of the credit for the 1755 victory to the Connecticut troops. See Milton W. Hamilton, "Battle Report: General William Johnson's Letter to the Governors, Lake George, September 9-10, 1755," *Proceedings of the American Antiquarian Society* 74 (Part 1, 1964): 28-29.

3. Defeat at Fort William Henry

1. Anderson, 170; See also Gipson, 6:207.

2. Anderson, 174.

3. Ibid., 185.

4. Stanley M. Gifford, *Fort William Henry: A History* (Lake George, N.Y.: Fort William Henry Museum, 1955), 32; On October 16, 1756, Dr. Cutter noted that "the Fleet consists of 1 sloop about 40 tons, 2 smaller about 20 tons each, another sloop on ye Ways ready to Launch of ye Bigness of former." Ammi Ruhamah Cutter, "Dr. A. R. Cutter's Journal of his Military Experience, 1756-1758," in *A History of the Cutter Family of New England*, by William Richard Cutter (Boston: David Clapp & Son, 1871), 66; See also William Hervey, *Journals of Hon. William Hervey* (Bury St. Edmund's: Paul & Mathew, Butter Market, 1906), 38.

5. *Boston Gazette and Country Journal*, 13 September 1756; Nathan L. Swayze, *Engraved Powder Horns* (Yazoo City, MS.: Gun Hill Pub. Co., 1978), 219; One of the vessels on the lake in 1756 was a sailing barge, see Jeduthan Baldwin, "Journal Kept by Capt. Jeduthan Baldwin While on the Expedition Against Crown Point, 1755-56," *Journal of the Military Service Institute* 39 (July-August 1906): 129.

6. Bougainville , 35.

7. Luther Roby, *Reminiscences of the French War; Rogers' Expeditions and Maj. Gen. John Stark* (Concord, N.H.: Luther Roby, 1831), 22-23.

8. Bougainville, 46; Roby, 31.

9. Roby, 43.

10. Thomas Mante, *The History of the Late War in North—America* (1772; reprint ed., New York: Research Reprints Inc., n.d.), 84.

11. Bougainville, 97.

12. Ibid.

13. *NYCD*, 10: 545.

14. Bougainville, 119.

15. Ibid., 142.

16. Ibid., 138.

17. Ibid., 140.

18. *NYCD*, 10: 647; James Montresor, "Journals of Col. James Montresor," *Coll. NYHS* 14 (1881): 22.

19. *NYCD*, 10: 599.

20. Bougainville, 142.

21. Mante, 85; *The London Magazine* (September 1757): p.n.a.

22. *NYCD*, 10: 592.

23. *NYCD*, 10: 734; See also Seth Tinkham, "Diary of Seth Tinkham," in *History of Plymouth County, Massachusetts*, comp. by D. Hamilton Hurd (Philadelphia: J.W. Lewis & Co., 1884), 996.

24. Bougainville, 143.

25. Reuben Gold Thwaites, ed., *Travels and Explorations of the Jesuit Missionaries in New France* (Cleveland: The Burrows Brothers Company, 1900), Volume 70, 125.

26. Ibid., 155.

27. Bougainville, 144.

28. Eckert, 454; See also George Bartman, "The Siege of Fort William Henry, Letters of George Bartman," *Huntington Library Quarterly* 12 (August 1949): 418.

29. *NYCD*, 10: 606-7; Bougainville's figures in his journal (152, 153) differ slightly from his official report.

30. Bougainville, 146.

31. Ibid., 147.

32. Ibid., 156.

33. Pouchot, 86; Bougainville, 158; Mante, 90; *NYCD*, 10: 611.

34. Mante, 91; See also Joseph Frye, "A Journal of the Attack of Fort William Henry," Parkman Papers 42: 140-41, MASS HS.

35. Anderson, 95.

36. Francis Parkman, *France and England in North America* (Boston: Little, Brown, and Company, 1885), 496.

37. Bartman, 419.

38. Eckert, 463; Parkman, *France and England*, 497.

39. Frye, 143; See also Bartman, 420-21; Mante, 92; Bougainville, 163.

40. "A Journal Kept During the Siege of Fort William Henry, August, 1757," *Proceedings of the American Philosophical Society* 37 (1898): 147.

41. Bougainville, 166-67.

42. "Journal During the Siege," 148.

43. Francis Parkman, *Montcalm and Wolfe* (1884; reprint ed., New York: Atheneum, 1984), 291-92.

44. Bartman, 423.

45. D. Clark, *Phineas Lyman*, 34-35; See also M.A. Stickney, "Massacre at Fort William Henry, 1757," *EIHC* 3 (1861): 81.

46. Frye, 146; "Journal During the Siege," 149; See also Lawrence Henry Gipson, *The Great War for the Empire: The Victorious Years, 1758-1760* (New York: Alfred A. Knopf, 1949), 7: 83.

47. Pouchot, 88; Mante, 93-94.

48. Bougainville, 170.

49. Thwaites, 179.

50. Frye, 152; See also Thwaites, 179; Seth Metcalf, *Diary and Journal of Seth Metcalf* (Boston: The Historical Records Survey, 1939), 10; *The London Magazine* (October 1757): 494.

51. Frye, 152; See also Jonathan Carver, *Travels Through the Interior Parts of North America in the Years 1766, 1767, and 1768* (1778; reprint ed., Minneapolis: Ross & Haines, Inc., 1956), 318.

52. Parkman, *France and England*, 510.

53. Thwaites, 181, 187, 189.

54. Bougainville, 174; See also Luke Gridley, *Luke Gridley's Diary of 1757* (Hartford, CT.: Acorn Club, 1906), 49.

55. The numbers are low considering the number of troops that had been at Fort William Henry. According to Bougainville's journal, there were 2,339 men at the fort when the garrison finally surrendered. The troops included 713 regulars from the 50th and 60th Regiments, 798 from the Massachusetts militia, 302 from New Jersey, 231 from New Hampshire, 57 from New York, 113 from two independent militia companies, 30 from the Royal Artillery and 95 Rangers. Bougainville, 176.

56. Captain John Knox, *An Historical Journal of the Campaigns in North America*, Volume 1, (1769; edited by Arthur G. Doughty, 1914-1916; reprint ed., Freeport, N.Y.: Books for Libraries Press, 1970), 68.

57. *NYCD*, 10: 605.

58. Montresor, 37.

59. Bougainville, 177.

4. Abercromby Expedition

1. Horatio Rogers, ed., *Hadden's Journal and Orderly Books: A Journal Kept in Canada and Upon Burgoyne's Campaign in 1776 and 1777* (1884; reprint ed., Boston; Gregg Press, 1972), 104.

2. William Parkman, "Journal of William Parkman," *Proceedings of the Massachusetts Historical Society* 7 (1879-80): 243.

3. E. C. Dawes, ed., *Journal of Gen. Rufus Putnam 1757-1760* (Albany: Joel Munsell's Sons, 1886), 66.

4. J. Knox, *An Historical Journal*, 1: 181.

5. Mante, 145.

6. Anderson, 76; Amos Richardson, "Amos Richardson's Journal, 1758," *BFTM* 12 (September 1968): 274.

7. *Boston Gazette and Country Journal*, 20 November 1758.

8. William Sweat, "Captain William Sweat's Personal Diary of the Expedition Against Ticonderoga," *EIHC* 93 (1957): 42.

9. Dr. James Searing, "The Battle of Ticonderoga, 1758," *Proceedings of the New-York Historical Society* 5 (1847): 113; Peter Pond, an 18-year-old provincial from Connecticut, later noted that the fleet also included "Gondoloes, Rogalleys & Gunboats." Peter Pond, "Experiences in Early Wars in America," *The Journal of American History* 1 (1907): 91; Colonel Melancthon Taylor Woolsey only mentions the "900 bateaux, 135 whale-boats, artillery on flat-boats." Melancthon Taylor Woolsey, *Letters of Melancthon Taylor Woolsey* (Champlain, N.Y.: Moorsfield Press, 1927), 12; A contemporary letter reported "two floating castles," *New-York Mercury*, 24 July 1758.

10. Parkman, *Montcalm and Wolfe*, 357; Gipson, 7: 218.

11. Roby, 69.

12. J. Knox, *An Historical Journal*, 1: 190.

13. *NYCD*, 10: 747.

14. Robert Rogers, *Journals of Major Robert Rogers* (1765; reprint ed., Ann Arbor, MI.: University Microfilms, Inc., 1966), 113-14.

15. David Perry, "Recollections of an Old Soldier," *BFTM* 14 (Summer 1981): 5.

16. Joseph Nichols, "Joseph Nichols Military Journal 1758-59," Henry E. Huntington Library, HM 89, 20.

17. S. H. P. Pell, *Fort Ticonderoga, A Short History* (Ticonderoga, N.Y.: Fort Ticonderoga Museum, 1978), 29; Howe's body was sent on to the southern end of Lake George, contrary to nineteenth-century reports that he was buried in Ticonderoga, see Samuel Thompson, *Diary of Lieut. Samuel Thompson*, ed. by William R. Cutter (Boston: Press of David Clapp & Son, 1896), 9.

18. Rogers, *Journals*, 114; See also PRO 272, 34/30, fol. 22.

19. *NYCD*, 10: 726.

20. Winslow C. Watson, *The Military and Civil History of the County of Essex, New York* (Albany: J. Munsell, 1869), 89; *NYCD*, 10: 739; Pond, 92; Woolsey, 14; PRO 272, 34/30, fol. 23; *The Universal Magazine* (August 1758): 97.

21. A. G. Bradley, *The Fight with France for North America* (New York: E. P. Dutton and Company, 1900), 246; E. P. Hamilton, *French and Indian Wars*, 220-21; *NYCD*, 10: 727.

22. Montresor, 63.

23. Abel Spicer, "Diary of Abel Spicer from June 5th Until September 29th, 1758," in *History of the Descendants of Peter Spicer*, comp. by Susan Spicer Meech and Susan Billings Meech (Boston: F. H. Gilson, 1911), 395; Benjamin Jewett similarly observed that the regulars were "cut down amazin." Benjamin Jewett, "The Diary of Benjamin Jewett-1758," *National Magazine* 17 (1892-93): 63.

24. Perry, 6; See also Archelaus Fuller, "Journal of Col. Archelaus Fuller of Middleton, Mass., in the Expedition Against Ticonderoga in 1758," *EIHC* 46 (1910): 214.

25. Dawes, 69; See also Benjamin Glasier, "French and Indian War Diary of Benjamin Glasier of Ipswich, 1758-1760," *EIHC* 86 (1950): 76; Spicer, 394; *NYCD*, 10: 749.

26. J. Knox, *An Historical Journal*, 1: 192.

27. Spicer, 395; Parkman, *Montcalm and Wolfe*, 366.

28. Pouchot, 118-19.

29. Eleanor S. Murray, "Manuscripts As Resources," *Vermont Quarterly* 20 (April 1952): 92.

30. *NYCD*, 10: 740.

31. Bradley, 254-56; E. P. Hamilton, *French and Indian Wars*, 225; Ralph Nading Hill, *Lake Champlain: Key to Liberty* (Montpelier, VT.: Vermont Life Magazine, 1976), 61-63; Parkman, *France and England*, 433-36; Parkman, *Montcalm and Wolfe*, 561-63; Wallace E. Lamb, *Lake George: Facts and Anecdotes* (Glens Falls, N.Y.: Glens Falls Post Co., 1938), 133-35; Carroll V. Lonergan, *Ticonderoga: Historic Portage* (Ticonderoga, N.Y.: Fort Mount Hope Society Press, 1959), 47-53; Frederick B. Richards, *The Black Watch* (Ticonderoga, N.Y.: Fort Ticonderoga Museum, 1926), 34-60.

32. Bougainville, 233.

33. Gertrude Selwyn Kimball, ed., *Correspondence of William Pitt* (New York: The Macmillan Company, 1906), Volume 1, 300; *NYCD*, 10: 727; See also PRO 272, 34/30, fol. 23; *The Universal Magazine* (August 1758): 97.

34. Perry, 6-7; Abner Barrows had the same observation as Perry. "I fear a great many Wounded men fell Into the hands of our Enemy & the Slain all Lay on the spoot." Abner Barrows, "Diary of Abner Barrows," in *History of the Town of Middleboro*, by Thomas Weston (New York: Houghton Mifflin, 1906), 97.

35. Fuller, 214.

36. Spicer, 407; See also Pond, 91.

37. Nichols, 24.

38. Lemuel Lyon, "Military Journal for 1758," in *The Military Journals of Two Private Soldiers, 1758-1775*, by Abraham Tomlinson (1854; reprint ed., New York: Books for Libraries Press, 1970), 23; See also Joseph Smith, "Journal of Joseph Smith, of Groton," *Connecticut Society of Colonial Wars Proceedings* 1 (1896): 307.

39. Dawes, 71-72.

40. John Cleaveland, "The Journal of the Rev. John Cleaveland," *EIHC* 12 (July 1874): 185-86; See also *Scots Magazine* (August 1758): 439.

41. Cleaveland, 13 (1877): 63.

42. Kimball, 300; See also PRO 272, 34/30, fol. 23.

43. *NYCD*, 10: 744; Bougainville, 236; See also *Scots Magazine* (August 1758): 491.

44. Perry, 7.

45. George Francis Dow, *History of Topsfield, Massachusetts* (Topsfield: The Topsfield Historical Society, 1940), 161-62.

46. Bougainville, 249.

47. Pouchot, 121; *NYCD*, 10: 725.

48. Bougainville, 235; *NYCD*, 10: 725, 733, 746, 753, 848.

49. Allan Rogers, *Empire and Liberty* (Berkeley, CA.: University of California Press, 1974), 72.

50. Brian Connell, *The Savage Years* (New York: Harper & Brothers Publishers, 1959), 159.

51. D. Clark, *Phineas Lyman*, 41.

52. Douglas Edward Leach, *Roots of Conflict: British Armed Forces and the Colonial Americans, 1677-1763* (Chapel Hill, N.C.: The University of North Carolina Press, 1986), 131.

53. D. Clark, *Phineas Lyman*, 41.

54. Cleaveland, 12 (1874): 185.

55. Dawes, 72.

56. Rogers, *Journals*, 119; Bougainville, 261.

57. For more details on the ordeal of Putnam see Parkman, *Montcalm and Wolfe*, 377-78; See also Mante, 159; Pouchot, 123; Rogers, *Journals*, 117-19.

58. Samuel Cobb, "The Journal of Captain Samuel Cobb," *BFTM* 14 (Summer 1981): 20; Cobb's journal was first published in 1871 with a notation that the author was unknown, "Journal of a Provincial Officer, in the Campaign, in Northern New York, in 1758," *The Historical Magazine* 10 (July 1871): 113-22.

59. Henry Champion, "The Journal of Colonel Henry Champion," in *Champion Genealogy*, by Francis Bacon Trowbridge (New Haven, CT.: F. B. Trowbridge, 1891), 420; See original "Accounts & Journal of Captain Henry Champion of Colchester, Campaign of 1758," CSL.

60. Caleb Rea, "The Journal of Dr. Caleb Rea, Written During the Expedition Against Ticonderoga in 1758," *EIHC* 18 (1881): 107, 102, 111, 113; See also Asa Foster, "Diary of Capt. Asa Foster of Andover, Mass.," *NEHGR* 54 (January 1900): 185; Joseph Holt, "Journals of Joseph Holt, of Wilton, N.H.," *NEHGR* 10 (January 1856): 307; A. Fuller "Journal," 215-16; Glasier, 75, 77-78.

61. Abercromby to Pitt, 19 August 1758, MASS HS, Parkman Papers 42: 253.

62. *Boston Gazette and Country Journal*, 28 August 1758; Spicer, 402; On August 28 during the celebration of the capture of Louisbourg by Amherst, Dr. Rea noted that the "Sloop fired 21 Guns," Rea, 190; See also Shubael Griswold, "Journal During Service in French and Indian Wars," CSL.

63. Bougainville, 279; *NYCD*, 10: 853.

64. Cobb, 24; See also Glasier, 81; Rea, 184, 186; Nichols, 74.

65. Rea, 191; See also *Phineas Lyman*, 42.

66. John Cleaveland, "Journal of Rev. John Cleaveland Kept While Chaplain in the French and Indian War 1758-1759," *BFTM* 10 (no. 3, 1959): 277; Harrison Bird, *Navies in the Mountains* (New York: Oxford University Press, 1962), 232.

67. PRO 281/2, 34/46B, fol. 1.

68. Cleaveland, *BFTM*, 229; *Boston Gazette and Country Journal*, 8 October 1759; See also Samuel Niles, "A Summary Historical Narrative of the Wars in New-England with the French and Indians, in Several Parts of the Country [1760]," *Collections of the Massachusetts Historical Society* 6 (3rd Series) (1837): 524.

69. Champion, 431.

70. Rea, 199.

71. Christopher Comstock, "Diary of Christopher Comstock 1758-59," Connecticut Historical Society.

72. Sweat, 54; On October 18, Dr. Rea recorded that "Two of the Row Gally missing, I suppose sunk," Rea, 203; Abel Spicer noted on October 3 that "one of the row gallies out of the lake loaded on a pair of wheels," Spicer, 405.

73. Cobb, 30; Abel Spicer in September had mentioned the planned construction of a vessel "50 foot long and 20 foot wide," Spicer, 404.

74. Cobb, 30.

75. Ibid.

76. John Noyes, "Journal of John Noyes of Newbury in the Expedition Against Ticonderoga, 1758," *EIHC* 45 (1909): 76; Rea, 203; Nichols 86; Cleaveland, *BFTM*, 229; Holt, 310.

77. Champion, 433.

78. Bougainville, 292.

79. Ibid.

80. PRO 272, 34/30, fol. 36.

81. Ogden J. Ross, *The Steamboats of Lake George* 1817 to 1932 (Albany: Press of the Delaware and Hudson Railroad, 1932), 33; Captain E. S. Harris, *Lake George: All About It* (Glens Falls, N.Y.: Glens Falls Republican, 1903), 27; See also B. F. DeCosta, *Lake George: Its Scenes and Characteristics* (New York: Anson D. F. Randolph & Co., 1869), 63.

82. Charles H. Possons, *Possons' Guide to Lake George, Lake Champlain and Adirondacks* (Glens Falls, N.Y.: Chas. H. Possons, Publisher, 1888), 77-78.

83. *LGM*, 5 August 1960; *The Times-Union*, 31 July 1960; *The Saratogian*, 30 September 1960.

84. *LGM*, 10 June 1893.

85. *LGM*, 12 August 1960.

86. PRO 160, 34/57-58, fol. 17.

87. John Gardner, "Bateau 'Reconstructed' from Remains, Drawing," *National Fisherman*, August 1967, 8-A; See also George F. Bass, ed., *Ships and Shipwrecks of the Americas* (New York: Thames and Hudson, 1988), 133, 136-37.

88. *New York Times*, 27 June 1965.

89. PRO 291, 34/75-76, fol. 251; PRO 285/1, 34/64, fol. 208.

90. Sweat, 54.

5. Amherst Sweeps the Lakes

1. Bougainville, 246.

2. Henry True, *Journal and Letters of Rev. Henry True* (Marion, OH.: Star Press, 1900), 18; William Henshaw, "William Henshaw's Journal," *Proceedings of the Worcester Society of Antiquity* 25 (1909): 56; See also Samuel Warner, "Extracts from Samuel Warner's Journal," in *An Historical Address — Town of Wilbraham*, by Rufus P. Stebbins (Boston: George C. Rand & Avery, 1864), 210; PRO 293, 34/80, fol. 114.

3. Francis Grant, "Journal from New York to Canada, 1767," *Proceedings of the New York State Historical Association* 30 (1932): 321.

4. J. Clarence Webster, ed., *The Journal of Jeffery Amherst* (Toronto: The Ryerson Press, 1931), 128.

5. Lemuel Wood, "Diaries Kept by Lemuel Wood, of Boxford," *EIHC* 19 (1882): 143; This is probably the same vessel that Captain Philip Skene, who would play a significant role in the settlement of Lake Champlain, discovered in the lake: "We have weighed a large boat that was sunk at the close of the campaign in forty fathom water." (The depth was actually 40 feet.), J. Knox, *An Historical Journal*, 1: 492.

6. Gary Zaboly, "A Royal Artillery Officer With Amherst: The Journal of Captain-Lieutenant Henry Skinner, May 1-July 28, 1759" (manuscript, 1991), 15; See also forthcoming *BFTM* 15; *The Universal Magazine* (November 1759): 265-69, (December 1759): 284-88.

7. Montresor, 98.

8. Zaboly, "Skinner," 10.

9. J. C. Webster, *Journal of Jeffery Amherst*, 141.

10. *BFTM* 6 (January 1942): 84.

11. Zaboly, "Skinner," 18; One Massachusetts provincial in referring to the *Invincible* recorded that "They call it an Ark of Redoubt." James Henderson, "James Henderson's Journal," in *The First Century of the Colonial Wars in the Commonwealth of Massachusetts* (Boston: Society of Colonial Wars, Mass., 1944), 204.

12. Zaboly, "Skinner," 17.

13. "Diary of a Soldier at Crown Point, etc., 1759," French and Indian War Collections Octavo 2, AAS; Montresor, 83; See also John Woods, "John Woods His Book," French and Indian War Collections, Octavo, Vol. 1, AAS.

14. PRO 285/1, 34/64, fol. 175; See also PRO 283, 34/50, fol. 6; Journal of Major Salah Barnard, MS, Fort Ticonderoga Museum, Ticonderoga, N.Y.

15. J. Knox, *An Historical Journal*, 1: 485; Jonathan Knap, "Journal of Jonathan Knap of Killingly, Connecticut," CSL, mentions "2-12 pounders" on the vessel.

16. J. C. Webster, *Journal of Jeffery Amherst*, 138.

17. PRO 285/1, 34/64, fol. 182.

18. Mante, 210; See also the following sources for details on the sailing order of the fleet: J. Knox, *An Historical Journal* 1: 501-2; Commissary Wilson, *Commissary Wilson's Orderly Book*, 1759 (Albany: J. Munsell, 1857), 88; John Hawks, *Orderly Book and Journal of Major John Hawks 1759-1760* (n.a., N.Y.: Society of Colonial Wars, 1911), 42; *Boston Gazette and Country Journal*, 30 July 1759; PRO CO 5/56.

19. *NYCD*, 10: 1055; J. Knox, *An Historical Journal*, 1: 503.

20. S. H. P. Pell, *Fort Ticonderoga*, 49.

21. J. C. Webster, *Journal of Jeffery Amherst*, 144; See also L. Wood, "Diaries," 19: 148.

22. Robert Webster, "Robert Webster's Journal," *BFTM* 2 (July 1931): 133.

23. Mante, 213.

24. S. H. P. Pell, *Fort Ticonderoga*, 51.

25. L. Wood, "Diaries," 19: 185-86; See also *Scots Magazine* (August 1759): 439.

26. J. C. Webster, *Journal of Jeffery Amherst*, 146.

27. Ibid., 148.

28. Huden, "The Admiral of Lake Champlain," 66.

29. As early as May, Amherst had informed Loring that he needed "Two Briggs. . .and. . . two Snows, capable of Mounting Eighteen Six Pounders" for Lake Champlain. PRO 285/1, 34/64, fol. 198, see also fol. 196.

30. L. Wood, "Diaries," 19: 149.

31. S. H. P. Pell, *Fort Ticonderoga*, 51.

32. J. C. Webster, *Journal of Jeffery Amherst*, 151.

33. Henderson, 206.

34. Parkman, *Montcalm and Wolfe*, 445.

35. PRO 285/1, 34/64, fol. 212.

36. L. Wood, "Diaries," 20: 156; Skinner on July 23 reported that the army "discovered in the Lake a sloop with eight guns." Zaboly, "Skinner," 20; In 1761 Captain John Wrightson mentioned "a large French Boat at the Landing which could be Easily repaired." PRO 283, 30/50, fol. 58; See "Scows," PRO 293, 34/81, fol. 37, 40.

37. J. C. Webster, *Journal of Jeffery Amherst*, 174; For information on the building materials and problems involved in the construction of the radeau *Ligonier* see PRO 285/1, 34/64, fols. 152, 155, 207-8, 212.

38. PRO 285/1, 34/64, fol. 157; See also D. Clark, *Phineas Lyman*, 47; For some details on arming and manning the brig and sloop on Lake Champlain see PRO 285/1, 34/64, fols. 164-65, 215, 218.

39. PRO 285/1, 34/64, fol. 212.

40. *NYCD*, 10: 1055.

41. Thomas M. Charland, "The Lake Champlain Army and the Fall of Montreal," *Vermont History* 28 (October 1960): 294.

42. PRO 285/1, 34/64, fol. 225.

43. Samuel Merriman, "Journal of Samuel Merriman," in *A History of Deerfield*, by George Sheldon (1895-96; reprint ed., Somersworth, N.H.: New Hampshire Publishing Company, 1972), 666; A newspaper account noted "5 Row Gallies, which mount

18 Pounders, each of them one; the Gun is placed fore and aft, and fires out at the Head, they row with 14 Oars on each side, carry 30 Men each." *Boston Gazette and Country Journal*, 8 October 1759.

44. Burt Garfield Loescher, *Genesis: Rogers Rangers, The First Green Berets* (San Mateo, CA.: B. G. Loescher, 1969), Volume 2, 65; See also L. Wood, "Diaries," 20: 290, 296.

45. PRO 272/1, 34/30, fol. 87.

46. J. C. Webster, *Journal of Jeffery Amherst*, 180.

47. PRO 272/1, 34/30, fol. 88; To retrieve the cannon, the French set a pattern of anchors and cables which could be snagged later with a drag line. George F. Bass, ed., *A History of Seafaring* (New York: Walker Publishing Co., Inc., 1972), 288-89.

48. J. C. Webster, *Journal of Jeffery Amherst*, 183.

49. Ibid., 185; PRO 272/1, 34/30, fol. 86; Comstock, p.n.a.

50. Ebenezer Dibble, "Diary of Ebenezer Dibble," *Society of Colonial Wars in the State of Connecticut Proceedings* 1 (1903): 318.

51. PRO 283, 34/50, fol. 8; For information on the debate on winter protection for the vessels see fols. 5, 160 and PRO 285/1, 34/64, fol. 229.

52. J. C. Webster, *Journal of Jeffery Amherst*, 197.

53. P. M. Woodwell, ed., *Diary of Thomas Moody* (South Berwick, ME.: The Chronicle Print Shop, 1976), 18.

54. Samuel MacClintock, *Rev. Samuel MacClintock's Journal. 1760* (Crown Point, N.Y.: Crown Point Road Association, Inc., 1972), 11; For a report of the on-going construction at Fort Ticonderoga in 1760 which included barracks, a hospital, a sewage system that emptied into the lake, redoubts, and the covered way, see PRO 283, 34/50, fol. 23.

55. Woodwell, 24; Samuel A. Green, ed., *Three Military Diaries* (Cambridge, MA.: John Wilson & Son, 1901), 59; See also MacClintock, 14.

56. John Bradbury, "Diary of Old John Bradbury," in *Bradbury Memorial*, comp. by William Berry Lapham (Portland, ME.: Brown Thurston & Company, 1890), 275.

57. True, 29; L. Wood, "Diaries," 20: 291; Bradbury, 276; MacClintock, 14; Woodwell, 26; Jacob Bayley, "Capt. Jacob Bayley's Journal," in *History of Newbury, Vermont*, by Frederic P. Wells (St. Johnsbury, VT.: The Caledonian Company, 1902), 379.

58. Green, 61; The captured vessels were listed differently in other journals, see L. Wood, "Diaries," 20: 293; MacClintock, 16; True, 30; John Frost, Jr., "Expedition Against Canada," *Old Eliot* 8 (1908): 115; Samuel Jenks, "Samuel Jenks, his Journal of the Campaign in 1760," *Proceedings of the Massachusetts Historical Society* 5 (2nd Series) (1889-90): 371, see also 374.

59. Woodwell, 31; See also Green, 61-62.

60. Bougainville, 326.

61. J.C. Webster, *Journal of Jeffery Amherst*, 262.

62. Woodwell, 39.

63. PRO 283, 34/50, fols. 83, 86.

64. Ibid., fol. 83; At the end of his command at Ticonderoga, Grant recommended sinking some of the vessels and removing "the most valuable stores to the fort." fol. 140.

65. PRO 287/2, 34/69, fols. 36, 38; True, 22.

66. F. Grant, "Journal," 319.

67. Ammi R. Robbins, "Journal of the Rev. Ammi R. Robbins," in *History of Norfolk*, comp. by Theron Wilmot Crissey (Everett, MA.: Massachusetts Publishing Company, 1900), 101.

68. F. Grant, "Journal," 320.

69. Haldimand Papers, "Misc. Papers Relating to the Provincial Navy, 1775-1780," NAC, Microfilm H-1649, Volume 1, B144, fol. 99.

70. PRO 283, 34/50, fol. 59.

71. Ibid., fols. 58, 65; See also PRO 285/1, 34/64, fol. 175; James Walker, "Capt. James Walker's Journal," in *History of Bedford New Hampshire* (Concord, N.H.: Town of Bedford, 1903), 477.

72. Haldimand Papers, "Misc. Papers Relating to the Provincial Navy, 1775-1780," NAC, Microfilm H-1649, Volume 1, B144, fol. 99.

73. *Plattsburgh Evening News*, 18 December 1908; See also *LGM*, 1 July 1922.

74. "Arnold's Ships," *BFTM* 9 (Winter 1954): 227; See also "The Revenge," *BFTM* 1 (July 1928): 6-11.

75. Peter Barranco, April 15, 1970, personal communication; *Albany Times-Union*, 16 September 1954.

76. Edwin Rich, "Arnold's Fleet 1771-1790," (unpublished paper, 1964), 64.

77. *BFTM* 14 (Fall 1985): 335-440; Bass, *Ships and Shipwrecks*, 142-47.

78. J. Knox, *An Historical Journal*, 3: 74.

79. James T. Hays, David E. Mize, and Richard W. Ward, "Guns Under Lake Champlain," *York State Tradition*, Winter 1969, 10.

80. *Plattsburgh Press Republican*, 14 April 1987.

81. André Lépine, "An 18th Century Wreck in the Richelieu River, Quebec, Canada," *The International Journal of Nautical Archaeology and Underwater Exploration* 8.4 (1979): 340-46; André Lépine, "A Wreck Believed to Be a French 'Bateau' Sunk During Action in 1760 off Isle-aux-noix in the Richelieu River, Quebec, Canada," *The International Journal of Nautical Archaeology and Underwater Exploration* 10.1 (1981): 41-50.

6. From Champlain to Canada

1. *NDAR*, 1: 162.

2. Ibid., 267; See also Thomas Jones, *History of New York* (New York: The New-York Historical Society, 1879), Volume 1, 546-47.

3. *NDAR*, 1: 316.

4. Ibid., 314, see also 312-13, 751-52.

5. Royal R. Hinman, comp., *A Historical Collection of the Part Sustained by Connecticut* (Hartford: E. Gleanson, 1842), 29.

6. Aaron Barlow, "The March to Montreal and Quebec, 1775," ed. by Charles Burr Todd, *American Historical Register* 2 (1895): 644.

7. *NDAR*, 1: 313.

8. Ibid., 364-67; See also "Journal Kept by Eleazer Oswald on Lake Champlain," *BFTM* 13 (1977): 341.

9. Haldimand Papers, "Misc. Papers Relating to the Provincial Navy, 1775-1780," NAC, Microfilm H-1649, Volume 1, B144, fol. 99; *NDAR* 1: 319; See also Oscar E. Bredenberg, "The American Champlain Fleet, 1775-77," *BFTM* 12 (September 1964): 249-51.

10. *NDAR*, 1: 539.

11. Ibid., 366, 358.

12. "Benedict Arnold's Regimental Memorandum Book," *BFTM* 14 (Winter 1982): 77.

13. *NDAR*, 1: 808.

14. Ibid., 763.

15. Don R. Gerlach, *Proud Patriot — Philip Schuyler and the War of Independence, 1775-1783* (Syracuse, N.Y.: Syracuse University Press, 1987), 10, 21.

16. *NDAR*, 1: 1217.

17. Benjamin Trumbull, "A Concise Journal or Minutes of the Principal Movements Towards St. John's," *Coll. Conn. HS* 7 (1899): 146; Bredenberg, "Champlain Fleet," 257; Oscar R. Bredenberg, "The Royal Savage," *BFTM* 12 (September 1966): 138.

18. John Joseph Henry, *Account of Arnold's Campaign Against Quebec* (1877; reprint ed., New York: The New York Times & Arno Press, 1968), 94; Charles Bracelen Flood, *Rise, And Fight Again* (New York: Dodd, Mead & Co., 1976), 46.

19. *NDAR*, 1: 1044, 1043, 1055, 1215.

20. B. Trumbull, "Concise Journal," 139; "The Montgomery Expedition, 1775," *BFTM* 1 (January 1927): 12, 141.

21. B. Trumbull, "Concise Journal," 143.

22. *NDAR*, 2: 150-51.

23. Ethan Allen, *A Narrative of Colonel Ethan Allen's Captivity* (1930; reprint ed., Rutland, VT.: Vermont Heritage Press, 1988), 19-20; See also George F. G. Stanley, *Canada Invaded* (Toronto: A. M. Hakkert Ltd., 1973), 44-48.

24. R. N. Hill, *Lake Champlain*, 88.

25. "Papers Relating to the Surrender of Fort St. Johns and Fort Chambly," in *Report of the Work of the Public Archives for the Years 1914 and 1915*, ed. by Arthur G. Doughty (Ottawa: Public Archives of Canada, 1916), 20.

26. B. Trumbull, "Concise Journal," 146; See also a rendition of the *Enterprise* and *Liberty* carved on a powder horn in 1775 shown in Swayze, 141, 212.

27. Henry Livingston, "Journal of Major Henry Livingston, 1775," ed. by Gaillard Hunt, *The Pennsylvania Magazine of History and Biography* 12 (1898): 17.

28. *NDAR*, 2: 891.

29. See B. Trumbull, "Concise Journal," 171; Stanley, 59-60; See also John Fassett, "Diary of Lieutenant John Fassett," in *The Follett-Dewey, Fassett-Safford Ancestry*, by Harry Parker Ward (Columbus, Ohio: Champlin Printing, 1896), 225-28.

30. B. Trumbull, "Concise Journal," 156.

31. *NDAR*, 2: 1390.

32. Bredenberg, "The Royal Savage," 134, 137, 138-39; See also Livingston, 17-18; Livingston's journal indicated that the vessel had been brought to Ticonderoga. Livingston, 32.

33. *NDAR*, 2: 431.

34. Henry Dearborn, *Revolutionary War Journals of Henry Dearborn, 1775-1783*, ed. by Lloyd A. Brown and Howard H. Peckham (1939; reprint ed., New York: Da Capo Press, 1971), 50; See also Henry, 59-60.

35. Edwards Park, "Could Canada Have Ever Been Our Fourteenth Colony," *Smithsonian*, December 1987, 46; Jeremiah Greenman, *Diary of a Common Soldier in the American Revolution, 1775-1783*, ed. by Robert C. Bray & Paul E. Bushnell (DeKalb, Ill.: Northern Illinois University Press, 1978), 18; Henry, 71-72.

36. Doyen Salsig, ed., *Parole: Quebec; Countersign: Ticonderoga — Second New Jersey Regimental Orderly Book, 1776* (Cranbury, N.J.: Associated University Presses, Inc., 1980), 26.

37. B. Trumbull, "Concise Diary," 162.

38. "The Montgomery Expedition, 1775," *BFTM* 1 (July 1928): 33; See also B. Trumbull, "Concise Diary," 167; Alan S. Everest, ed., *The Journal of Charles Carroll of Carrollton* (Fort Ticonderoga, N.Y.: The Champlain–Upper Hudson Bicentennial Committee, 1976), 52.

39. *NDAR*, 2: 1056; The two gondolas *Hancock* and *Schuyler* were also referred to as "row gallies," see Barlow, 645.

40. Flood, 51.

41. Henry Knox, "Knox's Diary During His Ticonderoga Expedition," *NEHGR* 30 (1876): 323; See also Wm. L. Bowne, *Yᵉ Cohorn Caravan, The Knox Expedition in the Winter of 1775-76* (Schuylerville, N.Y.: NaPaul Publishers, Inc., 1975), 21.

42. H. Knox, "Diary," 323.

43. *NDAR*, 3: 251; See also Willard M. Wallace, *Traitorous Hero* (1954; reprint ed., Freeport, N.Y.: Books for Libraries Press, 1970), 81-82.

44. *NDAR*, 3: 315; See also Henry, 108; and "Journal in Quebec," *Coll. NYHS* 13 (1880): 188.

45. James Melvin, *The Journal of James Melvin — Private Soldier in Arnold's Expedition Against Quebec in the Year 1775*, ed. by Andrew A. Melvin (Portland, ME.: The Wardwell Press, 1902), 61; See also Charles Porterfield, "Memorable Attack on Quebec, December 21, 1775," *MAH* 21 (April 1889): 319.

46. Dearborn, 68.

47. Ibid., 68-69.

48. Melvin, 61; See also Henry, 114-15.

49. Melvin, 62.

50. Henry, 135.

51. Ibid., 132.

52. *NDAR*, 3: 1072.

53. Everest, *Journal of Carroll*, 30-31.

54. Ibid., 32.

55. Ibid., 34.

56. "John Trumbull at Ticonderoga from His Autobiography," *BFTM* 3 (January 1933): 5.

57. Everest, *Journal of Carroll*, 37-38.

58. Boylan, 67.

59. Beebe, 327; See also *NDAR*, 5: 22; Charles Henry Jones, *History of the Campaign for the Conquest of Canada in 1776* (1882; reprint ed., New York: Research Reprints, Inc., 1970), 44.

60. Elizabeth Cometti, ed., *The American Journals of Lt. John Enys* (Syracuse, N.Y.: The Syracuse University Press, 1976), 12.

61. *NDAR*, 4: 1456; George M. Wrong, *Canada and the American Revolution* (New York: The Macmillan Company, 1935), 313.

62. Lewis Beebe, "Journal of a Physician on the Expedition Against Canada, 1776," *The Pennsylvania Magazine of History and Biography* 59 (October 1935): 328.

63. Salsig, 113.

64. *NDAR*, 5: 390.

65. One American participant, however, suggested that the incursion into the swamp occurred only after the battle had started when the Americans were "exposed to a very galling fire from all the vessels, seventeen in number." John Almon ed., *The Remembrancer; Or Impartial Repository of Public Events* (London: J. Almon, 1776), Part 2, 304; See also Joshua Pell, Jr., "Diary of Joshua Pell, Junior," *MAH* 2 (1878): 43; R. Lamb, *Journal of Occurrences During the Late American War* (Dublin: Wilkinson & Courtney, 1809), 107-8.

66. Cometti, 14.

67. *NDAR*, 5: 444.

68. Beebe, 331, 342.

69. Ibid., 336; *NDAR*, 5: 614, 694; See also Elisha Porter, "The Diary of Mr. Elisha Porter of Hadley," *MAH* 29 (1893): 197.

70. Cometti, 16.

71. Beebe, 336; See also William Chamberlin, "Letter of General William Chamberlin," *Proceedings of the Massachusetts Historical Society* 10 (2nd Series) (1896): 498.

72. R. Lamb, *Journal,* 109; Almon, 305.

7. Battle of Valcour Island

1. *NDAR*, 5: 701, see also 873.

2. Ibid., 731.

3. Ibid., 710.

4. *NDAR*, 6: 3; See also *NDAR*, 5: 309-10, 498, 988, 1088-89, 1113.

5. Henry Steele Commager and Richard B. Morris, ed., *The Spirit of 'Seventy-Six* (Indianapolis, IN.: The Bobbs-Merrill Company, Inc., 1949), Volume 1, 221.

6. Salsig, 163.

7. Ibid., 165.

8. *AA5*, 1: 376; Others, however, claim that the gondolas did correspond to the "Delaware mould," *AA5*, 1: 682.

9. *AA5*, 1: 512; Dorothy U. Smith, "Historic War Vessels in Lake Champlain and Lake George," *New York State Museum Bulletin*, No. 313 (October 1937): 124.

10. D. Smith, "Historic War Vessels," 125; *AA5*, 1: 649.

11. *AA5*, 1: 582.

12. Ibid., 649, see also 51, 340, 512; Christopher Ward, *The War of the Revolution* (New York, The Macmillan Company, 1952), Volume 1, 388; Supervision of the construction of the vessels at Skenesborough was accomplished through a mixture of officers during the spring and summer of 1776. Initially, Assistant Deputy Quartermaster General Harmanus Schuyler (no relation to Philip Schuyler) began the gondola construction; later Colonel Cornelius Wynkoop, commander of a New York infantry regiment, helped oversee a good deal of the shipbuilding and work at the sawmills. After arriving on July 14, Brigadier General David Waterbury from Connecticut, who had served during the 1775 St. Jean campaign, was sent by Gates to Skenesborough to command the militia arriving there and eventually participated in the supervision of naval construction.

13. *NDAR*, 5: 1282.

14. Wallace, 103.

15. Ibid.; See also Allan S. Everest, *Moses Hazen and the Canadian Refugees in the American Revolution* (Syracuse, N.Y.: Syracuse University Press, 1976), 44-45; *AA5*, 1: 1273-75.

16. Bayze Wells, "Journal of Bayze Wells," *Coll. Conn. HS 7* (1899): 268.

17. *NDAR*, 6: 215.

18. Ibid., 1073.

19. Many accounts of the fleet suggest that the *Revenge* was built at Ticonderoga. Ward, 387; Frederic F. Van De Water, *Lake Champlain and Lake George* (Indianapolis, IN.: The Bobbs-Merrill Company, 1946), 191; "A List of Ships in the American and British Fleets in the Battle of Valcour Island," *BFTM* 1 (July 1928): 13.

20. *AA5*, 1: 1268.

21. *NDAR*, 5: 1168.

22. The dimensions of the British vessels may be found in the Haldimand Papers, "Misc. Papers Relating to the Provincial Navy, 1775-1780," NAC, Microfilm H-1649, Volume 1, B144, fols. 15, 142 and Microfilm C-3242, Volume 722A, fol. 20.

23. *NDAR*, 1: 1271; *NDAR*, 6: 1341; Howard I. Chapelle, *The History of the American Sailing Navy* (New York: Bonanza Books, 1949), 103.

24. "A Journal of Carleton's and Burgoyne's Campaigns," Part 1, *BFTM* 11 (December 1964): 256; See also William L. Stone, trans. and ed., *Letters of Brunswick and Hessian Officers During the American Revolution* (Albany, N.Y.: Joel Munsell's Sons, Publishers, 1891), 51.

25. Eleanor M. Murray, "The Burgoyne Campaign," *BFTM* 8 (January 1948): 6.

26. *AA5*, 1: 826.

27. *NDAR*, 6: 734.

28. Ibid., 735.

29. *AA5*, 2: 113.

30. Ibid., 440; See also Rufus Wheeler, "Journal of Lieut. Rufus Wheeler of Rowley," *EIHC* 68 (October 1932): 373.

31. Ibid., 591.

32. Ibid., 440.

33. *NDAR*, 6: 1237.

34. Ibid., 1117.

35. *AA5*, 2: 421.

36. *NDAR*, 6: 1081; *AA5*, 2: 566; Intelligence reports include *AA5*, 2: 421, 481-82, 835, 982; General James Wilkinson, *Memoirs of My Own Times* (1816; reprint ed., New York: AMS Press Inc., 1973), 87.

37. *AA5*, 2: 933.

38. Ibid., 834.

39. John Schank, John Starke, and Edward Longcroft, "An Open Letter to Captain Pringle," *BFTM* 1 (July 1928): 18; J. Robert Maguire, "Dr. Robert Knox's Account of The Battle of Valcour, October 11-13, 1776," *Vermont History* 46 (Summer 1978): 148.

40. William L. Stone, trans. *Memoirs, Letters, and Journals of Major General Riedesel* (1868; reprint ed., New York: The New York Times & Arno Press, 1969), Volume 1, 70; *NDAR*, 6: 1277, 858; Wells, 283. Arnold reported two British gondolas carrying three cannon each, Lieutenant Wells on the Providence reported observing two

British sloops in addition to the four larger ships at Valcour, and Sergeant Eli Stiles, reconnoitering St. Jean in September, also noticed two gondolas.

41. *AA5*, 2: 1224; Palmer, 227.

42. Arnold saw 28 gondolas—*NDAR*, 6: 1277; Pascal De Angelis observed 30 sail in the whole fleet—Charles M. Snyder, "With Benedict Arnold at Valcour Island: The Diary of Pascal De Angelis," *Vermont History* 42 (summer 1974): 198; 28 gunboats and 4 armed longboats were on a September 1776 British list—*NDAR*, 6: 883-84; Captain George Pausch mentioned 27 armed bateaux (gunboats) - William L. Stone, ed., *Journal of Captain Pausch* (Albany, N.Y.: Joel Munsell's Sons, 1886), 82; An anonymous British journal listed 29 gunboats—"A Journal of Carleton's and Burgoyne's Campaigns," 256; Lieutenant James Hadden listed 22 gunboats—Horatio Rogers, ed., *Hadden's Journal and Orderly Books: A Journal Kept in Canada and Upon Burgoyne's Campaign in 1776 and 1777, by Lieut. James M. Hadden, Roy. Art.* (1884; reprint ed., Boston: Gregg Press, 1972), 16; both Sergeant R. Lamb and Lieutenant John Enys noted 20 gunboats—R. Lamb, *Journal*, 110, and Cometti, 18; Captain Charles Douglas reported 20 gunboats and 4 armed longboats—*NDAR*, 6: 1344.

43. Synder, 198; E. Vale Smith, *History of Newburyport* (Newburyport, MA.: pub.n.a., 1854), 357.

44. *NDAR*, 7: 123.

45. H. Rogers, *Hadden's Journal*, 23.

46. W. Stone, *Journal of Pausch*, 83-84.

47. Arnold recorded that two British gondolas sank and one blew up—*NDAR*, 6: 1277; William Briggs, a seaman on the *Washington,* said that two English gunboats sank—*AA5*, 2: 1028; Joshua Pell, Jr., an officer with the British army on Lake Champlain but not at Valcour, noted 2 British gunboats sank—Joshua Pell, Jr., "Diary of Joshua Pell, Junior," *MAH* 2 (1878): 46; General Burgoyne, General Carleton, Lieutenant Digby, Lieutenant Hadden and Dr. Knox mentioned that only one gunboat sank—*Plattsburgh Republican*, 25 December 1897 (Burgoyne, Canadian Archives); *NDAR*, 6: 1272-74 (Carleton); James Phinney Baxter, ed., *The British Invasion from the North, The Campaigns of Generals Carleton and Burgoyne from Canada, 1776-1777, With the Journal of Lieut. William Digby* (Albany, N.Y.: Joel Munsell's Sons, 1887), 159; H. Rogers, *Hadden's Journal*, 23; Maguire, 148 (Knox).

48. Edward Osler, *The Life of Admiral Viscount Exmouth* (London: Smith Elder & Co., 1835), 12-13; See also Philip Stephens, "A British View on the Battle of Valcour," (letter, Canadian Archives) *North Country Notes,* April 1963, 3; Wells, 284.

49. Schank, Starke, and Longcroft, 18.

50. W. Stone, *Journal of Pausch*, 83.

51. Schank, Starke, and Longcroft, 18.

52. *NDAR*, 6: 1235.

53. W. C. Watson, "Arnold's Retreat After the Battle of Valcour," *MAH* 6 (June 1881): 414-17; Palmer, 111; Gardner W. Allen, *A Naval History of the American Revolution* (New York: Russell & Russell, Inc., 1913), 173; Most British officers believed the Americans passed through their lines - see Cometti, 20; H. Rogers, *Hadden's Journal*, 24; Schank, Starke, and Longcroft, 19; "Carleton's Prize," Melvin Barnes, *Reprint of a Short Biography of Colonel Ebenezer Allen* et al. (Plattsburgh, N.Y.: J. W. Tuttle Book and Job Printer, 1852), 26-27.

54. *AA5*, 2: 1224; Pascal De Angelis also noted "that night we ran through the British fleet." *History of Oneida County, New York* (Philadelphia: Everts & Fariss, 1878), 569.

55. *AA5*, 2: 1069.

56. Schank, Starke, and Longcroft, 19.

57. W. Stone, *Memoirs of Riedesel*, 71.

58. Cometti, 20; Hadden's journal also states that the Americans were "scarcely out of sight" the next morning. H. Rogers, *Hadden's Journal*, 26.

59. Wells, 284.

60. *AA5*, 2: 1079.

61. Ibid., 1224; See also *NDAR*, 7: 1295.

62. Snyder, 198.

63. E. Smith, *History of Newburyport*, 358.

64. *AA5*, 2: 1079.

65. Wells, 284.

66. *AA5*, 2: 1180; "Journal of Carleton's and Burgoyne's Campaigns," 257; Baxter, 162; *NDAR*, 6: 1245; Haldimand Papers, NAC, Microfilm C-3242, Volume 722A, fol. 21.

67. Wilkinson, 91.

68. "A View of the New England Arm'd Vessels on Valcure Bay on Lake Champlain, 11 October 1776," NAC, water colour no. C-13202; See also *BFTM* 1 (January 1929): 16-17.

69. Mark Mayo Boatner III, *Encyclopedia of the American Revolution* (New York: David McKay Company, Inc., 1966), 1207.

70. Cometti, 20, 22; Waterbury's account of February 26, 1777, stated that "the Enimy Came Down Under the West Shore," *NDAR*, 7: 1295.

71. *AA5*, 2: 1080; For the departure time of the British fleet see H. Rogers, *Hadden's Journal*, 28; Enys noted the fleet left early on October 13, Cometti, 20; See also Maquire, 148.

72. *AA5*, 2: 1069; R. Lamb, *Journal*, 110.

73. Wells, 284.

74. *NDAR*, 6: 1258, 1245; Cometti, 22; W. Stone, *Memoirs of Riedesel*, 10.

75. *AA5*, 2: 1079.

76. Ibid., 1224.

77. E. Smith, *History of Newburyport*, 358.

78. *History of Oneida County*, 569.

79. Wilkinson, 91; Morris F. Glenn, *The Story of Three Towns* (Ann Arbor, Mich.: Braun-Brumfield, 1977), 102-3.

80. *AA5*, 2: 1069; R. Lamb, *Journal*, 110; Maguire, 148; E. Smith, *History of Newburyport*, 358.

81. Persifer Frazer, "Letters from Ticonderoga, 1776," *BFTM* 10 (January 1962): 453; Sewall also "Heard a cannonading down the lake in the morning," Henry Sewall, "The Diary of Henry Sewall," *Historical Magazine* 10 (August 1871): 132; Ingalls recorded firing "till 2 or 3 o'clock," Phineas Ingalls, "Revolutionary War Journal, Kept By Phineas Ingalls of Andover, Mass.," *EIHC* 53 (1917): 90; Dr. Beebe noted "incessant fire from daybreak, till afternoon," Beebe, 354; At 11:30 A.M., Colonel Thomas Hartley at Crown Point stated that the enemy "have been firing, for two hours past, a few heavy guns," Thomas Hartley, "Hartley, Thomas – to General Gates," *BFTM* 4 (July 1938): 46.

82. *NDAR*, 7: 1295; Snyder, 199; See also Stephens, 3.

83. E. Smith, *History of Newburyport*, 358-59.

84. *AA5*, 2: 1080.

85. Wilkinson, 91.

86. Maguire, 148.

87. W. Stone, *Memoirs of Riedesel*, 80.

88. Max Von Eelking, *The German Allied Troops in the North American War of Independence 1776-1783*, trans. J. G. Rosengarten (Albany: Joel Munsell's Sons, Publishers, 1893), 96.

89. Art Cohn, "An Incident Not Known to History: Squire Ferris and Benedict Arnold at Ferris Bay, October 13, 1776," *Vermont History* 55 (Spring 1987): 108-10; P. C. Tucker, Esq., *General Arnold and the Congress Galley* (Vergennes, VT.: booklet originally written, 1861), 3.

90. Samuel Swift, *History of the Town of Middlebury* (Middlebury, VT.: A. H. Copeland, 1859), 89; See also Rowland E. Robinson, *Vermont, A Study of Independence* (Boston: Houghton Mifflin Company, 1892), 136.

91. Wells, 284-85.

92. *AA5*, 2: 1080.

93. Jeduthan Baldwin, *The Revolutionary Journal of Col. Jeduthan Baldwin 1775-1778*, ed. Thomas Williams Baldwin (Bangor, ME.: De Burians, 1906), 80.

94. Hartley, 46; *AA5*, 2: 1028.

95. Schank, Starke, and Longcroft, 19.

96. Baxter, 160-61.

97. John Trumbull, *Autobiography, Reminiscences and Letters of John Trumbull from 1756 To 1841* (New Haven, CT.: B. L. Hamlen, 1841), 35-36.

98. Baldwin, *Revolutionary Journal*, 81.

99. *AA5*, 2: 1040-41; *NDAR*, 6: 1257-58.

100. *AA5*, 2: 1041; Cometti, 20, 22; Haldimand Papers, NAC, Microfilm C-3242, Volume 722A, fol. 21; Most sources suggest the *Lee* was found on the western shore, but some secondary accounts placed the vessel on the eastern shore, see Thomas H. Canfield, "Discovery, Navigation, and Navigators of Lake Champlain," in Abby Maria Hemenway, ed., *The Vermont Historical Gazetteer* (Burlington, VT.: A. M. Hemenway, 1867), Volume 1, 665.

101. *NDAR*, 6: 1258; "A View of the New England Arm'd Vessels," NAC, water colour no. C-13202; "A Journal of Carleton's and Burgoyne's Campaigns," 257; Baxter, 162.

102. *AA5*, 2: 1080.

103. Ibid., 1186.

104. Beebe, 355.

105. Baldwin, *Revolutionary Journal*, 82.

106. *NDAR*, 6: 1336.

107. Frazer, "Letters from Ticonderoga, 1776," 455.

108. Ibid.; See also Persifer Frazer, "An Account of a Skirmish on or Near Lake Champlain," 28 Oct. 1776, NYSL, #14007: 5; See also Wells, 286; Baldwin, *Revolutionary Journal*, 84; Sewall, 133; AA5, 2: 1314-15; Wheeler, 376; Nathaniel Dodge, "A Letter and Diary of 1776," *Vermont Quarterly* 21 (1953): 35; Micah Hildreth, "Micah Hildreth of Dracutt His Book," in *History of Dracut*, by Silas R. Coburn (Lowell, MA.: Press of the Courier-Citizen Co., 1922), 150; Simon Mudge, "A Journal of the

March to Continental Army," in *Memorials: Mudge,* by Alfred Mudge (Boston: Alfred Mudge & Son, 1868), 205.

109. J. Trumbull, *Autobiography*, 36.

110. Baxter, 176.

111. Anthony Wayne, *Orderly Book of the Northern Army at Ticonderoga and Mount Independence, from October 17th, 1776, to January 8th, 1777* (Albany, N.Y.: J. Munsell, 1859), 134, the *New York* gondola was also mentioned on 110.

112. *AA5*, 2: 1192.

113. Ibid., 1143.

114. *NDAR*, 7: 29.

115. Paul David Nelson, "Guy Carleton versus Benedict Arnold: The Campaign of 1776 in Canada and on Lake Champlain," *New York History* 57 (July 1976): 361.

116. W. Stone, *Memoirs of Riedesel*, 83.

117. A. T. Mahan, *War of American Independence* (Boston: Little, Brown, and Co., 1913), 25.

8. Invasion of the Lakes

1. *NDAR*, 7: 621.

2. Ibid., 784.

3. *NDAR*, 8: 528.

4. Van De Water, 204.

5. *NDAR*, 7: 1190.

6. James Thacher, M.D., *Military Journal of the American Revolution* (Hartford, CT.: Hurlbut, Williams & Company, 1862), 80.

7. *NDAR*, 8: 187-88; See also *NDAR*, 7: 1255-56, 627.

8. Gerlach, *Proud Patriot*, 222.

9. Sources for the vessels include: Haldimand Papers, "Misc. Papers Relating to the Provincial Navy, 1775-1780," NAC, Microfilm H-1649, Volume 1, B144, fols. 15, 142 and Microfilm C-3242, Volume 722A, fols. 20-25, 30-31; *NDAR*, 7: 830-31; *NDAR*, 8: 986; *NDAR*, 9: 331-33; Rich, 42-43; J. Pell, "Diary," 107; H. Rogers, *Hadden's Journal*, 53.

10. Thomas Anburey, *Travels Through the Interior Parts of America* (Boston: Houghton Mifflin Company, 1923), Volume 1, 181-82.

11. W. Stone, *Memoirs of Riedesel*, 1: 108-9.

12. "The Trial of Major General Schuyler, October 1778," *Coll NYHS* 12 (1879): 14.

13. Anburey, 187.

14. "The Trial of Major General St. Clair, August 1778," *Coll NYHS* 13 (1880): 116.

15. "Trial of Schuyler," 158.

16. Ibid., 13.

17. "Trial of St. Clair," 69; See also Baldwin, *Revolutionary Journal*, 108; Enos Stone, "Capt. Enos Stone's Journal," *NEHGR* 15 (January 1861): 300; Thomas Blake, "Lieutenant Thomas Blake's Journal," in *History of the First New Hampshire Regiment*, by Frederic Kidder (Albany: Joel Munsell, 1868), 26.

18. Anburey, 190.

19. Thacher, 82.

20. Wilkinson, 184.

21. "Trial of St. Clair," 55.

22. Ibid., 111.

23. Thacher, 83.

24. Ibid.

25. Anburey, 192-93.

26. W. Stone, *Memoirs of Riedesel*, 1:113; H. Rogers, *Hadden's Journal*, 85; Blake, 29.

27. "A Journal of Carleton's and Burgoyne's Campaigns," Part 2, *BFTM* 11 (September 1965): 312; See also James Minor Lincoln, *The Papers of Captain Rufus Lincoln of Wareham, Mass.* (1904; reprint ed., Arno Press, Inc., 1971), 14; Pell, "Diary," 108; H. Rogers, *Hadden's Journal*, 91; Philip Skene Petition, NYSL, #7308.

28. "A Journal of Carleton's and Burgoyne's Campaigns," Part 2: 321; *NDAR*, 9: 225.

29. H. Rogers, *Hadden's Journal*, 89.

30. Thacher, 84; See also J. Lincoln, *Rufus Lincoln*, 14.

31. Anburey, 194.

32. Ibid., 199; See also J. Lincoln, *Rufus Lincoln*, 14; J. Pell, "Diary," 107-8; Boatner, 526-28; William L. Stone, *The Campaign of Lieut. Gen. John Burgoyne* (Albany: Joel Munsell, 1877), 22.

33. J. Lincoln, *Rufus Lincoln*, 15; See also Thacher, 85.

34. F. J. Hudleston, *Gentleman Johnny Burgoyne* (Garden City, N.Y.: Garden City Publishing Co., 1927), 162; Doris Begor Morton, *Philip Skene of Skenesborough* (Granville, N.Y.: The Grastorf Press, 1959), 54; R. N. Hill, *Lake Champlain*, 116; Van De Water, 213.

35. B. F. DeCosta, *Notes on the History of Fort George During the Colonial and Revolutionary Periods* (New York: J. Sabin & Sons, 1871), 45; See also a summary of debate on the issue in H. N. Muller and David A. Donath," 'The Road Not Taken': A Reassessment of Burgoyne's Campaign," *BFTM* 13 (1973): 272-85.

36. DeCosta, *Fort George*, 38; See also *NDAR*, 8: 1000.

37. *NDAR*, 9: 331-32; See also Anburey, 213; William Gordon, *The History of the Rise, Progress, and Establishment of the Independence of the United States of America* (New York: Samuel Campbell, 1794), Volume 2, 210.

38. H. Rogers, *Hadden's Journal*, 103.

39. Ibid., 107.

40. W. Stone, *Memoirs of Riedesel*, 1:296.

41. DeCosta, *Fort George*, 36-37.

42. Palmer, 129.

43. Gerlach, *Proud Patriot*, 283-84; Muller and Donath, 276; Lawrence Cortesi, "The Tragic Romance of Jane McCrea," *American History Illustrated*, April 1985, 10-15.

44. Bruce MacGregor, "A Failure to Communicate," *American History Illustrated*, October 1985, 19.

45. Wilkinson, 198.

46. "Trial of St. Clair," 67, 68, 76, 83, 108, 111, 120, 171; "Trial of Schuyler," 6-182.

47. W. Stone, *Memoirs of Riedesel*, 1:130.

48. Roby, 250.

49. Ibid., 192.

50. Robert T. Pell, "John Brown and the Dash for Ticonderoga," *BFTM* 2 (January 1930): 32; Peter Nelson, "The Battle of Diamond Island," *Quarterly Journal of the New York State Historical Association*, (January 1922): 43.

51. "Brown's Attack of September 1777," *BFTM* 11 (July 1964): 212.

52. R. T. Pell, "John Brown," 31.

53. Ibid., 36.

54. "General Powell to Sir Guy Carleton, 19 September 1777," *BFTM* 7 (July 1945): 30.

55. *NDAR*, 9: 939.

56. Jn. Starke, "Remarks on Affairs at the Portage Between Ticonderoga and Lake George, and the Mount Independence, in Sept. 1777," *BFTM* 11 (July 1964): 207-8.

57. Ibid., 209.

58. "Powell to Carleton," 32.

59. *NDAR*, 9: 968.

60. P. Nelson, "Diamond Island," 48; Captain Lemuel Roberts, *Memoirs of Captain Lemuel Roberts* (1809; reprint ed., New York: The New York Times & Arno Press, 1969), 62.

61. Roberts, 62.

62. R. T. Pell, "John Brown," 39.

63. "General Powell to Sir Guy Carleton, 27 September 1777," *BFTM* 7 (July 1945): 34.

64. *NDAR*, 9: 968.

65. "Powell to Carleton, 27 September 1777," 34; "A Journal of Carleton's and Burgoyne's Campaigns," Part 3, *BFTM* 7 (March 1966): 32, reported the "principal vessel, and gun boats were retaken."

66. Thomas Reeves Lord, *Stories of Lake George, Fact and Fancy* (Pemberton, N.J.: Pinelands Press, 1987), 36; Rod Canham, "New York's Lake George, Queen of American Lakes," *Skin Diver Magazine*, October 1983, 43.

67. W. Stone, *Memoirs of Riedesel*, 1:134, 274, 276; *NDAR*, 9: 969; Rev. B. F. DeCosta, *The Fight at Diamond Island, Lake George* (New York: J. Sabin & Sons, 1872), 9.

68. Richardson, 284; See also Benson Lossing, ed., *The Military Journals of Two Private Soldiers 1758-1775* (Poughkeepsie, N.Y.: Abraham Tomlinson, 1855), 24.

69. Alexander Monypenny, "Monypenny Orderly Book," *BFTM* 7 (October 1970): 444; See also Champion, 421, 426, 433, which mention the "first Island" in the lake as "Diamond Island."

70. Benjamin Silliman, *Remarks Made on a Short Tour Between Hartford and Quebec in the Autumn of 1819*, 2nd ed. (New Haven, CT.: S. Converse, 1824), 153.

71. Elizabeth Eggleston Seelye, *Lake George in History*, 2nd ed. (Lake George, N.Y.: Elwyn Seelye, 1896), 107; W. Lamb, Lake George, 42; See also Henry Marvin, *A Complete History of Lake George* (New York: Sibells & Maigne, Printers, 1853), 54-56; W. Max Reid, *Lake George and Lake Champlain* (New York: G. P. Putnam's Sons, 1910), 331.

72. Gerlach, *Proud Patriot*, 319.

73. W. Stone, *Letters*, 128.

74. Ibid., 129.

75. Haldimand Papers, NAC, Microfilm C-3242, Volume 722A, fols. 30-31, Microfilm H-1649, Volume 1, B144, fol. 142.

76. Ibid.

77. Ida H. Washington and Paul A. Washington, *Carleton's Raid* (Canaan, N.H.: Phoenix Publishing, 1977), vii.

78. For the Ferris story see Samuel Swift, *History of the Town of Middlebury* (Middlebury, VT.: A. H. Copeland, 1859), 89-93; See also Washington and Washington, 56, 65, 67, 69.

79. Cometti, 46-47; Brian Burns, "Carleton in the Valley or the Year of the Burning," *BFTM* 13 (Fall 1980): 404.

80. Cometti, 46.

81. Ibid., 48.

82. Oscar E. Bredenberg, *Military Activities in the Champlain Valley after 1777* (Champlain, N.Y.: Moorsfield Press, 1962), 30.

83. Ibid., 30-31; See also Don R. Gerlach, "The British Invasion of 1780 and 'A Character. . .Debased Beyond Description,' " *BFTM* 14 (Summer 1984): 316.

84. Charles A. Jellison, *Ethan Allen, Frontier Rebel* (Syracuse, N.Y.: Syracuse University Press, 1969), 283-84; See also Van De Water, 236.

85. Jellison, 285.

9. The Search for the Valcour Fleet

1. Bredenberg, "The Royal Savage," 149.

2. Palmer, 109.

3. *Plattsburgh Republican*, 21 March 1868.

4. *Glens Falls Daily Times*, 23 October 1908.

5. John B. Ferguson, "Whatever Happened to the Royal Savage," *Yankee*, November 1975, 269.

6. Horace Sawyer Mazet, "Lake Champlain Yields Historic Relics," *Motor Boating*, February 1935, 294.

7. Robert G. Skerrett, "Wreck of the Royal Savage Recovered," *U.S. Naval Institute Proceedings*, (November 1935): 1652.

8. Sidney Ernest Hammersley, *The Lake Champlain Naval Battles of 1776-1814* (Waterford, N.Y.: Col. Sidney E. Hammersley, 1959), 21.

9. L. F. Hagglund, *A Page from the Past*, 2nd ed. (Lake George, N.Y.: Adirondack Resorts Press, 1949), 20.

10. *NDAR*, 6: 1276, 1389.

11. *AA5*, 2: 1179.

12. John R. Spears, *The History of Our Navy* (New York: Charles Scribner's Sons, 1897), Volume 1, 109.

13. *AA5*, 2: 1143.

14. *NDAR*, 6: 1245; Baxter, 162; "A Journal of Carleton's and Burgoyne's Campaigns," Part 1, *BFTM* 11 (December 1964): 257 (original in West Point Library); "An Account of the Expedition of the British Fleet on Lake Champlain under the command of Captain Thomas Pringle & the Defeat of the Rebel Fleet commanded by Benedict Arnold on the 11 & 13 of October 1776," NYSL, #1008.

15. Cometti, 20, 22.

16. Snyder, 198.

17. *NDAR*, 7: 1295.

18. Spears, 109.

19. Philip K. Lundeberg, *Search for Continental Gunboats at Schuyler Island, Lake Champlain, New York* (Washington, D.C.: National Geographic Society Research Reports, 1968 Projects, 1976), 223.

20. *Valley News*, 2 March 1988.

21. "A View of the New England Arm'd Vessels on Valcure Bay on Lake Champlain, 11 October 1776," NAC, water colour no. C-13202.

22. Ibid.

23. "A Journal of Carleton's and Burgoyne's Campaigns," Part 1: 257.

24. Baxter, 162.

25. W. Stone, *Memoirs of Riedesel*, 1: 80.

26. Zadock Thompson, *History of Vermont* (Burlington, VT.: Chauncey Goodrich, 1842), Part 3, 135.

27. Hemenway, 1: 80.

28. Philip C. Tucker, *General Arnold and the Congress Galley* (Vergennes, VT.: pub., n.a., 1861), 6.

29. Mazet, 101.

30. Reid, 357.

31. *New York Times*, 23 November 1952.

32. *Lake Placid News*, 28 May 1954.

33. Lundeberg, 215.

34. *Ticonderoga Sentinel*, 16 November 1911; See also *LGM*, 2 September 1910.

35. Doris Begor Morton, *Birth of the United States Navy* (Whitehall, N.Y.: Whitehall Times, 1982), 14; "The Trial of Major General St. Clair, August, 1778," 92, 94; Rich, 57.

36. "A Journal of Carleton's and Burgoyne's Campaigns," Part 2: 321.

37. J. Lincoln, *Rufus Lincoln*, 14.

38. Haldimand Papers, "Misc. Papers Relating to the Provincial Navy, 1775-1780," NAC, Microfilm H-1649, Volume 2, B145, fol. 55.

39. Ibid., 120; See also John W. Krueger, ed., "Simon Metcalfe's 'Little Book,' " *BFTM* 15 (Winter 1988): 30.

40. Bredenberg, "The American Champlain Fleet," 263.

41. H. N. Muller III, *The Commerical History of the Lake Champlain–Richelieu River, 1760-1815* (Ph.D. diss., University of Rochester, N.Y., 1968), 101.

42. André Lepine, *La Richelieu Archeologique* (Montreal: La Societé du Musée Militaire et Maritime, 1983), 29-30.

43. Edward P. Hamilton, "An Historic Mortar," *BFTM* 10 (February 1960): 299-303.

10. War Of 1812: Plattsburgh Bay

1. Hugh Ll. Keenleyside, *Canada and the United States* (Port Washington, N.Y.: Kennikat Press, 1971), 79.

2. Allan S. Everest, *The War of 1812 in the Champlain Valley* (Syracuse, N.Y.: Syracuse University Press, 1981), 45; H. N. Muller III, *Commercial History*, 210; Doris B. Mor-

ton, *Whitehall in the War of 1812* (Whitehall, N.Y.: Washington County Historical Society, 1964, Mimeographed), 2; Walter Hill Crockett, *Vermont: The Green Mountain State* (New York: The Century History Co., 1921), 43.

3. Rodney Macdonough, *Life of Commodore Thomas Macdonough* (Boston: The Fort Hill Press, 1909), 108; William S. Dudley, *The Naval War of 1812: A Documentary History* (Washington, D.C.: Department of the Navy, 1985), Volume 1, 319.

4. Everest, *War of 1812*, 64; Dudley, 325; *The Battle of Plattsburgh: What Historians Say About It* (1914; New York State Commission Plattsburgh Centenary; reprint ed., Elizabethtown, N.Y.: Crown Point Press, Inc., 1968), 60.

5. Walter Hill Crockett, *A History of Lake Champlain 1609-1909* (Burlington, VT.: Hobart J. Shanley & Co., 1909), 293; H. N. Muller III, *Commerical History*, 159, 264.

6. Dudley, 371.

7. Everest, *War of 1812*, 92; See also Wallace E. Lamb, *The Lake Champlain and Lake George Valleys* (New York: The American Historical Company, Inc., 1940), Volume 1, 312-13 .

8. Dennis M. Lewis, "An Expedition Upon Lake Champlain: Murray's Raid, 1813," *Proceedings of the Champlain Valley Symposium*, edited by Bruce P. Stark (Plattsburgh, N.Y.: Clinton County Historical Association, 1982), 31; Macdonough, 116.

9. Macdonough, 116.

10. Charles G. Muller, *The Proudest Day* (New York: The John Day Company, 1960), 343; For the British version see NAC, Record Group 8, Microfilm C-3502, Volume 1170, fol. 226.

11. Macdonough, 120.

12. Glenn, *Story of Three Towns*, 340; Everest, *War of 1812*, 120; Crockett, *Lake Champlain*, 293.

13. Van De Water, 251; Bird, 268, 276.

14. NAC, Record Group 8, Microfilm C-3173, Volume 679, fol. 291.

15. Everest, *War of 1812*, 116.

16. Macdonough, 123.

17. NAC, Record Group 8, Microfilm C-3173, Volume 679, fol. 341.

18. Macdonough, 126; Chapelle, *American Sailing Navy*, 275-76; NRCNA, Record Group 45, Microcopy 147, Roll 5, Part 2, fol. 144.

19. K. Jack Bauer, *The New American State Papers: Naval Affairs* (Wilmington, DE.: Scholarly Resources, Inc., 1981), Volume 4, 385; Byron N. Clark, *A List of Pensioners of the War of 1812* (Burlington, VT.: Research Publication Company, 1904), 60; Chapelle, *American Sailing Navy*, 298, 532-33, 545; Theodore Roosevelt, *The Naval War of 1812* (New York: G. P. Putnam's Sons, 1882), 377.

20. Everest, *War of 1812*, 135.

21. NRCNA, Record Group 45, Microcopy 149, Roll 11, fol. 63; See also Chapelle, *American Sailing Navy*, 274-76.

22. NRCNA, Record Group 45, Microcopy 149, Roll 11, fol. 223.

23. Ibid.

24. A. Bowen, *The Naval Monument* (Boston: George Clark, 1830), 152; *Niles' Weekly Register*, 1 October 1814; Clark, *Pensioners*, 60; Chapelle, *American Sailing Navy*, 298, 532-34, 541, 556.

25. Kevin J. Crisman, *The Eagle* (Shelburne, VT.: The New England Press, 1987), 19.

26. Kevin James Crisman, *The History and Construction of the United States Schooner Ticonderoga* (Alexandria, VA.: Eyrie Publications, 1983), 4; Macdonough, 144.

27. Crisman, *Ticonderoga*, 13.

28. NRCNA, Record Group 45, Microcopy 147, Roll 5, Part 2, fol. 115.

29. NAC, Record Group 8, Microfilm C-3174, Volume 683, fol. 160, Microfilm C-3526, Volume 1219, fol. 89; See also Joyce Gold, *The Naval Chronicle* (London: Joyce Gold, 1814), Volume 32, 157.

30. NRCNA, Record Group 45, Microcopy 147, Roll 5, Part 2, fol. 128; Macdonough, 142.

31. Glenn, *Story of Three Towns*, 245; See also Palmer, 183.

32. Macdonough, 147.

33. Glenn, *Story of Three Towns*, 215; "Essex: An Architectural Guide," Essex Community Heritage Organization, pamphlet, 1986, 1; Alfred H. Trost and Robert C. De-Long, eds., *A History Celebrating the 150th Anniversary of the Town of Essex, N.Y. 1805-1955* (Malone, N.Y.: The Industrial Press, 1955), p.n.a.

34. Crisman, *Eagle*, 28-31.

35. H. N. Muller III, "A 'Traitorous and Diabolical Traffic': The Commerce of the Champlain–Richelieu Corridor During the War of 1812," *Vermont History* 44 (Spring 1976): 83.

36. Everest, *War of 1812*, 139, 151-52.

37. J. F. C. Fuller, *Decisive Battles of the U.S.A.* (New York: Harper & Brothers Publishers, 1942), 117; A. T. Mahan, *Sea Power in Its Relations to the War of 1812* (Boston: Little, Brown, and Company, 1905), Volume 2, 364.

38. H. N. Muller III, *Commerical History*, 311.

39. Mahan, *Sea Power*, 363.

40. Macdonough, 150; H. N. Muller III, "Diabolical Traffic," 90; C. G. Muller, *Proudest Day*, 254-55; Everest, *War of 1812*, 152; Joel Abbot Papers, Microfilm no. 25, Special Collections, Nimitz Library, U.S. Naval Academy, Annapolis, MD., fol. 173.

41. B. Clark, *Pensioners*, 61; Bowen, 153; William James, *Naval Occurrences* (London: T. Egerton, 1817), 409; William Wood, *Select British Documents of the Canadian War of 1812* (Toronto: The Champlain Society, 1926), Volume 3, Part 1, 402, 406, 429-30, 433, 450, 459, 476; The *Tecumseh* was listed by Macdonough as a British galley that had participated in the battle; the number of gunboats was listed as 12 in NAC, Record Group 8, Microfilm C-3840, Volume 1709, fol. 116, Microfilm C-3526, Volume 1219, fol. 279.

42. *Niles' Weekly Register*, 1 October 1814; James, 420; Bauer, 385.

43. J. Mackay Hitsman, *The Incredible War of 1812* (Toronto: University of Toronto Press, 1965), 217; William Wood, *Select British Documents of the Canadian War of 1812* (Toronto: The Champlain Society, 1920), Volume 1, 121.

44. Crisman, *Eagle*, 48.

45. NRCNA, Record Group 45, Microcopy 147, Roll 5, Part 3, fol. 12.

46. James MacGregor Burns, *The Vineyard of Liberty* (New York: Alfred A. Knopf, Inc., 1981), 213; Frank B. Latham, *Jacob Brown and the War of 1812* (New York: Cowles Book Company, Inc., 1971), 99.

47. Macdonough, 158.

48. Everest, *War of 1812*, 166.

49. Hitsman, 215.

50. NAC, Record Group 8, Microfilm C-3527, Volume 1222, fols. 194-95.

51. Leonard F. Guttridge and Jay D. Smith, *The Commodores* (New York: Harper & Row, Publishers, 1969), 257; J. F. C. Fuller, *Decisive Battles*, 117.

52. Everest, *War of 1812*, 158; Hitsman, 219.

53. Everest, *War of 1812*, 164.

54. B. Clark, *Pensioners*, 49, 53; Everest, *War of 1812*, 167; W. Wood, *Select British Documents*, 1: 117; Byron N. Clark, "Accounts of the Battle of Plattsburgh, 11 September, 1814," *The Vermont Antiquarian* 1 (March 1903): 79.

55. Everest, *War of 1812*, 178; C. G. Muller, *Proudest Day*, 347.

56. Crisman, *Eagle*, 61.

57. W. Wood, *Select British Documents*, 3: 378, 461-62, 469.

58. Ibid., 380.

59. W. Wood, *Select British Documents*, 1: 125, see also 3: 414, 441-42, 459, 463, 470.

60. Ibid., 3: 47; See also NAC, Record Group 8, Microfilm C-3526, Volume 1219, fol. 280.

61. B. Clark, *Pensioners*, 57; W. Wood, *Select British Documents*, 3: 369, 482, 495; NRCNA, Record Group 45, Microcopy 125, Roll 39, fol. 51; See also Joyce Gold, *The Naval Chronicle* (London: Joyce Gold, 1815), Volume 33, 255.

62. W. Wood, *Select British Documents*, 3: 381, see also 396; Macdonough, 171.

63. John M. Stahl, *The Battle of Plattsburg; A Study in and of the War of 1812* (Illinois: The Van Trump Company, 1918), 117-18; Everest, *War of 1812*, 181.

64. Joseph Allen, *Battles of the British Navy; From A.D. 1000 to 1840* (London: A. H. Baily & Co., 1842), Volume 2, 481; Everest, *War of 1812*, 185.

65. Bowen, 159; *What Historians Say*, 38; Roosevelt, 390; Macdonough, 178; *Niles' Weekly Register*, 1 October 1814.

66. James, 410; C. G. Muller, *Proudest Day*, 349; W. Wood, *Select British Documents*, 3: 374.

67. W. Wood, *Select British Documents*, 3: 369, 407, 423, 426, 497.

68. Everest, *War of 1812*, 185.

69. C. H. J. Snider, *In the Wake of the Eighteen–Twelvers* (1913; reprint ed., London: Cornmarket Press Limited, 1969), 218-19; James Russell Soley, *The Boys of 1812* (Boston: Estes and Lauriat, 1887), 288; B. Clark, *Pensioners*, 48; Macdonough, 182.

70. W. Wood, *Select British Documents*, 3: 402, 406, 429, 433.

71. Ibid., 406, 429-33, 462, 490-91; James, 409.

72. W. Wood, *Select British Documents*, 3: 483.

73. Ibid., 473.

74. Ibid., 483, see also 496.

75. NRCNA, Record Group 45, Microcopy 125, Roll 39, fol. 55; W. Wood, *Select British Documents*, 3: 384.

76. Crisman, *Eagle*, 74.

77. Bowen, 157-58.

78. NRCNA, Record Group 45, Microcopy 125, Roll 39, fol. 51; Bowen, 148; Captain Daniel Pring's report noted that the movement of the *Eagle* "enabled us to direct our fire against the division of the enemy's gunboats and ship [*Saratoga*]." *Naval Chronicle*, 33:255.

79. W. Wood, *Select British Documents*, 3: 384, 422.

80. Ibid., 374.

81. Ibid., 375.

82. Ibid., 375, 474.

83. NRCNA, Record Group 45, Microcopy 125, Roll 39, fol. 51; Bowen, 148; James, 412.

84. W. Wood, *Select British Documents*, 3: 351; See note 41, the galley *Tecumseh* appears in American records; NAC, Record Group 8, Microfilm C-3840, Volume 1709, fol. 116, Microfilm C-3526, Volume 1219, fol. 279.

85. Bess H. Langworthy, *History of Cumberland Head* (Plattsburgh, N.Y.: pub., n.a., 1961), 23.

86. *What Historians Say*, 39-40.

87. Crisman, *Eagle*, 79-80; Bowen, 149, 154; NRCNA, Record Group 45, Microcopy 125, Roll 39, fol. 51.

88. NRCNA, Record Group 45, Microcopy 125, Roll 39, fol. 51; Bowen, 149; W. Wood, *Select British Documents*, 3: 408, 413; See also James, 415; Macdonough, 168; Roosevelt, 379.

89. Bowen, 152; Everest, *War of 1812*, 185; James, cixii; W. Wood, *Select British Documents*, 3: 479; Oscar Bredenberg, *The Battle of Plattsburgh Bay* (Plattsburgh, N.Y.: Clinton County Historical Association, 1978), 21.

90. NAC, Record Group 8, Microfilm C-3526, Volume 1219, fol. 280; Prevost's letter of September 16, 1814, reasoned that "the impracticability of carrying on any operations without a sufficient Naval cooperation has caused me to turn the whole of my attention to upper Canada," Microfilm C-3527, Volume 1222, fol. 195; See also W. Wood, *Select British Documents*, 3: 352, 359; Fuller, 122; Everest, *War of 1812*, 186; B. Clark, *Pensioners*, 54-55.

91. W. Wood, *Select British Documents*, 3: 360.

92. Ibid., 400.

93. NRCNA, Record Group 45, Microcopy 125, Roll 40, fol. 105.

94. Macdonough, 185; NRCNA, Record Group 45, Microcopy 125, Roll 39, fol. 38.

95. Macdonough, 185.

96. Ibid., 190; See also *Naval Chronicle*, 33:257.

97. W. Wood, *Select British Documents*, 3: 402, 458, see also 385-86, 440, 447, 486; *Naval Chronicle*, 33:254.

98. W. Wood, *Select British Documents*, 402, 459, see also 440, 491.

99. Mahan, 381.

100. Roosevelt, 398-99.

101. NRCNA, Record Group 45, Microcopy 149, Roll 11, fol. 492.

102. Crisman, *Eagle*, 98-101.

103. Silliman, 192-93.

104. Ibid., 192.

105. Crisman, *Eagle*, 107-10.

106. Morton, *Whitehall*, 8.

107. Silliman, 208.

108. Hammersley, 24.

109. Morton, *Whitehall*, 9; Crisman, *Eagle*, 128; interviews with local residents.

110. Russ Bellico, "The Battle of Plattsburgh," *Adirondack Life*, September/October 1977, 48.

111. Crisman, *Eagle*, 118, 151, 235-43; Bass, *Ships and Shipwrecks*, 185-86; Arthur B. Cohn, ed., *A Report on the Nautical Archeology of Lake Champlain: Results of the 1982 Field Season of the Champlain Maritime Society* (Burlington, VT.: The Champlain Maritime Society, 1984), 47-71; R. Montgomery Fischer, ed., *A Report of the Nautical Archeology of Lake Champlain: Results of the 1983 Field Season of the Champlain Maritime Society* (Burlington, VT.: The Champlain Maritime Society, 1985), 13-19.

11. Champlain Canal Boats

1. Fred Copeland, "Champlain Canal Days," *The Vermonter*, August 1941, 157.

2. Everest, *Journal of Carroll*, 24.

3. See Ronald E. Shaw, *Erie Water West* (Lexington, KY.: University of Kentucky Press, 1966), 12-16; Alvin F. Harlow, *Old Towpaths* (New York: D. Appleton and Company, 1926), 29-32; *A Canalboat Primer on the Canals of New York State* (Syracuse, N.Y.: The Canal Museum, 1981), 5.

4. Jonathan Hughes, *American Economic History* (Glenview, IL.: Scott, Foresman and Company, 1983), 175.

5. Gertrude E. Cone, "Studies in the Development of Transportation in the Champlain Valley to 1876," (M.A. thesis, The University of Vermont, 1945), 74.

6. G. W., "A Sketch of the Great Northern or Champlain Canal," 1823, Special Collections, NYSL, 7.

7. R. S. Styles, *A Descriptive and Historical Guide to the Valley of Lake Champlain and the Adirondacks* (Burlington, VT.: R. S. Styles' Steam Printing House, 1871), 29.

8. See Richard Garrity, *Canal Boatman* (Syracuse, N.Y.: Syracuse University Press, 1977), 50; and Capt. Frank H. Godfrey, *The Godfrey Letters* (Syracuse, N.Y.: The Canal Society of New York State, 1973), 29-30, for details on canal boat operations.

9. Andrew G. Meiklejohn, "The Champlain Canal—Remarks of Hon. Andrew G. Meiklejohn," 5 April 1864, Special Collections, NYSL, 2-3; See also Thomas X. Grasso, *Champlain Canal* (Syracuse, N.Y.: The Canal Society of New York State, 1985), 4.

10. Ethel M. Springer and Thomas F. Hahn, *Canal Boat Children* (Shepherdstown, W. VA.: The American Canal & Transportation Center, 1981), 34.

11. Martha Robbins Juckett, *My Canaling Days*, ed. Dorothy M. Parker (reprint, Whitehall, N.Y.: Historical Society of Whitehall, 1972), 10.

12. Juckett, 8.

13. Springer and Hahn, 8; See also James Lee, ed., *Tales the Boatmen Told* (Exton, PA.: Canal Press Incorporated, 1977), 101.

14. Ibid., 9.

15. Harlow, 352.

16. Ibid.; See also Lamb, *Lake Champlain and Lake George*, 2: 578.

17. John E. O'Hara, "Erie's Junior Partner," (Ph.D. diss. Columbia University, 1951), 186.

18. Ibid., 175; Henry Wayland Hill, *Waterways and Canal Construction in New York State* (Buffalo, N.Y.: Buffalo Historical Society, 1908), 145.

19. O'Hara, 175.

20. Ibid., 176.

21. Ibid., 219.

22. Meiklejohn, 4.

23. Godfrey, *Godfrey Letters*, 27.

24. Fischer, 21-24; Russell Bellico, "The General Butler," *Skin Diver*, September 1985, 100, 104-8.

25. *Boston Globe*, 17 November 1978.

26. See Cohn, 1982 *Field Season*, 31-39; and Fischer, 27-35, for more details.

27. Morris F. Glenn, *Glenn's History of Lake Champlan: Occasional Lists of Shipping on Lake Champlain* (Alexandria, VA.: Morris F. Glenn, 1980), Volume 2, 18; See also Giovanna N. Peebles and David C. Skinas "Vermont's Underwater Historic Preserves: Challenges, Benefits, Problems, and Process," *Underwater Archaeology Proceedings*, 1989, 51; For the dimensions of many canal boats and other sailing vessels on Lake Champlain see W. S. Rann, ed., *History of Chittenden County Vermont* (Syracuse, N.Y.: D. Mason & Co., Publishers, 1886), 314.

12. Steamboats of Lake Champlain

1. Thomas H. Canfield, "Discovery, Navigation, and Navigators of Lake Champlain," in Abby Maria Hemenway, ed., *The Vermont Historical Gazetteer* (Burlington, VT.: A. M. Hemenway, 1867), Volume 1, 688; Glenn, *Occasional Lists*, 2: 8; Rann, 39.

2. Canfield, 670; Palmer, 164; Crockett, *Lake Champlain*, 291, 293; H. N. Muller III, *Commercial History*, 159; Glenn, *Story of Three Towns*, 340.

3. For details on early steamboat history see James Thomas Flexner, *Steamboats Come True* (New York: The Viking Press, 1944), 16, 68-69; Thompson Westcott, *Life of John Fitch* (Philadephia: J. B. Lippincott & Co., 1857), 177-78, 180, 184-85, 198; Ralph Nading Hill, *Sidewheeler Saga* (New York: Rinehart & Company, Inc., 1953), 3-45.

4. David J. Blow, "*Vermont I*: Lake Champlain's First Steamboat," *Vermont History* 34 (April 1966), 117-18; Crockett, *Lake Champlain, 294;* Ogden J. Ross, *The Steamboats of Lake Champlain 1809 to 1930* (Albany: Press of the Delaware and Hudson Railroad, 1930), 24.

5. Hill, *Sidewheeler Saga*, 47.

6. Lake Placid News, 28 May 1954; Barney Fowler, *Adirondack Album*, (Schenectady, N.Y.: Outdoor Associates, 1974), 31.

7. Rebecca Davison, ed., *Phoenix Project* (Burlington, VT.: Champlain Maritime Society, 1981), 7.

8. Canfield, 690.

9. Fred Erving Dayton, *Steamboat Days* (New York: Frederick A. Stokes Company, 1925), 91, 93.

10. Ronald A. Anderson, *Government and Business*, 4th ed. (Cincinnati: South-Western Publishing Co., 1981), 124.

11. Silliman, 191.

12. Dayton, 92; Ross, *Steamboats of Lake Champlain*, 35.

13. Allen Penfield Beach, *Lake Champlain As Centuries Pass* (Burlington, VT.: Lane Press, 1959), 64.

14. Ross, *Steamboats of Lake Champlain*, 50.

15. Ell B. Rockwell, "Various Recollections," Captain E. Rockwell Papers, Special Collections, Bailey-Howe Library, University of Vermont, Burlington, VT.

16. Canfield, 707.

17. Caroline Halstead Royce, *Bessboro: A History of Westport, Essex Co., N.Y.* (Elizabethtown, N.Y.: C. H. Royce, 1904), 417.
18. Champlain Transportation Company Papers, Carton 1, Folder 188, Special Collections, Bailey-Howe Library, University of Vermont, Burlington, VT.
19. Ibid., Carton 1, Folder 242.
20. Rockwell Papers, "Various Recollections."
21. *The Daily Free Press*, 27 April 1866.
22. Crockett, *Lake Champlain*, 305; Canfield, 703.
23. Ross, *Steamboats of Lake Champlain*, 61; See also Canfield, 696.
24. Ross, *Steamboats of Lake Champlain*, 63.
25. State of New-York. No. 64. In Assembly, January 22, 1841, 1, author collection.
26. *Plattsburgh Republican*, 6 August 1841; See also *A Century of Progress: History of the Delaware and Hudson Company 1823-1923* (Albany, N.Y.: J. B. Lyon Company, 1925), 710.
27. See the *Plattsburgh Republican*, 5 September 1846, for the Champlain Transportation Company's explanation of the unsuccessful agreement.
28. For a list of steamers which includes dimensions and final disposition see Canfield, 707; Rockwell Papers, "Various Recollections"; F. H. Wilkins, "Lake Champlain Steamers," *The Vermonter* 21 (January 1916): 14-15.
29. Cone, "Studies," 60.
30. Ross, *Steamboats of Lake Champlain*, 125.
31. *Plattsburgh Sentinel*, 23 July 1875; Royce, 576.
32. Rockwell Papers, "The Story of the Wreck," 2; R. N. Hill, *Sidewheeler Saga*, 266; Lynn H. Bottum, "*Oakes Ames/Champlain*: The Biography of a Lake Champlain Steamboat," *Vermont History* 51 (Summer 1983): 133.
33. Champlain Transportation Company Papers, Report of Abijah North to Directors, Carton 8, Folder 21, 7, Special Collections, Bailey-Howe Library, University of Vermont, Burlington, VT.
34. *Plattsburgh Sentinel*, 23 July 1875.
35. Ibid.
36. Ibid.
37. Rockwell Papers, "The Wreck of the 'Champlain' in 1875," 4.
38. Rockwell Papers, "The Story of the Wreck," 4.
39. Rockwell Papers, "The Wreck of the 'Champlain' in 1875," 3.
40. *Plattsburgh Sentinel*, 23 July 1875.
41. Ross, *Steamboats of Lake Champlain*, 128.
42. Russ Bellico, "Historic Preservation: The Wreck of the *Champlain*," *Adirondack Life*, July/August 1989, 26-28.
43. R. N. Hill, *Sidewheeler Saga*, 268.
44. Ibid.
45. Fischer, 56-61, for measurements of the sunken steamers.
46. Merritt Carpenter, "The Wrecks of Shelburne Harbor," *Champlain Maritime Society Soundings*, August 1981, 2.
47. Morris F. Glenn, *Lake Champlain Album* (Alexandria, VA.: Morris F .Glenn, 1979), Volume 2, 25, 27; Assorted materials, Vermont Collection, Bixby Library, Vergennes,

VT.; Gordon C. and Elsie L. Sherman, *An Illuminating History of the Champlain Valley and Adirondack Mountains*, 1814-1929 (Elizabethtown, N.Y.: Denton Publications, Inc., 1977), Volume 2.

48. Ralph N. Hill, "Shelburne Shipyard," *Vermont Life*, Autumn 1953, 8-13, 60.

49. Ralph Nading Hill, *Two Centuries of Ferry Boating* (Burlington, VT.: Lake Champlain Transportation Co., Inc., 1972), 33; See also Sherman, 42-45, 64-80.

50. For more information on the *Juniper* see Russ Bellico, "The Cruise of the *Juniper*," *Adirondack Life*, May/June 1978, 38-40.

51. Lynn Watt, "Is Champlain Doomed?" *Vermont Life*, Spring 1969, 46-50.

52. Lori Fisher, "The Battle of Burlington: Sewage Hits the Beaches," *Lake Champlain Committee Newsletter*, Summer/Fall 1987, 2.

13. Steamboats of Lake George

1. Stuart D. Ludlum, *Exploring Lake George Lake Champlain 100 Years Ago* (Utica, N.Y.: Brodock & Ludlum Publications, 1972), 3.

2. F. Grant, "Journal," 320; Betty Ahearn Buckell, *Old Lake George Hotels* (Lake George, N.Y.: Buckle Press, 1986), 66.

3. Cometti, 47; Silliman, 150; Buckell, *Hotels*, 30.

4. Silliman, 151.

5. Marvin, 32.

6. *GFR*, 19 May 1857.

7. Silliman, 155; The tavern mentioned in Silliman's book was probably the Lake House, first built in 1800 on the present site of Shepard Park in Lake George Village, see Buckell, *Hotels*, 25.

8. *GFR*, 19 May 1857.

9. Ibid.

10. Harris, 26; See also Ross, *Steamboats of Lake George*, 53; Canfield, 693; S. R. Stoddard, *Lake George: A Book of To-day* (Albany: Van Benthuysen & Sons, Printers, 1880), 59.

11. *GFR*, 19 May 1857; Harris, 26.

12. Data on the dimensions of the steamer *William Caldwell* vary considerably, see *GFR*, 19 May 1857; Ross, *Steamboats of Lake George*, 57; Canfield, 693.

13. Ross, *Steamboats of Lake George*, 63.

14. Harris, 10.

15. *LGM*, 26 August 1893.

16. *GFR*, 5 August 1856.

17. Ibid.

18. *LGM*, 26 August 1893.

19. *GFR*, 5 August 1856.

20. Stoddard, 60.

21. *GFR*, 5 August 1856.

22. *GFR*, 19 May 1857.

23. Ross, *Steamboats of Lake George*, 81.

24. Charles H. Possons, *Possons' Guide to Lake George, Lake Champlain and Adirondacks* (Glens Falls, N. Y.: Chas. H. Possons, Publisher, 1888), 46.

25. *LGM*, 8 July 1893.

26. Ross, *Steamboats of Lake George*, 101.

27. Lord, 91.

28. *LGM*, 6 July 1892; For more information on the *Island Queen* see *Glens Falls Daily Times*, 14 November 1892; See also *Glens Falls Daily Times*, 29 August 1901; *LGM*, 18 July 1891; Fred T. Stiles, "Tales of Lake George," *York State Tradition*, Summer 1963, 50; For additional details on Everett Harrison's operation see *LGM*, 18 July 1891; *LGM*, 2 September 1893; *LGM*, 1 June 1895.

29. Possons, 47; See also T. E. Roessle, *Lake George: A Descriptive and Historical Sketch* (Lake George, N. Y.: T. E. Roessle, 1887), 16.

30. *LGM*, 13 August 1892; *LGM*, 5 September 1896; *LGM*, 12 June 1897; *LGM*, 3 June 1899; Dorothy Backus Offensend, *The Sexton Boatbuilders of Hague* (Pawlet, VT.: D. B. Offensend, 1982), 56, 64, 65, 71, 90, 94, 98.

31. *LGM*, 7 July 1923.

32. *LGM*, 12 August 1893; See also *Glens Falls Daily Times*, 4 August 1893.

33. *Glens Falls Daily Times*, 29 August 1901; See also *LGM*, 31 August 1901.

34. Lape, 208; telephone interview with Dr. George Peter Cook of Ticonderoga whose father helped remove the wreckage in 1902.

35. Buckell, Bernard. Interview by Russell Bellico, 28 August 1988.

36. *LGM*, 17 July 1915; Harris, 15; For other details on the *Scioto*'s subsequent career see *LGM*, 15 July 1922; *LGM*, 4 September 1926; *LGM*, 2 July 1927; *LGM*, 30 June 1934; *LGM*, 16 July 1937; Glens Falls newspapers also carried stories on the *Scioto II* in June 1938 and June 1939.

37. Frederick C. Thorne, *Pilot Knob Story: An Historical Report of Its Life and Times* (Pilot Knob, N. Y.: F. C. Thorne, 1977), 38; Burleigh, Captain Gordon. Interview by Russell Bellico, 25 July 1990.

38. For more information on the *Iroquois* see *LGM*, 6 June 1902, 9 August 1902, 23 August 1919, 21 July 1923.

39. *LGM*, 2 July 1927.

40. *LGM*, 28 July 1939.

41. Some details on the *Ranger* may be found in the *LGM*, 28 June 1946; *LGM*, 27 June 1947; Arthur S. Knight, ed., *Vacationland : In Picture, Story and History* (Lake George, N. Y.: Adirondack Resorts Press, Inc., 1950), 74.

42. *Abandoned Historic Shipwreck Protection Act*, H. R. 2071, lines 17-22.

43. *The Plan for the Future of the Lake George Park* (Lake George, N. Y.: The Task Force for the Future of the Lake George Park, 1985), 5.

Photo by the author.

Select Bibliography

Journals and Primary Sources

Abbot, Joel. Papers. Special Collections, Nimitz Library, U.S. Naval Academy, Annapolis, MD. Microfilm 25.

Alexander, Thomas. "Ens. Alexander's Diary." In *History of Northfield, Massachusetts*, by J. H. Temple and George Sheldon. 303-5. Albany: Joel Munsell, 1875.

Allen, Ethan. *A Narrative of Colonel Ethan Allen's Captivity*. 1930; Reprint. Rutland, VT.: Vermont Heritage Press, 1988.

Almon, John, ed. *The Remembrancer; Or Impartial Repository of Public Events*. Part 2. London: J. Almon, 1776.

Amherst Papers, Public Record Office, London, 22 vols.

Anburey, Thomas. *Travels Through the Interior Parts of America*. Vol. 1. Boston: Houghton Mifflin Company, 1923.

[André, John.] "Papers Relating to the Surrender of Fort St. Johns and Fort Chambly." In *Report of the Work of the Public Archives for the Years 1914 and 1915*, edited by Arthur G. Doughty. 3-25. Ottawa: Public Archives of Canada, 1916.

"The Anonymous Journal of the French and Indian War." *BFTM* 12 (September 1968): 291-97.

Arnold, Benedict. "Benedict Arnold's Regimental Memorandum Book." *BFTM* 14 (Winter 1982): 71-80.

Baldwin, Jeduthan. "Journal Kept by Capt. Jeduthan Baldwin While on the Expedition Against Crown Point, 1755-56." *Journal of the Military Service Institute* 39 (July-August 1906): 123-30.

Baldwin, Thomas Williams, ed. *The Revolutionary Journal of Col. Jeduthan Baldwin 1775-1778*. Bangor, ME.: DeBurians, 1906.

Bangs, Nathaniel. *Orderly Book Kept by Nathaniel Bangs at Fort Edward, 1758*. MASS HS

Barlow, Aaron. "The March to Montreal and Quebec." *The American Historical Register* 2 (September 1894–February 1895): 641-49.

Barrows, Abner. "Diary of Abner Barrows." In *History of the Town of Middleboro*, edited by Thomas Weston. 95-98. New York: Houghton Mifflin, 1906.

Bartman, George. "The Siege of Fort William Henry, Letters of George Bartman." *Huntington Library Quarterly* 12 (August 1949): 415-24.

Bauer, K. Jack, ed. *The New American State Papers: Naval Affairs*. Vol. 4. Wilmington, DE.: Scholarly Resources, Inc., 1981.

Baxter, James Phinney., ed. *The British Invasion from the North, The Campaigns of Generals Carleton and Burgoyne from Canada, 1776-1777, With the Journal of Lieut. William Digby*. Albany: Joel Munsell's Sons, 1887.

Bayley, Jacob. "Part of the Journal of Capt. Jacob Bayley, in the Old French War." In *History of Newbury, Vermont*, by Frederic P. Wells. 376-80. St. Johnsbury, VT.: The Caledonian Company, 1902.

Beebe, Lewis. "Journal of a Physician on the Expedition Against Canada, 1776." *The Pennsylvania Magazine of History and Biography* 59 (October 1935): 321-61.

Benson, Adolph B. ed. *Peter Kalm's Travels in North America*. New York: Dover Publications, Inc., 1937.

Benzel, Adolphus. "Remarks on Lake Champlain, 1772." *BFTM* 12 (December 1969): 358-64.

Biggar, H. P., ed. *The Works of Samuel De Champlain*. Vol. 2, 1608-1613. Toronto: The Champlain Society, 1925.

Blake, Thomas. "Lieutenant Thomas Blake's Journal." In *History of the First New Hampshire Regiment in the War of the Revolution*, by Frederic Kidder. 25-56. Albany: Joel Munsell, 1868.

Bougainville, Louis Antoine de. *Adventure in the Wilderness. The American Journals of Louis Antoine de Bougainville 1756-1760*. Translated and Edited by Edward P. Hamilton. Norman, OK: University of Oklahoma Press, 1964.

Bowen, A. *The Naval Monument*. Boston: George Clark, 1830.

Bradbury, John. "Diary of Dea. John Bradbury." In *Bradbury Memorial*, comp. by William Berry Lapham. 261-95. Portland, ME: Brown Thurston & Company, 1890.

Burk, John. "John Burk's Diary." In *History of the Town of Bernardston*, by Lucy Cutler Kellogg. 40-47. Greenfield, MA.: Press of E. A. Hall & Co., 1902.

Burr, Asa. "Diary of Asa Burr, 1758." Octavo Volume 1, AAS.

Bushnell, Charles I., ed. *The Narrative of Ebenezer Fletcher, A Soldier of the Revolution*. 1866. Reprint. Freeport, N.Y.: Books for Libraries Press, 1970.

Calfe, John. "Capt. John Calfe's Journal, 1777." In *A Memorial of the Town of Hampstead, New Hampshire*, by Harriette Eliza Noyes. 288-95. Boston: George B. Reed, 1899.

"Campaign in Canada & c Under G. Carleton." *BFTM* 11 (December 1964): 235-69; 11 (September 1965): 307-35; 12 (March 1966): 5-37.

Carleton, Major. "Articles of Capitulation. . .at Fort George." *BFTM* 7 (July 1946): 25.

Carver, Jonathan. *Travels Through the Interior Parts of North America in the Years 1766, 1767, and 1768*. 1778. Reprint. Minneapolis: Ross & Haines, Inc., 1956.

Chamberlin, William. "Letter of General William Chamberlin." *Proceedings of the Massachusetts Historical Society* 10, Second Series (1895, 1896): 490-504.

Champion, Henry. "The Journal of Colonel Henry Champion." In *Champion Genealogy*, by Francis Bacon Trowbridge. 417-38. New Haven: F. B. Trowbridge, 1891.

Chandler, Samuel. "Extracts from the Diary of Rev. Samuel Chandler." *NEHGR* 17 (October 1863): 346-54.

Clark, Byron N. "Accounts of the Battle of Plattsburgh, 11 September, 1814." *Vermont Antiquarian* 1 (March 1903): 75-93.

_____. ed. *A List of Pensioners of the War of 1812*. Burlington, VT.: Research Publication Company, 1904.

Clark, William Bell and William James Morgan, eds. *Naval Documents of the American Revolution*. 9 vols. Washington, D.C.: Naval History Division, Department of the Navy, 1964-86.

Cleaveland, John. "The Journal of the Rev. John Cleaveland." *EIHC* 12 (April 1874): 85-103; (July 1874): 179-96; 13 (1877): 53-63.

_____. "Journal of Rev. John Cleaveland Kept While Chaplain in the French and Indian War, 1758-1759." *BFTM* 10 (No. 3, 1959): 192-234.

Cobb, Samuel. "The Journal of Captain Samuel Cobb." *BFTM* 14 (Summer 1981): 12-31.

Cometti, Elizabeth, ed. *The American Journals of Lt. John Enys*. Syracuse, N.Y.: Syracuse University Press, 1976.

Comstock, Christopher. "Diary of Christopher Comstock 1758-59." Connecticut Historical Society.

Cutter, Ruhamah Ammi. "Dr. A. R. Cutter's Journal of his Military Experience 1756-1758." In *A History of the Cutter Family of New England*, by Richard Cutter. 60-72. Boston: David Clapp & Son, 1871.

Cutter, William R., ed. *Diary of Lieut. Samuel Thompson*. Boston: Press of David Clapp & Son, 1896.

Dawes, E. C., ed. *Journal of Gen. Rufus Putnam 1757-1760*. Albany: Joel Munsell's Sons, 1886.

Dearborn, Henry. *Revolutionary War Journals of Henry Dearborn, 1775-1783*. Edited by Lloyd A. Brown and Howard H. Peckham. 1939. Reprint. New York: Da Capo Press, 1971.

"Diary of a Soldier at Crown Point 1759." French and Indian War Collection. AAS.

Dibble, Ebenezer. "Diary of Ebenezer Dibble." *Proceedings of the Society of Colonial Wars in the State of Connecticut* 1 (1903): 313-29.

Dodge, Nathaniel Brown. "A Letter and Diary of 1776." *Vermont Quarterly* 21 (1953): 29-35.

Douglas, Charles. "A British View on the Battle of Valcour." *North Country Notes*, April 1963, 2-3.

Dudley, William S. *The Naval War of 1812: A Documentary History*. Vol. 1. Washington, D.C.: Department of the Navy, 1985.

Dwight, Nathaniel. "The Journal of Capt. Nathaniel Dwight of Belchertown, Mass., During the Crown Point Expedition, 1755." *The New York Genealogical and Biographical Record* 33 (1902): 3-10, 65-70.

Everest, Allan S., ed. *The Journal of Charles Carroll of Carrollton*. Fort Ticonderoga, N.Y.: The Champlain-Upper Hudson Bicentennial Committee, 1976.

Fassett, John. "Diary of Lieutenant John Fassett." In *The Follett-Dewey, Fassett-Safford Ancestry*, by Harry Parker Ward. 225-28. Columbus, OH.: Champlin Printing, 1896.

Fitch, Jabez, Jr. *The Diary of Jabez Fitch, Jr. in the French and Indian War 1757*. 3rd ed. Fort Edward, N.Y.: Rogers Island Historical Association, 1986.

Forbush, Eli. "Camp at Ticonderoga or Fort Carillon, Aug. 4, 1759." In *Fort Ticonderoga, A Short History*, by S. H. P. Pell. Ticonderoga: N.Y.: Fort Ticonderoga Museum, 1978.

Force, Peter, ed. *American Archives*. Fourth Series, Vol. 3, Vol. 4. Washington, D.C.: M. St. Clair Clarke and Peter Force, 1840, 1846; and Fifth Series, Vol. 1-3. Washington, D.C.: M. St. Clair Clarke and Peter Force, 1848-53.

Foster Asa. "Diary of Capt. Asa Foster of Andover, Mass." *NEHGR* 213 (1900): 183-88.

Frazer, Persifer. "Letters from Ticonderoga, 1776." *BFTM* 10 (January 1962): 450-59.

French and Indian War Collection 1754-1774, "A Soldier at Fort William Henry, 1756." Octavo Volume 2, AAS.

Frisbie, Judah. "Journal as a Soldier in the Revolution." In *History of the Town of Wolcott*, by Rev. Samuel Orcutt. 306-11. Waterbury, CT.: Press of the American Printing Company, 1874.

Frost, John Jr. "Diary of Lieut. John Frost, Jr., 1760." *Old Eliot* 8 (1908): 109-17.

Frye, Joseph. "A Journal of the Attack of Fort William Henry." *Parkman Papers* 42: 137-62. MASS HS

Fuller, Archelaus. "Journal of Col. Archelaus Fuller of Middleton, Mass." *EIHC* 46 (1910): 209-20.

_____. "The Journal of Archelaus Fuller May–Nov. 1758." *BFTM* 13 (December 1970): 5-17.

Gilbert, James. "Journal Kept by James Gilbert." *Magazine of New England History* 3 (1893): 188-95.

Glasier, Benjamin. "French and Indian War Diary of Benjamin Glasier of Ipswich, 1758-1760." *EIHC* 86 (1950): 65-92.

Godfrey, Richard. "A Journal of the March of Captain Richard Godfrey's Company, 1755." In *History of Taunton, Mass.*, by Samuel H. Emery. 419-24. Syracuse, N.Y.: D. Mason, 1893.

Gold, Joyce. *The Naval Chronicle*. Vol. 32, 33. London: Joyce Gold, 1814 & 1815.

Goodrich, Josiah. "The Josiah Goodrich Orderbook." *BFTM* 13 (Fall 1980): 410-31.

Graham, John. "The Journal of the Rev. John Graham." *MAH*, Part 1 (1882): 206-12.

Grant, Francis. "Journal from New York to Canada, 1767." *Proceedings of the New York State Historical Association* 13 (1932): 181-322.

Grant, W. L., ed. *Voyages of Samuel De Champlain 1604-1618*. New York: Charles Scribner and Sons, 1907.

Green, Samuel A., ed. *Three Military Diaries*. Cambridge, MA.: John Wilson & Son, 1901.

Greenleaf, Samuel. *Account Book and Journal*, 1756. MASS HS.

Greenman, Jeremiah. *Diary of a Common Soldier in the American Revolution, 1775-1783*. Edited by Robert C. Bray and Paul E. Bushnell. DeKalb, IL.: Northern Illinois University Press, 1978.

Gridley, Luke. *Luke Gridley's Diary of 1757*. Hartford, CT.: The Acorn Club, 1906.

Guild, Joseph. "Journal of Captain Joseph Guild." *The Dedham Historical Register* 7 (1896): 43-47.

Haldimand Papers. National Archives of Canada, Ottawa. "Misc. Papers Relating to the Provincial Navy, 1775-1780." Microfilm H-1649, Vol. 1, B144, Vol 2, B145; Microfilm C-3242, Vol. 722A.

Hardy, Constantine. "Extracts from the Journal of Constantine Hardy." *NEHGR* 60 (1906): 236-39.

Hawks, John. *Orderly Book and Journal of Major John Hawks 1759-1760*. New York: Society of Colonial Wars, 1911.

Hawley, Elisha. "Capt. Hawley's Journal." In *History of Northampton, Massachusetts*. Vol. 2. by James R. Trumbull. 254-59. Northampton, MA.: Press of Gazette Printing Co., 1902.

Haynes, Thomas. "Memorandum of Collonial French War A.D. 1758-." *BFTM* 12 (October 1967): 193-203.

Henderson, James. "James Henderson's Journal." In *The First Century of the Colonial Wars in the Commonwealth of Massachusetts*, 195-209. Boston: Society of Colonial Wars, Mass., 1944.

Henry, John Joseph. *Account of Arnold's Campaign Against Quebec*. 1877. Reprint. New York: The New York Times & Arno Press, 1968.

Henshaw, William. "William Henshaw's Journal." *Proceedings of the Worcester Society of Antiquity* 25 (1912): 43-64.

Hervey, William. *Journals of the Hon. William Hervey.* Bury St. Edmund's: Paul & Mathew, Butter Market, 1906.

Hildreth, Micah. "Micah Hildreth of Dracutt His Book." In *History of Dracut, Massachusetts*, by Silas R. Coburn. 147-52. Lowell, MA.: Press of the Courier-Citizen Co., 1922.

Hill, James. "The Diary of a Private on the First Expedition to Crown Point." edited by Edna V. Moffett. *New England Quarterly* 5 (1932): 602-18.

Holden, David. "Journal of Sergeant Holden." *Proceedings of the Massachusetts Historical Society* 4, Second Series (1887-1889): 384-409.

Hollister, Josiah. *The Journal of Josiah Hollister.* Illinois: Romanzo Norton Bunn, d.n.a.

Holt, Joseph. "Journals of Joseph Holt, of Wilton, N.H." *NEHGR* (1856): 307-11.

Hurlbut, John, Jr. "The Journal of a Colonial Soldier." *MAH* 39 (1893): 395-96.

Ingalls, Phineas. "Revolutionary War Journal, Kept by Phineas Ingalls of Andover, Mass, April 19, 1775 - December 8, 1776." *EIHC* 53 (1917): 81-91.

Jewett, Benjamin. "The Diary of Benjamin Jewett–1758." *National Magazine* 17 (1892-93): 60-64.

"A Journal Kept During the Siege of Fort William Henry, August, 1757." *Proceedings of the American Philosophical Society* 37 (1898): 143-50.

"Journal of a Provincial Officer in the Campaign in Northern New York in 1758." *The Historical Magazine* 10 (July 1871): 118-22.

Jenks, Samuel. "Samuel Jenks, his Journal of the Campaign in 1760." *Proceedings of the Massachusetts Historical Society* 5, Second Series (1889-1890): 353-91.

"Journal in Quebec." *Coll. NYHS* 13 (1880): 173-236.

Kimball, Gertrude Selwyn, ed. *Correspondence of William Pitt.* Vol. 1. New York: The Macmillan Company, 1906.

Knox, Captain John. *An Historical Journal of the Campaigns in North America.* 3 vols. 1769. by Arthur G. Doughty 1914-1916. Reprint. Freeport, N.Y.: Books for Libraries Press, 1970.

Knox, Henry. "Knox's Diary During His Ticonderoga Expedition." *NEHGR* 119 (July 1876): 321-27.

___. "Diary of Henry Knox." In *Ye Cohorn Caravan*, by Wm. L. Bowne. Schuylerville, N.Y.: NaPaul Publishers, Inc., 1975.

Kruger, John W., ed. "Simon Metcalfe's 'Little Book.' " *BFTM* 15 (Winter 1988): 28-36.

Lamb, R. *Journal of Occurrences During the Late American War.* Dubin: Wilkinson & Courtney, 1809.

"Letters of Benedict Arnold, Guy Carleton, Horatio Gates, Thomas Hartley et al." *BFTM* 4 (July 1938): 20-56.

"Letters of General Gates, 1776." *BFTM* 5 (January 1939): 9-34.

"Letters of General Powell, 1777." *BFTM* 7 (July 1945): 29-35.

Lincoln, Charles Henry, ed. *Correspondence of William Shirley.* Vol. 2. New York: The Macmillan Company, 1912.

Lincoln, James Minor. comp. *The Papers of Captain Rufus Lincoln of Wareham, Mass.* 1904. Reprint. New York: Arno Press Inc., 1971.

Livingston, Henry. "Journal of Major Henry Livingston 1775." edited by Gaillard Hunt. *The Pennsylvania Magazine of History and Biography* 22 (1898): 9-33.

Lyon, Lemuel. "Military Journal for 1758." In *The Military Journals of Two Private Soldiers 1758-1775*, by Abraham Tomlinson. 11-45. 1854. Reprint. Freeport, N.Y.: Books for Libraries Press, 1970.

MacClintock, Samuel. *Rev. Samuel MacClintock's Journal*. 1760. Crown Point, N.Y.: Crown Point Road Association, Inc., 1972.

Maguire, Robert J. "Dr. Robert Knox's Account of the Battle of Valcour, October 11-13." *Vermont History* 46 (Summer 1978): 141-50.

Melvin, James. *The Journal of James Melvin — Private Soldier in Arnold's Expedition Against Quebec in the Year 1775*. Edited by Andrew A. Melvin. Portland, ME.: The Wardwell Press, 1902.

Merriman, Samuel. "Journal of Samuel Merriman." In *A History of Deerfield*, by George Sheldon. 661-68. 1895. Reprint. Somersworth, N.H.: New Hampshire Publishing Company, 1972.

Metcalf, Seth. *Diary and Journal of Seth Metcalf*. Boston: The Historical Records Survey, 1939.

Montresor, James. "Journals of Col. James Montresor." *Coll. NYHS* 14 (1881): 17-111.

Monypenny, Alexander. "Monypenny Orderly Book." *BFTM* 12 (October 1970): 434-61.

Mudge, Simon. "Journal of the March to Continental Army." In *Memorials: Mudge*, by Alfred Mudge. 204-5. Boston: Alfred Mudge and Son, 1868.

National Archives of Canada, Ottawa. Record Group 8. British Military and Naval Records. Microfilm C-3173, Vol. 679; Microfilm C-3174, Vol. 683; Microfilm C-3233, Vol. 690; Microfilm C-3243, Vol. 730; Microfilm C-3502, Vol. C.1170; Microfilm C-3526, Vol. 1219; Microfilm C-3527, Vols. 1222 and 1225; Microfilm C-3840, Vol. 1709.

Naval Records Collection of the Office of Naval Records and Library. Washington, D.C.: National Archives. Record Group 45, Microcopys 125, 147, 149.

Nichols, Joseph. "Joseph Nichols Military Journal 1758-59." HM 89. Henry E. Huntington Library, San Marino, California.

Nourse, Henry S. *The Military Annals of Lancaster, Massachusetts 1740-1865*. Lancaster, MA.: Henry S. Nourse, 1889.

Noyes, John. "Journal of John Noyes of Newbury in the Expedition Against Ticonderoga, 1758." *EIHC* 45 (1909): 73-77.

O'Callaghan, Edmund B. ed. *The Documentary History of the State of New York*. 4 vol. Albany: Weed, Parsons & Co.; Charles Van Benthuysen, Public Printer, 1849-51.

_____. *Documents Relative to the Colonial History of the State of New York*. 10 vol. Albany: Weed, Parsons and Company, 1853-1858.

Oswald, Eleazer. "Journal Kept by Eleazer Oswald on Lake Champlain." *BFTM* 13 (1977): 341.

Parkman Papers. Vol. 42. MASS HS.

Parkman, William. "Journal of William Parkman." *Proceedings of the Massachusetts Historical Society* 17 (1879-80): 243-45.

Pell, Joshua, Jr. "Diary of Joshua Pell, Junior." *MAH* 2 (1878): 43-47, 107-11.

Perry, David. "Recollections of an Old Soldier." *BFTM* 14 (Summer 1981): 4-11.

Pomeroy, Seth. *The Journals and Papers of Seth Pomeroy*. Edited by Louis Effingham De Forest. New York: Society of Colonial Wars in the State of New York, 1926.

Pond, Peter. "Experience in Early Wars in America." *The Journal of American History* 1 (1907): 89-93.

Porter, Elisha. "Diary of Mr. Elisha Porter of Hadley." *MAH* 29 (1893): 185-206.

Porterfield, Charles. "Memorable attack on Quebec, December 21, 1775." *MAH* 21 (1889): 318-19.

Pouchot, M. *Memoir Upon the Late War in North America Between the French and English* 1755-60. Translated and Edited by Franklin B. Hough. Roxbury, MA.: W. Elliot Woodward, 1866.

Rea, Caleb. "The Journal of Dr. Caleb Rea, Written During the Expedition Against Ticonderoga in 1758." *EIHC* 18 (1881): 81-120, 177-205.

Revolutionary War Manuscripts. Albany: New York State Library and Archives. Documents #224, 671, 1008, 1382, 1477, 1484, 1570, 1572, 1633, 7308, 7312, 11107, 14007.

Richardson, Amos. "Amos Richardson's Journal, 1758." *BFTM* 12 (September 1968): 267-91.

Ritzema, Rudolphus. "Journal of Col. Rudolphus Ritzema." *MAH* 1 (1877): 98-105.

Robbins, Ammi R. "Journal of Rev. Ammi R. Robbins, A Chaplain in the American Army." In *History of Norfolk,* by Theron Wilmot Crissey. 97-121. Everett, MA.: Massachusetts Publishing Company, 1900.

Roberts, Lemuel. *Memoirs of Captain Lemuel Roberts*. 1809. Reprint. New York: The New York Times & Arno Press, 1969.

Roby, Luther. *Reminiscences of the French War; Roger's Expeditions and Maj. Gen. John Stark*. Concord, N.H.: Luther Roby, 1831.

Rockwell, Ell B. Papers. Special Collections, Bailey-Howe Library, University of Vermont, Burlington, VT.

Rogers, Horatio, ed. *Hadden's Journal and Orderly Books: A Journal Kept in Canada and Upon Burgoyne's Campaign in 1776 and 1777*. 1884. Reprint. Boston: Gregg Press, 1972.

Rogers, Robert. *Journals of Major Robert Rogers*. 1765. Reprint. Ann Arbor, Mich.: University Microfilms, Inc. 1966.

Schank, John, John Starke, and Edward Longcroft. "An Open Letter to Captain Pringle." *BFTM* 1 (July 1928): 14-20.

Searing, James. "The Battle of Ticonderoga, 1758." *Proceedings of the New-York Historical Society* 5 (1847): 112-17.

Sewall, Henry. "Diary of Captain Henry Sewall of the Army of the Revolution, 1776-1783." *The Historical Magazine* 10 (July 1871): 128-35.

_____. "The Diary of Henry Sewall." *BFTM* 11 (September 1963): 75-92.

Smith, E. Vale. "Diary of Colonel Edward Wigglesworth." In *History of Newburyport*, 357-59. Newburyport, MA.: pub.n.a., 1854.

Smith, Joseph. "Journal of Joseph Smith, of Groton." *Proceedings of the Society of Colonial Wars in the State of Connecticut* 1 (1903): 305-10.

Snyder, Charles M. "With Benedict Arnold at Valcour Island: The Diary of Pascal De Angelis." *Vermont History* 42 (summer 1974):195-200.

Spaulding, Leonard. "French and Indian War Record." In *The Vermont Historical Gazetteer*. Vol. 5. edited by Abby Maria Hemenway. 28-33. Brandon, VT.: Carrie E. H. Page, 1891.

Spicer, Abel. "Diary of Abel Spicer from June 5th Until September 29th, 1758." In *History of the Descendants of Peter Spicer*, by Susan Spicer Meech and Susan Billings Meech. 388-409. Boston: F. H. Gilson, 1911.

Starke, Jn. "Remarks on Affairs at the Portage Between Ticonderoga and Lake George, and the Mount Independence, in Sept. 1777." *BFTM* 11 (July 1964): 207-10.

Stickney, M. A. "Massacre at Fort William Henry, 1757." *EIHC* 3 (1861): 79-84.

Stone, Enos. "Capt. Enos Stone's Journal." *NEHGR* 15 (January 1861): 299-303.

Stone, William L., ed. *Journal of Captain Pausch*. Albany: Joel Munsell's Sons, 1886.

_____. trans. and ed. *Letters of Brunswick and Hessian Officers During the American Revolution*. Albany: Joel Munsell's Sons, Publishers, 1891.

_____. trans. *Memoirs, Letters, and Journals of Major General Riedesel*. 2 vols. 1868. Reprint. New York: The New York Times & Arno Press, 1969.

Sullivan, James, ed. *The Papers of Sir William Johnson*. 2 vol. Albany: The University of the State of New York, 1921-1922.

Sweat, William. "Captain William Sweat's Personal Diary of the Expedition Against Ticonderoga, May 2–November 7, 1758." *EIHC* 93 (1957): 36-57.

Thacher, James. *Military Journal of the American Revolution*. Hartford, CT.: Hurlbut, Williams & Company, 1862.

Thompson, Samuel. "Diary of Lieut. Samuel Thompson of Woburn." In *The History of Woburn*, by Samuel Sewall. 547-59. Boston: Wiggin and Lunt Publishers, 1868.

Thwaites, Reuben Gold, ed. *Travels and Explorations of the Jesuit Missionaries in New France*. Vol. 70. Cleveland: The Burrows Brothers Company, 1900.

Tinkham, Seth. "The Diary of Seth Tinkham." In *History of Plymouth County, Massachusetts*, by D. Hamilton Hurd. 944-98. Philadelphia: J. W. Lewis & Co., 1884.

"The Trial of Major General St. Clair, August 1778." *Coll. NYHS* 13 (1880): 1-171.

"The Trial of Major General Schuyler, October 1778." *Coll. NYHS* 12 (1879): 1-181.

True, Henry. *Journal and Letters of Rev. Henry True*. Marion, OH.: Star Press, 1900.

Trumbull, Benjamin. "A Concise Journal or Minutes of the Principal Movements Towards St. John's." *Coll. Conn. HS* 7 (1899): 137-73.

_____. "The Montgomery Expedition, 1775." *BFTM* 1 (January 1927, July 1927, July 1928): 11-18; 26-33; 21-35.

Trumbull, John. *Autobiography, Reminiscences and Letters of John Trumbull from 1756 to 1841*. New Haven, CT.: B. L. Hamlen, 1841.

_____. "John Trumbull at Ticonderoga from His Autobiography." *BFTM* 3 (January 1933): 3-12.

Walker, James. "Capt. James Walker's Journal." In *History of Bedford New Hampshire*. 474-49. Concord, N.H.: The Town of Bedford, 1903.

Ware, Joseph. "Expedition Against Quebec." *NEHGR* 6 (April 1852): 129-45.

Warner, Samuel. "Extracts from Samuel Warner's Journal Kept on the Expedition to Crown Point, 1759." In *An Historical Address Delivered at the Centennial Celebration of the Incorporation of the Town of Wilbraham*, by Rufus P. Stebbins. 208-13. Boston: George C. Rand & Avery, Printers, 1864.

Warren, Benjamin. "Diary of Capt. Benjamin Warren on Battlefield of Saratoga." *The Journal of American History* 3 (1909): 201-16.

Wayne, Anthony. *Orderly Book of the Northern Army at Ticonderoga and Mount Independence, from October 17th 1776, to January 8th, 1777*. Albany: J. Munsell, 1859.

Webster, Clarence J., ed. *The Journal of Jeffery Amherst*. Toronto: The Ryerson Press, 1931.

Webster, Robert. "Robert Webster's Journal." *BFTM* 2 (July 1931): 120-59.

Wells, Bayze. "Journal of Bayze Wells." *Coll. Conn. HS* 7 (1899): 239-96.

Wheeler, Rufus. "Journal of Lieut. Rufus Wheeler of Rowley." *EIHC* 68 (1932): 371-77.

Wild, Ebenezer. "A Journal of a March from Cambridge, on an Expedition against Quebec in Colonel Benedict Arnold's Detachment, Sept. 13, 1775." *Proceedings of the Massachusetts Historical Society* 2, Second Series (1885-1886): 267-85.

Wilkinson, James. *Memoirs of My Own Times*. 1816. Reprint. New York: AMS Press Inc., 1973.

Williams, Thomas. "Correspondence of Doctor Thomas Williams, of Deerfield, Mass., A Surgeon in the Army." *The Historical Magazine* 7 (April 1870): 109-216.

Wilson, Commissary. *Commissary Wilson's Orderly Book, 1759*. Albany: J. Munsell, 1857.

Wood, Lemuel. "Diaries Kept by Lemuel Wood, of Boxford." *EIHC* 19 (1882): 61-80, 143-92; 20 (1883): 156-60, 198-208, 289-96; 21 (1884): 63-68.

_____. "Extract from the Diary of Lemuel Wood in Colonel Willard's Regiment of Massachusetts Militia." *BFTM* 2 (July 1932): 252-53.

Wood, William. *Select British Documents of the Canadian War of 1812.* Vol. 1, 3. Toronto: The Champlain Society, 1920-1926.

Woods, John. "Diary of John Woods June 10, 1759–November 4, 1759." Octavo Vol. 1, AAS.

Woodwell, P. M., ed. *Diary of Thomas Moody.* South Berwick, ME.: The Chronicle Print Shop, 1976.

Woolsely, Melancthon Taylor. *The Letters of Melancthon Taylor.* Champlain, N.Y.: Moorsfield Press, 1927.

Zaboly, Gary. "A Royal Artillery Officer With Amherst: The Journal of Captain-Lieutenant Henry Skinner, May 1 - July 28, 1759." manuscript 1991; forthcoming *BFTM* 15 (Winter 1992)

Books And Monographs

Allen, Gardner W. *A Naval History of the American Revolution.* New York: Russell & Russell, Inc., 1913.

Allen, Joseph. *Battles of the British Navy; From A.D. 1000 to 1840.* Vol. 2. London: A. H. Baily & Co., 1842.

Anderson, Fred. *A People's Army — Massachusetts Soldiers and Society in the Seven Years' War.* New York: W. W. Norton & Company, 1985.

Auld, Joseph. *Picturesque Burlington.* 2d. ed. Burlington, VT.: Free Press Association, 1894.

Barkley, Alexander. *Rival Routes from the West.* Albany: Report of Canal Commissioner, 1875.

Barnes, James. *Naval Actions of the War of 1812.* New York: Harper & Brothers Publishers, 1896.

[Barnes, Melvin.] *Reprint of a Short Biography of Colonel Ebenezer Allen . . .Lieutenant Samuel Allen.* Plattsburgh, N.Y.: J. W. Tuttle, Book and Job Printer, 1852.

George F. Bass, ed. *A History of Seafaring.* New York: Walker Publishing Co., Inc., 1972.

_____. *Ships and Shipwrecks of the Americas.* New York: Thames and Hudson, 1988.

The Battle of Plattsburgh — What Historians Say About It. Albany: J. B. Lyon Company, Printers, 1914.

Beach, Allen Penfield. *Lake Champlain As the Centuries Pass.* Burlington, VT.: Lane Press, 1959.

Bielinski, Stefan, ed. *A Guide to the Revolutionary War Manuscripts in the New York State Library.* Albany: New York State American Revolution Bicentennial Commission, 1976.

Bird, Harrison. *Navies in the Mountains.* New York: Oxford University Press, 1962.

Boatner, Mark Mayo, III. *Encyclopedia of the American Revolution.* New York: David McKay Company, Inc., 1966.

Boylan, Brian Richard. *Benedict Arnold — The Dark Eagle.* New York: W. W. Norton & Company, Inc., 1973.

Bradley, A. G. *The Fight with France for North America.* New York: E. P. Dutton and Company, 1900.

Bredenberg, Oscar E. *Military Activities in the Champlain Valley after 1777.* Champlain, N.Y.: Moorsfield Press, 1962.

_____. *The Battle of Plattsburgh Bay*. Plattsburgh, N.Y.: Clinton County Historical Association, 1978.

Brown, William H. ed. *History of Warren County New York*. Glens Falls, N.Y.: Board of Supervisors of Warren County, 1963.

Buckell, Betty Ahern, ed. *No Dull Days at Huletts*. Glens Falls, N.Y.: Guy Printing Co., Inc., 1984.

_____. *Old Lake George Hotels*. Lake George, N.Y.: Buckle Press, 1986.

_____. *Lake George Boats*. Lake George, N.Y.: Buckle Press, 1990.

Burns, James MacGregor. *The Vineyard of Liberty*. New York: Alfred A. Knopf, Inc., 1981.

Butler, B. C. *Lake George and Lake Champlain*. Albany: Weed, Parsons and Co., 1868.

A Canalboat Primer on the Canals of New York State. Syracuse, N.Y.: The Canal Museum, 1981.

Canfield, Thomas H. *Discovery: Navigation and Navigators of Lake Champlain*. 1859. Reprint. Burlington, VT.: Burlington Savings Bank, 1959.

Carpenter, Warwick Stevens. *The Summer Paradise in History*. Albany: The Delaware and Hudson Company, 1914.

A Century of Progress: History of the Delaware and Hudson Company 1823-1923. Albany, J. B. Lyon Company, 1925.

Chapelle, Howard I. *The History of American Sailing Ships*. New York: W. W. Norton & Company, Inc., 1935.

_____. *The History of the American Sailing Navy*. New York: W. W. Norton & Company, Inc., 1949.

Chidsey, Donald Barr. *The French and Indian War*. New York: Crown Publishers, Inc., 1969.

Child, Hamilton. *Gazetteer and Business Directory of Addison County Vt*. Syracuse, N.Y.: pub.n.a., 1882.

Clark, Delphina L. H. *Phineas Lyman — Connecticut's General*. Springfield, MA.: Connecticut Valley Historical Museum, 1964.

Clark, Raymond C. *A View of Westport, N.Y. on Lake Champlain*. Elizabethtown, N.Y.: Denton Publications, Inc., 1972.

Coggins, Jack. *Ships and Seamen of the American Revolution*. Harrisburg, PA.: Promontory Press, 1969.

Cohn, Arthur B., ed. *A Report on the Nautical Archeology of Lake Champlain: Results of the 1982 Field Season of the Champlain Maritime Society*. Burlington, VT.: The Champlain Maritime Society, 1984.

Commager, Henry Steele and Richard B. Morris, ed. *The Spirit of 'Seventy-Six*. Indianapolis, IN.: The Bobbs - Merrill Company, 1949.

Cone, Gertrude E. "Studies in the Development of Transportation in the Champlain Valley to 1876." Master's Thesis, The University of Vermont, 1945.

Connell, Brian. *The Savage Years*. New York: Harper & Brothers Publishers, 1959.

Cook, Joseph and Edward J. Owen. *Extracts from Sketches of Ticonderoga; Burial of Lord Howe*. Ticonderoga, N.Y.: n. d.

Coolidge, Guy Omeron. *The French Occupation of the Champlain Valley from 1609 to 1759*. 1938. Reprint. Harrison, N.Y.: Harbor Hill Books, 1979.

Cooper, J. Fenimore. *The History of the Navy of the United States of America*. Vol. 1. Philadelphia: Lea & Blanchard, 1839.

Copeland, Fred. *Lake Champlain*. Rutland, VT.: Charles E. Tuttle Co., 1950.

Coughlin, Richard. *The Adirondack Region*. Watertown, N.Y.: Samway Photo-Craft Company, Inc., 1921.

Crisman, Kevin J. *The History and Construction of the United States Schooner Ticonderoga*. Alexandria, VA.: Eyrie Publications, 1983.

_____. *Of Sailing Ships and Sidewheelers*. Montpelier, VT.: Division of Historic Preservation, 1986.

_____. *The Eagle*. Shelburne, VT.: The New England Press, 1987.

Crockett, Walter Hill. *A History of Lake Champlain 1609-1909*. Burlington, VT.: Hobart J. Shanley & Co., 1909.

_____. *Vermont: The Green Mountain State*. New York: The Century History Co., 1921.

Cuneo, John R. *Robert Rogers of the Rangers*. New York: Oxford University Press, 1959.

Currier, John J. *History of Newburyport, Mass. 1764-1905*. Newburyport, MA.: John J. Currier, 1906.

Davison, Rebecca, ed. *Phoenix Project*. Burlington, VT.: Champlain Maritime Society, 1981.

Dayton, Fred Erving. *Steamboat Days*. New York: Frederick A. Stokes Company, 1925.

DeCosta, B. F. *A Narrative of Events at Lake George*. New York: B. F. DeCosta, 1868.

_____. *Lake George; Its Scenes and Characteristics*. New York: Anson D. F. Randolph & Co., 1869.

_____. *Notes on the History of Fort George During the Colonial and Revolutionary Periods*. New York: J. Sabin & Sons, 1871.

_____. *The Fight at Diamond Island, Lake George*. New York: J. Sabin & Sons, 1872.

Diamant, Lincoln. *Bernard Romans*. Harrison, N.Y.: Harbor Hill Books, 1985.

Donaldson, Gordon. *Battle for a Continent Quebec 1759*. Garden City, N.Y.: Doubleday & Company, Inc., 1973.

Dow, George Francis. *History of Topsfield, Massachusetts*. Topsfield, MA.: The Topsfield Historical Society, 1940.

Doyle, Russell T., Jr. "A History of the Naval Operations in the Champlain Valley During the American Revolution." Master's thesis, State University College of Plattsburgh Arts and Science, 1982.

Eckert, Allan W. *Wilderness Empire*. Boston: Little, Brown and Company, 1969.

Eller, E. M. *Riverine Warfare: The U.S. Navy's Operations on Inland Waters*. Washington, D.C.: Naval History Division, Department of the Navy, 1969.

Everest, Allan S. *Moses Hazen and the Canadian Refugees in the American Revolution*. Syracuse, N.Y.: Syracuse University Press, 1976.

_____. *The War of 1812 in the Champlain Valley*. Syracuse, N.Y.: Syracuse University Press, 1981.

Favreau, J. Arthur. *La Grande Semaine*. Worcester, MA.: Société Historique Franco-Américaine, 1909.

Fischer, Montgomery, ed. *A Report of the Nautical Archeology of Lake Champlain: Results of the 1983 Field Season of the Champlain Maritime Society*. Burlington, VT.: The Champlain Maritime Society, 1985.

Flexner, James Thomas. *Steamboats Come True*. New York: The Viking Press, 1944.

_____. *Mohawk Baronet*. 1950. Reprint. Syracuse, N.Y.: Syracuse University Press, 1989.

Flood, Charles Bracelen. *Rise, And Fight Again*. New York: Dodd, Mead & Co., 1976.

Folsom, William R. *Vermonters in Battle and Other Papers*. Burlington, VT.: Lane Press, 1953.

Forbes, Esther. *Paul Revere & the World He Lived In*. Boston: Houghton Mifflin Company, 1942.

Fowler, Barney. *Adirondack Album*. Schenectady, N.Y.: Outdoor Associates, 1974.

_____. *Adirondack Album*. Vol. 3. Schenectady, N.Y.: Outdoor Associates, 1982.

Fowler, William M. Jr. *Rebels Under Sail*. New York: Charles Scribner's Sons, 1976.

Fuller, J. F. C. *Decisive Battles of the U.S.A.* New York: Harper & Brothers Publishers, 1942.

Gardner, John. *The Dory Book.* Mystic, CT.: Mystic Seaport Museum, Inc., 1987.

Garrity, Richard. *Canal Boatman.* Syracuse, N.Y.: Syracuse University Press, 1977.

Gerlach, Don R. *Proud Patriot — Philip Schuyler and the War of Independence, 1775–1783.* Syracuse, N.Y.: Syracuse University Press, 1987.

Gifford, Stanley M. *Fort William Henry: A History.* Lake George, N.Y.: Fort William Henry Museum, 1955.

Gilchrist, Helen Ives. *Fort Ticonderoga in History.* Ticonderoga, N.Y.: Fort Ticonderoga Museum, n.d.

Gipson, Lawrence Henry. *The Great War for the Empire: The Years of Defeat, 1754-1757.* Vol. 6. New York: Alfred A. Knopf, 1946.

_____. *The Great War for the Empire: The Victorious Years, 1758-1760.* Vol. 7. New York: Alfred A. Knopf, 1949.

_____. *The Great War for the Empire: The Culmination, 1760-1763.* Vol. 8. New York: Alfred A. Knopf, 1954.

_____. *The Coming of the Revolution 1763-1775.* New York: Harper & Brothers Publishers, 1954.

Glenn, Morris F. *The Story of Three Towns.* Ann Arbor, MI.: Braun-Brumfield, 1977.

_____. *Lake Champlain Album.* Vol. 2. Alexandria, VA.: Morris F. Glenn, 1979.

_____. *Glenn's History of Lake Champlain: Occasional Lists of Shipping on Lake Champlain.* Vol. 2. Alexandria, VA.: Morris F. Glenn, 1980.

_____. *The Capture and Burning of the Sloop Essex.* Alexandria, VA.: Morris F. Glenn, 1981.

_____. *Glenn's History of Lake Champlain: Canal Boats.* Vol. 4. Alexandria, VA.: Morris F. Glenn, n.d.

Godfrey, Frank H. *The Godfrey Letters.* Syracuse, N.Y.: The Canal Society of New York, 1973.

Gordon, William. *The History of the Rise, Progress, and Establishment of the Independence of the United States of America.* Vol. 2. New York: Samuel Campbell, 1794.

Grasso, Thomas X. *Champlain Canal.* Syracuse, N.Y.: The Canal Society of New York State, 1985.

Guttridge, Leonard F. and Jay D. Smith. *The Commodores.* New York: Harper & Row, Publishers, 1969.

Hahn, Thomas F., ed. *The Best from American Canals.* York, PA.: The American Canal and Transportation Center, 1980.

Hamilton, Edward P. *Lake Champlain and the Upper Hudson Valley.* Ticonderoga, N.Y.: Fort Ticonderoga Association, 1959.

_____. *The French and Indian Wars.* Garden City, N.Y.: Doubleday & Company, Inc., 1962.

_____. *Fort Ticonderoga — Key to a Continent.* Boston: Little, Brown and Company, 1964.

Hamilton, Milton W. *Sir William Johnson.* Port Washington, N.Y.: Kennikat Press, 1976.

Hammersley, Sidney Ernest. *The Lake Champlain Naval Battles of 1776-1814.* Waterford, N.Y.: Col. Sidney E. Hammersley, 1959.

Harlow, Alvin F. *Old Towpaths.* New York: D. Appleton and Company, 1926.

Harris, Captain E. S. *Lake George: All About It.* Glens Falls, N.Y.: Glens Falls Republican, 1903.

Hatch, Robert McConnell. *Major John André.* Boston: Houghton Mifflin Company, 1986.

Haviland, William A. and Marjory W. Power. *The Original Vermonters.* Hanover, N.H.: University Press of New England, 1981.

Hemenway, Abby Maria, ed. *The Vermont Historical Gazetteer.* Vol. 1. Burlington, VT. A. M. Hemenway, 1867.

Hill, Henry Wayland. *Waterways and Canal Construction in New York State*. Buffalo, N.Y.: Buffalo Historical Society, 1908.

_____. *The Champlain Tercentenary 1909*. 2 vols. Albany: J. B. Lyon Company, State Printers, 1913.

Hill, Ralph Nading. *Sidewheeler Saga*. New York: Rinehart & Company, Inc., 1953.

_____. *Two Centuries of Ferry Boating*. Burlington, VT.: Lake Champlain Transportation Co., Inc., 1972.

_____. *Vermont Album*. Brattleboro, VT.: The Stephen Greene Press, 1974.

_____. *Lake Champlain: Key to Liberty*. Montpelier, VT.: Vermont Life Magazine, 1976.

Hinman, Royal R. comp. *A Historical Collection of the Part Sustained by Connecticut*. Hartford: E. Gleason, 1842.

History of Oneida County, New York. Philadelphia: Everts & Fariss, 1878.

Hitsman, J. MacKay. *The Incredible War of 1812*. Toronto: University of Toronto Press, 1965.

Hogan, Matthew P. comp. *Underwater Archaeology Diver's Manual*. Syracuse, N.Y.: Canal Museum, 1981.

Horsman, Reginald. *The Causes of the War of 1812*. New York: A. S. Barnes and Company, 1962.

Huden, John C., comp. *Archaeology in Vermont*. Rutland, VT.: Charles E. Tuttle Company, 1971.

Hudleston, F. J. *Gentleman Johnny Burgoyne*. Garden City, N.Y.: Garden City Publishing Co., 1927.

James, William. *A Full and Correct Account of the Chief Naval Occurrences of the Late War Between Great Britain and the United States of America*. London: T. Egerton, 1817.

Jellison, Charles A. *Ethan Allen, Frontier Rebel*. Syracuse, N.Y.: Syracuse University Press, 1969.

Jones, Charles Henry. *History of the Campaign for the Conquest of Canada in 1776*. 1882. Reprint. New York: Research Reprints, Inc., 1970.

Jones, Thomas. *History of New York*. Vol. 1. New York: The New-York Historical Society, 1879.

Keenleyside, Hugh Ll. *Canada and the United States*. Port Washington, N.Y.: Kennikat Press, 1971.

Kellogg, Lewis. *A Sketch of the History of Whitehall*. Whitehall, N.Y.: S. B. Fairman, Printer, 1847.

Kimball, Francis P. *New York — The Canal State*. Albany: The Argus Press, 1937.

Knight, Arthur S., ed. *The Adirondack Guide — Vacationland: In Picture, Story and History*. Lake George, N.Y.: Press of Lake George Printing Co., 1929.

_____. *Vacationland: In Picture, Story and History*. Lake George, N.Y.: Adirondack Resorts Press, Inc., 1946-1960.

Krueger, John W. *A Most Memorable Day: The Battle of Lake George, September 8, 1775*. Saranac Lake, N.Y.: North Country Community College Press, 1980.

Lake Champlain Tercentenary. Albany, N.Y.: New York State Education Department, 1909.

Lamb Wallace E. *Lake George: Facts and Anecdotes*. Glens Falls, N.Y.: Glens Falls Post Co., 1938.

_____. *The Lake Champlain and Lake George Valleys*. Vol. 1 and 2. New York: The American Historical Company, Inc., 1940.

_____. *Historic Lake George*. Glens Falls, N.Y.: The Glens Falls Post Company, 1946.

Langworthy, Bess H. *History of Cumberland Head*. Plattsburgh, N.Y.: pub.n.a., 1961.

Lape, Jane M., ed. *Ticonderoga — Patches and Patterns from Its Past*. Ticonderoga, N.Y.: The Ticonderoga Historical Society, 1969.

Latham, Frank B. *Jacob Brown and the War of 1812*. New York: Cowles Book Company, Inc., 1971.

Leach, Douglas Edward. *Roots of Conflict: British Armed Forces and the Colonial Americans, 1667-1763*. Chapel Hill, N.C.: The University of North Carolina Press, 1986.

Lee, James, ed. *Tales the Boatmen Told*. Exton, Pa: Canal Press Incorporated, 1977.

Lépine, André. *La Richelieu Archeologique*. Montreal: La Societé du Musée Militaire et Maritime, 1983.

Loescher, Burt G. *The History of Rogers Rangers*. Vol. 1. San Francisco: Burt G. Loescher, 1946.

_____. *The History of Rogers Rangers: Officers and Non-commissioned Officers*. Vol. 3. Burlingame, CA.: Burt Garfield Loescher, 1957.

_____. *Geneis: Rogers Rangers the First Green Berets*. Vol. 2. San Mateo, CA.: B. G. Loescher, 1969.

Lonergan, Carroll Vincent. *The Northern Gateway*. Ticonderoga, N.Y.: C. V. Lonergan, 1939.

_____. *Ticonderoga: Historic Portage*. Ticonderoga, N.Y.: Fort Mount Hope Society Press, 1959.

Lord, Thomas Reeves. *Stories of Lake George, Fact and Fancy*. Pemberton, N.J.: Pinelands Press, 1987.

Lossing, Benson J. *The Pictorial Field-Book of the Revolution*. Vol. 1. 1851. Reprint. Freeport, N.Y.: Books for Libraries Press, 1969.

_____. *The Life and Times of Philip Schuyler*. Vol. 2. New York: Sheldon & Company, 1873.

Ludlum, Stuart D. *Exploring Lake George Lake Champlain 100 Years Ago*. Utica, N.Y.: Brodock & Ludlum Publications, 1972.

Lundeberg, Philip K. *The Continental Gunboat Philadelphia and the Northern Campaign of 1776*. Washington, D.C.: Smithsonian Institution, 1966.

MacDonald, James N., ed. *Historical Sketches of the Town of Plattsburgh*. Elizabethtown, N.Y.: Denton Publications, 1975.

Macdonough, Rodney. *Life of Commodore Thomas Macdonough*. Boston: The Fort Hill Press, 1909.

Mahan, A. T. *Sea Power in Its Relations to the War of 1812*. Vol. 2. Boston: Little, Brown, and Company, 1905.

_____. *War of American Independence*. Boston: Little, Brown, and Co., 1913.

Mahon, John K. *The War of 1812*. Gainesville, FL.: University of Florida Press, 1972.

Mante, Thomas. *The History of the Late War in North-America*. 1772. Reprint. New York: Research Reprints, Inc., n.d.

Marvin, Henry. *A Complete History of Lake George*. New York: Sibells & Maigne, Printers, 1853.

Mason, Richard A., ed. *Exploring Rogers Island*. Fort Edward, N.Y.: The Rogers Island Historical Association, 1969.

McKelvey, William J., Jr. *Champlain to Chesapeake*. Exton, PA.: Canal Press Inc., 1978.

Millar, John F. *American Ships of the Colonial and Revolutionary Periods*. New York: W. W. Norton & Company, Inc., 1978.

_____. *Early American Ships*. Williamsburg, VA.: Thirteen Colonies Press, 1986.

Morton, Doris Begor. *Philip Skene of Skenesborough*. Granville, N.Y.: The Grastorf Press, 1959.

_____. comp. *Day Before Yesterday*. Whitehall: Town Board of Whitehall, 1977.

Mountain Steamboats. Lake George, N.Y.: The Lake George Steamboat Company, 1981.

Muller, Charles G. *The Proudest Day*. New York: The John Day Company, 1960.

Muller, H. N. III. *The Commerical History of the Lake Champlain-Richelieu River Route 1760-1815*. Ann Arbor, MI.: University Microfilms, 1969.

Murray, W. H. H. *Lake Champlain and Its Shores*. Boston: DeWolfe, Fiske & Co., 1890.

Nelson, Paul David. *General Horatio Gates*. Baton Rouge, LA.: Louisiana State University Press, 1976.

Nutting, Wallace. *New York Beautiful*. Garden City, N.Y.: Garden City Publishing Co., Inc., 1927.

O'Brien, Kathryn E. *The Great and the Gracious on Millionaires' Row*. Sylvan Beach, N.Y.: North Country Books, 1978.

Offensend, Dorothy Backus. *The Sexton Boatbuilders of Hague*. Pawlet, VT.: D. B. Offensend, 1982.

O'Hara, John E. "Erie's Junior Partner." Ph.D. diss., Columbia University, 1951.

Osler, Edward, Esq. *The Life of Admiral Viscount Exmouth*. London: Smith Elder & Co., 1835.

Palmer, Peter S. *History of Lake Champlain*. 1886. Reprint. Harrison, N.Y.: Harbor Hill Books, 1983.

Papp, John. *Erie Canal Days*. Schenectady, N.Y.: Historical Publications, 1975.

Parkman, Francis, *Montcalm and Wolfe*. 1884. Reprint. New York: Atheneum, 1984.

_____. *France and England in North America*. Boston: Little, Brown, and Company, 1885.

Paullin, Charles Oscar. *The Navy of the American Revolution*. 1906. Reprint. New York: Haskell House Publishers Ltd., 1971.

Pell, S. H. P. *Fort Ticonderoga, A Short History*. Ticonderoga, N.Y.: Fort Ticonderoga Museum, 1978.

Possons, Charles H. *Posson's Guide to Lake George, Lake Champlain and Adirondacks*. Glens Falls, N.Y.: Chas. H. Possons, Publisher, 1888.

Powers, M. J. *A Summer Paradise*. Albany: The Delaware and Hudson Railroad, 1932.

Randall, Willard Sterne. *Benedict Arnold: Patriot and Traitor*. New York: William Morrow and Company, Inc., 1990.

Rann, W. S., ed. *History of Chittenden County Vermont*. Syracuse, N.Y.: D. Mason & Co., 1886.

Reid, Max W. *Lake George and Lake Champlain*. New York: G. P. Putnam's Sons, 1910.

Richards, Frederick B. *The Black Watch*. Ticonderoga, N.Y.: Fort Ticonderoga Museum, 1926.

Robinson, Rowland E. *Vermont, A Study of Independence*. Boston: Houghton Mifflin Company, 1892.

Robison, S. S. and Mary Robison. *A History of Naval Tactics From 1530 To 1930*. Annapolis, MD.: The United States Naval Institute, 1942.

Roessele, T. E. *Lake George: A Descriptive and Historical Sketch*. Lake George, N.Y.: T. E. Roessele, 1887.

Rogers, Allan. *Empire and Liberty*. Berkeley, CA.: University of California Press, 1974.

Roosevelt, Theodore. *The Naval War of 1812*. New York: G. P. Putnam's Sons, 1882.

Ross, Ogden, J. *The Steamboats of Lake Champlain 1809 to 1930*. Albany: Press of the Delaware and Hudson Railroad, 1930.

_____. *The Steamboats of Lake George 1817 to 1932*. Albany: Press of the Delaware and Hudson Railroad, 1932.

Royce, Caroline Halstead. *Bessboro: A History of Westport, Essex Co., N.Y.* Elizabethtown, N.Y.: C. H. Royce, 1904.

Salsig, Doyen, ed. *Parole: Quebec: Countersign: Ticonderoga — Second New Jersey Regimental Orderly Book, 1776*. Cranbury, N.J.: Associated Presses, Inc., 1980.

Seelye, Elizabeth Eggleston. *Lake George in History*. 2nd ed. Lake George, N.Y.: Elwyn Seelye, 1896.

_____. *Saratoga and Lake Champlain in History*. Lake George, N.Y.: Elwyn Seelye, 1898.

Shaughnessy, Jim. *Delaware & Hudson*. Berkeley, CA.: Howell - North Books, 1967.

Shaw, Ronald E. *Erie Water West*. Lexington, KY.: University of Kentucky Press, 1966.

Sherman, Gordon C. and Elsie L. Sherman. *An Illuminating History of the Champlain Valley and the Adirondack Mountains, 1814-1929*. Vol. 2. Elizabethtown, N.Y.: Denton Publications, Inc., 1977.

Silliman, Benjamin. *Remarks Made on a Short Tour Between Hartford and Quebec in the Autumn of 1819*. 2nd ed. New Haven, CT.: S. Converse, 1824.

Smith, Edgar Newbold. *American Naval Broadsides: A Collection of Early Naval Prints (1745-1815)*. New York: Philadephia Maritime Museum and Clarkson N. Potter, Inc. Publisher, 1974.

Smith, H. P., ed. *History of Warren County*. Syracuse, N.Y.: D. Mason & Co. Pub., 1885.

_____. *History of Addison County*. Syracuse, N.Y.: D. Mason & Co. Pub., 1886.

Smith, R. P. *Historical and Statistical Gazetteer of New York State*. Syracuse, N.Y.: R. P. Smith, 1860.

Smith, William Henry. *The Life and Public Services of Arthur St. Clair*. Cincinnati, OH.: Robert Clarke & Co., 1882.

Snider, C. H. J. *In the Wake of the Eighteen-Twelvers*. 1913. Reprint. London: Cornmarket Press Limited, 1969.

Soley, James Russell. *The Boys of 1812*. Boston: Estes and Lauriat, 1887.

Spears, John R. *The History of Our Navy*. New York: Charles Scribner's Sons, 1897.

Springer, Ethel M. and Thomas F. Hahn, *Canal Boat Children*. Shepherdstown, W. VA.: The American Canal & Transportation Center, 1981.

Stahl, John M. *The Battle of Plattsburgh; A Study in and of the War of 1812*. Illinois: The Van Trump Company, 1918.

Stanley, George F. G. *Canada Invaded*. Toronto: A. M. Hakkert Ltd., 1973.

Steinback, Elsa Kny. *Sweet Peas and a White Bridge: On Lake George When Steam Was King*. Burlington, VT.: The George Little Press, 1974.

Stevenson, Robert Louis. *Ticonderoga: A Legend of the West Highlands*. 1887. Reprint. New York: The Fort Ticonderoga Museum, 1947.

Stoddard, S. R. *Ticonderoga: Past and Present*. Albany: Weed, Parsons and Company, Printers, 1873.

_____. *Lake George: A Book of To-day*. Albany, N.Y.: Van Benthuysen & Sons, Printers, 1880.

_____. *Lake George and Lake Champlain a Book of To-day*. Glens Falls, N.Y.: S. R. Stoddard, 1900, 1901, 1906.

Stone, R. G. *An Account of the Anniversary of the Battle of Plattsburgh*. Plattsburgh, N.Y.: Plattsburgh Republican, 1843.

Stone, William L. *The Campaign of Lieut. Gen. John Burgoyne*. Albany: Joel Munsell, 1877.

Stott, Earl E. *Exploring Rogers Island*. Fort Edwards, N.Y.: The Rogers Island Historical Association, 1969.

Styles, R. S. *A Descriptive and Historical Guide to the Valley of Lake Champlain and the Adirondacks*. Burlington, VT.: R. S. Styles' Steam Printing House, 1871.

Swayze, Nathan L. *Engraved Powder Horns*. Yazoo City, MS.: Gun Hill Pub. Co., 1978.

Swift, Samuel. *History of the Town of Middlebury*. Middlebury, VT.: A. H. Copeland, 1859.

Taylor, Daniel T. *The Shores of Champlain*. Champlain, N.Y.: Moorsfield Press, 1979.

Thompson, Zadock. *History of Vermont*. Part 3. Burlington, VT.: Chauncey Goodrich, 1842.

_____. *History of the State of Vermont*. Burlington, VT.: Smith & Co., 1858.

Thorne, Frederick C. *Pilot Knob Story: An Historical Report of Its Life and Times*. Pilot Knob, N.Y.: F. C. Thorne, 1977.

Todish, Timothy J. *America's First World War*. Grand Rapids, Mich.: Suagothel Productions Ltd., 1982.

Trost, Alfred H. and Robert C. DeLond, eds. *A History Celebrating the 150th Anniversary of the Town of Essex, N.Y. 1805-1955*. Malone, N.Y.: The Industrial Press, 1955.

Tyrell, William G. *Champlain and the French in New York*. Albany: The University of the State of New York, the State Education Department, 1959.

Van De Water, Frederic F. *Lake Champlain and Lake George*. Indianapolis: The Bobbs-Merrill Company, 1946.

Van Doren, Carl. *Secret History of the American Revolution*. 1941. Reprint. New York: Viking Press, Inc., 1968.

Von Eelking, Max. *The German Allied Troops in the North American War of Independence 1776-1783*. Translated by J. G. Rosengarten. Albany: Joel Munsell's Sons, Publishers, 1893.

Wallace, Willard M. *Traitorous Hero*. 1954. Reprint. Freeport, N.Y.: Books for Libraries Press, 1970.

Ward, Christopher. *The War of the Revolution*. New York: The Macmillan Company, 1952.

Warner, C. B. and C. Eleanor Hall. *History of Port Henry*. Rutland, VT.: The Tuttle Co., 1931.

Washington, Ida H. and Paul A. Washington. *Carleton's Raid*. Canaan, N.H.: Phoenix Publishing, 1977.

Watson, Winslow C. *The Military and Civil History of the County of Essex, N.Y.* Albany: J. Munsell, 1869.

Westcott, Thompson. *Life of John Fitch*. Philadelphia: J. B. Lippincott & Co., 1857.

Whitehall Bicentennial. Whitehall, N.Y.: Whitehall Bicentennial Association, 1959.

Whittemore, Charles P. *A General of the Revolution, John Sullivan of New Hampshire*. New York: Columbia University Press, 1961.

Whittier, Bob. *Paddle Wheel Steamers and Their Giant Engines*. Duxbury, Ma.: Seamaster Boats, Inc., 1983.

Wright, Wyllis E. *Colonel Ephraim Williams: A Documentary Life*. Pittsfield, MA.: Berkshire County Historical Society, 1970.

Wrong, George M. *The Conquest of New France*. New Haven, CT.: Yale University Press, 1921.

_____. *Canada and the American Revolution*. New York: The Macmillan Company, 1935.

Wyld, Lionel D. *40' x 28' x 4': The Erie Canal – 150 Years*. Rome, N.Y.: Oneida County Erie Canal Commemoration Commission, 1967.

Wynkoop, William. "The Wynkoop Family." In *A Collection of Papers Read Before the Bucks County Historical Society*, edited by Harman Yerkes et al. Riegelsville, PA.: B. F. Fackenthal, Jr. 1909.

Zarzynski, Joseph W. *Champ – Beyond the Legend*. Port Henry, N.Y.: Bannister Publications, 1984.

_____. *Monster Wrecks of Lock Ness and Lake Champlain*. Wilton, N.Y.: M-Z Information, 1986.

MAGAZINES, PAMPHLETS, PERIODICALS, and UNPUBLISHED PAPERS

Barker, Elmer Eugene. *The Story of Crown Point Iron*. Ironville, N.Y.: The Penfield Foundation, 1969.

Bellico, Russell. "Gateway in the North: Lake Champlain." *Skin Diver*, March 1973.

_____. "Sails and Steamers in the Mountains." *Aquarius*, Fall 1974.

_____. "Diving into History." *Adirondack Life*, Fall 1976.

_____. "The Battle of Plattsburgh." *Adirondack Life*, September/October 1977.

_____. "The Cruise of the Juniper." *Adirondack Life*, May/June 1978.

_____. "The Search for Arnold's Navy." *Adirondack Life*, September/October 1980.

_____. "Beneath Lake George: Underwater Paradise." *Lake Champlain Waterways*, June 1982.

_____. "The Abercromby Expedition." *Adirondack Life*, July/August 1983.

_____. "Battle on Lake Champlain." *American History Illustrated*, March 1985.

_____. "The Search for Benedict Arnold's Navy." *American History Illustrated*, March 1985.

_____. "The *General Butler*," *Skin Diver*, September 1985.

_____. "Littered With History." *Scubapro Diving*, Summer 1986.

_____. "Lake Champlain, A Storehouse of Marine History." *Scubapro Diving*, Fall 1987.

_____. "Historic Preservation: The Wreck of the *Champlain*." *Adirondack Life*, July/August 1989.

_____. "Ghost from the Depths." *American History Illustrated*, March/April 1992.

Blow, David J. "*Vermont I*: Lake Champlain's First Steamboat." *Vermont History* 34 (April 1966): 115-22.

Bottum, Lynn H. "*Oakes Ames/Champlain* — The Biography of a Lake Champlain Steamboat." *Vermont History* 51 (Summer 1983): 133-57.

Bredenberg, Oscar E. "The American Champlain Fleet, 1775-77." *BFTM* 12 (September 1964): 249-63.

_____. "The Royal Savage," *BFTM* 12 (September 1966): 128-49.

Burns, Brian. "Carleton in the Valley or the Year of the Burning." *BFTM* 13 (Fall 1980): 398-411.

Carroll, Hanson. "Skin Diving." *Vermont Life*, Summer 1960.

Charland, Thomas M. "The Lake Champlain Army and the Fall of Montreal." *Vermont History* 28 (October 1960): 293-301.

Cohn, Arthur B. "The Fort Ticonderoga King's Shipyard Excavation: 1984 Field — Season Report." *BFTM* 14 (Fall 1985): 337-55.

_____. "An Incident Not Known to History: Squire Ferris and Benedict Arnold at Ferris Bay, October 13, 1776." *Vermont History* 55 (Spring 1987): 108-10.

Cone, Gertrude E. "Early Sailing Craft on Lake Champlain." *North Country Life,* Winter 1950.

Cook, Joseph. *An Historical Address*. Ticonderoga, N.Y.: Ticonderoga Historical Society, 1864.

Copeland, Fred. "Champlain Canal Days." *The Vermonter,* August 1941.

Cortesi, Lawrence. "The Tragic Romance of Jane McCrea." *American History Illustrated*, April 1985.

Crisman, Kevin J. "The Construction of the Boscawen." *BFTM* 14 (Fall 1985): 357-70.

_____. "The Fort Ticonderoga King's Shipyard Excavation: The Artifacts." *BFTM* 14 (Fall 1985): 375-436.

Dawson, Henry B. "The Battle of Bennington." *The Historical Magazine* 7 (May 1870): 289-305.

Dechame, Roger R. P. "The First Fort at Fort Ticonderoga." *BFTM* 15 (Winter 1988): 8-14.

DeCosta, B. F. "The Fight at Diamond Island." *NEHGR* 26 (April 1872): 147-52.

Dufour, Madaleine M. "Samuel De Champlain and the Discovery of the Lake." *BFTM* 14 (Summer 1984): 271-76.

Farmer, Edward G. "Skenesborough: Continental Naval Shipyard." *The Naval Institute Proceedings* 90 (October 1967): 160-62.

Frise, Joseph R. "A Trumbull Map of Fort Ticonderoga." *BFTM* 13 (June 1971): 129-36.

Gardner, John. "Famous Boat Type in Transitional Stage." *National Fisherman*, May, August 1967.

Gerlach, Don R. "The British Invasion of 1780 and 'A Character. . . Debased Beyond Description.' " *BFTM* 14 (Summer 1984): 311-21.

_____. "The Fall of Ticonderoga in 1777: Who Was Responsible." *BFTM* 14 (Summer 1982): 131-57.

Gordon, Robert. "Still Steaming. . ." *Adirondack Life*, Summer 1973.

Hagglund, L. F. *A Page from the Past*, 2nd ed. Lake George, N.Y.: Adirondack Resorts Press, 1949.

Hamilton, Edward P. *The Champlain Valley in the American Revolution*. Albany: New York State American Revolution Bicentennial Commission/Champlain Valley Committee for the Observance of the Bicentennial of the American Revolution, 1976.

_____. "An Historic Mortar." *BFTM* 10 (February 1960): 299-303.

Hamilton, Milton W. "Battle Report: General William Johnson's Letter to the Governors, Lake George, September 9-10, 1755." *Proceedings of the American Antiquarian Society* 74 (Part 1, 1964): 19-36.

Hays, James T., David E. Mize, and Richard W. Ward. "Guns Under Lake Champlain." *York State Tradition,* Winter 1963.

Hill, Ralph N., Jr. "Shelburne Shipyard." *Vermont Life*, Autumn 1953.

_____. "Sidewheeler for Shelburne." *American Heritage*, April 1955.

_____. "Gateway Struggle." *Vermont Life*, Summer 1959.

_____. "Indian Legacy." *Vermont Life*, Summer 1959.

_____. "The One. . .The Only Ti." *Vermont Life*, Summer 1961.

_____. "A New Era for Lady Ti." *Yankee*, November 1983.

Huden, John C. "The Admiral of Lake Champlain." *Vermont History* 30 (January 1962): 66-69.

Juckett, Martha Robbins. *My Canaling Days*. Edited by Dorothy M. Parker. Reprint. Whitehall: N.Y.: Historical Society of Whitehall, 1972.

Kane, Roberta. "The Fort That Almost Lived Twice." *Adirondack Bits 'n Pieces*, Winter 1983-84.

Kellogg, Lewis. *A Sketch of the History of Whitehall*. Whitehall, N.Y.: S. B. Fairman, Printer, 1847.

Krueger, John W. "Troop Life at the Champlain Valley Forts During the American Revolution." *BFTM* 14 (Summer 1982): 158-64; (Fall 1983): 220-49; (Summer 1984): 277-310.

Lépine, André. "An 18th Century Wreck in the Richelieu River, Quebec, Canada." *The International Journal of Nautical Archaeology and Underwater Exploration* 8.4 (1979): 340-46.

_____. "A Wreck Believed to Be a French 'Bateau' Sunk During Action in 1760 off Isle-aux-noix in the Richelieu River, Quebec, Canada." *The International Journal of Nautical Archaeology and Underwater Exploration* 10.1 (1981):41-50.

Lewis, Dennis M. "An Expedition Upon Lake Champlain: Murray's Raid, 1813." *Proceedings of the Champlain Valley Symposium*, edited by Bruce P. Stark. Plattsburgh, N.Y.: Clinton County Historical Association, 1982.

_____. "The Naval Campaign of 1759 on Lake Champlain." *BFTM* 14 (Fall 1983): 203-16.

Lundeberg, Philip K. *Search for Continental Gunboats at Schuyler Island, Lake Champlain, New York*. Washington, D.C.: National Geographic Society Research Reports, 1976.

MacGregor, Bruce. "A Failure to Communicate." *American History Illustrated*, October 1985.

Mazet, Horace Sawyer. "Lake Champlain Yields Historic Relics." *Motor Boating*, February 1935.

Meiklejohn, Andrew G. "The Champlain Canal—Remarks of Hon. Andrew G. Meiklejohn." 5 April 1964, NYSL.

Miksch, Heidi. "The Fort Ticonderoga King's Shipyard Excavation: The Conservation Program." *BFTM* 14 (Fall 1985): 371-74.

Mize, David E. *Scuba Explorers Research*. Plattsburgh, N.Y.: Clinton County Historical Association, 1967.

Morton, Doris Begor. *Birth of the United States Navy*. Whitehall, N.Y.: Whitehall Times, 1982.

_____. "Birth of a Navy." *Adirondack Bits 'n Pieces*, Winter 1983-84.

_____. *Whitehall in the War of 1812*. Whitehall, N.Y.: Washington County Historical Society, 1964.

Muller, H. N. and David A. Donath. " 'The Road Not Taken': A Reassessment of Burgoyne's Campaign." *BFTM* 13 (1973):272-85.

Muller, H. Nicholas, III. and Marchall M. True. "All Unquiet on the Waterfront." *Vermont Life*, Summer 1985.

Muller, H. N., III. "A 'Traitorous and Diabolical Traffic': The Commerce of the Champlain—Richelieu Corridor During the War of 1812." *Vermont History* 44 (Spring 1976):78-96.

Muratori, Marisa. "The Lac du Saint Sacrement." *Adirondack Life*, September/October 1989.

Murray, Eleanor S. "The Burgoyne Campaign." *BFTM* 8 (January 1948):4-16.

_____. "The Invasion of Northern New York." *BFTM* 7 (July 1946):3-21.

_____. "Manuscripts as Resources." *Vermont Quarterly* 20 (April 1952): 89-104.

_____. "Resume of the Court Martial of General St. Clair Resulting from the Evacuation of Fort Ticonderoga and Mount Independence July 6, 1777." *BFTM* 7 (July 1947):3-19.

Nelson, Paul David. "Guy Carleton versus Benedict Arnold: The Campaign of 1776 in Canada and on Lake Champlain." *New York History* 57 (July 1976): 339-66.

Nelson, Peter. "The Battle of Diamond Island." *Quarterly Journal of the New York State History Association* (January 1922): 36-53.

_____. "John Brown and the Dash for Ticonderoga." *BFTM* 2 (January 1930): 23-40.

Niles, Samuel. "A Summary Historical Narrative of the Wars in New-England with the French and Indians, in Several Parts of the Country [1760]." *Collections of the Massachusetts Historical Society*. 6, Third Series (1837): 154-279; 5, Fourth Series (1861): 309-589.

Noble, Henry Harmon. *A Sketch of the History of the Town of Essex, New York*. Champlain, N.Y.: Moorsfield Press, 1940.

Olsen, Godfrey, J. "Archaeology of Ticonderoga." *Proceedings of the New York State Historical Association* 32 (1934): 407-11.

Osler, Edward. "The Battle of Valcour Island." *BFTM* 2 (January 1932):163-68.

Paltsits, Victor H. and W. Max Reid. "Rock Inscription at the Ruins of Old Fort St. Frederick at Crown Point." *Proceedings of the New York State Historical Association* 10 (1911):107-13.

Park, Edwards. "Could Canada Have Ever Been Our Fourteenth Colony." *Smithsonian*, December 1987.

Peebles, Giovanna N. and David C. Skinas. "Vermont's Underwater Historic Preserves: Challenges, Benefits, Problems, and Process." *Underwater Archaeology Proceedings* (1989):49-53.

Pell, John H. G. "General George Washington's Visit to Fort Ticonderoga in July 1783." *BFTM* 14 (Fall 1983): 260-62.

Pell, Robert T. "John Brown and the Dash for Ticonderoga." *BFTM* 2 (January 1930): 23-40.

Pines, Paul. "Lake George: Milfoil, Moratoriums and Controversy." *Adirondack Life*, July/August 1987.

Pollard, Louise. "The Champlain Transportation Company." *The Vermonter*, February 1933.

"The Revenge." *BFTM* 1 (July 1929):6-11.

Rich, Edwin. "Arnold's Fleet 1771-1790." unpublished paper, 1964.

Shomette, Donald G. "Heyday of the Horse Ferry." *National Geographic,* October 1989.

Skerrett, Robert G. "Wreck of the Royal Savage Recovered." *U.S. Naval Institute Proceedings* (November 1935): 1646-52.

Smith, Dorothy U. "Historic War Vessels in Lake Champlain and Lake George." *New York State Museum Bulletin* 313 (October 1937): 123-36.

Stephens, Philip. "A British View of the Battle of Valcour." *North Country Notes*, April 1963.

"Steamboats on Lake Champlain and Lake George." *North Country Life-York State Tradition*, Winter 1962.

Stiles, Fred T. "Tales of Old Canal Days." *North Country Life*, Winter 1959.

_____. "Recollections of the Knapp Estate." *North Country Life*, Fall 1960.

_____. "Tales of Lake George." *York State Tradition*, Summer 1963.

Trumbull, J. H. *The Origin of the Expedition Against Ticonderoga in 1775*. Hartford, CT.: J. H. Trumbull, 1869.

Tucker, Philip C. *General Arnold and the Congress Galley*. Vergennes, VT.: pub., n.a., 1861.

"Was Washington to Blame for the Loss of Ticonderoga in 1777?" *BFTM* 11 (September 1963): 65-74.

Wagner, John. "Au Plaisir." *Adirondack Life*, January/February 1988.

Watson, W.C. "Arnold's Retreat After the Battle of Valcour." *MAH* 6 (June 1881):414-17.

Watt, Lynn. "Is Champlain Doomed?" *Vermont Life,* Spring 1969.

Webb, Stephen Saunders. "The Strange Career of Francis Nicholson." *The William and Mary Quarterly* 23 (October 1966):513-48.

W. G. "A Sketch of the Great Northern or Champlain Canal." Albany: New York State Library, 1823.

Wilkins, F. H. "Lake Champlain Steamers." *The Vermonter*, January 1916.

Zaboly, Gary. "The Battle on Snowshoes." *American History Illustrated*, December 1979.

Zarzynski, Joseph et al. *The Atlantic Alliance for Maritime Heritage Conservation 1987 Lake George, New York Underwater Archaeology Workshop and Field Report*. AALGBRT, 1987.

Newspapers, Newsletters, and Contemporary Magazines

Boston Gazette and Country Journal
Burlington Free Press
Champlain Journal
Champlain Maritime Society Soundings
Daily Free Press (Burlington)
Glens Falls Daily Times
Glens Falls Republican
Lake Champlain Committee Newsletter
Lake George Mirror
London Magazine
New-York Mercury
New York Times

Niles Weekly Register
Plattsburgh Daily Press
Plattsburgh Evening News
Plattsburgh Press-Republican
Plattsburgh Sentinel
Post-Star (Glens Falls)
Scots Magazine (Edinburgh)
Times-Union (Albany)
Universal Magazine (London)
Valley News (Elizabethtown)
Vergennes Enterprise
Warrensburg News

Detail of "Line of Vessels on Lake George under General Amherst, 1759" showing the English flat-bottomed boat, radeau *Invincible*, and rafts with cannon.
(Public Record Office, London)

INDEX

Reviewers' comments on
SAILS AND STEAM IN THE MOUNTAINS
A Maritime and Military History of Lake George and Lake Champlain

"Bellico fully traces the roles played by Lake George and Lake Champlain in the French and Indian War, the American Revolution, and the War of 1812, then moves beyond to the canal boats and steamships that plied them in more peaceful pursuits during the nineteenth and twentieth centuries."—*American History*

"What makes Bellico's work stand out from the literature in the subject is his extensive use of original diaries and journals of the soldiers who fought the battles at the lakes. At points it achieves the narrative flow and high drama of the new hit movie *The Last of the Mohicans*." —*Times Union*, Albany

"Bellico draws on a vast fund of research and documentation to bring to life the early explorations, naval and military actions of the French and Indian wars, the Revolution, and the War of 1812. . . . This massive work is substantiated by an impressively extensive bibliography."—*Vermont Sunday Magazine*

"Attractively illustrated, handsomely printed and bound, this new history of maritime and military affairs on Lake Champlain and Lake George gives a thorough review of the exploration and early, crucially important military history of the Champlain Valley."
—*Vermont Life Magazine*

"No one who claims interest in the history of the Lake George/Lake Champlain region, who expresses a fascination with the richness of underwater history and a desire to see it preserved, or who just enjoys envisioning the past in modern landscape, should find their library without this book."—*Sea History Magazine*

"Now in its second printing in two years, this popular and very readable history of two significant Adirondack lakes and the events and ships involved through the years is the most comprehensive account of the area. Meticulously documented, it takes the reader into the early history of the strategic waterway into Canada, and right down to present time and the boats currently plying the lakes."—*Steamboat Bill* (Journal of the Steamship Historical Society)

"Offering a wealth of new details culled mainly from primary sources: journals, orderly books, letters, newspaper reports, etc.—this book provides a fresh retelling of the 17th, 18th, and 19th century battles waged along the 152-mile water chain linking what is now the United States and Canada. . .author Bellico has laced the book not infrequently with colorful anecdotes, observations by participants, and sections discussing archaeological discoveries related to the campaigns."—*Military Collector and Historian*

"The maritime and military history of Lake George and Lake Champlain springs to life in the pages of this compelling reference."—*Adirondack Life Magazine*

"Bellico's book meticulously traces the history of these two lakes. In all of this material Bellico presents much primary data as well as a complex synthesis of events. . .the volume also offers copious textual and citation footnotes and additional page-end comments. . .Exquisite photographs provide a counterpoint to the historical illustrations in the text."
—*American Neptune: A Quarterly Journal of Maritime History*